Route of
De Soto's Army
through
La Florida
1539–1543

The
FLORIDA
of
THE INCA

Hernando de Soto
Governor and Captain General
of the Kingdom of Florida

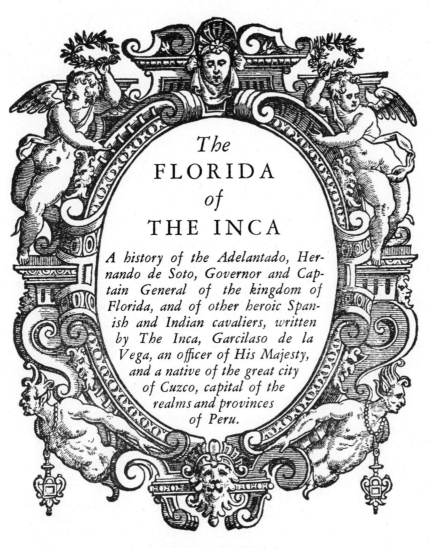

The
FLORIDA
of
THE INCA

A history of the Adelantado, Hernando de Soto, Governor and Captain General of the kingdom of Florida, and of other heroic Spanish and Indian cavaliers, written by The Inca, Garcilaso de la Vega, an officer of His Majesty, and a native of the great city of Cuzco, capital of the realms and provinces of Peru.

Translated and Edited by

John Grier Varner
and
Jeannette Johnson Varner

1951 · UNIVERSITY OF TEXAS PRESS · AUSTIN

Drawings for frontispiece and end-papers
by Reese Brandt.

PREFACE

T JUST what date the Inca Garcilaso de la Vega first became obsessed with the idea of recording the events of Hernando de Soto's conquest of that vast area of the North American continent which the Spaniards referred to as Florida is not certain, but from his own words we can ascertain that he was playing with the thought as early as 1567 and had completed a fourth of *The Florida* by 1587. Two years later he wrote the King that he was in the process of compiling a final draft of this history, and in 1591 he recorded within the pages of his manuscript that he was bringing the work to a close. The acquisition of new information necessitated revisions, and *The Florida* was not actually completed until 1599. Then five more years elapsed before this book received the approvals necessary for publication, and it was 1605 before it actually appeared in print.

The first edition of *The Florida* was published by Pedro Crasbeeck at Lisbon under the title, *La Florida del Ynca. Historia del Adelantado Hernando de Soto, Governador y capitan general del Reyno de la Florida, y de otros heroicos cavalleros Españoles è Indios.* A reprint of this edition with emendations was made at Madrid in 1723 under the editorship of Andrés González Barcia Carballido y Zúñiga, who in this instance used the pseudonym "Gabriel Daza de Cárdenas." Other reissues have appeared, but the best known of the Spanish editions is that of 1723.

Almost three hundred and fifty years have gone by since *The Florida* first reached the book marts of Portugal and Spain, and though translations of it have appeared in several languages, no complete rendition in English from the original Spanish has heretofore been made available to the public. Theodore Irving, at the suggestion of his celebrated uncle, Washington Irving, did a translation from an early Spanish edition, but, before publishing his results in 1833, he interpolated material from other sources and omitted some of *The Florida*. Again, Barnard Shipp published an English version in 1881, but unfortunately he avoided the original Spanish and worked from the abbreviated French version of Pierre Richelet. It has seemed wise therefore to prepare a translation of this ever beguiling and significant old chronicle which will enable English readers to see the whole of Garcilaso's picture.

In the present rendition we first used the Madrid edition of 1723 and then collated our results with the Lisbon edition of 1605. Our text is complete and without alterations other than those required by the process of translation, for our sole purpose has been to present clearly and accurately the meaning and feeling the Inca was trying to convey. In the main we adhered fairly closely to the syntax of the original, but when such procedure resulted in cumbersomeness, grotesquerie or obscurity, we sought a form which would be agreeable and at the same time uninjurious to sense and tone. In the process of translation, words of course present significant problems; for, dependent as they are in their meaning upon time, geographical location and even context, they must be carefully chosen. We attempted, therefore, to find those words which would preserve as much as possible of the music and thought of the Inca's Spanish while conveying his message without offense to a modern audience. And finally, aware that the products of Garcilaso's mind were cast in the golden mold of sixteenth-century Spain, we sought to acquaint ourselves adequately with the man and his environment, and to interpret his story as we feel it should be interpreted—in the light of the age which produced it.

With the text of *The Florida,* we have included only that prefatory material to be found in the Lisbon edition, and some few annotations designed to provide the reader with supplementary data of importance. Much of the latter information has been drawn from three other early accounts, i.e., the Ranjel, the Biedma, and the Elvas. But the primary purpose of our annotations is simply to heighten the interest of the Inca's story, and to leave the reader with a clearer idea of the approximate route of the Spanish army. We are not attempting to estimate the relative value of the early reports or to establish time sequences and geographical locations. Such points in question have been thoroughly explored by a number of reliable historians, and their results are readily available. In this particular, we would call the reader's special attention to the scholarly report of the De Soto Expedition Commission, cited frequently in our annotations.

The kind assistance and encouragement of a number of persons have made our translation possible. We are under special obligation to Mr. John Cook Wyllie, Curator of Rare Books at the Alderman Library of the University of Virginia, and to Mr. R. E. Banta, well-known author and publisher of Crawfordsville, Indiana. Mr. Wyllie not only has made available for our use valuable materials from the McGregor Library of Americana with which he is charged, but throughout the process of our work has continued to review our efforts and to offer scholarly criticism and suggestions which have proved of great worth. Mr. Banta has given us confidence as well as excellent advice, and because of his keen perception of the true literary and historical value of *The Florida* has spared no effort to assist us in bringing our translation to light. Our indebtedness extends likewise to various administrative officials as well as members of the faculty and staff of The University of Texas, among whom we would call especial attention to the following: to Dr. Carlos Castañeda and Dr. Pablo Max Ynsfran for their sympathetic interest and able assistance in matters pertaining to historical background and interpretation; to Dr. R. H. Williams, Dr. Ramón Martínez-López, and Dr. Daniel Lee Hamilton for erudite advice concerning unusual problems of translation; and to Dr. Nettie Lee Benson, Miss Fannie Ratchford, and others of the library staff who facilitated our use of materials in their care. And in conclusion, we are mindful of the many friends and acquaintances in Venezuela and Mexico who, during our years of residence in those two republics, gave us a better understanding of the Spaniard, the Indian, the creole and the mestizo—an understanding which we trust has contributed to a more accurate and a more sympathetic interpretation of the Inca, Garcilaso de la Vega.

JOHN GRIER VARNER, PH.D.
Associate Professor of English
The University of Texas

JEANNETTE JOHNSON VARNER, PH.D.
Reference Librarian
Austin Public Library

From "The Land of the Herdsmen"
January 1, 1951

TABLE OF CONTENTS

THE FIRST BOOK

Of the History of Florida by the Inca presents a description of the land and the customs of its natives; a record of its first explorer and of those explorers who went there afterward; an account of the people who accompanied Hernando de Soto in his expedition; the strange events that occurred on their voyage, the supplies which the Governor ordered and provided in Havana, and his embarkation for Florida.
It contains fifteen chapters, which are as follows.

THE FIRST PART
OF THE SECOND BOOK

Of the History of Florida by the Inca treats of the Governor's arrival in that land and his discovery there of traces of Pámphilo de Narváez; his finding of a Christian captive who describes the tortures and cruelties imposed upon him by the Indians as well as the hospitalities extended him by a certain Indian lord of vassals; the further preparations which the Spaniards made for the expedition and the events that occurred in the first eight provinces they explored; and the extraordinary bravery in both words and deeds of a bold cacique. It contains thirty chapters, which are as follows.

THE SECOND PART
OF THE SECOND BOOK

Of the History of Florida by the Inca wherein will be seen the many fierce struggles that occurred under difficult circumstances between the Indians and the Spaniards in the great province of Apalache; the hardships the Spaniards suffered in finding the sea; the events and incredible anxieties experienced in the going and coming of thirty cavaliers who returned for Pedro Calderón; and the fierceness of the Indians of Apalache, the capture and strange flight of their Cacique, and the fertility of that great province. It contains twenty-five chapters, which are as follows.

THE THIRD BOOK

*Of the History of Florida by the Inca tells of the departure of
the Spaniards from Apalache; the fine reception offered them
in four provinces; the hunger they suffered in some of the
uninhabited lands; the infinity of pearls and other grandeurs
and riches which they found in a temple; the generosities of
the Lady of Cofachiqui and of other caciques, lords of
vassals; a very bloody battle which the Indians under the
guise of friendship perpetrated upon the Spaniards; a mutiny
which certain Castilians discussed; the laws of the Indians
against adulteresses; and another very fierce battle
which was waged at night. It contains thirty-
nine chapters, which are as follows.*

THE FOURTH BOOK

Of the History of Florida by the Inca treats of the battle at the fort of Alibamo; the death of numerous Spaniards for want of salt; the arrival at Chisca and the crossing of the Great River; the solemn procession made by both the Indians and Spaniards to adore the cross and beseech God's mercy; the cruel war and pillage between Capaha and Casquin; the Spaniards' discovery of a means for making salt; the fierceness of the Tulas both in stature and in arms; and the comfortable winter which the Castilians passed in Utiangue. It contains sixteen chapters, which are as follows.

THE FIRST PART
OF THE FIFTH BOOK

Of the History of Florida by the Inca where mention is made of a Spaniard who remained among the Indians; the efforts exerted to regain him; a long journey of the Castilians across eight provinces; the enmity and cruel war between the Guachoyas and Anilcos; the lamentable death of the Governor Hernando de Soto and the two burials that his men gave him. It contains eight chapters, which are as follows.

THE SECOND PART
OF THE FIFTH BOOK

Of the History of Florida by the Inca tells of how the Spaniards decided to abandon Florida, and the long journey they made in an effort to do so; the unbearable hardship they suffered both in going and returning until they came once again to the Great River; the seven brigantines they constructed for the purpose of leaving that kingdom; the league of ten Caciques formed against the Spaniards and the secret information which they obtained concerning this league; the promises of General Anilco and the fine qualities of this man; a severe rise in the Great River; the efforts involved in making the brigantines; a challenge of General Anilco to the Cacique Guachoya and the reason for this challenge; and the punishment inflicted upon the messengers of the league.
It contains fifteen chapters, which
are as follows.

THE SIXTH BOOK

Of the History of Florida by the Inca contains an account of the selection of the captains for the navigation; the multitude of canoes opposing the Spaniards; the order and the manner of their fighting, which continued for eleven days without ceasing; the death of forty-eight Castilians because of the mad action of one of them; the return of the Indians to their homes; the arrival of the Spaniards at the sea and a skirmish they had with the people on the coast; the events of their fifty-five days of navigation before reaching Pánuco; the many quarrels which took place among them there, and the reason for these quarrels; the fine reception given them by the Imperial City of Mexico; the way in which they dispersed through different parts of the world; and the wanderings and hardships of Gómez Arias and Diego Maldonado, with which our history ends. It contains twenty-two chapters, which are as follows.

End of the Table of Contents

INTRODUCTION

ARLY in the month of April of the year fifteen hundred and thirty-eight, a fleet of tall-masted ships slid over the treacherous sand bar at San Lúcar de Barrameda and turned its prows toward a fabulous kingdom in the west which Ponce de León had poetically dubbed *La Florida* or the land of flowers. Hernando de Soto, swollen with the riches of Cajamarca and honored with a writ from his Caesarean Majesty, Charles the Melancholy, had set forth to explore and exploit the unlimited reaches of the North American continent. Never previously had there been assembled such an impressive array of ships, men, dogs and horses for any expedition to the Indies, and the hearts of these cavaliers burned with expectancy, for rumor persisted that this new kingdom would yield more gold, silver and precious gems than had all the lands of either Mexico or Peru. Moreover, for those fired with a messianic zeal, there was additional temptation since the pagan domains of the Indies offered unlimited possibilities for the enrichment of the Church as well as the Crown.

But once again the hardships of the great North American wilderness were to convert a resplendent dream of exploration and conquest into a doleful reality; De Soto's vast enterprise was destined for dismal failure. By the year fifteen hundred and forty-three, the deep forests and broad savannas of Florida were strewn with Spanish dead; the fever-ridden body of De Soto himself had been lowered to a watery sepulchre in the depths of the Mississippi; and the last of that gallant band of horses, the very sinew of the Spanish army, had been ignominiously sacrificed to facilitate the escape of those men fortunate enough to survive. In the end several hundred lean, naked, and half-starved stragglers fought their way down the Mississippi and on to the shores of Mexico while two faithful captains sailed the American coast from Nombre de Dios to the Land of the Cod in a vain search for their commander. And the Indians of Florida? Not as yet having received the waters of baptism, they went on, as in centuries past, worshipping the sun and the moon.

Survivors of the De Soto expedition were quick to tell their story in whatever parts of the world they happened to land, and their tales must soon have become incorporated into the folk culture of Spain and Portugal as well as all of the Spanish speaking regions of the newly discovered Indies. To some of these same eyewitnesses is to be traced the bulk of our present day knowledge of a tremendously important phase of early American history. We have, for instance, the day-by-day record of Luis Hernández de Biedma, who served as factor to the expedition, and the invaluable diary of Rodrigo Ranjel, who traveled as De Soto's official secretary. Again, one of the Portuguese contingent, who preferred to be known to his contemporaries and to posterity simply as "A Fidalgo of Elvas," published as early as 1557 what he described as "A true relation of the vicissitudes attending the Governor Don Hernando de Soto and some nobles of Portugal in the discovery of the province of Florida." But the account which is of specific interest to us in this study is that poured by an anonymous Spanish cavalier into the ears of a Peruvian mestizo who bore the baptismal name of Gómez Suárez de Figueroa. This story, supplemented by excerpts from the manuscripts of two additional eyewitnesses, Juan Coles and Alonso de Carmona, is known to us today as *The Florida of the Inca,* and its Peruvian compiler has identified himself as the Inca, Garcilaso de la Vega, a name which he apparently assumed in his more mature years.

Garcilaso, from time to time both in Peru and in Spain, encountered men who had participated in De Soto's expedition, but on several occasions he declares that the material for *The Florida* was derived solely from the three above mentioned sources. The account of Alonso de Carmona, he tells us, was received from the author himself, and that of Juan Coles he found in a somewhat battered condition at the establishment of a printer in Cordova. But the bulk of his facts came to him orally from the aforementioned noble Spaniard, whom he eventually cornered in Las Posadas. The identity of this man he for some reason leaves shrouded in mystery; nevertheless there is sufficient evidence for speculation, and historians in general have concluded that he was none other than Gonzalo Silvestre, a native of Herrera de Alcántara, whose fine horsemanship and exceptional boldness displayed as he gallops through the pages of *The Florida* threaten at times to eclipse the glory of the Adelantado himself.

Strong reasons for believing that Silvestre occupied this important role are to be seen in the text of *The Florida.* For here many of his more trivial words and conversations are quoted, and here we find anecdotes concerning him which only he would have been likely to consider of sufficient importance to remember. Moreover, he fits comparatively well into the description which the Inca has offered of his source, and, whereas he is ignored by other commentators, his is one of the names most frequently encountered in *The Florida.* But more conclusive evidence, it would seem, is to be found in the movements of this man after the conquest and in his subsequent association with Garcilaso himself. For when the wretched and disgruntled survivors of the expedition began to disperse, Silvestre found his way down into Peru and became embroiled in the same civil wars which occupied so much of the attention of Garcilaso's own father. Then when some years later he refused to obey the Viceroy's order to settle down and espouse one of the ladies of questionable virtue whom the King had sent out for the pleasure and comfort of his subjects, the old conquistador was shipped back to Spain, where at Las Posadas, according to records, he had some dealings with the future author of *The Florida.* Garcilaso himself tells of Silvestre's return to Spain, and he several times acknowledges having received from this man personally information which he incorporated into his history of Peru. Since this history and *The Florida* were in the process of composition simultaneously, we can suppose with some confidence that the old warrior was relating the story of De Soto's struggle through North America at the same time he was telling of the turmoil in Peru.

But of more interest to us than this spinner of tales is the man who took these tales and wove them into the fabric of early American history. For in the Inca, Garcilaso de la Vega, we have a chronicler who, because of the unusual circumstances of his birth and early environment as well as the unique associations he enjoyed through a long life, was able to give a sympathetic view of the De Soto story from several levels: first, from that of the invading Spaniard who had set forth upon an adventure or a crusade for God, the Crown, and incidentally, Mammon; second, from that of the Indian who found himself confronted with strange white men, demanding at the point of the sword that he shift his way of life, his faith, and his allegiance; and finally, from that of the scholar and historian touched with a zeal to see the culture and faith of old Spain bestowed upon the pagan realms of the far-flung Indies.

The Inca, Garcilaso de la Vega, who, as stated, bore the baptismal name of Gómez Suárez de Figueroa, was born at Cuzco on the twelfth of April in the year fifteen hundred and thirty-nine. He was the only son of a "second" conquistador, Don Sebastián Garcilaso de la Vega Vargas, and an Indian princess, Chimpa Ocllo, a niece of Huayna Capac, last of the legitimate rulers of the Inca empire. Hence there flowed through the veins of this mestizo not only the blood of the great Spanish lords of Sierrabrava and Feria, but also that of pagan emperors who from remote antiquity had held sway over the Children of the Sun.

Don Sebastián had wandered into Peru with the lusty and covetous band of Pedro de Alvarado, and then, joining forces with Francisco Pizarro, he had launched into a career which was to keep him embroiled for much of the remainder of his life in the turbulent civil wars and rebellions of the land. It was possibly while a prisoner of Diego de Almagro at Cuzco that he first formed his liaison with the native girl who was to become the mother of the author of *The Florida.* This union was destined never to receive the sanction of the Church, for marriage between conquistadors and Indian maidens was not usual and concubinage was respectable. Nevertheless, either because of a true conversion to the Faith or because a certain delicacy of taste among cavaliers dictated such procedure, Chimpa Ocllo did receive the waters of baptism and was christened Isabel.

After the defeat of Almagro, Don Sebastián received the bounty of his chieftain, which consisted, among other things, of extensive and productive farms and, in addition, a large house at Cuzco. During the early childhood of Garcilaso, this house was presided over by his mother, and here under her care and amid the ruins of the fast-fading Inca empire, he passed one of the most significant periods of his entire life. For Chimpa Ocllo, though a heretic among her people, was visited regularly by numbers of her kinsmen, who filled the ears of the little mestizo with the ancient lore of Peru. Hence at an early age he began to absorb information which was to bring him renown as an outstanding authority on the Inca civilization. Moreover, he began to develop a pride and sympathy which was to extend to all of the Indians of the New World, a warmth of feeling which he continued to manifest in his writing and his course of action throughout his life. Repeatedly in *The Florida* he proclaims that he is a Peruvian and furthermore that he is an Indian, and though he at times does so modestly, his modesty is feigned. And he would have us feel that the Indian, given an equal chance, would not prove himself inferior physically, mentally, or spiritually. In scene after scene, he reminds us that the Spaniard, when deprived of his horse and his armor, was but a poor match for his native antagonist; once in a burst of ecstasy over the intellectual possibilities of his Indian and mestizo companions, he pictures his Latin master, the good Canon of Cuzco, as yearning to see a dozen of these young

Peruvians exposed to the academic wonders of Salamanca; and he makes as the basis of his principal plea in *The Florida* the fact that the mind of the Indian is ready and competent to receive and absorb the cultural and spiritual splendors of Christianity. Moreover, when in his later years he laid aside his baptismal name to take that of a renowned ancestor, he did not become simply Garcilaso de la Vega, but Garcilaso de la Vega, el Inca.

On the other hand, Garcilaso's excessive pride in his Indian background was mingled strangely and almost paradoxically with a similar pride in the noble blood and daring achievements of his father's people. From Don Sebastián and other kinsmen he gleaned reports of what Spaniards had accomplished in all parts of the world, and within the ranks of his own ancestors he found names which had become fixed in the heroic legends of old Spain. Such, for instance, was that of Garcí Pérez de Vargas, who in 1348 had helped Ferdinand the Holy wrest Seville from the Moors and thus came to have his name spelled upon the walls of the ancient city and within the poetry of the land as well. Then there was an early Garcí Lasso who brought just retribution to a pagan upon the plains of Granada when that dastard appeared with an Ave Maria draped conspicuously across the rump of his steed. This spectacular incident had added a Hail Mary to the family escutcheon and accounts for the Vega in the Lasso name. But much of Garcilaso's pride sprang from a continuous panorama of bold achievements which was unfolding before his youthful eyes, for both his father and an uncle, Don Juan de Vargas, were fighting the battles of Peru, and he frequently found himself sharing the glories and miseries of their victories and defeats. Once he pictures himself as a very small boy riding by his father's side in a triumphal procession to Cuzco. But again, he tells of a time when he and his mother huddled within the great house at Cuzco while its walls resounded to the thud of enemy shells; and in another instance he speaks of a hairbreadth escape over house tops and down narrow streets when he himself helped his father elude the forces of Francisco Hernández Girón.

He was trained in the saddle, he tells us modestly, to the detriment of his nominatives, and he knew personally those men whose swords were hewing the destiny of Peru, counting among his playmates some of their very sons.

Equal in significance to what this boy actually saw and experienced in the travail of his land are the contacts which he made, undoubtedly through his father and uncle, with those adventurers who wandered into Peru from other regions of the Indies, bringing with them prodigious stories of giants and pygmies, monsters, Amazonian women, gold, silver, pearls, and far-away realms without limit. For among these tale bearers were men who had followed Lucas Vázquez de Ayllón and Hernando de Soto through the North American wilderness. Garcilaso names some of these men and we can be sure that in their number was the cavalier who later was to prove such a rich source of information at Las Posadas.

Don Sebastián appears to have veered with the wind in his loyalties, attaching himself usually to those forces which he felt were to his best advantage; but in the main his sympathies lay with the King's regents and he consequently was able to pass his riper years in comparative wealth, peace and power. Some time before he was to die, he was named Corregidor of Cuzco and while occupying this position was able to ennoble himself with a number of beneficent acts. Meanwhile, however, his domestic affairs had shifted, for when new laws for the Indies made it necessary for him to seek a more conventional union, he married Doña Luisa Martel de los Ríos, a creole from Panama, and Chimpa Ocllo became the legitimate bride of Juan del Pedroche, a merchant of sorts, whom her son never saw fit to mention.

With the death of his father in 1559 Garcilaso began to make plans to sail for Spain. Some say that his decision had been instigated by Don Sebastián himself, who had provided for the journey in his will; and others have suggested that it was an idea of Philip II who was beginning to fear the rising influence of this young mestizo among the Children of the Sun. Be that as it may, Garcilaso no doubt felt a natural yearning to witness the splendors of the Spanish court; and the very modest circumstances in which he now found himself moved him to seek substantial recognition for his father's services to the Crown. And so it was that in 1560, when scarcely twenty years of age, he gave his mother the annuities from a farm in exchange for a few pesos of gold and set out for Europe, going first to Lisbon and Seville, and then to Estremadura, the land of his father's people.

Don Sebastián had left influential friends and relatives in Spain who could come to the aid of his mestizo son. A brother, Alonso de Vargas y Figueroa, from whom Garcilaso later was to inherit comfortable annuities, had fought at the side of Charles V throughout Europe and on to the shores of Africa; and the head of his mother's family, the Duke of Feria, had been of sufficient importance to accompany Philip II to England, where he, like the King, obtained an English bride. And of those who came to his aid, Garcilaso makes particular mention of Alonso Fernández de Córdoba y Figueroa, Marquis of Priego, and Francisco de Córdoba, son of the Count of Alcaudete. One is not surprised therefore to find him at Madrid in 1561 preparing to lay his petition before the King and his Council. But the spectacle of a mestizo at court must have been novel and the outcome of his mission does not lead us to believe that he was received with warm sympathy. Here, we are told, he fell in with Hernando Pizarro and Bartolomé de las Casas, but by this time Pizarro was old and an object of pity, and Las Casas, on learning that Garcilaso was not a Mexican, treated him with coolness. Furthermore, the petition to the Council of the Indies, though at first favored, was, after several years, denied, the councilors having been apprised of certain discrepancies in Don Sebastián's loyalties at the battle of Huarina. Garcilaso's disappointment was no doubt keen, for soon after we find him contemplating a return to Peru.

And now there was to come a short interlude in the life of the Inca which is partially shrouded in mystery and which marks his last efforts to share in the affairs of the Crown. He entered the army. It may be that he was attempting to strengthen his case with the Council, or that he was simply seeking a livelihood in an activity which had occupied the attention of many of his forebears and which was considered requisite to the education of a man of station. And apropos of the latter, it is interesting to note that during this interlude he possibly passed some time in Italy, that "Utopia of irregularity," whose culture was to impregnate the cultures of France, England and Spain. Here he could have acquired the knowledge of Tuscan needed to translate León Hebreo, and here he could have developed his taste for the *novellieri* and other forms of Italianism which show a marked influence upon his literary style. Be that as it may, he was again in Spain in 1568, for when the Moriscos of Alpujarras were forced into rebellion by the obstinacy of the King, Garcilaso took part in their subjugation, assuming two commands under Philip II and two under his brother, Don Juan of Austria. Thus this half-Indian descendant of the famed Garcí Lasso found himself, like his progenitor, fighting the Moors in the vicinity of Granada, and one wonders if it were not here that he resolved to be known as the Inca of the Vega.

Garcilaso had served the King well, but he was to realize even more acutely that merit did not always receive its just reward in the high councils of Spain. At one point in his *Comentarios* he declares that because of the old reproach against his father he was unable to obtain satisfactory recognition for his own military service and as a result left the army so naked and impoverished that he dared not appear again at Court. Even lands of his mother which had escheated to the Crown were beyond recovery. His experience during the past few years had brought disillusionment and resignation, and when urged by friends to present another petition to the Council under more auspicious circumstances, he declined to make the effort. The extent to which he felt his failure is to be detected in several subtle barbs in *The Florida* which he obviously is directing at Philip II and the Council of the Indies; and of some interest in this connection is the fact that whereas the first production of his pen carries dedications to the King, his later writings are directed either to Portuguese princes or to the Queen of Heaven.

During his first decade in Spain, the Inca had spent some time in Seville perfecting his Latin with Pedro Sánchez de Herrera and arranging for the reburial of his father's remains in the old church of San Isidoro of that city. On leaving the army, however, he had retired to Cordova, where in 1671 he received news of the death of his mother. But he could have felt no impulse to remove the remains of this woman to Spain as he had done in the case of his father, for though Chimpa Ocllo as the years rolled by had adopted more and more the habits and the character of the Spaniard, even signing her will as Isabel Suárez, she was ever to her son a symbol of the vanishing glories of the Inca empire. Only through the adoption of the Christian Faith, he declares, had she made herself more noble than she already was as a daughter of the earliest monarchs of Peru. It takes but little reasoning, therefore, to understand Garcilaso's reluctance to discuss her marriage to a "son of nobody" in the Indies.

The retirement to Cordova was not accompanied by the penury and solitude which Garcilaso's words lead us to believe he was to experience, for he spoke figuratively and comparatively. This old Moorish stronghold was still the busy haunt of all types of men, and in addition to what he already possessed, Garcilaso was to inherit eventually from the estate of his father's brother, Alonso de Vargas, who resided at Montilla. There were to be some inconveniences in collecting annuities, particularly from the Marquis of Priego, who never permitted monetary problems to destroy a warm friendship, but Garcilaso in the meantime was able to ease his economic situation with stipends which he received as major-domo of the Hospital of the Immaculate Conception. Nevertheless the retirement to Cordova did mark his retreat from the world and his entrance into the life of the scholar and religious. For here he began to devote much time to pious duties, forming fast friendships with the Jesuits as well as various other ecclesiastics, and eventually assuming the austere habit of the cleric. And here also he began to apply himself more and more to his literary activities, writing feverishly, in what he thought was a race with death, in order to bring to a conclusion his monumental record of the accomplishments of Spaniards, Indians, mestizos, and creoles in the Indies. And when several years before his death, he completed the final lines of the last thing he was to write, he closed this work significantly with an "Amen, Jesus, a hundred thousand times, Jesus."

Possibly the literary production for which Garcilaso is best known is the book which he concluded last; i.e., the *Comentarios Reales,* the second part of which is usually referred to as the *Historia General del Perú.* In its two parts, this book treats of the history of Peru from the origin of the Inca empire through the conquest and subjugation of that kingdom by the Spaniards. Garcilaso's initial literary essay, however, was a work of a different nature, a translation from the Tuscan of *The Dialogues of Love* by Judas Abrabanel, who used the pseudonym of León Hebreo. This romantic discourse on a popular subject had been several times translated by Spaniards, and was of sufficient importance to bring the condemnation of the Holy Office as well as the mockery of Cervantes. The only additional work, other than *The Florida,* which Garcilaso is known to have written is the *Relación de la Descendencia de Garcí Pérez de Vargas,* an account, as is manifest, of one branch of his father's distinguished family.

In the year 1616, on the twenty-second day of April, the same month which had witnessed his birth, the author of *The Florida* made his confessions and departed this life. His body was laid within the great cathedral at Cordova, in the Chapel of the Souls of Purgatory, which he some time previously had purchased and prepared for his sepulchre. In his last testament he had provided funds for the upkeep of the chapel, and, among other things, annuities for one Diego de Vargas, a man who came eventually to serve as its sacristan. It is of some significance that Garcilaso throughout his life apparently made no effort to acknowledge the true identity of this man, because he too, though the natural son of a serving girl at Montilla, bore in his veins the blood of high lords of Spain as well as that of ancient Peruvian potentates. For records of the ecclesiastical *Cabildo* at Cordova have revealed that Diego de Vargas was the Inca's own son.

Washington Irving, in his *Knickerbocker History of New York* has humorously accused the romantic historians of feeling that they can color both characters and events to suit their fancy so long as they do not tamper with certain incontrovertible facts. And this tendency, although not always intentional, is especially evident in *The Florida* since it is a history which has been twice processed, first by the narrator and then by the scribe. For Silvestre was glancing nostalgically back over the years, and Garcilaso, in spite of his insistence that his role was no more than that of an amanuensis, was tinting the picture with his personality, his erudition, and a well-defined literary style. Therefore, in searching for the truth of history in *The Florida,* we should be mindful of the character of all sources, and we especially should not lose sight of certain obvious facts concerning the man who gave this story its final form. First, his excessive pride in the two races which contributed to his being, made him overzealous about depicting both the Spaniard and the Indian in a splendid and equally valiant light. Second, he wrote with a burning purpose. As yet the vast wilderness of North America remained uncolonized and un-Christianized, and he sought to persuade Spain that it was her duty, as the one Catholic nation uncontaminated by the heresies of Luther, to bring the true Faith to the pagans of Florida and while doing so to enrich her domains with some of the most extensive and productive lands in the Indies. Third, though at times chiding explorers and conquerors for their omissions and procrastinations, he felt a genuine urge to sing the glory of their deeds, often in such a way as to disclose that the merits of these men exceeded the recognition they received from the Crown. And finally, Garcilaso, as an historian, was a product of the thought and the literature of the Spanish Renaissance. His was an age when fact was likely to be confused with fiction and serious chroniclers were prone to give credence to the marvelous. Moreover, cavaliers were well-versed in the chivalric cycles and frequently sought to imitate in reality the role of some legendary hero. Hence a correct picture of these adventurers sometimes required that they be presented in a gilded frame.

A rather trustworthy key to the sources of Garcilaso's erudition and literary style is to be found in an inventory of the books with which he surrounded himself at Cordova. Here among Bibles, breviaries, holy treatises, moral reflections and all the necessary equipment for a man of piety, one may see long lists of Greek and Roman classics, the poetry and prose of the Italian Renaissance, philosophies, histories both ancient and modern, including the works of outstanding figures on the Indies, contemporary Spanish writers, books on equitation and military science, and many other titles which one would expect to find in the library of a sixteenth-century scholar. We do not have to look far to discover patterns and sources for Garcilaso's Byzantine and Italianesque scenes, the classical speeches and harangues of his Indians, his historical references, and the many maxims and proverbs, which, when touched with the art of the mestizo, add such charm to his book. But strangely and disappointingly, this library seems not to have yielded a single tome of Miguel de Cervantes, and though rich in the names of the Italian *novellieri* and even possessed of a manual of chivalry, it apparently was barren of the *libros de caballería*. Furthermore, with the possible exception of the fact that *The Florida* abounds in such incidents as Cervantes was burlesquing and the additional fact that Garcilaso a number of times would appear to be depicting chivalric scenes with his tongue in his cheek, we can find no trace of his having known this man who, in the same year that *The Florida* was published, was to administer the *coup de grâce* to the books of chivalry. On the other hand, we do know that at an early age Garcilaso had been exposed to these so-called "lying histories"; for not only does he tell us so, somewhat penitently, but he records that his godfather at confirmation was none other than Diego de Silva, son of Feliciano de Silva, whose *Don Florisel de Niquea* was to equal the *Amadís de Gaula* in its power to stimulate chivalric tastes.

Because of the presence of so much of the romantic in Garcilaso's account, many historians, while admitting its essentiality to a study of De Soto's expedition, have been careful to warn readers to regard it with suspicion, admonishing them to beware of the poetic passages and probe deep for the truth—an admonition which it of course is wise to heed even in the case of many better known and more generally recognized historical classics. And it would appear that this suspicion has blinded some to the true worth of *The Florida*. For while adhering in general to what others have reported of geography and events, it reflects, in its very romanticism, the true heart and soul of those cavaliers who in imitation of Amadís, Palmerín, or Roland set forth to brave unknown perils and explore mystic and pagan lands. Thus in *The Florida,* which represents the most lengthy of the early accounts of De Soto's expedition, we find not only innumerable trustworthy details of a vast area of what is now the United States, but in addition a most accurate picture of the spirit and temper of the age which witnessed the discovery of these lands. Moreover, laying aside its value as a chronicle, we still may see in its pages a splendid specimen of sixteenth-century literary art. And so it is that this first truly American work, along with the well-known *Comentarios Reales,* has won for Garcilaso the distinction of being the first American to attain pre-eminence in literature.

THE INCA'S DEDICATION

To the Very Excellent Señor Don Theodosio of Portugal, Duke of Braganza and of Barcelos, etc.

URING my childhood, Most Serene Prince, both my father and his kinsmen told me of the heroic virtues and magnanimous deeds of the kings and princes of glorious memory who were Your Excellency's forebears, and of the military prowess of the nobility of this celebrated kingdom of Portugal. Then later in the course of my life I read of the accomplishments of the Lusitanians, not only in Spain but in Africa and in the great India to the east; of the long and amazing voyages and hardships which these men suffered both in their conquests and in the dissemination of the Holy Gospel; and of the magnificent provisions that their kings and princes made for carrying out these various undertakings. In consequence, I always felt a desire to serve the people and the sovereigns of your realm. This desire later developed into a feeling of obligation, for on coming to Spain from my native Peru, the first places I visited were the Portuguese islands of Fayal and Tercera, and the imperial city of Lisbon. The royal ministers and inhabitants of that city as well as the people of the islands were most kind and charitable, offering me the finest reception and welcoming me as if I had been a native son. But not wishing to tire Your Excellency, I shall refrain from telling of the particular favors bestowed upon me by these people, other than to say that one of them eventually was to save me from death.

Being then on the one hand so indebted and on the other so consumed with admiration, I have been ignorant as to how I might repay my obligation and show my esteem unless it were by committing the audacity of offering and dedicating my history to Your Excellency. For an Indian this is a presumption, but a presumption which has been inspired no little by the deeds related in my account of the native Portuguese cavalier hildalgos who went on the conquest of the great Florida; for it is right that the acts of these men be appropriately and worthily used and dedicated, so that under the protection of Your Excellency they may be remembered, esteemed, and honored as they deserve.

I beseech Your Excellency, therefore, to deign to accept this small service with the affability and approbation consistent with your royal blood, and to look favorably upon the desire I have always had and still have of seeing my name placed among those of the subjects of Your Excellency's royal household. Should you grant me this favor, as I trust you will, I shall be more than humored in my fondness, and I shall at the same time be able to repay an obligation to the natives of this most Christian kingdom, for through Your Excellency's generosity I shall become as one of them. May Our Lord preserve Your Excellency for many happy years as a refuge and protection for the poor and needy. Amen.

The Inca Garcilaso de la Vega.

THE INCA'S PREFACE

ONVERSING over a long period of time and in different places with a great and noble friend of mine who accompanied this expedition to Florida, and hearing him recount the numerous very illustrious deeds that both Spaniards and Indians performed in the process of the conquest, I became convinced that when such heroic actions as these had been performed in this world, it was unworthy and regrettable that they should remain in perpetual oblivion. Feeling myself therefore under obligation to two races, since I am the son of a Spanish father and an Indian mother, I many times urged this cavalier to record the details of the expedition, using me as his amanuensis. And although it was the desire of us both to accomplish the task, we were prevented from doing so by such circumstances as that of my going to war and the long absences which occurred between us. Thus more than twenty years elapsed. But as time passed, my desire to preserve this story increased, and I began to fear more and more that if something should happen to either of us, our whole project would vanish. For were I to die, this man would have no one to encourage him or serve as his scribe; and on the other hand, were I to lose him, I should be ignorant as to whom I might turn for the facts that he was able to provide. I determined therefore to overcome the obstacles and delays then existing by simply abandoning the position and advantages I enjoyed in the town where I was then living and moving to where he resided. Here we devoted ourselves most carefully and industriously to recording all that had happened from

the beginning to the end of the expedition. And this we did, not alone for the honor and renown of the Spanish nation, which has accomplished such great things in the New World, but no less for that of the Indians who are revealed within our story, for they too appear worthy of the same praise.

In addition to the brave deeds performed and the hardships suffered by the Christians both individually and generally, and the notable things discovered among the Indians, we present in this history a description of the many extensive provinces found throughout the great kingdom of Florida by the Governor and Adelantado Hernando de Soto and the numerous other cavaliers who hailed from Estremadura, Portugal, Andalusia, Castile, and all the rest of the lands of Spain. Our purpose in offering this description has been to encourage Spain to make an effort to acquire and populate this kingdom (now that its unsavory reputation for being sterile and swampy, as it is along the coast, has been erased) even if, without the principal idea of augmenting the Holy Catholic Faith, she should carry forward the project for the sole purpose of establishing colonies to which she might send her sons to reside just as the ancient Romans did when there was no longer space in their native land. For Florida is fertile and abundant in all things necessary to human life, and with the seed and livestock that can be sent there from Spain and other places, it can be made much more productive than it is in its natural state. As will be seen in the course of our history, it is a region well adapted to such things.

In recording the details of this history I have taken the greatest care to present them chronologically and accurately. And since my principal purpose is to bring about the acquisition of Florida through the statements I make concerning it, I have attempted to elicit from the person who provided me with this record all that he saw on the expedition. He was a noble hildalgo and as such prided himself on speaking the truth in all matters. Many times I saw the Royal Council of the Indies call upon him as a man worthy of confidence to verify acts that had occurred in the expedition to Florida as well as in other expeditions in which he had served. He was a very fine soldier, performing frequently as a leader; and since he participated in each of the events of the conquest, he was able to supply me with complete details of the history as they occurred. There are people who would brand as cowards and liars those men who give a good description of specific deeds that have occurred in battles in which they themselves have participated. These people customarily inquire as to how it is that such men could have seen everything in a battle if they were fighting in it, or how they could have fought if they were occupied in watching, since two such activities as watching and fighting cannot well be carried on simultaneously. And if someone should now ask such a question, my answer is that it was a common custom among these soldiers, as it is in all of the conflicts of the world, to relate the most notable events of a battle afterward in the presence of the general and the other officers. And often when some captain or soldier told of a very brave deed which was difficult to believe, those who heard him went out to see what actually had been done and to verify the report with their own eyes. It was in this manner that my author was able to obtain all of the information that he gave me to write down; and the many questions which I put to him repeatedly concerning the details and qualities of that land helped him no little to recall these facts to mind.

But in addition to the authority of my author, I have the sworn testimony of two other soldiers who were on the same expedition, and who consequently were eyewitnesses. One of these men is Alonso de Carmona, a native of the village of Priego. After having wandered through Florida during the six years of this expedition and later for many years in Peru, this man returned to the land of his birth, where he wrote of these two peregrinations, as he called them, simply for the pleasure he derived from recollecting his previous experiences. Unaware that I was engaged in writing this history, he sent me both accounts of his travels to examine, and I was much pleased with them, for his record of the expedition to Florida, although very brief and without order as to time and events and with a few exceptions without names of provinces, does tell, by skipping from one place to another, the most notable events of our history.

The second soldier was Juan Coles, a native of the village of Zafra. This man wrote another brief and disorganized account of the expedition, and he too related the most valiant things that occurred. His details he set down at the request of Friar Pedro Aguado, a Provincial of a district in the Indies called Santa Fe and one of the brotherhood of the Seraphic Father San Francisco. In his desire to serve the Catholic king, Philip II, this friar had gathered many diverse accounts from trustworthy people concerning the discoveries they had seen accomplished in the New World, and he had made a particular collection of stories about the first exploration of the Indies, as they call all of the Windward Islands, Vera Cruz, Tierra-Firme, Darien, and other provinces of those regions. But leaving his stories in the hands of a printer in Cordova, he had hastened to perform other duties in the service of his ecclesiastical order, thus abandoning his records, which still were not in a proper form for printing.

I saw these records. They had been very badly treated and were half-consumed by moths and rats. They consisted of more than a ream of paper and were set down in separate notebooks just as each author had written them. Among them I found, only a short time after Alonso de Carmona had sent me his story, the account which I have said Juan Coles left. It is a fact that I had already completed my history, but when I discovered that these two eyewitnesses were so in accord with what I had written, I felt it wise, on rewriting, to name them both in their respective places and in many instances to quote their words verbatim. For it was my opinion that by thus presenting two witnesses who confirmed the statements of my own author, I would show that all three accounts were really one and the same.

The truth is that except in the beginning, these men observe no chronological sequences and no order of events in what they relate.

Some occurrences they place before their proper time, and others they place after. Again, they name only a few of the provinces, and these they name without continuity. They simply tell the outstanding things that they saw as they remembered them. Nevertheless, the events which they do mention, when compared with those of my own history, are seen to be the same, although they do relate some things with greater awe and exaggeration than I, as will be seen in the passages quoted from them. The inadvertencies of these men must have sprung from the fact that they were not writing with any intention of publication. Such at least was true in the case of Alonso de Carmona, for he wished no more than that his kinsmen and neighbors read of the things he had seen in the New World. Thus it was that he sent his accounts to me as an acquaintance who had been born in the Indies so that I too might peruse them. The reason for Juan Coles' not arranging his material in an historical manner must have been also that he did not want to bother with putting it in order, since it was not to be published in his name. He told what he remembered more as an eyewitness than as the author of the work, believing that the Provincial Father who had asked for the story would arrange it suitably for printing. Thus his account is composed in a legal style, so that it appears that another person wrote what he told; for sometimes he says "this witness states this and this," and at other times he says "this person declared that he saw such and such a thing." Yet, on still other occasions, he speaks as if he himself had written the passage, saying "we saw this and we did this, etc." Both accounts are very short. The one of Juan Coles consists of no more than ten pages of a very diffuse and legal style of handwriting; whereas that of Alonso de Carmona contains eight and a half pages written in a very compact hand.

Some of the things that these men tell, although they merit recording, I have not included in my history. Such for instance is the statement of Juan Coles that while traveling about with some other footsoldiers (no doubt without the General's order) he found a temple which housed an idol adorned with many pearls and seed pearls and holding in its mouth a precious red stone a half-foot long and as thick as a thumb, and that he took this stone without anyone's seeing him, etc. This and similar stories I have not mentioned because of not knowing in what province they took place; for, in the matter of naming the lands through which they passed, both of these men, as I have already stated, were very lax, and Juan Coles was especially so. In conclusion I would say that these two soldiers recorded none of the incidents I mention other than those in which they themselves are included, but the incidents that they did tell are outstanding, and I am happy to refer to them in their proper places so as to be able to claim that I have based my history upon the statements of three authorities whose facts are in agreement.[1]

In addition to the three aforementioned accounts, I have in my support a great favor bestowed upon me in writing by a chronicler[2] of the Catholic Majesty, who among other things has the following to say: "I have compared your history with an account in my possession, the one comprising the statements made to Don Antonio de Mendoza in Mexico by the survivors among the followers of that excellent Castilian who entered Florida; and I find that your history is true and conforms to the said account, etc."

[1] The accusation has been made (see *Proemio* of the 1723 edition of *The Florida*) that Garcilaso followed the *Relaçam Verdadeira* published by the anonymous "Gentleman of Elvas" at Evora in 1557, or at least tried to bring his account into accord with that of the Portuguese. Since the Elvas story had been published so early, and since the sources of the *Florida* are obscure, such an assumption is within the realm of possibility, but it seems highly improbable in the light of the Inca's pride in his sources, and for that matter his expressed desire to honor the Lusitanians. It appears more probable that had Garcilaso been acquainted with the Elvas narrative, he would have used it openly and boasted of having drawn his material from four authorities instead of three.

[2] This chronicler, according to Edward Gaylord Bourne, *Narratives of the Career of Hernando de Soto* (New York: 1922), I, x–xi, was no doubt Antonio de Herrera, who testified to his approval of Garcilaso's work by making it the basis of his own account of De Soto in his *Historia General de las Indias*. Bourne adds that Herrera may have had another brief source and "did not care to acknowledge the extent to which he had exploited Garcilaso's work, submitted in a friendly way." It could be, however, that the same man who gave the Inca his material had given a similar report to Antonio de Mendoza some forty-odd years earlier.

This is sufficient evidence for one to believe that I do not record fictions, and indeed it would be unlawful for me to do so since my history must be presented to the entire Spanish republic, which would have reason to be provoked with me should I give a dishonest and false report. Neither would I fail to displease gravely the Eternal Majesty (who is the one we should fear most), if with the idea of inciting and persuading Spaniards by my history to acquire the land of Florida for the augmentation of Our Holy Catholic Faith, I should deceive with fictions and falsehoods those of them who might wish to employ their property and life in such an undertaking. For indeed, to tell the whole truth, I have been moved to labor and to record this history solely by a desire to see Christianity extended to that land which is so broad and so long; and I neither aspire nor hope for temporal favors in recompense for my lengthy toil since I long ago lost faith in aspirations and despaired of hopes because of the inconsistency of my fate.

Yet examining my lot dispassionately, I ought to be very grateful to Fortune for having treated me so ill; for had it shared its wealth and its favors with me copiously, perhaps I would have gone down other roads and paths that would have led me to worse precipices or destroyed me altogether on that great sea with its waves and storms, as almost always it is accustomed to destroy those whom it has favored and elevated into the lofty positions of the world. But since I have experienced the disfavors and the persecutions of fortune, I have been forced to retire from this world and to conceal myself in the haven and shelter of the disillusioned, which are the corners of solitude and poverty. Here consoled and content with the paucity of my scanty possessions, I live a quiet and peaceful life (thanks to the King of Kings and Lord of Lords) more envied by the rich than envious of them.

In this serene existence, to avoid an idleness more wearisome than labor and to obtain greater peace of mind than wealth can bring, I have engaged in other projects and ambitions, for instance the translating of the three *Dialogues of Love* by León Hebreo.[3] After publishing these translations, I occupied myself with writing this present history; and with the same pleasure I am fabricating, forging, and polishing a history of Peru,[4] wherein I shall tell of the origin of the Inca kings, their ancient customs, their idolatry and conquests, and their laws and order of government both in peace and war. And now with God's help, I have almost reached the end of all this. There have been obstacles and not small ones, but still I value my labor more highly than the gifts Fortune might have bestowed upon me, even though it had treated me most favorably and propitiously; for I aspire to attain another and better end, and I trust in God that my works will bring me more honor and greater renown than I would have gained from the entailed estate that Lady Fortune might have bequeathed me from her store of worldly goods. Thus I am rather a debtor than a creditor of Fortune, and as such I give her many thanks; for in spite of herself she is now forced by divine clemency to permit me to offer this history to the entire world.

My history is compiled in six books, each of which corresponds to one of the six years of the expedition. Since there were more oc-

[3] Garcilaso's translation was published at Madrid in 1590. It is of some interest to note that Cervantes, in his "Author's Prologue" to *Don Quixote*, ridicules those writers who turned to Judas Abrabanel (León Hebreo) for information on the subject of love, and that the Holy Office in an effort to stem the current enthusiasm for romance placed the work on the Index. See Julia Fitzmaurice-Kelly, *El Inca Garcilaso de la Vega* (Oxford: 1921), p. 35; also *"Prólogo a los Indios, Mestizos y Criollos de los Reynos y Provincias del grande y riquísimo Imperio del Perú,"* attached to Part II of Garcilaso's *Comentarios Reales,* a description of which will be found in note 4, below.

[4] This history, which was published in two parts, is commonly known as the *Comentarios Reales.* The first part was published at Lisbon in 1609 under the title *Primera Parte de Los Comentarios Reales.* The printing of the second part was completed in Cordova on November 17, 1616, and some copies were released within the year. There was a suspension of publication, however, apparently because of economic difficulties, and as a result most copies of the second part bear the date 1617. Although the second part carried the running head *La Segunda Parte de los Comentarios Reales* the title pages of both the 1616 and 1617 issues read *Historia General del Perú.* See Aurelio Miró Quesada y Sosa, *El Inca Garcilaso* (Madrid: 1948), pp. 209–210.

currences worthy of mention in the second than in any other year, it seemed wise to divide the second book into two sections so that no one part of the history would be too long and consequently tiring to the eyes. In this way each of these sections would be in proportion to the other books, yet the events of this year still would form only one complete book. A division was made also in the fifth book in order to separate the deeds of the Governor and Adelantado Hernando de Soto from those of Luis de Moscoso de Alvarado, who succeeded him in executive power. Thus in the first section of the fifth book, the narrative proceeds as far as the death and the two burials of Hernando de Soto; and then in the second section it treats of those things which the Governor's successor did and ordered to be done after his death until the end of the expedition, which came in the sixth year.

I plead now that this account be received in the same spirit as I present it, and that I be pardoned its errors because I am an Indian. For since we Indians are a people who are ignorant and uninstructed in the arts and sciences, it seems ungenerous to judge our deeds and utterances strictly in accordance with the precepts of those subjects which we have not learned. We should be accepted as we are. And although I may not deserve such esteem, it would be a noble and magnanimous idea to carry this merciful consideration still further and to honor in me all of the mestizo Indians and the creoles of Peru, so that seeing a novice of their own race receive the favor and grace of the wise and learned, they would be encouraged to make advancements with similar ideas drawn from their own uncultivated mental resources. I trust therefore that the noble in understanding and the liberal in spirit will offer their favor most generously and approvingly to both my people and myself, for my desire and willingness to serve them (as my poor works, both past and present reveal, and as my future works will show) well deserve their consideration. Our Father, etc.

The
FLORIDA
of
THE INCA

THE

FIRST

BOOK

Of the History of Florida by the Inca presents a description of the land and the customs of its natives; a record
of its first explorer and of those explorers who went
there afterward; an account of the people who accompanied Hernando de Soto in his expedition; the strange
events that occurred on their voyage, the supplies which
the Governor ordered and provided in Havana,
and his embarkation for Florida. It
contains fifteen chapters.

CHAPTER I

Hernando de Soto requests permission of Em-
peror Charles the Fifth to make a con-
quest of Florida. His Majesty
grants him this
favor.

T IS for the glory and honor of the Most Holy
Trinity, God Our Lord, and with a desire to aug-
ment His Holy Catholic Faith and the Crown of
Spain that we now attempt to record in these
pages the story of many cavalier Spaniards and
Indians, and especially that of Hernando de Soto, Governor and
Captain General of the provinces and seigniories of the great king-
dom of Florida.[1]

Hernando de Soto participated in the first conquest of Peru and
in the seizure of the despot, Atahuallpa, that bastard son who stole
the Inca throne from its legitimate heir and was the last of his race
to rule the empire. Because of the tyrannies and cruelties of this
man, the severest of which he used upon his own flesh and blood,

[1] The syntax of the Inca's first page, or paragraph, or sentence (they are
all the same), defies imitation in English. Garcilaso starts his book, as we
do the second paragraph, with Hernando de Soto's name. We have set
first a parenthetical *Ave Iglesia,* not only because it must go somewhere, but
also because the whole book is in a way a genuflection to the Church with
the Crown of Spain running a close second to the Holy Roman Faith. God
and gold were the passions of Garcilaso's day.

the kingdom of the Incas was lost;[2] or at least because of the division and discord which his rebellions and atrocities produced among the natives, the Spaniards found it possible to conquer his realm with the ease that they did, as with divine favor I shall reveal elsewhere.[3] The ransom exacted of the Incas for their king, as is well known, was so large, rich and dazzling that it exceeded anything one can believe in the history of mankind. According to the records of an auditor of His Majesty's possessions in Peru, who first determined the value of the king's fifth[4] and from this computed the worth of the whole (he reduced it to the monetary standards of Castile by allowing three hundred and seventy-five *maravedís*[5] for each ducat), the entire ransom amounted to a few coins more than three million, two hundred and ninety-three thousand ducats, and this figure did not include another great sum which was squandered because the Spaniards did not succeed in dividing it into fifths. Hernando de Soto's share of this ransom, combined with the profits he received as an officer of such importance and with the gifts that were presented him both by the Indians of Cuzco when he and Pedro del Barco went alone to that city, and by Atahuallpa himself, who admired this first Spaniard he had ever seen and spoken to, amounted in all to more than one hundred thousand ducats.[6]

[2] Garcilaso was a second cousin of Atahuallpa, and according to his own story had reason to resent the cruelties of this king. For he reported in the *Comentarios Reales* that Atahuallpa, in his effort to exterminate the whole of the royal race so that he might rule without dispute the land of his father Huayna Capac, drove all the women and children on to a big plain north of Cuzco and there had them unmercifully slain. Garcilaso's mother and her brother, Francisco Huallpa Tupac Inca Yupanqui, who were little children at the time, succeeded with others in escaping through the lines.

[3] In Garcilaso's *Comentarios Reales*, Part I, Book IX, chapters xxxv–xxxviii.

[4] *el quinto*, or the king's fifth, was the income tax of the day.

[5] *maravedí*—an old Spanish coin of the smallest value; worth about one-sixth of a cent or one-third of a farthing.

[6] The variation in monetary standards makes it difficult to estimate the true value of sixteenth-century fortunes. But since the ducat was worth about two dollars and twenty-five cents, De Soto's "haul" must have amounted to several hundred thousand dollars, a sum worth considerably more in his day than at the present.

This was the sum that Hernando de Soto possessed when he and sixty other conquistadors came to Spain with the allotments and spoils they had received at Cajamarca. And with this treasure he could have bought more estates in his own province of Villanueva de Barcarrota than could be obtained now at the same price, for money had a greater value at that time, since so much treasure had not as yet arrived from the Indies, and property was not valued so highly as it is today. But he had no desire to purchase property. On the contrary, his thoughts and his spirit being elated by memories of what had been accomplished through his efforts in Peru, he could no longer be content with his former exploits but was filled with a yearning to undertake other tasks of equal if not greater consequence, if such were to be found. So he went to Valladolid, where the Emperor, Charles the Fifth, King of Spain, maintained his court, and he begged that sovereign to grant him permission to make a conquest of the kingdom of Florida (a region so called because its coast was discovered on the day of *Pascua Florida*[7]), a conquest which he expressed his willingness to undertake at his own risk and expense, and to pay for with his own fortune and life in order to serve His Majesty and increase the power of the Spanish Crown.[8]

Hernando de Soto was moved to make this request by an openhearted envy of and a magnanimous enthusiasm for the recent accomplishments of the Marquis del Valle Don Hernando Cortés in Mexico and those of the Marquis Don Francisco Pizarro and the Adelantado Don Diego de Almagro in Peru. The latter accomplishments he had seen and helped to make possible, but being a liberal and free-spirited man, it was not in his nature to serve as an

[7] *Pascua*—the common name for the three great feasts of the year: *Pascua de Espíritu Santo* (Whitsunday); *Pascua de Natividad* (Christmas); and *Pascua de la Resurrección* (Easter). The last named was sometimes referred to as *Pascua Florida* because generally in Spain flowers came up at that time of the year. We have left this term in Spanish rather than submit the reader to the indignity of "flowered" or "flowery feast."

[8] It is interesting to note at this point that De Soto enriched the royal purse with a loan from the spoils of Cajamarca, a circumstance which may have influenced His Caesarean Majesty considerably in his decision concerning the Florida appointment.

inferior, and indeed he was not inferior to the individuals mentioned, either in valor and strength in time of war or in wisdom and discretion in time of peace; so he forsook those noble exploits, important as they were, and set out upon others which for him proved to be of even more serious consequences, for in them he lost his life, not to speak of his previously earned fortune.[9]

Since almost all of the principal conquests of the New World have been accomplished under similar conditions, some people, moved by malice and excessive envy, have accused Spain of having bought dominion over the whole of the New World at no greater outlay of fortune than the expenditure of stupid and persistent madmen. But such malicious and envious persons fail to consider that these same stupid and persistent individuals have been the sons of Spain, a nation whose best fortune lies in the men she has produced, men reared to conquer the New World and at the same time to make themselves feared by the Old.

In the discourse of this history I have employed both the terms "Spanish" and "Castilian"; therefore, be advised that I am using these words to mean one and the same thing.

CHAPTER II

*A description of Florida and an account of the
first, second, and third explorers
of that land.*

IT WILL be difficult for us to paint as complete a picture of the vast land of Florida as we should like because, this region being as yet unexplored and unconquered, its confines are still a mystery. A most certain fact, which we cannot ignore, is that to the south of it lie the ocean sea and the great island of Cuba; but even though

---

[9] "*y emprendió estotra para él mayores, pues en ellas perdió la vida, y la hacienda, que en las otras avía ganado*"—The muted overtone of the relative worth of life and fortune is the Inca's, not the translators'.

it is said that Hernando de Soto penetrated a thousand leagues into its interior (as we shall see later), we are still ignorant as to whether or not it is limited on the north by more lands or by the sea itself. To the east, it is cut off at a place called the Land of the Codfish,[10] but a certain French cosmographer states that between Florida and this land there lies another which he even calls New France.[11] On the west, it is bound by the Provinces of the Seven Cities,[12] so called by their discoverers who found them in the year 1539, having left Mexico by order of the Viceroy, Don Antonio de Mendoza, and under the captaincy of Juan Vásquez Coronado,[13] a resident of that city. By the term resident, one understands in the Indies a person with an allotment of Indians. The name came to have this significance because such people were obliged to maintain their residence wherever they held the Indians; and only with permission of the king could they come to Spain and remain away from their Indians for so much as two years without forfeiting their allotment. Juan Vásquez Coronado discovered extensive and excellent lands, but he was unable to colonize because of the great inconveniences he encountered. In consequence he returned to Mexico, very much to the disappointment of the viceroy who had provided horses and people for this fruitless expedition. On the west, Florida is bound

[10] Throughout the text, with the exception of one or two names like *Nombre de Dios* and *Tierra-Firme,* which have become fixed in English, we are translating Spanish geographical names and then giving the original in a footnote for the sake of readers who may want to consult early maps. The Land of the Codfish is *Tierra de los Bacallaos.* The reader should not be too quick to suppose that this is Cape Cod, so named by Gosnold in 1602, though the Cape was a well-known landmark for early explorers before Hernando de Soto's time. It is not always easy to distinguish between Newfoundland and Cape Cod on the early charts. On the Wolfenbüttel-Spanish map, for example, the "Tierra Nueva de los Bacallaos" could very well be Newfoundland. See the facsimile of this map, facing page 378, NS Volume 19 (1909), *Proceedings of the American Antiquarian Society.*

[11] *Nueva Francia.*

[12] *Las Provincias de las Siete Ciudades.*

[13] The error is the Inca's. *Francisco* Vásquez de Coronado led the expedition to Cíbola.

likewise by the land of the Chichimecas,[14] a most valiant people who dwell along the borders of Mexico.

The first Spaniard to explore the land of Florida was Juan Ponce de León, a native of the kingdom of León. This noble man was serving as Governor of the island of San Juan de Puerto Rico; but since in those days Spaniards occupied themselves solely in the exploration of new territories, he armed two caravels and went in search of an island named Bimini (called by others Buyoca), where, according to fables of the Indians, there was a fountain that rejuvenated the aged.[15] Juan Ponce de León wandered fruitlessly for many days seeking this land,[16] and eventually was driven by storm to a coast that lay north of the island of Cuba. This coast he named Florida because it was Easter Day when he first came upon it.[17] The year was 1513, and according to some computers, Easter was celebrated that year on the twenty-seventh of March.

Just the realization that he had discovered land was sufficient for Juan Ponce de León, and without taking pains to determine whether it were the mainland or merely an island, he came to Spain to petition the right to govern and conquer it. Their Catholic Majesties permitted him this favor; and, according to Francisco López de Gomara, he set out for the Indies with three ships in the year fifteen. Others say that it was in the year twenty-one, but the exact date is of little consequence. After undergoing some misfortunes at sea, Juan

[14] According to Don José Pichardo, these were the Indians of Coahuila and Nuevo León. See Charles Wilson Hackett (ed.), *Pichardo's Treatise on the Limits of Louisiana and Texas* (Austin: 1931), I, 91.

[15] *una fuente que remozaba a los viejos*—Spanish writers never refer to the hypothetical fountain as "The Fountain of Eternal Youth," but simply as "the fountain which rejuvenates" or "the fountain which converts old men into youths."

[16] For the kind of map he used, see Peter Martyr's map of 1511, a copy of which is in the McGregor Library of the University of Virginia. Bimini appears on it in a Latinized form.

[17] *Día de Pascua de Resurrección* is the expression used here. Herrera says that Ponce de León called the land La Florida partly because of its wealth of flowers and partly because of the church festival. See above, note 7.

Ponce de León landed in Florida. Here the Indians came out and fought valiantly until they had defeated him, slaying almost all of the men who had accompanied him. He himself escaped with only six of his companions, and together they sailed for the island of Cuba, where all died of the wounds they had received. Thus unhappily ended the expedition of Ponce de León, the first to explore the land of Florida, and it would appear that he left his misfortune as a heritage to those who succeeded him in this same search.

A few years later a navigator named Miruelo, master of a caravel, while trading among the Indians was blown by storm to the coast of Florida or to some other region. Just what place is not known. The natives received this Spaniard peacefully, and in his dealings with them, they offered him some little pieces of silver and small quantities of gold. Taking these gifts, he returned quite pleased to the island of Santo Domingo without having determined the latitude and marked off the land as any good navigator should have done. It would have been well had he done so, for thus he would have been saved from a plight in which he afterward found himself because of this negligence.

At the same time, seven rich men of Santo Domingo formed a company. In their group was one Lucas Vázquez de Ayllón, a special Judge of the Audiencia[18] and also of the Appellate Court that had been appointed for the island of Santo Domingo before the Audiencia had been founded. This company armed two ships and sent them out among the islands to seek and capture Indians in whatever manner they could, so as to throw them to work in their gold mines. The vessels proceeded on their pretty[19] mission but because of unfavorable weather landed by chance at a cape which they named Santa Elena, it being the day of this saint. Afterward they came to a river called Jordan in memory of the sailor who first

[18] A royal tribunal. The word is common enough in English for a peculiarly Spanish institution, so we leave it as it stands.

[19] *Los navíos fueron a su buena empresa.* The Inca's Indian blood leaves little doubt as to his ironical use of the word "good."

saw it. Here they landed, and the Indians approached in great fear to see such strange vessels, the like of which they had never beheld before. And they were amazed at the sight of bearded men who wore clothing. Nevertheless each treated the other in a friendly manner, and gifts were exchanged. The Indians offered the Spaniards some very fine and fragrant marten furs, some seed pearls, and some small quantities of silver, whereas the latter in turn presented them with articles brought for barter. When such courtesies had been exchanged and the ships had taken on supplies of wood, water and other provisions, the Spaniards embraced their new friends and invited them to come on board to examine their vessels and the cargo carried in their holds. Trusting in the loyalty of men who had treated them so kindly and desiring to see things so novel, more than one hundred and thirty natives entered the ships. Then when the Spaniards saw such a good haul below deck, they weighed anchor and set sail for Santo Domingo. On the voyage to that land, however, one of the two vessels was lost, and even though the other arrived safely, all of the Indians aboard had perished of sorrow and starvation, for being angry at the deception done them under the guise of friendship, they had refused to eat.

CHAPTER III

Other explorers who have gone to Florida.

THOSE Castilians who had sailed for Florida in the ships of the seven rich men of Santo Domingo told of what they had seen when they came again to that island; meanwhile, Miruelo's story was being circulated in the same place. Now when these accounts reached the ears of the Judge, Lucas Vázquez de Ayllón, he came to Spain to petition the conquest and government of Chicoria,[20] one of the many provinces of Florida. Not only did the Emperor favor his request, but he honored him with knighthood in

---

[20] Chicora. Somewhere in the region of present day South Carolina.

the order of Santiago. So returning to Santo Domingo, this man fitted out three large vessels in the year 1524, and taking Miruelo as his navigator, sailed for that land which the latter had discovered earlier, for it was rumored to be richer than Chicoria. But persistently as he tried, Miruelo could never locate the spot he had previously visited and as a result fell into such a melancholia that in a few days he lost his reason and expired.

The Licenciate Ayllón now proceeded in search of the province of Chicoria. At the river Jordan he lost his flagship, but with his two remaining vessels, he sailed toward the east and landed on the coast of a peaceful and delightful region near Chicoria where the natives received him with much festivity and praise. Believing that all now was in his power, he commanded two hundred Spaniards to disembark and inspect a village three leagues inland. The Indians directed these men to that place, but one night, after they had feasted them for three or four days and given assurances of loyalty, they slew them all. Then at dawn they made a sudden attack on the few who had remained at the coast to guard the ships, and when they had killed or wounded the majority, they forced the others, including the Judge, to embark and return, broken and defeated, to Santo Domingo. Thus they avenged the Indians betrayed on the previous voyage. Among the few who managed to escape with Lucas Vázquez de Ayllón was a cavalier named Hernando Mogollón, a native of the city of Badajoz. This man, whom I knew personally, later came to Peru and told at length what we have given in resumé.

After Judge Lucas Vázquez de Ayllón, the next explorer in Florida was Pámphilo de Narváez, who went there in the year 1537. As Alvar Núñez Cabeza de Vaca, who accompanied him as Treasurer of the Royal Purse, tells us in his *Naufragios*, this captain and all of his men except Cabeza de Vaca himself, three other Spaniards and one Negro, were miserably lost. Our Lord God was so merciful to the five who escaped that they succeeded in performing miracles in His name and thus gained such a reputation and esteem among the Indians that they were worshipped as deities. Nevertheless they did not want to remain in this land, and as soon as they were able to do so, left very hastily and came to Spain to solicit new governorships. They succeeded in obtaining their desire, but many things occurred which were to bring them to a sad end, according to this same Alvar Núñez Cabeza de Vaca, who died in Valladolid after returning in chains from the Río de la Plata where he had gone as Governor.

When Pámphilo de Narváez went to Florida he took on the journey as navigator another Miruelo who was a relative of the aforementioned one and equally as unfortunate in his profession, for he never succeeded in finding the land his uncle had discovered. From his kinsman's account he had received information concerning that land, and it was for this reason that Pámphilo de Narváez had taken him with him.

After the unfortunate Pámphilo de Narváez, the Adelantado Hernando de Soto went to Florida, entering it in the year thirty-nine. It is our intention to record his history along with that of numerous other famous Spanish and Indian cavaliers,[21] to give an account of the many great provinces he explored up until the termination of his life, and moreover to tell of what his captains and soldiers did after his death until they abandoned that land and came to a halt in Mexico.

CHAPTER IV

Still others who have made the same journey to
Florida. The customs and common
weapons of the natives of
that country.

A S SOON as the news of the death of Hernando de Soto became known in Spain, many candidates appeared to ask for the governorship and conquest of Florida; but the Emperor Charles V

[21] *cavalleros Españoles e Indios*—This passage could be translated "Spanish cavaliers and Indians," but wherever it occurs we give deference to the Inca's insistence that, though horseless, the Indians numbered among them persons sufficiently noble to be called cavaliers.

refused them all, sending instead at his own cost in the year 1549 a group of Dominicans led by one of their order, Luis Cancer de Balbastro. These friars had offered to convert the Indians to the Evangelical faith with their preaching, but when they arrived in Florida and disembarked for the purpose, the natives, who had learned a lesson in their previous contact with the Spaniards, refused to listen. Instead they fell upon them and slew Friar Luis as well as two of his companions. The remainder of the brothers then took refuge in their ship and, returning to Spain, proclaimed that people so barbarous and inhuman as Indians had no desire to hear sermons.

In the year 1562, a son of the judge, Lucas Vázquez de Ayllón, asked for this same conquest and governorship, and his petition was granted. But this man died in Hispañola while searching for a crew, his sickness and death having been caused by sorrow and anxiety over an undertaking that had little possibility of completion and was consequently becoming more difficult each day. Since then, others have gone to Florida, among whom was the Adelantado Pedro Meléndez de Valdés; but I shall not write of these men because I do not have complete information relative to their accomplishments.

Although brief, this is the most accurate account that it has been possible to give concerning the land of Florida and those who have gone there to explore and conquer it. But before we continue, it will be well to describe some of the customs which in general the Indians of that great kingdom observe, at least those which the Adelantado Hernando de Soto discovered to be common to practically all of the provinces that he visited. And if in some other place in the process of our history customs differ, we shall take care to note the fact. In general, however, all Indians observe essentially the same mode of living.

The Indians are a race of pagans and idolaters; they worship the sun and the moon as their principal deities, but, unlike the rest of heathendom, without any ceremony of images, sacrifices, prayers, or other superstitions. They do have temples but they use them as

sepulchres and not as houses of prayer. Moreover, because of the
great size of these structures, they let them serve to hold the best
and richest of their possessions. Their veneration for the temples
and burial places, therefore, is most profound. On the doors of
them they place the trophies of victories won over their enemies.

Among the common people a man marries only one woman and
she is obliged to be faithful to her husband under penalty of laws
that have been ordained for the punishment of adultery. In certain
provinces this punishment is cruel death, and in others it is something very humiliating, as we shall show in its place. The lords,
by royal prerogative, have license to take whatever women they
please, and this law or liberty of the nobility is observed in all of
the Indies of the New World, but ever with the distinction of the
principal legitimate wife; the other women, who act as servants, are
more concubines than wives, and their offspring, being illegitimate,
are not equal in honor or inheritance to those of the principal wife.

Throughout Peru, the common man marries only one woman, and
he who takes two does so under penalty of death. But the Incas,
who are those of royal blood, and the curacas, who are lords of
vassals, have license to possess all the women they desire or can
maintain, although with the distinction stated above between the
legitimate wife and the concubines. As heathens they claim that
this dispensation is permitted because it is necessary that they have
many wives in order to produce many children, for it being the
nobility who are wasted and destroyed in battles, there is a need for
additional people of this class to wage wars and to augment and
govern the republic. There are more than enough of the base-born
to carry burdens, till the soil and perform the duties of serfs, they
say, for not being people who can be used as the nobility in times
of peril, they increase extensively regardless of how few are born.
Persons of this second class are of no value to the government, and
it is unlawful and even an insult for them to offer their services for
such work, since governing and administering justice are the duties
of cavalier hidalgos and not plebeians. But let us return to the
natives of Florida.

The basic food of these people is corn[22] rather than wheat, and their general fare consists of beans, the type of squash known as Roman squash, and many of the fish indigenous to their rivers. There being no tame animals in large numbers, they have a scarcity of beef;[23] but with their bows and arrows, they shoot much wild game such as stags, roedeer and bucks, which are larger and more numerous than those of Spain. They also kill a great variety of birds, first to eat the flesh, and then to obtain different colored feathers with which to decorate their heads; for the adornments they wear on their heads are sometimes half a fathom in height, and by means of them the nobles are differentiated from common people in time of peace, and the soldiers from non-combatants in time of war. Whatever meat and fish they do eat must be well baked and boiled, and their fruit must be very ripe. In no wise will they partake of green or half-ripe fruit, and they ridicule the Spaniards for eating green grapes. Their drink is clear water as nature gives it, without mixture of anything.

People who say that the Indians eat human flesh attribute this practice to them falsely, at least to those of the provinces our Governor discovered. They on the contrary abominate this practice, as Alvar Núñez Cabeza de Vaca notes in his *Naufragios,* chapters fourteen and seventeen. Here he states that certain Castilians who were camped apart died gradually of hunger and that those of them who remained alive devoured the dead until the last one of them had perished, there being none left to eat him.[24] Because of this

[22] The Inca's Spanish word is, of course, *"maíz,"* which is consistently represented in this translation by the word "corn," rather than "Indian corn," or even "maize."

[23] The word used here is *carne,* a word which includes the meat from all types of domesticated animals. But since in some present day Latin American markets one calls for *carne* when beef is desired, and since the Inca in certain instances is obviously referring to beef, we sometimes take the liberty of translating it thus.

[24] All of the group mentioned in Chapter XIV did perish, but of the group described in Chapter XVII, one man survived. Hernando de Esquivel, by drying and preserving the flesh of a man named Soto-Mayor, was able to keep alive until he could rejoin the Indians. Soto-Mayor was a brother of Vasco Porcallo de Figueroa, later De Soto's lieutenant general in Florida.

incident, he says, the natives were scandalized and wanted to destroy all of the Spaniards who had remained in the other camp. It may be, however, that the Indians do eat human flesh in places where our men did not penetrate, for Florida is so broad and long that there is space enough within it for anything to happen.

The Indian men go naked, wearing only certain little cloths of varicolored chamois, something like extremely short pants, which modestly cover all parts of their bodies necessary to conceal, both in front and behind. Instead of cloaks they have robes which are fastened at the neck and extend to the middle of the legs. Some are made of very fine marten fur and smell of musk, whereas others are of cowhide and different small skins of such animals as bucks, roes, stags, bears, lions, and various species of cats. These skins they dress to the utmost perfection, preparing a cowhide or bearskin without removing the hair. Thus it remains soft and smooth, and can be worn as a cloak or can serve at night on their beds. Their hair they permit to grow, wearing it caught up in a large knot on the head. As an adornment, they use a thick skein of thread, of whatever color they wish, which encircles the head and falls over the forehead. In the ends of the skein they tie two half knots, so that each end hangs over a separate temple down to the bottom of the ears. The women dress in chamois, keeping their whole body modestly covered.

The weapon which the Indians commonly carry is the bow and arrow. It is true that they do possess and are skillful in the use of other arms such as pikes, lances, darts, halberds, slings, clubs, broadswords, sticks and the like, if there are more such weapons; but they do not understand and thus cannot use the arquebus and the crossbow. Yet with all their various types of arms, they generally employ only the bow and arrow, because it is more dressy and more ornamental for those who carry it. For this same reason ancient pagans painted their most beloved gods such as Apollo, Diana and Cupid with bows and arrows; for in addition to what such arms signified among them, they were very beautiful and increased both grace and elegance in the one who bore them. But the Indians have found also that they can obtain a better effect with this weapon either at a distance or near at hand, whether they are fleeing or attacking, or whether they are fighting or taking recreation in hunting. In all the New World, therefore, it is a very much used weapon.

The bows are of the same height as the men who carry them, and since the natives of Florida are generally tall, theirs are more than two yards in length and are thick in proportion. They make them of oak and of their other different woods which are strong and heavy. Thus they are so difficult to bend that no Spaniard, regardless of how much he persisted, was able to draw a bowstring back as far as his face. The Indians, on the other hand, because of their skill and constant use of this weapon, draw the cord with great ease, even to the back of the ear; and they make very fierce and frightful shots, as we shall see later.

The bowstrings are made with thongs of deerskin. Taking a strip two fingers wide from the tip of the tail to the head of the deer, the Indians after first removing the hair, wet and twist this strip firmly. Tying one end to the branch of a tree, they suspend from the other end a weight of one hundred or one hundred and twenty-five pounds and leave it thus until it becomes like one of the heavy cords of the bass-viol and is very strong. In order to shoot with safety, so that the bowstring on being loosened may not injure the left arm, they trim that arm on the inner side with a half bracer of heavy feathers, in this way protecting it from the wrist to the elbow. This bracer is secured with a deerskin thong which encircles the arm seven or eight times at the place where the bowstring quivers with the greatest force.[25]

The above is what in sum may be said of the life and customs of the Indians of Florida. And now we return to Hernando de Soto,

[25] In telling of the customs of the Indians, Garcilaso uses the past tense until he has completed his description of the Incas and then he employs the historical present. Since North American Indians as well as remnants of the Inca civilization were still adhering to these customs at the time Garcilaso was writing, we have rendered the entire passage in the historical present.

who has asked for the conquest and governorship of that great
kingdom, a project which has been so unhappy and so costly to all
those who have undertaken it.

CHAPTER V

*Both the writs authorizing the conquest and the
great preparations for carrying it
forward are made known in
Spain.*

HIS Caesarean Majesty granted permission to Hernando de
Soto to undertake the conquest of Florida with the title of
Adelantado and Marquis of a state thirty leagues long and fifteen
leagues broad in whatever section he should designate of whatever
region he should conquer at his own expense;[26] and he specified
likewise that so long as this man should live he should be Governor
and Captain General, not only of the land of Florida but also of
the island of Santiago de Cuba. Hernando de Soto had very dis-
creetly petitioned the administration of this island since the position
was most important to him in making his explorations, conquests
and settlements in Florida; and the Emperor had honored his request, knowing that if he were Governor and Captain of these

---

[26] Actually the King's agreement, which was executed at Valladolid and
dated April 20, 1537, gave De Soto the authority to conquer, pacify and
populate all of the provinces of the *Tierra Nueva* which previously had been
assigned to the governorship of the Licentiate Ayllón, as well as those lands
lying between Florida and the province of the Río de las Palmas, lands
which once had been bestowed upon Pámphilo de Narváez. Moreover, he
was to have the titles of Governor, Captain General, Adelantado and High
Constable of whatever two hundred leagues of coast he should designate; he
was to have the lieutenancy of three stone fortresses which he should build
at his own cost within this land; he was to be given twelve leagues in square
of land; and he was to have the government of the island of Cuba. The
agreement makes no mention of the title of Marquis, although both Garcilaso
and Elvas do. For a detailed description of the agreement, see *The Final
Report of the United States De Soto Expedition Commission* (Washington:
1939), pp. 76–79.

people, they would obey and assist him more promptly in whatever
he might find it necessary to demand for his expedition.

The titles and charges were published throughout the realm, and
much fanfare was raised over this new enterprise in which Hernando
de Soto was to subjugate and acquire great provinces and kingdoms
for the Crown of Spain. Rumor spread to all corners of the empire
that the captain who was to undertake this project had been Conqueror of Peru, and that not content with the hundred thousand
ducats he had brought from that land, he now was investing his
fortune in a second conquest. All men consequently were seized
with enthusiasm and felt that this second venture would be much
better and richer in its rewards than had been the initial one.[27] So
from every part of Spain they flocked to join the enterprise. There
were many cavaliers of distinguished lineage, many hildalgos and
many experienced soldiers who had served the Crown in divers
parts of the world. Moreover there were civilians and laborers in
large numbers who had left their lands, friends, families and parents
because of the silver and gold and precious stones they had seen
brought in such great quantity from the New World, and because
of the fine reports they now heard of another conquest in preparation. Selling their possessions, all made ready and offered by letter
and in person to join this conquest, hoping, as had been promised,
that the rewards would be as rich as if not richer than had been the
two previous conquests, that of Mexico and that of Peru. And with
this same expectancy, six or seven of the conquistadors who we said

[27] Enthusiasm for this new conquest had been aroused considerably by
Alvar Núñez Cabeza de Vaca, who, after surviving the ill-fated expedition
of Pámphilo de Narváez, had returned to Spain. His initial reticence about
disclosing what he had seen, combined with hints of untold riches, fired
youthful imaginations. And finally when his disclosures to the King reached
the court by way of the royal "grapevine," cavaliers were not lacking for the
expedition. A quarrel with De Soto and a desire for a command of his own
moved Alvar Núñez to direct his steps to the Río de la Plata, but he did
not hesitate to advise his kinsmen, Baltasar de Gallegos and Cristóbal de
Espíndola, to join the expedition to Florida. We are told that whereas men
were usually lacking for expeditions to known lands, many men of good
condition who had disposed of their estates, remained behind in San Lúcar
for "lack of shipping."

had returned from Peru were now moved to venture upon the journey to Florida. Dissatisfied with their previous gains, they failed to note that the land they would seek could be no better than the one they had abandoned. It appears that their hunger for wealth had increased in conformance with their nature, which was insatiable. In the progress of this history we shall name these men and tell how they came to offer themselves.

As soon as the Governor had made public his need for provisions, he set about giving orders for the purchase of arms, munitions, supplies, ships, and all other materials pertaining to such a great enterprise as he had undertaken. He selected qualified persons for official positions, assigning each man his particular function; and he called together military men, naming captains and officers for the army, as we shall show in the following chapter. In sum, as a man with the desire and power to do so, he provided with complete munificence and largess all that was essential for his undertaking.

Since both the General and his officers and ministers assisted so liberally in the expenses of the enterprise, and since each worked so diligently to carry out his own particular assignment, preparations were concluded within a little more than a year after His Majesty had published the writ of authorization, and all met in San Lúcar de Barrameda, which had been designated as the port of embarkation. When the vessels had been assembled and when the men raised for the army had gathered on the appointed day, the spectacle was dazzling. Further ship stores finally were brought on board along with a great quantity of crude iron, steel, iron for saddlebows, spades, pickaxes, crates, ropes and baskets, all of which were necessary for colonization; and when everything was ready, the ships set out to sea, observing an order of navigation which will be given in the following chapter.

CHAPTER VI

The number of men and officers who embarked for Florida.

NINE hundred and fifty Spaniards of all ranks had gathered in San Lúcar de Barrameda to go on the conquest of Florida. All were young, for hardly was there one among them who had grey hair[28] (youth being a very necessary qualification for performing the tasks and overcoming the difficulties encountered in new conquests). To a number the Governor had given financial aid, sending each what he felt was due him according to the quality of his person and the company and servants he had brought. Many out of necessity had accepted this aid, whereas others out of respect and courtesy had not been willing to do so; for now that they saw the huge machinery of operations he bore upon his shoulders, they felt it more appropriate to assist him than to receive his help. With the arrival of the season of the spring tide, these men embarked in seven large ships and three small ones, each of which had been purchased in different ports of Spain.

The Adelantado sailed with his whole household, including his wife and family, in the *San Christóbal,* a ship of eight hundred tons burden which was to serve as the flagship of the armada. This vessel was well provided with artillery, munitions and men of war, as was fitting for the command ship of so illustrious a captain. Nuño Tovar, a native of Xerez de Badajoz, traveled in a vessel just as large called the *Madalena.*[29] One of the sixty conquistadors of Peru, this man now served as Vice Admiral[30] of the Fleet. With him he carried Don Carlos Enríquez, also a native of Xerez de Badajoz, who was a second son of a distinguished family of that

[28] The Inca later tells us that the only man with grey hair on the expedition was Juan Mateos.

[29] This ship is called the Madalena in the 1605 edition and the Magalena in the 1723 edition. Other authorities have referred to it as the Magdalena.

[30] *este cavallero iba por Teniente General*—literally, as Lieutenant General.

city. The cavalier, Luis de Moscoso de Alvarado, a native of Badajoz and resident of Zafra, who was the son of a knight commander,
Diosdado de Alvarado, was charged with the *Concepción*, a galleon
of more than five hundred tons burden. Also one of the sixty
conquistadors, he had been named Campmaster of the Army. In
the *Buena Fortuna*, a galleon just like the *Concepción*, Captain
Andrés de Vasconcelos, a native cavalier of Yelves, traveled with
a very splendid and brilliant company of Portuguese gentlemen, some
of whom had fought on the African frontiers. Diego García, son
of the Governor of Villanueva de Barcarrota, was Captain of another
heavy ship called the *San Juan*, and Arias Tinoco, who had been
appointed a Captain of the Infantry, was in command of still another
large ship called the *Santa Bárbara*. This man's brother, Alonso
Romo de Cardeñosa, who in addition was a Captain of the Infantry,
commanded a small galleon called the *San Antón*, and with him was
a third brother, Diego Arias Tinoco, who had been named as Ensign
General of the Army. These three brothers were relatives of the
Governor. Pedro Calderón, a gentleman who was a native of Badajoz, commanded a very beautiful caravel, and he was accompanied
by Captain Micer Espíndola, a cavalier of Genoa, who was in charge
of sixty halberdiers of the Governor's guard. Two brigantines[31]
were carried to service this fleet of eight vessels, and since they were
lighter and easier to manage than the heavy ships, they were to be
used as lookouts to keep watch on all sides of the armada while it
was at sea.

In these seven ships, one caravel and two brigantines, there traveled nine hundred and fifty soldiers in addition to sailors and people
necessary for the management and servicing of each vessel;[32] further-

[31] *vergantines*—The type of ship known as a pinnace is possibly more
like the vessels referred to here. We prefer, however, to use the cognate.
For an excellent discussion of the vessels employed in the conquest, see
Final Report, De Soto Commission, pp. 97–99.
[32] Luis Hernández de Biedma (in the manuscript record which he presented to the Council of the Indies in 1544) gives this number as six hundred and twenty; the anonymous "Gentleman of Elvas" (in his *Releçam
Verdadeira*, published at Évora in 1557) estimates it as six hundred;

more, the armada was accompanied by twelve priests, eight of whom were clerics, and four, friars. I remember the names of only four of the clerics.[33] They were Rodrigo de Gallegos, a native of Seville and relative of Baltasar de Gallegos; Diego de Bañuelos and Francisco del Pozo, both natives of Córdova; and Dionisio de París, a Frenchman born in the very city of Paris. The friars were as follows: of the Order of Saint Dominic there were Friar Luis de Soto, a native of Villanueva de Barcarrota, who was a relative of Governor Hernando de Soto, and Friar Juan de Gallegos, a native of Seville, who was a brother of Captain Baltasar de Gallegos; of the Order of Saint Francis, there was Friar Juan de Torres, a native of Seville; and of the Advocation and Insignia of the Holy Trinity, there was Friar Francisco de la Rocha, a native of Badajoz. All of these ecclesiastics were learned and exemplary men.

The Florida armada was accompanied by a second fleet of twenty heavy ships destined for Mexico. These vessels were to sail under the command of General Hernando de Soto as far as the island of Santiago de Cuba, at which point they were to separate and proceed to Vera Cruz under the captaincy of an illustrious cavalier named Gonzalo de Salazar. The latter was the first Christian born in Granada after it was taken from the Moors, and for this reason, although he was already a cavalier hidalgo, the Catholic Kings of glorious memory who vanquished that city gave him great privileges and made him grants, with which a mighty estate was founded for his descendants. One of the conquistadors of Mexico, he was now returning as Factor of the Imperial Resources of the City of Mexico.

In the order we have mentioned, the thirty ships of the two armadas hoisted their sails and passed over the bar of San Lúcar on the sixth of April in the year 1538; and they sailed that day and

---

Roderigo Ranjel (in his diary, which has been preserved in Oviedo's *Historia General y Natural de los Indios* [Madrid: 1851]) says there were seven hundred, including the sailors. For a full discussion of the above sources and convenient translations, see *Final Report, De Soto Commission,* pp. 4–11.

[33] An interesting sentence in that it identifies Garcilaso's friend, the chief first-hand source of this work, as non-clerical.

many other days with all the success and fair weather that could be desired. The Florida armada especially was so well provided with every kind of ship supplies that double rations were given to all who went with it, a nonsensical thing to do because they thereby wasted all their surplus, which was much. But the General traveled in such splendor, and he was so happy to be carrying in his company such brilliant and noble people that he counted everything as trivial in his desire to regale them.

CHAPTER VII

What happened to the armada on the first night of its navigation.

SHORTLY before nightfall of the first day that the armada sailed, the General summoned Gonzalo Silvestre,[34] a native of Herrera de Alcántara who was one of many he had chosen to have near him. "Be sure that you instruct the sentinels tonight as to how to stand watch," he said, "and warn your chief gunner to keep all of his artillery in readiness to fire on any enemy vessel that may appear. Furthermore, take care to maintain the order of navigation among the whole fleet that good sailing requires."

All of the Governor's commands were executed and the armada proceeded on its voyage with a favorable wind. But a little past midnight, it happened that the mariners of the vessel which was to become the flagship of the fleet destined for Mexico, and on which traveled the Factor, Gonzalo de Salazar, permitted their boat to move ahead of the entire fleet and to continue a cannon shot in advance and to the windward of the admiral's ship. It may be that they wished to demonstrate the speed of their craft or to boast that it too was a flagship like that of Hernando de Soto, but what is more probable is that, the weather being favorable, the pilot and the first

[34] It behooves the reader who is interested in discovering the name of Garcilaso's informant to watch the recurrence of this man's name.

mate had gone to sleep, and the sailor steering the vessel was unfamiliar with the laws of navigation. Nevertheless, for either of the two things they did, mariners are subject to the penalty of death.

Although he had stationed his sentinels, Gonzalo Silvestre, in order to give a good account of what had been charged him, had remained awake (as every good soldier and hidalgo such as he ought to do). So arousing his gunner, he now asked if the ship which was proceeding ahead belonged to the armada, or if it were that of an enemy. The gunner replied that it could not be one of their own number, for if so, it would not dare continue in its present position since the mariners responsible for it would realize that they were liable to the penalty of death. Thus, both men concluded that they were confronted with the vessel of an enemy and decided to fire upon it. Their first cannon shot pierced the center of all its sails from poop to prow, and their second tore away a part of its upper works. Then as they made ready to discharge a third, they heard people aboard shouting that they were friends and begging that their assailants be merciful and hold their fire.

The Governor was aroused by the noise, and the whole armada, being disturbed likewise, manned its guns and turned them toward the Mexican ship. Then since the wind was blowing through the rent left by the cannon ball in its sails, this vessel came falling to the leeward of the admiral's ship, which, being itself in pursuit, shortly overtook it. And now there was to befall a second and even more serious calamity, for the men aboard one ship, being confused and afraid because of their guilt, paid more attention to excusing themselves than to steering; whereas those of the other, being provoked by anger to believe that the act had been motivated by disrespect and not carelessness, resolved to punish and avenge it. Thus both vessels neglected to observe how or where they were going, and it became inevitable that they should meet side-on. And they were now so close together that those within, hoping thereby to succour themselves in this danger, and finding no more adequate remedy, seized with the utmost haste a great number of pikes and then leaning from one boat to the other, broke more than three hundred of these weapons in an effort to keep the vessels apart. The scene created a very fine effect and gave the impression of a most magnificent and unusual foot tournament. With these pikes and other sticks, they did manage to prevent a violent collision, but they could not keep the ships from laying across each other and entangling their rigging, sails and lateen yards in such a manner as to bring them to the very point of sinking. The cause of this situation was that both vessels were left without any support whatsoever. For the sailors, frightened as they were by such sudden and imminent danger, distrusted all remedy and did not know anything to do that would be of advantage; and when they could do something, the clamor of people now face to face with death was so great that they were unable to hear themselves, and the darkness of the night which had been increased by storms made it impossible for them to see what was best to be done. Moreover, those who had some courage and strength to command could not do so because there was no one to listen to or obey them, since everything now was weeping, shouting, screaming, howling and tumult.

The generals and their flagships had reached this point when Our Lord God came to their assistance in that the cutwater or the sickles[35] which the Governor carried on his lateen yards severed all of the ropes, rigging and sails of the Factor's ship. This being done, the Governor with the aid of the good wind that was blowing was able to pull away, and thus both vessels remained free.

The past danger in which he had just found himself, and his belief that the act responsible for it had been perpetrated out of disrespect and with malicious intent so angered Hernando de Soto that his inclination was to resort to violence and command that the Factor be deprived of his head. But the latter excused himself most humbly, pleading that he was blameless for anything that had occurred, and all of his men corroborated his statement. With this

[35] *trajamares (sic) ó navajas*—The *tajamar* is the cutwater, which divides the water before it comes to the ship's bow. A *navaja* is a razor or knife. Many ships of De Soto's day carried sickle-like knives in their yards for just such purposes as De Soto in this instance used his.

excuse and with the additional assistance of good mediators on the Governor's ship, he was absolved. Thus the Governor's anger was appeased and he pardoned the Factor, dismissing the whole incident. But Gonzalo de Salazar, as a man resentful of what had been done, found the matter more difficult to forget. Always after his arrival in Mexico when conversation was offered concerning the events of that night, he was accustomed to remark that it would give him great pleasure to meet Hernando de Soto on equal terms so that he could oppose him in combat, for then he would challenge him for the useless words uttered that night in excessive wrath concerning an incident for which he, Salazar, was blameless. And the truth is that he had not been at fault; but neither had the Governor said anything to him for which he should have been offended. Nevertheless, just as the one had suspected that the deed had been malevolent, so had the other become angry because he felt that the words had been abusive. The act was not committed with evil intent and the Governor's remarks were not insulting, but suspicion and anger rule men with powerful force, and especially strong men such as were our two commanders.

Gonzalo de Salazar's mariners now mended the breaks in their sails and rigging with all of the haste, industry and good skill that sailors ordinarily exert on such occasions, and then continued their voyage, giving thanks to Our Lord for having delivered them from such grave danger.

CHAPTER VIII

The armada arrives at Santiago de Cuba; what happened to the flagship at the entrance to that port.

WITHOUT further notable events, the Governor arrived on April 21, Easter Sunday, at Gomera, one of the Canary Islands. Here he was received by the lord of Gomera with great festivity and rejoicing.

Of this stage in the journey, Alonso de Carmona in his *Peregrina-*
ción has the following to say: "During the Lenten season of the
year thirty-eight, we sailed from the port of San Lúcar for the island
of Gomera where all ships go to take on water and renew supplies;
and when we had traveled for fifteen days we came in sight of that
land. I will tell of two incidents which occurred at that time on
my ship. First, two soldiers engaged in a fight and, seizing each
other by main force, fell overboard and were drowned. Neither
hair nor bone of them was ever seen again. Second, there was in
our company an hidalgo named Tapia, a native of Arévalo. This
man had with him a very fine and valuable greyhound, which also
fell overboard when we were something like twelve leagues from
port. As a fair wind was blowing, we could not stop to rescue the
animal and consequently left it in the sea while we continued on our
way into port. The following morning, Tapia, very much to his
surprise and happiness, beheld his dog on land and attempted to
regain it; but the man who now had possession of the animal prevented his doing so. It was found to be true that this greyhound,
after falling into the sea, had swum for five hours before being
discovered and brought aboard a vessel that was cruising among the
islands. Taking on new ship stores and other supplies, we continued
on our way, but while still in sight of Gomera, Tapia approached
the edge of his boat, and as he did so was struck by a sail and pushed
into the sea. He sank like lead and never appeared again. This
incident saddened the whole armada, etc."

I have taken these words verbatim from Alonso de Carmona and
used them here because the three incidents he relates are noteworthy,
and also because by means of them one may perceive how his story
conforms to ours. For instance, his statement concerning the year
and the first fifteen days of the voyage, and again his account of the
weather and the port to which the armada arrived are in accord
with what we have said. In the same manner I therefore shall quote
many other passages from his records as well as from those of Joan[36]

---

[36] The printer was no doubt responsible for this spelling of Juan.

Coles, an additional eyewitness, for both of these men were on the expedition along with my author.

Before proceeding on the journey, the fleet spent three days of the Easter season replenishing necessary supplies. During that interval Hernando de Soto many times besought the Count of Gomera to permit his seventeen-year-old natural daughter, Doña Leonor de Bobadilla,[37] to accompany the expedition so that in this new conquest a marriage might be arranged for the girl which would make her a great lady. Being very confident of the Governor's magnanimity and feeling that he would do even more than he promised, the Count acceded to the request and turned his daughter over to Doña Isabel de Bobadilla, the Governor's wife, who was to receive her as her own child and permit her to travel in her company. Hernando de Soto was very happy when on the twenty-fourth day of April he departed from the island of Gomera with Doña Leonor, whose beauty was extreme.[38]

A favorable wind continued to blow with the result that by the end of May the Governor caught sight of the island of Santiago de Cuba. Twelve days earlier, the Factor Gonzalo de Salazar had asked leave to depart with the Mexican fleet for Vera Cruz. He had been exceedingly anxious to obtain this permission, it being natural for a man to prefer commanding to obeying; and the Governor, aware of his great desire, had granted the request freely.

Then the Adelantado and those of his armada directed their course toward the port of Santiago de Cuba with much celebration and rejoicing, for they saw that their long journey was at an end and that they were approaching the land they had been so anxious to

[37] The Count of Gomera was a Bobadilla and a cousin of De Soto's wife. See Theodore Maynard, *De Soto and the Conquistadores* (New York: 1930), p. 132.

[38] There had been amorous peccadillos and even other Leonors in De Soto's past, and this maiden soon revealed that her virtue was not proof against attack. But men of our race and generation should not attempt to decide whether this present generosity on the part of the Adelantado was an evidence of the purest Spanish chivalry or the most guileless of love affairs. Either phenomenon would be misunderstood in this naughty age.

reach in order to provide from a closer range those things expedient for the exploration and conquest. But as they neared the island, they beheld a man on horseback whom the inhabitants of the city had sent out to them. He was running toward the mouth of the harbor and shouting in a loud voice to the flagship, which was on the point of entering: "To port, to port." For those who do not know it, these words, in the language of sailors, mean "to the right of the ship";[39] and this man used the expression purposely, so that both the flagship and those which followed would be wrecked on some very dangerous rocks and shoals lying to the right of the harbor.

The pilot and sailors, who must not have been sufficiently well acquainted with the entrance of that port (thus proving how important practice and experience are in their profession), steered their vessel in the direction the horseman indicated. And now with louder shouts and cries, as though he realized he had mistaken the armada for enemy vessels, this individual came back and told them just the contrary, advising them to turn to the starboard (which is to the left of the ship)[40] lest they be destroyed. To make himself better understood he dismounted suddenly and ran toward the right, while signaling with his arms and cloak and crying: "Return, return to the other side before all of you are lost." When the crew of the flagship had understood what he was saying, they swung their vessel hastily to the left, but, in spite of their efforts, could not prevent it from striking a rock. The blow was such that all on board thought the ship had been split and was doomed. Rushing to the pumps they drew up through them a great quantity of wine, vinegar, oil and honey, which came from numerous earthern jars that had been shattered by the collision. The sight of these liquids confirmed the people in their accumulated fear that the ship was

[39] *a babor a babor (que en lenguage de Marineros, para los que no lo saben, quiere decir, a mano derecha del Navío)*—This confusion in the use of nautical terms, like that in the paragraph below, is the Inca's and not the translators'.

[40] *decir en contra, a estribor, (que es a mano izquierda del Navío)*—See above, note 39.

doomed, and they hastily threw a skiff[41] into the water to take the Governor's wife and her young maidens and ladies-in-waiting[42] to land. Some of the fledgling cavaliers who were inexperienced in such perils accompanied the women. In their haste to leave the ship, these youths disregarded all courtesy due the feminine sex and rushed into the skiff first, for they felt that now was no time for courtesies. The General was urged to go ashore, but, being a good and experienced commander, he refused to do so before determining what damages had been wrought. It was his desire to be near to assist if necessary, and with his very presence to keep everyone from abandoning the ship. At this point many of the sailors rushed below deck where they discovered that no greater damage had been incurred than the breaking of the jars, and that the ship was still worthy and sound. They were further assured by the fact that the pumps delivered no more liquids. All rejoiced over this news, but those who had been so discourteous and diligent about going ashore were now filled with shame.

CHAPTER IX

A four day naval battle between two ships in the harbor of Santiago de Cuba.

IN ORDER to exonerate the inhabitants of Santiago, it is only just to explain why they gave the armada that damaging information which led to the events just recorded. Certainly by examining well the incident which provoked them to do so, and the

---

[41] *batel*—Because of its use here, we are tempted to translate this word as lifeboat, but a lifeboat would have been incomprehensible to the conquistadors, who did not overestimate the value of human life. The Spanish galleons carried small landing boats for more utilitarian purposes than saving lives, even of great ladies and seventeen-year-old beauties.

[42] Among the ladies were the wives of De Soto, Baltasar de Gallegos, Carlos Enríquez and Nuño Tovar. Also the names of several women appear in connection with the enlistments.

persistent stubbornness involved, one may see that it is worth remembering and that it in some respects excuses these people; for
they were driven by fear, and fear prevents common souls and the
masses of people from accepting wise counsel.

You must know therefore that ten days previous to the Governor's arrival at Santiago, there called at that port a magnificent ship
belonging to one Diego Pérez, a native of Seville. The quality of
this man's person is not known, but the nobility of his equipage and
the cavalier mien which he displayed in his conversation, manners
and business dealings revealed that he was by rights a gentleman,
for these are the things which constitute gentility.[43] Furthermore,
as we presently shall have occasion to observe, he was a very fine
soldier on both land and sea. At the time he was trading among
the islands and traveled in the character of a merchant, but he likewise kept his ship well supplied with arms, munitions and men just
in case it should become necessary to engage the corsairs who
infested those islands and waters.

This merchant captain had passed three days in the harbor of
Santiago when another ship no smaller than his own came into port.
It was the vessel of a French privateer out for an adventure. And
now for the sole reason that one was French and the other Spanish,
the two recognized each other as enemies and launched an attack.
Grappling, they fought throughout the whole day until darkness
forced them to separate; but once their struggle had ceased, these
captains exchanged greetings and, as if they were two very intimate
friends, sent each other most courteously worded communications
along with gifts and dainties of wines, preserves, and fresh and
dried fruits from their ship stores. Then for the future each pledged
himself to limit his hostility to the daytime and never attack at
night. Furthermore they agreed not to fire upon each other since
it was their feeling that fighting with swords and lances was much
more becoming to valiant men than fighting with missiles; to them,

---

[43] This is the ruling class of the Peruvians reflecting on the nature of the
ruling class of its conquerors. It should be remembered that when Garcilaso
wrote this he was not wealthy, but was still an Inca.

crossbows and arquebuses of themselves gave testimony of having been inventions of cowardly or needy souls. And by their refraining from the use of artillery, they said, the victor not only would enjoy the pleasure of fighting as a gentleman and conquering with his own strength and force of arms, but he also would gain a ship with its spoils that would be sound and unbroken and consequently of some benefit to him. Just what the real motive of these two gallants was in making such an agreement could not be ascertained, but it may have been that they feared both might perish without either being of any advantage to the other. Nevertheless, their truce remained inviolable. But in spite of their vows, each continued to keep watch at night and was on guard against a sudden attack; for a good soldier should never put faith in the word of an enemy and become careless about doing what is necessary for his health and life.

On the second day these men again fought obstinately, not ceasing until they were parted by hunger and fatigue. Then when they had eaten and caught their breath, they entered once more into the struggle, which continued until sunset. The battle over for that day, they retired to their separate positions and as before exchanged visits and gifts, each asking about the health of the other and offering medicines kept on hand for the wounded.

That night, Captain Diego Pérez sent a message to the citizens of Santiago in which he said that they had seen very clearly what he had done during those days to kill or overcome the enemy, and how his efforts had met with no success because of his having encountered great resistance; that he was begging them (since it behooved the city to rid its sea and coasts of such a corsair as this one) to favor him with a promise to restore to him or his heirs, in the event he by chance were vanquished in battle, the value of his ship minus one thousand pesos; that he would offer to fight with the enemy until he had either subdued him or met death at his hands; that he sought this recompense because he was poor and possessed no property other than his ship; that if he were rich he would be pleased to risk his vessel freely in their service; and finally that if he should be victorious, he would expect no recompense from them.

But the city of Santiago refused to concede this favor to Diego Pérez. Rather they sent a rude reply, declaring that he could act as he wished in the matter, but that they were unwilling to place themselves under any obligation. Perceiving the unjustness of their response and their ingratitude for his gracious intention, the Captain remarked that a man who can serve himself errs in serving others since the rewards of men are almost always such as these people had offered; and he resolved to continue his fight for his own honor, life and possessions, without hope for other gain.

The dawn of the third day of the conflict between these two brave commanders found Diego Pérez at the place of battle, and he now fell upon his enemy with the same spirit and gallantry demonstrated during the previous days, for he wished to make it clear to the people of Santiago that he was fighting, not because of any confidence in them, but because of his faith in God and in his own strength and purpose. Meanwhile, the Frenchman came forth to receive him with no less a desire to conquer or die on that day than on the previous days. Apparently the obstinacy of these men and their having made the fight a point of honor instigated them more than any gain that could come by the one despoiling the other, for apart from the ships themselves, what was in them was worth very little. Headstrong then, they fought throughout the whole of that day just as in the past two days, separating only to eat and rest when they felt much necessity to do so. And when they had refreshed themselves, they returned to the conflict as invigorated as if just starting, and always with greater wrath at not being able to conquer. Then daylight failing, they withdrew with many wounded and some dead on both sides. But as soon as they had done so, they exchanged visits and gifts in the customary manner as if nothing ill had gone on between them. Thus they passed the night while the whole city of Santiago was amazed that two individuals in search of an honest living should persist so obstinately in destroying each other when neither necessity nor obligation forced them to do so; for there was no more reward to carry off than that of having been killed and furthermore they could hope for no official gratification since neither was in the service or the pay of his king. Yet all this and more human passsions can bring about when they begin to reign.

CHAPTER X

*A continuation of the incident of the sea fight
until its close.*

WITH the arrival of the fourth day, both Frenchman and Spaniard shouted greetings from one ship to the other, as is customary with seafaring men. Then they returned to their stubborn quarrel with the same strength and zeal they had displayed during the past three days, this time however with fewer men since many were now tired and many sorely wounded. Nevertheless the lust for honor, which can accomplish so much in noble souls, gave those who came the vigor to endure such hardship. Consequently they struggled the entire day as they had done previously, separating only to eat, rest, or take care of the wounded, and then returning to fight until the coming of darkness put them at peace. Once again when they had retired they proceeded to exchange the customary gifts and flattery.

Two such contrary extremes of enmity and courtesy as passed between the captains during those four days merit recording, for it is a fact that although they fought as mortal enemies, eager to take one another's life and property, yet when they ceased fighting, all their enmity was converted into such friendship as might be found between brothers. For then they were eager to present each other as many regalements as possible in order to prove that they were no less courteous and affable in peace than valiant and ferocious in war, and that they wanted no less to conquer in one manner than in the other. But let us return to the affairs of the battle.

Diego Pérez had sensed a weakness that day in his adversary, so in the evening, along with fine words and presents, he sent a message expressing extreme desire to continue this conflict, which had lasted so long, until one of them had gained the victory, and beseeching the corsair with assurances of reward to meet him on the following day. Then to bind the Frenchman further and prevent his taking flight in the night, he placed him under the obligation of military law by issuing another challenge to do battle; and since this man had revealed himself to be such a fine and valiant commander in every thing that had occurred, he trusted him not to evade the challenge.

The Frenchman in turn made a great show of joy at this new challenge, responding that Diego Pérez should rest the whole night without worry so as to gain strength and vigor for the coming day, and that he could be certain that his invitation was accepted and that his opponent would await him on the morrow and on as many days thereafter as might be necessary to fulfill his desire and terminate the conflict, the end of which he himself wished to see no less than did his adversary. And at the same time, he besought Diego Pérez to be definite and sincere and not to issue his challenge as a device to make his opponent so confident and careless that the Spaniards could flee to their own safety in the night; for, he said, he desired this encounter for the purpose of exhibiting in his own person the courage of the French nation. Nevertheless, after making all of these boasts, this corsair, when he perceived the weather was favorable, weighed anchor and set sail with the utmost silence lest he have occasion to repent having fulfilled a promise given in prejudice and self harm. After all, the observance of one's word in such cases is very stupid, for it is a characteristic of wise men to change their minds, particularly in war since things pertaining to war are unstable and peace is uncertain, and since the ultimate end one seeks in war is simply to emerge victorious.

The sentinels of the Spanish ship heard some commotion among the French during the night, but they sounded no alarm or call to arms, for they believed that their opponents were merely preparing for the approaching battle and not for flight. Nevertheless, when day dawned they discovered that they had been duped. Captain Diego Pérez regretted exceedingly to see that his enemies had fled, because judging from the weakness he had sensed in them the previous day, he had been confident that victory was his. Eager still for this victory, he now took from the city of Santiago what he needed for his men and set out in search of the pirate.

CHAPTER XI

The festivities given in honor of the Governor at Santiago de Cuba.

SUCH a strange and remarkable conflict as that between Diego Pérez and the French corsair had greatly amazed and frightened the people of Santiago, and since it had taken place so few days before the arrival of Hernando de Soto at their port, they had been afraid that the Governor himself was the corsair, and that having gathered support he was returning to sack and burn the city. Their fear and confusion, therefore, had been responsible for their giving the malicious information we have just described, it having been their wish that the pirate ships should be ruined on the rocks and shoals lying at the entrance to the harbor.

The Governor disembarked and the whole city came out with great celebration and rejoicing to receive and congratulate him on his safe arrival, at the same time, however, excusing themselves for having angered him with their unfortunate message. Then they told more at length and more in particular of all that had occurred in the four days of battle between the merchantman and privateer, describing the exchange of visits and gifts. They begged forgiveness on the basis that their fear had driven them to send the misinformation that they did, but they made no plea for exoneration in regard to their rude and ungracious behavior toward Diego Pérez. Later when informed privately of their discourtesies, the Governor was no less surprised than he had been at the alternate courtesies and hostilities of the two captains. For it is a fact that besides having replied uncivilly to the terms Diego Pérez had offered, these people had been so uncompromising with him that even though the battle was being fought in their service and the whole city had gone out each day to witness it, they never once during the entire four days had shown the graciousness to assist their benefactor while he was fighting or to give him so much as a jug of water while he was at rest. Instead, they had treated him as scornfully as if he were of a nation and religion contrary to their own. And furthermore, they had refused to do anything against the Frenchman, even for their own welfare. Sending twenty or thirty men in a boat or raft, they could have made a show of attacking the corsair from another side and thus by simply diverting him could have bestowed victory upon their compatriot without coming to blows. For any assistance rendered, even though small, would have sufficed to bring him triumph since the forces of both combatants had been so equal that they had been able to struggle four days without any advantage being recognized on either side. Yet the residents of Santiago had behaved as though they were not Spaniards, refusing to render this or any other assistance either in behalf of themselves or of Spain, for they had feared that should the Frenchman conquer, he would sack and burn their city, bringing others of his cohorts with him, it being their suspicion that he had already brought them.

These people did not take into consideration the fact that the enemy of a nation or religion, being the victor, knows neither respect for ills withheld nor gratitude for good deeds rendered, and furthermore that he feels no shame in regard to broken promises, as is proved by examples both ancient and modern. So it is that in war, and especially in war with infidels, an enemy always should be regarded as an enemy and liable to suspicion, whereas a friend should be looked upon as a friend and held in good faith. Friends should be trusted, but enemies should be feared, and never should faith be put in their word. Rather than do so one should lose his life, for as infidels they take pride in breaking a promise and do so religiously, especially against the faithful.

As we were saying, the whole city now received the Governor with a great amount of festivity and general rejoicing, for good reports of his wisdom and affability having preceded him, these people had been very desirous of his presence. And to their happiness was added another of no less intensity which doubled their pleasure and joy; for accompanying the Governor in the same armada was the Bishop of the diocese, Friar Hernando de Mesa, a Dominican and a saintly man, who was the first prelate ever to visit that congregation. The Bishop, however, came near being drowned on disembarking, for when His Lordship sprang for the small landing boat, the ship moved back a little, and he, being unable to reach the second vessel because of his long robes, fell between the two. On emerging from the sea he struck his head against the ship and in consequence judged himself to have reached the end of his days. But the sailors plunged into the water and saved him.

Finding themselves now with two personages so essential for governing both the ecclesiastical and the civil estates, the city engaged in continuous celebrations for many days, sometimes with dances and masquerades which took place at night, and at other times with cane games[44] and bull fights in which they raced and hurled lances. On still other occasions they made merry by riding with long stirrups and running at the ring. Those who excelled in dexterity of arms and horsemanship, sharpness of wit in letters, novel inventions, and elegance of holiday attire, received rewards of honor, gold and silver trinkets, silk and brocades, all of which had been set aside for the occasion; and those with the least skill

[44] *juegos de cañas*—literally, cane-game or cane-play. According to R. B. Cunninghame-Graham *(Hernando de Soto, together with an Account of one of his Captains, Gonzalo Silvestre* [London: 1912], p. 69), this was the ancient game of jerid, brought by the Arabs from the East and continued in Spain until the close of the seventeenth century. It was played on horseback and though those participating cast only canes or reeds at each other, it simulated a battle of javelins.

were presented booby prizes.[45] There were no jousts or tourneys
either on horseback or afoot because of the lack of armor.[46] Many
of the cavaliers who accompanied the Governor participated in these
festivities and celebrations to demonstrate their skill in all things as
well as to amuse the inhabitants of the city, and happiness was
general.

In these entertainments the horses were a great asset, as they
always are in both play and work.[47] On the island there were a
great many of these fine animals, extremely good in shape, color,
and use; for besides possessing a natural excellence, the horses of
this region were bred with much curiosity and in great numbers.
Some individuals kept as many as fifty or sixty for trading purposes. For with the new conquests that had been made in Peru,
Mexico and other places, horses sold very well, and at that time
the biggest and best profits that the inhabitants of Cuba and its
vicinity realized, came from the sale of these animals.

[45] *premios de vituperio*—literally, prizes of vituperation, or awards of
scorn.
[46] *No huvo justas, ni torneos acavallo, ni apie, por falta de armaduras.*
Why no armor? Would the Inca have us believe that it was because this
was a real fighting unit with no fancy armor, good only for tournaments?
He is later somewhat scornful of the effectiveness of costly burnished steel
against savage arrows. A rather ironical passage from the Portuguese "Gentleman" would lead us to believe that the Castilians had set out more beauti-
fully arrayed than adequately prepared. When the Governor called a muster
at San Lúcar, the Portuguese contingent turned out in polished steel whereas
the Spaniards came in "silk over silk, pinked and slashed." On being ordered
to appear again the following day in more appropriate attire, they came in
sorry and rusty coats of mail, and even though they wore helmets, their
lances were poor. The Governor thereupon placed the glittering Lusitanians
near his standard bearer, and the possibly prejudiced narrator states that
some of the Spaniards sought to get among them.
[47] *burlas y veras*—literally, in jest and truth, or in acting and in real life.

CHAPTER XII

The supplies that the Governor procured in San-
tiago de Cuba. One notable circum-
stance concerning the natives
of those islands.

THERE was complete peace and harmony between the citizens
of Santiago and the people of the armada, and each made an
effort to offer the other the utmost friendship and hospitality. Consequently fiestas and celebrations continued for almost three months.
During this time, however, the Governor was occupied with more
serious matters. He visited other towns on the island, appointing
ministers of justice to remain as his deputies, and both he and his
leading men purchased numerous horses for the expedition. In
order for many to buy these animals it was necessary for him to
give a greater amount of help than he had offered in San Lúcar.
Meanwhile the natives of the island, who, as we have said, raise
horses in great number, had presented the Governor many of them.

At this time the island of Santiago de Cuba was prosperous and
rich, and there was a large Indian population; but a little later almost
all of the Indians hanged themselves. They were soft and lazy
and inclined to do little work, for all of that region of the earth is
hot and humid and the great fertility of the soil as well as the fruits
it bears makes it unnecessary to labor much in the planting and
harvesting of crops. No matter how little corn the Indians sowed,
each year they reaped more than they needed for their regular con-
sumption. As a result, they made no effort to do any other work.
Since they knew nothing about gold and did not value it as a thing
of wealth, they felt it wrong to take it from the streams or from the
face of the earth where it was nourished; and no matter how little
the Spaniards molested them, they were seriously grieved over any
trouble given them in regard to this metal. But the Devil incites for
his own gain, and he could do as he pleased with people so simple,

vicious and slothful as were these Indians. So it came to pass that
they took their own lives to avoid mining the gold which is so fine
and abundant in that island; and they did so in such a manner and in
such haste that in a single town fifty households of Indians, including
both women and children, hanged themselves one morning at dawn.
Scarcely a living being remained in that town, and it was the most
mournful sight in the world to see the bodies of these people suspended from the trees like thrushes when they are snared. The
Spaniards tried to prevent the suicides, but their efforts and remedies
were insufficient.[48] This abominable calamity was so extensive that
the natives of that island and its surroundings practically obliterated
themselves, so that today there is hardly an Indian left there. The
present high price of Negroes in that place grew out of this tragedy,
for it afterward became necessary to import Negroes to all parts
of the Indies to labor in the mines.

Among the things which the Governor did while in Santiago de
Cuba was to order Mateo Aceituno, a cavalier captain born in Tala-
vera de la Reyna, to go with other persons by sea and rebuild
Havana, for he learned that a few days previous to his arrival in
Santiago, the city of Havana had been sacked and burned by French
corsairs. These brigands had neither spared the church nor respected
the images within it, and the Governor and his whole company as
Catholics felt the desecration profoundly.

In sum, while in Santiago de Cuba, Hernando de Soto procured
everything that he felt was suitable for the conquest, and he was
benefited no little by a circumstance which we shall now relate. In
Trinidad, one of the towns of that island, there lived a very rich and
splendid cavalier named Vasco Porcallo de Figueroa, who was a

---

[48] An overseer of Vasco Porcallo de Figueroa seems to have found a
unique but effective means of eliminating these wasteful suicides. Awaiting
his slaves with cudgel in hand at the time and place of the proposed departure from this present life, he threatened to go with them for the purpose of
giving them even greater torment in their next existence. The slaves thereupon altered their plans.

close kinsman of the most illustrious house of Feria.[49] This noble man paid the Governor a visit in Santiago de Cuba, and being in that city for several days, he had occasion to observe the liveliness and gracefulness of so many cavaliers and such good footsoldiers as were going on the conquest. As a result, he was unable to contain himself, and his enthusiasm, which had already cooled for things of war, was now fired with new zeal for such. Thus he willingly offered to accompany the Governor on the conquest of that so-renowned kingdom of Florida. Vasco Porcallo was already over fifty years of age and had suffered many hardships both in the Indies and in Spain and Italy where in his youth he had been the victor in two duels. Moreover he had acquired great property through arms, and usually all men have a natural desire to enjoy their possessions. But such circumstances were insufficient to deter him, and laying everything else aside, he resolved to follow the Adelantado, offering him his person, life and property.[50] Thus the Governor, considering that a determination so heroic was instigated not by greed for property or desire for honor but by generosity itself and a bellicose spirit which this cavalier had always possessed, accepted his offer. Then having thanked and extolled him with words that corresponded within reason to the honor so great an act deserved, he named him Lieutenant General of his entire fleet and army; for many days before he had removed Nuño Tovar from that charge because of his having clandestinely married Doña Leonor de Bobadilla, daughter of the Count of Gomera.

Vasco Porcallo de Figueroa y de la Cerda as a very rich and generous man helped magnificently in the conquest of Florida. He

[49] One should remember that the Inca himself claimed a kinship with the illustrious house of Feria. One of his paternal grandfathers was Gómez Suárez de Figueroa, first Count of Feria. And coincidentally, Vasco Porcallo was accompanied on the expedition by an illegitimate son, who, like the Inca himself, bore the distinguished name of Gómez Suárez de Figueroa. See below, page 99.

[50] The miserable demise of his brother, who accompanied the ill-starred expedition of Pámphilo de Narváez, should in itself have deterred him from risking a similar fate, provided, of course, that he knew what had happened to his brother. See above, note 24.

carried with him on the journey many Spanish, Indian and Negro servants as well as other equipment and furnishings from his household; and he brought along thirty-six horses for his own use besides more than fifty others which he presented to individual cavaliers of the army. Furthermore, he provided a great supply of meat, fish, corn and cassava for the armada, not to mention other things they needed.[51] And finally, it was because of this man and in imitation of him that many Spaniards who were living in the island of Cuba became enthusiastic about the conquest and joined the expedition. These things all having been accomplished in a brief time, the Governor concluded matters of importance so that the armada and its men of war could depart for Havana.

CHAPTER XIII

The Governor goes to Havana. The preparations which he makes there for the conquest.

AT THE close of August of the same year of 1538, the General departed from the city of Santiago de Cuba for Havana. Setting out by land, he took fifty horsemen with him and gave orders for the remaining three hundred to follow in groups of fifty, leaving the city eight days apart so that they might travel more conveniently and be better provided for. The infantry, as well as his whole household and family, he commanded to travel by sea. They were to sail around the island, and all were to meet in Havana.

When the Governor arrived in Havana, he saw the destruction wrought by the corsairs upon that city, and with his own means he helped the inhabitants to rebuild their homes. Moreover, he restored to the best of his ability the churches and the images that the heretics had ravaged. Then just as soon as his ships came to Havana, he

---

[51] Many or all of the Governor's much valued swine were contributions of Vasco Porcallo.

ordered those men in the armada who were best acquainted with the sea to go in two brigantines under the command of Juan de Añasco and study the shores of Florida. They were to sail along the coast and note the creeks, ports or bays that might lie in that region.

Juan de Añasco, a cavalier who was a native of Seville, had come with the expedition as Comptroller of His Majesty's Imperial Exchequer, but he was a great mariner, cosmographer and astrologer. Departing from Havana with the two brigantines, he spent two months sailing up and down the coast of Florida. At the end of that time he returned to Havana with details of what he had seen, bringing with him two Indians whom he had seized on those shores. Taking note of the fine efforts of this man, the Governor ordered him to go again on the same mission and this time to make a meticulous observation of everything that lay along that coast so that the fleet would be able to sail straight to its destination and cast anchor without having to wander about in search of a place to land.

Juan de Añasco set sail on his second mission, and he explored the coast of Florida for three months with the utmost industry and care. At the end of that time he returned to Havana with a better documented account of what he had discovered and more information as to where ships might cast anchor and land. And from this voyage he brought with him two more Indians whom he had snared with effort and skillful trickery. The Governor and all of his people were now exceedingly pleased to have knowledge of definite ports where they would be able to disembark. At this point in the story, Alonso de Carmona says that because of their having been lost for two months on a desert island without anything to eat save sea snails and booby birds, which they killed with cudgels, and later on their return to Havana having risked great danger of being drowned, Juan de Añasco and all who came on that boat, when they landed, crawled on their knees from the very edge of the water to the church where a mass was said in their behalf. And he adds that when they had completed their pious offering, they were warmly received by the

Governor and his people, all of whom had been very much afraid that these men had been lost at sea, etc.

While in Havana preparing and providing necessities for his expedition, the Adelantado Hernando de Soto received word that the Viceroy of Mexico, Don Antonio de Mendoza, likewise was raising men for a conquest of Florida.[52] Not knowing to what place these people were to be sent, the Governor began to fear that the two expeditions would encounter and impede each other, thus causing such discord as there had been in Mexico between the Marquis del Valle Hernando Cortés and Pámphilo de Narváez, who had gone in the name of Governor Diego Velásquez to bring him an account of the people and the charge he had entrusted to Cortés. Similar quarrels had existed in Peru between the Adelantados Don Diego de Almagro and Don Pedro de Alvarado at the beginning of the conquest of that kingdom. For this reason and for the purpose of avoiding the opprobrium of buying and selling people as those captains were said to have done, Hernando de Soto felt that it would be wise to give notice to Don Antonio of the decrees and the commission with which His Majesty had favored him, that the Viceroy might be aware of them, and at the same time to beseech him not to raise people or hinder his expedition; then, if necessary, to threaten and persuade him with the King's orders. So for the purpose he dispatched to Mexico a Galician soldier named San Jurge,[53] who was industrious and skillful in everything that he did.

Shortly afterward, San Jurge returned with a message from Don Antonio de Mendoza stating that the Governor should by all means make his entrance into Florida and carry out his conquest as he had mapped it without fear that the two expeditions would meet; for, he said, he was sending his people to a place far distant from where the Governor was going, and Florida was so long and so wide that there was enough of it for all. He added likewise that he not only

---

[52] The reference here is to Mendoza's initial preparations for the expedition of Fray Marcos de Niza and Francisco Vásquez de Coronado to the Seven Cities of Cíbola.

[53] The Inca later spells this man's name as one word.

did not want to hinder the Governor but wished rather to help him if there should be need, and consequently was offering him his person, property, and anything he might be able to make available through his position and administration. This response satisfied the Governor and he was grateful for the Viceroy's offer.[54]

At this time, which was the middle of April,[55] all of the cavalry that had remained in Santiago de Cuba arrived in Havana, having traveled by very short marches the two hundred and fifty leagues more or less that lie between those cities. Seeing now that both cavalry and infantry were once more assembled, and that the time was approaching when he could sail, Hernando de Soto named as governess of that great island of Cuba his wife, Doña Isabel de Bobadilla, a woman of the utmost benevolence and discretion, who was the daughter of Governor Pedro Arias de Avila. As her chief deputy in Havana, he appointed Joan de Rojas, a noble and virtuous cavalier; and as her deputy in the city of Santiago, he named Francisco de Guzmán,[56] another of his cavaliers. These two men had ruled those cities before the General had arrived, and since his relations with them had been good, he left them in the same positions they had previously held.

The Governor now purchased the *Santa Ana*,[57] a very beautiful ship which came by chance to the port of Havana. In the conquest

[54] Mendoza's displeasure over the appointment of this new rival for power in America was increased by an order from his Queen not to poach on De Soto's preserves. Moreover, he was almost frantic lest news of rich discoveries to the north of him be relayed to the Adelantado by way of Cuba. Therefore when in August Fray Marcos returned to the capital with glowing stories of the wealth of Cíbola, a decree was proclaimed in the streets forbidding anyone to leave Mexico without license. By November the friar's stories had reached Havana, but De Soto was already submerged in the wilderness of Florida.

[55] April, 1539.

[56] See below, page 481 for further reference to a Francisco de Guzmán.

[57] According to the report of the United States De Soto Expedition Commission, the *Santa Ana* was apparently the boat which Hernán Ponce had brought to Havana, and Garcilaso's confusion resulted from the fact that other vessels arrived at Havana from Mexico just before the fleet sailed for Florida. Ponce's boat, it appears, was in such poor condition that it was

and discovery of the Río de la Plata, this vessel had served as the flagship of the Governor and Captain General Don Pedro de Zúñiga y Mendoza, who was ruined in that expedition and later while returning to Spain died of an illness at sea. His ship then had proceeded to Seville and afterward returned under the command of another to Mexico, from whence it was coming when Hernando de Soto bought it because of its great size and beauty. Eighty horses were carried in this vessel to Florida.

CHAPTER XIV

A ship arrives at Havana with Hernán Ponce,
a companion of the Governor.

THE Governor was now at the point of embarking on his conquest and was awaiting only the advent of favorable weather when a ship hailing from Nombre de Dios came to Havana. To all appearances, this vessel had been driven into port against its will by a powerful storm, for during the four or five days that it was seen resisting the wind, it came three times to the entrance of the harbor, only to return again as many times to the open sea as if it were making an effort to shun the place. But even though the principal passenger aboard may have promised great rewards to his mariners should they avoid this particular haven, they could not stand out against the raging tempest. No matter how much they hated to do so, they had to come into the harbor because there is no resisting the fury of the sea.

You must know that before Hernando de Soto left Peru for Spain, as we mentioned in our first chapter, he formed a pact and fraternity with Hernán Ponce whereby each was to share equally in the other's gains or losses during the whole of their lives, whether

---

scuttled and sunk on the Florida coast, and the *Magdalena* was returned to Havana for the express purpose of taking Ponce to Spain. See *Final Report, De Soto Commission*, pp. 97–98.

it were in allotments of Indians which His Majesty might give them or in things of honor and advantage that they might receive. For at the time of his departure from that land, it had been his intention to return and enjoy there the spoils which he had merited for services rendered in its conquest, although, as we have seen, his thoughts turned afterward to other places. This same kind of partnership was formed then and later among many cavaliers and individuals of importance in the conquest of Peru, and I myself came to know people who lived as brothers under such a pact, enjoying together the allotments they received without making any division of them whatsoever.

Now Hernán Ponce (whose lineage and place of birth I did not manage to learn, though I did hear that he was from the kingdom of León), after the departure of Hernando de Soto for Spain, held a very rich allotment of Indians in Peru, a favor granted him in His Majesty's name by the Marquis Don Francisco Pizarro. The Indians yielded him a great amount of gold, silver and precious stones; and with these things and whatever else he could realize from the value of his rich household ornaments and furnishings (for everything then sold by weight of gold), as well as from the collection of some debts his partner had left him, he now was returning as a very prosperous man to Spain. But when he learned in Nombre de Dios or in Cartagena that Hernando de Soto was at Havana with such a great provision of people and ships for the expedition to Florida, he resolved to by-pass that city completely lest he have to give the Governor an account of what was owned between them and consequently share with him the wealth he was bringing from Peru. For he feared that the Governor, as a needy man who had undertaken so much expense, would deprive him of everything. Thus it was that Hernán Ponce had refused persistently to enter the harbor at Havana so long as it was possible for him to avoid doing so; but Fortune, or the raging sea, disdains or favors whomever it wishes without heed or respect.

As soon as the ship came into port and the Governor learned that Hernán Ponce was aboard, he sent envoys to visit and congratulate him on his arrival as well as to offer him his home, goods, offices and titles; for as a partner and brother he considered that this man rightfully owned half of all that he himself possessed and commanded. Then he went afterward in person to greet his friend and bring him ashore.

Hernán Ponce did not relish so much civility and brotherhood. Nevertheless when he and the Governor had exchanged greetings with the usual expressions of courtesy, he hid his anxiety and excused himself from landing as best he could, saying that he was not yet prepared to disembark because of the great labor and loss of sleep suffered during those four or five stormy days at sea. Then he begged Hernando de Soto to permit him to remain aboard ship for at least that night, promising that should he feel better the following day, he would come ashore to kiss his lordship's hand and receive and enjoy the favor offered him. His request was granted, for the Governor longed to show the man that he had no desire to go against his will in anything; but he at the same time sensed the evil in Hernán Ponce and accordingly commanded that guards be stationed on land and sea to keep watch and observe how he conducted himself during the night.

And now since Hernán Ponce had no faith in the Governor's courtesy and was unable to comprehend as he did later how extensive it was, and since he took counsel solely with Avarice (whose advice is always prejudicial to the one accepting it), he decided to hide in a safe place on land a great quantity of gold and precious stones which he had brought from Peru, not noting that there could be no secure place for them in all that district on either land or sea—a place where there would be more hope for the courtesy of another than there would be in his own diligence. But the fearful and suspicious always choose a remedy which brings them the greatest damage and misfortune. Thus this cavalier, while leaving the silver on the ship for the purpose of making a show of it, now commanded his men to take all of the gold, pearls and precious stones, more than forty thousand pesos worth, which he had brought in two small chests, and at midnight to carry them to the house of some friend in the town or bury them near the shore, so that later, when the storm which he expected from Hernando de Soto had abated, he could return and recover his property.

But just the contrary came to pass. As the little boat containing Hernán Ponce's men approached land and its occupants unloaded their cargo, they were quietly watched by sentinels whom the Governor had stationed in the rugged forests of that port and along the coast itself; then when they had carried their cargo some distance ashore, these same sentinels fell upon them. Abandoning their treasure, all now fled toward their boat. Some succeeded in reaching it, whereas others, who failed to do so, plunged into the sea to save their lives or avoid capture. Without further ado, the guards seized the booty and carried it to the Governor, who was very much pained to find his companion so suspicious of his friendship and brotherliness as this act proved him to be. Meanwhile, however, he commanded that the treasure be hidden until it were possible to determine what Hernán Ponce would do about it.

CHAPTER XV

The issues between Hernán Ponce de León and
Hernando de Soto. How the Governor
embarked for Florida.

ON THE following day, Hernán Ponce disembarked, grieving exceedingly because of having lost his treasure in the very place he had hoped to secure it. But concealing his pain, he went to lodge with the Governor. When the two men were alone, they talked at length of matters pertaining to both the past and present, their conversation turning eventually to the incident of the preceding night. The Governor complained bitterly because Hernán Ponce had lacked faith in his loyalty and fraternity, and had been moved to conceal his possessions by fear that his partner would seize them. Then he added that he was going to do something which would reveal that his intentions were far from such. So saying he commanded to be brought before them all that had been removed from the boat on the previous evening, and presenting it to his friend, he begged him to examine everything so that if aught were missing it might be restored. Moreover, to prove how different his own feelings had been about dissolving their bonds, he declared that he could produce witnesses[58] who were present when the writs and decrees necessary for the conquest had been authorized, and that these same witnesses could certify that all expenditures for the project and even the petition to His Majesty for permission to undertake it had been executed with their pact in mind so that both could enjoy the honor and advantage of the expedition. Finally, to satisfy Hernán Ponce further, the Governor invited him to accompany the expedition and offered to renounce to him, regardless of his decision, whatever title or titles he most coveted from among those His Majesty had granted. Let Ponce but inform him, he said, of all that he might need for his pleasure, honor and profit, and contrary to his fears, he would find in him the kind of friend that he desired.

Hernán Ponce was humiliated by such great courtesy and by his own lack of faith. Dispensing with excuses, since he could find none that would exonerate him, he now begged that his past error be forgiven and that the Governor deem it wise to continue to strengthen and support the honor he had conferred upon him by calling him companion and brother. This title, he said, he considered himself fortunate in possessing, and he wanted no other since for him there was none better. All that he now desired, he continued, was that greater fame be given to their contracts of partnership by having them renewed and that his lordship should proceed on the conquest with much good fortune while permitting him to return to Spain; for God granting them health and life, they meanwhile would simply enjoy their fraternity, and later, if they wished

[58] The Governor may have had in mind Juan de Añasco, Luis de Moscoso de Alvarado, Nuño Tovar and Juan Rodríguez Lobillo, all of whom, according to the Elvas account, accompanied him to the Court of Charles V. Furthermore, all but Juan de Añasco had been with him in Peru.

to do so, divide their gains. He did plead, however, that at this time Doña Isabel de Bobadilla, the Governor's wife, be permitted to receive ten thousand pesos of the gold and silver he had brought from Peru; for, he said, although less than half the amount due the Governor according to their pact, this sum would serve as a contribution to the expedition and its acceptance would indicate that his lordship was still willing to take his share of the spoils.

It met with the Governor's pleasure to do what Hernán Ponce had requested. So both of them being in hearty agreement, they renewed the contracts of their partnership and fraternity,[59] and conducted themselves in accordance with these bonds during the whole time they remained in Havana. The Governor privately instructed his men and persuaded them by his own public example to make no distinction in their treatment of Hernán Ponce and himself. Thus all addressed that captain as Your Lordship and respected him even as they did the Adelantado.

Having concluded the events we have just described and feeling the weather now suitable for sailing, the Governor ordered that the ships be loaded as soon as possible with provisions and other things that they were to carry. Then when the supplies had been placed in the vessels as they were to go, the horses were brought on board. Eighty of these beasts were carried in the *Santa Ana;* sixty, in the *San Christóbal;* forty, in the *Concepción;* and seventy, in the three small boats, the *San Joan,* the *Santa Bárbara,* and the *San Antón.* In all a total of three hundred and fifty[60] horses were taken to Florida. Next, the men of war came aboard. Including the islanders who wanted to accompany the expedition but not counting the mariners of the eight ships, the caravel and the brigantines, there were one thousand men, all fine people and all provided with arms,

[59] Evidence of De Soto's sincerity is to be found in a document or will drawn up in Havana two days before he sailed for Florida. Here he reaffirms that one-half the estate he then possesses or should come to possess, belongs to his friend. The article states in addition that this partnership had been in existence for eighteen or nineteen years.

[60] One might note that only two hundred and fifty horses are allocated.

personal equipment and horses. So great was their number that never before nor since in any other expedition for the conquest of the Indians has such a goodly band of people and horses been seen in any one group.

In all details concerning boats, people, horses and fighting equipment, Alonso de Carmona and Juan Coles are equally in agreement in their accounts.

This multitude of ships, horses and fighting men, not to mention mariners, accompanied the Governor and Adelantado Hernando de Soto when he sailed from Havana on the 12th of May in the year 1539 to enter and make a conquest of the kingdom of Florida. And so adequately had this cavalier stocked his armada with all manner of supplies that it appeared to be established in a well-provided city rather than navigating across the sea. But we shall leave the fleet here and return to a new deed perpetrated by Hernán Ponce in Havana, where, on pretext of resting and awaiting more favorable weather for his voyage to Spain, he had remained until the Governor's departure.

Thus it was that eight days having elapsed after the Governor sailed, Hernán Ponce presented a document to Juan de Rojas, Lieutenant Governor of Havana, stating that because of his fear that Hernando de Soto as a person of power would seize all of the wealth he had brought from Peru, he had surrendered to that man ten thousand pesos in gold, which he did not owe him; and he now requested that the Governor's wife, Doña Isabel de Bobadilla, who had received the money, be commanded to refund it. Should she refuse to do so, he said, he would complain to His Majesty, the Emperor Our Lord.

When news of this demand reached the ears of Doña Isabel, she replied that there were many old and new accounts between her husband and Hernán Ponce which should be investigated, for according to the contracts of their partnership, it was evident that the latter was indebted to her husband for more than fifty thousand ducats as his portion of the outlay for the conquest. She thereupon instructed the magistrate to seize the man and hold him with great care until the records could be examined, and then she offered immediately to produce these records in her husband's name. But Hernán Ponce learned of the lady's reply before the magistrate carried out his duty (since deceitful spies can be purchased in all places); so to avoid any more such dangers and contingencies as he had just experienced, he raised sail and came to Spain without waiting for an investigation of those obligations which specified that he should share a great sum of money with Hernando de Soto.

Many times even rich and noble men are so blinded by selfish interests that they do things which serve no other purpose than to disclose the baseness and vileness of their souls.

End of the First Book.

THE
FIRST PART
OF THE
SECOND BOOK

Of the History of Florida by the Inca treats of the Governor's arrival in that land and his discovery there of traces of Pámphilo de Narváez; his finding of a Christian captive who describes the tortures and cruelties imposed upon him by the Indians as well as the hospitalities extended him by a certain Indian lord of vassals; the further preparations which the Spaniards made for the expedition and the events that occurred in the first eight provinces they explored; and the extraordinary bravery in both words and deeds of a bold cacique. It contains thirty chapters.

CHAPTER I

*The Governor arrives in Florida and finds traces
of Pámphilo de Narváez.*

GOVERNOR Hernando de Soto, who, as we have said, was sailing in search of Florida, first sighted land in that kingdom on the last day of May. He had been nineteen days at sea because of unfavorable weather, but his ships now anchored in a good, deep bay which the Spaniards named the Bay of the Holy Spirit.[1] It being late afternoon when the armada arrived, no one disembarked, but on the following day, which was the first of June, some went ashore in small boats. They returned with their vessels loaded with grass for the horses and with many unripe grapes from vines found growing wild in the forests. The grape is not cultivated by the natives of this great kingdom of Florida, and they do not care as much for it as do people of other nations, but they will eat it when it is very ripe or has been dried. Our men were extremely happy over these fine specimens of the fruit, for they were similar to those grown in Spain, the like of which they had not found in Mexico or in the whole of Peru.

[1] *La Bahía del Espíritu Santo.* They first sighted land on the 25th, the Feast of *Espíritu Santo;* i.e., Whitsunday. The earliest known map of the expedition labels Charlotte Harbor "b [aía] Honda," and many have thought that it was here that De Soto first landed, but the place is now generally conceded to have been Tampa Bay.

On the second of June, the Governor ordered three hundred foot-soldiers ashore to perform the solemn act of taking possession of Florida in the name of the Emperor Charles V, King of Spain. This procedure completed, these men passed the rest of the day walking along the coast, and that night slept on land. As yet they had seen nothing of the natives, but at the third or dawn watch, the Indians burst upon them with such audacity and force as to compel them to retreat to the edge of the water. Meanwhile, however, they sounded an alarm, and both men and horses came from the ships to aid them as quickly as if they too had been on land.

Lieutenant General Vasco Porcallo de Figueroa, who commanded the assistance, found these footsoldiers very much upset and confused, for like raw recruits, they had got in each other's way while fighting, and some already had been wounded by arrows. With the advent of help, however, all pursued the Indians for a good while and then returned to their quarters. But hardly had they arrived there when Vasco Porcallo's horse fell dead from the effects of an arrow. Striking above the saddle, the missile had passed through the cloth, saddle tree, and pack saddle; and more than a third of it had penetrated the ribs of the animal to the very cavity of its body. Vasco Porcallo, however, was exceedingly pleased that the first horse to be used in the conquest and the first lance to be employed in the first skirmish should have been his.[2]

On this and the following day, the Spaniards disembarked both animals and men. Then when they had rested for eight or nine days and had put everything in order pertaining to their ships, they marched inland a little more than two leagues to the town of a cacique known as Hirrihigua. When Pámphilo de Narváez had gone to conquer that province, he had waged war with Hirrihigua and later he had converted the Indian to friendship; then for some unknown reason, he had committed certain abuses against the

---

[2] *la primera lanza que en los enemigos se estrenó*—The word *estrenar* has a first-night implication that cannot be reproduced in English without some such expression as "first lance to make its debut among the enemy."

Cacique which are of too odious a nature to be told here.³ It suffices to say that because of those offenses, Hirrihigua was now so
fearful of the Spaniards and so consumed with bitterness toward
them that on learning of Hernando de Soto's arrival in his land,
he left both his house and village unprotected and fled to the
forest. And although the Governor sent him gifts, endearments
and promises by means of certain of his vassals whom the Spaniards had captured, still he refused to come out and make peace
or even listen to any messages. Instead his anger was aroused
at those of his vassals serving as envoys, and he ordered them to
refrain from doing so, since they were aware of the manner in which
he had been hurt and offended by the Spanish nation. He would
willingly receive the heads of these Castilians, he said, but he wanted
to hear nothing more of their names and words.

All such things and more abuse can bring about, particularly if it
is committed against someone who has given no offense. But in
order to present a better picture of the rage Hirrihigua felt for the
Castilians, it will be well to show here some of the cruelties and
martyrdoms⁴ he himself had inflicted upon four of Pámphilo de
Narváez' men whom he succeeded in capturing. To a certain extent
we may be digressing; yet we will not be leaving the main purpose
of the story, and the digression will contribute much to the value
of our history.

Know then that some days after Pámphilo de Narváez had done
what we have mentioned and had departed from the land of Hirrihigua, one of his ships, which had stopped elsewhere, happened
to call at this same bay in search of its captain.⁵ On ascertaining
the identity and purpose of the vessel, the Cacique resolved to seize

³ The Inca does tell some of them, though, in Chapter III, of this book.
He is our sole authority for Narváez' outrage upon this chieftain. It may be
that these cruelties were the work of one of Narváez' commanders.

⁴ *martyrios*—The idea of death is here, else our own more common word
"atrocities" would be better.

⁵ According to the Elvas account, this ship had returned to Cuba after
Pámphilo de Narváez landed, and from there had been ordered back to
Florida.

every man aboard and burn him alive. Therefore, with the idea of instilling confidence in them, he pretended to be a friend of their captain, sending them word that Pámphilo de Narváez had indeed been in that place, and moreover had left a message with him as to what their ship should do if it too should call there. Then to persuade them to belief, he disclosed from land two or three sheets of white paper and some old letters which he had obtained from Spaniards in former times by friendly means, or however it may have been, and in the interim had guarded very carefully.

But in spite of all of Hirrihigua's manifestations, the men aboard ship were very cautious and refused to disembark. Then the Cacique sent out a canoe with four principal Indians, saying that he was offering these lords and cavaliers as hostages and security so that those Spaniards who wished to come ashore and learn of their captain, Pámphilo de Narváez, might do so. (It seems inappropriate to employ the term cavalier, or *caballero,* in referring to Indians because they possessed no horses, or *caballos,* from which word the name is deduced; but since in Spain this term implies a nobleman and since there is a nobility among the Indians, it may be used likewise in speaking of them.) And he added that if they were not reassured thereby, he would send more pledges. On witnessing the apparent good faith of the chieftain, four Spaniards set out in the canoe with those Indians who had brought the hostages. The Cacique had hoped for all of them; still when he saw that only these few were coming, he resolved not to insist on more lest the four be offended and return to their ship.

As soon as the Indian hostages saw the Christians on land and in the hands of their people, they plunged into the sea, and diving far below the surface, swam like fish to the shore, thus fulfilling the instructions of their chieftain. Meanwhile, the Spaniards on board ship, finding themselves fooled,[6] sailed out of the bay before anything worse could befall them, very much grieved, however, at having lost their four companions so indiscreetly.

[6] *burlados*—literally, burlesqued; "laughed at" might be a better translation.

CHAPTER II

The tortures which an Indian chief inflicted
upon a Spaniard who was his slave.

THE Cacique Hirrihigua now ordered that the four Spaniards be guarded most cautiously so that with their death his Indians might solemnize a great feast which according to the rites of paganism they expected to celebrate within a few days. Then with the arrival of that festival, he commanded that the captives be taken naked to the plaza and there made to run in turn from one side to the other while the Indians shot arrows at them as if they were wild beasts. But to delay further the death and increase the agonies of their victims, and at the same time to prolong and enliven their own festivity and enjoyment, they were to discharge only a few arrows at a time.

Three of the Spaniards were tortured in this manner, and Hirrihigua received a great amount of pleasure and delight as he watched them flee in all directions, searching for a refuge which they found only in death. But when the Indians wanted to bring out the fourth, a native of Seville named Juan Ortiz, who was scarcely eighteen years of age, the Cacique's wife came with her three daughters and, standing before her husband, begged that he be content with the death of the three captives and pardon the fourth, since he and his companions had not come to that land with Pámphilo de Narváez and therefore were guiltless of the wickedness perpetrated by their predecessors. This particular boy, she said, was deserving of forgiveness because of his tender age, which gave proof of his innocence and pled for compassion; and since he had committed no crime, it was therefore enough that he remain with them as a slave and not be destroyed so cruelly.

In an effort to make his wife and daughters happy, the Cacique for the time being spared the life of Juan Ortiz; but afterward he tortured him so grievously and bitterly that the boy frequently was moved to envy his three dead companions. The ceaseless labor of carrying firewood and water was so strenuous, the eating and sleeping were so infrequent, and the daily slaps, blows, and lashes as well as other torments given him on feast days were so cruel that he many times would have sought relief in suicide had he not been a Christian. For in addition to daily tortures, Hirrihigua on numerous occasions of celebration, just as a diversion, ordered the boy to run continuously the entire day in the long plaza where his comrades had been slain. He himself went out to watch, taking his noblemen, who carried bows and arrows with which to kill the captive at any time he should pause. Thus Juan Ortiz began at sunrise and continued from one side of the plaza to the other until sunset, these being the time limits allotted by the Indians for him to run; and even when Hirrihigua went away to eat, he left his cavaliers to watch the youth so that they might slay him in the event he should stop. Then when the day was over, this sad boy lay extended on the ground, more dead than alive, as one can imagine. But on such occasions as these, he received the compassion of the chieftain's wife and daughters, who took him and clothed him and did other things which helped to sustain his life, although it would have been better had they deprived him of it and thereby freed him from his many tasks.

Hirrihigua now realized that such numerous and continuous torments were not sufficient to destroy Juan Ortiz, and his hatred for him increased by the hour. So to finish with the youth he gave the order on a certain feast day to kindle a great fire in the center of the plaza, and when he saw many live coals made, he commanded that they be spread out and that over them there be placed a grill-like wooden structure[7] which stood a yard above the ground, and upon which they should put his captive in order to roast him alive. Thus it was done, and here the poor Spaniard, after being tied to the grill, lay stretched out on one side for a long time. But at the

---

[7] *barbacoa*—Because of the nature of the torture, we have been tempted to leave the word in Spanish.

shrieks of the miserable youth, the wife and daughters of the Cacique rushed up, and, pleading with their lord and even scolding him for his cruelty, removed the boy from the fire, not, however, before he was half-baked and blisters that looked like halves of oranges had formed on one of his sides. Some of these blisters burst and much blood ran from them, so that they were painful to behold. Hirrihigua overlooked what his wife and daughters were doing because they were women whom he loved deeply, and possibly also because he wanted someone on whom he later might vent his wrath and exercise his vengeance. And although Juan Ortiz provided less occasion for vengeance than the chieftain desired, still he was amused with that little. Thus he many times expressed his regret that he had destroyed the other three Spaniards so precipitately. The women, on the contrary, had time and again repented of having saved Juan Ortiz from death on the first occasion, since they had seen how long and cruel his daily torments had been. But being moved to great compassion on beholding him in his present state, they took him to their lodging and treated him with the juices of herbs (for having no doctors, both Indian men and women are great herbalists). Hence after many days, Juan Ortiz recovered, although the burns from the fire left great scars.

Wishing to free himself from the sight of his captive as he now was and at the same time from the bother of the pleas of his wife and daughters, the Cacique ordered to be inflicted upon the youth another torment which, though not so grave as those in the past, would keep him from idleness. This was that day and night he should guard the remains of dead citizens placed in a designated section of a forest that lay at a distance from the town. These bodies had been put above the ground in some wooden chests which served as sepulchres. The chests had no hinges and could be closed only by covering them with boards and then placing rocks or beams of wood on top of the boards. Since the Indians were not cautious about guarding their dead, the lions, which are numerous in that country, sometimes robbed the chests and carried away the bodies, thus creating a situation which grieved and angered these people exceedingly. So it was that the Cacique now ordered Juan Ortiz to guard the place carefully, and he threatened and swore that should any corpse or any part of one be borne away, he would bake the Spaniard alive, this time without any remedy. Then as a means of protecting the sepulchres, he gave the youth four darts to throw at the lions or any other wild beasts that might come to desecrate the place.

Thanking God for having delivered him from the continuous presence of his master, Juan Ortiz now went to guard the dead, hoping to find with them a better life than he had found with the living. And he did watch these bodies with the utmost care, especially at night, since it was then that the risk was greater. But it happened that on one of these nights when he was thus occupied, he found himself unable to resist sleep and consequently succumbed in the dawn watch, this being the hour at which sleep ordinarily shows its greatest force against those who keep vigil. At this time a lion came to the place of the dead, and knocking down the covers of one of the chests, seized and bore away the body of a child which had been laid there only two days previously.

Juan Ortiz was awakened by the noise of the falling boards, and when on rushing to the chest he failed to find the body, he considered himself as good as dead. Nevertheless in his anxiety and anguish he did not waver in his duty and determined instead to go in search of the lion; for he vowed that on running across it, he would recover the remains of the child or die at the hands of the beast. At the same time, however, he commended himself to God, invoking His name and making his confessions, for he was confident that when the Indians came at dawn to visit the sepulchres and failed to find the body of the child, they would burn him alive. As he moved here and there through the forest, haunted by the fear of death, he came out upon a broad road and proceeded for a little while down the middle of it, for impossible as escape was, he had made up his mind to flee. Then in the woods not far from where he was walking, he heard a sound much like that of a dog gnawing bones. Listening carefully, he made certain of the sound, and suspecting that it might be the lion devouring the stolen corpse, groped his way through the underbrush toward the spot from whence it was coming. Presently in the light of the moon, which was shining, although dimly, he saw the beast nearby, feeding at its pleasure upon the remains of the child.

Calling upon God and mustering courage, Juan Ortiz hurled a dart. At the moment he did not see what kind of throw he had made because of the underbrush; still, he felt that his marksmanship had not been bad because his hand was salty,[8] and there was a saying among hunters that one's hands were thus when he had made a successful shot at wild beasts in the night. Encouraged now by this hope, slight as it was, and by the fact that he had not heard the lion flee from the spot to which he had directed his dart, Juan Ortiz now awaited the coming of dawn, trusting in Our Lord to succor him in his necessity.

CHAPTER III

*A continuation of the miserable life of the
captive. How he fled from his
master.*

WITH the light of day, Juan Ortiz verified the good throw made blindly in the night, for he discovered the lion lying dead, pierced through the center of its heart and entrails (as was afterward seen when its carcass was opened). The sight was more than he could believe, so with a joy that can be imagined more easily than described, he gathered up the uneaten remnants of the child's body and returned them to the chest. Then seizing the dead beast by one foot, he dragged it to his master without removing the

---

[8] *quedarle la mano sabrosa*—something like our expression, "to have a green thumb."

dart so that the Cacique could see the animal just as he himself had found it.

Hirrihigua and his whole village were greatly amazed at what Juan Ortiz had accomplished, for in that land it is generally considered miraculous to kill a lion, and he who happens to do so is treated thereafter with great veneration and respect. Since this creature is so savage, people everywhere should be held in high esteem for destroying it, especially if, as in the case of Juan Ortiz, they do so without benefit of arquebus or crossbow. It is true that the lions of Florida, Mexico and Peru are not so large or so wild as those of Africa, but after all they are lions and the name is enough. Even though there is a common saying to the effect that these animals are not so fierce as they are painted, nevertheless those who have found themselves in the proximity of them insist that live lions are much fiercer than painted ones, no matter how lifelike the painting may be.

With the good fortune of Juan Ortiz, the Cacique's wife and daughters became even more daring and courageous in their efforts to persuade their lord to exonerate the youth completely and give him tasks that would be both honorable and worthy of his strength and valor. And thenceforward for a few days, Hirrihigua did treat his slave better, being motivated as much by the admiration and esteem the people of his house and town had bestowed upon him as by the fact that he had performed a deed which was not only valiant but one that the Indians in their superstition had come to venerate as something sacred and even superhuman. Nevertheless outrage knows no forgiveness, and each time that Hirrihigua recalled that Spaniards had cast his mother to the dogs and permitted them to feed upon her body, and each time that he attempted to blow his nose and failed to find it, the Devil seized him with the thought of avenging himself on Juan Ortiz, as if that young man personally had deprived him of his nostrils. The very sight of this Spaniard always brought past offenses before his eyes, and such memories increased each day his anger and lust for retribution.

So although Hirrihigua for some time restrained these passions, he now was unable to resist them. Thus one day he informed his wife and daughters that he could no longer suffer the Christian to live. For, he said, he found the life of this man very odious and abominable and could not view him without experiencing a revival of past grievances and without feeling offended anew; and it was therefore his command that unless they were willing to share the same anger, they should in no manner intercede further for the Christian. Then he added that in order to end completely with his slave he had made up his mind that on such and such a feast day soon to be celebrated, the Indians should shoot the Spaniard with arrows and slay him just as they had slain his companions. This, he said, was to be done in spite of Juan Ortiz' bravery, for such bravery being that of an enemy should be abhorred rather than esteemed.

Perceiving the anger of the Cacique, the women realized that further intercession was useless, and moreover that it had been rude for them to importune and pain their lord so extensively in behalf of his slave. So they ventured no word in contradiction, instead hastening with female astuteness to agree that he should by all means proceed with his plan since such was his pleasure. But a few days before the approaching celebration, the eldest daughter, in order to carry out an idea of her own, secretly notified Juan Ortiz of her father's decision against him, warning at the same time that neither she nor her mother and sisters would or could prevail upon Hirrihigua since he had imposed silence upon them in regard to his prisoner and had threatened them should they violate his restriction. To this sad news, however, the maiden in her desire to encourage the Spaniard added some words of quite another character.

"Lest you lose faith in me and despair of your life or doubt that I will do everything in my power to save you," she said, "I will assist you to escape and find refuge if you are a man and have the courage to flee. For tonight, if you will come at a certain hour to a certain place, you will find an Indian in whom I shall entrust both your welfare and mine. This man will guide you to a bridge two leagues distant; but when you arrive there, you must command him to go no further and instead to return before dawn to this village lest he be missed and by revealing my rashness as well as his own cause both of us to suffer for having given you aid. Six leagues beyond the bridge there is another town, the lord of which is Mucozo, a man who loves me exceedingly and desires my hand in marriage. You will tell him that I am sending you in my name so that he may help you in your need. I know that, being the person he is, he will do everything he can for you, as you shall see. And now commend yourself to your God, for there is no more that I can do in your behalf."

Juan Ortiz threw himself at the feet of the maiden in gratitude for this favor and benefit as well as for all of her kindnesses both past and present. Then he made preparations to flee during the coming night. At the appointed hour, when everyone in the Cacique's household was asleep, he sought out the promised guide and they departed from the town without being heard. When they reached the bridge and the youth learned that there was no further possibility of his losing his way before coming to the town of Mucozo, he instructed his companion to return at once with the utmost caution to his home.

CHAPTER IV

*The magnanimity of the Curaca or Cacique
Mucozo to whom the captive was
entrusted.*

A FUGITIVE now, Juan Ortiz arrived before dawn at the place he was seeking, but he dared not enter lest he create a disturbance. Then when it was day he saw two Indians coming out of the town by the same path he himself was pursuing. These men wanted to shoot at him, for the people of Florida are always armed; but Juan Ortiz, being armed also, put an arrow to his bow to defend himself and even to take the offense. Oh, how much a small favor can do, especially if it be the favor of a lady; for we now see that he who only a short time previously feared death and knew not where to hide, now dared mete it out with his own hands simply because he had seen himself assisted by a beautiful, discreet and generous young maiden. But such a favor does exceed all other human kindness.

Mustering his courage and strength and even his arrogance, Juan Ortiz disclosed that he was no enemy but merely a messenger sent by a lady to the lord of that land. On hearing him, the Indians withheld their arrows and then conducted him to the town where they informed their Cacique that Hirrihigua's slave had come with a message for him.

This news having been made known to Mucozo (or Mocozo, for it is the same name), he came to the plaza to receive the Christian's words. Then Juan Ortiz, after having saluted the chieftain as best he knew how according to native customs, gave a brief account of the martyrdoms he had suffered at the hands of his master, in testimony of which he revealed the scars from the burns, blows, and other injuries he had received. He told how Hirrihigua at last had determined to kill him for the purpose of enlivening a certain feast day that was approaching, and how that Cacique's wife and daughters, who had saved him so many times previously, dared not speak now in his behalf since they had been forbidden to do so under penalty of incurring their lord's wrath. "But the eldest daughter," he continued, "not wanting to see me perish, commanded and gave me courage as a last resort to flee. She provided a guide to direct me to your town and your lodging, and told me to present myself before you in her name, saying that she begs Your Lordship, for the love that you bear her, to receive me under your protection and, being the person you are, to favor me as something she herself has entrusted to you."

Mucozo received the Christian affably and listened with compassion to his account of the sufferings and torments he had experienced, evidences of which were clearly revealed by the scars on his body, for he was dressed as the Indians of that land in no more than some loin cloths. At this point in the story Alonso de Carmona adds that the Cacique embraced Juan Ortiz and kissed him on the face as a sign of peace. Moreover, he assured him of his welcome and urged him to make an effort to forget the fear of his former existence; for, he said, in his house and company he would find life very different from what he had known previously. "In order to serve the one who sent you as well as yourself who have come to me and my house for protection," he continued, "I will do all that I can, as you shall see by my actions; and you may be certain that so long as I shall live, no one will take the occasion to molest you."

All the promises this good Cacique made in favor of Juan Ortiz, he fulfilled; and he did much more, for immediately he appointed him his chamberlain and carried him in his company day and night. He bestowed many honors upon him and increased these honors exceedingly when he learned that Juan Ortiz had killed a lion with a single dart. In sum he treated him as his own brother, but as a very much beloved brother (for there are some brothers who love each other like fire and water).

Hirrihigua suspected that his slave had fled to his neighbor for protection, and he many times asked for his return; but on each occasion Mucozo excused himself, finally telling the Cacique among other things that the loss of a slave so odious to him was a small loss indeed and that he should cease molesting that slave now that he had sought protection in his neighbor's house. Then Hirrihigua asked the assistance of Urribarracuxi, a brother-in-law of Mucozo, but when that chieftain sent messages concerning the release of the captive, Mucozo gave the same reply. Furthermore, he did not vary in his decision when Urribarracuxi, after finding his messages futile, came to him in person. On the contrary, he angrily informed his brother-in-law that it was unjust for a kinsman to demand that he do a thing so unbefitting his honor and reputation. And he added that if performing his duty meant delivering up an afflicted person who had been entrusted to his care just so that person's enemy might torture and kill him like a wild beast solely for entertainment and pleasure, then he would continue remiss in his obligation. Indeed this Cacique defended Juan Ortiz with such generosity against the two chieftains who sought him so persistently and obstinately that rather than return the slave to be slaughtered by his former master, he chose to abandon all possibility of a marriage with Hirrihigua's daughter, whom he ardently desired and subsequently lost, and at the same time to forfeit his friendship and kinship with Urribarracuxi. Moreover, he continued to hold the Christian in high esteem and to regale him until the coming of Governor Hernando de Soto to Florida.

Juan Ortiz was ten years among those Indians. For a year and a half he was in the power of Hirrihigua; but the remainder of the time he spent with the good Mucozo, who although a barbarian, behaved toward this Christian in a manner far different from that of the famous Triumvirate of Laino (a place near Bologna), which made a never-sufficiently abominated proscription and agreement to exchange relatives, friends and protectors for enemies and adversaries. And too, his behavior was much more admirable than that of other Christian princes who since then have made bargains equally odious, if not more so, when one considers the innocence of those delivered up, the rank of some of them, and the fidelity which their deliverers should have had and respected. For the betrayed were infidels, whereas their betrayers took pride in the name and doctrines of Christianity. Violating the laws and statutes of pagan realms, disrespecting the very existence and rank of kings and great princes, and valuing even less their sworn and promised fidelity (a thing unworthy of such a name), these Christians, solely to avenge their anger, exchanged people who had not offended them for those who had, thus giving up the innocent for the guilty. To this fact, both ancient and modern histories testify, but we shall abandon this subject lest we offend powerful ears and grieve the pious.

It suffices to represent the magnanimity of an infidel so that princes of the Faith may make efforts to imitate and if possible surpass him—not in infidelity, as some do who are undeserving of the title of Christian, but in virtue and similar excellences; for being of a more lofty estate, they are under greater obligations. In fact, when one has considered well the circumstances of this Indian's valiant deed, the people for whom and against whom it was performed, and the great amount he was willing to forego and forfeit, even proceeding contrary to his own love and desire by denying the aid and favor asked of and promised by him, it will be seen that he was born with a most generous and heroic spirit and did not deserve to have come into the world and lived in the barbarous paganism of Florida. But God and human nature many times produce such souls in sterile and uncultivated deserts to the greater confusion and shame of people who are born and reared in lands that are fertile and abundant in all good doctrines and sciences, as well as the Christian religion.

CHAPTER V

The Governor sends for Juan Ortiz.

ON ARRIVING at the Cacique Hirrihigua's village (where we now find him), the Governor had received a garbled version of the life of Juan Ortiz; moreover, while still in Havana, he had heard a less extensive report from one of the four Indians seized by the Comptroller Juan de Añasco at the time he was sent to explore the coast of Florida. Now when this Indian, who happened to be a vassal of Hirrihigua, was speaking of Juan Ortiz, he said only Ortiz, omitting the Juan since he knew nothing of this part of the name. But the pronunciation of the name was defective and the understanding of the good interpreters who were declaring what he desired to say was even worse. Therefore when those listening, whose principal aim was to go in search of gold, heard him say Orotiz, they asked for no further interpretation but understood him to declare flatly that in his land there was much *oro* or gold. Thus they were cheered and made merry just with hearing the word named, although with such different meaning and sense.

Having made certain that Juan Ortiz was indeed in the power of Mucozo, the Governor concluded that it would be wise to send for him; first, to remove him from the hands of the Indians, and then to provide the army with a much needed interpreter whom he could trust. For the purpose, he selected Baltasar de Gallegos, a native of Seville, who served as high constable of both the fleet and the army, but who because of his great virtue, strength and courage really deserved to command an even greater force than the present one. "Go now to Mucozo with a squadron of sixty lancers," he said to this cavalier, "and tell him how grateful I and my whole company of Spaniards are for the honors and benefits he has conferred upon Juan Ortiz, and how much I desire to be offered an occasion to requite them. Moreover say that since I have need of the Christian for some things of great import, I beseech that he be returned to me and that when the Cacique should find it convenient to come and visit me, I should be most pleased to know him and would regard him as a friend."

With his sixty lancers and an Indian guide, Baltasar de Gallegos thereupon left the camp to execute the Governor's command.

The Cacique Mucozo, for his part, having learned that Governor Hernando de Soto had arrived with a great force of men and horses to seize land near that of his own and fearing now that these Spaniards would do him harm, resolved, with prudence and good advice, to forestall the evil that might be visited upon him. So summoning Juan Ortiz, he addressed him as follows:

"You should know, my brother, that in the town of your good friend Hirrihigua there is a Spanish captain who comes with a thousand warriors and many horses to seize this land. You are indeed aware of what I have done for you, how in order to save you from that person who held you in slavery and wanted to deprive you of life, I chose to incur the enmity of my relatives and neighbors rather than comply with what they asked me to do to your harm. A time and occasion has now arisen wherein you can repay me for my hospitality, largess and friendship; and although I have never once done anything for you with expectancy of reward, Fortune makes it prudent that I at this time take advantage of the opportunity offered me in your person. Go therefore to the Spanish general and request in my name as well as your own, that as a recompense for the favor I have rendered him and all of his nation through my kindness to you (since I would do the same for each of them), he not deem it expedient to do me harm in this little land of mine, and that he deign to receive me into his fellowship and service. Say also that I henceforward offer him my person, house and state so that he may place my land under his protection and favor. And that you may be accompanied in a style befitting both your station and mine, take with you fifty gentlemen of my household and look out for them and for me as our friendship obligates you to do."

Rejoicing over this fortunate news and inwardly thanking God for it, Juan Ortiz expressed great pleasure that a time and occasion should have arisen wherein he might render service for the mercy and benefits bestowed upon him—not only for life itself but in addition for the extensive favor, esteem and honor he had received as a result of Mucozo's great virtue and courtesy. Then he promised to give a liberal account of all such things to the Spanish Captain and his men that they too might in turn express their gratitude and make recompense with what he at present was going to ask of them in the Cacique's behalf and also with whatever might arise in the future. He was quite confident, he said, that that Captain would comply with his request since the Spanish nation prided itself on being a people who felt gratitude for anything that might be done in the service of their countrymen. Surely, therefore, the Cacique might hope to succeed in the petition he was sending.

With that, the fifty Indians came whom Mucozo had ordered to be made ready, and together with Juan Ortiz set out on the highway joining the two towns. They departed on the same day that Baltasar de Gallegos left the camp to go in search of the captive.

Now it happened that when the Spaniards had traveled more than three leagues along this broad, straight road leading to the town of Mucozo, their Indian guide decided that it was not very clever for him to exercise so much fidelity with men who had come to deprive his people of their lands and liberty, and who from far back had shown themselves to be declared enemies, although the present army up until this point had caused them no grievances of which they could complain. So he changed his mind about directing these men, and the first path which he saw crossing and leaving the highway he took; then after pursuing this path for a short distance, he lost it, for it was not continuous. Thus for a great part of the day, he misled these Spaniards, directing them always in an arc toward the sea, for it was his purpose to come by chance upon some marsh, creek or bay where, if possible, he would drown them. Being unacquainted with the land, the Castilians were not aware of the deception until one of their number on arriving at a clear wood glanced through the trees and by chance saw the main topsails of the ships they had left behind in the bay. Realizing now that they were near the coast, this man hastened to inform the Captain of his discovery.

The perfidy of his guide having been disclosed, Baltasar de Gallegos threatened him with death and made a gesture as if to run him through with a lance. Fearing that the Spaniards might indeed kill him, the Indian, with whatever signs and words he could muster, indicated his willingness to take them once more to the main road, explaining, however, that it was necessary to go back over all of the places they had passed since leaving it. And this they did, returning through the same passages in search of the highway.

CHAPTER VI

What happened between Juan Ortiz and the Spaniards who were seeking him.

FOLLOWING the highway, Juan Ortiz came to the path where Baltasar de Gallegos and his cavaliers had been led astray. Then being suspicious of what had come to pass and feaful lest the Castilians had taken some other route and thus eventually would harm Mucozo's town, he consulted his companions as to what should be done. All agreed that they must hasten as quickly as possible along the tracks left by the horses, and that lest they wander aimlessly they should never deviate from these tracks until such time as they had overtaken the Spaniards.

Now since the Indians were following the Spaniards and since the latter were returning over the same route they had taken, each caught sight of the other upon a great plain which was fringed along one side by a dense forest. On beholding the Castilians, the Indians told Juan Ortiz that it would be wise for them to secure their lives and persons by taking refuge among the trees until such time as the Christians should recognize them as friends, for since these people regarded them as enemies, they might lance them in the open field. But Juan Ortiz refused to heed their good counsel, being confident that since he was a Spaniard, his countrymen would recognize him the moment they beheld him—as if he had been attired in Spanish clothes or something else that might differentiate him, instead of being equipped as he was like the natives with nothing but some loin cloths on his body, a bow and arrows in his hand, and for ornament, plumage half a fathom in height upon his head.

Inexperienced and anxious to fight, the Castilians, on catching sight of the Indians, assailed them in full force despite the shouts of their captain who sought vainly to hold them in check. But who can do anything with raw recruits when they are disordered?

Meanwhile the natives on perceiving with what boldness and deliberateness the Spaniards came after them, plunged into the forest, none of their group remaining except Juan Ortiz and a lone Indian who had been a little less hasty than his comrades about seeking shelter. This particular Indian was overtaken in the bushes skirting the edge of the forest and wounded with a lance blow in the loin by Francisco de Morales, a native of Seville who had seen service in Italy. Juan Ortiz, on the other hand, was attacked by Alvaro Nieto, a native of Alburquerque, who was one of the strongest and most robust men in the entire Spanish army. Closing with the captive, this Spaniard thrust vigorously at him with his lance, but Juan Ortiz possessed good fortune as well as skill; for beating down the weapon with his bow and at the same time leaping aside, he was able to avoid both the lance and an encounter with the horse of his assailant. Then perceiving Alvaro Nieto turning again upon him, he cried in a loud voice, "Xivilla, Xivilla," by which he intended to say, "Sevilla, Sevilla."[9]

In describing the incident, Juan Coles adds that failing in his efforts to speak Castilian, Juan Ortiz made a sign of the cross with his hand and his bow so that his opponent might recognize him as a Christian.

Since there had been little or no opportunity for Juan Ortiz to speak Castilian among the Indians, he had forgotten even so much as how to pronounce the name of his native land. But I shall be able to say the same of myself, for having found no person in Spain with whom I may speak my mother tongue, which is the one generally used in Peru (although the Incas have a special language that they employ in speaking among themselves), I have so forgotten it that I cannot construe a sentence of as many as six or seven words which will convey my meaning, and I cannot remember many

[9] Accounts of this incident vary. Ranjel says that Ortiz shouted: "Sirs, for the love of God and of Holy Mary, slay not me; I am a Christian like yourselves and was born in Seville, and my name is Juan Ortiz." Elvas has him say: "Do not kill me, cavaliers; I am a Christian! Do not slay these people, they have given me my life!" Biedma simply says that Ortiz identified himself by calling upon the name of Our Lady.

of the Indian terms necessary to name such and such an object. This language having been the idiom of the court, and the Incas having been the chief courtiers, they speak it most excellently and better than all others; and I, as the son of an Inca princess and the nephew of Inca princes, know how to speak it as well if not better and more eloquently than those Indians who are not Incas. But even though it is true that I would understand all that were said should I hear an Inca speak, since I would remember the meaning of forgotten words, still, try as I may, I cannot tell of my own accord what certain words are. Thus I have found through experience that one learns the words of a strange language by using them, but that he likewise forgets those of his own language by failing to use them.

But let us return to Juan Ortiz, whom we left in great danger of being destroyed by those who of all others desired to see him alive. When Alvaro Nieto heard the captive shout "Xivilla," he inquired if he were Juan Ortiz, and on the latter's answering in the affirmative, he seized him with one arm and threw him across the haunches of his horse as if he had been a child, for this good soldier was robust and strong. Overjoyed at having found the man he was seeking, he thanked God that he had not killed him, for he still had visions of having done so; then he carried him to Captain Baltasar de Gallegos, who received him with much happiness.

In their eagerness to destroy Indians, the other cavaliers were combing the woods for them as if they were deer, so that later all might meet and enjoy the good luck that had befallen them. But lest they unwittingly injure people who were their friends, the Captain ordered them to be recalled. Then Juan Ortiz entered the forest and shouted loudly for the Indians to come out and not be afraid. Many, however, kept on running until they had reached their town and informed Mucozo of what had occurred, but others who had not gone far did return in groups of three and four just as they happened to find themselves.

Each and every one of the Indians individually and angrily scolded Juan Ortiz for his rashness, and when they realized that their companion had been wounded because of the Christian, they were so angered that they could scarcely refrain from laying hands on him and would have done so but for the fact that the Spaniards were present. They did avenge their anger, however, with a thousand affronts, saying that he was a foolish, silly and nonsensical man who was neither Spaniard nor warrior, and that he had benefited little or nothing from his past afflictions, which had not been imposed upon him in vain since he had really deserved much worse. In sum, no Indian came from the forest without scolding him in almost identical words, all of which he, to his greater shame, interpreted for the rest of the Spaniards. Thus Juan Ortiz was thoroughly rebuked for having been so trustful, but in exchange he was completely compensated by the sight of himself once again among Christians. They in turn treated the wounded Indian and putting him on a horse, set out with Juan Ortiz and all of his companions for the camp, for they were anxious to bring the Governor such a prompt and satisfactory response to his orders. Before they departed, however, Juan Ortiz dispatched a messenger to Mucozo with an account of all that had actually occurred so that the Cacique would not be upset by what he might have learned from those of his people who had fled.

Both Alonso de Carmona and Juan Coles relate all of the facts we have reported concerning Juan Ortiz, but the former adds that worms fell into the sores acquired while the Christian was being roasted, and the latter says that the Governor immediately gave the man a suit of black velvet, but that since he had gone naked for so long a time, he could not bear to wear it and in consequence wore only a shirt, some linen pants, a cap and some shoes for twenty days while gradually accustoming himself to being dressed. Likewise, both of these eyewitnesses declare that in addition to other favors conferred upon the Christian, Mucozo made him his Captain General on both land and sea.

CHAPTER VII

*The entertainment which the whole army gave
Juan Ortiz. How Mucozo came to
visit the Governor.*

THE night was already far advanced when Baltasar de Gallegos and his companions entered the camp. On hearing them
the Governor experienced a sudden dread, for not expecting them
until the third day, he was apprehensive lest their having returned
so suddenly forebode some mishap. But when he was told the good
news that they brought, all of his dismay was converted into merriment and rejoicing, and he rendered thanks to the captain and his
soldiers for having performed their duty so well. Juan Ortiz, he
received as if he were his own son, with pity and sorrow at being
reminded of so many hardships and martyrdoms as the Christian
had related and indeed as his very body proved him to have endured, since the marks from the burns received while being roasted
were so extensive that one entire side of him was a solid scar. So
the Governor thanked God for having delivered Juan Ortiz from
such difficulties as well as from the peril of that day, a peril which
had not been the least of those he had experienced; and then after
having spoken kindly to the Indians who had accompanied the
Christian, he gave instructions that their wounded companion be
treated with especial generosity and care.

Within the same hour Hernando de Soto dispatched two Indians
to the Cacique Mucozo with messages of gratitude for benefits bestowed upon Juan Ortiz as well as for his willingness to return him
freely and to offer to the Spaniards his own person and friendship.
These gestures, he said, he now accepted not only in his own name
and that of the captains and cavaliers in his company, but in the
name of his master, the Emperor and King of Spain, who was the
first and greatest lord of all Christendom, and this he did so as to
thank and repay the Cacique for what he had done for each of

them in saving the life of his countryman. Then he added that since all wished to see and know Mucozo, it was their desire that he pay them a visit.

Juan Ortiz was feted individually and collectively by the officers and ministers of both the army and the Royal Exchequer, by the cavaliers, and indeed by all the rest of the soldiers; for that man who did not come forward to embrace and congratulate him on his arrival was not regarded as a friend. In this way they passed the entire night, and none slept because of the general demonstrations of joy. Then on the following day, the Governor summoned Juan Ortiz for the purpose of ascertaining what he knew of that region and of hearing the details of his experience while in the power of the two chieftains.

In regard to the land, Juan Ortiz replied that although he had been in that place for such a great length of time, he knew little or nothing about it; for while in the power of Hirrihigua, that Cacique, when not tormenting him with new afflictions, had not permitted him to deviate a step from the routine of carrying water and firewood for his entire household; and while with Mucozo, although at liberty to come and go as he pleased, he had not taken advantage of his freedom lest Hirrihigua's vassals find him separated from his protector and slay him as their master had commanded them to do. But he did assure the Governor that in spite of his inability to give a satisfactory report on the qualities of the land, he could say that he had heard that it was good, and that the further inland one penetrated, the better and more fertile he would find it to be.

Then Juan Ortiz explained that the life he had passed with the Caciques had varied between the two extremes of good and evil which one might experience in this world; for, he said, as his lordship already would have been informed, Mucozo had been as compassionate as Hirrihigua had been vengeful, and it was impossible to exaggerate sufficiently the virtue of the one or the cruelty of the other. And as a proof of the latter he again disclosed the marks still to be seen on his body and enlarged upon the story we have given of his life, telling of many more tortures he had endured, all of which moved his listeners to pity. But here let us leave him in order to avoid prolixity.

On the third day after his Indians had brought the Governor's message, the Cacique Mucozo came to the camp with many of his followers. He kissed the Governor's hands with the utmost veneration and respect and then spoke to the Lieutenant General, the Campmaster, and other captains and cavaliers present. First ascertaining from Juan Ortiz who this, that, and the other person was, he would address each individual according to his rank; and although informed at times, in his own language, that the one being honored was a mere soldier and not a captain or cavalier, he still would treat that person with much courtesy. The Spaniards did note, however, that his attitude toward the ministers and the nobility of the army was much more respectful than it was toward those of lesser rank. Finally, after having spoken to all present and given them occasion to address him, Mucozo again saluted the Governor with new gestures of esteem, and the latter, having already received the Cacique with friendliness and courtesy, thanked him for what he had done in behalf of Juan Ortiz and for having returned the Spaniard so amicably, assuring him that he thereby had placed both himself and the entire Spanish nation under an eternal debt of gratitude. To these words the chieftain replied:

"What I did in behalf of Juan Ortiz, I did in my own interest, for since he came in his need to commend himself to me and ask the assistance of myself and my house, I was obliged by the law of my people to act as I did, all of which appears insignificant to me since his virtue, strength, and valor alone (nothing else considered) merit much more. My returning him to Your Lordship was done to serve my own advantage rather than yours, for I sent him as a mediator and advocate who through his merits and intercession might obtain grace and favor and thereby prevent harm from being perpetrated in my lands. Your Lordship, therefore, has no cause to feel gratitude for either of my actions or to regard them as a favor; for, however they may have been, I am pleased to have chanced to do a thing for which Your Lordship, these cavaliers, and the whole Spanish nation, whose admiring servant I am, should be grateful and should show yourselves to have received contentment. I beseech Your Lordship, therefore, to receive me with the same good will into your service, and I hereby place under your protection my person, house and state, while recognizing the Emperor and King of Spain as my principal sovereign, and Your Lordship as my Captain General and the Governor of this kingdom. Should this favor be granted me, I would consider myself more advantageously repaid than I have merited for service in behalf of Juan Ortiz or for having returned him freely, an act which Your Lordship has esteemed so highly. For in this respect," he continued, "the privilege of seeing myself as I have today, favored and honored by Your Lordship and all of these cavaliers, I regard as being of more worth than all of the good deeds I have performed in my entire life. I solemnly declare, therefore, that I will make every effort from now on to perform similar acts in the service of the Spaniards, since those I have performed have turned out so much to my profit."

These and many other courteous remarks the Cacique uttered with all the graciousness and discretion that might be represented in an eloquent courtier, and the Governor as well as those with him were no less amazed by his words than they had been by the generous deeds performed in behalf of Juan Ortiz, deeds which his words imitated. Because of all these things, the Adelantado Hernando de Soto, the Lieutenant General Vasco Porcallo de Figueroa, and other individual cavaliers and admirers of the eloquence and virtue of the chieftain were moved by their appreciation of such goodness to make a suitable return with whatever each on his part was able to award. Thus they presented both the Cacique and the gentlemen who accompanied him many gifts and in consequence all were content.

CHAPTER VIII

The mother of Mucozo arrives in great anxiety
concerning her son.

TWO days after the events just related, Mucozo's mother came
to the camp, very uneasy and troubled that her son should
be in the power of the Castilians; for having been away from home,
she was unaware that he had gone to pay the Governor a visit and
would never have consented to his doing so. Thus her first words
to Hernando de Soto were that he should give back her son and
not do to him what Pámphilo de Narváez had done to Hirrihigua.
If he were thinking of such, she said, then he should set Mucozo
free and carry out his will upon her, since she was old and willing
to bear the pain alone for the two of them.

The Governor received the Indian woman with many kind words,
replying that because of his great goodness and judgment, Mucozo
deserved no maltreatment and that as a result all should serve him
and even herself since she was the mother of such a person. Therefore, he said, she should banish her fear because no harm would
be done either to herself or her son, or indeed to anyone else in
the whole land, but on the contrary all would receive whatever
pleasure and gratification it was possible to bestow upon them.
With such words he quieted the good old lady to some extent and
she remained three days among the Spaniards, but she was always
so suspicious and prudent that when eating at the Governor's table
she would ask Juan Ortiz if she dared accept what was given her;
for, she said, she feared and suspected the Spaniards might attempt
to poison her. Although the Governor and his whole company
laughed a great deal at her apprehension and assured her that she
could eat safely since their desire was to regale, not to kill her,
still she refused to trust the words of strangers, and would not eat
or even taste the food offered her from the very same plate of the
Governor unless Juan Ortiz had first tasted it for her. Observing
her caution in this respect, a Spanish soldier asked why it was that

since she had offered her life for her son just a short time before, she was now so wary about dying. She replied that she did not hate life and as a matter of fact loved it as intensely as the rest of mankind, but that she was willing to die for Mucozo at any time it were necessary because she loved him more than life itself. Therefore, she continued, she was begging the Governor to restore him to her, for not daring trust him to the Christians, she wanted to take him away.

The General replied that she was at liberty to go whenever she pleased, but that since her son was enjoying himself among those Spanish cavaliers who too were youths, soldiers and men of war, he wished to remain in their company for a few days. He assured her, however, that when Mucozo decided to do so, he could depart freely and completely unmolested. With this promise the aged woman left the camp; but she was unhappy at the thought of her son remaining in the power of the Castilians and on parting told Juan Ortiz that he should liberate Mucozo from that captain and his soldiers just as Mucozo had liberated him from Hirrihigua and his vassals. At that the Governor and the other Spaniards laughed very much, and the good Cacique himself joined them in jesting at the anxiety of his mother.[10]

Such incidents of laughter and gaiety having passed, Mucozo remained eight more days with the army. During that time he visited in their quarters the Lieutenant General, the Campmaster, the captains of the army and the officers of the Royal Exchequer, and in addition many individual cavaliers, since they too were of the nobility; and with all of these men, he spoke so familiarly, cheerfully and courteously that he seemed to have been reared among

---

[10] Although Garcilaso minimizes De Soto's cruelties, the good old mother had reason to fear him. According to the accounts of Ranjel, Elvas and the Inca himself, De Soto did cut off the hands and noses of Indians and did order some to be cast to the dogs. Another authority has stated that he cut off their lips and chins, leaving the face flat, and that he was known to have severed the heads of fainting carriers rather than bother to untie the collars by which they were led. Such accusations, however, are indignantly denied in the preface to the 1723 edition of the *Florida*.

them. He asked specific questions about the Court of Castile as well as the Emperor, and the lords, ladies and cavaliers who formed it; and he said that he would be most pleased to see that court if it were possible for him to go there. When the week had passed he returned to his home, but he came afterward at other times to visit the Governor and each time brought as gifts some of the things to be found in his land. This Cacique, who was twenty-six or twenty-seven years of age, was very handsome in both body and face.

CHAPTER IX

The preparations which were made for the exploration. How the Indians seized a Spaniard.

THE Governor and Adelantado Hernando de Soto was not idle while such things were going on among his men; on the contrary he was performing his office as commander and chief with both caution and industry. For at the moment he was occupied in unloading supplies and munitions, which he placed in Hirrihigua's town, it being near the sea and closest to the Bay of the Holy Spirit. Then when his eleven vessels were cleared, he ordered the seven largest of them back to Havana so that his wife, Doña Isabel de Bobadilla, could dispose of them there. The four smaller ones he kept for whatever use he might have for them at sea. Remaining were the ship, *San Antón,* a caravel and two brigantines, all of which were now placed under the command of Captain Pedro Calderón, who along with other fine qualifications had the distinction of having served as a very young man under the command of the great Captain Gonzalo Fernández de Córdoba.[11]

[11] Commonly known as "Gonzalo de Córdova, El Gran Capitán," a favorite subject with literary men.

Now it was the Governor's feeling that he could hope or fear that the other chieftains of this section of the country would follow the example of Hirrihigua; consequently, at this point, he was trying most assiduously and carefully to win that chieftain to peace and concord, so that through his particular friendship he might obtain the allegiance of all the caciques of Florida. If he could but reconcile and gain the good will of an Indian who had been so greatly offended by the Castilians, then, he reasoned, how much more quickly would he be able to obtain the allegiance of those Indians who had not been offended. But in addition to gaining such friendships, the Governor hoped that by placating this rabid enemy of his nation, he might strengthen his own reputation and honor in general among both the Indians and the Spaniards themselves. For this reason, therefore, if the Christians, in going about the country, happened to seize some of Hirrihigua's vassals, he would return these captives with gifts and finely worded messages. Thus he courted Hirrihigua with friendship, and because of a desire to do so, compensated him whenever possible for the abuses he had suffered at the hands of Pámphilo de Narváez.

Yet the offended Cacique refused to come out peacefully and accept the friendship of the Spaniards, and he would make no answer to any of the messages they sent. He did tell the envoys that his injury had made it impossible for him to give a favorable reply and that the Captain had been so courteous as not to deserve an unfavorable one. But never once did he utter another word on the subject. The admirable efforts of the Governor to obtain Hirrihigua's friendship did not therefore gain the ends he desired; nevertheless, they served to mitigate the anger and rancor which the chieftain held for the Spaniards, a fact which will be proved by what we have to say later.

Each day the domestics of the camp customarily went out to procure grass for the horses, taking with them fifteen or twenty footsoldiers as well as eight or ten of the cavalry for protection. It happened one day that the Indians ambushed and attacked these

people so suddenly and with so much yelling and shouting that
with no arms whatsoever and with their cries alone, they terrified
them. Being heedless and disorganized the Spaniards were thrown
into confusion, and before they could collect themselves, a soldier
by the name of Grajales had been seized. But then the Indians,
not wishing to do further harm, departed with their captive, rejoicing in the meantime over their success.

Slowly the Spaniards collected themselves, and one of the horsemen dashed to the camp to sound an alarm and inform the rest of
the army of what had occurred. On hearing his story, twenty
well-equipped cavaliers rushed forth and, locating the tracks of the
Indians, proceeded to follow them. Two leagues ahead they came
upon an extensive canebrake which the Indians had selected as a
secret and remote place in which to conceal their women and children. Here, all of them, both large and small, with much merriment and joy over their successful seizure, were feasting in utter
complacence and without regard for the fact that the Castilians
would take so much pains to rescue their lost comrade. The men
among them told Grajales to eat and forget his anxiety as they
were not going to give him the miserable life they had given Juan
Ortiz, and the women and children said the same, all of them
offering him the food set aside for themselves and begging that he
eat and be consoled since he was to be granted excellent courtesy
and fellowship.

On hearing the Indians, the Spaniards entered the canebrake
and at the same time raised a clamor as if their number were actually greater than it was, for they hoped thereby to frighten those
within and thus prevent their exerting any effort to defend themselves. And indeed, just as they had hoped, the Indian males, on
hearing the sound of the horses' hooves, fled through the paths they
had made on all sides for going in and out of the place, meanwhile
leaving their women and children in a space they had cleared for
them in the center. Thus the latter found themselves in the power
of the Spaniards, slaves now of the very man who but a short while

before had been their own captive. But the variety of the events and the inconstancy of the fortunes of war are such that at one point a person may recover what he has considered completely lost, and at another, lose what he has thought most secure.

When he recognized the voices of his friends, Grajales hastened out to receive them and then gave thanks to God for having delivered him so soon from his enemies. The Spaniards for their part hardly recognized their comrade since in the brief time he had been captured, the Indians had removed his clothes and dressed him in some loin cloths such as they themselves wear. But rejoicing together, they now collected all of the women and children from the canebrake and took them back to the camp. Here they were received gleefully by the Governor, not only because of the liberation of Grajales but also because of the seizure at the same time of so many of the enemy's people.

Grajales then told everything that had occurred. He said that on coming out of their ambush, the Indians had not wished to harm the Christians and had shot their arrows simply to frighten them. For had they so desired, he explained, they could have killed or wounded the majority of them, finding them as they did so careless and disorderly. As soon as they had taken him prisoner, however, they had been content to go away and leave the rest of the Castilians as they were. And all along the road as well as in their encampment among the reeds they had treated him well. Even the women and children had done so, all of them offering him words of consolation and the very food that had been set aside for themselves.

On being told these facts, the Governor ordered all of the prisoners—boys, girls, women and children—to be brought before him. Then he expressed his gratitude for the good treatment and the gracious words they had extended his countryman; and in recompense for their kindness, he gave them permission to go to their homes. He charged them, however, from that time forward not to flee or fear the Castilians, but to deal and traffic with them as if all were of the same nation; for, he said, he had not come to their land to mistreat the natives but to make friends and brothers of them. This message he instructed them to carry not only to their Cacique but likewise to their husbands, kinsmen and neighbors; and in addition to his adulation, he and his whole army gave them gifts and sent them away most content with the favors they had received.

During two other encounters, the same Indians captured two more Spaniards, one a large seaman named Hernando Vintimilla[12] and the other a boy called Diego Múñoz, who served as page for Captain Pedro Calderón; but they did not kill these men or even maltreat them as they had done Juan Ortiz. On the contrary, they permitted them to go about as freely as any one of themselves, and in consequence both cunningly contrived to escape in a boat driven by storm to the Bay of the Holy Spirit, as we shall tell later on.

Thus it was that by sending friendly messages to Hirrihigua and by doing good deeds for his vassals, the Governor eventually forced that Cacique to mitigate and extinguish the fire of rage which he carried in his heart for the Castilians. Beneficent acts have so much force that they can cause even the most savage of wild beasts to lose their natural fierceness.

CHAPTER X

How the exploration was begun. The entrance of the Spaniards into the interior of the land.

THESE things occurred within a period of a little more than three weeks. Then the Governor commanded Baltasar de Gallegos to take sixty lancers and a like number of footsoldiers, including arquebusiers, crossbowmen and shieldbearers, for the purpose of exploring the interior as far as the principal town of the Cacique Urribarracuxi, which was located in the province nearest the lands of Mucozo and Hirrihigua.

[12] The Inca sometimes spells this name Ventimilla.

The names of these provinces are not included here inasmuch as it is not known whether they were called after the caciques or vice versa. Further on in our story we shall see that in many parts of this great kingdom the lord and his lands as well as his principal village went by one and the same name.

To accompany him now, Captain Baltasar de Gallegos selected those same sixty lancers who had assisted in the search for Juan Ortiz, and then took in addition sixty footsoldiers, among whom was Juan Ortiz himself, who was to serve along the route as guide and interpreter. This group proceeded first to the village of Mucozo, who came out on the road to receive them and, with much joy at seeing them in his land, offered them entertainment and lodging for the night.

On the following day the Captain requested that his host provide an Indian to guide him to the village of Urribarracuxi; but Mucozo excused himself and begged that he not be commanded to do a thing that would sully his reputation and honor. For he said that it seemed unjust that he supply a person to direct strangers against his brother-in-law and neighbor, and should he do so, Urribarracuxi would complain with reason that a kinsman had conducted enemies to his house and land. Now that he was a servant and friend of the Spaniards, he explained, he did not want this relation to be prejudicial either to another person or to his own honor. And were Urribarracuxi a mere stranger and not his kinsman, he added, his conduct toward him would be the same, but being, as he was, such a near relation both by affinity and neighborliness, he was willing to do even more in his behalf. In the same manner, the chieftain then earnestly besought Baltasar de Gallegos not to attribute his reluctance to a lack of love or to any lessening of his wish to minister unto the Spaniards, for it was due simply to his desire not to perform an unjust act—an act for which he would be censured as a traitor to his kinsmen and neighbors as well as to his country. Even the Castilians, he added, would regard as evil a willingness on his part to carry out their orders in this instance or in any similar instance, although it were to their advantage, for after all he would be guilty of performing a dishonorable deed. Rather than do something that he ought not to do, he concluded, regardless of whom it might be against, he would choose first to die.

Then Juan Ortiz, by command of Captain Baltasar de Gallegos, informed Mucozo that they had no need for a guide to show them the road, it being well known that the highway over which they had come led to the village of his kinsman, but that they wanted a messenger to precede them and counsel Urribarracuxi lest that Cacique be annoyed by the coming of the Spaniards and apprehensive that they intended him harm. And in order that the chieftain might believe that the messenger was loyal and not a person to deceive him, they did not wish to send a stranger but one of Mucozo's vassals, for as such he would be more deserving of trust. This messenger was to declare on the part of Governor Hernando de Soto that neither he nor any of his people desired to inflict injury upon anyone. Moreover, he was to say on the part of Baltasar de Gallegos, the Captain who was coming to his land, that he and his soldiers bore the express command of their General to maintain peace and friendship with Urribarracuxi even though that Cacique might not desire to do so with them. And this, the messenger was to explain, they were doing not out of consideration for Urribarracuxi, whom they did not know and who had merited nothing from them, but out of love for Mucozo. For to Mucozo, the Spaniards and their Captain General wished to give happiness, and through him to all of his relatives, friends and neighbors, just as they had done in the case of Hirrihigua, who in spite of his rebelliousness, had as yet received no harm from the Spaniards and would receive none in the future.

Mucozo thereupon responded most gratefully that he kissed the hands many times of the Governor as the Son of the Sun and the Son of the Moon, and likewise of his captains and soldiers—and this he did for the grace and favor they had bestowed upon him with those words which indeed renewed his obligation to die in their behalf. And now that he was aware of the purpose for which they wanted the guide, he said, it would give him great pleasure to provide one; moreover, that this man might be a person in whom both Indians and Spaniards could place their confidence, he would send a noble Indian who in days gone by had been a great friend of Juan Ortiz.

So the Spaniards left Mucozo's village, very gay and happy and even surprised that a barbarian should be so considerate on all occasions. They traveled the distance of approximately sixteen or seventeen leagues to Urribarracuxi's village in four days; but on arriving there, they found the place abandoned, the Cacique and all of his vassals having fled to the forest, notwithstanding the fact that the Indian, who had been Juan Ortiz' friend, had carried them the most amicable message that could be sent. And although this Indian twice again took the same message to Urribarracuxi after the Spaniards had arrived at his village, the Curaca would never come out and make peace. He did not attack the Castilians, and he did not give them malicious answers, but he excused himself with courteous words and with reasons which, though frivolous and vain, he felt were sufficient.

The title "curaca" in the common tongue of the Indians of Peru signifies the same as "cacique" or "lord of vassals" in the language of Hispañola and its neighboring islands. Since I am a Peruvian Indian and not from Santo Domingo or its vicinity, I feel it my privilege to introduce into this work certain words of my own language so as to make it clear that I am a native of Peru and not of some other land.

All along the twenty-five leagues that Baltasar de Gallegos and his companions traveled between the town of Hirrihigua and that of Urribarracuxi, they found many species of trees which they had known in Spain; but here, as we have said before, these trees grew wild. There were walnuts, mulberries, cherries, pines, liveoaks and oaks; and the country, which was made up as much of woods as of fields, was indeed peaceful and delightful. Some marshes were encountered, but fewer and fewer as they left the seacoast and went inland.

Captain Baltasar de Gallegos now sent four horsemen, among whom was Gonzalo Silvestre, to the Governor with an account of what they had seen and with a report that there was sufficient food in Urribarracuxi's village and its vicinity to sustain the army for several days. These men covered the distance of twenty-five leagues in two days without experiencing anything along the way worthy of recording. But here we shall leave them and tell what has occurred in the meanwhile at the camp.

CHAPTER XI

What happened to the Lieutenant General while on his way to seize a Curaca.

ONE day while the Governor was in Hirrihigua's village, he received definite news that the Cacique had retired into a wood not far from where the army was encamped. At that, Lieutenant General Vasco Porcallo de Figueroa, who was bellicose and desirous of honor, resolved to go in pursuit of the Indian so as to enjoy the glory of having fetched him by either friendly means or otherwise. And it was of no avail that the Governor should try to dissuade him by saying that he would send another captain, for Vasco Porcallo had determined to go himself. So naming the horsemen and footsoldiers whom he judged expedient to take in his company, he sallied forth with great lustiness and with even greater hope of returning with the Curaca either as a prisoner or a friend.

Having been informed in the meantime by his spies that the Lieutenant General and many other Castilians were coming to where he was now encamped, Hirrihigua sent an envoy to his pursuers begging them to advance no further and assuring them that they could not reach him regardless of how hard they might try since he was in a secure place and they would encounter difficulty in crossing the many streams, marshes and woodlands that lay between them. And he even pled that they return to their camp lest they enter some region from which they could not extricate themselves and thus become the victims of ill fortune. He had not been moved to give this advice by any fear that he might be taken prisoner, he explained, but by his desire to repay the Spaniards for refraining from doing the harm to his land and vassals that they could have done.

This same communication was sent so many times that the Cacique's envoys almost overtook each other; but the more the messages multiplied, the more Vasco Porcallo desired to advance, for he had persuaded himself that Hirrihigua had been moved to persist in his warnings, not by courtesy or friendship, but by fear of his own inability to escape. With such delusions, he quickened his speed, prodding his men on until they came to a large and treacherous swamp. Then when all of them raised difficulties about continuing through this place, he urged them forward and persuaded them to enter it by setting the example. As an experienced soldier, he was aware that the most satisfactory means for a captain to command obedience in difficult situations is to lead the way himself, even though he display rashness in doing so. Thus he gave the spurs to his mount, and rushing into the marsh was followed by a number of his companions. He had proceeded only a few steps, however, when his horse fell with him at a spot where both stood a chance of being drowned. Here, because of the mud and slime, no one could swim out quickly to help him, and again because of the possibility of their sinking into the mire also, neither horsemen nor footsoldiers could wade through the water to give him aid. Indeed all risked the same danger, but that of Vasco Porcallo was much greater since he was loaded with arms and enveloped in mud and in addition had caught one leg beneath his horse in such a way that the animal was drowning him without affording him an opportunity to save himself.

Vasco Porcallo escaped from the present danger more through divine intercession than human efforts. And now seeing himself as he was, covered with mud and destitute of all hope of capturing the chieftain, and ashamed and humiliated as well as intensely grieved that he should have been conquered by this Indian who had not even bothered to come out and meet him in open combat but instead had merely challenged him with friendly words, he ordered his men to return to the camp. And then in the midst of his anger at his misfortune, there came visions of his great property and the ease and comfort he had enjoyed at home. He began to realize that he was no longer young, and that the major part of his life had already passed. All of the future labors of the conquest, he now reasoned, would be like those he had just experienced or even worse; and there was no necessity for him to continue voluntarily with these hardships since he already had experienced sufficient. Hence, he resolved to return to his home and leave that expedition to the young men who had come with it.

Such thoughts continued to run through the mind of Vasco Porcallo all the way back to the camp; sometimes he would mutter them to himself, and at other times aloud. Frequently he would repeat the names of the two Curacas, Hirrihigua and Urribarracuxi, breaking them down into syllables and changing some of the letters so that the sounds would come out more appropriate for what he wished to infer.

"Hurri, harri, hurri, higa, burra coja, hurri, harri," he would say; "may the Devil take the land where the first and most continuously spoken names I have heard are so vile and infamous.[13] I swear to

[13] Vasco Porcallo has provided us with the most effective bit of profanity that the Inca records, and there can be little doubt that his words were punctuated with equally picturesque gestures. *Hurri* and *harri* as Porcallo used them are simply a breaking down of those tongue-twisting Indian names, Hirrihigua and Urribarracuxi. But when he shouted *burra coja*, he had reference to a she-ass and a lame one at that. The word *higa* has a pornographic significance which sometimes found expression in an amulet hung about children to guard them from evil. This article was a hand doubled up with the thumb poking vulgarly between the fingers. Hence, *dar una higa* was to double the hand in such a way and hold it out at a person, thus expressing excessive scorn. It is easy to believe therefore that this cavalier, while uttering the word, was making the physical gesture and thereby enjoying somewhat the same satisfaction that one receives today in "thumbing the nose."

God,[14] one cannot expect good measures or results from such princes, nor good events from such omens. Let that man labor who must in order to eat or to win esteem. As for myself, I have enough property and honor for this life as well as for that which is to come."

Repeating these and similar remarks many times, the Lieutenant General came once more to the camp, where he immediately asked the Governor's permission to return to the island of Cuba. His petition was granted with the same liberality and grace with which his offer to join the conquest had been accepted, and after being given the small ship, *San Antón,* he departed.

As a very rich and noble man, Vasco Porcallo had carried excellent equipment, so now according to his best judgment, he divided his arms and horses as well as the rest of his provisions and domestic furnishings among the cavaliers and soldiers. All of the supplies and seafaring gear which he had brought from his estate for both himself and his kinsmen, he bequeathed to the army, and after commanding Gómez Suárez de Figueroa, his illegitimate son by an Indian girl in Cuba, to continue with the Governor on the expedition, he bestowed upon this youth two horses, arms and whatever else was necessary for him in the conquest. Being the offspring of such a sire, this young man continued throughout the whole expedition as a very fine cavalier and soldier, serving with great promptness on all occasions that presented themselves. Later when Indians killed his horses, he traveled afoot, and even when he found himself wounded and in dire necessity, he would not accept the loan or gift of a horse or anything else from the General or any other person, for he felt that all gifts offered him were insufficient to recompense what his father had done individually and collectively

[14] *Voto a tal,* which we have translated "I swear to God," means literally "I swear to such." It was a mild oath in which *tal* was substituted for some stronger word like *Dios* or *Diablo* so as to avoid taking the name of the Deity in vain or invoking the devil. Here Vasco Porcallo tempers his oath to the extent of employing the *tal* (although one is tempted to believe Garcilaso has edited this phrase) but only after consigning the whole land to the devil in *"doy al diablo la tierra."*

for the whole army. Because of Vasco Porcallo's generosity, the Governor was anxious to please and regale this youth, but being of a strange and disdainful nature, he would accept nothing from anyone.

CHAPTER XII

The account which Baltasar de Gallegos sent of what he had discovered.

THE things we have just related were concluded in a very brief time, and Vasco Porcallo embarked for Cuba, taking with him all of the Spaniards, Indians and Negroes he had brought in his service. In deserting the expedition he did not leave the impression that he was a coward, for he had shown no such spirit; but the feeling of the whole army was that he was irresolute. This same feeling, however, he had created in Cuba at the time he had offered himself for the conquest, for then he had been over-ambitious and willing to leave his home, property and comforts unprotected just to obtain new things for which he had no need.[15] But always when a man makes decisions in serious matters without considering the wise advice of friends, he is likely to end in violent and even desperate repentance, the victim of much infamy and harm. It follows that had this cavalier carefully considered beforehand those conditions which afterward made him want to return to Cuba, he would not have incurred the censure he did, and he would not have been discomforted either by the diminution and loss of reputation, or by

[15] The Elvas account asserts that Porcallo's real purpose in coming to Florida had been to obtain slaves for his plantation and mines, and that on finding that no seizures could be made because of the bogs and forests, he determined to return to Cuba, thus giving rise to a hostility between himself and the Governor which made it impossible for them to address each other kindly. Ranjel says that once this clash was settled, it was agreed that the Cuban should return to his home and provide the army later with whatever it might need.

the waste of property which he now suffered. For with more wisdom and better council he could have used his worldly goods for the expedition and at the same time have won praise and honor for himself.

But who is to control a wild beast? Or who is to counsel the free and powerful, confident of themselves and persuaded that wisdom accompanies material wealth, and confident that he who enjoys an advantage of riches over one who has gained nothing, enjoys the same advantage in wisdom and discretion, things that are not learned? Such a person does not seek advice, does not want to receive it, and cannot abide those who are willing to give it.

On the day following the departure of Vasco Porcallo, the four cavaliers whom Baltasar de Gallegos had ordered back to the camp arrived with a report of what their captain had seen and heard in the lands through which he had passed. These men gave a very exact account which brought great joy to the Spaniards since with one exception everything that was told was favorable to their ambition and conquest. The exception was that beyond the village of Urribarracuxi there lay a very extensive swamp which was most difficult to cross. But all were joyful over the news and in regard to the swamp declared that God had given man ingenuity and skill to flatten out and pass over those difficulties which confronted him. On receipt of the report, the Governor published an order for the army to prepare to march within three days. Then he instructed Gonzalo Silvestre to return with twenty other horsemen to advise Baltasar de Gallegos that the army would follow when four more days had passed.

In departing from Hirrihigua's village, it was necessary for the Governor to leave a garrison of soldiers and other persons to defend and protect the weapons, supplies and munitions of the army, since he had brought a great quantity of these things, and at the same time to guard the caravel and two brigantines which lay at anchor in the bay. He therefore named Captain Pedro Calderón to remain in charge of everything that was left behind on both land and sea, giving him for his defense forty lancers and eighty footsoldiers in addition to the sailors who belonged to the ships. These men, he said, were not to move to any other location until he should send to command them to do so, and they were to endeavour to maintain peace at all times with the natives of that district. In no manner were they to quarrel with the Indians, even though they suffered their disdain, and furthermore they were to be at special pains to regale Mucozo and maintain with him the most cordial relationship. These orders Pedro Calderón as a good captain and soldier respected.

At length the Governor left the Bay of the Holy Spirit and the village of Hirrihigua, traveling now toward the town of Mucozo, where he arrived on the morning of the third day. That Cacique knew in advance of his coming and went out to receive him. Shedding many tears and manifesting great sorrow at his lordship's departure from his land, he begged him to remain with him for that day; but the Governor, not wishing to burden the Indian with so many people, replied that, his time being limited, it was expedient that he continue on his way. Then he commended Mucozo to God and requested that the Cacique consider himself the guardian of the Spanish captain and soldiers whom he had left in Hirrihigua's village. He thanked him once more for what he had done for himself, his army and Juan Ortiz, and afterward he embraced him with deep tenderness and with manifestations of the great love which the goodness of this notable Indian deserved.

Kissing the hands of the Governor, the chieftain shed many tears, although he tried to refrain from doing so. Among those remarks with which he now signified his pain at the Governor's departure, he said that he could not estimate which was the greater, his happiness in having known Hernando de Soto and having accepted him as his lord, or his sorrow at seeing him leave without being able to follow him; then imploring the Governor as a last favor to remember him and bidding him farewell, he turned to the other officers and noblemen and, as an appropriate conclusion, told them of the sadness and solitude in which they left him and expressed his wish that the Sun might guide and prosper them in all that they did. With these words the good Mucozo ended, and the Governor continued his journey to the village of Urribarracuxi without experiencing anything further of note along the way.

From the Bay of the Holy Spirit to the village of Urribarracuxi, the Spaniards traveled always to the northeast, that is to say to the north and turning a little toward where the sun rises. This direction and any other that you will find in the course of my history, I must warn you not to take precisely lest you blame me if contrary information should appear after, God being served, the land is won; for although I have taken the utmost care to be able to write with certainty, it has not been possible for me to do so. The first idea in the minds of these cavaliers was to conquer that kingdom and seek gold and silver, and they paid no attention to anything that did not pertain to these metals. Thus they failed to accomplish other things of more import such as tracing out the limits of the land. Their negligence, therefore, suffices to exonerate me for my failure to write with the certainty which I have desired and which I know to be essential.

CHAPTER XIII

Twice the Spaniards cross the great swamp
uselessly. The Governor sets out to
search for a passage and
finds it.

HAVING arrived at the town of Urribarracuxi, where Captain Baltasar de Gallegos was awaiting him, the Governor sent messengers offering friendship to the Cacique, who in the meantime had withdrawn to the woods; but no effort was sufficient to persuade the Indian to come out in peace. Aware now of this fact, the

Governor bothered him no further and set about sending out runners in three directions to find a passage through the swamp.

This swamp, which lay three leagues from the town, was broad and very troublesome to cross, for besides being a league in width and very deep at its banks, it contained a great amount of *cieno* or slime (from whence it takes the name *ciénaga* or swamp). Two-thirds of its area, along the edges, was mud, and the other third, which was its center, consisted of water that was too deep to be forded. Notwithstanding these obstacles, the guides found a passage and at the close of eight days returned to announce that they had done so and that the passage was very good.

With the receipt of this report, the Governor and all of his people set out from the town and in two days arrived at the swamp. Then since the passage was indeed good, they crossed over the swamp with ease, but because of its breadth, it required the entire day for them to do so. Once across, however, they encamped on a good plain half a league beyond. The following day the same explorers, who now had gone out to see which direction they must proceed from this point, returned to say that the army could by no means move forward because of the numerous marshes formed by streams that ran out of the main swamp and flooded the countryside. Thus it was that even though the main swamp might be crossed satisfactorily by means of the aforementioned passage because of the great amount of water flowing over it from the channel of the river, one still found it impossible to travel through the surrounding areas.

Since in matters so laborious and dangerous the Governor could not be satisfied with the report of another, he now resolved to make his own exploration. Having reached this decision he selected a hundred horsemen and a hundred footsoldiers to accompany him, and leaving the rest of his army where they were in charge of the Campmaster, returned once more to the other side of the swamp so as to cross it elsewhere. Then for three days he traveled up one side of it, sending out individual scouts at intervals to ascertain if any new passage might be located.

During these three days, Indians were never lacking. Emerging from the forests lining the banks of the swamp, they would rush up and fire their arrows at the Spaniards only to take refuge again among the trees. Some, however, were snared and killed or captured. Then to free themselves from the hardships and afflictions the Spaniards bestowed upon them while demanding the way and passage to the swamp, those who were seized offered to serve as guides, but being hostile, merely led their captors into difficult passes and places where Indians lying in ambush came out to hurl arrows at them.

On sensing the malice of their guides, the Spaniards permitted the dogs to kill four of them. In consequence, another whom they had seized was moved by fear of death to offer to direct his captors faithfully, and this he did, taking them from their present unfortunate location to an open, flat and broad road that lay far from the swamp. Then when they had traveled four leagues along this road, they turned once again toward the marshes where they found another passage. This passage had no mud at its entrance and exit, and could be waded for a distance of one league in water that came only to the chest. For a space of a hundred feet in the center of the channel, the water was too deep to ford, but here the Indians had constructed a rude bridge of two large fallen trees. Where these trees did not join, they had added long pieces of wood, some tied to others and smaller ones laid crosswise in the form of rails. Two years previously Pámphilo de Narváez had passed along this same route with his ill-fated army.

Happy at having discovered a new passage, the Governor issued an order to two soldiers, *mestizos,*[16] who were natives of the island of Cuba. In all of the West Indies, those of us who are born of a Spanish father and an Indian mother or vice versa are called *mestizos,* just as in Spain those who are born of a Negro father and an

[16] The expressions in this paragraph are all common in English: mestizo, mulatto, creole, quadroon. The Inca adds to the list in his *Comentarios Reales, Part I* (Book IX, chapter xxxi) and speaks of his own great pride in the name mestizo. Since he is defining Spanish words, we have left them in the easily comprehended original.

Indian mother or vice versa are called *mulatos*. The Negroes designate all persons *criollos* who have been been born in the Indies of either pure Spanish or pure Negro parents, thus indicating that they are natives of the Indies and not of Spain. Likewise, the Spaniards have already introduced the word *criollo* into their language, attaching to it the same significance. The man who is a fourth part Indian, such as the son of a Spanish father and a *mestiza* mother or vice versa is known as a *quateron* or *quatralvo,* whereas a native of Guinea is simply called a Negro, and a native of Spain, a Spaniard. All of these names, as one can surmise, are used in the Indies to distinguish intruding from indigenous races.

But as we were saying, the Governor commanded the two islanders, whose names were Pedro Morón and Diego de Oliva, to take axes and clear away some branches that were obstructing the bridge, moreover to do everything else they thought necessary for the convenience of those who were to use it. Thus these two soldiers, both of whom were very good swimmers, made haste to execute his command, but while working furiously and diligently, they beheld Indians who had been hidden among the many cattails and reeds near the banks coming out with great fury to shoot arrows at them. So throwing themselves headfirst from the bridge and plunging beneath the water, the *mestizos* now swam back to their people, arriving only slightly wounded since the arrows did not penetrate far beneath the surface of the water. This sudden attack having been made, the Indians retired from the pass without inflicting additional damage and betook themselves to where they were seen no more. Thus without further interference the Spaniards repaired the bridge and then three shots of a crossbow above that passage found another which was very good for the horses.

Now that he had located the coveted passage, the Governor thought it wise to give notice of his success to Luis de Moscoso, his Campmaster, so that he could bring up the army, after having first sent biscuits and cheese; for those people with the Governor, not having expected to travel far, had brought few provisions and consequently were suffering from a want of food. Therefore, with this end in view, he summoned Gonzalo Silvestre, and in the presence of everyone said to him:

"The fact that the best horse in the whole army has fallen to your lot must work to your greater hardship, for we find it necessary to entrust to you the most difficult transactions which confront us. Have patience therefore and be advised that it is essential to our life and conquest that you return to the camp this night to inform Luis de Moscoso of what you have seen and to instruct him to follow us with the whole army, since we have found a passage through the swamp. But on your arrival say that we are in need of sustenance and that he is first to send you back with two loads of biscuits and cheese with which we may feed ourselves until additional food can be found. And that you may return with more security than you go, request that he provide thirty lancers to protect you along the way. I will await you in this same spot until tomorrow night, by which time you should have arrived here. Although you may feel that the road is too long and difficult and that the time is brief, I know to whom I entrust the deed. But lest you have to travel alone, take with you whomever you think best as a companion. Go now at once, for it is advisable that you reach the camp before dawn, since the Indians may kill you if daylight overtakes you before you have crossed the swamp."

Without a word, Gonzalo Silvestre departed from the Governor and mounted his horse. Then as he was proceeding along the road, he encountered one Juan López Cacho, a native of Seville, who was a page of the Governor and possessed a fine horse. To this youth he said:

"The Governor commands that you and I be at the camp with a message of his by dawn; therefore follow me at once, for I am now on my way."

"By your life," Juan López replied, "take someone else, for I am weary and cannot go there."

"But the Governor has ordered that I select a companion, and you are the one I choose," Gonzalo Silvestre replied. "So if you wish to come with me, come willingly; if not, it is all the same to me. For the danger will not be lessened by there being two of us, nor will the hardship be increased by my going alone."

With these words Gonzalo Silvestre gave the spurs to his horse and continued on his way, while Juan López, as much as it pained him to do so, mounted and followed after him. Thus both youths, neither of whom had passed his twentieth year, rode forth at the hour of sunset from where the Governor was to await them.

CHAPTER XIV

*What the two Spaniards experienced on their
journey before coming to the camp.*

THESE two vigorous and spirited young Castilians made no attempt to evade the task to be accomplished, even though they realized that it was so excessive, nor did they fear the danger, imminent as it was. On the contrary, as we have seen, they offered themselves for these hardships and perils most readily and promptly. The first four or five leagues of the journey they traveled without any difficulty whatsoever, for the road was clear of woods, streams and marshes, and during this time they did not perceive a single Indian. But once beyond this point, they were confronted with the same obstructions and tedious passages that they had encountered in coming there; for now there were trees and marshes and those streams which flowed in and out of the main swamp. There was no escape from these treacherous passages because there was no open road; and being ignorant of the land, they found it necessary, in order not to lose their way, to return by the same trail they had made three days previously in coming to this place. In doing so they were guided solely by their ability to recognize landmarks noted before.

The danger which they now ran of being killed by the Indians was so inescapable that no precaution they might have taken would have been sufficient to save them had not God in His mercy come to their aid by means of the natural instincts of their horses. For these beasts now thrust their noses to the ground like hounds or bird dogs and, as if possessed of human intelligence, set about tracing and following the path left by the Spaniards in coming there. Not comprehending the intention of the animals, the riders at first drew in their reins, but the horses would not lift their heads from the trail and, to find it when it was lost, gave great puffs and snorts which alarmed their masters exceedingly lest the Indians hear them. At length, however, Gonzalo Silvestre recognized the intention and excellence of his horse in lowering its head to seek the trail, and in consequence he permitted the animal free rein, not contradicting it in any way, for thus they traveled more easily.

In keeping the trail and especially in locating it again after it once had been lost, Gonzalo Silvestre's mount was much more reliable than that of Juan López. But this excellent talent as well as other fine qualities possessed by his horse need not surprise us, for it had the natural markings and color common to horses which are extremely good in both peace and war. It was a pitch-dark chestnut with a stockinged left foot and a stripe on its forehead with which it drank.[17] Such markings as these give more promise of excellence and loyalty in a horse than do any others, whether they are found in work horses or ponies. Furthermore, of all colors, the chestnut, and especially the very dark chestnut, is the best in mud and dust and for use in work or sport. The horse of Juan López, for instance, was a "toasted bay" (a color sometimes called vulpine) with a black mane and tail, and was a most excellent animal; but it failed to measure up to the chestnut, which now guided both its master and his companion.

With the difficulties we have described and others which can be more easily imagined than recorded, these two brave Spaniards

---

[17] *y lista en la frenta, que bebía con ella*—We have translated this literally. This expression, common in Mexico today, means that the stripe extended over the horse's nose into his mouth.

traveled the entire night without a road. They were exhausted by lack of sleep and by fatigue, and dead from hunger, for the only thing they had eaten in two days was some corn stalks planted by the Indians. The horses too were in the same condition, for they had not been unsaddled in three days, and hardly once had their bits been removed for them to feed. But the fact that they must look death in the eye if they did not overcome their hardships gave the two youths strength to go forward. On both sides of where they were traveling, they left behind them large bands of Indians who appeared in the light of their great fires to be leaping and dancing, eating and drinking, talking, shouting and singing in demonstrations of much merriment and rejoicing, all of which went on throughout the night. Whether they were celebrating some pagan festival or chattering about the strangers who so recently had come to their land is not known. But the cries and huzzas which they made in their merriment meant life itself to the two Spaniards who rode through their midst, for this great clamor prevented their hearing the passing horses or taking notice of the loud barking of the dogs, who, having perceived the horses, were yowling themselves to death.[18] All such things, however, were manifestations of Divine Providence, for had it not been for the noise of the Indians and the ability of the horses to find the trail, it would have been impossible for Gonzalo Silvestre and his companion to have traveled so much as one league, much less twelve, without having been heard and killed by the natives.

After they had ridden more than ten leagues under the difficult circumstances we have seen, Juan López said to his companion:

"I am exhausted from lack of sleep. Therefore, either permit me to rest a brief period or destroy me here on the road with your lance, since I can neither go forward nor hold myself on my horse."

Two times already, Gonzalo Silvestre had denied this same request, but overpersuaded now by the insistence of his companion, he replied:

[18] The expression is in the Spanish: *se mataban a alaridos.*

"Judging from the distance we have already covered, the entrance to the great swamp cannot be far from where we now are. The reasonable thing for us to do, therefore, is to get beyond that point before dawn, for should daylight overtake us on this side of the swamp, there will be no possibility of our escaping death. But since you prefer to have the Indians kill us rather than to stay awake for another hour, dismount and sleep as long as you wish."

Without waiting for further discussion, Juan López Cacho permitted himself to fall like a corpse to the ground. His companion thereupon took his lance from him and held his horse by the bridle. And then at that hour a great darkness came unexpectedly upon them and at the same time so much rain poured from the heavens that it appeared to be a deluge. But all of the water that fell on Juan López failed to awaken him, for the force that the passion of sleep has over the human body is very great and sleep, like food, is so necessary that it cannot be denied.

The ceasing of the rain, the dispersing of the clouds, and the appearance of daylight were all so simultaneous that Gonzalo Silvestre murmured that he had not seen the dawn break. But it could be that he himself had fallen asleep on his horse just as his companion had done on the ground. I once knew a cavalier in another group who likewise fell asleep while traveling and continued thus for three or four leagues. It was useless for his companions to address him, and at times he was in danger of being dragged along the ground by his horse. Gonzalo Silvestre, just as soon as he saw that the day was so light, made haste to awaken Juan López, and when his low, hoarse and muffled calls were insufficient to arouse the sleeping man, he availed himself of the butt-end of his lance and awakened him with some heavy blows, saying: "Behold what your sleeping has done. We have been caught in the broad daylight which we feared, and it is impossible to escape death at the hands of our enemies."

At that Juan López mounted his horse, and both men hastened forward with the utmost diligence, running now at a half speed, for these horses were so good that they bore the present hardship as well as the past. In the light of day, however, the Indians could not but see the cavaliers and presently raised an outcry and alarm. Those on one side of the swamp warned their friends on the other with such a buzzing and clamor, and with such a resounding noise of conch-shells, horns and drums as well as other rustic instruments that it looked as if they hoped to slay the Spaniards with no more than their racket. At the same moment, so many canoes issued from among the cattails and reeds that the Spaniards in speaking of the incident afterward, said, in imitation of poetic fables, that it seemed just as if the leaves which had fallen from the trees into the water had been converted into canoes. And these Indians now hastened with such effort and speed to the passage through the great swamp that they were already at the deep part awaiting the Christians when they arrived.

Although they saw themselves confronted with such imminent peril in the water at the end of so much hardship on land, the two companions came to the conclusion that their danger was more certain in fearing than in daring, so they plunged into the morass with great force and courage, setting their minds solely on the task of passing that one final league, which as we have said, was the width of this boggy area. But God willed that inasmuch as the horses were traveling beneath the water and the riders were well armed, all should escape without wounds, a circumstance which was regarded as no small miracle considering the infinity of arrows that had been hurled at them. Afterward when speaking of how Our Lord had bestowed His grace upon them at this particular moment by saving them from wounds and death, one of them remarked that when they had emerged from the water and he turned to see what had been left there, he found it covered with arrows in the same way that a street ordinarily is littered with sedge on the day of some great, solemn feast.

In the little that we have told here of these two Spaniards and in other similar occurrences which we shall see further on in our story, one will be able to note something of the valor of the Spanish race. Through the accomplishment of so many and such great undertakings as have been described and other even greater ones which have never been recorded because of carelessness, the Spaniards have obtained the New World for their sovereign. This gain has been a happy one for both races, for by means of it Castilians have won temporal riches and Indians spiritual ones.

When those Spaniards with the army heard the Indians shouting so strangely, they suspected their reason for doing so and, calling out to each other by name, more than thirty cavaliers rushed with the utmost haste to assist their two companions crossing the swamp. Far ahead of them all and riding furiously on a beautiful dappled grey was Nuño Tovar. The great ferocity and vigor of the animal, and the boldness and cavalier mien of the rider, a handsome horseman, were such that with just the gallantry and nobility of his person this good cavalier was able to offer assurance to the two men in such danger. For even though Nuño Tovar now suffered the disfavor of his Captain General, he never failed to display on all occasions the force of his personality and the strength of his spirit, always doing his duty to fulfill his obligation to his own nobility; at no time could the full force of the disdain he suffered make him do otherwise, for those who truly possess a noble spirit will not stoop to depravity. When tyrannous princes and powerful men feel, with or without reason, that they have been offended, they are seldom or never wont to grant the favor of reconciliation and pardon that generous spirits deserve. On the contrary it would seem that the more such a person insists on his virtues, the more he offends. Therefore, it appears to me in my poor judgment that he who sees himself in such a predicament should go, for the love of God, and beg his food wherever he may find it rather than persist in the service of this kind of master, for regardless of what miracles he may succeed in performing, they will not be sufficient to restore him to the grace of the one he has angered.

CHAPTER XV

Thirty lancers with a supply of biscuits set out in
pursuit of the Governor.

ALTHOUGH they saw that the two Spaniards were now out of
the water, the Indians continued to pursue them on land, and
being exceedingly angry because these men had traveled so many
leagues without having been heard, they hurled many arrows at
them. But the moment they beheld Nuño Tovar and the other
cavaliers galloping to the aid of their friends, they left off their
pursuit and returned to the woods and marshes to avoid receiving
harm from the horses, for these animals were no joking matter with
them in the open countryside.

The two companions were received with much gladness and rejoicing by their people, who were especially pleased to discover that
neither had been wounded. Then when the Governor's order had
been made known, Luis de Moscoso, the Campmaster, prepared
thirty cavaliers to return immediately with Gonzalo Silvestre, who
hardly had time to bolt the two mouthfuls of boiled, half-ripe
corn and the small amount of cheese they had given him. More
than this they could not offer because there was nothing else, and
the army itself was suffering from hunger. Nevertheless, two
mules were loaded with biscuits and cheese for the Governor,
rations which would have been scant enough for so many people
had not God provided food from another source, as we shall see
later. Thus supplied, Gonzalo Silvestre set out with his thirty companions in less than an hour after his arrival at the camp. Juan
López, however, remained where he was, saying: "The General
did not order me either to come here or to return."

Although they carried additional men from the army to assist
in the swamp in the event that they were needed, the thirty horsemen passed through this area without challenge, and they traveled
the whole day without seeing a single Indian. Regardless of the

fact that they made great haste, however, it was two hours after nightfall before they could reach the spot where the Governor had promised to await them. Once there, they discovered that he had moved forward through the swamp, and they were much distressed to find themselves alone with only thirty men in the midst of as many enemies as they now feared were upon them. Nevertheless, not knowing which direction the Governor had taken, they made no attempt to follow him, agreeing instead to remain in the encampment he had occupied the previous night. Then they arranged a certain order of procedure among themselves. This was that during the first third of the night, ten men were to make the rounds of the camp on horseback while ten others stood guard with their horses saddled and bitted and held by the reins, so that if necessary they could rush out and fight. Meanwhile, the third ten men were to keep the saddles upon their horses but remove the bits and permit them to feed. Thus by taking turns, with some working and others resting, they could carry out the duties of the night; and in this manner they did pass the night without hearing any sound from their enemies.

With the coming of day, they were able to see the trail the Governor had left in the swamp and accordingly moved on through it, quite happy that there were no Indians present to obstruct them. And indeed it would have been a severe task to have had to gain the passage by fighting in water up to their chests, without any opportunity to attack or flee and with no firearms to stop their enemies at a distance; for the Indians at the same time would have been able to come upon them in their canoes and retreat with the greatest agility while hurling arrows at them from near and far.

In fact one must consider why it was that on this occasion as well as similar ones in the course of our history, some of the same Indians in their own territory and with an opportunity to do so would fight on certain days with such great anxiety and desire to slay the Castilians, whereas on other days they would have no concern whatsoever about these strangers. I have no reason to offer other than to say that, whether fighting or not, there were certain pagan super-stitions which they had to observe, just as was the case with other nations in the time of the great Julius Caesar, and again that they may have permitted the Spaniards to go unmolested because they saw that they were simply passing through their land with no in-tention of stopping. But however it may have been, the thirty horsemen were fortunate and continued along the track left by the Governor, whom, after six more leagues, they found encamped among some very beautiful vales of corn, so fertile that each stalk bore three or four ears. Without dismounting, they now plucked the corn and to satisfy their hunger ate it raw, at the same time giving thanks to God Our Lord for having succored them so bountifully. When a man is in need, anything he receives seems abundant.

The Governor greeted the thirty cavaliers most cordially and praised them with magnificent words. Gonzalo Silvestre he lauded exceedingly for his fine efforts and for the great danger and intol-erable hardships he had borne, saying at length that no human being could have done more. He offered to reward this youth in the future for such great merit and at the same time asked his pardon for not having awaited him as he had agreed to do. His excuse, he said, was first that he was forced to advance because of the unendurable hunger of his men, and then that he had not been sure than Gonzalo Silvestre would return, since he had feared that, the danger being so great, the Indians might have killed him.

This very fertile province where the Governor was found en-camped was called Acuera. It lies some twenty leagues from the province of Urribarracuxi on a line running more or less north and south. The lord of the place, who also was called Acuera, on learn-ing of the arrival of the Spaniards in his land, fled with all of his people to the forest.

Luis de Moscoso, the Campmaster, set out with the main body of the army on the same day that he received the General's order. They crossed the swamp with ease, since the Indians gave them no opposition, and continued along the road. In three more days they came to the second passage, and since the ford at this place was wider and carried more water than the other, they spent three additional days in crossing it. But during the whole time they were in the swamp and traveling the twelve leagues along its banks, not a single native was seen. Thus the Indians did the army no small favor, for regardless of how little they might have opposed them, they would have increased the hardships for them extremely, since the passages alone were so difficult. While Luis de Moscoso was crossing this swamp, his men suffered from hunger. The Governor therefore sent them a great deal of corn with which they satiated themselves. Eventually all arrived at the place where Hernando de Soto was encamped.

CHAPTER XVI

The insolent reply of the lord of the province of Acuera.

THE whole army had now reassembled in the province of Acuera, and eventually both men and horses were able to assuage the great hunger they had suffered during the past days. Then with his customary clemency, the Governor sent messages to the Cacique Acuera by some of his own vassals whom the Spaniards had captured. In these communications, he begged that chieftain to come out peacefully and accept the Castilians as his friends and brothers, since they too were warriors and people of valor. Then he warned: "Should you fail to do so, my men can cause much damage to your vassals and your lands. But I would have you know and rest assured that we come with no intention of harming anyone and have not harmed anyone in the provinces we have left behind. Instead we have extended cordial friendship to those desiring to receive it. Our principal purpose is to reduce by peaceful and friendly means all the provinces and nations of this great kingdom to the obedience and service of our lord, the mighty Emperor and King of Castile, whose servants all Spaniards are. It is for the purpose of discussing such things more at length and of informing you of the command that my sovereign and master has asked me to communicate to the rulers of this land that I now desire to see and talk with you."

The Cacique Acuera's reply to the Governor's message was insolent. "I have long since learned who you Castilians are," he said, "through others of you who came years ago to my land; and I already know very well what your customs and behavior are like. To me you are professional vagabonds who wander from place to place, gaining your livelihood by robbing, sacking, and murdering people who have given you no offense. I want no manner of friendship or peace with people such as you, but instead prefer mortal and perpetual enmity. Granted that you are as valiant as you boast of being, I have no fear of you, since neither I nor my vassals consider ourselves inferior to you in valor; and to prove our gallantry, I promise to maintain war upon you so long as you wish to remain in my province, not by fighting in the open, although I could do so, but by ambushing and waylaying you whenever you are off guard. I therefore notify and advise you to protect yourselves and act cautiously with me and my people, for I have commanded my vassals to bring me two Christian heads weekly, this number and no more. I shall be content to behead only two of you each week since I thus can slay all of you within a few years; for even though you may colonize and settle, you cannot perpetuate yourselves because you have not brought women to produce children and pass your generation forward."

In reply to what was said about his rendering obedience to the King of Spain, the Cacique continued: "I am king in my land, and it is unnecessary for me to become the subject of a person who has no more vassals than I. I regard those men as vile and contemptible who subject themselves to the yoke of someone else when they can live as free men. Accordingly, I and all of my people have vowed to die a hundred deaths to maintain the freedom of our land. This is our answer, both for the present and forevermore."

Then apropos of the subject of vassalage and the Governor's statement that the Spaniards were servants of the Emperor and King of Castile, for whose empire they now were conquering new lands, the Cacique retorted: "I should congratulate you warmly, but I hold you in even less esteem now that you have confessed that you are servants and that you are working and gaining kingdoms so that another may rule them and enjoy the fruits of your labor. Since in such an undertaking you are suffering hunger, fatigue and other hardships as well as risking your lives, it would be more to your honor and advantage to acquire things for yourselves and your descendants rather than for someone else. But being so contemptible and as yet unable to rid yourselves of the stigma of servitude, you should never at any time expect friendship from me, for I could not use my friendship so basely. Furthermore, I do not wish to know what your sovereign demands, for I am well aware of what has to be done in this land, and of what manner I am to use in dealing with you. Therefore, all of you should go away as quickly as you can if you do not want to perish at my hands."

On hearing the Indian's reply, the Governor was astonished that a barbarian should manage to say such things with so much arrogance and loftiness of spirit. In consequence he persisted even more in his efforts to win the friendship of this man, sending him from then on many affectionately and courteously worded communications. But the Curaca told all subsequent messengers who came to him that he had given his answer and never intended to give any other. And he never did.

The army remained twenty days in this province while recovering from the hunger and fatigue of the previous journey and making necessary preparations for advancing. Meanwhile, the Governor tried to obtain information concerning the province, and for the purpose sent out runners to all parts of it, instructing them to observe and record carefully and diligently whatever good qualities it might possess. These men carried out their mission and returned with favorable news.

During these twenty days, the Indians never slept and were always on the alert. In order to fulfill the fierce threats of the Curaca and to prove that his promises to the Castilians had not been made vainly, they ambushed their enemies so cautiously and skillfully that not a single Spaniard who strayed so much as a hundred yards from the camp escaped being shot and beheaded at once. And in spite of the great haste our men made to assist their companions at such times, they always found them decapitated, for the Indians had carried the heads to their Cacique in obedience to his command. The Christians buried their dead where they found them, but during the night the Indians returned and after digging them up, cut them into pieces, which they hung on the trees where the Spaniards could see them. Thus they fulfilled well the Cacique's command that he be brought two Christian heads each week. Indeed they fulfilled it so well that in two days they carried him four heads (two each day); and during the time that the Spaniards were in their land, they took him in all fourteen heads. Moreover, they wounded many of our men.

When the Indians came out of the forest to attack, they were very cautious about their own security, staying so near their lurking place that they could do all harm possible without letting a single opportunity slip and then return unhampered to safety. Thus our Spaniards began to realize that there was some truth in the threats made by the natives all along the road through this great marshy area when they shouted at them: "Advance, thieves and traitors, for here in Acuera and further on in Apalache you will be treated as you deserve, since all of you, after being quartered and cut into pieces, will be hung on the largest trees along the road."

Because of the vigilance and caution of the Indians in their ambushes, the Spaniards, regardless of how persistently they tried, were unable to slay more than fifty of them during the whole time they were in the province of Acuera.

CHAPTER XVII

The Governor arrives at the province of Ocali.
What befell him there.

AT THE end of twenty days, the Governor departed with his men from the province of Acuera, having avoided doing any damage to either towns or fields lest the Spaniards be looked upon as cruel and inhuman. They were now searching for a province called Ocali which was about twenty leagues distant. Proceeding toward the north, yet turning a little to the northeast, they traveled for some ten or twelve leagues through an uninhabited region where there was a great forest of walnut and pine as well as other trees not known in Spain. All looked as if they had been planted by hand, being so far apart that the horses could safely run between them. The result was a very light and peaceful wood.

Already the swamps and muddy passages were becoming less frequent in this province than in the others the Spaniards had traversed since it was further from the coast and not penetrated by the salt marshes and bays which had been formed elsewhere by the sea. For those other regions were so low and flat that the ocean had flowed into them in some places thirty, forty, fifty, and even sixty leagues, and in others more than a hundred. Thus great swamps and morasses had formed which were difficult and at times even impossible to pass. Some of them the Christians found to be so treacherous that when they put foot on them the land shook for twenty or thirty feet around. Since on the surface they were dry and gave no evidence of water or mud beneath, they looked as if the horses might tread upon them; but once they did and that surface was broken, both horses and riders sank and were drowned without recourse. The Spaniards therefore had been put to much pains to overcome such passages.

The province of Ocali likewise was found to offer more abundant provisions than others we have described; first, because there were more people to cultivate it, and then because it was more naturally fertile. And in all of the provinces of this great kingdom through which the Spaniards passed, they found that the further inland and the more distant the land lay from the sea, the more populated and the more naturally fertile and productive it was. But in the four provinces we have mentioned, as well as in the others we shall describe later, that is to say, in all of the land of Florida that these particular Spaniards explored, they felt a great necessity for beef. In no place did they find it, since the Indians are without domesticated animals. Nevertheless, throughout the region there were many red deer and fallow deer which the natives kill with their bows and arrows. The stags were like great bulls, and indeed all of the red deer were almost as large as the stags of Spain. In this land there are also large bears, and, as we have already said, brown lions.

Having crossed over the twelve leagues of wilderness, the army now passed through seven leagues of an inhabited area where there were a few houses scattered throughout the countryside, but no towns. At the end of this distance, however, they came to the principal town of the district, which like the province and its chieftain, was called Ocali. Here they found that the Cacique and all of his people had gathered up their household possessions and fled to the woods. They therefore entered the town and proceeded to take lodging in the six hundred dwellings that comprised it. Within these houses they found a great store of corn and other grains, vegetables, and fruits such as prunes, raisins, nuts and acorns.

Once encamped, the Governor immediately dispatched Indians to Ocali, requesting his presence with peace and friendship. The Curaca asked courteously to be excused for the time being, saying that he could not leave his place of hiding so soon. Six days later, however, he did join the Spaniards peacefully, but they suspected his intentions; for never during the entire time he was with them did he act honestly. Still the Governor and his men received him with many affectionate words and concealed the fact that they sensed evil in him so as not to add to the irritation which his own malicious design already was producing within him, as we shall see later.

Near the village lay a large river[19] which carried a great amount of water and which the Spaniards could not ford even though it was now summer. On both sides of this stream there were banks twenty-eight feet in height which were as sheer as a wall. In all of Florida, since there is little or almost no rock in the soil, the rivers cut away much earth and leave deep ravines. But this particular river I am describing more in detail than others, since mention is to be made later of a notable act performed within its waters by thirty Spaniards.

It being necessary to construct a wooden bridge before this river could be crossed, the Governor brought up the matter with the Curaca, who thereupon commanded his vassals to build it. Then one day he and the Curaca went out to see where the structure could be located, and as they were strolling along and planning the bridge, more than five hundred native archers rushed out from the bushes growing on the opposite bank and shouted: "So you thieves, vagabonds, and foreign immigrants want a bridge. You will not see it built with our hands." And with these taunts they cast a sprinkling of arrows toward where the Governor and the Cacique Ocali stood. Thereupon the Governor asked his companion how he could permit this shameful behavior once he had pledged his friendship. At that the Indian replied that he was powerless to remedy the situation, and was not to blame for the deed; for many of his vassals on seeing him inclined to the friendship and service of the Spaniards had refused him further obedience and, as they had just demonstrated, no longer looked upon him with respect.

On firing their arrows the Indians had raised a shout which provoked a greyhound to dash forward. Dragging to the ground one

[19] This was the river of Ocali which the Spaniards sometimes referred to as The River of Discords *(El Río de las Discordias),* possibly because of the hostility displayed in the following paragraph of the text.

of the Governor's pages who was holding it by the collar, the dog now freed itself and plunged into the water, refusing to return in spite of the repeated commands of its masters. Then as the animal swam the stream the Indians hurled their arrows so skillfully that more than fifty of them penetrated its head and shoulders, which were above the water. Even so, the dog succeeded in reaching land, only to fall dead immediately on leaving the water. The Governor and all of his companions were much grieved at the loss of this particular greyhound, for it was a rare hunter and very necessary for the conquest. Within the short span of its life, it had made skillful and admirable attacks on the Indians both by day and by night. One of these attacks, I shall describe since it reveals just what kind of an animal this dog was.

CHAPTER XVIII

Other events which occurred in the province of Ocali.

DURING the six days in which the Cacique Ocali had withdrawn into the woods and was refusing to come out amicably, the Governor had taken care to send him three and sometimes four messengers daily with overtures of peace, just to keep him informed that the Spaniards still bore him in mind. These envoys would return with the Curaca's reply; but on one occasion a certain messenger brought back four young Indian noblemen, their heads bedecked with many feathers, since these are the Indians' principal ornaments of dress. They had come to the camp for the sole purpose of seeing the Spanish army and taking note of what kind of people these newcomers were, what order of rank they observed, what manner of dress and arms they used, and what the horses were like which had so dazzled them. In sum they came to verify the truth or falsehood of the stories they had heard of the ferocity of the Spaniards.

The Governor was aware that the four Indians were noblemen, and that it was only their curiosity to see the army that had brought them to his camp; so he received them affably and took the opportunity of winning their friendship as well as that of their Cacique by presenting them gifts he had brought from Spain. Then he ordered his men to take them to another part of the camp and give them refreshments.

The Indians ate in complete tranquility, but when the Castilians were feeling most carefree about them, all four arose simultaneously and raced as fast as they could to the forest. In fact they traveled so swiftly that the Christians doubted their ability to overtake them on foot, and they were unable to ride after them since the horses were not at hand. Meanwhile, however, a greyhound chanced to be close by, and on hearing the Spaniards shout to the Indians and seeing the latter in flight, he set out in pursuit. Then just as if possessed of human understanding, this dog rushed by the first three Indians he came to and on reaching the fourth, who was in advance of the others, threw a paw to his shoulder and knocked him to the ground, holding him there until the next man approached. And now as each successive Indian came near and attempted to pass, the animal released the one he was holding and tossed another to the ground. And when he had thrown the last, he went back and forth among the four of them with such skill and trickery, turning loose one to hurl down another who was attempting to rise and frightening them all with great barks as he lay his paw upon them, that he was able to detain them until the Spaniards arrived and took them back to the camp.

There had been some fear that the flight of the Indians might have been a prearranged signal for treachery. Therefore on their return to the camp, the Spaniards questioned them separately as to why they had fled in such a fashion when there had been no occasion for them to do so. Their replies were identical, for all answered that the sole reason for their flight was that they had been struck with the vain idea that it would be a great feat and a fine proof of much gallantry and swiftness for them to escape thus from the midst of the Castilians; and with this noble action they had hoped to glorify themselves afterward among their people. In their opinion, they said, they would have enjoyed a signal victory but for the fact that the greyhound Bruto, as they called the dog, had seized it from their hands.

In giving some of the details of the incident we have just related, Juan Coles tells of another feat of this same Bruto. He declares that before the Spaniards came to Ocali, they were talking peacefully one day with some natives on the bank of a river in another province when a bold Indian, such as many of them are, struck a Spaniard viciously with his bow, for no reason whatsoever, and then plunged into the water, followed by his companions. Being nearby, this same greyhound Bruto witnessed the deed and darted after the Indians. Some of them he soon overtook, but he did not seize a single one until he came to the individual who had delivered the blow. Then striking this man with his paw, he proceeded to tear him to pieces in the water.

In addition to his other offenses against the natives, Bruto had guarded the army at night so that no hostile Indian could enter the camp without being destroyed at once. Hence, as I have said, the Indians now avenged themselves against this greyhound by taking his life. For having identified him by rumor, they shot at him most eagerly, and in doing so revealed their skill in the use of the bow and arrow.

In the conquest of the New World, greyhounds have accomplished feats that are worthy of great respect. For instance, in the island of San Juan de Puerto Rico, the Spaniards manifested their admiration for a dog named Becerrillo by giving him a part of their winnings, or rather by leaving the dog's portion with his master, a crossbowman, who as a result received a share and a half of the amount due a man of his profession. Furthermore, Leoncillo, a son of Becerrillo,[20] received five hundred pesos in gold as his share in one of the divisions made after the famous Vasco Núñez de Balboa had discovered the Sea of the South.[21]

CHAPTER XIX

The Spaniards construct a bridge and cross the Ocali river. They come to the province of Ochile.

SEEING now that the Cacique Ocali commanded little respect and less obedience from his people, the Governor realized that by holding him he had little or nothing to gain either in his project for building a bridge or in any other enterprise he might undertake; and further, he perceived that there was danger of irritating the rest of the lords of the vicinity because of their suspicion that Ocali was being held against his will. He decided, therefore, to give the man his freedom and return him to his people. So summoning him one day, he told him that he had always regarded him as a free man and treated him as a friend, that he did not want him to lose the respect of his vassals because of this friendship, and again that he wished to avoid additional rebellions on the part of the Indians because of the belief that their Curaca was being held in bondage. With that he begged the Cacique Ocali to go again to his people whenever he wished, and he gave him the liberty, once there, of deciding for himself as to whether or not he should return to the Spaniards.

[20] Becerrillo or Bezerrico belonged to Ponce de León, and was said to have been able to distinguish between a peaceful Indian and a warrior. Leoncillo or Leonzico, a red bloodhound with a black nose, was Balboa's own dog, and according to Oviedo gained for his master more than two thousand pesos in gold. This same author records that in addition to gold, dogs received allotments of slaves as well as other things of importance. See Arthur Strawn, *Sails and Swords* (New York: 1928), pp. 203, 312.

[21] *Mar del Sur*—The Pacific Ocean.

The Curaca received these words joyfully, replying that he did desire to return to his vassals for one sole purpose, and that was to reduce them to obedience so that all might come afterward and minister unto the Governor. He swore, however, that should he not be able to bring them with him, he would come alone so as to prove his allegiance to his lordship. Such promises and many more, the Cacique Ocali made to the Governor, but he never fulfilled any of them, and never did he return as he swore to do. But there are few captives who, on leaving prison under oath, have done what Atilius Regulus did.

When the Cacique had departed, the Spaniards, employing the ingenuity of Maestro Francisco, a Genoese engineer, drew geometrical plans for a bridge and then proceeded to build it. First they threw great beams of wood across the river, binding them together with heavy ropes which had been brought along for just such occasions. Then to join and secure the beams they laid thick boards over the top of them, there being so much wood in that vicinity that they could use all they wished. Thus this structure was completed in a few days, and it was so well built that both men and horses passed over it very much as they pleased.

But before the army crossed the river, the Governor commanded his men to ambush and seize as many natives as possible, for those few who had come along to serve the Castilians had now fled with the Cacique Ocali, and guides were needed. Accordingly they took thirty Indians, counting both children and adults. Then coaxing the captives on the one hand with flattery, gifts and promises of reward should they do their duty, and on the other with great threats of cruel death should they fail in it, they persuaded them to direct their search for another province sixteen leagues distant from that of Ocali.

The region which lay between the two provinces was unpopulated and peaceful. It was filled with many forests and with streams which ran through very flat country that would have been quite fruitful had it been cultivated. The first eight leagues of this land the army crossed in two days, but when they had completed a half of the third day's march, the Governor took a hundred cavalrymen and a hundred footsoldiers and went in advance of the army for the remainder of that day and all of that night. At dawn of the next day he arrived at Ochile, the principal village of Vitachuco, a large province with more than fifty leagues of road in the part through which the Spaniards passed.

The province of Vitachuco had been divided among three brothers. The eldest, who ruled five-tenths of this land, bore the same name as the province and its principal village, as we shall see later; the second, whose name is omitted because of its having been forgotten, ruled three-tenths; and the youngest, who was lord of the village of Ochile and had the same name as his village ruled the remaining two-tenths. Just why or how such a division may have come about was not learned, for in the other provinces through which the Spaniards passed, the first-born by right of primogeniture always inherited the land, and no part of it was given to another. It could be that the different sections of this particular province had been united by marriage with the provision that it was to be divided again among the succeeding children. It is also possible that relatives dying without the necessary heirs and desiring to be remembered had left their land to the parents of the three brothers with the same stipulation that it should be divided eventually among their successors. The desire for immortality through the preservation of one's fame is a natural instinct among men of all nations no matter how barbarous they may be.

But as we were saying, the Adelantado arrived at dawn in Ochile, a village consisting of fifty houses which were large and substantially built since it was situated on the frontier and served as an outpost against the adjoining province through which the Spaniards had just passed. For these two provinces, like almost all the others in the kingdom of Florida regarded each other with hostility. Coming suddenly upon the village, the Governor commanded his men to play their martial instruments— trumpets, fifes and drums— so that with this noise they might frighten the natives all the more.

Thus they were able to take many Indians, for those people had never heard such a clamor, and because of the very novelty of it, came forth in fright from their houses to see what it might be.

The Governor next laid siege to the habitation of the Curaca. This was a magnificent structure which consisted primarily of one large sala more than a hundred and twenty feet in length and forty feet wide. Opening to the four winds were four separate doors, and attached to it around the exterior were many rooms communicating with it, like apartments. Within this house was the Cacique himself, surrounded by the numerous warriors whom he, as a man possessed of enemies, customarily kept in his presence. With him also were many people who had rushed there from the town when the Spaniards made their unexpected attack. The Cacique gave an order to sound the alarm and would have gone out to fight, but he was unable to do so, for in spite of the haste he and his warriors had made to arm themselves and leave the house, they discovered that the Christians had already gained the four entrances and now forbade their exit.

The Spaniards threatened to burn the Indians alive if they did not surrender but at the same time offered them peace, friendship and the best treatment if they should do so. But neither threats nor cajolery prevailed upon the Curaca to yield until, the sun having come out, they brought before him many of his own people who were now captives. These Indians assured him that the Castilians were numerous and could not be overcome with arms, but that he should trust in their friendship since they had not mistreated any of their prisoners. Then they added that, there being no other remedy, the Cacique should conform to the present necessity. So it was that the Cacique Ochile was persuaded to surrender, and the Governor received him affably. Moreover, he commanded that his men treat the Indians most kindly, and then retaining only the Curaca, he set the remainder of the captives at liberty, an act which gratified both the chieftain and his vassals.

The victory won, the General now noticed that in a beautiful valley on the other side of the town, there was a large settlement of houses scattered in clusters of four and five, sometimes more and sometimes less. There being a great number of Indians in the settlement, he felt it unsafe to remain where he was until nightfall, for should these Indians come together and see just how few Spaniards there were, they might be so bold as to seize their Curaca and make some kind of uprising with the assistance of all the other lords of the vicinity. So taking the Curaca with him, the Governor set out for the place where his army was encamped. Three leagues from the town, he found his people, most anxious now because of his absence; and all rejoiced exceedingly when he arrived with such good booty, for the Cacique Ochile was accompanied by many servants as well as Indian warriors who had come with him of their own accord.

CHAPTER XX

*The brother of the Curaca Ochile comes in
peace. They send emissaries to
Vitachuco.*

ON THE following day the army entered the village of Ochile in battle formation with both infantry and cavalry assembled in squadrons and playing their trumpets, fifes and drums so as to make the Indians realize that the Spaniards were not people with whom they could trifle. Then when they had pitched camp, the Governor arranged for the Curaca Ochile himself to send envoys with words of peace and friendship to his two brothers, since from him those chieftains would receive messages with greater confidence and thus be more apt to believe them than if they came from the Spaniards. Accordingly the Cacique forwarded individual communications to his brothers. Devising the best words and arguments he knew, he told them of how the Spaniards had come to their land with a desire to make friends and brothers of the Indians, and of how they were just passing through on their way to other provinces.

They were doing no harm to places through which they traveled, he said, and were content with taking just such food as they needed, especially if received peacefully; but if the natives did not come out to serve them, they laid waste the villages, using wood from the houses as firewood instead of going to the forest for it, and scattering lavishly whatever provisions they found while partaking freely of more than they needed. Furthermore, they did other things that one ordinarily would do in the land of enemies. But, the Cacique explained, his brothers could avoid these things altogether by accepting the peace the Spaniards offered and receiving them as friends; and he assured them that they should do so if for no other reason than that of their own self-interest.

The second brother, who dwelt nearest Ochile and whose name I do not know, answered immediately and thanked his kinsman for the information he had sent. He declared that he was very pleased that the Castilians had come to his land, and that he felt a desire to see and know them; and he explained that he did not return immediately with the messengers because he was making the necessary preparations for serving the Spaniards more adequately and receiving them with the greatest festivity possible. But he promised to come within three or four days to kiss the Governor's hands and pledge obedience to him; and he begged that his brother in the meantime accept and confirm the peace and fellowship of the Spaniards; for, as he said, he of course looked upon them as lords and friends.

When three days had elapsed, this brother arrived at the camp in the company of many noble and very brilliant people. First kissing the Governor's hands, he then spoke most cordially to the other captains, ministers, and individual cavaliers of the army, asking in turn who each of them was. In truth he conducted himself as freely as if he had been reared among the Spaniards; and they for their part made much of this Cacique and all of his warriors. But the General and his ministers always regaled with great attention and care those chieftains and their Indians who came to them in peace. Moreover, they did no damage to the towns or property of those who were rebellious other than to take from them the food they required, and this they could not avoid doing.

The third brother, who was the eldest and most powerful in estate, would not answer Ochile's message; rather, he detained the messengers and refused to allow them to return. Consequently on the persuasion and insistence of the Governor, both of the other brothers sent him additional envoys with the same message. To this communication, however, they added very decorous words in praise of the Christians and warned him not to fail to receive the peace and friendship they offered.

"We would have you know," they said, "that these are not people with whom one can presume to win in war, for they are very brave in character and call themselves invincible. By their very lineage, quality and nature they are indeed sons of our own gods, the Sun and the Moon, and as such have come from where the Sun rises, bringing with them some animals called horses, which are so swift, brave and strong that we cannot escape them through flight or resist them with either physical strength or arms. For this reason, and as brothers who desire your health and life, we beseech you not to refuse that which is so much to your advantage, for to do so is only to seek ill and harm for yourself as well as for your vassals and lands."

Vitachuco responded very strangely and with a boldness never heard of or even imagined in an Indian; for it is a fact that if such violent and fierce threats as he made and such arrogant remarks as he uttered could be written as the messengers related them, none of the words of the bravest cavaliers introduced into the works of the divine Ariosto and his predecessor, the very illustrious and enamoured Count Matheo Maria Boiardo or of other sagacious poets would equal the words of this Indian.[22] Because of the long time that has elapsed since they were spoken, many of his remarks have

[22] Here as well as in numerous other passages of the *Florida* we find something of the genesis of the "noble savage" who later was to play a prominent role in both American and European literature.

been forgotten, and the order in which they were uttered has been lost. But those that can be recalled and that we can guarantee to be the actual ones which he sent his brothers in answer to their message will be told in the following chapter.

CHAPTER XXI

The arrogant and foolish reply of Vitachuco.
How his brothers go to persuade
him to peace.

"FOR you to say what you have said about these Spaniards would make it appear that you are mere boys lacking in judgment and experience. You praise them extensively as virtuous people who have done no harm or damage to anyone, and you proclaim them to be very valiant men who are sons of the Sun and as such merit whatever service may be rendered them. The bondage in which you have placed yourselves and the vile and cowardly spirit that you have assumed in the brief time since giving yourselves up to serve as slaves of Spaniards make you talk like women, praising as you do people whom you ought to vituperate and abhor. Do you not see that since these Christians are of the same government and race as those who perpetrated so many cruelties among us in the past, they can be no better? You take no note of their treason and perfidies. If you were men of good judgment you would perceive that their very lives and deeds reveal them to be sons of the devil rather than sons of our gods, the Sun and the Moon, for they go from land to land killing, robbing and sacking whatever they find, and possessing themselves of the wives and daughters of others without bringing any of their own. They are not content to colonize and establish a site on some of the land that they see and tread upon because they take great pleasure in being vagabonds and maintaining themselves by the labor and sweat of others. If, as you say, they were men of virtue, they would not have left their own country, for there they could have employed their strength in sowing the land and raising cattle to sustain their lives without damage to others and without increasing their own infamy. But they have made highwaymen, adulterers, and murderers of themselves without shame of men or fear of any god. Warn them, therefore, not to enter my land, for I promise that no matter how valiant they may be, if they put foot upon it, they shall never leave it, since I shall destroy them all. Half of them I shall bake, and the other half, I shall boil."

This was the initial reply that the messengers brought from Vitachuco, but he afterward sent many others. Two or three of his men came each day to the camp, always blowing their trumpets and uttering new warnings which were even greater and fiercer than the previous ones. Thus the Cacique sought to frighten the Spaniards by threatening them with different manners of death imagined in his ferocious mind. Sometimes he instructed his messengers to say that when our men came to his province, he was going to cause the earth to open up and swallow them all, and again that he was going to command the hills, which lay along the route they would travel, to come together, and catching their victims between them, bury them alive. Once he promised that when the Christians should be passing through the woods of pine and other tall and thick trees which bordered the road, he would command such strong and furious winds to blow that the trees would be uprooted and thrown upon them, so that all would be destroyed. And at another time he said that he would order a great multitude of birds with venom in their beaks to fly over the intruders and drop this venom upon them so that they should rot and their flesh become corrupt without any remedy. And still again he threatened to poison the waters, grasses, trees, fields, and even the air in such a way that not a man or a horse of the Christians would be able to escape with his life. Thus, he declared, he would warn those who in the future might have the audacity to come to that land against his will.

These and similar extravagant threats Vitachuco sent simultaneously to his brothers and the Spaniards, thus revealing the fierceness of his nature. The latter, however, laughed and jested at his words, for to them they seemed the stupid and silly utterances which his deeds afterward proved them to be, as we shall see later; still, they were aware that these had not been mere words, but expressions of the very ardent desires of a heart as brave and proud as his was, and that they had not been born in foolishness or simplicity, but in an excess of boldness and ferocity. With such messages, renewed each day, the Spaniards were detained by the Cacique for eight days, during which time they went over the estates of the two brothers who now ministered unto them and regaled them with all their strength and good will, giving them to understand that they desired to please. And in the meantime these Caciques labored persistently and solicitously to bring their elder brother to the obedience and service of the General. When they saw that their messages and persuasions gained them little or no advantage, they agreed to seek him out in person. Informing the Governor of this decision, they requested his permission to put it into effect, and he not only granted their petition but gave them many gifts and offerings of friendship to convey to Vitachuco.

The presence of his brothers and the great amount that they had to say in their own as well as the Governor's behalf, and moreover the knowledge that the Spaniards were already in his land and could do him harm if they so desired, made it appear wise to Vitachuco to lay aside his malice and hatred until a more propitious time and occasion should arise. This he hoped to find in the carelessness of the Spaniards and in the confidence they would place in the cordiality that he would feign. Thus under the guise of friendship he would be able to annihilate them more easily and less dangerously than he could in an open war. With such an evil design in mind, he now changed the harsh words which he had spoken previously into others that were more suave and gentle. Accordingly he informed his brothers that he had not realized that the Castilians were people of such fine quality and condition as those chieftains had pictured them, and that he would be very pleased to have their peace and friendship. But, he said, he wished first to know how many days they would be in his land, what quantity of supplies he was to give them when they left, and what other things they needed for their journey.

These questions the two brothers sent by an envoy to the Governor, and in answer to them the latter replied that his army would remain no longer in Vitachuco's land than the Cacique wished, that they desired no more supplies than he should consider it wise to give them, and that they wanted nothing other than the Cacique's friendship, for with that they would have everything they needed.

CHAPTER XXII

Vitachuco comes out in peace. He plans a betrayal of the Spaniards and confides in the interpreters.

VITACHUCO feigned contentment with the Governor's reply and to hide his evil designs left the impression and made public statements to the effect that his desire to visit the Spaniards for the purpose of serving them increased each day, as they themselves would discover. Then he commanded that his nobles make ready to go out and receive the Governor and that his village be well supplied with food, water and firewood for the Spanish people as well as grass for their horses. And lest these Castilians lack anything whatsoever for their service and comfort, he gave orders for supplies to be collected in his village from all the other villages of his estate.

Juan Coles says that the Indians claimed the province of the three brothers to be two hundred leagues in length.

Provisions having been assembled, Vitachuco set out from his village, accompanied by his two brothers and five hundred noble Indian cavaliers, all of them magnificently arrayed in plumage of different colors and armed with most highly polished and elegant bows and arrows, which they fashion for their greater adornment and fine dress. And when the Cacique had traveled two leagues, he came upon the Governor who was encamped with his army in a beautiful valley; for he had journeyed to this place in short daily marches after learning that the Indian had resolved to come out to the road to kiss his hands. This honor the Cacique now proceeded to render with a manifestation of complete peace and friendship; and afterward he begged the Governor to forgive the abusive words uttered in his slanderous description of the Castilians, saying that now that he was undeceived concerning them, he would show by deeds how much he really desired to minister unto his lordship and all of his nation, and in the same manner he would give satisfaction for the offenses his remarks might have occasioned. That he might do so with better reason, he added, he would pledge both himself and his vassals to obey and recognize his lordship as their sovereign.

The Governor received and embraced Vitachuco with much fidelity and then declared that he had forgotten the aforementioned words since he had not listened with the idea of remembering them; and he added that he was much pleased with the present friendship of the Curaca and would be happy to know his will, so that in the future likewise he might satisfy and not offend him. Then the Campmaster and other officers as well as the ministers of His Majesty's Exchequer, and in general all of the Spaniards spoke to Vitachuco and welcomed him with manifestations of joy. He was a man of approximately thirty-five years of age and of very good stature, as for the most part all of the Indians of Florida are, and the fierceness of his spirit was clearly revealed in his countenance.

On the following day the Castilians entered the principal village of Vitachuco in battle formation. This place, which went by the same name as its chieftain, contained two hundred large, strong houses in addition to many small ones which lay about like suburbs. The Christians took quarters in various of these dwellings, and the Governor together with the personnel of his guard and service as well as the Curacas were lodged in Vitachuco's own house, which being large provided ample accommodation for everyone. Here in the company of all three brothers, the Spaniards passed two days amid much fiesta and rejoicing. But on the third day, the two younger Caciques asked leave of the Governor and of Vitachuco to return to their homes; and when they had received permission to do so, along with gifts which the General bestowed upon them, they went away in peace and were happy over the fine treatment they had received at the hands of the Spaniards.

For four days after his brother's departure, Vitachuco continued to make a great show of serving the Spaniards in order to render them careless and thus give himself more assurance about putting into effect the plans he had desired and dreamed of carrying out against them; for his purpose was to destroy them all without exception. So ardent and so passionate was this desire that it blinded him, and as a result he would neither examine nor consider the means he ought to employ for its fulfillment. On this subject he refused to consult with his captains and vassals or to procure advice from relatives or friends who might have told him dispassionately what he should do; for he felt that such people would only hinder and not help him in his fine scheme, and that all that was necessary for the success of the enterprise was for him to desire and plan it. The only advice that he sought and accepted, therefore, was that of persons who told him what he wanted to hear without considering obstacles and without using prudence or judgment; and thus he avoided the people who could have counseled him wisely. Such is the custom, however, of men who have confidence in themselves, and the result is that their own deeds punish them for their imprudence as they did this chieftain, who was poor in understanding and lacking in reason.

Not being able to suffer longer the fires of his passion and his desire to kill the Castilians, Vitachuco, on the fifth day after his brothers had departed, secretly summoned four of the Indians whom the Governor carried as interpreters. Since different languages are spoken in the separate provinces of Florida, it was necessary to have an interpreter for almost every one of them so that each interpreter might declare successively to the other what the first had said. The Cacique informed these four men of his violent intentions and declared that he had determined to destroy the Spaniards, who, because of their great faith in his friendship, apparently trusted both himself and his vassals and in consequence were becoming very careless. He now had in readiness, he said, more than ten thousand chosen warriors whom he had ordered first to conceal their arms in the nearby forest and then to come into the village with water, firewood, grass, and all of the other things that the Christians needed, so that, seeing these people unarmed and subservient, they would be indiscreet and trust them completely. Then when two or three more days had passed he was going to invite the Governor to come out into the open countryside on pretense that he wished to show him his vassals in battle formation that he might see the power of the Indians and the number of warriors that could be provided for the service of the Spaniards in their future conquests.

"Since we are friends," the Cacique continued in his reasoning, "the Governor will come out carelessly. Therefore, I shall command a dozen strong and spirited Indians to go along near him, so that when he approaches my squadron, these men can carry him off bodily, whether he be mounted or on foot, and then attack him in the midst of the Indians. At the same time my warriors will hurl themselves against the rest of the Spaniards, who being unprepared and upset by the seizure of their captain, will be very easily taken and killed. On those who are captured, I plan to inflict all the modes of execution I have threatened them with in order that they may see that my warnings were sincere and not the foolishness and mad ravings they judged them to be and laughed at as such. Some I shall roast alive, and some I shall boil. I shall bury some alive with just their heads remaining above the ground, and others I shall poison with a mild poison so that they will be able to see themselves in a state of decomposition and decay. Still others I shall hang by the feet on the highest trees to provide food for the birds. There will be no manner of cruel death that I shall not carry out upon these people."

Vitachuco now charged the four Indians to give their opinion and guard his secret. Then he promised that should they wish to remain in his land after the undertaking was completed, he would bestow upon them eminent duties and positions as well as noble and beautiful wives and all the other distinctions, honors and liberties that the most favored persons in his province enjoyed; and he assured them in addition that should they wish to return to their own lands, he would see that they were well guarded and protected along the road they must traverse between his province and their homes. Let them take note, he said, of how the Christians had brought them to where they were by force and made slaves of them, and remember that these same men now would take them so far from their country that, even though they might later receive their liberty, they would be unable to return to their homes. And let them consider not only their own personal danger but also the common peril of all of the people of that great realm. For, he assured them, the Castilians were not going to do the Indians any good; on the contrary they would deprive them of their ancient liberties and make of them vassals and tributaries. They would take from them the most beautiful of their wives and daughters and the best of their lands and properties, while each day imposing upon them new taxes and tributes. These things, he declared, should not be tolerated, but should be prevented in time and before they had taken place and root among them. And since the matter was one which concerned all of the Indians, he begged and charged them, he said, to assist him with their industry and counsel, and at the same time to regard his purpose as just, his determination as courageous, and his plan and method as proper.

The four interpreters responded that the undertaking was worthy of Vitachuco's spirit and valor and that all he had proposed appeared to them wise. Such an excellent plan, they assured him, could not but result successfully, as they indeed expected it to do. The whole kingdom, therefore, was indebted to him for having defended and protected the life, property, honor and liberty of all its inhabitants; and as for themselves, they would carry out his commands while keeping his secret and praying to the Sun and the Moon to put into motion and to favor his deed as he had planned and ordained it. Only through their spirit and will would they be able to serve him, they said, but if their strength could just equal their desire, then his lordship would have need for no servants other than themselves to complete his excellent and noteworthy scheme.

CHAPTER XXIII

*Vitachuco commands his captains to conclude
the betrayal, and he begs the Governor
to come out and review his
people.*

WITH great inner happiness the proud Vitachuco and the four Indian interpreters separated after the consultation, the latter hoping to see themselves soon free and possessed of great charges as well as noble and beautiful wives, and the former visualizing himself already triumphant in the enterprise he had conceived badly and planned worse. Even now he could picture himself adored by the surrounding nations and indeed by the whole of that great kingdom for having liberated them and saved their lives and property. Already he fancied that he heard the plaudits his people would bestow upon him for such a memorable act; and he even dreamed of the songs that the women and children would sing in their groups as they danced before him—songs composed in praise and memory of his prowess; for such was a very general custom among the Indians of that land.

Growing more and more arrogant each hour because of these and similar visions, which imprudent and mad persons as a rule conceive for their greater ill and perdition, Vitachuco now assembled his captains to tell them his vain thoughts and insane ideas, not that they might contradict his plan and counsel him as to what he should do, but simply that they might obey him and carry out his desire. They should make haste, he said, to put into effect the commands he had given so many days previously for exterminating the Christians, and not delay for him the honor and glory of this deed which he even now enjoyed in his imagination and looked upon as having already been accomplished through their efforts and valor. And he charged that they relieve him of those cares which gave him such pain and fulfill for him the hopes which he regarded as so certain.

The captains responded that because of their great love for Vitachuco, they were prepared to obey and serve him as their lord. They were holding their warriors in readiness, they said, for the day he might wish to see all of them together and were waiting only for the hour to be designated in which they were to execute what he had ordained. This response made the chieftain very happy and he thereupon dismissed them, saying that he would advise them beforehand of what they must do.

Meanwhile, however, the four Indian interpreters had reconsidered the substance of the Curaca's communication, this time with more wisdom. To them the undertaking now appeared difficult and a victory in it impossible, first because of the strength of the Spaniards who had shown themselves to be invincible, and then because of their feeling that the Spaniards had never been so poorly prepared and careless as to be taken by treachery, or again so simple as to permit Vitachuco to deceive them as he had thought and planned to do. Their certain and present fear therefore conquered a doubtful and distant hope, for it appeared to them that, as participants in this treason, they too would die if the Castilians discovered the plot before they themselves had revealed it. Agreeing therefore to revise their decision, they broke their promise to maintain secrecy and informed Juan Ortiz of the planned betrayal so that he might reveal to the Governor the long account of all that Vitachuco had communicated to them.

When the Governor learned of the wickedness and perfidy of the Curaca, he discussed it with his captains, who now felt it wise to dissimulate with the chieftain and thus lead him to believe that they were ignorant of his plan. Accordingly they ordered their comrades to proceed cautiously and on advice, while making a show of carelessness in order not to frighten the Indians. It seemed to them likewise that the best and most justified procedure for capturing Vitachuco was the same that he himself had devised for the Governor, for in this way the Indian would fall into his own trap. They therefore held in readiness a dozen very strong soldiers to accompany their general and seize the Cacique on the day that he should invite the Spaniards to review his army. Such things were arranged in secret, and the Castilians now kept on the alert for what Vitachuco himself was doing.

Everything having been made ready which he thought necessary to carry out successfully his evil intentions and the day having arrived which he so desired, Vitachuco came that morning to the Governor and with much humility and veneration said: "I beg Your Lordship to agree to do me and all of my vassals the great favor of coming out to the open plain where we are waiting, in order that you may see us arranged in squadrons and in battle formation. For thus favored by your sight and presence, all will be obligated to assist Your Lordship with greater spirit and promptitude on whatever future occasion may be offered us. I myself should like for you to see my people in battle array so that you may have a clear idea of what they are like and be apprised of the number with which I can serve you, and also that you may decide if the Indians of this land can form a squadron like those of other nations, which, I have heard, are skilled in military art."

Feigning ignorance and carelessness, the Governor replied that he would be very pleased to review the Indians as Vitachuco had suggested, but that in order further to enhance the field and to give the natives likewise something to see, he would command his own Spanish cavalry and infantry to go out in squadron formation and hold a friendly skirmish in which they would enjoy themselves while exercising in a playful but at the same time serious way.

The Curaca did not welcome so much ceremony and ostentation, but because of his obstinacy and blind faith in his ultimate success, he did not reject the skirmish, it appearing to him that his own strength and valor as well as that of his vassals would be sufficient to conquer and defeat the Castilians regardless of how well prepared they might be.

CHAPTER XXIV

*How they seized Vitachuco. The outbreak of
the battle which occurred between the
Spaniards and the Indians.*

THE people having been ordered out from both sides, as has been stated, the Spaniards sallied forth magnificently decorated and armed, their squadrons arranged in battle formation with the horsemen divided from the footsoldiers. The Governor, in order further to conceal his knowledge of the treason of the Indians, had resolved to accompany the Curaca on foot.

Near the village there was a great plain, on one side of which was a tall, dense and extensive forest, and on the other, two lagoons. The first lagoon was small, measuring only a league in circumference, but it was clear of underbrush and mud, and so deep that at three or four steps from its bank, one could not find footing. The second, which was farther from the town, was very large, for it was more than half a league in width and so long that it looked like a great river, and they had no idea as to where it ended. Between the forest and the two lagoons, the Indians placed their battalion in such a way that water lay to their right and trees to their left. There must have been almost ten thousand of these warriors, all of whom were chosen people, valiant and well disposed. On their heads were their finest adornments, some large feather ornaments, prepared and worn in such a way as to rise a half-fathom high and thus make the wearers appear taller than they actually were. Their bows and arrows they had laid on the ground and covered with grass so as to leave the impression that as friends they were un-armed; their squadron they had arranged in the utmost military perfection, not squared but elongated, with the rows straight and somewhat open, and with two flanks on each side of the command-ing officers. Indeed their battalion was so excellently organized that it was a beautiful sight to behold. In this manner, they waited for their lord Vitachuco and Hernando de Soto to come out to review them. And eventually these two men did approach on foot, each accompanied by twelve of his own soldiers and each harboring the same motive and desire against the other. To the right of the Gov-ernor marched the Spanish battalions, the infantry remaining close to the forest and the cavalry holding to the middle of the plain.

When they came to the place where Vitachuco had promised to give a signal for his Indians to seize the Governor, the latter, who was playing the same game, gave his signal first lest his opponent win over him by a hand; for it was with this signal that the stakes between them were to be won. So it was that the Governor now had a crossbow fired, this being the indication that his men were to act. (Alonso de Carmona says that the signal was the blowing of a trumpet, and it could have been either the one or the other.) With that, the twelve Spaniards who were near Vitachuco seized the Cacique in spite of the fact that the Indians accompanying him made an effort in his defense.

Being secretly armed, Hernando de Soto now mounted one of the two horses standing nearby. This was a dappled gray called Acey-tuno, after Mateo de Aceytuno who had presented it to the Gover-nor. (We have told before how this man had gone to rebuild Havana. Remaining there, he became warden of a fortress which he himself founded, and which is the one that at present protects the city and port, although in his time it was not so large and majestic as it is today.) It was a very brave and beautiful animal and was indeed worthy of having had such masters. Once mounted, the Governor attacked and penetrated the squadron of Indians before any other Castilian had an opportunity to do so, for this valiant captain was nearest the foe, and furthermore he prided himself on being first always in each of the battles and encounters that were offered him by day or by night in both the conquest of Florida and that of Peru. And indeed he was one of the four best lancers that could have come or did come to the West Indies. Many times his captains complained about his subjecting himself to such risk and danger, since in the preservation of the life and health of the head of the army lay the safety of the army itself; and although it is possible that he realized that they were right, still he could not curb his bellicose spirit, and he disliked victories unless he were the first in gaining them. Leaders should not be so audacious.

The Indians who at this point already had their arms in their hands, received the Governor with the same spirit and gallantry that he himself displayed; and they did not permit him to break many lines of their battalion, for, of the numerous arrows which they discharged when he reached the first line, eight struck his horse. As we shall see in the process of this history, the Indians always tried to kill the horses first because of the advantage these animals gave the cavaliers. Thus they nailed the General's horse with four arrows through the chest and four in the knees, two on each side; and they did so with such skill and ferocity that, just as if hit in the forehead with a piece of artillery, the animal fell dead without so much as moving a foot.

Meanwhile the Spaniards, having heard the shot from the crossbow, followed the lead of their Captain General and rushed at the squadron of Indians. Their horses passed so near the Governor that they were able to assist him before the enemy could do further harm. At this time one of the Governor's pages, an hidalgo called something-or-other Viota, who was a native of Zamora, dismounted and, offering the Governor his horse, helped him upon it. Then both the Governor and his men fell upon the Indians once more, and the latter being without pikes were unable to resist the combined impact of the three hundred cavalrymen. Consequently they turned their backs without making further proof of their strength and valor, which was quite contrary to what they and their Cacique had thought it to be a short while before, when it had appeared to them impossible for so few Spaniards to conquer so many and such valiant Indians as they prided themselves on being.

Their squadron broken, the Indians fled to the nearest shelters they could find. A great band of them saved their lives by entering the forest; whereas many others escaped by plunging into the large lagoon. But some of the rearguard not near shelter fled forward across the plain, where a few of them were captured, while more than three hundred were lanced and killed. Those of the advance guard who were the best soldiers and as such are accustomed always to pay in battle for everyone else, were less fortunate because they received the first encounter and the greatest impact of the cavalry. Not being able to take refuge in the woods or in the large lagoon, which were the best shelters, more than nine hundred of them threw themselves into the small lagoon. This first demonstration of Vitachuco's bravery took place at nine or ten o'clock in the morning.

The Spaniards pursued the Indians in every direction, even entering the woods and the large lagoon; but when they saw that all of their perseverance was not resulting in their taking a single Indian, they rushed back to the small lagoon, within which, as we have said, more than nine hundred men had sought shelter. With these men, they fought the entire day, more with threats and terror, however, than with arms since they merely wished to make them surrender. Hence in firing their crossbows and arquebuses, it was not their intention to kill but to frighten, for they were loath to harm men who were exhausted and unable to flee.

The Indians for their part continued to discharge arrows throughout the day, not ceasing until their supply was gone. Because of the depth of the water they were unable to stand, and in order to fire one man would mount three or four of his companions as they swam and, suspended thus in the air, shoot until he had used up the

ammunition of his team. In this manner, they occupied themselves
for the entire day without any one of them surrendering. Then
when night came groups of Spaniards stationed themselves at short
intervals so that no one could escape in the darkness—the cavalry
being arranged in pairs and the infantry in groups of six. And
now they continued to torment the Indians, never once letting them
set foot on the shore, for when they heard them near, they shot
at them and drove them away, hoping that they would become
exhausted by the swimming and as a result give up the more
quickly. Thus they threatened with death those who would not
surrender, at the same time offering pardon, peace and fellowship
to those who were willing to receive them.

CHAPTER XXV

*The gradual surrender of the conquered In-
dians, and the constancy of seven
of them.*

REGARDLESS of how much the Castilians afflicted the Indians
in the lake, they could not do enough to keep them from
showing their spirit and strength; for even though these men realized that they were without hope of help in the hardships and danger
they were experiencing, they chose death as a lesser evil to that of
showing weakness in adversity. This obstinacy they maintained
until twelve o'clock that night, for there was not one of them who
would yield in spite of the fact that all had spent fourteen hours
in the water. From that time on, however, because of the many
persuasions of Juan Ortiz and the four Indian interpreters with him
who promised and assured them of their lives, the weakest began
to come out and surrender one at a time and in pairs, but with such
reluctance that by dawn not more than fifty had done so. Then,
persuaded by their comrades who had yielded and seeing that they
had not been killed or harmed but on the contrary well treated,

those remaining in the water now surrendered in greater numbers, although with so much hesitation and so much urging that many, after they were near the bank, returned to the depth of the lagoon. But eventually the will to live brought them once again to the shore. In this manner they continued, fearing to come out and submit, until ten o'clock in the day when those who remained, about two hundred in all, yielded in a body. They had been swimming twenty-four hours, and it was a great pity to see them emerge from the lagoon, half drowned and swollen by the large amount of water they had swallowed, and transfixed by the toil, hunger, fatigue and lack of sleep they had suffered.

Only seven Indians now remained in the water. They were so obstinate that the pleas of the interpreters, the promises of the Governor, and even the example of those who had yielded, were insufficient to persuade them to do the same. On the contrary they appeared to have absorbed the spirit that the others had lost and to prefer death to being conquered. Thus, forcing themselves to answer what was said to them as best they could, they responded that they neither wanted the promises of the Spaniards nor feared their threats or even death itself. With this constancy and strength, they remained in the lagoon until three o'clock in the afternoon and would have ended their lives there but for the fact that at that hour the Governor decided it was inhuman to permit men of so much magnanimity and virtue (which even in enemies inspires our admiration) to perish. He therefore ordered twelve Spaniards who were great swimmers to go with their swords in their mouths (in imitation of Julius Caesar at Alexandria, Egypt, and of the few Spaniards who did likewise on another occasion in the river Albis, when they conquered the Duke of Saxony and all of his league) and take those seven valiant Indians from the lagoon. At that the swimmers plunged into the water and seizing the men by the leg, arm or hair, dragged them out and threw them on the ground, more drowned than alive, for they were almost unconscious. Thus they remained stretched on the sand in a condition one may well imagine of men who had struggled in water for almost thirty hours without having put foot on dry land (as it appeared) or received any other relief. Their performance was indeed incredible, and I would not dare tell of it were it not verified by the testimony of so many cavaliers and illustrious men who spoke of it in the Indies and in Spain, as well as of others who saw it in this conquest, and in addition by the authority and truthfulness of the individual who related this history to me, a person who is worthy of faith in all respects.

Since we have mentioned the River Albis, it is not right to pass on without referring to a very Catholic story told, after the rout which occurred there, by Alonso Vivas (a brother of good Doctor Luis Vivas) who was Campmaster at the time and charged with guarding the person of the Duke of Saxony. It happened that one day when Alonso Vivas was speaking in the presence of that very gross and fierce Saxon of the many miracles performed by images of Our Lady in divers parts of the world, the Duke, who had been poisoned by the heresies of Martin Luther, said: "In one of my towns there was an image of the Virgin Mary which was rumored to have performed miracles. I had this image cast into the river Albis, but it performed no miracle."

The Campmaster, pained by such profane words, answered hastily: "What more miracle do you wish, Duke, than the fact that you were defeated in that same river in a manner so very contrary to your own hopes as well as those of your league?" Lowering his face until his beard was thrust on his chest, the Duke did not lift it again that day, and did not leave his room for three days, so abashed and humiliated was he because this Catholic Spaniard had proved his infidelity and heresy by showing that the image of Our Lady had indeed performed on his very person a miracle which had been to his harm.

This story and others of those times as well as of earlier and later times were told me by Don Alonso de Vargas, my uncle, who was present on the occasion and served throughout the whole German expedition as a sergeant major with a regiment of Spanish infantry, calling himself Francisco de Plasencia. Later he became a captain in the cavalry.

Moved to pity and compassion by the hardship the seven Indians had suffered in the water, and admiring the strength and constancy of spirit they manifested, the Spaniards now carried them to their camp and did everything possible to recall them to life. Because of these attentions as well as of their own good spirits the miserable ones were revived during the night, but it required the whole of the night to free them from danger. Then when morning came, the Governor commanded that all seven of them be brought before him; and feigning anger, he ordered them to be questioned as to the cause of their persistence and rebellion, and as to why, seeing themselves in such a circumstance and without hope of help, they would not surrender as the rest of their companions had done. Four of these Indians, who were approximately thirty-five years of age, responded. They talked in turns, first one and then the other, this one taking up the account where that one, because of being nervous or not happening to relate it well, had left off. At other times one who had been silent would supply a word that the speaker happened to omit, it being their custom to assist each other in discourse with serious persons before whom they feared they would be ill at ease. Thus maintaining this style of communication, they answered the Governor in many long discourses, the sum of which was understood to be as follows. They had realized that they were in danger of losing their lives and had had no hope of assistance, but in spite of this fact, had felt and confidently believed that in surrendering themselves, they would not be complying in any manner with the obligations of the military offices and charges which they exercised. Their lord and prince had selected them in time of prosperity and had honored them with the titles and insignia of captain because he had looked upon them as men of strength, spirit and constancy; therefore, they said, it was only just that in times of adversity they should fulfill the obligations of their offices and thus show themselves worthy of those charges lest their Curaca and lord feel that he had erred in choosing them. But in addition to satisfying the military obligations which they owed their lord, they added, they wished likewise to set an example for their sons and successors and for all soldiers and fighting men as to how they should act in similar circumstances, especially in the position of captain and superior; for as such their deeds of spirit and strength or of weakness and cowardice were more conspicuous to those who would honor or censure them than they would be were they base plebeians with no responsibility or charge to fulfill. For this reason, they said, even though they had experienced and survived what his lordship had witnessed, they were not satisfied that they had done their duty or fulfilled their obligations as chiefs and leaders, and it would have been a greater favor and honor for the Governor to have permitted them to perish in the lagoon than to have given them their lives. Hence they refused to recognize any beneficence in his act, and they begged his lordship to command that they be killed, since, not having died for their lord Vitachuco, who had honored and esteemed them so very much, they would not dare appear before him again and would live in the world in great infamy and shame.

CHAPTER XXVI

What the Governor did with the three Indians,
lords of vassals, and with the Curaca
Vitachuco.

THE four Indian captains having responded with what we have told in the preceding chapter, the Governor, not without admiration for their reasoning, now cast his glance toward the other three prisoners who had remained silent. These were men of tender age, none being more than eighteen years old, who were sons and heirs of lords of vassals of the region and neighborhood of Vitachuco. In order to hear what they would say, he asked why it was that they, not being captains themselves and thus not having the obligation of the other four, had acted with the same obstinacy and stubbornness. The youths, with a spirit that was very strange for prisoners and with a semblance as lofty as if they were at liberty, answered in their own tongue, each helping the other. Interpreted in Spanish, their words are as follows:

"The principal motive that took us from the houses of our fathers, whose eldest sons we are and the heirs of whose estates and realms we were to have been, was not altogether a desire for your death or the destruction of your captains and your army, although our aim could not have been realized without doing harm to you and to all of your people. Neither were we moved by self-interest, which generally motivates those who participate in war, nor by the gain which one customarily receives in the sacking of conquered towns and armies. Furthermore we did not go forth to serve our princes in order that, pleased and obligated with our future services, they should grant us favors befitting our merits. All such motives were lacking in us, for we had no need of any of these things.

"We left our homes to join in the battle just finished solely out of ambition for glory, for our fathers and our teachers have taught us that this is the thing gained in war which is of greater value and esteem than anything else in this world. With prospects of such fame our neighbors and fellow citizens invited and incited us to join them, and because of it, we placed ourselves in the toil and danger in which you saw us yesterday, and from which you, through your clemency and compassion, have removed us, thus making us your slaves today.

"Then when fate took from us the victory in which we had hoped to achieve that glory to which we aspired, and gave it to you as the ones who better deserved it, while subjecting us on the contrary to the misfortunes and hardships that the conquered are wont to suffer, it appeared to us that we could gain glory in these very adversities by enduring them with the same spirit and force we had manifested in prosperity; for our elders have taught us that the vanquished one who is faithful and who minimizes the value of his life for the honor of preserving the liberty of his country as well as his own personal liberty, deserves no less than the triumphant conqueror who uses his victory well.

"In all of these things and many others we were instructed by our fathers and relatives. For this reason, although we came with no official duties or military offices, it appeared to us that our responsibility was no less than that of the four captains and on the contrary was even greater and more obligatory, as fate had selected us for greater pre-eminence and estate. Since we were to become lords of vassals, we wished to make our future subjects realize that we aspired to succeed to the estates of our fathers and ancestors by the same steps by which they had risen to be lords—those of fortitude, constancy and other virtues that they possessed—and with which they had sustained their estates and princely realms. We likewise wished to console our fathers and kinsmen with our own death, for by perishing in the line of duty we would thus reveal ourselves to be their true relatives and sons.

"These, oh invincible Captain, were the reasons for our having found ourselves in this undertaking, and for the rebellion and obstinacy that you say we have shown, if thus one can call the desire for honor and fame and the wish to fulfill our obligation and natural debt, a debt which because of their higher quality and estate is greater in princes, lords and cavaliers than in common people. And now if this explanation is sufficient for our exoneration, pardon us, Son of the Sun; for our obstinacy was not due to any desire to treat you with disrespect, but to the reasons which you have heard. If we do not deserve pardon, you see here our throats; do with our lives what may most please you, for we are yours, and to the conqueror, nothing is denied."

Many of the surrounding Spaniards on hearing the concluding words of these young men and seeing such noble and tender youths so afflicted and speaking thus of their fate, could not refrain from showing their pity and tenderness, which eventually was revealed in their eyes. And the Governor, who likewise was of a compassionate nature, also became tender, and, standing up, embraced all three of the youths together and afterward each one separately, as if they were his own sons. Among other very affectionate words, he told them that the fortitude they had displayed in battle and the prudence they had shown outside it, made it very clear who they were, and that such men deserved to be lords of great estates. He added that he was much pleased to have known them and to have saved them from death, and moreover that he would be glad to set them at liberty soon so that they might be happy and lose the pain which their adversity had occasioned them.

After the aforementioned conversation, the Governor kept these young men with him for two days, and during this time, in order to attract their fathers to his friendship and devotion, he showered the youths with gifts and endearments and seated them at his table, an honor which they esteemed exceedingly. When the two days had passed, he gave them gifts of linens, silks, mirrors and other things from Spain, which they were to carry to their mothers and fathers, and then sent them to their homes accompanied by some of the captured Indians whom he had found to be of their people. And he bade them tell their parents what a good friend he had been and that he would extend his fellowship to them if they so desired.

When they had given thanks to the Governor for having spared their lives and for the favors he now was granting, the youths returned content to their lands, carrying something indeed to tell their people. But the Governor ordered the four captains to be held in prison so that he might reprimand them along with their Cacique. Then on the day after the youths had departed, he commanded these five Indians to be called before him and with severe words told them how malicious it had been for them under the guise of peace and friendship to try to kill the Castilians, who had done them no ill. For this reason, he said, they deserved death so that they might serve as an example to resound throughout the world; but in order to prove to the natives of all that great kingdom that he did not wish to avenge himself for his injuries but rather to have peace and friendship with everyone, he was going to pardon them their past transgressions with the understanding that in the future they should be good friends. Now, he added, since he on his part had proved himself to be amicable, he begged and charged that they, without remembering the past, should make an effort to preserve their lives and property by not attempting anything else, for if they did so they would have no more success than they had had previously.

In order to mitigate the hatred and rancor that Vitachuco held for the Christians, the Governor told him many things privately in very affectionate words, and he commanded him to eat again at his table, for until that time he had punished him by placing him at a distance and making him eat elsewhere. But these speeches, caresses and gifts, which were offered with a manifestation of tenderness, did not have a satisfactory effect upon Vitachuco who was obstinate and blind in his passion; on the contrary, they incited him to greater madness and foolhardiness, because, enslaved as he was to fury and temerity, he was incapable of counsel and of all reason, and he was ungrateful and unmindful of the pardon and beneficent acts of the Governor. Dominated by his passions, he was like a lost soul; and he did not stop until he realized the destruction and death of both himself and his vassals, as we shall see later.

CHAPTER XXVII

An objection or counter-view is answered.

BEFORE my readers proceed with this history, it will be well to answer an objection which could be raised to the effect that such deeds and speeches of the Indians as I relate here are not to be found in other histories of the West Indies. For in general these people are looked upon as a simple folk without reason or understanding who in both peace and war differ very little from beasts and accordingly could not do and say things so worthy of memory or praise as some of those which I have described up to this point, and which, Heaven willing, I shall tell further on in my story. Thus I may be accused of having written as I have either to fictionize or to lavish praises upon my own people since all of these lands and regions, though far apart, are regarded as the Indies.

To this first objection, my answer is that the opinion ordinarily held of the Indians is unreliable and in all respects contrary to what one should believe, as the Very Venerable Father Joseph de Acosta notes, argues and proves most successfully in the first chapter of the sixth book of his *Historia Natural y Moral del Nuevo Orbe.*[23] I would refer all who wish to see his opinion to this book, a book in which one may find also other admirable things written by so worthy a master. But in regard to what concerns our particular Indians and the truth of my history, as I said in the beginning, I have simply recorded the words of another who witnessed and supervised the writing personally. This man was so anxious to be accurate that he corrected each chapter as it was written, adding what was lacking or deleting what he himself had not said, for he would not consent to any word other than his own. I, therefore, as the author contributed no more than the pen, and can truthfully declare that this account is not a fabric of my imagination. In fact all of my life I have been an enemy of such fiction as one finds in books of knighthood and the like, good poetry excepted.[24] For this attitude I am indebted to the illustrious cavalier, Pedro Mexía de Sevilla, since with the censure that he applies in his heroic treatise on the

[23] The success of this work earned for its author the designation of the "Pliny of the New World." Its first two books were composed while Father Acosta was serving on the faculty of the University of San Marcos in Lima.

[24] There was ample opportunity for Garcilaso to become well acquainted with chivalric literature. Prohibitory decrees had failed to stem the flow of popular fiction to the New World and the Inca's godfather was none other than Diego de Silva, whose *Crónica de don Florisel de Niquea* eventually attained a popularity unsurpassed even by the *Amadís de Gaula.* See Irving A. Leonard, *Books of the Brave* (Cambridge: 1949), *passim,* and particularly pp. 23–24.

Caesars[25] to those who occupy themselves with reading and composing such books, he took from me the love that I had for them as a boy and thus made me abhor them forever.

But to say that I exaggerate my praise of the race because I myself am an Indian is indeed a falsehood, for I confess with shame on my part that instead of finding myself with an excess of words to overstate what did not occur, I lack sufficient words to present in their proper light the actual truths that are offered me in this history. Such a deficiency is a result of the unfortunate circumstances of my childhood, for at that time there were no schools of letters and there was an excess of schools of arms for training both infantry and cavalry, and especially men in horsemanship. Since our land was won in the saddle, my fellow students and I were trained so much in these schools from our childhood on that many or all became notable cavalrymen without having learned very much of the nominatives. For this reason, I consider myself very unfortunate today, although the fault is neither ours nor our fathers but that of our fate, which at that time had no more to offer us because our land had been so recently won, and because of the civil wars that then followed one after the other from those of the Pizarros and Almagros to those of Francisco Hernández Girón. Under such conditions, maestros of science were scarce and there was an excess of maestros of arms. But in these present times, through the mercy of God, the contrary is true, for the Fathers of the Holy Company of Jesus have planted so many schools of all sciences that the universities of Spain are no longer missed.

But returning to our original purpose, to certify upon the word of a Christian that we have written the truth in the past, and that with the favor of the Highest Truth, we shall write it in the future, I shall tell what happened at this point in the story between me and the one who gave me my facts. If I did not hold this man to be

[25] Pedro Mexía's *Historia Imperial y Cesarea*, published at Seville in 1545, represented one of the numerous efforts to stem the tide of interest in the *libros de caballería*—efforts which were to find a fruitful culmination in *Don Quixote*.

such an hidalgo and the trustworthy person he is, as later in other passages I shall speak of him as being, I would not pride myself on having written as much truth as I have, and moreover would not guarantee it as such. I say then that when we had come to the previously mentioned reply of the four Indian captains to the Governor, and then to the one of the three youths who were sons of lords of vassals, it appeared to me that (according to the general opinion held of the Indians) their reasoning was superior to that of barbarians,[26] and I thereupon remarked: "According to the universal reputation of the Indians, one is not to believe that these were their actual words."

"You well know," he replied, "that that opinion is false, and one must disregard it; moreover it will be only right to destroy it by showing just what truth there is in it. As you yourself have seen and known, there are Indians of very fine understanding who in peace and war, and in adverse and prosperous times, are able to speak like the people of any nation of much wisdom. These Indians did answer in substance what I have told you, and furthermore they made many other magnificent speeches which I do not recall, but which I would not be able to repeat as they were said even if I should remember them. Nevertheless these speeches were so eloquent that the Governor and those who accompanied him were more surprised by the utterances of the Indians than they were by their having permitted themselves to swim almost thirty hours in the water. And when many Spaniards well read in history heard them, they asserted that the captains appeared to have been influenced by the most famous officers of Rome when that city dominated the world with its arms, and that the youths, who were lords of vassals, appeared to have been trained in Athens when it was flourishing in moral letters. Consequently, as soon as they responded and the Governor had embraced them, there was not a captain or a

[26] The Inca rather carefully avoids referring to the Indians as barbarians. For this reason we have not used in our translation the word most commonly applied to the earliest inhabitants of America, i.e., savages.

soldier of any importance who did not embrace them likewise with very great rejoicing and enthusiasm at having heard them.

"Write what I have told you, therefore, with all the exaggeration that you can, for I promise that regardless of how much you may sharpen your pen in praise of the generosities and excellencies of Mucozo, and of the strength, constancy, and wisdom of these seven Indians, both captains and lords of vassals, and no matter if you enlarge more and more upon the savagery and ferocities of Vita-chuco and other chieftains to be encountered later, you will not reach the height they attained in their greatness and heroic deeds. So write what I tell you without scruple, regardless of whether it is believed or not, for with having told the truth of what happened, we shall have fulfilled our obligation, and to do otherwise would be to wrong the parties concerned."

All this, just as I have told it, occurred between me and my author, and I put it here in order that one may understand and believe that we were boldly attempting to write the truth, not with an excess of hyperbole but rather with a lack of the eloquence and rhetoric necessary to give the deeds their proper place of honor, for that place was not reached. And since in the pages ahead it will be necessary for me to bolster faith in my veracity when I tell of other things as great and greater than those in the past, I shall say no more at present. Instead, let us return to our history.

CHAPTER XXVIII

*A foolhardy action which Vitachuco ordained
for the purpose of destroying the
Spaniards, and which re-
sulted in his own
death.*

BY ORDER of the Governor, the more than nine hundred Indians who came out of the small lagoon and surrendered were held captive and, as a punishment for their treason, distributed among the Castilians as slaves. This measure was taken, however, for the sole purpose of intimidating and putting a check on the inhabitants of the district, who had learned of the late uprising, lest they too dare commit similar offenses; and the Spaniards fully intended to give the captives their liberty as soon as they themselves had departed from the province.

Vitachuco was now sequestered in his house in the role of a prisoner, but he learned of these circumstances, and being blinded by his passion, this miserable man thought day and night of nothing other than what means he could employ to annihilate the Spaniards. Already his obstinacy and shortsightedness had made him hasty, and it appeared to him that since these nine hundred men represented the most noble, valiant and select people of his nation (according to an accurate report brought by four little pages who served him), they would be sufficient to accomplish individually all of those things that they had failed to accomplish collectively; for now that they more or less equalled the Christians in number, each of them could kill one Castilian just as he himself planned to do. And he further persuaded himself that when the time came for the Indians to carry out such a scheme, they would be at an advantage, since the Christians would be eating, heedless and unconcerned about men who had surrendered and were unarmed slaves. Having conceived this foolish idea, he rushed into it without gathering information as to whether or not the Indians were at liberty or had weapons, for he felt that since with just his own strong arms he himself was adequately equipped, all of the others would be likewise.

By means of his pages Vitachuco advised the leaders among the nine hundred Indians of this very hasty and foolhardy decision, commanding that they treat the matter secretly but pass the word from one to the other of his vassals that at noon sharp on the third day to come, each was to be prepared to slay that Spaniard whom it had fallen to his lot to serve, for it was at this hour that he himself would destroy the Governor. And he said that as a signal for them to begin, he would give a cry on killing the General that would be loud enough to be heard throughout the whole village. Since the Cacique issued this order on the same day that the Governor had reprimanded and restored him to his friendship and grace, one may see by his behavior just how ingrates show their appreciation for beneficences offered them.

Although they realized the rashness of their Cacique's command, the miserable Indians obeyed and replied that they would do what he had ordered with all their strength or die in the attempt. But the Indians of the New World hold their lords and kings in such veneration and respect that they obey and worship them as gods rather than as men, and in obedience to their commands will throw themselves as readily into fire as water. They think of life or death only in so far as these things concern the fulfillment of the precepts of their lord, in whom they have placed their happiness; and it was because of this sacred duty (for as such they held it) that Vitachuco's Indians obeyed him with such simplicity and without a word in reply.

Seven days after the recent skirmish and rout, just at the moment when the Governor and Vitachuco had finished eating (for the Governor had granted the Cacique all possible courtesies in order to win his friendship), the latter sat bolt upright in his chair and, turning his body from one side to the other, extended his arms in both directions with his hands closed and then brought them back again until his fists rested upon his shoulders. Then he shook his arms once or twice with such force and violence as to cause both bones and joints to crack like breaking canes. The purpose of these gestures was to awaken and call up the force to carry out his plan, and the procedure is a common one which is done almost spontaneously by the Indians of Florida when they wish to accomplish something that requires strength. Having completed these movements, the Cacique rose to his feet with all imaginable savagery and fierceness and in an instant closed with the Adelantado, on whose right he had been seated. Seizing him by the collar with his left hand, he gave him such a blow over the eyes, mouth and nose with his right fist that he knocked down the chair in which he was seated and stretched him out unconscious on his back as if he had been a child. Then in order to finish with his victim, he let himself fall upon him, while at the same time giving such a tremendous roar that it could be heard for a quarter of a league around. But when those cavaliers and soldiers who chanced to be eating with the General saw him so badly used and his life so endangered by such a strange and unexpected performance, they grasped their swords and attacked. Then ten or twelve of them pierced the body of the Indian simultaneously, and he fell dead, blaspheming heaven and earth because he had failed in his wicked attempt.

The assistance which these cavaliers rendered their captain was most timely and fortunate; had they not been on hand or had they delayed just long enough for the Indian to strike another blow, he would have succeeded in killing the Governor. For the blow which the Governor did receive was so fierce that he was unconscious for more than a half hour, and he bled through the eyes, nose, mouth, gums, and upper and lower lips as if he had been struck with a large club. Furthermore both his front and back teeth were so tormented that they almost fell out, and for upwards of twenty days he could eat only food that could be taken with a spoon and nothing that had to be chewed. Indeed during this whole time his nose and lips remained so swollen that it was necessary to apply plasters.

As we have said, Vitachuco proved himself to be too strong and fierce to live. Thus one may deduce that those terrible threats—and such strange threats they were—which he had made from the first, had been born of a savageness and fierceness of spirit which, because of its rarity, had not admitted the consideration, prudence and counsel that great deeds require.

In addition to what we have said of the blow which Vitachuco struck with his fist, Juan Coles adds that with it, the Cacique knocked out two of the Governor's teeth.

CHAPTER XXIX

*The strange battle which took place between
the captive Indians and their masters.*

WHEN the Indians heard the cry of their Cacique, which, as
we said, he had given as a signal to his vassals for the desperate act that caused his own death as well as that of the remainder
of his men, incidents occurred in the camp between them and the
Spaniards which were no less cruel and frightful than they were
ludicrous. For at that moment, each captive fell upon his master
with the intention of either killing or wounding him. As weapons,
they used the burning wood from the fire or other things found at
hand; for lacking the desired arms, they simply converted into offensive implements whatever they discovered in front of them. Thus
many struck their masters in the face and burned them with pots
of boiling food; others hit them with plates, crocks, jars and pitchers,
while still others used benches, chairs, and tables if they were to be
had, and if not, anything else that came to hand. As one can
imagine would be true in such a case, their actions served for no
better purpose than to disclose their desire to destroy the Spaniards;
but they did do more damage with the burning pieces of wood than
with the other weapons, and it could be that these had been prepared
for the purpose, since the majority came out with them in their
hands. One Indian gave his master a blow on the head with a burning brand, and then rushing at him with two or three of his comrades, dashed out his brains. Many Spaniards came out of the fray
with their brows and noses broken and their arms mutilated by the
burning wood; whereas others received great slaps and blows from
fists, stones and sticks, each according to what fate held for him
from such an arsenal as was afforded the Indians offhand within
their houses.

One Indian, after having maltreated his master with sticks and
beaten him with his fists until his lips were swollen thick, fled from

the Castilians who came to assist their comrade. Seizing a lance which he had found against the wall and climbing a hand ladder to an upper room, he proceeded to defend the door in such a way that his enemies could not reach him. At the cry which arose, a cavalier named Diego de Soto, who was a relative of the Governor, rushed up with a loaded crossbow and prepared to fire at the man from the patio. Nevertheless the Indian made no attempt to preserve his life but sought rather to sell it at the best price possible, and, even though he saw the Spaniard aiming at him, would not flee. Placing himself in front of the door so as to be able to throw well, he hurled his lance at the same moment that the Spaniard fired his crossbow. The weapon missed its mark but passed so close to the left shoulder of the Spaniard as to strike him a great blow and bring him to his knees; then driving itself half a fathom into the earth it remained there vibrating. Diego de Soto, on the other hand, was more successful in hitting his mark, for his arrow struck the Indian in the chest and thus brought his life to a close.

Having witnessed this effrontery and daring on the part of the Indians and being aware of how badly the Governor had been hurt by the blow from Vitachuco's fist, the Spaniards lost patience and gave themselves over to getting revenge through the destruction of their foes. And those men especially who had been injured by blows or affronted by slaps, now most angrily destroyed every Indian they encountered. Others, who did not feel that they had been offended, considered it unworthy of their rank and person to slay men who had surrendered and were slaves in both appearance and name. These men therefore took their captives to the plaza and turned them over to the halberdiers of the Governor's guard, who were there to judge them, and who killed them with their halberds and partisans. And for the purpose of pledging the interpreters and other Indians in the service of the army who had been brought from the provinces already passed and to make them enemies of the inhabitants of this land so that they would not dare attempt an escape in the future, the Spaniards commanded them to shoot the captives with arrows and thus help to destroy them. This order these Indians carried out.

One Castilian, a small and very neat person named Francisco de Saldaña, did not relish the task of slaying the Indian who had fallen to his lot in the distribution of the slaves, so tying a cord about the man's neck, he led him to the judges. Now when this Indian caught sight of the plaza and perceived what was transpiring there, he was so enraged that he came up from behind and seized his master with one hand on his collar and the other on the seat of his trousers. Lifting him in the air as he would a child, he turned him upside down and without the Spaniard's being able to help himself, struck him so hard on the ground that he was stunned. Then he jumped on him with his feet so angrily as to almost burst him open with his kicks. Those Spaniards who witnessed the incident rushed with sword in hand to assist their companion, but the Indian seized the sword which his master wore at his waist and received them so savagely that, in spite of the fact that there were more than fifty to resist, he detained them in a great circle about him. Swinging the weapon in both hands with great velocity of body and desperation of spirit, he showed well that he preferred killing Castilians to having them kill him, and they, not desiring to receive injuries in exchange for slaying a desperate man, drew back. Thus fenced in on all sides, this Indian continued to attack everyone without any of them being willing to accept his challenge until long-handled weapons were brought, with which they succeeded in killing him.

These and many similar incidents occurred in this more than domestic riot in which four Spaniards were killed and many others seriously injured. And it was very fortunate for our men that most of the Indians were in chains or other confinements; for they were valiant and spirited people, and had they found themselves free, would have done more harm. With all that, imprisoned as they were, they tried to do everything they could; and for this reason the Spaniards killed each of them, not permitting a single one to live, which was a great pity.

The rashness and arrogance of Vitachuco, born of a spirit more ferocious than prudent and spawned in excessive presumption and lack of counsel, thus terminated in his having brought about without any purpose his own death as well as that of a thousand and three hundred of his vassals, who were the best and noblest of his state— and all because he had not taken counsel with some of his own people as he did with those strangers who later proved to be his enemies. And furthermore his rashness was responsible for the death of the four good captains who had escaped from the small lagoon, they being slain in turn along with the other Indians; for one of the greatest tragedies of this life is the fact that the prudent who are obliged to obey the commands of a madman come to an evil end.

CHAPTER XXX

The Governor continues to Osachile. Herein is described the manner in which the Indians of Florida build their towns.

AFTER the battle just described, which was ludicrous although bloody and cruel for the poor Indians, the Governor remained four days in Vitachuco's town repairing the damage that he and his men had received. On the fifth day, however, they went in search of a nearby province called Osachile. Having marched four leagues, they pitched camp on the bank of a great river marking the boundary of the two provinces. Since this river could not be forded, it was necessary to construct another bridge similar to the one built at the river of Ochile. But when the framework was completed and ready to cast into the water, a band of Indians rushed up on the opposite shore to prohibit the work and defend the pass. The Christians thereupon left off the construction of the bridge and made six large rafts in which they ferried a hundred men, including arque-busiers, crossbowmen, and fifty armed cavaliers bearing the saddles of their horses. When these men had landed, the Governor, who was present at all times in spite of the fact that his face was swathed in plasters, commanded that fifty horses be driven into the river and made to swim across.

The Spaniards on the opposite bank, having received and saddled the horses, rushed with the utmost haste to the plain. Then when the Indians saw the horses in places clear of trees, they left the site undefended and permitted the Christians to continue the construction of the bridge, which they now threw into the river and with their customary diligence completed in a day and a half.

The army thereupon crossed the river and traveled two leagues through a treeless land, coming eventually to a place where they found great fields of corn, beans, and a type of squash known in Spain as Roman squash. Beginning with these fields there were settlements which were not arranged as villages but were separated and spread out over the distance of four leagues that remained to the principal town, which was called Osachile. This place contained two hundred large and good houses and was the seat and court of the Curaca and lord of that land, who likewise was called Osachile.

The Indians had not dared await the Spaniards along the two leagues of open, flat terrain, but as soon as they saw them among the fields, they returned and, concealing themselves in the corn, hurled many arrows at them. Attacking from all sides they seized every time, place and occasion offered to do them harm, and thus they wounded many. But they did not continue to glorify themselves, for the Christians, seeing the shamelessness and rabid anger of these infidels in their efforts to kill or wound, began to cast their lances at them whenever they found them in the open, pardoning none and taking very few prisoners. Thus this rigorous game went on throughout the whole of the four leagues of sown fields with losses now on one side and now on the other, as is always the case in time of war. Between the village of Vitachuco and that of Osachile, there are ten leagues of level, pastoral land.

The Spaniards found the town of Osachile unprotected, for the Curaca and his people had withdrawn to the forest. The Governor now selected men from among the few Indians captured in that land and sent them at once to the Curaca with overtures of peace and friendship, but Osachile neither came out nor answered the messages, and furthermore none of the messengers returned. This circumstance must have been due to the little time that the Spaniards spent in that town, for they were not there more than two days. During this time, however, they arranged an ambush and captured many Indians, for once having surrendered, these people made good domestics, even though they had proved to be ferocious when armed.

Because this province was small, although well populated and supplied with food, and because the Spaniards spent only a brief time within it, few events occurred there worthy of relating other than those already told. In order, however, not to leave the subject of this province so soon, it is fitting that we describe the location and plan of the town of Osachile with the idea of giving some conception of the site and arrangement of the rest of the towns of this great kingdom called Florida. Since all of the land of this realm is practically identical in kind and quality and is flat with many rivers running through it, its inhabitants live, dress, eat and drink in somewhat the same manner. Even in their idols and their rites and ceremonies of paganism (of which there are but few), and in their weapons, their social distinctions and their ferocity, they differ little or nothing from each other. Thus having seen one town we shall have seen practically all of them, and it will be unnecessary to draw a specific picture of any of the others unless some particular one is offered which is so different that we shall feel obligated to give it a special account.

You may know therefore that the Indians of Florida always try to dwell on high places, and at least the houses of the lords and Caciques are so situated even if the whole village cannot be. But since all of the land is very flat, and elevated sites which have the various other useful conveniences for settlements are seldom found, they build such sites with the strength of their arms, piling up very large quantities of earth and stamping on it with great force until they have formed a mound from twenty-eight to forty-two feet in height. Then on the top of these places they construct flat surfaces which are capable of holding the ten, twelve, fifteen or twenty dwellings of the lord and his family and the people of his service, who vary according to the power and grandeur of his state. In those areas at the foot of this hill, which may be either natural or artificial, they construct a plaza, around which first the noblest and most important personages and then the common people build their homes. They make an effort not to be far distant from the site upon which the dwelling of their lord is located.

In order to reach the house of the Curaca, the Indians build two, three or more streets, according to the number that are necessary, straight up the side of the hill. These streets are fifteen or twenty feet in width and are bordered with walls constructed of thick pieces of wood that are thrust side by side into the earth to a depth of more than the height of a man. Additional pieces of wood just as thick are laid across and joined one to the other to form steps, and they are worked on all four sides so as to provide a smoother ascent. The steps are four, six or eight feet apart and their height depends more or less on the disposition and steepness of the hill. Because of the width of these steps, the horses went up and down them with ease. All of the rest of the hill is cut like a wall, so that it cannot be ascended except by the stairs, for in this way they are better able to defend the houses of the lord.

Osachile had built his town and house according to the plan and structure described, but he had abandoned them because to him the forest still appeared to be a stronger fortification. And there he remained, unwilling either to accept the friendship of the Spaniards or to answer their messages.

End of the First Part
Of the Second Book

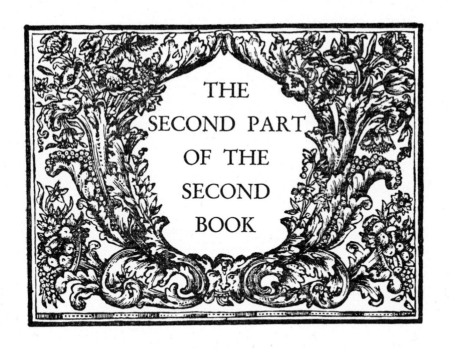

THE
SECOND PART
OF THE
SECOND
BOOK

Of the History of Florida by the Inca wherein will be seen the many fierce struggles that occurred under difficult circumstances between the Indians and the Spaniards in the great province of Apalache; the hardships the Spaniards suffered in finding the sea; the events and incredible anxieties experienced in the going and coming of thirty cavaliers who returned for Pedro Calderón; and the fierceness of the Indians of Apalache, the capture and strange flight of their Cacique, and the fertility of that great province. It contains twenty-five chapters.

CHAPTER I

The Spaniards come to the famous province
of Apalache. The resistance of
the Indians.

T THE village of Osachile, the Governor and his captains had learned that they were near the province of Apalache of which they had heard such lavish praise because of its extent and fertility and the brave feats and military accomplishments of its people. All along the road, the natives had warned them of the ferocity and valor of the inhabitants of Apalache, saying that they would shoot them with arrows, quarter, burn and destroy them. So the Spaniards were determined to see this land, and, if it were as fertile as it had been represented, to pass the winter there. For this reason they would stop no longer than two days in the village of Osachile, and at the end of that time departed.

Traveling without opposition for three days through the twelve leagues of wilderness that lie between the provinces, they came at noon of the fourth day to an extensive swamp which was difficult to cross, for the water alone, not counting the forests on both sides, was a half-league wide and as long as a river; and skirting the edge of this swamp, was a jungle of tall, thick trees, intertwined with a great undergrowth of brambles and other low bushes, so dense that they looked like a strong wall. Through this entanglement and mud there was no passage except that of a small footpath made by the Indians, so narrow that two men could hardly walk along it abreast.

Before coming to the first wooded area, the Spaniards encamped on a good plain; but it being early in the day, the Governor commanded a hundred footsoldiers (including crossbowmen, arquebusiers and shieldbearers), thirty cavalrymen and twelve swimmers (who were designated to determine the depth of the water) to go out and reconnoiter the passage through the swamp that they might advise him wisely concerning the difficulties it held. Thus the army would have some foreknowledge of what obstacles to expect when they set forth on the following day. Accordingly these men departed, but a few steps after entering the wood, encountered Indians prepared to prohibit their advance. And now since the path was narrow, only the two foremost of each band could fight; consequently, the best armed of the Christians stationed themselves in front with their swords and shields while two crossbowmen and two arquebusiers followed along closely behind. In this manner they confronted the infidels throughout the whole of the forest until coming to the water. Here since all could spread out, a great battle ensued and many very accurate shots were made from one side to the other with the result that both groups found themselves burdened with numerous dead and wounded.

Because of the great resistance offered in the water, the Christians were unable at the moment to determine the depth of the channel; and when they informed the General of this fact, he came in person to assist them, bringing with him the best footsoldiers in the army. But the Indians likewise rushed many additional men into the fray, and with these reinforcements the battle quickened and became even more sanguine and cruel. Both sides now continued to fight amid great difficulty and asperity, for the water came half-way up to their thighs and waists and underneath it was a tangle of brambles, bushes and fallen trees. But regardless of these obstacles, the Spaniards saw that it would be unwise to turn back without first having discovered a crossing, so making a great assault on their foes, they drove them completely out of the water. Then they found that the whole stream was fordable in water up to the waist or thigh except for a space of about forty feet in its center, which, because of its great depth, had to be crossed by a bridge made of two fallen trees and pieces of wood that had been fastened together. Moreover, they discovered that underneath the water, there was a path which was free of the plants and brambles growing on both sides of it just as the one through the forest had been. But when they had crossed to the opposite bank, they found a second forest as dense as the one we have just mentioned and through which a person could proceed only by means of a narrow footpath that had been cut out by hand. These two forests and the swamp itself were each a half-league across; thus in all, the distance amounted to a league and a half.

Having examined the passage well and considered the difficulties it entailed, the Governor returned with his men to their encampment in order to make plans for the coming day, plans which would be in accord with what he had seen and noted. Then when he had consulted with his captains concerning the inconveniences and dangers involved, he commanded a hundred cavalrymen to be made ready since they were better armed than the footsoldiers and hence always received less damage from arrows. As horses were useless in such terrain, these men were to go ahead on foot and thus form a protection for a hundred of the infantry, including crossbowmen and arquebusiers, who would follow. Instructions were given likewise for all to be provided with axes, hatchets, and other implements with which to clear an area in the forest on the far side of the swamp. For since it was necessary that everyone cross in single file because of the narrowness of the path, and that along the passage they resist the Indians who at that time had shown themselves to be so ferocious, the Governor felt that it would be impossible for the army to travel through both forests in one day. Therefore, he had determined to provide himself with quarters in the second wood by dint of arms, this being the only way in which he could have them.

CHAPTER II

The Spaniards gain the passage to the swamp.
The great and fierce struggle which
occurred therein.

WITH the preparations and arrangement described, two hundred of the most select Spaniards left the camp, each carrying in his breast his ration for that day, which consisted of no more than a little roasted or boiled corn. Two hours before dawn they entered the passage through the forest and, following it as silently as possible, came eventually to the water. Finding that the path which continued beneath the water was free of underbrush, they followed it to the bridge which had been built of fallen trees and bound pieces of wood over the deepest part of the channel. This bridge they crossed without opposition, for the Indians, not feeling that the Spaniards would dare enter the dense part of the forest or the brambly depths of the water by night, had been lax about rising early to defend the passage. But seeing the dawn and hearing that their enemies had already passed over the bridge, they rushed forth in great fury, howling and shouting at each other to dispute that portion of the water and swamp which still remained for the Christians to traverse—a distance of a quarter of a league. Angry at themselves for having so carelessly overslept, they charged with great ferocity and impetus. But the Spaniards were well prepared, and not wanting to consume much time with this battle, met the attack vigorously.

At this point both groups were proceeding in water up to their waists. Then the Spaniards drove the Indians from the water into the passage to the second wood where because of the density of the trees they could not disperse but were forced to move in single file along a narrow pathway. With their enemies shut off in this passage which because of its narrowness required but few men to guard it, the Spaniards agreed to employ one hundred and fifty of their

number in clearing a camp site while fifty stood watch against anyone who might attempt to disturb their activity. There being just the
one entrance to this area, the few Christians who were on guard
were sufficient to protect the whole of it. Thus the entire day passed
with the Indians whooping and shouting in order to upset their
enemies with noise now that they could not do so with arms, and
with some of the Castilians defending the entrance while others
cut wood and still others burned what had been cut so as to clear a
place to pitch camp. And when darkness came upon them, each
Spaniard remained where he was, none of them sleeping any part
of the night because of the shouts and numerous assaults of their
foes.

At daybreak, the remainder of the army began to move across the
swamp. They suffered no opposition from the enemy, but were
impeded by the extreme narrowness of the path and the underbrush
in the water which made it necessary to advance in single file and
thus prevented their progressing as they wished. Being so greatly
delayed, they were satisfied that day just with having arrived in time
to pitch camp in the clearing. But they enjoyed no more sleep
during that night than they had the previous one because of the
noise and assaults of the Indians; and they had to provide food for
those who were guarding the entrance to the wood by handing it
from one to the other until it had reached the foremost in the line.

With the dawn of a new day, the Spaniards advanced along the
path through the wood, pushing back the Indians, who continued to
fire arrows at them and to withdraw only a little at a time since they
were unwilling to yield any more space than could be gained with
the blow of a sword. In this way they won the remaining half-
league of dense forest and entered a lighter and more open area.
Here, since the Indians could spread out and come and go among
the trees, they caused great affliction, attacking from both sides of
the road and shooting many arrows; and they attacked with uniformity and system, those on one side waiting until the others had
departed before releasing their arrows in order not to wound their

own men. With that, however, the arrows were so numerous that they looked like rain falling from the heavens.

As we have said, the forest in which the struggle now ensued was not so dense as the previous one, yet it was not sufficiently open for the horses to race through it. Consequently, the infidels were so daring that they came and went among the Christians without paying them any heed whatsoever, even when crossbowmen and arquebusiers came out to resist; for while a Spaniard was firing one shot and reloading for another, an Indian fired six or seven times. And these Indians fired so skillfully and close together that they had hardly released one arrow before they had placed another in the bow.

In the open sections of the forest through which the horses might have run, the Indians had secured themselves by fastening long pieces of wood between the trees; and in that part through which they themselves had not been able to pass, they had cleared areas with entrances and exits which permitted them to fall upon the Christians without receiving any attacks in return. These precautions they had taken in advance, for they had known that the great density of trees in the swamp would not permit their harassing their enemies as they wished or as they might have done had that part of the forest been as open as the one through which the Spaniards were now passing. And when they did find themselves at a point of vantage because of their location, they, in their anxiety to kill or wound the Christians, never ceased to use every effort, stratagem or deceit they could against them.

As the Castilians advanced, they were more intent on defending themselves than attacking, for the obstacle of the forest prevented their taking advantage of their horses. Thus they were harassed more by their own rage than by the weapons of their opponents. Observing their confusion, the Indians increased their attacks on all sides, anxious now to break and destroy them. Moreover they gathered new strength and spirit in recalling that it had been in this identical swamp, although not the same pass, that ten or eleven

years previously they had routed and destroyed Pámphilo de Narváez; and they at this time reminded the General and his men of
their previous deed, adding among other impertinent remarks and
affronts that they would do the same with their present foes.

Struggling in this manner with the difficulties of the road and
the afflictions bestowed upon them by their enemies, the Spaniards
traveled the two remaining leagues through the wood, coming
eventually to clear, open terrain; and now thanking God, who had
released them from their confinement, they loosed the reins of
their horses and demonstrated clearly the hatred they felt for the
Indians; for in the more than two leagues that remained of open
land before they reached the cornfields, they killed or captured
every one they encountered. They slew in particular those who
made a show of resistance, not permitting any to escape. The result
was that the mortality that day was great, for they seized few and
killed many. So it was that they avenged the insult and damage
which Pámphilo de Narváez had suffered at the hands of the inhabitants of Apalache, and they disillusioned these people of their
arrogant idea that they might destroy these Castilians as they had
their predecessors.

CHAPTER III

*The continuous fighting which lasted until the
arrival at the principal town
of Apalache.*

IT APPEARED to Governor Hernando de Soto that for this day
he should be satisfied with having emerged from the forest
where so much opposition had been met, and with having punished
the Indians in part. And he felt no desire to go any farther but
wished instead to bivouac his army in that plain since the ground
was free of underbrush. For this reason, he pitched camp near a

small village that marked the beginning of the fields and settlements of the province of Apalache which was so famous throughout that land.

The Indians refused to rest that night because they did not want the Christians to recuperate from the troublesome days and nights given them since their arrival in the swamps. So they continued to hoot and shout, and at all hours to launch sudden attacks in which they hurled numerous arrows into the camp. Thus amid such noises the entire night passed without either side coming to blows. Then at dawn, the Spaniards marched on through some great fields of corn, beans, squash and other vegetables which had been sown on both sides of the road and were spread out as far as the eye could see across two leagues of the plain. Among these fields there were sprinklings of settlements with houses set apart from each other and not arranged in the order of a town. From both the houses and fields, the Indians, still obstinate in their desire to kill or wound their foe, poured forth with the utmost haste to hurl arrows at them. Their continuous manifestation of anger and stubbornness enraged the Castilians, who, losing patience, lanced them pitilessly in the cornfields, hoping now with military severity either to dominate or punish them. Nevertheless, all was in vain, for it appears that as the anger of the Indians was increased, their desire for revenge grew even more intense.

After having advanced two leagues through the fields, the Spaniards came to a deep ravine containing a great quantity of water and fringed on both sides with dense woods. The passage through this place was tedious; and the Indians, recognizing the fact, had foreseen an opportunity to fall upon their opponents here. But observing the obstacles and defenses offered, the best armed of the cavaliers dismounted and, some with sword and shield and others with axes, gained the passage and knocked down the barricades and fences which had been constructed to keep the horses from advancing or their riders from attacking. At this point, the natives charged with their greatest impetus and fury, for the passage being difficult, they had placed their last hope of conquering the Christians here. Thus the battle raged and many Spaniards were wounded and some killed, for their enemies fought boldly, making their final effort as people will who are desperate. Nevertheless, they were unable to realize their malicious desire, and the Castilians, because of the courage and strength they showed and the great effort they made to keep the damage from being as extensive as they had feared it would be in such a difficult place, emerged triumphant.

Once across the ravine, the army moved on two more leagues through country devoid of both fields and towns. The Indians no longer molested them since they could have no advantage where horses were used, and they feared to encounter these animals in open country. Therefore when the Christians pitched camp, they were permitted to sleep throughout the remainder of the day, and they did indeed need rest since they had labored and watched during the whole of the previous four days and three nights. But when this day was over, they slept just as little as they had before, for the infidels now trusted in the darkness, even though the ground was clear, and throughout the whole of the night continued to shout and make assaults upon all parts of the camp. Never would these people of Apalache permit the Castilians to rest, for they did not wish to forfeit the opinion and reputation they had gained among all their neighbors and fellow citizens as the most valiant and warlike people of their race.

As soon as the army resumed its march on the following day, which was the fifth day after they had crossed the swamp, the Governor went in advance with two hundred horsemen and a hundred footsoldiers, for he had learned from prisoners that the town of Apalache was only two leagues distant, and that he was awaited there by the Cacique and a great number of very valiant men whose intention it was to kill and quarter all of the Spaniards. His captives had used these very words in threatening him, for even though they were in the power of their enemies, they never once lost pride in the fact that they were natives of Apalache. So the General and his companions galloped their horses across the intervening two leagues, lancing every Indian encountered on both sides of the road. Arriving at the town, they found that the Curaca and his people had left it undefended, but knowing that these Indians had not gone far, they pursued them for two leagues beyond the place. Many of them they killed and captured, but never did they succeed in overtaking Capafi, as this Cacique was called. (This is the first Cacique we have encountered whose name differed from that of his province.) In consequence, the Adelantado returned to the village, which consisted of two hundred and fifty large and good houses. Finding his whole army lodged now in these houses, he himself took quarters in the habitations of the Cacique, which were located on one side of the town and as royal dwellings had advantages over all of the others.

In addition to the principal town, there were many more scattered throughout the vicinity at a half-league, one, one and a half, two and at times three leagues apart. Some comprised fifty or sixty dwellings and others a hundred more or less, not to mention another great number which were sprinkled about and not arranged as a town. The site of the whole province was peaceful, and the land was fertile; for it produced a great abundance of food, and in addition there were many fish which the natives caught and kept prepared throughout the year for their subsistence.

The Governor and his captains and ministers of the Royal Exchequer rejoiced at seeing the fertility and other fine qualities of that land. For good as were all of the provinces they had left behind, this one had an advantage over the rest because its people were unconquerable, and, as has been seen, boldly militant. Later we shall record some of the notable incidents which occurred in particular and in general between the Spaniards and Indians here, although to avoid prolixity we shall not give an account of them all. But by those we do tell, one will be able to obtain a clear picture of the ferocity of the people of Apalache.

CHAPTER IV

*Three captains go to explore the province of
Apalache. The report which
they bring.*

ALTHOUGH the enemy continued their alarms and sudden
attacks day and night, the army rested a few days and recuperated somewhat from the great toils of the past. Meanwhile the
Governor sent out chosen officers with soldiers on horseback and
afoot to penetrate inland for fifteen or twenty leagues in order to
see what there was to be found in the surrounding country. Two
of these officers, Captain Arias Tinoco and Captain Andrés de
Vasconcelos, took different routes toward the north, but returned
without having experienced anything worthy of note, one of them
eight days and the other nine, after they had left the camp. The
reports of both were almost identical, for each said that he had
found many populous villages as well as land that was abundant
in food and clear of swamps and extensive forests. On the other
hand, Captain Juan de Añasco, who had gone at the same time
toward the south, reported that he had discovered a very rough and
difficult terrain, almost impossible to traverse because of its woody
undergrowth and swamps, and he added that the farther south he
traveled the worse he found the land to be.

Having called attention to the fact that some of this land was
very good and some very bad, I feel it wise not to continue my
story without pausing to touch upon what Alvar Núñez Cabeza de
Vaca writes of the province of Apalache in his *Comentarios*. Here
he describes the country as rough and craggy; covered with forests,
swamps, rivers, and troublesome passages; and poorly populated
as well as sterile. Since all of these characteristics are contrary to
what we are writing, and since what this gentleman records is trustworthy, we are led to believe that his expedition took place near
the seacoast, and that he did not go so far inland as did Governor

Hernando de Soto. This supposition would account for his saying
that he found the country so rough and so filled with woods and
swamps; for Captain Juan de Añasco, as we shall see later, found
it to be the same when he left the principal village of Apalache to
go in search of the sea, and the truth is that he was fortunate in
not having been lost a great number of times, in view of the roughness of the terrain he encountered.

Since the settlement we have referred to as the principal village
of the province was such as we have described, I am of the opinion
that the one which Cabeza de Vaca called Apalache, and to which
he said Pámphilo de Narváez came, was not the same that Hernando
de Soto discovered but some one of the many others of that province.
It must have been nearer the sea, and being under the jurisdiction of
the province of Apalache, could have been called by the same name.
It should be noted, however, that a great part of Alvar Núñez'
description of that land is what the Indians themselves gave him,
and, as he himself says, those Castilians never saw it. For being
few in number and almost or completely exhausted, there was no
possibility for them to subject it and see it with their own eyes or
to look for food there. Indeed most of them were left to perish
of hunger. Also worthy of consideration is the fact that the Indians
would have given the Spaniards an unfavorable rather than a favorable account of their land, so that in discrediting it they would
discourage them from coming there. Accordingly, our story does
not give the lie to the cavalier, Alvar Núñez.

CHAPTER V

*The hardships which Juan de Añasco experienced
in his effort to find the sea.*

I HAVE said that one of the captains who set out to explore
the neighborhood of Apalache was Juan de Añasco, but in
order that more in particular may be known of the trouble which

ensued, I should tell you that he was accompanied by forty horsemen and fifty footsoldiers. Among his companions was Gómez
Arias, a fine soldier and cavalier who was a relative of the Governor's wife, and who was very useful wherever he happened to be;
for with his excellent military skill, his industry, his good advice,
and his very great prowess as a swimmer (a valuable and necessary
accomplishment in conquests), he overcame all difficulties he encountered on both land and water. Once this man had been a slave
in Barbary and while there had learned to speak the Moorish language so properly that he was able to travel from many leagues in
the interior out to the Christian frontier without any of the Moors
he happened to meet being aware that he was a slave. And now
both he and the others we have mentioned accompanied Juan de
Añasco to the south in search of the sea, which they had been told
was fewer than thirty leagues from Apalache. With them they
took an Indian who had offered himself as a guide and appeared
to be a very faithful friend of the Christians.

Marching six leagues a day for two days along a very excellent
road, both wide and flat, these men, after crossing a couple of small
and easily forded rivers, came to a village called Aute. Finding
the place uninhabited but well stocked with food, they provided
themselves with sufficient rations for the next four days and continued their quest along the same fine road. On the second day,
however, their guide began to mislead them, feeling now that it was
shameful to serve enemies so well. He took them away from the
good, wide road they had been following for such a long time and
brought them through some dense, rough woods where there were
many fallen trees and neither roads nor paths. It is true that they
did meet with some plots of land that were level and bare, but so
marshy that both cavalry and infantry sank into the mire even though
it was covered over with grass and looked like firm ground that
could be trodden on safely. In this path, or rather wood, they encountered a kind of bramble with long, thick branches which spread
out over the ground and covered much of the land. The long,

straight thorns of this plant cruelly injured both horsemen and footsoldiers, and in spite of all efforts to protect themselves against it, they were unable to do so, for in addition to being very abundant it was extended between two layers of soil and covered with mud, sand or water.

With these hardships and such others as can be imagined, the Castilians strayed from their road for five days, turning now one way and then another, in whatever direction the Indian according to his whim wished to take them, it being his purpose to trick or lead them to where they would never come out again. But when the food which they had taken from the town of Aute was exhausted, all agreed to go back and replenish their supplies before persisting in their search. Their return was more fraught with hardships than the journey out had been, for they were obliged to retrace their steps to avoid becoming lost, and since the earth along the road previously passed over was now trampled, both horsemen and foot-soldiers bogged in the mire even more than when it was fresh.

While suffering these hardships and toils, the Castilians were well aware that the Indian had purposely led them astray. For in those woods, they found themselves three times so near the sea that they could hear the surf; but whenever this sound reached the ears of their guide, he turned once again inland, hoping thereby to trap them in a place where because of their inability to escape, they eventually would perish of hunger. And even though conscious that he too might perish, he was content so long as the Spaniards died with him. All of these things the Christians knew, but they dared not permit the Indian to discover their feelings since they had no one else to direct them, and they did not want to make this man worse than he already was of his own accord.

They arrived in Aute dead with hunger as anyone would be who had eaten nothing but grass and roots for four days, but there they found an abundance of supplies, and taking sufficient rations for another five or six days, set out once again, not by better roads than those they had traveled in the past but by others even worse if such were possible, or if the guide in his malice were able to find the kind he desired for them.

One night while they were sleeping in the forest this Indian reached the conclusion that he could no longer endure the length of time it was taking to destroy these Christians, and seizing an ember from the fire he injured one of them with a blow in the face. The others thereupon resolved to kill him for his shamelessness and audacity, but the Captain forbade their doing so, saying that they must bear with him somewhat since he was their only guide. But within an hour after they had retired again to rest, the Indian committed the same offense against another Spaniard. This time they chastised him with a great number of kicks, slaps and blows, but he learned nothing from the experience and before dawn had struck a third victim in the same manner. Not knowing just what to do with the culprit, the Spaniards contented themselves for the present by beating him well with cudgels and entrusting his shackles to one of their men who was to give him special attention.

With the coming of the dawn, they resumed their journey, sorely afflicted by the roughness of both the past and the present road, and enraged by the perfidiousness of their guide. When they had traveled but a short distance, the Indian, conscious now that he was in the power of his enemies and could neither kill nor escape them, began to despair of life and in consequence assailed the soldier who was leading him by a chain. Throwing his arms about this man from behind and lifting him in the air, he cast him to the ground. Then before he could rise, he leaped upon him with both feet and kicked him over and over again. Such insolence being beyond endurance, the Castilians and their captain bestowed so many slashes and thrusts upon the Indian that they left him for dead. A strange thing was noted, however: this was that their swords and the points of their lances had cut and pierced the man so little that he appeared to bear a charm, for the many strokes given him left no more wounds than did the lashes which they customarily inflicted with a rod of quince or wild olive. Juan de Añasco was so angered thereby that he stood up in his stirrups and with his lance grasped in both hands struck the Indian with all his force; but strong and robust as he was, he did not succeed in thrusting so much as half the head of his weapon into that creature's body. This circumstance, on being noted by the Spaniards, left them in amazement, and they thereupon loosed a greyhound to finish killing the Indian and gorge itself upon his flesh. Thus this malicious and shameless guide was left to the fate he deserved.

CHAPTER VI

Captain Juan de Añasco arrives at the Bay of Aute. What he found there.

THE Castilians had not advanced fifty feet beyond the Indian, whom they now presumed to be dead and already devoured, when they heard great yowls and complaints from the greyhound as if he too were being slain. Rushing back to ascertain the reason for this noise, they found that the Indian with the little life left in him, had placed his thumbs on both sides of the dog's mouth and was tearing it apart without the animal's being able to help itself. One of the Spaniards, on beholding this scene, stabbed the man many times and thus finished killing him, and another cut off his hands with a forest knife. But even after the hands were severed, they could not be pried loose from the dog's mouth, so firmly had they grasped it.

With this incident the Spaniards resumed their journey, amazed that a single Indian could have given them so much trouble. But they now were ignorant as to which way to turn, and confused as to what they should do. Nevertheless, in their bewilderment, Fate came to their assistance in the person of an Indian whom they had captured on their return to the village of Aute and brought along with them. It is true that before the death of their guide, they had asked this captive many times if he knew the way to the sea and he had feigned muteness, never answering a word because the other Indian had threatened to kill him should he do so. But seeing this impediment removed since he was free of his companion and fearing that the Spaniards might condemn him to the same fate that the guide had suffered, he now spoke and answered all questions asked him. With signs and occasionally comprehensible words, he said that he would lead his captors to the sea and to the very same place where Pámphilo de Narváez had built his ships and embarked. He insisted, however, that it would be necessary first to return to the village of Aute since from there they could follow the road straight to their destination. And even though our men reminded him that he should take into consideration the fact that they were already sufficiently near the sea to hear the dashing and breaking of the billows on its shore, he answered that never in all their lives would they be able to reach it by the route they had in mind since their guide had led them to where they were because of the underbrush and many swamps in the woods which lay between them and the coast. He insisted therefore that they must return to the village of Aute, and they accordingly retraced their steps, after having wasted not only much personal toil but also five days of time on this second trip in addition to the ten days they had spent on the first. It was this loss of fifteen days that they regretted most because of the anxiety the Governor would be occasioned at their delay.

On their journey back, Gómez Arias and Gonzalo Silvestre, who went in advance of the others to reconnoiter the land, seized two Indians whom they found near the town. When these people were questioned as to whether or not they would be able to guide their captors to the sea, they answered in the affirmative, and their statements coincided in all respects with what the other captive had said. So with such encouragement, the Spaniards rested, somewhat happier this night than they had been the fifteen previous ones.

On the following day, all three Indians led the Christians along a peaceful, flat and open road which lay through some large and good stubble, and which became even broader and more open when it emerged from the stubble. Along the whole of this route they failed to encounter a single difficult passage, with the exception of one narrow swamp which was easy to cross because the horses did not sink even to their pasterns in the mire. When they had traveled a little more than two leagues, they came to a very broad and spacious bay which they skirted until arriving at the place where Pámphilo de Narváez had camped. There was a great amount of charcoal around the site where he had built his forge to make the assortment of nails necessary for ships, and there also were some thick beams which had been hollowed out like bread troughs to serve as cribs for horses.[1] The guides now pointed out the spot where the Indians had killed ten of those Christians (as Alvar Núñez Cabeza de Vaca tells us in his history), and they led their captors step by step through all of the places where Pámphilo de Narváez had traveled, pointing out where such and such a thing occurred and eventually giving by signs and words, some well and some poorly understood, an account of all the remarkable things that worthy cavalier had done at the bay. Some spoke in Castilian, for the people along that entire coast prided themselves on their knowledge of that language and made every effort possible to learn even isolated words, which they repeated again and again.

And now Captain Juan de Añasco and his soldiers searched in the hollows and under the bark of trees in an earnest attempt to ascertain if letters had been left which would disclose what their predecessors had seen and noted, it being a very usual custom for the discoverers of new lands to leave such announcements for those to come, and many times these announcements had been of major importance. But they found no such messages, and their effort completed, they continued along the coast of the bay to the sea, which lay three leagues distant. There they discovered some old canoes which had been grounded, and when the tide was low, ten or twelve swimmers rowed out to test the depth of the bay in the middle of its channel. Finding it capable of receiving heavy vessels, they placed

---

[1] Here, according to the Elvas account, the Spaniards found the skulls of horses, and they afterward referred to this place as *La Bahía de Caballos,* or the Bay of the Horses. This is in the region of Apalachee Bay.

signs in the tallest trees of the vicinity so that anyone who might be sailing along that coast would be able to recognize the spot. This was the place where Pámphilo de Narváez had embarked in his five ships, which had been so ill fated that none of them had ever come to light again.

Having made the aforementioned provisions and kept a memorandum of them so that anyone who later came that way might not err in the place, these cavaliers returned to their camp and gave the Governor an account of all that they had experienced and done. He was very pleased to see them because of his concern over their delay; and he was happy to know that there was an available port for his ships.

CHAPTER VII

Thirty lancers make preparations to return to the Bay of the Holy Spirit.

WHILE the three explorer captains were going out and bringing back details of what each had discovered, Governor Hernando de Soto was neither dallying nor resting. On the contrary he was continuing with the utmost caution and vigilance to study and contemplate those things which were best for his army. Having noted that cold weather was setting in, since it was already October, he felt it wise to discontinue his exploration for the year and to winter in the province of Apalache where provisions were abundant; and it occurred to him also that he should send for Captain Pedro Calderón and the other Spaniards who remained in the province of Hirrihigua in order that they too might join him since they were doing nothing of importance where they were. With such ideas in mind, he ordered his men to collect all possible supplies and build many new houses in addition to those that the town already afforded, so that there might be comfortable quarters for his entire army. And then for greater security, he had the place fortified to the extent that he felt was necessary. Meanwhile he never ceased to send envoys to Capafi, the lord of the province, with gifts and kind messages in which he begged that Cacique to come out peacefully and be his friend. But Capafi refused all favors and ensconced himself within a rugged wood, full of swamps and difficult passages, which he had chosen for the defense and shelter of his person.

When all the things we have mentioned had been planned and executed, the Governor instructed the Comptroller Juan de Añasco to prepare to return to the province of Hirrihigua, for it seemed to him that from the beginning of the expedition this cavalier had been his luckiest captain, drawing better lots than any of the other men; and he felt that a person who combined such good fortune with the excellent military qualifications that this particular man possessed was now essential in order to survive the perils and hardships he was going to offer him. With this consideration in mind, he gave an order for the Comptroller to return to Hirrihigua's village with twenty-nine other lancers who were now ready (he himself making the thirtieth), using the same route the army had previously traveled. Once there, he was to inform Captain Pedro Calderón and the rest of the soldiers of what their General had commanded concerning them.

The assignment was a most rigorous one for these cavaliers since they were to retrace their steps over almost a hundred and fifty leagues of terrain peopled by valiant and cruel enemies and obstructed by woods, swamps, swollen rivers and difficult passes in which the army already had encountered grave danger. And the present risk would be even greater because there were only thirty of them, and they must of necessity find the Indians not only better prepared than when the Governor had crossed their lands but angrier and more anxious to avenge themselves of the injuries they had received. But all such circumstances were insufficient to deter those thirty noble men who had been summoned to carry out the expedition; on the contrary they offered with the utmost promptitude to obey. And now since they were men of such great courage and strength, and since we shall see them passing through so many hardships and dangers, it is only just that their names be recorded, and that I mention here those that have been remembered. And may the others, whose names are lacking, forgive my omission and accept my good will, for I would that I might have knowledge of them and of all men who have gone out to conquer and win the New World, and that at the same time I might attain the classic eloquence of the greatest Caesar so as to be able to pass my entire life relating and commemorating their magnificent deeds. For these deeds have been so much nobler than those of the Greeks, Romans and peoples of other nations although the Spaniards have been much less fortunate in having a suitable person to write of them. And it is indeed no small misfortune that the task of recording such accomplishments should fall to the lot of an Indian where they will appear minimized and mutilated rather than as they actually occurred and deserve to be seen. For it has been my fate to be more abundant in eagerness to serve than in force and skill; but with having done my best, I shall have complied with my obligation.

Those cavaliers who were summoned for the expedition were the Comptroller and Captain, Juan de Añasco, a native of Seville; Gómez Arias, a native of Segovia; Juan Cordero and Alvaro Fernández, natives of Yelves; Antonio Carrillo, a native of Yllescas and one of the thirteen men who along with Francisco Hernández Girón rose in rebellion with the people of Cuzco in the year 1553; Francisco de Villalobos and Juan López Cacho, both citizens of Seville; Gonzalo Silvestre, a native of Herrera de Alcántara; Juan de Espinosa, a native of Ubeda; Hernando Athanasio, a native of Badajoz; Juan de Abadía, a Biscayan; Antonio de la Cadena and Francisco Segredo, natives of Medellín; Bartolomé de Argote and Pedro Sánchez of Astorga; Juan García Pechudo, a native of Alburquerque; and Pedro Morón, a mestizo who was a native of the city of Bayamo in the island of Cuba. This last named soldier had the rare gift of being able to scent a track better than a bloodhound. Many times on the island of Cuba, it happened that when he and others were searching for Indians who had been carried off or had fled, he tracked them to the bushes, tree hollows, or caves in which they had hidden. Likewise, he could smell fire at a distance of more than a league, and often during the discovery of Florida, without having seen flame or smoke, told his companions to be prepared since there was a fire nearby. And they would indeed find it within half a league or a league. As we have said before, he was a fine swimmer and was accompanied by his friend and compatriot, Diego de Oliva, a mestizo who likewise was a native of the island of Cuba.

CHAPTER VIII

What the thirty cavaliers did before arriving at Vitachuco and what they found there.

THESE twenty cavaliers[2] and ten others whose names are lacking to conclude the number of thirty, left the village of Apalache on the twentieth day of October in the year 1539 to return to the province of Hirrihigua where Pedro Calderón remained. They bore an order, which will be disclosed later, as to what was to be done on both land and sea, and all traveled lightly, with no more than helmets and coats of mail over their clothes and lances in their hands. On their saddles were great saddlebags in which they took some nails, horseshoes, and whatever food supplies they could fit in them for both the men and horses.

It was a good while before dawn when they left the camp, and in order to prevent the news of their departure from preceding them, thereby giving the Indians time to come out and occupy the passes, they traveled as rapidly as possible, running whenever it was feasible to do so. On this day they lanced and killed two Indians encountered along the road, lest by some outcry these men warn the other Indians scattered throughout the countryside to be on guard; and as they traveled on, they continued to observe this same precaution so that

[2] Note that in the previous chapter the Inca names only eighteen cavaliers.

news of their coming should not precede them. Thus they covered that day the eleven leagues which lie between Apalache and the swamp. Then they crossed this swamp without opposition from the enemy, and they were not a little fortunate in being able to do so, for had just a few Indians appeared they would have sufficed to hurl arrows at the horses along a path so narrow as the one which lay through the trees and the water. When night fell, they slept on an open plain away from the forest, having run and walked that day more than thirteen leagues. But while resting, they watched over each other in thirds, or, as we have explained previously, in groups of ten.

Before daybreak they continued their journey across the twelve leagues of unpopulated land between the swamp of Apalache and the village of Osachile, but still fearful that Indians might learn of their approach and come out to obstruct their passage, they proceeded slowly, awaiting nightfall. Then near midnight they rushed through the village at a half-speed, and when they had ridden a league beyond the town, rested for the remainder of the night at a place off from the road, a third of the group at a time, as we have said, keeping watch over the others. On this day they had traveled another thirteen leagues.

At the crack of dawn they were on their way, again running at a half-speed because there were people in the fields; and they continued to travel thus when moving through populated regions in order that news of their approach might not precede them, a possibility which constituted their greatest fear. The whole five leagues from where they had slept to the river of Osachile they covered in this manner and at the expense of their horses, but these animals were so fine that they bore it all. Then as they approached the river, Gonzalo Silvestre, who was in the lead, since he had forced his mount to run faster than the others, glanced toward the stream with justifiable fear lest he find it larger than when the army had crossed, but God willed that there should be less water here now than before. Happy at the sight the cavalier plunged into the river, and swimming to the opposite bank came out onto the plain. His companions, on seeing him there, were exuberant since they too had suffered his same fear. All now crossed over without any misfortune whatsoever, and, with much fiesta and rejoicing at having done so, began their lunch. Afterward, they traveled at a moderate pace the four leagues lying between the river of Osachile and the town of Vitachuco where the Cacique Vitachuco had made his bold coup.

These Spaniards had held some misgivings as to whether or not they would find the town of Vitachuco as they had left it, and they had feared that if it were necessary to engage its inhabitants and gain admittance by force of arms, it could happen that the Indians would kill or wound some man or horse and thereby double for them the difficulties of the road. Hence they agreed among themselves that no one should stop to fight, and that each should make an effort to pass forward without permitting himself to be delayed. It was with this determination that they came to the town, but their anxiety was dispelled when they discovered that the entire place had been laid waste and burned. Its walls had been leveled to the ground and all of the bodies of the Indians who had died on the day of the battle and of those who had been killed at the time the Cacique Vitachuco had struck the Governor were now piled up in the fields, for their people had resolved not to bury them. The town had been destroyed and abandoned, as the Indians later explained, because it had been founded in an unpropitious and doomed place; and the dead had been left without sepulchre to serve as food for birds and wild beasts because they were ill-starred men who had not succeeded in their purpose. For among the Indians this was a most infamous punishment, which, according to their pagan custom, was bestowed upon those who were unlucky and unsuccessful in war as well as those who were accursed and nefarious. In this manner, therefore, they had rewarded both the town and those who died there, for since there had been so few Spaniards to oppose so many and such valiant Indians, they had felt that the calamity which occurred in that place had been caused more by the evil nature of the site and the malevolent fate of the men than by the strength and courage of their enemies.

CHAPTER IX

The journey of the thirty lancers continues to the River of Ochile.[3]

AMAZED at what they had seen, the Spaniards passed on through the town. Hardly had they left it, however, when they came upon two Indian gentlemen[4] who were sporting with their bows and arrows, without thought of seeing Christians that day. As the cavaliers came into view, these men sought shelter beneath a large walnut tree that stood nearby; one of them, however, not trusting much in this protection, fled on in an attempt to gain a forest that lay to the side of the road. Immediately he was pursued by two Castilians, very much against the will of their captain, and before he could reach his goal, they had lanced him—a very ignominious thing for two cavaliers to do.

The other Indian, who had shown more courage by waiting beneath the tree, enjoyed better luck; for the daring, being people who merit favor, are protected by Fortune. Putting an arrow to his bow, this man faced the Spaniards and, as they galloped toward him at a half-speed and in single file, gave them to understand that he would fire at anyone who approached. At that, some of the cavaliers, angered by his boldness and effrontery, or envious at seeing such rare spirit and courage, wanted to dismount and attack on foot with their lances. But Juan de Añasco would not consent to their doing so, saying that at a time when both horses and men were so sorely needed and equipment for treating the injured was so inadequate,

[3] In the table of contents and in the chapter headings of both the 1605 and the 1723 editions, this word is given as Ochile and in the context of the chapter as Ochali. In each case it should be Ocali. See note 5, below.

[4] *dos Indios gentiles hombres* —This may of course mean simply "two tall or well-made Indians."

it was neither valiant nor wise to take a chance on anyone's being wounded or slain just for the purpose of killing a rash and desperate person. Then being in the lead, he made a great swerve away from the road lying near the tree lest the Indian fire arrows as they passed and wound some horse, this being the possibility most feared.

As the first Spaniard rode by, the Indian aimed at his face with a loaded bow and threatened to shoot, and afterward made the same gesture toward each of the other Spaniards respectively until all had passed. And when he realized that they were fleeing and not attacking, he began to heap insults upon them, calling them cowards and pusillanimous creatures who in spite of there being thirty of them on horseback, dared not engage a single Indian on foot. Bragging in this manner, he remained beneath his tree with greater honor than one might gain through fame. This the Castilians admitted as they rode away shamed by the imprecations leveled at them.

And now a great outcry and clamor was heard from the natives in the fields along both sides of the road as they called to each other to cut off the way. But the Spaniards were saved by the swiftness of their horses, for running continuously they left the Indians behind. Then when this third day of their journey was already quite dark, they came to a good plain which was clear of underbrush. Here they rested, having run or walked that day seventeen leagues, the last eight of which had been in the province of Vitachuco. On the fourth day they continued for seventeen leagues more through this same province. When the natives saw that there were so few of them, they resolved to avenge the injuries and insults suffered in the previous battle, and for the purpose formed relays to carry news ahead that their enemies were approaching, hoping thereby to summon certain of their people to intercept them by seizing some narrow passage. But divining their intention, the Spaniards pursued the would-be messengers with such swiftness that none of them escaped. Accordingly seven Indians felt the lance that day.

At nightfall, having come to a place which was clear of brush, the Castilians deemed it wise to rest since they heard no noise to indicate that there were Indians in the surrounding district. But a little past midnight, they started out again and after traveling five more leagues came at sunrise to the river of Ochali[5] where, as we have said, the Indians slew the greyhound Bruto. They had held some hope of finding this river like that of Osachile with less water than when they previously had crossed it; but they found just the contrary, for a good while before arriving there they could see that the bluffs, which, as we have said, were twenty-eight feet high, were completely covered with water which now overflowed into the fields. The river was so wild and turbid and there were so many whirlpools everywhere that just the sight of it, much less the necessity of swimming it, filled them with fright. And added to this difficulty and danger was another even greater. This was that the Indians on both sides of the river had raised a hue and cry on seeing the Christians approach and had called out to each other to kill them as they attempted to cross.

Realizing that their salvation lay in their strength, perseverance and courage, the cavaliers came to an agreement at once as to what course they should take in their peril. Just as if all were captains with a prearranged decision, they called out to each other by name and commanded the twelve best swimmers among them to plunge into the river (wearing no more than helmets and coats of mail over their shirts so as to leave the horses unhampered in their swimming), and with lances in their hands, to seize the opposite shore before the Indians arrived. The danger was greater there since the Indians were more numerous and were now rushing from their village toward the river. Thus it was necessary to keep that shore unencumbered in order to prevent the Indians from hurling arrows at the Castilians with ease while they were swimming the river. The twelve men selected, on seeing that they were going

[5] Although spelled Ochali in both early editions, this word should be Ocali, for the greyhound Bruto was slain in the river of Ocali.

into such imminent danger, gave each other courage by crying out simultaneously: "Succeed if you can and die if you must, for we see now that nothing else can be done." Likewise fourteen men were ordered to cut five or six thick logs as quickly as possible from the trees lying fallen and dry on the shore and with them to construct a small raft on which to ferry the saddles, saddlebags and clothing, as well as those men among them who were unable to swim. And meanwhile the remaining four men were to try to resist the Indians who on this side were hastening furiously from both upstream and downstream to prevent their crossing.

The twelve Spaniards chosen to swim to the opposite shore immediately put their scheme into action exactly as they had planned it. Ridding themselves of their clothes, they plunged at once into the water. Eleven of them reached land successfully through a great gap in the opposite bluff, but the twelfth, Juan López Cacho, failed to make the exit because his horse fell a little short of the gap and was unable to breast the fury of the water sufficiently to reach it. He then permitted himself to drift downstream to see if there were another opening through which he might escape; but even though he made many attempts to gain the land by climbing the bank, he could not succeed since it was cut like a wall and his horse was unable to find a firm footing. It became necessary therefore for him to return to where he had started, and since his horse had swum so long without resting and was extremely fatigued, he made a plea for help from those of his companions who were cutting wood for the raft. On witnessing his plight, four fine swimmers plunged into the water and brought both man and beast to shore. So exhausted were they by what they had experienced that this assistance was of no small consequence to them. But here we shall leave these men in order to tell what the Governor was doing in the meantime at Apalache.

CHAPTER X

The Governor seizes the Curaca of Apalache.

WHILE the Comptroller and Captain, Juan de Añasco, and his thirty cavaliers were accomplishing the journey we have described, the Adelantado Hernando de Soto was not idle. But being now in Apalache, he saw how anxious its inhabitants were to kill or wound the Castilians, and that they lost no occasion offered either by day or by night to do so. He felt, therefore, that if he could have the Curaca in his power, the intrigues and treasons of the Indians would cease. So he took great pains to find out secretly where Capafi was, and in a few days received positive information from his spies to the effect that the Cacique had gone to some large and very rugged mountains where, although not more than eight leagues from the camp, he felt himself to be secure because of the abundance of underbrush and the difficulty of the road, swamp and forest which protected the site, and also because of the many good people he had with him for his defense.

Now when the General learned positively of these things, he determined to make an expedition to that place in person; so taking all of the horsemen and footsoldiers he needed as well as the same spies for his guidance, he left for the Cacique's hideout. After traveling eight leagues over a period of three days and experiencing a great amount of hardship because of the difficulties of the road, he came eventually to a place which the Indians had fortified in the following manner. In the center of a very large and dense wood, they had cleared a spot for the Curaca and his men to set up their camp. Then as an entrance to this place they had opened a narrow path of more than a half-league in length; and at intervals of a hundred feet along the path they had constructed strong ramparts of thick pieces of wood, thus cutting off the passage. Special guards had been chosen to defend each of these obstructions, and no exit had been cleared on the other side of the fortification because of the belief that even if the Spaniards should reach the place, it was in itself so strong and the people who defended it so numerous and valiant that there would be no possibility of its being taken. Within the fortification, the Cacique Capafi had ensconsed himself with a goodly number of people, all of whom were determined to die rather than see their lord in the power of his enemies.

On reaching the entrance to the passage the Governor found the Indians well prepared for its defense. The Castilians struggled bravely, though because of the narrowness of the path only the two foremost of them could fight. But midst a rain of arrows they gained the first and second barricades simply with the work of their swords. Meanwhile it was necessary to cut the willow cables and other cords with which the wooden crosspieces were tied, and as they did so, they received further damage from the Indians. With all such difficulties, however, they gained the third enclosure and then each of the rest. Thus regardless of the great and obstinate resistance of the Indians, they won the path handbreadth by handbreadth to the very clearing where the Curaca was. But here the battle became intense, for when the Indians saw their lord in danger of being slain or captured they struggled desperately, and when they could not kill or wound their assailants otherwise, came out and encountered them amidst their very swords and lances. The Christians, for their part, on seeing the coveted prize so near, continued to fight as much as possible in order not to waste the efforts they had made by permitting the Curaca to slip from their hands. In the ensuing struggle, both sides, first the one and then the other, for some time revealed the strength of their courage; but the Indians for lack of defensive arms eventually came out the worse. The Governor himself, in his desire to capture Capafi, now that he felt him so within reach, fought like the very valiant soldier he was. As a good captain, he gave courage to his men by calling their names aloud, and when he did so, they made such a tremendous onslaught upon their foes and wounded them with such ferocity and cruelty as to almost annihilate them.

The Indians had done as much as naked people could do, so those few who remained gave up their weapons and surrendered; first, because they saw that they could no longer defend the Cacique and they wanted to prevent their enemies from surrounding and killing him, and again, because Capafi himself had shouted for them to do so. Kneeling now before the Governor, all begged that he take their own lives while sparing that of their lord. But the Governor received them compassionately, and answered that he forgave both them and their lord for their past disobedience on condition that in the future they should be his trusted friends. Then the Cacique himself, who was unable to walk, came in the arms of his vassals to kiss the hands of the Governor, who received the Indian affably because of the happiness it gave him to have this man in his power.

The Cacique Capafi was very fat, in fact so much so that the habitual indisposition and impediments which generally accompany excessive weight handicapped him in such a way as to make it impossible for him to take a single step or even to stand. Hence his vassals carried him about on a litter, and always in his house he crawled on his hands and knees. It was for this reason that he had not gone farther from the camp of the Spaniards than he had; and too, he had believed that the distance to his fastness, as well as the barricades and underbrush along the path which protected it, was sufficient to secure him. Nevertheless he found himself deceived in his confidence.

CHAPTER XI

The Cacique of Apalache goes by order of the Governor to subdue his Indians.

HAVING captured the Cacique, the General returned to the town of Apalache, much elated because it was his belief that with the seizure of the lord, the rash and shameless acts of the

vassals would come to an end. Ever since the Castilians had first
entered that town, its inhabitants had never once ceased to torment
them day and night with frequent alarms and unexpected attacks,
and they had laid their ambushes so skillfully and diligently that
no matter how short a distance a Spaniard might stray from the
camp, he was immediately set upon or wounded. And now the
General felt that with the Curaca in his power, all such mischief
would end. His hopes came to naught, however, for the Indians
with the loss of their leader grew even more bold, impudent and
persevering in their annoyances. Having no lord to defend and
serve, all directed their energies more obstinately than before toward molesting and injuring the Christians. The Adelantado, angered by their activities, spoke one day to Capafi of the displeasure
he felt at the great insolence of these vassals and their obvious lack
of appreciation for the leniency he had shown in sparing both themselves and their Curaca the evil and hurt they had merited as a
punishment for their obstinacy. Instead, he said, he had treated
them as friends even though they had angered him, and he had not
ordered his men to kill or wound any of them or to damage their
fields and towns, although he might have laid waste and burned
their whole province, comprised as it was of the lands and dwellings of such perverse enemies. And he thereupon told Capafi
to command his people to put an end to their treachery and shameless activities unless they wanted the Spaniards to ravage them
with both sword and flame; and he reminded the Cacique to reflect
that he himself was at present in the power of the Spaniards, and
that even though he was being honored with much respect and
generosity, it was possible for the great arrogance and disrespect
of his vassals to bring about his own death as well as the total
destruction of his land.

The Curaca responded with great humility and manifestations of
deep feeling:

"I am extremely displeased," he said, "by the failure of my vassals to act in accord with the obligation they owe Your Lordship

for the favor you have bestowed upon them, and to serve as I have desired and tried to persuade them to do since I have fallen into your power. I have sent messengers to command them to cease angering and afflicting the Castilians, but my messages have had no effect because the Indians do not believe that they come from me. Furthermore they cannot understand that Your Lordship has granted me both favor and generosity, and that I am at liberty; rather they suspect that I am being badly used and am a prisoner in irons. And now because of this suspicion, you should be even more solicitous and persistent in your artifices than previously, and I therefore beg Your Lordship to order your captains and soldiers to carry me with great caution to a place I shall show them five or six leagues distant. For there in a spacious forest, the noblest and most illustrious of my vassals have retired. Once arrived I shall shout their names day and night, and they on hearing the voice of their master, will hasten to my call, and having been undeceived of their evil suspicions will be pacified and agreeable to whatever is commanded of them, as you will see by the result itself. The quickest and most certain way to subdue the Indians to the service of Your Lordship is through the respect and veneration they naturally hold for their Curaca, and you will accomplish nothing, nor succeed in bringing about any negotiation with them by means of messengers, because they will answer that the messages are false and emanate from their enemies instead of their Cacique."

With these words and a very pained expression, Capafi persuaded Hernando de Soto of the advisability of sending him to the place mentioned, and thus his plan was ordered and put into effect. Two companies of soldiers went with the Curaca, one of cavalry and the other of infantry, and they were especially urged to guard and keep him in security lest he escape. With this charge they left the camp before dawn and traveled six leagues south, arriving about nightfall at the place where the Cacique had said his men had withdrawn into the forest.

As soon as Capafi reached the appointed spot, three or four of the Indians who had accompanied him entered the forest and a short time later ten or twelve other Indians emerged. The Curaca then commanded these men to assemble all of the principal Indians in the forest and appear before him on the following day; for, he said, he wished to give them news in person of matters which were very important to the honor, health, and general welfare of everyone. This message the Indians carried back to the forest, and that night the Castilians, after stationing sentinels and placing a special guard on the person of the Cacique, lay down to rest singularly pleased with their undertaking, for it seemed to them that it was progressing in such a fashion that they would return from this expedition with honor and glory. But these Spaniards failed to take note of the fact that the greatest hopes with which men personally flatter themselves are wont to be vain, as indeed their own turned out to be.

CHAPTER XII

The Cacique of Apalache, being handicapped, flees from the Spaniards on hands and knees.

WITH great happiness and general rejoicing, our Castilians, both officers and soldiers, lay down to rest; for it was their belief that on the morrow they would return to their Captain General in victory and triumph, bringing to him each of the principal Indians of that province converted now to his friendship and service. Thus all had thought to continue in peace and tranquility when they found that their visions had mocked them, for with the arrival of dawn, it became evident that they were minus both the Cacique and the few Indians who had come with him. Greatly astonished at this turn of events, they now questioned each other as to what the Cacique could have done with himself, and all agreed that the only possible explanation for his disappearance was that he had conjured up demons who had spirited him away through the air; for the sentinels vowed that there had been no carelessness on their part by means of which he could have escaped.

The truth of the matter is that all of the Castilians, both those on guard and those who were not, had become careless and fallen asleep, not only because of the fatigue brought on by the long journey of the previous day, but also because of the confidence they had gained from Capafí's fine words and friendship as well as from his impediment and lameness. Seeing them asleep and recognizing a good opportunity, the Curaca had ventured to steal away, putting his boldness into execution by crawling on all fours through the midst of the sentinels. His Indians, who were not sleeping, but laying an ambush for the Spaniards, had then run across him and borne him off on their shoulders. That these infidels did not return and cut the throats of the Christians was a blessing of God, for they could have done so very easily, since they were ferocious and our men were asleep. They were content, however, with seeing their lord delivered from the power of the Castilians, and they made an effort to put him in a place of greater security than he had been before lest he fall once more into their hands. Accordingly they carried him to where he never then nor afterward was seen again.

The two captains (whose names we are quiet about because of their honor) and their good soldiers made extensive searches in the forest throughout that whole day, hunting for Capafí as they would a wild beast. Nevertheless they found no trace of him, for one recovers with difficulty the bird escaped from the net.

Having put their Curaca in a safe place, the Indians came out and offered the Christians a thousand affronts, taunting and ridiculing them; but not wishing to fight, they did no further harm and permitted them to return to their camp. There they arrived very much ashamed that an Indian so closely guarded should have escaped from them on his hands and knees. To the General and the other officers they told a thousand tales in exoneration of their carelessness and in defense of their honor. All affirmed that they had heard very strange noises that night, and they vowed that the only way the Cacique could have eluded them was to have fled through the air with devils. Any other mode of escape, they swore, would have been impossible, since they had watched him so carefully.

The Governor realized that his men had not taken sufficient precaution and that their error was without remedy; but not wanting to insult these captains and soldiers to their faces, he pretended to believe what they said and supported their statements by asserting that the Indians were such expert sorcerers that they could do even more than they had done in that instance. Still, he did not fail to regret their carelessness.

But let us return to the thirty cavaliers whom we left struggling to pass the swollen river of Ocali. Those of them who were occupied in cutting wood soon completed the raft, for having anticipated just such necessities, they were well equipped with axes and with ropes of great length. Two such ropes were attached to the vessel, which they now threw into the water, and then two good swimmers carried one rope to the opposite shore. Thus by means of the two ropes the raft could be tugged from one side of the water to the other. All of these things had already been done when the Indians of Ocali approached the river in a great rush of violence and noise and with their minds set on killing the Christians.

The eleven cavaliers on the far side of the river now closed with these Indians with great boldness and determination, lancing the first of them that they encountered. Because the land was clear of underbrush as well as tall trees, they were masters of the field, and as a result the Indians dared not await them, but withdrew and kept at a distance, contenting themselves with shooting many arrows at them from afar. Meanwhile the four cavaliers who had remained on the near side of the river where there were fewer enemies ran up and down the bank, two going each way, for the Indians came from both directions. Thus by confronting the infidels they were able to keep them from reaching the place where the raft lay.

While men on horseback defended both shores of the river, the raft made five trips across. On the first, it carried the coats of the eleven cavaliers, who were now demanding them loudly, for a north wind had risen and they were freezing with the cold since they were wet and naked except for their coats of mail and the shirts which they wore beneath. In the four remaining trips, the saddles, reins, saddlebags, and those few men who were unable to swim were ferried across. Those who could swim, did so in order that time not be lost in making more trips than were necessary. As each man reached the opposite shore, he went out upon the plain to help resist the Indians who were increasing hourly. Two, however, stayed at the river to tow the raft and receive what was in it.

For the last trip there remained only two men on the near side of the river, Hernando Athanasio and Gonzalo Silvestre. While his companion was driving his mount into the water and boarding the raft, Gonzalo Silvestre rode out to detain the Indians; then when he had pushed them back a good run of his horse, he returned at full speed to where the other cavalier was waiting. Without removing the saddle or reins he drove his horse into the water and boarded the raft, having first untied the rope with which it was secured to the land. And now since the Indians were approaching at great speed to shoot arrows at these two Castilians, their friends on the opposite shore tugged with great effort and pulled the vessel to the middle of the river where it was safe.

After being led into the water, the horses had gone ahead willingly without being forced or guided. Just as rational human beings they seemed to be aware of the harm that the enemy would do them and thus hastened to obey orders, not refusing to enter or leave any place they were urged. Their obedience was no small relief to the Spaniards, who even followed their example and hastened with greater promptitude to the work when they saw that the beasts had not refused it.

*** *** ***
*** ***
***

CHAPTER XIII

*An account of the journey of the thirty cavaliers
until they reached the great swamp.*

IMPEDED by the hardships and obstacles we have described as
well as many others which we shall not tell here, since it is
impossible to record all of the sufferings that occur in such journeys,
the thirty strong and valiant cavaliers crossed the river of Ocali,
Our Lord God having favored them so compassionately that not a
single man or horse of them came out wounded. It was already
two o'clock in the afternoon when all had reached the other side,
and they now went to the town, it being necessary to stop there
because Juan López Cacho had been frozen by the extreme cold of
the water in which he had worked so long, and like a wooden statue
was unable to move either hand or foot.

The Indians, on seeing the Spaniards approach the town, stationed
themselves to defend its entrance, not for the purpose of preventing
their coming and staying there as they wished, but of detaining
them until the women and children could flee to the forest. Then
when they felt that their people would be able to escape capture,
they retired and left the place unprotected. With that the Castilians
entered and encamped in the middle of the plaza, for they dared
not go into the houses lest their enemies on finding them separated
should surround and take them by hemming them in. Four large
fires were now kindled in the square, and in the midst of this heat,
Juan López was placed, after first having been wrapped well in all
of the coats of his companions. One man even gave him a clean
shirt which he had been carrying for his own use, and all marveled
that at such a time more shirts were to be found among them than
were actually being worn. This was the greatest gift that could
have been bestowed upon the youth.

They remained in this town for the rest of the day with great
anxiety and fear because of Juan López. They did not know whether

he would recover sufficiently for them to travel that night, or delay them so much that the Indians would warn one another to join and cut them off from their road. But they determined that, come what might, the health of their companion would be considered before all of the harm and danger that might befall them. Thus resolved, they stuffed the horses, each in its turn, with corn; then fifteen of the men ate while the others were making the rounds of the camp and drying the saddles and clothing that had been wet in the river. Also they repacked the saddlebags with food which they found in the town, but even though there was an abundance of raisins, dried prunes and other fruits and vegetables, they made no attempt to take anything except corn, for their principal concern was that there should be food for the horses, and the corn provided sustenance for both men and beasts.

With the coming of night, pairs of mounted sentinels were placed on guard and commanded to ride around at a great distance outside the village so as to have time and opportunity to warn the rest in the event that the enemy should return. Two of these men, at some time near midnight, heard a low noise as of people approaching, and while one rushed back to inform the rest of their companions, the other remained to investigate more thoroughly and assure himself as to what the noise might be. Then in the clearness of the night, he beheld a great, dark cloud of people moving toward the village with a ferocious and low, muttering sound; and on looking more closely, he verified them to be an organized band of the enemy. So he took the news immediately to the rest of the Spaniards, and they, seeing that Juan López was somewhat improved, wrapped him well and placed him upon his horse, tying him to the saddle, however, because he as yet could not support himself by his own strength. Thus he resembled Ruy Díaz, the Cid, as he rode out dead to win the famous battle of Valencia. A companion then took the reins of the horse in order to guide the animal, for Juan López was not ready to do even so much as that. In this manner and with the utmost secrecy possible, the thirty Spaniards left the town of

Ocali before their enemies arrived, and they traveled at such a good pace that they were six leagues beyond the place by dawn.

These men continued their journey always with the same diligence, posting through the inhabited districts to avoid having news of their approach precede them, and lancing the Indians whom they encountered near the roads to prevent their giving notice of them. And through the unpopulated regions where there were no Indians, they cut their pace to allow the horses to rest and get breath to run when there was need for them to do so. In this way they passed the sixth day of their journey, either running or walking for almost twenty leagues, a part of which lay in the province of Acuera, a land inhabited by many warlike people.

On the seventh day after their departure from the camp, a man named Pedro de Atienza fell sick and, a few hours later while still traveling, died upon his horse. His companions buried him with great pity at such a death, for in order not to lose time in their journey, they had refused to believe his complaints when he had suddenly become ill. They made him a sepulchre with the axes which they carried to cut wood but which served well even for this purpose; and then they passed on, grieved at having lost one of their number at a time when there were so few.

At sunset they came to the passage across the great swamp, having run and walked twenty more leagues just as they had done on the day before. People who have not participated in the conquests of the New World or in the civil wars of Peru find it difficult to believe that there are horses and men who can accomplish such long marches, but, by the code of hidalgos, I swear to the truth of the fact that in seven days these cavaliers traveled the one hundred and seven leagues, one more or less, which lie between the principal village of Apalache and the great swamp. This swamp they found to consist of a sea of water with many arms which flowed in and out of it so rapidly and fiercely that any one of them would have been sufficient to make the crossing difficult, but the great number of them and above all the deep channel of the river made it even more so.

I hold the opinion, which is in agreement with that of all Spaniards in the Indies whom I have heard mention the subject, that the principal explanation for the ability of horses to endure the excessive labor to which they have been and are being subjected in the conquests of the New World, may be found in the excellent nourishment received from the corn they consume. This grain offers much sustenance and is greatly enjoyed by horses and indeed by all animals. My belief may be substantiated by the fact that the Indians of Peru give corn to the llamas, which serve them as mounts, in order to enable these animals to bear their excessive loads, for their ordinary burden weighs as much as a man. The llamas are fed corn, but all other animals, even though they may carry a load befitting their strength, are sustained with just the food they find in the fields.

That night the Spaniards slept or, more properly speaking, kept watch on the edge of the swamp. It had suddenly turned extremely cold because of the rising of the north wind, which in all that region is most frigid. They therefore kindled great fires, and with the heat thereof were able to endure the weather, but they were fearful lest the Indians rush to the light of the flames. And indeed had as many as twenty of them come, that number would have been sufficient to block the passage and even to kill them all, for the Indians in their canoes could have taken the offensive safely from the water since the Spaniards would have been unable to employ their horses in returning the attack and furthermore would have had neither arquebuses nor crossbows with which to drive their enemies to a greater distance from them. So it was that with this anxiety and with a third of them at a time keeping watch, they lay down to rest, aware now of the work to be done on the coming day.

CHAPTER XIV

The intolerable hardships that the thirty cava-
liers experienced in crossing the
great swamp.

OUR Spaniards had rested but a few hours when they were
subjected to an unexpected calamity, not a calamity occasioned by the enemy but one caused by the excessive toil suffered
on the road. For it happened that near midnight Juan de Soto, a
comrade of Pedro de Atienza, whom they had left buried along the
way, died very suddenly. Now there was a man among them who
fled with all speed while shouting in a loud voice: "Cursed be he
who has given us the plague, for two of us have died so suddenly
and in such a brief time." But Gómez Arias, who was prudent
and discreet, cried out to the man as he fled: "You already carry
enough pestilence with you in your flight not to be able to escape
it, no matter how much you may try. If you flee from us now, where
do you propose to go? You are not on the sandy beach of Seville,
nor are you among its hills."

On hearing these words the man who was fleeing returned and
helped say the prayers offered for the dead, but he would not go with
his comrades to bury the body, for he still insisted that Juan de
Soto had been a victim of the plague.

With this help for their labors, the Castilians passed the night.
Then when morning came, they gave the order to cross the swamp,
which they perceived carried less water than on the previous day, a
circumstance that afforded them no small comfort because of the
difficulty they had anticipated. Eight of them who could swim
repaired the balustrade of the bridge of fallen trees which spanned
the deepest part and then carried across the saddles and the clothes
of all their companions. Meanwhile the other twenty, naked as they
were born, made an effort to drive the horses into the water, but
these animals because of the extreme cold were reluctant to enter

the area where they had to swim. So tying long ropes to the halters, four or five men swam to the center of the current and proceeded to pull while others applied cudgels, but the horses joined all four feet and remain stationary, preferring to be killed by blows rather than enter the water. And although some were forced to start out and swim a short distance, they were unable to bear the chill and fled again to land dragging the swimmers with them, for these men could not hold them and those on land could not stop them. Now we speak of the latter as being on land, but they were actually in water up to their waists and chests.

For more than three hours by the clock, the twenty Spaniards continued to belabor the horses, and even though they changed them from time to time, taking some and leaving others, to see if there were not at least one that would cross, all of their efforts were not sufficient to persuade a single animal to do so. Then at the end of the three hours, two of them, impelled by the great force, did cross; one being the horse of Juan de Añasco and the other that of Gonzalo Silvestre. But in spite of their example, the others would not follow, since they had gathered so much fear of the cold-ness of the water. Consequently, those horsemen who could not swim saddled and remounted their steeds so as to be prepared to do whatever they could in the event the enemy should arrive.

The leader of the comrades who were in the water was Gómez Arias, and he it was who labored the hardest. But all twenty of them had remained there more than four hours suffering cold that even the horses could not endure; hence their bodies were numb and so livid that they looked like Negroes. When these men per-ceived that their combined efforts and hardships (and anyone can imagine what they were) availed them naught since the horses would not pass over to the other side, they were almost in despair of their lives. Then just at this time Juan de Añasco, who, as we have said, had saddled his mount, rode through that part of the water that could be forded up to the deep channel. He was vexed that more horses had not crossed and was unmindful of the fact that this circumstance was not due to any lack of effort on the part of the men in the water. Furthermore he took no notice of the sad plight these men were in, but angered by his belief that they had lost the respect due him as their leader, shouted in a loud voice: "Gómez Arias, many curses upon you for not having finished bringing the horses across!"

Gómez Arias saw the condition of both himself and his companions, all of whom appeared to be more dead than alive, and he realized that they could no longer endure the bodily and spiritual torment they were now suffering—and indeed the difficulties which these twenty-eight companions, and especially those in the water, experienced on that day cannot be over-estimated or even adequately told. So he felt that Captain Juan de Añasco did not appreciate the intolerable hardship both he and his companions had suffered, and in his contempt for such ingratitude, he cried:

"Cursed be you and the lewd bitch prostitute who whelped you! You sit there on your horse finely dressed and wrapped up in your coat, taking no note of the fact that we have been in the water more than four hours, frozen with cold and doing all that we can. Get down off your horse, confound you, and come here; then we shall see if you are worth any more than we are."

To these words he added others which were no milder; for anger, when once kindled, knows no restraint.

But Juan de Añasco held himself back, not only because of what Gómez Arias as spokesman for his comrades had said, but also because he realized that he himself had spoken without reason and that the severity of his own evil disposition had caused both the dissension and consequent disrespect for his person. For many times on this errand as well as on others in which he participated, he found himself humiliated and his reputation diminished because of his failure to consider first what he should say in such cases. All men, and especially those who are leaders and superiors in time of war, ought to note that it is well for them to use gentleness and affability with subordinates and to persuade them to their tasks by example rather than words. And when it becomes necessary to employ words, let them be kind, for it is very easy to see what can be gained by good words and what can be lost by bad ones—and after all, the one is no more costly than the other.

CHAPTER XV

*An account of the journey of the thirty cavaliers
until their arrival a half-league from
the village of Hirrihigua.*

AS SOON as the dissension was settled, the Spaniards returned to their work. Since it was nearly midday, the heat of the sun slightly tempered the chill of the water, and the horses began to cross with less reluctance than previously, but not so quickly as was necessary, for it was already past three in the afternoon before all had reached the opposite shore.

The sight of these Castilians as they emerged from the water, crushed and broken by their long toil, was a most piteous one. They were consumed by the cold, endured for almost an entire day, and were so weak and fatigued that they could hardly support themselves. One should remember also that they had received little or no gratitude to restore them from the ills they had suffered. But they considered themselves fortunate since they were now beyond this evil swamp which had caused them so much anxiety. Thus they gave thanks to God that their enemies had not rushed up to obstruct their passage, because they felt that this particular circumstance had been an evidence of divine mercy. For if to the difficulties we have said they suffered, there had been added that of having to fight and defend themselves against no more than fifty Indians, what would have been their fate? The reason the Indians had not come out to meet them must have been that this swamp was far from the populated areas, and again that winter had already set in, for going as they do without clothes, these people are not accustomed to leave their houses very much at this season of the year.

The Spaniards agreed to pitch camp that night on a great plain which lay just beyond where they were, for both men and horses had emerged from the swamp in such a condition as not to be fit to travel another step. They kindled fires to warm themselves and took consolation in the thought that from this place on to Hirrihigua, which was their destination, they would encounter no more difficult terrain. Then when darkness arrived, they slept with the same precaution they had observed during previous nights.

Before dawn they were on their way, and when they came upon five Indians, they ran them through with their lances lest news of their approach be carried forward. The horses belonging to the two dead comrades were turned loose without their saddles and reins being removed, and they followed the other horses, many times going in advance since they had no need for the guidance of their masters. On this day our men traveled thirteen leagues, coming at length to an excellent plain where they could sleep in their accustomed order. Then at dawn of the following day they were off again, and a little past sunup came to the town of Urribarricuxi, which they did not want to enter and therefore left to one side in order to avoid an encounter with its inhabitants. On this tenth day of their journey they traveled fifteen leagues and then pitched camp just three leagues from the town of Mucozo.

A little past midnight, they awoke and set out once again. When they had advanced two leagues, they saw fire burning in a forest near the road. More than a league before they had reached this point, the mestizo Pedro Morón had said: "Be on the alert. I smell fire not far from where we are heading." A league farther on he added: "We are now very near the fire." Then after traveling for a short distance, they discovered this fire. Amazed at such a strange thing, the Castilians approached the fire. Here they found numerous Indians with their wives and children baking skates for their lunch. They agreed to seize as many of these people as possible even though they were Mucozo's vassals, and then to hold them until they could determine if peace had been maintained with Pedro Calderón; for if the Indians of that region had not kept their truce, it was their intention to send to Havana all of them that they could capture, along with evidence of their triumphs.

So with this determination, the Spaniards rushed toward the fire. Terrified by the noise and trampling of the horses, the vagrant Indians fled forward into the woods, but our men succeeded in capturing eighteen or twenty women and children from among those whom they were able to head off, many others having escaped because of the darkness of the night and the presence of brambles and briars in the forest. Those taken wept and shouted, and in loud voices called out the name Ortiz. Without uttering another word, they repeated this name many times as if wishing to remind the Spaniards of the numerous benefits they and their Cacique had conferred upon that Christian. But their shouting was of no avail in deterring their captors from holding them prisoner, those persons being few who remember to show gratitude for favors already received. Instead, the Spaniards without dismounting, ate the skates, which in the scramble of Indians and horses, had been filled with sand; and they did not even bother to remove the sand, for they said that in their great hunger, it tasted to them like sugar and cinnamon.

The cavaliers now proceeded over a trail far from the village of Mucozo, and when they had traveled five leagues that morning, the horse belonging to Juan López Cacho became exhausted. We have forgotten to mention this man again since the incident in the town of Ocali when his comrades bound him to his steed. You should know therefore that because of the great shock he received that night when the Indians returned, and because of the vigor accompanying his robust age, for he was little more than twenty years old, he regained both consciousness and bodily warmth. Thus he recovered from the indisposition caused by the cold and the great hardship experienced that day; and afterward he labored throughout the whole journey just like the rest of his companions.

The horse belonging to Juan López Cacho, having struggled so hard in crossing the river of Ocali, was now exhausted, and although no farther than six leagues from the town to which they were going, the men could do nothing to make this animal continue. Hence they left him in a good meadow where there was a great quantity of grass for his sustenance, first removing his saddle and reins and placing them in a tree so that whoever might wish to use him could take him away with all of his equipment. But they pitied the animal, for they feared that as soon as the Indians happened upon him, he would become a target for their arrows. With this painful thought they had traveled for almost five leagues when the suspicion of a still greater tragedy caused them to forget the present one. Coming to a place a little more than a league from the town of Hirrihigua where Captain Pedro Calderón had remained with the forty horsemen and eighty footsoldiers, they examined the ground, hoping to find horse tracks, for this place being so near the town and so free of underbrush, it seemed reasonable to expect that their compatriots would have ridden over it up to that point and even farther. Fnding no manner of footprints or other signs of horses, they were exceedingly pained and worried, fearing now that their companions either had been killed by the Indians or had sailed away in the caravel and brigantines left to their care. If those men were still in this land of Hirrihigua, they reasoned, it would be impossible for there not to be horse tracks this near the town.

With such suspicion and the ensuing confusion as to what they should do in the event that one or the other possibility had occurred, they deliberated upon their future action, for they found themselves isolated in such a manner that they had no boat in which to leave the land and go away by sea, nor anything with which to construct one; and in the light of what they had experienced in coming to this place, it appeared impossible for them to return to where the Governor was. In the midst of their fears and misgivings, all emerged with equal courage and determination, resolving that should they not find their companions in Hirrihigua, they would enter into some secret part of the forest where grass might be found for the horses. Here while recuperating, they would slaughter the extra horse for jerked meat to supply them on the road, and then having permitted the other animals to rest for three or four days, venture to return to where the Governor was. For, they said, should they lose their lives on the way, they would have ended them as good soldiers who had performed their duty in the assignments of their Captain General; and if on the other hand they should come out safely, they would have completed the task with which they had been charged. This then was the ultimate resolution of all twenty-eight of these Spaniards as to what they were to do in the future in the event that they failed to find Pedro Calderón in Hirrihigua.

CHAPTER XVI

The thirty cavaliers come to where Captain Pedro Calderón is. The manner in which they were received.

HAVING once reached this heroic decision, the cavaliers continued on their way, and the farther they went the more confirmed they became in their suspicion and fears, for they found no tracks of horses whatsoever and in fact no other signs to indicate that Spaniards had come in that direction. Eventually, however, they arrived at a small lagoon which was less than half a league from the town of Hirrihigua, and there they saw not only fresh horse tracks but evidence that water had been boiled with ashes for the purpose of washing clothes. These signs gave them great joy; and their horses on scenting the tracks of the other animals became so animated and took on so much new fire that they acted as if they were just coming out of their stables after twenty days of leisure. With such happiness as one may imagine, and with new inspiration, they now galloped forward at great speed, pushing back on the earth in such leaps and bounds that their masters could neither calm nor restrain them. So excellent were these beasts that when thought to be too exhausted to support themselves they still performed in such a manner. Thus it was that at sunset, after having traveled for an entire day without covering so much as eleven leagues, our men caught sight of the village of Hirrihigua, this being the shortest day's march they had accomplished on the whole trip.

As they approached the town, a mounted patrol came out two by two with their lances and bucklers to watch over and guard the camp in the night. At that, Juan de Añasco and his comrades grouped themselves likewise in pairs, and then just as men who at the start of a game of canes enter the race track with great shouts, halloos and festivity, they rushed forward to the town with the utmost fury, maintaining such regularity, however, that when the first men were stopping, the second were moving at half-speed, and the third were just leaving their posts. All ran thus, and the order they observed appeared magnificent. This was a happy and joyous celebration and the termination of a journey which had been as laborious as we have pictured it.

The shouts of the running men brought Captain Pedro Calderón and all of his soldiers from the town, and they were exceedingly pleased at the fine entrance made by their comrades as they approached. All therefore received them with open arms, and there were many embraces and much celebration in general. It is worth noting, however, that the first words uttered by the men who had remained at Hirrihigua were not inquiries concerning the army or the Governor or indeed of any other particular friend; but one and all, at practically the same time, asked most anxiously if there were much gold in the land. The great hunger and lust for this metal frequently moves men to put off and deny both relatives and friends.

So it was that these twenty-eight cavaliers, after having survived many more toils and dangers than we have told, came to the close of their journey. This, however, was not to be the end of their difficulties; rather, it was to mark the beginning of greater and more lengthy ones, as we shall see later. They had passed eleven days on the road, one of which had been spent in crossing the river Ocali, and another in crossing the great swamp. In only nine days, therefore, they had traveled one hundred and fifty leagues, which is a few more than there are between Apalache and the Bay of the Holy Spirit with its neighboring settlement of Hirrihigua.

By means of the few details I have recorded concerning the incidents of this brief journey, one will be able to perceive and pass judgment on what all the other Spaniards must have experienced in conquering a new world, a world which in itself is so large and austere, not to mention the ferocity of its inhabitants; for by the finger of the giant we may deduce the magnitude of his body. Nowadays, however, the conquerors of that world are ridiculed by those people who have not seen it; for partaking of its fruits as they do without having undergone the pain and labor of the men who won it, such people think that it was gained with the same ease with which they are now enjoying it.

As soon as he reached the town of Hirrihigua, Captain Juan de Añasco inquired of Captain Pedro Calderón as to whether the Indians of that province and those of Mucozo had maintained peace, and on learning that they had, he ordered his men to release at once the women and children whom he had brought as prisoners. Then he loaded these people with gifts and sent them to their homes, requesting them to tell the Curaca Mucozo to come to the camp with vassals to carry back the ship stores and many other things that the Spaniards intended to abandon on their departure. Also, he instructed them to tell that chieftain to hold in trust the horse which had been left in his land because of its exhaustion. At that the women and children departed, happy now to bear such a good message.

On the third day the good Mucozo arrived at the camp with his cavaliers and gentlemen. With him also was the horse, but his vassals carried the saddle and reins on their shoulders since they were ignorant as to how to use them. After embracing Captain

Juan de Añasco and all of his men most happily and affectionately, he inquired of each individually concerning his health and then asked about their lord the Governor and all of the other captains, cavaliers and soldiers who had accompanied him. Having satisfied his curiosity as to the condition of the army in general, he requested particulars concerning the journey of the cavaliers, what battles and skirmishes they had fought, and what hunger, toils and other necessities they had suffered. Then at the close of his inquiry, which was very long and pleasant, he assured them that he would be very pleased to impress his spirit and will upon all of the other Curacas and lords of that great kingdom so that they too might serve the Governor and his Castilians as they deserved and as he himself would like to see them served.

Without having failed to take note of the great difference in the manner of reception offered by the Curaca and that of their comrades, who had inquired only about gold, the Comptroller and Captain, Juan de Añasco, now spoke in the name of his people, rendering thanks to Mucozo for his love. Then acting in behalf of the General he gave numerous messages of gratitude to the Cacique and all of his Indians for the peace and friendship they had preserved with Captain Pedro Calderón and his soldiers, and for the affection they had always shown the Spaniards. Many other courteous and affectionate expressions were offered on both sides, but those uttered by Mucozo, since they were planned and spoken with a purpose, amazed the Spaniards. And this Indian was indeed possessed of all the excellent qualities that one might find in some cavalier who had been reared in the most polite courts of the world; for in addition to his bodily endowments of good proportion and facial beauty, he possessed those of the spirit. His virtues and discretion in deeds as well as words were such that our Castilians rightly marvelled at him, for they realized that he had been born and reared in that wilderness; and they very justly loved him for his fine understanding and exceeding goodness.

Thus it was a great pity that the Curaca Mucozo was not invited to accept the waters of baptism, for because of his good judgment, few persuasions would have been necessary to turn him from his paganism to our Catholic Faith. And the conversion of this man would have been a fine beginning, since one can expect such grain to produce many ears and bear much corn. But we must not blame these Christians, for they had determined to preach and administer the sacraments of our Law of Grace after having conquered and settled the land, and it was this determination that held them back from performing such sacraments at once. And let this be said here in order to exonerate these Castilians for exercising the same carelessness in similar instances which we shall see later; for certainly very propitious occasions were lost for the Gospel to be preached and received. And let those who forfeit such opportunities not be surprised that they are lost.

CHAPTER XVII

The things that Captains Juan de Añasco and
Pedro Calderón ordained in fulfill-
ment of what the General
had commanded
them.

THE Curaca Mucozo was entertained by Juan de Añasco and the other Spaniards for four days, during which time as well as during the rest of the period that our men were in Hirrihigua, his Indians came and went like ants, never ceasing to take back to their land all that the Spaniards were unable to carry with them. And this amounted to a great deal, for there were more than twenty-five tons of cassava alone (the bread used in the islands of Santo Domingo and Cuba, and their surroundings) besides a large number of cloaks, loose coats, doublets, breeches, hose and all kinds and weights of footwear such as shoes, buskins and sandals.[6] And of arms, there were many cuirasses, bucklers, pikes, lances and steel

[6] *alpargates*—a kind of shoe or sandal made of hemp.

helmets. Since the Governor was a man of wealth, he had brought a great abundance of each of these things in addition to such necessary ship supplies as sails, tackle, pitch, oakum, tallow, ropes, panniers, hampers, anchors, cables and quantities of iron and steel. It is true that he had taken what he could of these materials with him, but much still remained; and since Mucozo was a friend, the Spaniards were pleased to have him carry away what was left. This his Indians did and were thereby made rich and happy.

Juan de Añasco bore an order from the Governor to take the two brigantines remaining at the Bay of the Holy Spirit and sail along the whole of the coast to the west until coming to the Bay of Aute, which he himself, as we have seen, had discovered and marked so laboriously in order to be able to recognize it when he should return that way by sea. And now for the purpose of fulfilling his mission, he visited the brigantines, which were not far from the town, and then spent seven days repairing them, procuring supplies, and readying the people who were to accompany him. Meanwhile he gave notice to Captain Pedro Calderón of the Governor's instruction as to what was to be carried on the trip across the land, and then after having bid farewell to the rest of his comrades, he set out in search of the Bay of Aute where we shall leave him until the proper time.

The Governor had commissioned the good cavalier Gómez Arias to sail to Havana in the caravel. There he was to visit Doña Isabel de Bobadilla and the city of Havana as well as the whole of the island of Santiago de Cuba for the purpose of relating all that had occurred to the Spaniards up until that time and rendering an account of the fine qualities which they had seen in the land of Florida. Moreover he was to treat of other important matters, of which I give no record here since they do not concern our history. Hence, Gómez Arias commanded his men to examine and repair the vessel and in addition to provide it with people and supplies. Then raising sail, he came safely in a few days to Havana where he was well received by Doña Isabel and the inhabitants of the island of Cuba, all of whom welcomed with much festivity the account of the progress being made in the discovery and conquest of Florida. And they rejoiced also over the news that the Governor was in good health, for everyone, both individually and collectively, loved this man and desired for him the greatest happiness just as if he were the father of them all. And he had indeed merited their affection.

Back in the first book of this history, we mentioned that on two chance occasions two Spaniards were captured in the province of Hirrihigua, more through their own fault than through any desire on the part of the natives to do them harm. Although incidents of little importance, it will be well to tell of them here since they did occur during the time Captain Pedro Calderón remained in that province after the Governor's departure, and since no affair of greater moment happened to him there.

You should know that these Indians had constructed great enclosures of dry rock in the Bay of the Holy Spirit so as to be able to enjoy the skates and many other fish that came in with the high tide and remained there trapped and almost dry when the tide was low. In this manner they caught many fish which the Castilians with Captain Pedro Calderón likewise enjoyed. Thus it came to pass that one day two Spaniards, Pedro López and Antón Galván, both of whom were natives of Valverde, desired very earnestly to go fishing, and although they had no permission from the Captain to do so, they set forth in a small canoe, carrying with them a fourteen- or fifteen-year-old boy named Diego Múñoz who was a native of Badajoz and a page of the Captain himself. While these men were fishing in a great enclosure, twenty Indians approached them in two canoes, and in the meantime many others waited for them on the land. Entering the enclosure these twenty men addressed the Christians kindly, some speaking in Spanish and some in their own tongue. "Friends, friends," they said, "let us all enjoy the fish."

Pedro López, who was a crude and arrogant individual, replied: "Dogs! We don't have to traffic with dogs." With that he grasped his sword and wounded an Indian who had come near. Then the other Indians, on perceiving the unreasonableness of these Spaniards, hemmed them in from all sides, and striking them with their bows and arrows as well as their oars, they killed Pedro López, who had caused the fracas, and left Galván for dead with his head laid open and his whole face torn by the force of the blows. Diego Múñoz, they took prisoner but did him no further harm because of his extreme youth.

Shouting, the Castilians in the camp ran to the canoes in the hopes of giving aid to their companions; but they arrived too late, for they found two of them dead[7] and the third a captive of the Indians. Pedro López they buried; but when they perceived that Antón Galván was still breathing, they gave him succour and thus restored him to this life. He was thirty days, however, in recovering from his wounds, and for many months after the parts of his body had healed he was like a fool, stunned still by the blows he had received on the head. Even when in normal health, he was not the cleverest of their rustics, and always in telling of what had happened on that day, he would say among other stupid things: "When the Indians slew me and my comrade, Pedro López, we did this and that." Once his companions teased him by saying: "They slew Pedro López, not you. How can you say they slew you when you are still alive?"

"They slew me also," Antón Galván insisted, "and if I am alive today, it is because God gave me back my life."

Just for the sake of hearing these stupid and clownish remarks, the soldiers made this man repeat his tale many times, and since he persevered in using elegant language and telling the story always in his own way, he afforded his companions pleasure and laughter.

On another chance occasion similar to the one we have just described, the Indians seized in the same province of Hirrihigua a

---

[7] In the next sentence the Inca reveals that Galván was not dead; but Galván himself always insisted that he was.

large Spanish seaman called Hernando Vintimilla. One evening when the sea was at low tide, this man inadvertently walked down the shore of the bay to gather shell fish and shrimp, wandering carelessly until he was hidden by a forest which lay between the town and the water. Here there were Indians concealed, and when they saw him alone, they came out and addressed him in a friendly manner, remarking that he should share with them the cockles that he carried. Vintimilla replied scornfully and tried to intimidate them with his words so that on seeing that he did not fear them they would not dare do him harm. But it enraged the Indians for a single Spaniard to speak thus arrogantly to the ten or twelve of them who were there, so they closed with him and took him away captive, although they did him no other manner of harm.

Now the Indians of this province kept these two Spaniards with them for ten years, and they permitted them to go about as freely as one of themselves. Then in the year 1549 the ship of the Dominican Friar, Luis Cancer de Balbastro, who had come to preach to the people of Florida, was forced by a storm to take port in the Bay of the Holy Spirit. This priest the Indians killed, as well as two of his companions; and those of his associates who had remained aboard ship thereupon fled to the open sea. But in their flight, they again were overtaken by a storm and forced to re-enter the bay to escape the fury of the waves. When the tempest had abated, the Indians came out in many canoes to attack them, and they, not having men of war aboard, withdrew once more to the open sea. But the Indians persisted in following them and with these Indians came the two Spaniards, Diego Múñoz and Vintimilla, who had cast off in a canoe with the idea of eluding their captors and escaping to the ship if it could be persuaded to await them. Thus all were pursuing that vessel when the north wind chanced to rise, and the Indians, fearing that it might attain the velocity that it customarily reaches in that region and consequently cast them out to the sea where they would be in danger, decided upon the wisdom of returning to land. The two Spaniards, however, astutely made themselves stationary, while leading their companions to believe that being alone they were unable to row against the wind. Then when they saw the Indians somewhat apart from them, they directed the prow of their canoe toward the ship, and as men who desired liberty and were risking their lives for it, proceeded to row as furiously as possible, pleading loudly in the meantime for those on board to wait for them. Seeing that a single canoe approached and perceiving at once that its occupants were people in distress, the men on the ship did lower their sails and wait. And with the arrival of the canoe they received the two Spaniards in exchange for those companions they had lost. Thus Diego Múñoz and Vintimilla returned to the protection of the Christians at the close of the ten years they had spent in the power of the Indians who inhabit the province of Hirrihigua and the Bay of the Holy Spirit.

CHAPTER XVIII

Pedro Calderón sets out with his men. The events of his trip until he comes to the great swamp.

AS SOON as Juan de Añasco and Gómez Arias had sailed, one for the Bay of Aute and the other for the island of Havana, Captain Pedro Calderón put into readiness the people who remained with him. There were seventy lances and fifty footsoldiers, for Juan de Añasco and Gómez Arias had taken the other thirty men in the caravel and brigantines so as not to have to travel with just the mariners. Then the Captain left the town of Hirrihigua and its fresh gardens which the Castilians as a pastime had planted with lettuce, radishes and other vegetables since they had come prepared with seed against the time that they should make a settlement.

On the second day of their journey, these men arrived at the village of the good Mucozo, who came out in person to receive them. That night he extended them very excellent hospitality and on the following day accompanied them beyond the boundaries of his land. When the time came for leave-taking, he spoke with much tenderness and sentiment.

"My Lords," he said, "until now your presence in that fortress has led me to expect that I might see my lord the Governor once more, and I have enjoyed the thought of serving him as I have always desired to do; but now I lose all hope of ever seeing him or his men again, and without any consolation shall mourn his absence for the remainder of my days. I beg you therefore to tell him what I have said, and that I beseech him to accept my words in the same spirit as I send them."

With these remarks and with many tears by which he revealed his affection for the Spaniards, Mucozo bade them farewell and returned to his house.

Captain Pedro Calderón and his one hundred and twenty companions traveled in daily marches until they came to the big swamp without anything happening to them worthy of remembering unless it is an incident which occurred one night before they arrived there. They had encamped on a plain near a forest, out of which many Indians emerged at all hours to make sudden forays, even entering the encampment and coming to blows. And when the Spaniards retaliated, they fled to the forest, only to return later and molest them once more. On one of these chance occasions, a cavalier charged an Indian who appeared to be more daring than his companions. This man thereupon fled but when he perceived that he was being overtaken, turned to receive his pursuer with an arrow placed in his bow. He was at such close range, however, that at the same time he released his arrow, the Spaniard struck a blow with a lance and killed him. Nevertheless, the Indian did not ill avenge his death, for the arrow caught his assailant's horse in the chest, and in spite of the close range was so forceful that the animal with both front and hind legs outstretched and without another step or move, tumbled over dead at the man's feet. Thus Indian, horse and rider all three fell together, one on top of the other.

This was the famous steed that belonged to Gonzalo Silvestre, but all of its fine qualities failed to achieve the respect of an infidel.

Astonished that an animal so gallant, hardy and spirited as a horse should have been slain so suddenly by a single arrow fired at such close range, the Spaniards, as soon as it was dawn, resolved to see what had been the nature of the shot. On opening the horse, they found that after entering the chest, the arrow had passed through the center of the heart, the stomach and the intestines, and finally had stopped in the bowels.

The natives of the great kingdom of Florida are in general very brave, strong and skillful in shooting arrows, but there is no reason for us to be surprised at their prowess if we will note the practice they have at all ages in this activity. The children for instance, when they are three years of age and even less, in fact as soon as they are able to walk, are moved by their natural inclination and by the sight of what their parents do, to ask for bows and arrows. When denied these things, they themselves make them of little sticks which they can obtain, and with such implements go unendingly in search of the disgusting reptiles which they run upon in their houses. If by chance they happen to see some mouse or little lizard entering its hole, they will wait for it to come out again for three, four and six hours with the greatest imaginable attention and with their arrows set in their bows ready to kill it, never resting until they have fulfilled their purpose. And when they fail to find anything else to shoot at, they go about shooting at the flies that they see on the walls and floors. On account of such continuous exercises and the consequent habit the Indians have formed in shooting arrows, they are skillful and ferocious in the art and thus make very amazing shots as we shall note in the course of our history.

And now since the following case is apropos even though it did occur in Apalache where the Governor at present is, it will be well to mention it here so that when we come again to that province, we will not have failed to tell of the valiant deeds of its inhabitants. Thus it was that in one of the first skirmishes which the Spaniards had with the Indians of Apalache, the Campmaster Luis de Moscoso was struck in the right side by an arrow which penetrated a leather jacket and the hauberk which he wore underneath as well. This particular hauberk was so highly burnished that it had cost him one hundred and fifty ducats in Spain, and it was the type which many rich men wore and highly esteemed. The arrow had continued through a quilted doublet and wounded him, though not fatally since it came at a slant.

The Spaniards were amazed at such an unusual shot, and they wanted now to see just how much protection was actually afforded by these most highly polished coats of mail in which they had put so much confidence. Therefore, on arriving at the village, they placed a basket in the plaza—a kind of receptacle which the Indians make of reed and use for harvesting—and after choosing the most valued hauberk from among those which they carried, they dressed it on the basket, which of itself was very strong because of the way it was woven. Then they loosed from his chains one of the Indians of Apalache, and giving him a bow and arrow, ordered him to shoot at the hauberk, which they had placed at a distance of fifty feet.

Having shaken his arms with his fists clenched in order to awaken strength, the Indian released the arrow, and it penetrated both hauberk and basket so freely and violently that it would have gone on through a man had there been one on the other side. Seeing now that a single hauberk afforded them little or no protection against an arrow, the Spaniards wished to determine what two of them would do. So they commanded that another very valuable hauberk be placed over that which was already on the basket, and giving the Indian a second arrow told him to shoot it as he had done the first in order that they might see if he were man enough to pass the missile through two coats of mail.

Shaking his arms again as if asking for new strength since the opposing defense had been doubled for him, the Indian loosed an arrow which hit the hauberk at the center of the basket and after passing through the four thicknesses of mail, remained crossed therein with an equal portion of the arrow protruding on each side. On seeing that his missile had not come clear on the far side, the Indian manifested great wrath and said to the Spaniards: "Permit me to shoot again, and if I do not pass an arrow through both hauberks as cleanly as I sent it through the one, then hang me immediately; for this second arrow did not come out of the bow for me as well as I wished and consequently failed to clear the hauberks as did the first."

The Spaniards would not grant that request because they did not want to see greater affront done their arms, but thenceforward, they were quite undeceived as to how much protection from the arrows these very esteemed coats of mail could afford them. Thus those who owned them jested about them, calling them Flemish linens; and to use instead, they devised quilted cloaks three or four fingers thick, with long folds that covered the chests and haunches of the horse. These cloaks, which were made of blankets, resisted arrows more effectively than any other of their defensive arms; and even those thick and quilted hauberks which they had held of no value, regardless of what protection they put beneath them, resisted arrows better than the very fine and highly burnished ones. The result was that those arms which had been scorned previously came to be esteemed, whereas those which had been valued were now thrown aside.

Later, in places where they occur, we shall mention other noteworthy shots which were made in this discovery, for there were indeed admirable ones. But in the end when we consider that these Indians are engendered and born among bows and arrows, and are reared and nourished on those things which are killed by these implements, and furthermore are so practiced in the use of them, we have no reason to be so astonished.

CHAPTER XIX

*Pedro Calderón crosses the great swamp and
arrives at the swamp of Apalache.*

TAKING up again the thread of our story, we shall say that
the Indians who had come out of the forest to annoy the
Spaniards in their encampment were satisfied with having slain
Gonzalo Silvestre's horse and lost the man who killed it, a man
who must have been of some importance among them, for when
they saw him dead, they withdrew at once and did not return. On
the day following this incident, the Castilians came to the passage
across the great swamp. Here they spent the night and on the next
day made the crossing without any opposition from the enemy or
indeed any trouble other than that afforded by the swamp itself,
which was great enough. They now continued through the province
of Acuera, making their daily marches as long as possible. To
relieve the infantry of the burden of traveling on foot, the horsemen
dismounted and permitted them to ride a part of the time. This
they did instead of taking them on the haunches of their horses
lest the animals be tired when they had need of them. With such
effort and care they traveled until reaching the village of Ocali
without having received any more opposition from the enemy than
if they had been passing through a deserted land. Here the Indians
had abandoned the village and gone to the woods, so the Spaniards
took what food they needed and moved on to the river which they
crossed in skiffs they themselves had constructed and without there
being a single Indian on either bank to shout at them.

They next entered the town of Ochile and then advanced through
the whole province of Vitachuco until coming to the site where
the death of the proud Vitachuco and his men had occurred. This
incident the Castilians referred to as "the slaughter." The province
of Vitachuco behind them, they proceeded to the river of Osachile
which was crossed in boats and without their seeing a single Indian

who might have said a word to them. From here they went to the town of Osachile, which had been abandoned by its inhabitants just as had been all the others they had left behind them. So, replenishing their supplies, they passed on through the wilderness that lies before the swamp of Apalache and came eventually to the swamp itself, after having traveled almost a hundred and thirty-five leagues with all the peace and quiet in the world; for with the exception of the one night when the Indians killed Gonzalo Silvestre's horse, they gave them no trouble whatsoever on the whole of this long road. We find no reason to offer at present for their peacefulness, nor could one be reached at the time.

The Indians of the province of Apalache, however, were more bellicose than the previous ones, and they sought to make amends for the carelessness and deficiency of the others in the matter of molesting and injuring the Spaniards, as we shall see later. Having come to the dense forest that borders the swamp, our men slept outside in an open part of the plain and then at dawn proceeded through the wood by the narrow path, which, as we have said, was a half-league in length. They entered the water and reached the bridge with the railings, and when they had replaced three or four fallen logs, the footsoldiers crossed this structure while the horsemen swam the deepest part of the channel.

Captain Pedro Calderón, seeing that his men were now beyond the deepest and most dangerous part of the water, and desiring that they advance through the rest of the swamp with greater speed and safety, ordered ten of his cavalry to take five crossbowmen and five shieldbearers up behind them and press forward to seize the narrow path in the forest lying on the opposite shore. In compliance with the Captain's instruction, these men hastened as quickly as possible through the water in order to reach land, but as they did so, many Indians emerged from different parts of the forest, where until that point they were lying in ambush behind the underbrush and large trees. With a great hue and cry, they fell upon the ten horsemen who were carrying the footsoldiers behind them; and discharging many arrows, they succeeded in wounding five horses in addition to killing the mount of Alvaro Fernández, a Portuguese, who was a native of Yelves. For since the attack was so sudden and since they were so heavily loaded in addition to being in water up to their chests, these animals turned and bolted without their masters' being able to check them. Thus the ten footsoldiers were spilled in the water and almost all of them badly wounded; for when the horses swung around, the Indians assailed them from the rear, shooting their arrows at them as they pleased. Then seeing the men fallen in the water, they rushed up with the utmost fury to behead them, meanwhile shouting their triumph to their companions so that they too might hasten forward with great force and spirit to enjoy the victory.

The suddenness with which the Indians attacked, the flight of the horses and consequent dumping of the footsoldiers into the water, and the great number of enemies who rushed up to contend with them, left the Castilians in great confusion, and they even began to fear that they might be conquered and destroyed; for the battle being waged in water, the speed of their horses served them no purpose either in assisting their friends or attacking their enemies. The Indians, on the other hand, had gathered new spirit and boldness when they perceived how well they had succeeded in their initial attack and as a result made an even greater effort to slay the footsoldiers who had fallen into the water. But other Spaniards now rushed forward to aid their comrades, growing more valiant as they found themselves nearer the fray. The first to arrive were Antonio Carrillo, Pedro Morón, Francisco de Villalobos, and Diego de Oliva, who, once they had crossed over the bridge, stationed themselves in front of the Indians and prevented their slaying the footsoldiers.

And now on the left of the Castilians a great band of Indians were hastening forward to enjoy the victory the first group had sung. More than twenty feet in advance of them all came a man wearing a large feather headdress and walking with all the audacity and courage that one can imagine. It was his purpose to seize a large tree which stood between the two adversaries, and from which the Indians, should they gain it, could do much damage to the Spaniards and even prevent their crossing the swamp. Observing this fact, Gonzalo Silvestre, who was nearest the tree, shouted to the aforementioned Antón Galván. Though he had been wounded and was one of those who had fallen from the horses, this cavalier, as a good soldier, had not lost his crossbow; so putting a shaft to his weapon, he now strode along behind Gonzalo Silvestre, who protected him with a half shield that he had found in the water and at the same time persuaded him not to fire upon anyone other than the Indian who walked in front and appeared to be the captain general. And in truth he was, although the Spaniard had said so with some misgivings. Thus these two men came to the tree, and when the advancing Indian saw that they, because of being nearer, had gained it, he fired three arrows in the twinkling of an eye. But Gonzalo Silvestre received these missiles on his shield, which being wet, was able to resist their force.

In order not to waste his shot, Antón Galván had waited for the enemy to come closer, and seeing him now in such a vulnerable position, he fired at him with such accuracy as to strike him in the center of the chest. Since the miserable man wore no more than hides for his protection, the entire shaft passed through his body. The Indian was not felled by the shot, but turning around cried out to his comrades: "These perfidious wretches have slain me." Then his companions seized him in their arms and, passing him from one to the other with a great murmur, bore him away along the same route they had come.

CHAPTER XX

Pedro Calderón continues along the way,
fighting constantly with the enemy.

THE fighting was no less cruel and bloody in other places. On the right flank of the battle, a large band of Indians rushed upon the Christians with great violence and furor. A brave soldier named Andrés de Meneses, who was a native of Almendralejo, went out with ten or twelve other Spaniards to resist this attack, but the Indians charged with such savagery and ferocity that they felled this man to the water with four arrows, which they drove through his thighs and genitals; for on seeing his body protected by a shield, they had aimed at his most vulnerable spot. In the same manner they wounded five of the others who accompanied him.

With such rage and cruelty, the struggle continued wherever the two adversaries were able to come in contact with each other. The Indians had redoubled their efforts and courage in order to finish the battle in triumph, for they were sure of the victory and were vain because of the accurate shots they had placed. The Spaniards, on the other hand, were being forced to defend their lives with their good courage, and indeed they fought now for no other reason. Meanwhile they were getting the worst of the battle, for since it was taking place in the water, the horsemen could be of no benefit to their friends or damage to their enemies, and as a result the Spanish defense consisted of no more than the fifty footsoldiers. But at this point the sad news that their captain general had been mortally wounded spread among all the Indians, and the fire and rage with which they had fought until that moment abated somewhat. Hence little by little they began to retire, never ceasing, however, to discharge arrows at their foes.

Reorganizing themselves and maintaining the best order possible, the Castilians now pursued the Indians until they had driven them completely out of the water and the swamp into the path which penetrated the dense forest lying on the opposite bank. Thus they gained from them the site that we have said the Spaniards had cleared for their encampment when the Governor passed that way with his army. This site the Indians had fortified and used for their own camp, but they had abandoned it to rush to the aid of their captain general. So the Spaniards remained here for the night, for this was a strong, enclosed square where their enemies could do them no harm except by the path, and since they guarded this path, they were secure. They treated their wounded as best they could, almost all of them being badly injured; and they kept watch throughout the night because the Indians with their shouts and alarms did not permit them to rest.

Our Lord saved these men with the accurate shot Antón Galván chanced to place that day, for indeed had his marksmanship not been such, and had the victim not been the captain general, it is feared that the Indians, who were powerful and triumphant and very numerous, would have made a great ravage upon our men or destroyed them all, since they were few and most of them mounted. For the fight being in the water, they were neither masters of themselves nor of their horses, either in an offense or defense. And because of the fact that the footsoldiers were fighting alone, all of them came very near to being lost. So it was that many times afterward when speaking before the Governor of that day, these men invariably gave to Antón Galván the honor of being the person who prevented the Indians from conquering and killing them all.

As soon as day broke, the Castilians followed the narrow path through the dense wood, pushing the enemy back until they had driven them into a lighter and more open forest two leagues across. Here on both sides were great barricades which either had been constructed by these particular Indians or were the same ones that had been made when Governor Hernando de Soto passed that way. From these protections the enemy now emerged to shoot innumerable arrows, meanwhile observing system and accord in order not to attack from both sides at the same time and thereby wound each other with their own weapons. Under such conditions, the Castilians covered the two leagues of forest, but the Indians wounded more than twenty of them, and they were unable to inflict any damage in return since they could do no more than protect themselves against the arrows. Nevertheless, when they had passed through this wood, they came onto an open plain, where their enemies, out of fear of the horses, dared not attack or even await them. Thus they were permitted to travel with less affliction.

When they had advanced five leagues, the Christians halted to camp on the plain, for the wounded of that and the previous day were fatigued by the continuous fighting they had endured. As soon as night fell, a large number of Indians came and attacked on all sides with a great clamor and outcry. The men on horseback went out to resist them, observing no order, however, but each rushing to where he heard the nearest foes. Seeing the horses, the Indians kept at a distance, but they continued to discharge arrows, with one of which they severely wounded the mount of Luis de Moscoso. Then throughout the night they never ceased to shout at the Christians, saying, "Whither are you wretches going now that your Captain and all of his soldiers are dead? We have quartered them and put them on the trees, and we will do the same with you before you arrive there. What do you wish? Why do you come to this land? Do you think that we who inhabit it are so vile as to abandon it and become your vassals and serfs and slaves? Let it be understood that we are men who will kill all of you as well as those of your people who remain in Castile."

These and similar persuasions the Indians uttered as they continued to fire their arrows until dawn.

CHAPTER XXI

By persisting in the struggle, Pedro Calderón comes to where the Governor is.

WITH the arrival of day our men resumed their journey, coming eventually to a ravine which was deep and very difficult to pass, and which the Indians had blocked with enclosures and strong walls placed at intervals. After investigating the crossing to see what had been done to it and taking advantage of the experience of those who had passed there at another time, the Spaniards commanded the men on horseback to dismount, since they were better armed. Taking shields, swords and axes, thirty of these men formed a vanguard to gain and break down the ramparts and defenses; and twenty of them formed a rearguard so that the enemy would find opposition in the event that they should attack from behind. Meanwhile the most poorly armed mounted the horses (since they were of no benefit at this point) and followed along in the center with the clothing and the servants. In this order all entered the wood which lay in front of the ravine.

When the Indians saw the Castilians in a place where horses, which they had feared above everything else, were of no avail, they charged with the greatest violence, ferocity and clamor to shoot them with arrows, for they intended to kill all of them now that they were few in number and the passage was difficult. Meanwhile, the Christians made an effort to defend themselves since the narrowness of the place prevented their taking the offensive. In this manner they came to the enclosures where a most disputed and persistent fight ensued, for one group was trying to clear a way through which to pass while the other sought to prevent their doing so, and as a result each wounded the other cruelly. At length by some of the Spaniards resisting with swords and others applying axes to the ropes and *bejucos*[8] (which are like long vines and are used by the Indians to tie whatever they wish), they won the first and second enclosures and eventually all the rest. Nevertheless, their success cost them very severe wounds, which most of them suffered, and also a horse which received an arrow through the chest. The animal belonged to Alvaro Fernández, a Portuguese who was a native of Yelves. Thus this hidalgo lost two good horses, one in the ravine and one in the swamp just passed.

Amid these evils and harms, the Spaniards crossed that difficult passage and then traveled with less affliction through the plain where there was no undergrowth, for wherever the ground was free of entanglement, the Indians, out of fear of the horses, left the Christians alone. But wherever there were thick growths of trees near the road, there were always Indians in ambush who came out

---

[8] *bejucos*—flexible twigs or branches.

suddenly upon our men to attack them with arrows, while shouting repeatedly: "Since we have already slain your captain and all of his soldiers, where are you thieves going now?" And they persisted so much in these taunts that the Castilians were ready to believe them, for even though sufficiently near the town of Apalache for the cry that they raised to be heard in that place, no one had come out to help them, and they had not seen any people or horses or any signs which might lead them to believe that their companions were there. Skirmishing in this manner throughout the whole day, these one hundred and twenty Spaniards traveled on to Apalache, which they reached at sunset, for even though this day's march had not been so long as previous ones, they had moved slowly because of their many wounded. Later ten or twelve of these men died, and among them was that valiant soldier, Andrés de Meneses.

Arrived in the greatly desired presence of their Captain General and beloved companions, these Spaniards were received with such pleasure and joy as one may imagine, for they had been given up as dead. The Indians, in order to inflict pain and sorrow upon the Governor and his men, had told them many times that they had destroyed their comrades along the road, and this assertion was credible because the Governor himself had encountered grave dangers and necessities while passing through those same provinces and difficult crossings with his more than eight hundred men of war. Hence it was easy to believe that since there were only a hundred and twenty of those who now came, they might very well have been lost. For this reason they were received and feted by their companions both individually and collectively just as if they had been returned to life, and all gave thanks to God for having delivered them from so many dangers.

The Governor welcomed his captain and soldiers as would a loving father, joyfully embracing and questioning each of them individually as to how he felt and how he had withstood the journey. Those who were wounded, he ordered to be made much of and their injuries treated with great care. In sum, he praised these men lavishly, and made evident his gratitude for the hardships and dangers each and every one of them had suffered both in going and coming. For when the occasion was offered, this noble and good Captain could behave with much virtue, discretion and prudence.

CHAPTER XXII

Juan de Añasco arrives at Apalache. The provisions the Governor made for finding a port along the coast.

YOU must know that when Captain Pedro Calderón reached the village of Apalache, the Comptroller Juan de Añasco, who had gone out from the Bay of the Holy Spirit with the two brigantines to look for the Bay of Aute, had just six days previously arrived at his destination without having experienced anything at sea worthy of remembering. He had disembarked in Aute without opposition since the Governor had more or less computed the time required for the trip, and twelve days before he was due, had dispatched one company of horsemen and another of footsoldiers to make safe for him both the port and the road to the camp. These troops were replaced every four days so that when some were arriving others were returning. And while at the port they attached flags to the highest trees where they could be observed from the ocean. Juan de Añasco saw these flags and came with two companies of men to the camp, leaving a good defense, however, on the brigantines which lay at anchor in the bay.

Now when the two captains, Juan de Añasco and Pedro Calderón, found themselves united once again in the company of the Governor and his other captains and soldiers, they rejoiced and were exceedingly pleased, for the companionship of friends offers a solace and relaxation in time of anxiety; and they felt that being together now in their tasks, they would accomplish them with ease no matter how great they might be. With this mutual happiness, the Spaniards passed the winter in the village and province of Apalache where there were some incidents which it will be well to relate without observing any order or time sequence other than to say that they occurred in this encampment.

The Governor was never idle but was always scheming within his own mind concerning those things which appeared to him to be most appropriate for the discovery, conquest and later settlement of the land. Thus it was that a few days after what has been told, he commanded the cavalier Diego Maldonado (a native of Salamanca in whom he had the utmost confidence, and who as a captain of the infantry had served to the great satisfaction of the whole army in everything that had offered itself up to that time) first to turn his company over to his great friend and comrade, Juan de Guzmán (a cavalier who was a native of Talavera de la Reyna), and then to go to the Bay of Aute, where he was to take the two brigantines left by the Comptroller Juan de Añasco and coast along the shore toward the west for a distance of a hundred leagues. Meanwhile he was to examine with the utmost diligence and care all of the ports, coves, gulfs, bays, creeks and rivers that he found so that he could bring back a satisfactory account of the shoals and everything else that might lie along that coast. It was well to have knowledge of all such things, the Governor said, because of what would be offered them further on; and he set a time limit of two months for this cavalier to go and return.

Captain Diego Maldonado proceeded first to the Bay of Aute from whence he set sail to carry out his mission. Then after following the coast for two months, he returned with a long account of what he had discovered. Among other things, he said that about sixty leagues from the Bay of Aute, he found a magnificent harbor called Achusi,[9] which was sheltered from all winds, was capable

[9] Achusi is known to have been either Pensacola Bay or Mobile Bay, but the Achusi of De Soto, judging by its distance from the Apalachee port and Garcilaso's description, was probably Pensacola.

of receiving many ships, and had such good depth even up to its shores that he was able to bring his ship close to land and disembark without casting open the hatch.[10]

The Captain brought with him from this voyage two Indians who were natives of that same port and province of Achusi. One of them was a lord of vassals whom he had seized with a trickery and astuteness unworthy of cavaliers. For when he had arrived at the port of Achusi, the Indians had received him peacefully and invited him with many endearing words to disembark and partake of whatever he needed as if he were in his own land. But Diego Maldonado dared not accept their invitation because he had no faith in unknown friends. Perceiving his distrust, the Indians gave themselves over to treating freely with all the Castilians in order to allay completely their fears and suspicions. Thus they went in groups of three and four to the brigantines to visit Diego Maldonado and his companions, carrying to them whatever they requested. And now because of the affability of these people, the Spaniards ventured out in their little boats to sound and examine the bay and all that there was in the port; and when they had seen it and laid in the supplies they needed for navigation, they raised their sails and came away, bringing with them the two aforementioned Indians who happened to be the Curaca and one of his kinsmen. For confident in the good friendship that had been formed between the infidels and the faithful (although to the Indians the Castilians were not that), and moved by the account of the brigantines brought them by other Indians as well as by a desire to see new things, they had dared enter the ships and visit the Captain and his soldiers, who, on learning that one of them was a cacique, had joyfully carried him away.

[10] *sin echar compuerta*—The word *compuerta* can mean a hatch or portcullis. Here the Inca no doubt refers to an opening in the side of the ship used for disembarkation.

CHAPTER XXIII

The Governor sends an account of his discovery
to Havana. The temerity of an Indian
is described.

THE Castilians were exuberant over the account that Diego
Maldonado brought of the whole coast and of the fine port
he had discovered at Achusi. It seemed to them that, according to
the plans the General had made, the first and second stages of their
discovery and conquest were progressing well so far as concerned
their intention of populating and establishing a settlement in that
kingdom. For the main thing that the Governor and his men had
desired in order to colonize had been to locate a port such as had
now been found where they might anchor the ships that were to
bring people, horses, cattle, seed, and other things requisite for new
settlements.

A few days after the arrival of Captain Diego Maldonado, the
Governor ordered him to sail for Havana with the two brigantines
under his command, and once there to visit Doña Isabel de Bobadilla
for the purpose of providing her with information of what until
that time the army had seen and done on both land and sea. And
he ordered likewise that the same information be sent to all other
cities and towns on the island. Then during the coming October
(for this was the close of February of the year 1540), this captain
was to return to the port of Achusi with the two brigantines, the
caravel which Gómez Arias had carried away, and some other ship,
or ships, if such could be purchased. And in these vessels he was
to bring whatever was available of crossbows, arquebuses, lead and
powder; quantities of sandals and all kinds of articles to cover the
legs and feet; and other supplies needed by the army. A written
memorandum of these things was presented him with instructions
as to what he must do; and by the time he returned, the Governor
was expecting to be at the port of Achusi, after having made a

great swerve inland and explored the provinces in that place which might provide a start for a settlement, it being expedient, however, to occupy the port first, since it was so necessary for matters concerning both land and sea. The Captain was commanded also to tell Gómez Arias to come with him at the appointed time, for because of the great wisdom of the latter in matters of administration as well as his fine industry and extensive experience in warfare, it suited the Governor to have him in his company.

With this order and commission, Captain Diego Maldonado sailed out of the Bay of Aute for Havana. Because of the good news he bore concerning the prosperity and success the Governor and his army had enjoyed until then and as a result expected to enjoy in the future, this captain was welcomed by Doña Isabel de Bobadilla and all the citizens of Havana. The same news was relayed to the rest of the cities of the island, all of which celebrated their Governor's prosperity with exuberance. And great preparations were made to provide him, at the time specified, assistance in the form of men, horses, arms, and other materials necessary for colonization. Each of these things the cities collectively and the men of wealth individually assembled, all exerting themselves proportionately to send or carry the most and best that they could in order to demonstrate their affection for their Governor and Captain General, and to obtain the rewards which they expected. But we shall leave them in these preparations so as to return to an account of some of the particular incidents that occurred in the province of Apalache. By these incidents, one may perceive the savagery and at the same time the audacity of the Indians of that province, for certainly their actions proved that they knew to dare and not to fear. This fact we will reveal in the following case as well as in others to be told, but we shall excuse ourselves from relating most of the things that came to pass lest we become verbose.

It happened that one day in the month of February, 1540, the Comptroller Juan de Añasco and six other cavaliers were riding in a group through Apalache. When they had passed along all the streets of this town, they resolved to go out into the surrounding countryside, but for a short distance only because of the Indians who hid behind each bush and made the place unsafe. And since they were not going far from the town, they felt that they could travel without weapons, or at least without defensive weapons; therefore each, with the exception of a native of Yelves called Estévan Pegado, sallied forth with no more than his sword. This cavalier, however, happened to be armed, for he wore a helmet and carried a lance. Traveling in a group, they beheld two Indians, a man and a woman, who were going about gathering kidney beans that had been sown the previous year in the cleared part of the forest lying near the town. They no doubt were doing so, not because of any necessity they might have had for the beans, since, as we have said, the country was replete with all food supplies, but because of a desire to amuse themselves while waiting to ascertain if some Castilian would venture from the town. On seeing these people, the Spaniards rushed forward to capture them, and the woman, perceiving the horses, stopped short and was unable to run; but seizing her in his arms, her husband carried her quickly toward the nearby trees. Then when he had attained the first bushes, he gave the woman two or three heavy blows and told her to go on into the forest. This done, he could have escaped with her, but he had no desire to do so. Instead he rushed back to where he had left his bow and arrows, and having collected them, went out to receive the Castilians with as much determination and good daring as if they like himself were just another single Indian. And his behavior was such that the Spaniards were forced to agree that they should take him alive, for it seemed to them a despicable thing that seven Spaniards on horseback should slay one single Indian on foot. Moreover they felt that an infidel who manifested such gallant spirit was undeserving of death and instead should be shown all mercy and honor. Unanimous in this conclusion, they approached the Indian, who because of the shortness of the interval, had not been able to fire a single arrow; and then they trampled him in an effort to overcome him before he could regain his feet. First one and then another assailed him, always just as he was going to rise, and each shouted at him to surrender.

But the more he was pressed, the more ferocious the Indian proved to be. Fallen thus as he was, he sometimes placed an arrow in his bow and fired it to the extent that it was possible to do so and at other times pricked the bellies and thighs of the horses. In this way he injured all seven of them, but with slight wounds since he was denied sufficient space to enable him to inflict more severe ones. Escaping eventually from beneath the feet of the horses, he stood up and, seizing his bow in his hands, dealt Estévan Pegado (the man who had harrassed him the most with the blows of his lance) such a fierce blow on the forehead as to half-stupify him and cause the blood to burst out over his brow and run down his face. This Portuguese Spaniard, on finding himself thus injured and abused, cried out in his anger: "Such things considered, is it wise for us to wait until this lone Indian kills all seven of us?" With that he thrust his lance completely through the man's chest and knocked him down dead. Afterward the Spaniards examined their horses and found them all wounded, though superficially. Then they returned to the camp, astounded at the temerity and strength of the barbarian and ashamed to admit that a single Indian had stopped seven cavaliers in such a manner.

CHAPTER XXIV

Two Indians offer to guide the Spaniards to a
place where they may find much
gold and silver.

DURING the whole time that Governor Hernando de Soto was wintering in the camp and the town of Apalache, he was always careful to inquire as to what lands and provinces lay to the west of him in that part of the kingdom which he had planned to explore the coming summer. Keeping this intention ever before him, he went about at all times obtaining information both from the Indians who had been servants in the army from days past and from those who had been captured only recently, insisting that they tell him what they knew of that land and its divisions. And while he and all his captains and soldiers were being so solicitous and assiduous, it chanced that those of them who were reconnoitering the country took among other captives a youth of sixteen or seventeen years of age who was already known to some of the domestics who ministered unto the Spaniards and loved their masters. By means of those whom they served, these slaves informed the Governor that this youth had been brought up by Indian traders who in buying and selling their wares were accustomed to travel many leagues inland, and that in consequence he had seen and learned what the Governor was trying so hard to ascertain. (Let it be understood that these merchants did not seek gold or silver but merely traded certain articles for others that the Indians exchange, for to them money was of no value.) Being thus advised, the Governor asked the youth what he knew, and the latter replied that it was true that he did have knowledge of provinces he had visited with the merchants he served, and that he would venture to guide the Spaniards on a twelve- or thirteen-day journey along the road through the part of the country he had seen. The Governor then turned this Indian over to a Spaniard with instructions to guard him with special caution lest he escape, but the boy himself dispelled their anxiety, for in a brief time he made himself so much a friend and familiar of his captors that he appeared to have been born and reared among them.

A few days after the seizure of this Indian, the Spaniards took another of about the same age or a little older, and the first captive, being acquainted with the second, said to the Governor: "My Lord, this boy has seen the same lands and provinces that I have, as well as others which lie farther on, for he has traveled with merchants who are wealthier than my masters."

The more recently captured Indian confirmed what the first boy had said, and he likewise offered willingly to lead the Spaniards through the provinces where he and his masters had gone, provinces which he assured them were many and great. Then they asked what he had seen in those lands, and if gold or silver or precious stones were to be found there, this being the information they desired most; and they showed him gold jewelry and pieces of silver and fine stones from the rings of some of the captains and more illustrious soldiers so that he might have a better understanding of what they had inquired of him. The boy replied that in the last province he had visited, a place called Cofachiqui,[11] there was much metal like the yellow and the white, and that the principal business of the merchants whom he served was that of buying and selling such metals in other lands. Moreover, he said, great quantities of pearls were to be found there; and for the purpose of making himself clear, he pointed to a pearl he had observed in one of the rings shown him. Our Spaniards were exuberant over this news and yearned to see themselves at once in Cofachiqui that they might possess this wealth of gold and silver and precious pearls.

But let us return to the individual incidents which occurred among the Indians and Spaniards in Apalache. Thus it was that the month of March having already begun, it happened that twenty horsemen and fifty footsoldiers went out from the camp to bring corn from the principal village of another district one league distant. In all the little villages throughout that region there was an abundance of corn, in fact such an abundance that during the entire time that the Spaniards were in Apalache, they never went so far as a league and a half from the principal town for the purpose of providing themselves with the corn and other grains and vegetables that they ate. Now when these men had gathered the food they were to carry back, they concealed themselves in the same town with the intention of capturing Indians in the event that some came there. A guard

[11] Biedma gives this name as Cofitachique; Elvas, as Cutifachiqui; and Ranjel, as Cofitachequi. These names are more commonly known today than the one used by the Inca.

was stationed in the highest part of a house which was very different from all the others and appeared to be a temple, and when a considerable time had elapsed, this guard gave notice that an Indian was looking about to see if there were something in the main plaza.

The Governor's nephew, a cavalier named Diego de Soto, one of the best soldiers in the army and a magnificent horseman, galloped out to seize the Indian, more through a desire to display his skill and valor than through any need that he might have for him. On beholding the horse, the Indian raced against it with great speed to determine if he could escape in flight, for the natives of this vast kingdom of Florida are swift runners and pride themselves on their skill. But when he perceived the animal gaining ground, he stationed himself under a nearby tree, this being the type of shelter that pedestrians for lack of pikes are always accustomed to take as a protection against horses; and putting an arrow to his bow (for, as we have said on other occasions, the Indians carry their arms with them continuously), he waited for the Spaniards to come within range. Diego de Soto, not being able to ride beneath the tree, passed to one side of it and made a thrust with his lance over his left arm to see if he could reach the man in this way. Guarding himself from the blow, the Indian shot an arrow at the horse as it came abreast and succeeded in hitting the animal between the cinch and the knee with so much force and skill that it stumbled forward fifteen or twenty feet and fell dead without moving a foot. At this point there hastened up at half-speed a cavalier named Diego Velásquez, who was an equerry of the Governor and no less valiant and skillful in horsemanship than the other Spaniard. He had followed Diego de Soto so as to give him assistance if such were necessary. Seeing the shot that the Indian had made, he quickened the speed of his horse; but being unable to pass beneath the tree, he too rode to one side of it while striking a lance blow similar to that of his companion. But the Indian now enjoyed the same fortune as before, for when this horse came abreast of him, he loosed a second arrow which pierced the animal's knee, and as in the first instance caused it to tumble over and over until falling dead at the feet of its mate. Both Spaniards now arose as quickly as possible and with lance in hand made at the Indian to avenge the death of their horses; but he being content with the two feats accomplished so luckily and quickly, fled to the wood while jeering at them and turning his face to make grimaces and gestures. And keeping their pace, since he did not wish to run as fast as he could, he shouted: "Let us all fight on foot and then we shall see which of us are the best men."

With these and other words which he spoke in vituperation, he put himself in safety, leaving the two Spaniards very much pained over such a great loss as that of their horses. For perceiving the advantage that the Spaniards had over them when mounted, these Indians tried first to destroy the horses, and they were more pleased with killing one of these animals than they were with killing four Christians. Thus it was that they took the utmost care and diligence to shoot at the horse instead of the rider.

CHAPTER XXV

Some dangerous fighting which occurred in Apalache. The fertility of that province.

A FEW days after the unfortunate experience of Diego de Soto and Diego Velásquez, another incident occurred which was equally adverse. It happened that two Portuguese, Simón Rodríguez, a native of the town of Maruán, and Roque de Yelves, a native of Yelves, rode out on their horses to gather fresh fruit from the forest lying near the village. Although these men were able to pick fruit from the lower branches while mounted, nothing would do but that they dismount and climb the tree in order to obtain that on the top branches, for they felt that it was the best. Now the Indians never lost any occasion to kill or wound Castilians, and when they observed these two Portuguese Spaniards aloft in the trees, they came out to where they were. Roque de Yelves sighted them before his companion, and after giving an alarm, threw himself from the tree and ran to mount his horse. But one of the Indians pursued him and shot a flint-headed arrow into his back, a quarter of it passing on through his chest. The blow knocked him to the ground and he was unable to rise. Simón Rodríguez they did not even permit to descend, but shooting at him where he was as if he were some wild beast that had climbed there, they brought him down dead with three arrows piercing him from side to side. Hardly had he fallen when they cut off his head, or rather I should say all the scalp in a circle,[12] and carried it away as a testimony of what they had done. (It is not known by what skill the Indians remove the scalp so easily from a person.) Roque de Yelves they left prostrate and did not take his scalp, for a relief of mounted Spaniards who had not been far away was now coming too close to permit them to do so. Nevertheless, after giving his companions a brief account of what had occurred, this cavalier presently called for confession and expired.

The two horses belonging to the Portuguese, at the noise and sudden attack of the Indians, fled toward the camp; but the Spaniards who had come out to assist, succeeded in recovering them both. Finding that one had a drop of blood on its thigh, they carried it to a veterinary surgeon for treatment, but when the surgeon perceived that the wound was no greater than that of a lancet, he said that there was nothing to treat. On the following day, however,

[12] *todo el casco en redondo*—literally, "all the skull in a circle." There is no word in Spanish similar to our transitive verb "to scalp," and even in present-day Spanish it is necssary to have some such circumlocution as *"quitar el pericráneo con la cabellera como hacen los indios."* Since history has taught us that it was the scalp which the Indians took, and since the Inca himself tells us that these prizes were used to decorate the arms of their bows (see below, note 13), we are convinced that he means scalp when he says *casco* and are translating it accordingly. R. B. Cunninghame-Graham (*op. cit.*, p. 120) has suggested that the scalping of Simón Rodríquez was the first case of scalping witnessed by white men in America.

the horse was dead. Suspecting that the wound had been inflicted by an arrow, the Castilians opened it, and after following signs through the length of the animal's body, did find a shaft which had passed through the thigh, bowels and intestines and lodged in the chest cavity, lacking less than four fingers of flesh of having come out through the breastplate. They were amazed, for in their opinion the ball of an arquebus could not have penetrated so far.

Although of small consequence, these specific incidents have been disclosed here because they occurred in this encampment and because of the remarkable ferocity they reveal. And now since it is appropriate that we bring to a conclusion those things which happened in the principal village of Apalache, we shall say in summary (since it would be very wordy to tell everything) that during the entire time that the Spaniards were wintering in this land, its inhabitants were very bellicose and solicitous; and they had the caution and diligence to attack the Castilians without ever losing an opportunity (regardless of how insignificant it might be) of wounding or killing those who strayed from the camp, even though it were for a very short distance.

Alonso de Carmona, in his *Peregrinación,* makes particular mention of the ferocity of the Indians of the province of Apalache, saying the following, which is taken to the letter:

"These Indians of Apalache are gigantic in stature and are very valiant and spirited. For just as in the past they came and fought with Pámphilo de Narváez' men and forced them to leave the land (as much as those Spaniards hated to do so), they now engaged us in daily skirmishes. But since our Governor was very valiant, strong, and experienced in fighting Indians, they could gain nothing from us, so they agreed to prowl around the woods in groups. Then when our men went into the forest to cut firewood, these Indians rushed up at the sound of the ax and slew them. They removed the chains from the Indians who had been brought along to carry the wood on their backs, and they took the crown of each Spaniard (this being the thing they most prized), to decorate the arm of the bow with which they fought.[13] At the hue and cry which they raised, we ran forward only to find the evil collection already made. This sort of thing occurred many times, and in this way more than twenty of our soldiers were slain. I remember that one day seven horsemen left the camp to *ranchear* (that is, to look for food) and to kill some little dog, for in that land all of us were accustomed to eating these animals and held the day fortunate when a portion of one fell to our lot. Not even pheasants tasted better to us. As they went about looking for such things, these men ran upon five Indians who awaited them with bows and arrows, and who after drawing a mark upon the ground, threatened to kill those who should cross it. Not relishing mockery, our Spaniards closed with their challengers, who thereupon took their bows from their arms and killed two horses, wounded two more and severely injured one man. One of the Indians was slain, but the others escaped on foot, for these people are truly very swift and are not hampered by clothes. In fact their going naked is a great help to them."

Here end the words of Alonso de Carmona.

Besides keeping a vigilance against those who wandered, the Indians watched the whole army, upsetting it with the alarms and sudden attacks which they made day and night. They would not offer to fight in squadrons but attacked from ambushes. Concealing themselves in the underbrush and little thickets, regardless of how small, and in places where it was least thought they might be, they would come out like footpads to do what damage they could.

But enough has been told of the valor and ferocity of the natives of the province of Apalache. Now as to its fruitfulness. As we have already said, it is very fertile. It is abundant in maize or corn, many species of beans and squash (which in the Peruvian language is called *zapallu*), and other varieties of vegetables; fruits common to Spain, such as various kinds of cherries; and three types

[13] *y quitavan al Español la corona, que era lo que ellos más preciavan, para traerla al brazo del arco con que peleavan*—It is our opinion that the Inca has used the word *corona* here to mean scalp. See above, note 12.

of nuts, one of which is all oil. Moreover, both the oak and liveoak produce such a great quantity of acorns that they fall on the ground and remain at the base of the trees from one year to the next; for since the Indians have no livestock to consume these acorns, they have no need for them and thus leave them to spoil.

In order that one may judge of the productivity and fruitfulness of the province of Apalache, we will say in conclusion that, during the more than five months they were wintering in this encampment, the whole Spanish army and their Indian servants, in all about fifteen hundred men and more than three hundred horses, fed upon the food which they gathered when they first arrived there; and when they needed more, they found it in the neighboring hamlets in such quantity that they never went so far as a league and a half from the principal village to obtain it.

In addition to this fruitfulness of the harvest, the land is very suitable for raising all kinds of livestock. It contains good forests, pasture lands with fine streams, and swamps and lagoons with quantities of rushes for cattle, which thrive on such things and need no grain when eating them. And now to conclude our account of what there is to be found in this province, it suffices to say that one of its fine qualities is its ability to produce much silk because of the great number of mulberry trees. And furthermore it is possessed of many excellent fish.

End of the Second Book

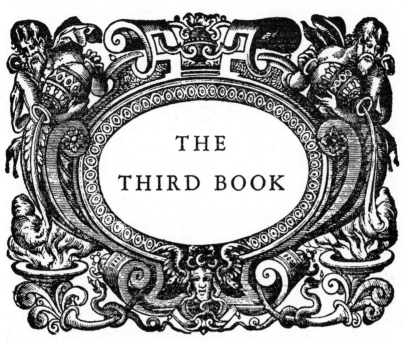

THE
THIRD BOOK

Of the History of Florida by the Inca tells of the departure of the Spaniards from Apalache; the fine reception offered them in four provinces; the hunger they suffered in some of the uninhabited lands; the infinity of pearls and other grandeurs and riches which they found in a temple; the generosities of the Lady of Cofachiqui and of other caciques, lords of vassals; a very bloody battle which the Indians under the guise of friendship perpetrated upon the Spaniards; a mutiny which certain Castilians discussed; the laws of the Indians against adulteresses; and another very fierce battle which was waged at night. It contains thirty-nine chapters.

CHAPTER I

*The Governor leaves Apalache. There is a bat-
tle of seven against seven.[1]*

AVING dispatched Captain Diego Maldonado to
Havana for reasons explained above, and having
commanded that food supplies and other necessities be made ready for leaving Apalache now
that it was time to go, the Governor and Adelantado Hernando de Soto led his army out of the encampment during
the closing days of March in the year fifteen hundred and forty. He
traveled three days toward the north in that same province without
encountering any enemies; had he done so, he might have been
molested because the Indians of that land were both hostile and
warlike. On the third day, his Castilians pitched camp in a small
town that formed a peninsula, it being almost completely surrounded by a swamp of more than a hundred feet in breadth and
with so much mud that it came up to the middle of the thighs. Over
this swamp, wooden bridges had been placed at intervals to afford
exits in all directions. The town itself was situated on an eminence
from which could be seen a great expanse of land as well as the
many other small villages sprinkled throughout that beautiful
valley.

Here in this town, the foremost of that valley and of all the
province of Apalache, the army made a halt for three days. Now it

[1] *y dá una Batalla de siete a siete*—In the table of contents the Inca gives
this as *y una Batalla que huvo de siete a siete.*

happened that at noon of the second day there went out from the camp five halberdiers of the Governor's guard and two other soldiers, both natives of Badajoz. The names of these two men were Francisco de Aguilar[2] and Andrés Moreno; but the latter bore the nickname of Angel Moreno, for being happy and always jovial, he without any reason whatsoever mixed the word "angels" into everything he said. These seven men had not been ordered by the ministers of the army to leave the principal village but had set out for the sole purpose of seeking recreation and seeing what the other little villages afforded. The five guards wore their halberds, Andrés Moreno carried his sword girded to his side and his lance in his hand, and Francisco de Aguilar had both a sword and a shield. Armed in this manner, all seven came out of the town, unmindful of the great vigilance and pains the Indians of that province always took to kill those who strayed.

Crossing the swamp and a strip of forest less than twenty feet wide, they came to some clear land where there were many fields of corn. But hardly had they separated themselves two hundred feet from the camp when they were attacked by the Indians, who, as we have seen, did not sleep while lying in wait for those who might stray. At the shouts raised by both groups as they struggled, the clashing of arms and the cries for help, many Spaniards rushed forth from the village to defend their companions; and lest they lose time searching for a passage to the swamp, they crossed it at the nearest point, only to discover themselves in water and mud up to their waists and chests. And then for all their haste, they found the five halberdiers dead, each with ten or twelve arrows transfixed in his body. Andrés Moreno, however, was alive; but in addition to other arrows which he had received, one with a flint harpoon had gone from his chest through his back, and he died just as soon as it was removed to give him treatment. Francisco de Aguilar, who was stronger and more robust than the others and as a result had defended himself more effectively, was also alive, although he came

---

[2] Here and in some other places the Inca spells this name Aguilera. We adhere to the spelling he most frequently used.

out with two arrows penetrating both thighs, and many blows which the Indians had rained upon his head and indeed his entire body with their bows. For he had succeeded in closing with them after they had spent their arrows; and they on seeing him alone had held their bows in both hands and beaten him so strenuously that they had broken his shield into pieces and left him clasping no more than its handles. Then they had struck him across the forehead with a slanting blow that tore off all the flesh down to the eyebrows and laid bare his skull.

Leaving the seven Spaniards in this condition, the Indians had fled to a place of safety before the arrival of assistance, for they had heard people approaching. The Christians consequently were unable to determine how numerous the enemy had been, but Francisco de Aguilar asserted that there were more than fifty of them, and that the reason for their killing his companions in such a brief time was that there had been so many of them fighting against so few. Nevertheless he afterward revealed from day to day things about the skirmish which threw a favorable light on the Indians. Thus more than twenty days later when his wounds had healed, although he was still emaciated and convalescent, the other soldiers jested with him concerning the beating the Indians had given him, inquiring if he had counted the blows, if they had been very painful, and if he intended to avenge his injuries and challenge his enemies to meet him singly so as to avoid their having the advantage of being many against one. Moreover they asked other similar and amusing questions such as soldiers customarily put to each other in their banter, and he in reply had the following to say:

"I took no count of the blows because the Indians did not inflict them slowly enough for me to do so. As to whether they pained me much or little, you yourselves will know when they bestow similar blows upon you, for I promise that the day will come for you to receive them. But now to speak truthfully and to make you realize just who the Indians of this province are, I want to tell you, with all joking aside and without adding or detracting anything to or from the dead (even though what I say may be against me), of the courtesy and valor which the Indians displayed with us on that day.

"I would have you know that, as I have said, more than fifty Indians came to take a look at us, but when they perceived that we were no more than seven and had no horses for our defense, seven of their number stepped out from the squadron which they had formed, while the others retired to a distance and refused to fight. These seven and no more attacked us. Then since we carried neither crossbows nor arquebuses with which to frighten them, and since they were lighter and swifter than we, they jumped about in front of us and derided us, while shooting arrows at us whenever they pleased, just as if we were wild beasts that had been tied and would not be able to harm them in return. In this manner they killed my companions, and then on seeing me alone, all seven closed with me, and with their bows in both hands put me, lest I glorify myself, in the condition you found me. And now since they spared my life, I pardon them the blows, and I do not plan to challenge them because they might ask what such a challenge were worth, since they would merely leave me in the same condition that they left me before. For the sake of my honor I have kept quiet about everything, and only now have I told it. But this is how it really happened, and I pray that God may keep you from straying lest a similar misfortune befall you."

The companions and friends of Francisco de Aguilar were amazed at what they heard, for they had never dreamed that the Indians were inclined to be so chivalrous as to want to fight singly with the Castilians when they could attack at an advantage. But all of the Indians of this kingdom do presume so much upon their courage, strength and speed that they refuse to recognize any superiority in the Spaniards when they do not see their horses. On the contrary, they assume that they themselves have the advantage, especially if the Christians happen to be as lacking as they in defensive arms.

CHAPTER II

The Spaniards arrive in Altapaha.[3] *The manner
in which they were received.*

WITH the misfortune and loss of the six Spaniards, the Governor left this peninsular town of the province of Apalache, and when he and his army had journeyed two more days, making five in all that were spent in their effort to quit this province, they came to the boundary of another called Altapaha. Now the Adelantado resolved to be the first to examine this new land because he wished to ascertain if its inhabitants were as cruel and warlike as those of Apalache, and again because it was a carefully guarded custom of his to go in person when there was a new exploration to be made, for he was never satisfied with the accounts of others and had to see things with his own eyes. So for the purpose he selected forty horsemen and sixty footsoldiers. Twenty of the latter bore shields; twenty, arquebuses; and twenty, crossbows; for always, regardless of their mission, the footsoldiers were armed in this manner.

Traveling with these men for two days, the Governor came at dawn of the third day to the first town of the province of Altapaha. Here he found that the Indians had withdrawn to the forest with their wives, children and possessions. But his Castilians ran through that town and seized six of its inhabitants, two of whom were cavaliers and military captains remaining there to evacuate the common people. All six were carried before the Governor that he might learn from them what there was in the province. But ere he could make any inquiries, the two Indian noblemen asked what it was he wanted in their houses and if he sought peace or war. And they spoke without revealing any affliction at seeing themselves in the power of another. Instead their bearing was lofty and they behaved as if they were at complete liberty and talking with their neighbors.

[3] The expedition is now in southern Georgia.

Then by means of his interpreter, Juan Ortiz, the General answered that he did not desire war with anyone but rather peace and friendship with all, that his men were seeking certain provinces which lay ahead and needed supplies for their journey since they could not avoid eating, and that they were causing only this inconvenience and no other along the roads since they wanted food and nothing more.

The principal Indians thereupon replied: "Then for this purpose, there will be no necessity for you to detain us, for here we shall provide all appropriate supplies for your journey, and we shall give you better treatment than you received in Apalache, for we are well aware of how you fared there."

Having made this statement, both of the Indian cavaliers ordered two of the four captives who had been seized along with them to go as quickly as possible and give notice to their chieftain of what they had seen and heard among the Castilians, and also to inform the inhabitants whom they encountered along the road so that they too might pass word from one to another that each without hesitation must serve the Christians who were in their land since they were friends and had not come to make war upon them. The Governor, having heard the good response of the Indians, believed them; and perceiving that things were working out more favorably than otherwise, he commanded that these people be released at once and treated as friends.

Two of the Indians bore the message while the others remained with the General. These four now advised his lordship to turn back to another village, which was better than the present one, and promised to guide him along a more peaceful road than the one he had been following. Since he would be drawing near to his army, the Governor was pleased to accept their suggestion, and he thereupon ordered one of them to carry word to the campmaster to come straight to this second town and not take the roundabout route which he himself had followed.

When the Castilians arrived at the village to which the Indians were directing them, they were greeted with manifestations of great affection. The Cacique, on being informed of this new friendship, came to kiss the Governor's hands; and words of courtesy and affability were passed between the two men. With this Curaca were all of his vassals and their wives and children, who had withdrawn to the fields and were now returning to their homes. Meanwhile the army arrived and pitched camp both inside and outside the town. And during the entire time that the Spaniards spent in this province, the Indians maintained the finest peace and loyalty with them, a circumstance which our men considered of no small consequence in the light of the extensive warfare they had suffered at the hands of the inhabitants of Apalache.

Having rested three days in Altapaha, the Castilians left this village and traveled for ten days upstream along the bank of a river. Here all of the land appeared as fertile as that of Apalache and even more so. Furthermore its people were domesticated and peaceful, and our men preserved with them that peace which they had promised from the beginning. Hence the Indians received no annoyance other than that of having to expend their food, and even of this the Spaniards took very little so as not to offend. In the province of Altapaha, they found very large mulberry trees; although they had seen them elsewhere, the others were nothing in comparison to these.

At the end of this ten-day journey made upstream and to the north,[4] the Spaniards departed from the province of Altapaha, leaving the Curaca and his Indians very happy over the friendship they had formed. And now they entered a province called Achalaque which was poor and unproductive. Here there were but few young Indians, for almost all of its inhabitants were old and near-sighted, and many of them were blind. Since the presence of such a goodly number of the aged in a town or province may indicate that the young are even more numerous, the Spaniards were amazed

---

[4] *caminaron Norte Sur, el Río arriba.*

when they did not find the latter, and they were even suspicious that they might have rebelled and were hiding somewhere for the purpose of doing them harm. On investigation, however, they were convinced that everything could be seen and that nothing was concealed. Hence they made no inquiry as to why there were so many old people and so few youths.

Long marches were made through this province of Achalaque in order to depart from it quickly, first because it was so barren of food, and then too because they were eager to reach the province of Cofachiqui; for according to information received, much gold and silver were to be had in that place, and it was their intention to load themselves with great treasures and return to Spain. Such a desire inspired them to double their marches, and they now could do so easily since the land was flat and there were no woods, mountains or rivers to interrupt their long strides. Thus they crossed the province of Achalaque in five days. They left the Curaca and natives of this land with a profound feeling of peace and friendship for the Castilians. To keep his memory alive among these people, the Governor gave them along with other gifts a male and a female hog so that they would be able to breed these animals. This same contribution he had made to the chief of Altapaha and to the lords of all those provinces who had come out in peace to accept his friendship.

Although we have not mentioned previously that the Governor brought swine to Florida, it is a fact that he did have with him more than three hundred head, both sows and boars. These animals multiplied exceedingly and were of great benefit in times of necessity during the exploration. And because of the natural propensity of this great kingdom for raising livestock, one might believe that many swine are to be found there today, unless, of course, the Indians (abhorring the memory of those who brought these animals more than esteeming the benefits thereof) have consumed them all. For in addition to those particular animals which the Governor presented his friends among the curacas, many others, even though carried with great care, since troops of horsemen took turns guarding them while en route, were lost along the way.[5]

CHAPTER III

The province of Cofa, its Cacique and a piece of artillery which the Spaniards left for him to guard.

IT WAS always the Adelantado's custom, when passing from one province to another, to send messengers ahead to notify the cacique of his coming. This he did for two reasons: first, to persuade the Indians with terms of peace and reassure them concerning any fear they might experience on seeing strange people in their land; and again, to detect in their replies the good or evil intent which dominated them. And when the Indians dared not go from one province to another because of some enmity existing among them, or when some unpopulated district lay between, then the Governor himself, as we have seen earlier, made the exploration in the best way he could. So, following his custom, he sent messengers before he left the province of Achalaque to the bordering province of Cofa to inform the Curaca there that he was coming to his land to recognize him as a friend and treat him as a brother, just as he had done all of the lords of vassals who had received him peacefully. And he commanded the Indians who carried this message to take care at the same time to inform the Cacique Cofa of the fine treatment their own Curaca Achalaque and all the natives of his province

[5] Garcilaso is the only authority who has anything to say about how the swine were handled on the long journey. Strong evidence that these animals did survive is to be seen in the statement of both Garcilaso and Elvas that when the Spaniards returned to the Mississippi after their futile attempt to reach Mexico by land, they encountered pigs dropped by some left with the Indians the summer before (See Book V, Part II, chapter VI). This statement, according to the findings of the United States De Soto Expedition Commission, creates a presumption that swine were permanently introduced by De Soto into the Southwest, but so far few references are to be found in proof of the fact.

had received from the Spaniards as a result of their having accepted them peacefully and maintained friendly relations with them at all times.

The Cacique Cofa and all of his vassals manifested great pleasure at the message. With the common consent of everyone and amidst great festivity and rejoicing, they replied that his lordship and his entire army would be most welcome to their homes and state, where they were waiting anxiously to see and know them in order to serve them with all their resources. And for that reason, they said, they begged him to make haste.

Content with this agreeable response, the General and his soldiers quickened their journey with the result that on the fourth day after leaving the province of Achalaque, they approached the foremost town of the province of Cofa. Here the Cacique was awaiting them with all of those people whom he had assembled to display the grandeur of his court and others whom he had mustered for the service of his guests. When he learned that the Castilians were nearing his village he came out a third of a league to receive them. Then he kissed the Governor's hands while reiterating his reply to the message, and the Governor in turn embraced him with a great show of love. Afterward the Spaniards entered the town with both horsemen and footsoldiers arranged in squadrons.

The Curaca lodged the Governor in his own house and the army within the town. He himself designated the quarters for the various troops, accommodating all according to their rank as if he were their campmaster. His behavior pleased the ministers of the army exceedingly for he thereby disclosed himself to be a man of war. When he had finished quartering the army, he went by permission of the Governor to another town, something like two shots of an arquebus distant.

This province of Cofa is fertile and abounds in such foods as are produced in that land. And like the other places we have mentioned it has all the additional fine characteristics of forests and clearings essential for raising livestock and planting; and it is inhabited by many good people, both domestic and affable. Here in the first village the Governor and his men rested and were entertained for five days, for the Curaca would not consent to their leaving sooner, and the Governor acquiesced for the sake of friendship.

We have not mentioned previously a piece of ordnance which the Governor carried in his army, and the reason for our omission is that this is the first occasion in the whole of the expedition that has been offered us to do so. Having observed that this weapon served only as a burden and an affliction, and that both men and mules had to be employed for its care and transportation, the Adelantado decided to let it remain in the protection of the Curaca Cofa. And in order to demonstrate just what he was leaving him, he ordered the piece to be aimed from the Cacique's very house toward a large and exceedingly beautiful liveoak growing outside the town. Then much to the surprise of both the chieftain and his people, the whole tree was destroyed with two shots. Meanwhile the Governor informed the Indians that as a manifestation of his love and a recompense for the kind fellowship and hospitality they had extended, he wanted to leave them this highly esteemed piece, and that they should guard and keep it in safety for him until he returned that way or sent to request it. The Cacique and all principal Indians present greatly appreciated the confidence the Governor had shown by trusting them with such a signal article, and after they had rendered thanks with the choicest words they could utter (first for the confidence and then for the cannon), they gave orders for the weapon to be guarded with much caution. And one may believe that until this day they still hold it in great veneration and esteem.

Having rested five days, the army left Cofa for a province called Cofaqui which belonged to the Cacique Cofa's elder brother, a man who was richer and more powerful than his kinsman. Taking his warriors and servants, the Curaca Cofa accompanied the Governor for one day, and he would have remained with him during the whole journey through his land, but the Governor would not consent to his going farther and insisted that he return to his home. Having perceived the Governor's will, the Cacique kissed his hands with great tenderness and sorrow at parting, and then said: "I entreat Your Lordship to remember my love and my desire to employ myself in your behalf, for I am your very affectionate servant." The Governor thanked the chieftain graciously and in this manner they took leave of each other.

The Curaca very carefully bade farewell to the Campmaster and the other captains, and likewise to the ministers of the Imperial Exchequer, addressing all as if they were old acquaintances. Then as soon as he had completed his leavetaking, he called his own captains and told them that they and the warriors and servants with them should continue to minister unto the Governor and his entire army, and that they should consider themselves fortunate because the Castilians had accepted them as friends and subjects. And he likewise commanded an Indian nobleman to go in advance and inform his brother Cofaqui that the Spaniards were coming to his land and that since they deserved favorable treatment, he begged his brother to accept them peacefully and serve them as he himself had done. Along with this message, the Governor sent another in which he personally offered peace and friendship to the Curaca Cofaqui. Such things having been provided for, the Cacique returned to his home. Then the Adelantado continued his exploration and at the end of six more days of marching departed from the province of Cofa, a land which, as we have said, was fertile and abundant, and was inhabited by the most docile and communicative people that our Spaniards up to that point had seen.

CHAPTER IV

Treats of the Curaca Cofaqui and the great
hospitality he offered the Spaniards in
his land.

A S SOON as the Curaca Cofaqui received the messages of his brother and the Governor, he commanded that everything necessary be made ready, both in the way of noblemen to display the splendor of his house and of provisions and servants to entertain the Spaniards. And before the Governor entered his land, he dispatched four illustrious cavaliers with a retinue of many people to welcome and felicitate him upon his arrival, to offer the obedience due him, and to say that all awaited him in complete peace and friendship and with a desire to serve and regale him to the utmost extent of their ability.

Since it was the custom of the Spaniards to solicit friends through kindness rather than force, the General and all his people were pleased with this message and thus marched on until reaching the boundary of Cofaqui. Here they gave permission to the Indians of the province of Cofa, both warriors and servants, to return to their homes, and in the meantime the people of Cofaqui fetched others to take their places in carrying the loads. Then the Governor came to the first town in the province where he was awaited by the Cacique himself. And when that chieftain learned of his approach from the tower watchman, he came outside the town to receive him in the company of many noblemen magnificently arrayed with bows and arrows and large feathers as well as rich mantles of marten and various other skins, which were as nicely dressed as the best of those to be found in Germany. Many fine words were exchanged between the Governor and the Curaca as well as between the principal Indians and the cavaliers and captains of the army, all of whom made themselves understood by both words and signs. So it was that amidst great festivity and joy on the part of the Indians our men entered the town.

After personally lodging the Spaniards, the Cacique, with the Governor's permission, withdrew to a nearby settlement to which he had removed his household in order to leave the first town free for the army. Then very early on the following day, he came to visit the Governor, and when he had passed a long time with him reporting things which concerned the province, he said: "My Lord, I would know your will—whether it be to remain here, where we wish to serve you, or to pass forward—so that accordingly provisions may be made in advance which will be agreeable to your needs."

The Governor responded that he was seeking other provinces which he had been informed lay ahead, one of which was called Cofachiqui, and that he could not establish a settlement or stop anywhere until he had visited and seen all the lands of Florida. Then the Curaca informed him that the province of Cofachiqui touched upon his own boundaries, but he said that between the one place and the other there lay an immense wilderness which required seven days to cross. And now for the journey he offered his lordship all the warriors and servants necessary to wait upon and accompany him to wherever he might wish to take them. And he likewise offered all the supplies needed for the trip, begging the Governor to ask for and even demand whatever he might wish to carry just as if he were in his own land; for, he explained, all his nation was subject to the Governor's will and desired very much to render him assistance.

The Governor expressed his appreciation for this offer, and then added that since the Cacique as an experienced captain and as the ruler of that land was acquainted with the route they were to travel and in consequence knew what supplies would be necessary, he himself should provide as if the cause were his own. For, he said, the Spaniards needed nothing but food, and in leaving everything to the will and pleasure of his host, he wished to show how little or no trouble they desired to give him. The Governor had spoken thus, for by placing such confidence in the chieftain, he had obliged him to do more than he would have done had he been asked specifically for what was needed. Immediately the Indian commanded that supplies and porters for carrying them be assembled with great care and solicitude, and his order was complied with so promptly that within the four days the Spaniards rested in the town of Cofaqui four thousand native domestics gathered to transport the food and clothing of the Christians and four thousand warriors came to guide and accompany the army.

Wherever they found themselves, the principal food secured by the Castilians was corn, a grain which means the same to all the Indies of the New World as wheat does to Spain. But along with the corn, the Indians now supplied a great amount of such dried fruit as we have talked about previously—fruit which the land produces of itself and without cultivation. They brought prunes and raisins, nuts of two or three varieties, and acorns of the liveoak and the oak. They offered no meat, however, because, as we have already said, they have none from livestock but only that which they kill while hunting in the forest.

Now even though these people had assembled to serve him, the Governor and his army, on beholding such a multitude, were cautious, keeping more than the ordinary vigil both day and night lest the Indians while feigning friendship find them careless and venture to do them harm. But in truth, the Indians themselves were heedless and were far from making an attack. On the contrary, they directed their attention toward serving and pleasing with their whole strength and spirit; for, as we soon shall see, they desired, with the favor and protection of the Spaniards, to avenge themselves of the injuries and damage received from their enemies, the people of Cofachiqui.

One day before the time set for the departure of the Spaniards, the Curaca, who was in the plaza of the town with the General and other captains and illustrious cavaliers of the army, summoned before him an Indian whom he had selected for his captain general in all matters that might arise concerning war, and who at present was to accompany the Governor in this same capacity. Then when this man appeared before him, he said: "You are well acquainted with the hostility and perpetual enmity that has always existed between our parents, grandparents, and other ancestors, and the inhabitants of the province of Cofachiqui where you are to go in the service of our Governor and these cavaliers. And the many grievances, evils and harms that the natives of that land have continuously made and still make on the people of our nation are indeed notorious. It is only right, therefore, that fortune having offered such a good occasion as the present for vengeance, we should not lose it. So you, my Captain General, as we have agreed, are to go in the company and service of the Governor and his invincible army, with whose favor and support you will do everything that you can think of against our enemies in satisfaction of our injuries and wrongs. And since I realize that there is no necessity for me to waste many words in charging you as to your duties, I rely upon your spirit and volition, which I know will conform with my purpose and with what in this case is commensurate with our honor."

CHAPTER V

Patofa promises his Curaca vengeance. A strange story is told about what happened to an Indian guide.

THE Indian *apu* (which in the language of Peru means the captain general or supreme in any office) whose name was Patofa, was so very handsome in body and countenance that his appearance gave proof of the Cacique's wisdom in naming him his Captain General as well as assurance that he would do everything wisely in both peace and war. Rising to his feet and throwing aside a mantle of cat skins which he wore as a cape, he grasped a broadsword of palmwood borne behind him by a servant as a sign of his rank, and leaping from one side to the other in the presence of the Cacique and the Governor, made many fine flourishes with a skill, gracefulness and rhythm that no fencing master of renown could have excelled. Indeed his gestures greatly astonished our Spaniards. After sporting in this manner for some time, he paused and with the sword still in his hand, approached the Curaca. Then making a sweeping bow according to native custom, which differs little from our own, said what the interpreters translated as follows:

"Our Prince and Lord, as your servant and as Captain General of your armies, I pledge to Your Greatness my faith and word to attain in fulfillment of what you have commanded all that my strength and industry will permit; and I promise that with the support of these valiant Spaniards, I shall avenge completely the injuries, deaths, damages and losses that we and our elders have suffered at the hands of the people of Cofachiqui. My vengeance will be such that with much satisfaction to your fame and greatness you will be able to erase from your mind those memories which now offend you because of things not yet avenged. And the most definite indication that you can have that your command has been fulfilled will be that I, having performed my task satisfactorily, will venture to return to present myself before you. On the other hand, should my fate be contrary to my expectations, neither your eyes nor those of the Sun will ever behold me again, for in case my enemies should refuse to destroy me with their own hands, I shall bestow upon myself the punishment of death that my cowardice or small fortune will merit."

Rising to his feet, the Curaca Cofaqui embraced his general and replied:

"I hold your promises to be as certain as if I had already seen them fulfilled, and I thus shall manifest my appreciation for them as if the service which I desire so much were already accomplished."

Saying this, he took off a mantle of very fine marten skins and with his own hands placed it upon the shoulders of Patofa as a recompense for those services yet to be accomplished. So excellent were these skins that the Spaniards judged this particular mantle to be worth two thousand ducats in Spain. Moreover, for a lord to favor a servant by presenting him his mantle, his feather headdress, or any other adornment from his person, especially if in order to do so he himself removed it, was a gesture of such honor and esteem among all the Indians of the great kingdom of Florida that no other reward could equal it. But this is a sentiment which conforms to good reason and should exist likewise among all nations.

Everything that was necessary had now been provided for the journey of the Spaniards, and the night before they were to depart, a strange thing occurred which caused them to marvel. As we have already mentioned, our Castilians had seized in the province of Apalache two young Indians who had offered to serve them as guides. One of these youths whom the Christians called Marcos, although they had not baptized him, had by now led them through all of the road that he knew. The other, who was called Pedro, although likewise unbaptized, was to guide them to the province of Cofachiqui, where, he had assured them, they would find quantities of gold, silver and precious pearls. This second lad went about among the Spaniards as familiarly as if he had been born in their midst. Now it happened that at almost twelve o'clock of the night before their proposed departure, Pedro was heard to cry out loudly for help, saying that he was being murdered. At that, the entire army rushed forth in the belief that the Indians had betrayed them; and sounding an alarm, they very quickly arranged themselves for battle in organized squadrons of horsemen and footsoldiers. Then perceiving no enemies, they proceeded to investigate the source of the alarm, only to find that it had been caused by the supplications of the Indian Pedro, whom they discovered trembling with fear and half dead. On their questioning this boy as to what he had seen or heard to make him cry out so strangely for assistance, he explained that a demon with a frightful visage had come to him in company with many of his imps, forbidding him under pain of death to guide the Spaniards where he had promised to take them. Moreover, that creature while uttering these words had shaken him and dragged him about his quarters, at the same time tormenting all parts of his body with a rain of blows that had left him crushed and broken and unable to bestir himself. According to the way he was being maltreated, he added, it was his belief that he would have been bereft of his life had not those two Spaniards who chanced to come to his aid entered his quarters so precipitately; for on seeing these men, the big demon had fled at once with all his imps trailing after him.

Thus Pedro had come to understand that devils fear Christians, and he in consequence desired to accept the Faith. So he besought his masters for the love of God to baptize him at once lest the demon return to destroy him; for having seen that spirit fleeing the Christians, he knew that if he too were baptized he would be safe and the demon would not touch him. These things the catechumen Indian Pedro told in the presence of the Governor and other Spaniards, all of whom were amazed when they heard him; and they realized that his story was not feigned since the discolorations, contusions and swellings which they found on his face and indeed on the whole of his body bore witness to the blows that had been bestowed upon him.

The General ordered the priests, clerics and friars to be summoned, and he told them that in this particular instance they should do whatever they felt wise. They, having heard the Indian's story, gave him the waters of baptism at once and remained with him throughout that night and the following day, confirming him in the Faith and strengthening him in his health; for he had said that the blows he received had crushed and broken him.[6] Because of his indisposition, the army failed to march until the second day, and then they carried Pedro for two days on horseback since he was unable to support himself on his feet.

By what we have related concerning the Indian Pedro, one can see how easy it was to convert these Indians and all of the others of the New World to the Catholic Faith, and I as a native of Peru and an eyewitness of the Indians of that land venture to remark that just the Indian Pedro's preaching of what he had seen would have been sufficient to convert all of the people of his province and to make them ask as he did for baptism. But our men, whose intention it was to spread the gospel after they had won and pacified the land, did no more at this time than what we have said.

[6] Ranjel states that the Christians actually believed that this Indian had been possessed of the devil, and that Friar John the Evangelist said that it was so.

When the army left the town of Cofaqui, it was accompanied by the Curaca for two leagues. He would have gone farther but for the fact that the Governor begged him to return to his home. On bidding the Spaniards farewell, he as a friend revealed his sorrow at parting. And when he kissed the hands of the Governor and his leading men, he once more delegated to Captain General Patofa the duty of ministering unto the Spaniards. Patofa in turn replied that by his accomplishments the Cacique would see how sincerely he accepted the responsibility of all that his master had commanded. At that the Cacique Cofaqui set out for his home, and the Spaniards continued in their search for the much coveted province of Cofachiqui.

CHAPTER VI

The Governor and his army find themselves in
great confusion on seeing that they are
lost and without food in
some uninhabited
lands.

THE army of the Christians traveled apart from the Indians in organized squadrons of infantry and cavalry; and those four thousand chosen warriors who, as has been said, were accompanying Captain General Patofa marched likewise in a squadron, with both vanguard and rearguard forming a protection for their carriers and servants. Thus these two peoples, so dissimilar, followed the same military procedure, for it afforded them much pleasure to observe the fine order and concord that each bore in competing with the other. And the Indians would recognize no superiority on the part of the Spaniards in matters pertaining to the science of war.

With the coming of night, the Indians and Spaniards camped apart, and the four thousand native porters, as soon as they had delivered supplies to our men, withdrew to sleep among their own people. Both armies stationed sentinels, each guarding against the other as if they were declared enemies. The Christians were particularly vigilant, being rendered cautious by the sight of so much uniformity and agreement among the infidels; but the latter were quite innocent of all malice and showed instead a desire to please the Spaniards in every respect. Their placing of sentinels with corps of guards as well as their observation of other regulations was done more to reveal themselves as men of war than to guard against the Spaniards. Nevertheless, all did travel with vigilance and care as long as they were together.

The region through which they now passed happened to be that of the narrowest part of the province of Cofaqui; they emerged from it, therefore, after two days of travel and on the second night slept where that great wilderness which lies between the provinces of Cofaqui and Cofachiqui begins. Then as they marched on for six more days through this wilderness, they observed that all of its terrain was pleasant, and that the mountains and forests encountered were not rough and dense but such as could be traversed with ease. During this journey, they crossed, in addition to some small streams, two large and swift rivers which carried a great amount of water. But since this water was diffused, they managed to ford both streams by forming a wall of the horses from one bank to the other, in this way breaking the fury of the current which was so strong at those places where it reached the waists of the footsoldiers that none could stand up against it. But by seizing hold of the horses all on foot, both Indians and Spaniards, were able to ford these rivers safely.

In the middle of their seventh day, both Spaniards and Indians found themselves in utter confusion, for the road which they had taken up to that point and which appeared to be a broad highway came to an end; and when they proceeded along the many narrow paths through the woods, they very soon lost sight of them. Thus it was that after having made many efforts, they found themselves enclosed in a wilderness with no knowledge whatsoever as to how to escape. Moreover the forests were different from previous ones, for they were more lofty and dense, and could be passed through only with difficulty.

But the Indians whom the Governor had brought as domestics and those who accompanied General Patofa were likewise bewildered, there being none among them who was acquainted with the road or who could say to which side they should turn in order to make a quicker exit from the forests and waste lands. So calling Captain Patofa before him, the Governor questioned this man as to why it was that under the guise of friendship he had brought them to these wilds which afforded no road out in any direction, and how it could be possible or even credible that there was not a single Indian among the eight thousand with him who knew where they were or by what means one might reach the province of Cofachiqui, even though it were by cutting through the forests by hand. It was not to be believed, he said, that, having waged perpetual warfare among themselves, they should not know both the public and secret roads passing from one province to the other.

Captain Patofa replied that neither he nor any of his Indians had ever previously been in this place, and that the wars waged by those two provinces had never assumed the nature of pitched battles in which one of two powers invaded enemy territory, but had simply occurred while each hunted and fished in the forests and streams through which the Spaniards had just passed. Meeting thus, they as enemies had slain and captured one another; but since the Indians of Cofachiqui were superior and always enjoyed many advantages in these battles, his own Indians had become intimidated, and like defeated people had not dared expand or go beyond their own boundaries. For this reason, he explained, they did not know at present either where they were or how to leave this region. "But should Your Lordship suspect," he continued, "that I have brought you to this wilderness by cunning and deception that you might perish here with your army, then be undeceived, for both my lord

Cofaqui and I pride ourselves on being men of truth; and having received you as friends, we would not imagine such a thing, much less do it. But to assure yourself of the veracity of what I have said, take whatever hostages you wish, and if my head is sufficient to satisfy you, I will willingly permit you to deprive me of it at once. Moreover you may take the heads of those Indians who accompany me, for all are subject to my will and command both by military law, since I am their captain general, and by the special order of our Curaca and lord, who has said that they must obey me in all things even unto death."

On hearing the fine words of Patofa and seeing the passionate spirit in which he uttered them, the Governor, to prevent his committing a desperate act, assured him that he believed what he said and was convinced of his loyalty. Then they called the Indian Pedro, whom as we have said a demon had maltreated in Cofaqui. From the province of Apalache until that very day he had guided the Spaniards with such excellent knowledge of the land that he could inform them the night before of all that they would encounter along the road on the ensuing day. But now this boy, like the rest of the Indians, had lost his knack, and he said that since he had not passed along that route for four or five years, he had so completely forgotten it that he was utterly lost and as a result did not know the road and would not venture to guess which direction they might take to reach the province of Cofachiqui. Many Spaniards on seeing this Indian close himself up and decline to trust his own knowledge, asserted that it was because of his fear of the demons who had maltreated and threatened him that he now refused to guide them or to say in what direction they might proceed to find their way out of the wilderness.

Therefore, confused and ignorant as to which way to turn, our Spaniards traveled the remainder of the day without a road, passing instead through that part of the forest which they found clear and open. Wandering in this manner, they came at sunset to a great river, which was even larger than the two they had already en-countered and could not be forded because of the enormous quantity of water it carried. The sight of this river gave them greater concern since they lacked both rafts and canoes for crossing it, and, what pained them more, provisions to eat while building such things; for the ration they had brought from Cofaqui had been doled out for the seven days specified as the time needed to pass through the wilderness. It is true that they had brought four thousand Indian porters, but the loads of these men were so light as to amount to less than half the ordinary ones, and an Indian at best can carry no more than a half-bushel of corn. Moreover, these Indians had not let the fact that they were loaded prevent their bearing arms like those of their people who traveled as men of war. All had left their homes to avenge themselves on the inhabitants of Cofachiqui, and since they would have to pass through strange and hostile lands, they did not want to return with their hands on their chests. For the above mentioned reasons and again because there were almost ten thousand men and nearly three hundred and fifty horses to consume the corn, the food had already disappeared by the close of the seventh day of the journey. A decree had been published on the previous day to the effect that because of the danger that more food would not be found soon, what they had should be guarded and handed out in small quantities, but it was already too late, for there was no longer anything to guard.

Thus our Spaniards discovered themselves without guide, road, or supplies; lost in barren lands with their route cut off in front by a surging river, behind by the long wilderness they had just passed, and on the sides by their confusion as to when or where they could get out of these places in which the ground was so craggy and full of brambles. But that which above everything else afforded them the greatest anxiety was their lack of something to eat.

CHAPTER VII

Four captains go out to explore the land. Pa-
tofa inflicts a strange punishment upon
an Indian.

HAVING considered the difficulties and inconveniences in which the army now saw itself, the Governor felt that it was safer and even imperative not to travel farther until he had found a road out of these wastes. With the dawn of the following day, he therefore ordered four groups, two of horsemen and two of footsoldiers, to go out and see if by one way or the other they might find some road or settlement. Two of the groups were to proceed upstream and two down, and they were so arranged and counseled that while one was adhering to the bank of the river, the other should pursue the same course a league inland, and each was to return within five days with an account of what he had found. The captains selected for this mission were Juan de Añasco, Andrés de Vasconcelos, Juan de Guzmán and Arias Tinoco.

Unwilling to remain in the camp, General Patofa accompanied Captain Juan de Añasco, who happened to be traveling upstream along the bank of the river. Also with this captain went the Indian Pedro; abashed at having lost his intuitive power, he felt that by making this journey he must of necessity succeed in bringing the Spaniards, as he had promised, to the province of Cofachiqui. And finally with each company there went a thousand Indians, whose duty it was to spread out through the woods and attempt to find some road.

The Governor stayed on the bank of the river to await whatever news his men might bring, and here he and his army suffered an extreme want of food, for they had nothing to eat other than the tendrils of young vines found growing in the woods and streams. Meanwhile, however, four thousand Indian servants who had remained with him went forth at daybreak to search the countryside for food, returning at night with edible herbs and roots and a few birds and small animals killed with their bows. Some brought fish, for they spared no possible diligence in their efforts to find sustenance. And all that they did obtain, they conveyed to the Spaniards and divided in their presence without touching or hiding any part of it, for they were so faithful and held our men in such veneration that they would fall dead of hunger rather than take anything without having first offered it to them. The Spaniards, on the other hand, were overcome by their courtesy and returned the greater part of what they had brought, all of which was as nothing for so many people.

Now when they had passed three days in that camp, the Governor perceived that such excessive hunger (which indeed cannot be overestimated) could no longer be endured. Hence he commanded that they kill some of the swine reserved for breeding purposes and dole out eight ounces of this meat to each Spaniard as a fresh ration —a ration which served more to increase hunger than allay it.[7] Even so, the Spaniards shared this food with the natives to make it clear that they desired no advantage over them in any respect, but wished rather to endure the hardship with them equally.

It was a matter of the greatest joy for the soldiers to witness the fine attitude the Governor himself demonstrated toward his men in this affliction by strengthening and helping them to endure their hunger as if he were not privileged in any way and were the least of them all. But they too acted in like manner toward their captain, for to relieve him of his pain (which he in the role of a good father felt on seeing his men in such trouble), they concealed their hunger, feigning less need than they actually suffered and exhibiting in their countenances the joy and happiness of men blessed with complete abundance and prosperity.

We have forgotten to mention previously and in its place an exemplary punishment which Captain Patofa inflicted upon one of

[7] According to the Elvas account, the thirteen sows which the Governor brought to Florida had increased to three hundred swine. Ranjel states that each man was given a ration of one pound of flesh.

his Indians for behaving so oddly. This incident should not be
forgotten and will fit in well wherever it is put. It happened that on
the fifth day that they were traveling through the wilderness, one
of the Indian porters (in the language of Hispañola such people
are called *tameme*), without having received any grievance, but
moved by cowardice or by a desire to see his wife and children or
by the Devil's having informed him of the hunger all were to suffer,
or by some other motive which he alone knew, decided to flee. Now
when the Spaniard in charge of this man found him missing, he
reported his absence to General Patofa, who thereupon commanded
four young Indian noblemen to pursue him with the utmost speed
and not to pause until they had overtaken him and brought him
back in chains. These Indians made such haste that in a brief time
they seized the fleeing man and returned to the camp to deliver
him to his captain.

And now Patofa, in the presence of all his soldiers decried this
man's cowardice and pusillanimity, his discourtesy to his prince and
Curaca, his little respect for his captain general, and his treason
and perfidy against his companions and indeed the whole of his
nation. Next addressing the fugitive he said: "I shall not permit
your transgression and iniquity to go unpunished lest others imitate
your base example." With that he ordered his men to carry the
victim to a small stream flowing through the camp, and, while he
himself was still present, to remove all the scant clothing from the
Indian's body except some loin cloths. Then when at his instructions
many tree branches of more than a fathom in length had been
brought, he said to the culprit: "Throw yourself upon your chest in
that stream and drink it dry; and do not stop until you have done
so." To enforce these commands, four vagabonds were told to
strike the Indian whenever he lifted his head and to continue to do
so until he began drinking again, meanwhile disturbing the water
to make it more difficult to swallow.

Thus forced to this torture, the Indian drank until he could
swallow no more; but when he paused, his executioners beat him

cruelly and continuously from head to foot until he began to drink again. Some of his relatives on perceiving the severity of his punishment and that he would be forced to drink until he was dead, hastened to the Governor and, casting themselves at his feet, begged that he take pity on their wretched kinsman. The Governor thereupon told Captain Patofa by messengers that he should be satisfied to cease this punishment, so justly inflicted, and not persist in his anger. With that they left this Indian already half-dead, who without thirst had consumed so much water.

CHAPTER VIII

*A special story about the hunger the Spaniards
suffered. How they found food.*

RETURNING to the hunger and necessity that the Governor and his army experienced during those days, I think it wise to tell of a special incident that occurred among some of the most privileged soldiers in the camp so that by means of this incident one may see and consider what the suffering in general must have been. For to tell each thing in particular would be never to end and to make our history very prolix. It happened that on one of those days when their hunger was most intense, four of the most illustrious and valiant soldiers, since they were such, were making witty remarks and feigning laughter at the toil and necessity they were undergoing. All being members of a partnership, they resolved to ascertain how much they possessed among them. This they found to be scarcely a fistful of corn. To divide this corn, they first cooked it so that it would increase somewhat, and then, equally shared, their separate portions amounted to eighteen grains. Three of the men, Antonio Carrillo, Pedro Morón and Francisco Pechudo, ate their portions at once. The fourth, who was Gonzalo Silvestre,[8] wrapped

[8] This story is one of the clearest evidences of the identity of the Inca's chief informant.

his eighteen grains in a handkerchief and put them in his breast. A little later he ran into Francisco de Troche, a Castilian soldier who was a native of Burgos, and this man said to him, "Have you anything to eat?" Gonzalo Silvestre then jokingly answered, "Yes, I have some very good marchpanes made just recently and brought to me from Seville." Instead of being angered, Francisco de Troche laughed at the nonsense. At this point another soldier, Pedro de Torres, who was a native of Badajoz, addressed a question to those who were talking of marchpanes. "You have something to eat?" he said, for they discussed nothing else in those days. "Yes," Gonzalo Silvestre responded, "I have a very soft and delicious Utrera bun, recently taken from the oven. If you wish some of it, I will share with you copiously." All laughed at this second impossibility just as they had laughed at the first. Then Gonzalo Silvestre said to them: "In order to prove to you that I have not lied, I will offer you something which will taste to one man like marchpanes if he has a desire for such and to another like a Utrera bun if that is what he longs for." Saying this, he took out the handkerchief with its eighteen grains of corn and gave six grains to each person, keeping six for himself. All three now ate the corn at once lest their companions increase and their share be lessened. Then having eaten, they repaired to a nearby stream and satiated themselves with water since they could not do so with food. And thus they passed that day with no more food, for there was no more.

It was with such hardships as these and not with eating marchpanes or Utrera buns that this New World was won from whence each year twelve and thirteen millions of gold and silver and precious stones are brought to Spain. Hence I take great pride in the fact that I am the son of a conquistador of Peru whose arms and labors contributed so much honor and advantage to Spain.[9]

[9] The Inca's father set out for the Indies at some time between 1525 and 1530. In 1531 he followed Pedro de Alvarado to Peru and served in the numerous conquests and rebellions which took place in that land. Apparently he veered with the winds of fortune and assisted that side which promised most, but in the main he was loyal to the forces of the King. At one

Returning to the four captains who went out to seek roads, let me say that they traveled for six days while undergoing the same hunger and necessity as the Governor and his army. Three of them found nothing noteworthy except hunger and more hunger. Only the Comptroller Juan de Añasco had better success, for when he had proceeded for three days, always upstream and never leaving the river, he discovered a town situated along its bank on the same side that he was traveling. Here he found few people but an abundance of food for such a small town, there being in a single depository five hundred bushels of meal made from toasted corn, not to mention a great quantity of other grain. As can be imagined, both Indians and Spaniards were exuberant with this discovery, and after seeing what there was within the houses, climbed to the roofs of the highest dwellings from whence they perceived that from this place on up the river the land was settled with numerous towns, both large and small, and there were many fields on all sides. For their good fortune, they gave thanks to God while both they and the Indians proceeded to allay their hunger. Past midnight they dispatched four horsemen at top speed to the Governor with information of what they had discovered, and in order to be believed, these messengers carried with them many ears of corn and some cow horns. The Spaniards could never learn where the Indians had obtained the latter, for in all the regions passed through in the land of Florida, never did they find cows. It is true that in some parts they did discover fresh beef, but no cows were in evidence, and they were unable to tell where these animals were.

During the night that they slept in the town, General Patofa and his Indians, while observing the utmost secrecy and keeping the Spaniards entirely ignorant of their actions, sacked and robbed the temple that served solely for burial, where (as we shall tell

---

time he served as Corregidor of Cuzco and before his death in 1559 was responsible for a number of benevolent and notable acts. Garcilaso took great pride in his father's achievements even though he could not explain some of them to the satisfaction of the Spanish Crown. See Fitzmaurice-Kelly, *op. cit.*, pp. 2–21. Also Miró Quesada y Sosa, *op. cit.*, pp. 7–77.

later of other more famous temples) the Indians kept the best and richest of their possessions. Moreover they killed all of the people they could capture both inside and outside the town, making no exception for age or sex; and from those slain they took the scalps from the ears up with admirable skill and dexterity, carrying them away so that their Curaca and lord, Cofaqui, should see with his own eyes the vengeance they had wrought on his enemies for the injuries he had received. For, as was afterward seen, this town belonged to Cofachiqui, a province which the Spaniards had so desired and which it cost them so much hunger to find.

At noon of the following day, Juan de Añasco departed from the town with all of his Spaniards and Indians. They dared not await the Governor because they feared that the inhabitants of that land might set up an outcry and call together a great number of people. For according to the large settlement that lay up the river, it was possible for many to unite and, attacking, kill them all. Lacking sufficient power to resist the Indians, they felt it safer to turn back and join the Governor.

CHAPTER IX

The army comes to a place where there are pro-
visions. Patofa returns home; and
Juan de Añasco goes out to
explore the land.

THE four cavaliers whom we left on the road with the good news of their discovery of food and settlements, came again to the Governor's camp, having covered in one day on returning what they had covered in three on going, a distance of more than twelve leagues. They informed the Governor of what they had discovered, and he, as soon as it was dawn, commanded the army to march to wherever these men should guide them. The soldiers were so hungry and so anxious to reach a place where there was food that they rushed forward with reins loose, and it was impossible to persuade them to keep order or travel in squadrons as they were accustomed, for whoever could outstrip the others, did so. Moreover, they traveled with such speed that all had entered the town before noon of the following day.

It appeared wise to the Governor to pause for some days in this village, not only to permit his people to rest and recuperate from the previous hardships, but also to await the remaining three captains who had gone out in other directions to explore the land. Each of those men had continued on his journey for three days, and each had found an equally great number of roads and paths crossing the land in every direction. Along these roads they had seen the tracks of Indians, but being unable to seize anyone from whom they might obtain information or to find a town without going farther, and again being pressed for time, they returned to their post at the end of the fifth day after their departure. Here, failing to find the Governor, they followed the tracks left by the army and in two more days overtook him, after having endured such hunger and toils as one may imagine men would endure who had eaten nothing but herbs and roots and not even enough of these for more than eight days. And now in the presence of the Governor and all of their companions they told of their sufferings; then they were comforted and care was taken to restore them.

All of the hunger and necessity which we have said the Spaniards experienced in the wilderness, Alonso de Carmona describes at great length in his account. He gives the number of hogs killed to feed the people as four and declares that they were huge. "With these," he says, "we dined better than usual." But he must have been speaking ironically, for four hogs were such a small amount for so many people.

In this first village of the province of Cofachiqui where the entire army reassembled, the Governor stopped for seven days to permit his people to recover from their previous suffering. Here Captain Patofa and his eight thousand Indians, while again observing the utmost secrecy, did as much harm as they could to their enemies. They ran through four leagues of land and inflicted damage wherever possible. They killed all of the Indians, both male and female, that they could seize, removing their scalps to carry away as a testimony of their deeds; and they sacked all the villages and temples they could reach, not yielding to their desire to burn them, however, lest the Governor see the fires and thus become aware of what they were doing. In sum they did everything they could think of that might injure their enemies and satisfy their own thirst for vengeance, and their cruelty would have extended further had not news of their activities come to the attention of the Governor on the fifth day of his sojourn.

The Governor did not think it right that anyone enjoying his favor and protection should inflict injuries on another, and he believed it unwise to accumulate future enemies because of offenses committed by such persons without his consent, especially since his own policy was to win the Indians by peaceful rather than hostile means. Hence he resolved to dismiss Patofa so that the Indian might return with his men immediately to his land; and his decision he put into effect as follows. First he rendered thanks to the Captain for his loyalty and good friendship, and then he presented him for both himself and his Curaca pieces of woolens, silks and linens, as well as knives, scissors, mirrors and other articles from Spain which the Indians hold in high esteem. Thus Patofa was sent away joyful and content because of the grace and favor he had received, but this happiness was augmented still more by his realization that he had adequately fulfilled his pledge to avenge his lord upon their enemies and aggressors.

After the departure of Patofa and his Indians, the Governor rested two more days in the same town. But once his men had regained strength, he deemed it wise to continue upstream along the bank of the river in the direction the settlements extended. Thus the army marched on for three days, during which time they saw no living Indians, but did see many that had been slain and deprived

of their scalps. For this was the scene of Patofa's slaughter which
had driven the natives to seek inland retreats where they could not
be taken. In the towns, however, the Castilians found food, and
food was at present what they needed.

At the end of three days, the army came to a halt in a very pretty
place, cooled by great groves of mulberries and other trees heavy
with fruit. Here the Governor resolved to remain until he had found
out something about the disposition of the land. First, he provided
lodging for his men, and then commanding the Comptroller Juan
de Añasco to be called, he ordered him to continue with thirty footsoldiers along the same route they had been following (a route
which though narrow did continue) and make an attempt during
the coming night to seize an Indian who could tell him something
of the content of the land, the name of its lord, and all the rest of
those things necessary to know. And should he be unable to capture
an Indian, he was to bring some other report of value which would
enable the army to continue its march less blindly than previously.
Having completed his charge, the Governor then told Juan de
Añasco that he in particular had been chosen for this task because
of the success of each of his previous special military errands, and
that he therefore should strive for success in this mission which
was of such import to everyone.

Juan de Añasco and his thirty companions left the camp on foot
before night fell and, like people who go out on the roads to rob,
followed as silently as possible the route designated for them. And
the farther they traveled, the more this road broadened into a highway. Now when they had journeyed for almost two leagues, they
became conscious of a murmuring in the silence of the night as if
people were near, and proceeding a little further so as to come
out of a sleeve of woods which bore in front of them and cut off
their view, they saw lights and heard the barking of dogs, the crying
of children and the chatter of men and women. Our Spaniards
knew then that they had come to a town and therefore prepared
themselves to seize some Indian in its outskirts secretly and unheard,

each desiring to be the first to make a capture so as to enjoy the
honor of having been the most assiduous. All were proceeding
with this care when they found themselves mocked in their hopes,
for the river, which up until that place had flowed to the side of
them, now crossed over and passed between them and the town.
For a good while they remained along the bank of this river at a
place where there was a large beach and a landing for canoes, but
when they had eaten supper and rested, now that it was midnight,
they set out for the camp, arriving there a short time before dawn
to give an account to the Governor of what they had seen and heard.

At daybreak, the Governor went out with a hundred footsoldiers
and a hundred cavalrymen to see the town and ascertain what it held
both for and against his expedition. On arriving at the canoe landing, Juan Ortiz and Pedro, the Indian boy, shouted to people on the
opposite shore to come and receive a message they wished to give
them for the lord of that land. These Indians, on seeing a thing
so novel as the Spaniards and their horses, rushed into the town
to make known what had been said to them.

CHAPTER X

The mistress of Cofachiqui[10] *comes to talk with
the Governor, offering him both provisions and passage for his
army.*

A LITTLE after the news had been carried to the village, there
issued from that place six principal Indians who, from
what was understood, must have been town magistrates. All were
of goodly appearance and of about the same age, being between
forty and fifty years old. They entered a large canoe which was

[10] *La Señora de Cofachiqui*—literally, the lady of Cofachiqui. Other
translators have referred to her as the *Cacica*, but Garcilaso tells us that the
Spaniards simply called her "la Señora." We have used the word mistress to
indicate that she is a woman with authority.

managed by servants. Afterward, when the six of them stood before the Governor, they at one and the same time made three different and sweeping bows: the first to the Sun, as all turned their faces toward the east; the second to the Moon, as all turned toward the west; and the third to the Governor, as all addressed themselves to him. The Governor was seated on a chair known as a rest seat, which it was the custom to carry for his use wherever he went so that he might receive the curacas and emissaries with a gravity and embellishment befitting the grandeur of his station. Their salutations completed, the six Indians said to the Governor: "My Lord, do you seek peace or war?" Now you must know that it was a general rule for the Indians to make this their initial question, and that always when the Governor entered a new province these were the first words that he heard from its inhabitants.

The General replied that he wished peace and not war, and that he asked no more of them than passage and supplies to enable him to continue on his way to certain provinces for which he was searching. He said that since they knew that food was something that could not be done without, he hoped they would pardon him the bother occasioned in granting it; and promising that he would try to trouble them as little as possible, he begged that they provide him rafts and canoes to cross that river and moreover that they grant him their friendship while his army was passing through their lands.

The Indians responded that they accepted the peace but that they had little food because a great pestilence with many consequent deaths had ravaged their province during the past year, a pestilence from which their town alone had been free. For this reason the inhabitants of the other villages of that province had fled to the forests without sowing their fields. And now, although the disease had passed, these people had not yet been gathered to their homes and towns. They added, however, that they themselves were the vassals of a lady, a young maiden who had recently inherited and was ready for marriage; that they would return to this lady to acquaint her with what his lordship had requested and then apprise him at once concerning her response; and that he meanwhile should await with confidence because it was their belief that their lady, since she was a woman of discretion and of queenly heart, would do everything that she could in the service of the Christians.

Having spoken these words and then obtained the Governor's permission to withdraw, the Indians returned to their village to inform their mistress of what the Captain of the Christians had requested for their journey. They could scarcely have delivered their message when the Castilians observed them making ready two large canoes. Afterward, the mistress of the town[11] and eight of her ladies embarked in one of these canoes, which had been covered with a great canopy and adorned with ornaments. No one else traveled in this canoe, and it was towed by the second one which bore the six principal Indians and many oarsmen. In this manner all crossed the river and came to the place where the Governor was awaiting them.

Although less spectacular in grandeur and majesty, this scene indeed resembles that one in which Cleopatra went forth to receive Marc Anthony on the river Cydnus in Cilicia. There the fates altered in such a fashion that she who had been accused of the crime of *lèse majesté* eventually became the judge of the man who had come to condemn her; and an emperor and lord became the slave of his serf, rendered thus by force of love and by the excellencies, beauty and discretion of that most famous Egyptian. This scene is copiously and ornately described by the teacher of the great Spaniard, Trajan, a disciple worthy of such a master; and because of the similarity of events, I could pilfer useful material from that same master, as others have done, since he has sufficient for everyone. But I would fear that his rich brocade, if so openly exposed, would be detected against the background of my base sackcloth.

The mistress of the province of Cofachiqui came before the Governor and after paying her respects seated herself upon a chair

[11] Biedma says that this woman was only a niece of the ruling dowager. He speaks of her as "brown but well proportioned."

which her subjects had brought for her. She alone spoke with the Governor, no other man or woman of her people saying a word. She referred once more to the message delivered by her vassals and declared that the scourge of the previous year had robbed her of the supplies she would like to have had in order to minister to his lordship more adequately, but that she would do all possible in his service. And that he might judge of her sincerity by her actions, she offered him immediately one of two deposits in that town, in each of which there were six hundred bushels of corn that had been gathered for the relief of those of her vassals who had escaped the pestilence. She begged him, however, to agree to leave her the other deposit for her own great need, assuring him that should his lordship require corn further on, he could take what he wanted from a deposit of two thousand bushels which had been gathered in a nearby town for the same purpose. As for accommodations, she declared that she would vacate her own house for his lordship, command half the town to be emptied for his captains and most illustrious soldiers, and have constructed very pleasant bowers of branches in which the remainder of his people could be at ease, but that if the Governor desired she would clear the entire town of Indians and send them to another one nearby. And then she assured him that rafts and wooden canoes would be provided quickly for the army to cross the river, and that on the morrow there would be a complete supply of them so that his lordship might perceive with what promptitude and willingness she served him.

The Governor responded to the lady's fine words and promises with profound gratitude, for he was much impressed by the fact that at a time when her own land suffered from want, she should offer him more than he had requested. So in deference to her beneficence, he said that both he and his people would try to be satisfied with as little food as possible in order not to afford her so much inconvenience, and that her plans for lodging and other provisions were well ordained. He added, moreover, that in the name of his lord, the Emperor of the Christians and the King of

Spain, he received her kindness in service so that his sovereign might show gratitude in his own time and occasion; and he assured her that he on his own part as well as that of the army, was accepting her generosity as a particular favor never to be forgotten.

Besides these things, they talked of additional matters which concerned that and other provinces in the district; and all that the Governor asked, the lady answered to the great satisfaction of those present and in such a manner that the Spaniards were amazed to hear of such fine and well co-ordinated words, disclosing the wisdom of a barbarian, born and reared far from all good teaching and refinement. But those who possess natural excellence, wherever they may be, grow in wisdom and gentility of themselves and without training; whereas the foolish reveal their stupidity all the more with an increase of instruction.

Our Spaniards noted especially that the Indians of this province and of the two previous provinces were of a more gentle and affable disposition and less ferocious than all the others they found in their expedition. For even though the inhabitants of the other provinces offered and maintained peace, it was always suspected that in their gestures and harsh words, one might detect a friendship more feigned than real. But there was nothing false about the people of Cofachiqui or those of Cofaqui and Cofa; rather they seemed to have passed their entire lives among Spaniards. Not only were they subservient, but in all their actions and words they made an effort to disclose and demonstrate their sincere affection. And the fact that people who had never seen them before should be so cordial was indeed gratifying to our men.

CHAPTER XI

*The army crosses the river of Cofachiqui and
is quartered in the town.*[12] *Juan de
Añasco is sent to fetch a
widow.*

WHILE the mistress of Cofachiqui was speaking with the
Governor of those things we have mentioned, she was dis-
engaging little by little a large strand of pearls as thick as hazelnuts
which encircled her neck three times and fell to her thighs. And
after utilizing the entire period that the conversation lasted to remove these gems, she held them out to Juan Ortiz, the interpreter,
and told him to present them to his Captain General. Juan Ortiz
replied that her ladyship should make the presentation herself since
in that way the Governor would place greater value upon her gift.
But the woman answered that she dared not lest she violate that
modesty which must be observed by those of her sex. At that the
Governor asked Juan Ortiz what she was saying, and on learning,
instructed him as follows: "Inform her that I shall esteem the
honor of having received the pearls from her own hands more than
the value of the jewels themselves, and that such an act will not
entail any breach of decorum because this is a matter of peace and
friendship, things which are so legitimate and important among
strangers." Then the lady, having heard Juan Ortiz, arose to deliver
the pearls to the Governor, and he in like manner arose to receive
them, taking from his finger a gold ring set with a ruby, which he
now bestowed upon her as a symbol of the peace and friendship
they were discussing.

The Indian woman received the Governor's gift with much
civility and placed it upon one of her fingers. And when this incident had passed and she had asked permission to withdraw, she

[12] This town apparently was on the South Carolina side of the Savannah
River, not far below Augusta, Georgia, and at or close to the present site of
Silver Bluff.

returned to her village, leaving the Castilians much satisfied with her discretion and enamoured of her great beauty, which was perfect in the extreme. Indeed they were so charmed with her that then nor afterward did they ever attempt to learn her name, but contented themselves just with calling her Señora. And they were correct in this, for she was a lady in all respects. But since they did not ascertain her name I am unable to record it here. There were many such careless omissions in the exploration.

The Governor remained on the bank of the river to give organization to the army so that it might cross the more speedily, and he sent a command to his campmaster that all of his forces should be brought as quickly as possible to his present location. Meanwhile, the natives constructed great rafts and brought numerous canoes; and through the industry of both Indians and Castilians, the entire army crossed the river during the whole of the following day, although not without the misfortune of losing four horses, which were drowned through the carelessness of some of the officers in charge of the passage of the people. Since these animals were so necessary and of such consequence, everyone mourned their loss more than if they had been their own brothers. Alonso de Carmona states that the number of horses drowned was seven, and that the tragedy was due to their masters, who drove them precipitately into the water without knowing where they should cross, the result being that when they came to a certain part of the river they sank, never to appear again. There must have been some violent whirlpool which sucked them down.

Once over the river, the army pitched camp in that half of the village which the Indians had vacated. For those who were without habitation, great and cool bowers of branches were constructed, there being a large and very fine grove of trees from which to make them. Moreover there were among those bowers many varieties of fruit trees, which included mulberries larger and more luxuriant than any our Spaniards had previously seen. This tree we always make special mention of because of its stateliness and the utility of its silk, which is to be esteemed greatly everywhere.

On the following day, the Governor made efforts to inform himself of the natural fitness and other virtues of that province called Cofachiqui; and he found that it was fertile for everything that one might wish to plant, propagate or raise upon it. Moreover he learned that the mother of its mistress was retired as a widow twelve leagues from the village, and he thereupon instructed the daughter to send for her. This she did, dispatching twelve principal Indians to beg her parent to come and visit the Governor and behold a race of people such as she had never seen before, who brought with them some strange animals. But the mother refused to accompany these Indians, and on learning what her daughter had done, manifested great sorrow and appeared to have received much pain at her levity in agreeing to show herself so soon and so easily to these Castilians whom she admittedly had never previously known or seen. Furthermore she scolded the messengers severely for having consented to her daughter's behavior and in addition said and did other immoderate things such as prudish widows are accustomed to say and do.

All of this being made known to the Governor, he commanded the Comptroller Juan de Añasco since he had a good hand in such matters, to take thirty footsoldiers down the river by land until he came to a place outside the limits of the other towns where it was said the widow was to be found, and then to bring this woman back in complete peace and friendship; for he desired that all of the land that he should discover and leave behind might remain tranquil and reduced to utter devotion so that he might have less to pacify when establishing settlements.

Even though the day was already well begun, Juan de Añasco set out at once on foot, accompanied by his thirty companions and some domestics. With him also was an Indian cavalier whom the mistress of the town had assigned personally to serve as his guide and, when they should find themselves near her mother, to proceed in advance and inform that lady that the Spaniards had arrived to ask her to return with them peacefully, and that her daughter and all of her vassals begged her to do so. Now this illustrious youth was a close relative of the widowed mother and had been brought up in her very arms. Because of the fact, and especially because of his having turned out to be affable and very noble in character, the woman loved him more than if he were her own son. So, for this reason, the daughter had entrusted him with the message, hoping that the love of her mother for the bearer would render the communication itself less grievous.

The cavalier and generous spirit of this Indian showed well in the expression of his face and the proportion of his body; for where the one is, the other will be found, since they accompany each other like the fruit and the tree. From twenty to twenty-one years of age, with a handsome face and the figure of a gentleman, he made a most gallant ambassador for such a mission. He wore a headdress of many-colored feathers which added to his gentility, and instead of a cape, he had a mantle of fine chamois; for in the summer mantles with fur linings do not serve because of the heat, and if the Indians do sometimes wear them, they turn the fur outward. In his hands he carried a beautiful bow, which besides being good and strong had been treated with a wax that the people of Florida use to stain their weapons whatever color they wish, and that looks like fine enamel and causes the bow or any other wood to appear as if it were glazed. On his back he bore his sheath of arrows. Appareled thus, this youth set out with the Spaniards, and he was so happy to accompany them that his desire to serve and please was indeed clearly evident.

CHAPTER XII

The Indian ambassador destroys himself, and
Juan de Añasco continues on his way.

HAVING traveled almost three leagues of the road in the manner described, Captain Juan de Añasco and his thirty cavaliers paused to eat and, it being very hot, to rest awhile in the shade of some large trees. The Indian cavalier accompanying them as an ambassador had been very gay and joyous until that time and had entertained our Spaniards all along the way with his answers to questions concerning the things of his land and its vicinity; but now he began to grow morose and to sit contemplatively with his hand on his cheek. He gave some long and profound sighs which our men noted well although without inquiring as to the cause of his sorrow lest they afford him more anguish than he had of his own accord.

Then as he sat in the midst of the Spaniards, this Indian placed his sheath before him and began to remove his arrows one at a time and very slowly. Because of the polish and skill employed in making them, these arrows were admirable. All had shafts of reed. For heads, some had the tips of deerhorn worked to very great perfection with four corners like the point of a diamond; others, fish spines marvelously designed for their particular purpose; and still others, heads of palm and additional strong woods that grow in that land—heads with two and three harpoons which were carved as perfectly in the wood as if they were made of iron or steel. In sum, all of the arrows were exquisite, each in its own way, and those present were moved to take them in their hands for the pleasure of examining them closely. Captain Juan de Añasco and his companions took one apiece for this purpose, and all praised the neatness and fastidiousness of the owner. They noted especially that these arrows were feathered in a triangle so that they would leave the bow more accurately, and finally that each possessed a novel and different strangeness which gave it a particular beauty.

What we have told of this cavalier's arrows is not exaggeration; instead, we have fallen short in describing them, for all of the Indians of Florida, and especially the noblemen, stake their whole happiness upon the beauty and polish of their weapons. Those that they make for ornament and daily use, they fashion with all the skill they possess, each striving to outdo the other with some new invention or a finer polish, so that there is generally a very gallant and honest rivalry and emulation going on among them. The many others which they produce as ammunition for warfare are common and despised; but all serve in times of necessity, and at such times those which are polished and esteemed are no more respected than those which are unpolished and scorned.

The Indian ambassador, who as we were saying was taking his arrows one by one from the sheath, now removed from among the last of them a shaft with a flint head almost a sixth of a yard in length and fashioned with the point and edge of a dagger. Observing that the Castilians were not watching him but were engrossed in the examination of his arrows, he struck himself in the gullet in such a way as to inflict a mortal wound, and thus died instantly.[13] Such a strange act shocked the Spaniards and they regretted not having been able to save him. Desiring to know just why this man, who only a short time previously was so joyous and gay, had destroyed himself so grievously, they summoned their native attendants and asked if they were aware of the cause of the tragedy. With copious tears and profound sorrow at the death of their leader, not only because of their love for him but also because of their knowledge of how greatly his sad end would grieve their mistresses, both mother and daughter, these Indians replied that in their opinion there could be but one reason. This was that the cavalier had realized that the communication he bore was contrary to the pleasure and will of the old mother (she having made it clear through the first messengers sent her that she would not see the Castilians), and that he knew that his act of guiding and carrying these same people to her present location so that they might bring her back either with or without her consent was unworthy of the love she bore him or the upbringing she as a mother and a lady had bestowed upon him. Moreover, they said, he must have realized that if he failed to obey the mandates of the younger lady to guide

---

[13] *se hirió en la garganta, de tal suerte, que se degolló y cayó luego muerto* —"*Degollarse*" is to wound mortally, generally to decapitate, but after the expression "wounding himself in the gullet" with an arrow, the meaning is clear enough.

the Spaniards and carry the message (now that he so inconsiderately had been charged with it), he would fall into her enmity and lose her favor. And either of the transgressions, whether against the mother or the daughter, the Indians affirmed, must have been more painful to him than death itself. Seeing himself, therefore, in such a dilemma, and not knowing how to escape without giving offense to one of his mistresses, he had wished to show both that he desired to serve and please them, and that in order to avoid displeasing or angering either one of them (now that he had fallen into the first error and wished to escape the second), he had preferred to die and thus had taken his life with his own hands. It was their belief, they said, that this and nothing else had brought about the death of that poor cavalier; and to the Spaniards their conjecture did not seem unreasonable.

Although grieved at the death of their guide, Juan de Añasco and his thirty companions continued on their mission and the same afternoon traveled three more leagues along the road they had followed until that time, this road being the highway. Then on the next day, in order to move forward, they asked the Indians if they knew where the widow resided and how far it was to that place. These people answered that they were not sure since their deceased comrade had held the secret of her location, but that they would make an attempt to guide them wherever they might command. So in all of this uncertainty, the Castilians marched on, and when they had covered almost four more leagues and it was near noon with the sun shining down upon them most furiously, they discovered more Indians, and placing themselves in ambush, seized one man and three women, there being no more who came. From these four people they now determined to ascertain where the widow might be. But their captives answered sincerely that they had heard she had withdrawn to a place farther on from where she was at first, and that they were ignorant as to just where that place might be. They added, however, that if the Spaniards wished, they would join them and inquire about her from those persons whom they might encounter along the road; for, as they explained, it could be that she was near at hand, and it could be that she was far away. This is a common expression in the language of Peru.

CHAPTER XIII

Juan de Añasco returns to the army without the widow. What happened concerning the gold and silver of Co-fachiqui.

THE statement of the Indians left our Spaniards perplexed as to what they should do, and when they had received many diverse opinions, one of their company spoke more advisedly. "Gentlemen," he said, "for many reasons it seems to me that we are not acting very wisely in making this journey. For since this woman manifested displeasure at the first communication and was unwilling to return with the principal Indians who bore it, I am skeptical as to how she will receive our message. It is now clear that she does not want to come to the Governor, and it could be that, aware that we are going to force her, she will have her people prepared to resist and even to attack us. And whichever of the two she may attempt, we are equipped neither to oppose her nor defend ourselves and return in safety, for we have no horses, and it is horses that put fear into the Indians. And so far as concerns the purpose of our discovery and conquest, I do not see that a widow withdrawn into her retreat can be of so much importance that we all must risk our lives to bring her back when there is no need for her, and when we have her daughter who as the mistress of the province can negotiate with us concerning necessary matters. Furthermore, we know neither the way nor what is ahead of us, and we have no guide in whom we can trust. And over and above all else, the very unexpected death which the ambassador we were bringing with us inflicted upon himself yesterday, admonishes us to proceed with caution and not to advance without some consideration of the points I have mentioned. But in addition to such obstacles," he continued as he turned toward the captain, "I perceive that you are greatly fatigued by the weight of the numerous arms you bear, by the excessive heat of the sun, and by your own corpulence, for you are very fat. These circumstances, therefore, not only persuade us but compel us to return in peace."

Since what their companion had said seemed wise to the others, they by common consent returned to the camp and reported to the Governor all that had happened to them along the way. Then three days later an Indian offered to take the Castilians down the river by water to the retreat of the mother of the mistress of Cofachiqui; so with the counsel and consent of the daughter, Juan de Añasco obstinately set out once again, carrying with him twenty Spaniards in two canoes. On their first day, they discovered the four drowned horses athwart a fallen tree, and weeping for these animals anew, they continued their journey. At the termination of six days when they had made all possible efforts, they returned to say that the good old lady had been warned that at one time or another the Christians had come for her, and she consequently had gone inland to seclude herself among some large mountains where she would be secure from capture. The Governor therefore molested her no further and dismissed her from his mind.

While those things we have told of Captain Juan de Añasco were transpiring in the country, neither the Governor nor any of his people in the town were resting, primarily because of their long-harbored expectations of finding quantities of gold, silver and precious pearls in the province of Cofachiqui. Inspired now by the desire to see themselves rich and free of the anxiety of those hopes, they began to make inquiries a few days after their arrival as to just what there was in that land. They called before them the two Indian boys who in Apalache had described the wealth of Cofachiqui, and then these boys, by order of the Governor, spoke to the mistress of the town, telling her that she should order her people to fetch samples of those metals which their former masters, the traders, used to purchase in her land to carry off and sell elsewhere, these being the same materials for which the Castilians were searching.

Immediately the lady issued an order for all the metals in her land of the colors the Spaniards were seeking to be brought before them, that is, all which were yellow and white; for they had shown her rings of gold and pieces of silver, and had asked for pearls and stones such as those which were set in the rings. The Indians having heard the command of their mistress brought with the utmost haste a great quantity of very golden and resplendent copper[14] which was so superior to the brass[15] found thereabouts that the two youths who had served the merchants could reasonably have been deceived by the sight of it and thought it the same metal that the Castilians had shown them, for they were unable to distinguish between brass and gold. Instead of silver, these people fetched great slabs of iron pyrites which were as thick as boards. I do not know how to give a true and comprehensible picture of them other than to say that they looked white and shone like silver, and that although a yard in length and another in width, they did not weigh anything, and when taken in the hand crumbled like a clod of dry earth.

As for the precious stones, the lady declared that there were none in her land except pearls, but that if the Spaniards wanted these they should go to the upper part of the town. And pointing with her finger, for her hands were uncovered, she showed them a temple about the size of the usual ones to be found in Florida. "That structure," she said, "is the burial place of the nobility of this town. Within it you will find large and small pearls and in addition many seed pearls. Take what you want, and if you desire still more, they may be had in a place a league distant which is the residence and family seat of my own ancestors and the principal village of our province. In that town is a still larger temple which is the burial place of my kinsmen. Within it you will find so many seed pearls and pearls that you will never be able to remove them all even

[14] *cobre.*

[15] *azófar*—This word often signified copper, but since the Inca has used *cobre* above, and since he here very definitely refers to an alloy, we give the more common translation.

though you load each of your horses and as many of your own selves as may come. But take them, and if others are necessary, then we can obtain more and more each day in the pearl fishing that is done in my land."

With this fine news and with the extreme magnificence of the lady, our Spaniards were consoled somewhat for having been deceived in their hopes regarding the great quantities of gold and silver they had thought to find in this province, although it is true that many of them still persisted in saying that the copper or brass contained a mixture, and no small one, of gold. But not carrying acid or touchstones, they could neither make a test that would undeceive them completely nor one that would enable them to collect new and more certain hope.

CHAPTER XIV

The Spaniards visit the burial place of the
nobles and later that of the curacas of
Cofachiqui.

OUR Castilians now awaited the return of the Comptroller and Captain, Juan de Añasco, from his second expedition before going to see the pearls and seed pearls in the temple. Meanwhile the Governor ordered trustworthy persons to guard the place, and he himself roamed about it at night lest someone coveting the riches he had heard described should become rebellious and attempt to carry away in secret the best that there was in that sepulchre. Then as soon as the Comptroller rejoined them, the Governor and the officials of the Imperial Exchequer went to the temple with thirty additional cavaliers, including both captains and outstanding soldiers, to examine the pearls and other objects enclosed there. They found that along all four walls the Indians had set wooden chests similar to those of Spain except that they were without hinges and locks; and they were amazed that these chests were so well constructed since the Indians lacked the implements of European artisans. Within the chests, which rested on benches half a yard high, the infidels had entombed the bodies of their dead without any more preservatives against decomposition than if they were giving them burial in the earth, for these people were not bothered with the stench of decaying flesh since their temples served only as charnel houses and no one entered them to make a sacrifice or pray because, as we stated in the beginning, such ceremonies were not observed among them. But I shall say no more at present of these sepulchres lest I repeat myself in my description of the tombs of the lords curacas which we shall see soon, when it is proper to speak of them.

Besides the large chests serving as sepulchres, there were smaller ones; and in both these and some spacious baskets woven of cane (a material which the Indians of Florida work with great skill and subtlety into whatever they wish just as the people of Spain do willow), there were great quantities of pearls and seed pearls as well as much of such clothing as the native men and women wear. These garments were made of chamois and other small skins which the Indians prepare without removing the fur and with such perfection that as lining for the clothes of princes and great lords they would bring a high price in our Spain.

All now rejoiced to find so much wealth in one place, for it was agreed that here there were more than twenty-five thousand pounds of pearls and seed pearls. Later when the Governor wandered off to see what the rest of the house contained, the officials of the Royal Exchequer, being provided with a balance, very quickly weighed out five hundred pounds of the gems; but when the Governor returned he declared that it was useless for them to arrange such nonsensical and cumbersome loads for the army since it was his intention to take only fifty pounds of pearls and seed pearls. "These," he said, "I will send to Havana as a sample of their quality and degree of purity. As to quantity, those to whom we write about them will simply have to believe us. Therefore return the pearls to their places and take no more of them than fifty pounds."

But the officials thereupon pled that since the pearls had already been weighed and not even a dent had been left among those remaining, he should permit them to remove what they now had, so that the sample might be richer and more abundant. To this suggestion, the Governor acquiesced, and taking for himself a double handful gave the same amount to each of the captains and soldiers who had accompanied him, instructing them to make rosaries on which to pray. And indeed these pearls could have served adequately for such a purpose since they were as thick as fat chick-peas.

Having done no more harm than we have described, the Castilians left that temple with an even greater desire to see the one that the lady had described as the burial place of her parents and grandparents. And two days later the General and his officials as well as the rest of the captains and soldiers of rank—three hundred Spaniards in all—did visit that place. Along the way they journeyed a full league through garden-like lands where there were many trees, both those which bore fruit and others; and among these trees one could travel on horseback without any difficulty, for they were so far apart that they appeared to have been planted by hand.

During the whole of that long league, as the Spaniards traveled, they spread out over the countryside, gathering the fruit and noting the fertility of the soil. In this way they came to Talomeco, a town of five hundred houses situated on an eminence overlooking a gorge of the river. All of the dwellings here were large and were better and more distinguished than ordinary buildings; and the physical appearance of this town made it very evident that as the seat and court of a powerful prince, it had been built with more neatness and embellishment than the common villages. From a distance the habitations of the lord appeared because they were situated in the highest place, and they revealed themselves to be his by a size and construction superior to the others.

In the center of the town and in front of the chieftain's dwellings was the temple or place of burial which the Spaniards had come to see. Here there were things admirable in grandeur, richness, curiousness and majesty—things which were strangely made and composed. I would like very much to be able to describe them as my author wished. But you must accept my willingness and leave that which I do not happen to tell to the imagination of the wise who may supply with their minds what my pen fails to indite. For how true it is that in this picture especially, and in others likewise which will be found in this history, my description falls very far short of the real grandeur of such scenes and of that which is necessary to portray them as they were. Therefore, ten and ten times (a Peruvian expression which means simply many times), I beg you earnestly to believe that I am lacking in words and am hesitant rather than too free and audacious about relating what should be told.

CHAPTER XV

The splendors found in the temple and burial place of the lords of Cofachiqui.[16]

THE Castilians found no people in Talomeco because the previous pestilence had been more rigorous and devastating in this town than in any other of the whole province, and the few Indians who had escaped had not yet reclaimed their homes; hence our men paused but a short time in these houses before proceeding to the temple. Now this temple was large, being more than a hundred feet in length and forty in width. Its walls were high, conforming to the vault of the room, and its roof also was very lofty and drafty, for since the Indians had not discovered tile, they found it necessary to raise their roofs a great deal in order to keep the houses from leaking. The roof of the temple revealed that it was constructed of reeds and very thin canes split in half.

[16] Neither Biedma nor the Gentlemen of Elvas mentions this temple, though it is in Ranjel's account in less gaudy form.

With this material these Indians make neat and well-woven mats much like those of the Moors, and by throwing four, five or six of them on top of each other, they fashion a roof which is useful as well as beautiful both on the exterior and the interior, for neither sun nor water can penetrate it. From now on within this province the Indians for the greater part use cane mats instead of straw to cover their houses.

Over the roof of the temple many large and small shells of different marine animals had been arranged. The Spaniards did not learn how they had been brought inland, but it may be that they too are produced in the rivers of that land which are so numerous and so full of water. These shells had been placed with the inside out so as to show their greatest luster, and they included many conch shells of strange magnificence. Between them, spaces had been left, for each had been placed in its particular order and count; and in these spaces there were large strands (some of pearls and some of seed pearls) half a fathom in length which hung from the roof and descended in a graduated manner so that where some left off others began. The temple was covered on the outside with all these things, and they made a splendid sight in the brilliance of the sun.

To enter the temple, they opened some large doors which were in proportion to the size of the building. Close to these portals were twelve giants, carved in wood and copied from life with so much ferocity and vigor of posture that the Castilians paused and took a stand where they might examine them with care; and they were amazed to discover in such barbarous lands works which would have been prized exceedingly both for their grandeur and perfection had they been found in the most famous temples of Rome at the time of its greatest strength and empire. These giants were placed so as to guard and defend the entrance against those who might wish to come through it. Six were stationed on each side, one standing behind the other and all descending gradually from the largest to the smallest, for the first were four yards high, the second somewhat less, and so on down until the last.

In their hands the giants bore various weapons made in proportion to their bodies. The first two, which were the largest, stood on opposite sides and carried massive clubs, the upper fourth of which was spiked with diamond points and trimmed with strips of copper. They were constructed exactly like those seen in paintings of Hercules, and it would seem that they were copied from these paintings or vice versa. The giants held them upraised in both hands as if threatening to strike whoever might enter the door, and their gesture was so ferocious and so savage as to cause fright. The second giants, which likewise stood opposite each other (for this is the arrangement they all followed) carried broadswords made of wood in the same shape as those made in Spain of iron and steel. The third had sticks a fathom and a half in length, which were unlike clubs and more in the manner of small swingles used to brake flax, the first two-thirds of them being round and the end widening little by little until it assumed the shape of a shovel. The fourth group in the line held large battle-axes which were in conformity with their own stature. One of these weapons had a head of brass with a long and well constructed blade, on the back of which was a four-cornered point a handbreadth in length. The other had a head with exactly the same point and blade, but to the greater amazement and admiration of the Spaniards, it was made of flint. The fifth giants, in turn, held bows which were the length of their bodies and were arched with arrows placed as if they were shooting them. Both bows and arrows showed the extreme neatness and perfection that these Indians possess in making them. One arrow had a head of deerhorn carved with four sides, and the other, a head of flint which in form and size was like an ordinary dagger. The sixth and last of the giants carried very large and beautiful pikes with blades of copper.

All of these giants as well as the first ones appeared to be threatening to wound anyone who attempted to enter by the door. Those with clubs were placed so as to strike down from above; those with broadswords and pikes, to pierce; those with axes, to cut; those with sticks, to strike diagonally; and those with bows and arrows, to shoot from afar. Each one of them was in the most savage and ferocious posture that the weapon in his hand permitted; and what most amazed the Spaniards was to see the naturalness and life-likeness with which these images had been copied in all respects.

The ceiling of the temple, from the walls upward, was adorned like the roof outside with designs of shells interspersed with strands of pearls and seed pearls which were stretched so as to adhere to and follow the contour of the roof. Among these decorations were great headdresses of different colors of feathers such as those made for wear, and in addition to the pearls stretched along the ceiling and the feathers nailed to it, there were many others which had been suspended by some thin, soft-colored strings that could not be seen distinctly. Thus both pearls and feathers seemed to have been placed in the air at different levels so that they would appear to be falling from the roof. In this manner the ceiling of the temple was adorned from the walls upward, and it was an agreeable sight to behold.

CHAPTER XVI

The riches of the burial place and the store of arms that was in it.

GLANCING now from the roof downward, our captains and soldiers perceived that along the highest of the four walls of the temple there were two rows of statues, ranged one over the other. These were figures of men and women, and were of the normal size of the people of that land, who are as large as Philistines. All rested upon a base or pedestal, their order of arrangement being determined by their size; and they served no other purpose than to adorn the walls and prevent their appearing bare at the top, there being no tapestries. The male figures held all of the various weapons that we have named at other times, and these weapons were adorned with bands of pearls and seed pearls, each band being comprised of four, five or six strands. And for greater beauty they were decorated at intervals with exquisitely tinted fringes, for these Indians color everything they wish, and do it extremely well. The statues of the women held nothing in their hands.

On the floor along the walls were some wooden benches which were excellently carved, as was everything in that temple; and resting upon these benches were the chests which served as sepulchres for the lifeless bodies of the curacas who had been lords of the province of Cofachiqui, their children, their brothers and sisters, and their nieces and nephews, no one else being buried in that temple. These chests were well covered with lids, and a yard above each of them was a statue carved from wood and placed on a pedestal against the wall. This was a personal likeness of the man or woman within the chest and was made at the age he or she had attained at death. Thus these likenesses served as memorials for the deceased. The statues of the men held weapons in their hands, whereas those of the women and children held nothing.

The space between the images of the dead and the statues along the upper part of the wall was covered with large and small shields, some of which were round and some oblong. They were made of such strongly woven cane that they would stop the missile of a crossbow or that of an arquebus which will penetrate even more. Both the oblong and the round shields were matted with strands of pearls and seed pearls, and on their edges were fringes of colored thread which beautified them exceedingly.

Running lengthwise along the floor of the temple were three rows of large and small wooden chests placed on benches and so arranged that some rested on top of others, the largest first, then smaller ones, and afterward others still smaller. In this manner four, five and six chests were stacked in such a way that they ranged from the greatest to the least in the form of a pyramid. Between some of them there were aisles which ran the length of the temple and crossed from one side to the other, and by means of which one could walk without any hindrance throughout the whole building and see what there was in each part of it.

All the chests, both great and small, were filled with pearls and seed pearls. And these gems were separated and arranged according to size so that the largest were on the bottom in the first chests, those not so large were in the second, those still smaller were in the third, and so on gradually to the seed pearls which were in the little chests highest up. In this collection of chests, there was such a great quantity of both pearls and seed pearls that on seeing them the Spaniards confessed that what the Señora had said of the temple and burial place was neither presumption nor exaggeration but the truth, and that even though all might load both themselves and their horses (there being more than nine hundred men and upwards of three hundred beasts), they would never be able to remove from the temple all the pearls it contained. But the sight of such a quantity of these gems should not produce much amazement if one considers that the Indians never sold any of those that they found but brought them all to their burial places, and that they must have been doing this for many centuries. And in comparison, we might say (since it is seen each year) that if all the gold and silver that has been brought and is being brought to Spain from Peru were not removed from that land, the people there would be able to cover many temples with roofs of such metals.

Along with this splendor and wealth of pearls in the temple, there were likewise many enormous bundles of chamois. Some were white and some had been dyed various hues, and those which had been dyed were separated according to color. Furthermore there were great bundles of mantles of many colors that were made of chamois, and another great quantity made of skins dressed with their fur—skins of all the various animals both great and small which thrive in that land. Many were of different species and colors of cat, and others, of very fine marten, each of them being so well dressed that among the best of Germany or Muscovy one could not have found better.

All things pertaining to the temple—the roof as well as the walls and the floor—were arranged in the manner and order I have described. Each article was placed with the care and system that one might expect of the neatest people in the world. Moreover, everything was clean, without spiderwebs or dust; hence it would appear that there must have been many people to assist with the ministry and service of the temple—the cleaning and the arranging of each thing in its proper place.

Around the temple, there were eight salas (each separated from the other and arranged in its own order and pattern), which proved to be annexes and were for both ornament and service. The Governor and his cavaliers on resolving to see what these chambers contained, discovered that they were filled with arms arranged in the order we shall now describe. The first sala to be inspected held pikes and nothing else. All were very long and finely worked with blades of brass, which because of its resplendent color appeared to be gold; and all had bands of pearls and seed pearls of three and four rows each placed along them at intervals. In the center, where the pike falls over the shoulder and the point fits on the iron, many were adorned with sleeves of colored chamois, at the ends of which, both above and below, there were three, four, five and six rows of pearls or seed pearls, which enhanced them extremely.

In the second sala there was nothing but maces such as those which we said were held by the first giants at the door of the temple. These differed, however, in that, as weapons which had served as a portion of a nobleman's equipment, they were decorated with bands of pearls and seed pearls and with fringes of colored thread placed at intervals so as to blend with one another and in such a way that all in turn blended with the pearls. Those clubs[17] belonging to the giants were unadorned.

The third sala contained only battle-axes such as those which we have said the giants of the fourth order carried. Some had heads of brass, on one side of which was a blade a sixth of a yard in length

[17] *picas*—Apparently the Inca intends the word *porras* (maces) here.

and on the other, a point like a diamond a fourth of a yard long. The heads of many were of flint and were fastened firmly to their shafts with copper rings. Along these shafts were bands of pearls and seed pearls and fringes of colored thread.

In the fourth sala there were broadswords such as those which the giants of the second order carried. They were made of different kinds of strong woods, and all were decorated along their handles and along the first third of their blades with pearls and seed pearls and fringes.

The fifth sala had only truncheons such as those we said the giants of the third order possessed. These, however, were decorated likewise with their bands of pearls and seed pearls and with colored fringes along the entire shaft to the point where the shovel began. But in order to prevent this chapter from becoming disproportionate, we shall leave the rest until the chapter which follows.

CHAPTER XVII

The army leaves Cofachiqui in two sections.

IN THE sixth sala there was nothing but bows and arrows, all of which were worked with the utmost degree of perfection and exquisiteness that the Indians possess in making them. Their heads were fashioned of wood, of the bones of land and marine animals, of flint such as the one with which we said the Indian cavalier destroyed himself, and of copper such as those which are found on arrows in our Spain. Some bore harpoons of this same copper while others had small chisels, lances and darts which looked as if they too might have been fashioned in Castile. It was noted that the heads of flint differed from each other, for some were made in the shape of a harpoon and some like a chisel, whereas others were round like a puncheon and still others had two edges like the point of a dagger. The Spaniards marveled at all of these things and were amazed that such articles could be wrought from material as rough as flint. But when one considers what Mexican history reveals of the broadswords and other arms that the natives of that land made of flint, a part of the wonder of those weapons will be lost. The bows were exquisitely carved and enameled in the different colors given them with a certain wax, which makes them so shiny as to cast a reflection. In speaking of this temple, Juan Coles has the following to say: "And in a separate room there were more than fifty thousand bows with their quivers or sheaths filled with arrows." In addition to the luster which would have been sufficient for them, these bows had many strands of pearls and seed pearls arranged at intervals upon them. Such strands or rings began at the handles and extended in graduated order to the tips. Thus the first rings were of thick pearls and consisted of seven or eight strands; the second were of smaller pearls and fewer strands; and in this way they continued by degrees to those last ones near the tips which were made up of very small seed pearls. The arrows likewise had rings at intervals, but of seed pearls only and not of pearls.

In the seventh sala there was a great quantity of round shields made of wood and of cowhide that had been brought from distant lands, the one and the other being decorated with pearls and seed pearls and fringes of colored thread. And in the eighth sala were great numbers of oblong shields, all of which were of cane, woven with such precision and strength that few crossbows were found among the Spaniards capable of passing an arrow completely through them. Such an experiment was tried in places outside of Cofachiqui. The oblong shields like the round ones were also adorned with networks of pearls and seed pearls and colored fringes.

Thus the eight salas were filled with all offensive and defensive arms, and in each there was such a quantity of its particular kind of weapon that the Governor and his Castilians were amazed as much by the multitude of them as by the neatness and skill with which they had been fashioned and assembled.

Having seen and made note of the splendors, sumptuousness and wealth of the temple, and of the great quantity of arms and ornaments and the order in which each thing had been placed and arranged, the General and his captains asked the Indians what such magnificent equipment signified. The latter answered that the lords of that kingdom, and particularly of the province of Cofachiqui and others which they would see farther on, looked upon the ornamentation and luxury of their burial places as their chief greatness, and that they thus tried to magnify them with all the arms and riches they would hold, as the Spaniards had observed in that particular temple.

I have felt it wise to write so copiously of the things in this temple and burial place because it was the richest and most superb of all those that our Spaniards saw in Florida, and again because he who gave me the account ordered that I do so; for, as he said, this was one of the greatest and most magnificent of all the things he had beheld in the New World, and he had passed through the most and better part of Mexico and Peru. It is true, however, that when he traveled through the latter kingdoms they had already been sacked of their most precious riches, and their most majestic edifices had been leveled to the ground.

The officials of the Imperial Exchequer discussed the subject of carrying away His Majesty's fifth of the pearls, seed pearls and other riches in the temple. But the Governor informed these men that such nonsensical loads would serve only to encumber the army, which already was unable to bear even the necessary burdens of arms and ammunition, and that they therefore should leave everything as it was since they were not dividing the land but exploring it. Then he added that when this land should be apportioned and settled, he to whose lot it might fall could pay the fifth. Thus no one touched any of the things they had seen, and all returned to the mistress of Cofachiqui, bringing indeed something to relate of the majesty of her burial ground.

All that has been said of the town of Cofachiqui, Alonso de Carmona relates in his account, although not so much at length as

I do in mine. But he speaks especially of the province of Cofachiqui and of the reception which the Señora gave the Governor as
he crossed the river, declaring that she and each of her female
attendants wore great strands of thick pearls cast about their necks
and tied to their wrists, whereas the men wore them only at their
throats. He states also that these gems lose much of their beauty
and fine luster when extracted with fire, which leaves them black.
And he says that in the town of Talomeco, where the rich temple
and burial place was located, they found four large houses filled
with the bodies of people who had died of the pestilence. Up to
here, these are the words of Alonso de Carmona.

After examining the temple, the Adelantado spent ten more
days obtaining information as to what there was in the provinces
bordering on Cofachiqui, and he was told that all of them were
fertile and abundant in food and were thickly populated. On learning this, he gave the order to prepare to proceed with the explorations. Then accompanied by his captains, he took leave of the
Indian mistress of Cofachiqui and the principal people of her town,
thanking them profusely for the courtesy shown him in their land.
Thus he left them as friends and enthusiasts of the Spaniards.

The army departed from the town in two groups since they were
not carrying sufficient food for all to leave together. Because of
this shortage the General had issued an order for Baltasar de Gallegos, Arias Tinoco and Gonzalo Silvestre to go with a hundred
cavalrymen and two hundred footsoldiers to a place twelve leagues
hence where the Señora had stored six hundred bushels of corn
which she had offered the Spaniards. Here they were to take what
they could carry of the corn and then follow on foot and meet the
Governor, who would proceed by the highway to Chalaque,[18] this
being the next province along that route bordering on Cofachiqui.
Thus ordered, the three captains left with their three hundred soldiers, and the Governor and the rest of the army continued along

---

[18] In the west central part of South Carolina.

the highway for eight days, eventually reaching Chalaque without experiencing anything worthy of remembrance.

Afterward, the three captains had the following events to relate. When they arrived at the storehouse, they took only two hundred bushels of corn, this being all they could carry, and then they turned their steps toward that part of the road where the Governor was traveling. Proceeding in this direction for five days, they came to the main highway, only to observe by tracks left by the army that it had already passed on and was ahead of them. This realization annoyed the two hundred footsoldiers, and they made up their minds to disregard the orders of their captains and cover as much ground as possible until they had overtaken their General; for, they said, since they carried very little food and were ignorant as to how many days it would require to come up with him, it was well to anticipate in time what might happen and make haste to rejoin him before their provisions were exhausted and they had perished of hunger. These soldiers were inspired to speak thus by their fear of experiencing again what they had suffered in the wilderness before their arrival in the province of Cofachiqui.

CHAPTER XVIII

What occurred to the three captains on their journey. How the army came to Xuala.[19]

THE three captains were distressed at the rebellion being perpetrated, for three of their horses, on the previous day, had been seized with pains in the bowels and, thus hampered, could not travel to the extent the footsoldiers desired. So they told these men that it was foolish to abandon three horses just to gain one day more or less of travel when they were aware of how much aid these

---

[19] In the foothills of northwestern South Carolina, near the borders of Georgia and North Carolina.

animals afforded them against their enemies. But those on foot replied that the lives of three hundred Castilians were of more significance than the health of three horses, that they did not know whether the trip would last one day or ten or twenty or a hundred, and that it was therefore only just to consider the things of most importance rather than those of so little moment. Speaking thus, they now began mutinously to march with the utmost haste and in no order whatsoever. At that all three captains rushed forward while one of them, acting as their spokesman, said:

"Gentlemen! Please consider the fact that you are on your way to your Captain General, who, as you know, is a man so precise in military affairs that it will weigh very heavily upon him to learn that you have disobeyed and broken his order and command. It could be, and in my opinion it will be, that we shall overtake him today, or tomorrow or day after tomorrow at the very latest; for it is not to be believed that having left us behind, he will go far. This being so, we should fall into much disgrace if without having passed through extreme want, we should be so weak as to fear uncertain hunger to such an extent that through this fear alone we abandoned three of these animals which are so greatly esteemed. For, as you know, our horses are the nerve and sinew of our army, and because of them our enemies dread us and our friends do us honor. And since the loss of a horse is so much lamented when the Indians kill just one of them for us, how much more would be deplored the loss of three if we should abandon them because of our weakness and cowardice and without any necessity for doing so other than that which we imagine. And what I see in such behavior which is even more worthy of lamentation is the loss of both your reputation and ours, for the General and the other captains and soldiers will say, and very rightly so, that during the four days we traveled without them, we were not able to govern you, nor you to obey us. But when they will have learned just how the incident came about, they will realize that you only are to blame and that we had no obligation other than that of dissuading you with reasonable arguments.

Therefore, gentlemen, please desist from doing such an evil thing, for it would be more honorable for us to die as good soldiers because of having performed our duty, than to live in infamy because of having fled an imaginary danger."

With these words, the footsoldiers were placated and persuaded to halt, but not without having traveled five or six leagues, which was as far as the sick horses could go.

At noon of the day following the mutiny, while these soldiers were on the march, there suddenly arose a great storm of strong contrary winds accompanied by much thunder, lightning and thick hail; and had there not happened to be near the road some large walnut trees as well as other heavy foliage under which to find shelter, all would have perished, for the hail was so heavy that the largest stones were like hen eggs, and the smallest like nuts. Those who bore shields put them over their heads, but with all that, if a stone caught them uncovered, it injured them seriously. God willed, however, that the tempest be of brief duration, for had it lasted longer, their shelter would have been insufficient to save them from death; and in the brief time that it did last, it caused them so much damage that they were unable to travel further on either that or the following day. On the third day, however, they continued their journey, coming to some small settlements called Chalaques,[20] whose inhabitants had not dared wait in their homes for the Governor but had fled to the woods, so that now there remained only the old men and old women, almost all of whom were blind. Continuing for three more days beyond the settlements of Chalaques, they overtook the Governor, who was encamped in a beautiful valley of the province of Xuala; for on his arrival at this place two days previously he had resolved to halt for the purpose of awaiting those captains and three hundred soldiers who were trailing him.

Along this particular route which these Castilians took from the town of Cofachiqui, where the Señora remained, to the first valley

---

[20] Although the name is spelled here and in the sentence which follows with an *s*, it is without doubt the same as that used on page 325, above, to designate the province.

of the province of Xuala, there were probably a little more or less than fifty leagues. All of this land was flat and peaceful, and there were small rivers running through it at distances of three or four leagues apart. There were but few mountains here, and they were possessed of much grass for cattle; moreover they were easy to traverse either on horseback or afoot. All fifty leagues, both that which was already populated and cultivated and that which was yet to be tilled, had the common characteristic of being good land.

In the whole of that distance between the province of Apalache and that of Xuala where we now have the Governor and his army, our Castilians (unless I have calculated incorrectly) spent fifty-seven days on the road. Their journey was directed more or less toward the northeast but many days they marched toward the north. And those mariners who accompanied them said that the swollen river which passed through Cofachiqui was the same which on the coast was called the Santa Elena. They did not make this statement because of knowing it to be a fact, but because, according to their journey, it appeared to them to be so. This uncertainty, however, and many others about which our history maintains silence will be clarified when, Our Lord God being served, that kingdom is won for the advancement of His Holy Catholic Faith. But in the fifty-seven-day journey from Apalache to Xuala, we would estimate the Spaniards covered an average of four and a half leagues per day, although some days they traveled more and some less. So according to this computation, it was not quite two hundred and sixty leagues to Xuala. And since, as we have said, they journeyed a hundred and fifty leagues from the Bay of the Holy Spirit to Apalache, we may estimate that they now had traveled in all slightly less than four hundred leagues.[21]

In the towns under the jurisdiction and vassalage of Cofachiqui, through which our Spaniards passed, they found many natives of other provinces who had been enslaved. In order to secure these

[21] According to the Inca's figures he should have said "a little more than four hundred leagues."

people and to prevent their fleeing, the Indians had wounded each of them in one foot, cutting the tendons above the instep where the foot joins the leg, or above the heel. And when they were thus perpetually and inhumanly fettered, they had put them in the interior far from their own lands to till the soil and do other servile jobs. These were people, however, whom they had captured in ambushes made while hunting and fishing and not in open battles fought between two powers with organized forces.

Farther back we told how the Captain and Comptroller Juan de Añasco had gone twice for the mother of the mistress of Cofachiqui, but we failed to give the principal reason why so much persistent effort was made to obtain her. It was that the Spaniards had learned that she had in her possession six or seven loads of thick pearls which being unpierced were better than those seen in the burial places; for the latter, having been pierced with hot copper needles, had collected a certain amount of smoke and consequently lost much of their natural excellence and luster. Hence our men wished to learn if the unpierced pearls were as large and good as the Indians had claimed them to be.

CHAPTER XIX

Some of the great spiritual endowments of the Señora of Cofachiqui are described.

THE Governor and his army rested fifteen days in the town and province of Xuala (which belonged to this same Señora of Cofachiqui, although it was in itself a separate province) because they had discovered in this place and its neighborhood a great amount of corn and of all the other grains and vegetables that we have said were to be found in Florida. Moreover, it was necessary to remain this long period of time in order to refresh and restore the horses, for having received such a scant provision of corn in the province of Cofachiqui they were emaciated and debilitated. It was even believed that this was the reason the three horses mentioned further back had lacked strength, and that it was merely to alleviate a bad situation and placate the rebellious soldiers that the statement had been made that these animals were suffering with pains in the bowels.

The town of Xuala lay at the foot of a mountain on the bank of a river, which though not very large, flowed with great swiftness; and it was this river which marked the boundary of Cofachiqui. Here the Indians served and regaled the Governor and his entire army extensively, for this town likewise belonged to the Señora of Cofachiqui, and since she herself had sent the command for her Indians to do so, they were making every possible effort both to obey their lady and to please the Spaniards.

When fifteen days had elapsed and the horses had recovered, our Spaniards set out from Xuala, and on their first day passed through the many fine fields and tilled lands of that province. Then for the next five days they proceeded across an uninhabited but very pleasant range of mountains. Here they found a great quantity of oaks and some mulberries, extensive grazing lands, gullies, and streams which though shallow were swift, and finally, cool, delightful valleys. The section of the range crossed was twenty leagues wide.

But let us return to the Señora of Cofachiqui, for we still have not left her holdings. Since it is only right that the generous deeds of this woman be recorded, we will say that she was not content just with having served and entertained the General and his captains and soldiers in her own house and court, or with having provided the supplies needed for their journey, scant as provisions were in her land, or again with having sent Indian porters to minister to them along the fifty leagues to the province of Xuala; but she also instructed her vassals to carry willingly all that the Spaniards might request from Xuala, where there was so much food, through the twenty leagues of wilderness they must encounter before coming to Guaxule, and furthermore to give them servants and every provision as if to herself. Along with these things she arranged for four principal Indians to accompany the General for the purpose of governing and issuing orders to the servants so that the Spaniards might be more comfortable on their journey.[22]

All such arrangements the woman made for her own province, but you must know likewise that she was mindful of those provinces which were not hers and desired that the same provision be made in each of them. Accordingly she issued an order that the four principal Indians, after having entered the province of Guaxule, which lay along her borders on that route, should go forward as her emissaries and charge the Curaca of that land under threat of war with fire and blood to serve the Governor and his whole army just as she herself had done. This message the Governor knew nothing about until after they had passed the wilderness and the four principal Indians had begged permission to go in advance to deliver it. Then he and his captains were amazed and filled with new gratitude to see that this Indian lady had not been content merely to serve and entertain them with so much love and kindness in her own house and land, but in addition had arranged beforehand for the other provinces. Thus they came to understand more clearly the spirit and desire that she had always possessed to serve both the Governor and his Castilians; for it was a fact, which they perceived, that she was doing everything in her power to please them. Yet she always asked the General to pardon her for not being able to accomplish everything she desired to do in his service; and in truth she was so anguished and saddened by her inability to do more that it was necessary for the Spaniards themselves to console her. With these noble services of a generous spirit, and with others which she bestowed upon her vassals (according to what they divulged), this lady revealed that she was a woman truly worthy of the estates she held and of others even greater, and that she was undeserving of

---

[22] The Elvas account states that De Soto forced the Lady of Cofachiqui to accompany him and that she eventually escaped, thus causing the Spaniards considerable pain because of the fact that she carried away with her a small casket of unbored pearls.

such a fate as that of having to remain an infidel. But the Castilians did not invite her to receive baptism because, as has been explained, they were determined to propagate the faith only after they had made a settlement in that land; for traveling as they did from one province to another without stopping, the faith could ill be preached.

CHAPTER XX

Events which occurred in the army until its arrival at Guaxule and at Ychiaha.

WE HAVE already told how the Governor and his army had left Xuala and traveled for five days through the wilderness which they encountered before reaching Guaxule. But turning back in our story, I must inform you that on the same day that they departed from the town of Xuala, they missed three slaves who had fled during the previous night. Two of them, who were of Negro blood, were servants of Captain Andrés de Vasconcelos de Silva; whereas the third, who was a Moor from Barbary, belonged to Don Carlos Enríquez, a previously mentioned cavalier who was a native of Xerez de Badajoz. It was believed that the flight of these men and their desire to remain among the Indians was a result of an affection for women rather than anything else;[23] and although the Spaniards made an effort to recapture them, they could not do so, for in general it pleased the Indians of this great kingdom (as we shall see more clearly later) to have the people of the Spaniards[24] remain with them. Such evil behavior on the part of the Negroes caused amazement because they were considered to be good Christians and friends of their master; but of the Moor it came as no surprise

[23] According to the Elvas account, the Governor afterward received a report that the Lady of Cofachiqui and one of the escaped slaves of Andrés de Vasconcelos were living as man and wife.

[24] *cosas de los Españoles*—literally, things of the Spaniards.

and rather confirmed the opinion always held that he was a very malicious man in every respect.

Another incident occurred two days later while the army was traveling through this same uninhabited region. In the middle of the journey and during the day when the sun shone brightest, Juan Terrón, a footsoldier born in Alburquerque and indeed appropriately named,[25] approached a friend who was mounted, and removing from a knapsack a small canvas bag containing more than six pounds of pearls, he said: "I do not want these pearls; take them and carry them away."

But the horseman replied: "It is best that you keep them since your need for them is greater than mine. You can send them to Havana and purchase three or four horses and mares in order to save yourself the bother of having to travel on foot; for, according to what has been said, the Governor is resolved to send messengers there soon with news of what we have discovered."

Angered at his comrade's refusal to accept his gift, Juan Terrón cried: "Well, since you do not want the pearls, I swear to God that I will not take them either, so they will have to remain here."

With this remark, he untied the little bag and swinging it along the ground with a movement of his arm like that of a person sowing seed, strewed all the pearls in the woods and grass. This he did in order to avoid having to carry them on his back, although he was robust and strong enough to bear almost as much as a mule. The deed done, he returned the bag to his knapsack as if it were worth more than the pearls themselves, thus leaving in amazement not only his friend but all the others who witnessed his foolishness. They had not imagined that he would do such a thing, and had they even suspected it would have prevented him since the pearls were worth more than six thousand ducats[26] in Spain, each of them being as thick and large as a hazelnut or a fat chick-pea. And what was most prized about them was the fact that, being as yet unpierced,

[25] The word "terrón" means "a clod of earth."
[26] The ducat being worth about $2.25, Juan Terrón apparently had discarded more than $13,500.00 worth of pearls.

they possessed a perfect color and were not smoked. As many as thirty soldiers turned back to search for them among the grass and trees. And when they saw that they were so fine, these men were even more distressed by the loss incurred and in consequence composed the following refrain which they employed among themselves: "Pearls are not for Juan Terrón."

Juan Terrón would never tell where he obtained the pearls. But since his companions joked with him many times afterward about his loss and ridiculed him for his folly, which indeed well suited the rusticity of his name, he said to them one day when he was most miserable: "For the love of God, do not mention this matter to me again; I assure you that each time you remind me of my stupidity, I feel a desire to hang myself from a tree." But prodigality incites such feelings in those who are its slaves, for when they have once spilled their possessions in vanity, it moves them to desperate acts. On the other hand, generosity, as such an excellent virtue, gladdens with great gentleness those who embrace and practice it.

Having marched five days through the mountain range, without anything else happening to them that may be told, the Castilians came to the province and the town of Guaxule,[27] which was situated in the midst of many small rivers born among those mountains they had crossed as well as others lying further on. The lord of the province, who likewise was named Guaxule, came out a half a league from his town accompanied by five hundred noblemen, who, conforming to the general custom of all that land, were adorned with large feather headdresses and rich robes of different skins. With such pomp as this, he welcomed the Governor, showing him signs of love and addressing him with very courteous words, spoken with the most lordly semblance. Then he carried him to his town, which consisted of three hundred dwellings, and lodged him in his own house; for when he had received the message delivered by the emissaries of the mistress of Cofachiqui, he not only had cleared

---

[27] At the southwest tip of the present state of North Carolina.

his home for the Governor but also had prepared other things in order better to serve him. His habitation, like similar ones we have described, was situated on a high hill and was surrounded by a walk which six men could pass along abreast.

The Governor remained four days in this town to obtain information as to what there was in its vicinity. Then from here he marched five leagues a day for six more days to another town and province called Ychiaha, whose lord bore the same name. The road he traveled in this journey followed down the many little streams which passed through Guaxule and after a short time joined to form a river so powerful that at Ychiaha, only thirty leagues distant, it was larger than the Guadalquivir at Seville. The town of Ychiaha was situated on the tip of a great island more than five leagues in length, which had been formed by the river.[28]

The Cacique of this town came out to receive the Governor and made a great celebration for him with all the demonstrations of love and rejoicing that he could show; and the Indians whom he brought with him did the same with the rest of the army, being most pleased to see them. Taking them across the river in the many canoes and boats prepared for the purpose, they lodged them in their own houses as if they were blood brothers. And everything else for their service and entertainment was done with the same pleasure; for, according to what they themselves said, they desired that their very hearts should be opened and placed before the Spaniards that they might see with their own eyes how much they had enjoyed having known them.

At Ychiaha, the Governor exerted the same efforts as he had in the other towns to learn what there was in that land and its vicinity. In answer to the questions put to him, the Curaca said, among other things, that thirty leagues distant there were mines of the yellow metal which the Spaniards were seeking, and that to assure himself of this fact his lordship should dispatch two of his men,

---

[28] In southern Tennessee near the Alabama-Georgia line. The island was Burns Island.

or as many more as he pleased, to examine these mines. And he added that he would provide guides to conduct the men there and bring them back safely. On hearing the Curaca's remark, a couple of Spaniards offered to accompany the Indians. One was Juan de Villalobos, a native of Seville, and the other, Francisco de Silvera, a native of Galicia. They departed at once, preferring to go on foot, although they had horses, for they felt that in this way they could accomplish more in a shorter time.

CHAPTER XXI

How they extract the pearls from their shells. The report brought by those who went to seek the gold mines.

ON THE day after the two Spaniards left to examine the gold mines they had been so eager to find, the Curaca came to visit the Governor and made him a present of a beautiful strand of pearls, which, had they not been pierced with fire, would have been magnificent; for the strand itself was two fathoms in length and all of the pearls besides being like hazelnuts were practically identical in size. The Governor received the gift very gratefully and in recompense gave the Curaca pieces of velvet and other cloths of different colors, as well as additional things from Spain which that Indian greatly valued. And when asked if the pearls had been found in his land, the Cacique replied in the affirmative, adding that in the temple and burial place of that same town, which held both his parents and grandparents, there was a great quantity of them, and that if the Governor wished, he might carry away all or whatever part of them he chose.

The Adelantado expressed his appreciation for the Cacique's good will, but said that though he might want the pearls, he would not wish to desecrate the ancestral burial ground of the Indians, and that since he did not want them, he would be even more reluctant to do so. And he explained that he had received the pearls presented him in the strand simply because they were a gift from the Cacique himself. All he desired, he added, was to know how the pearls were extracted from the shells wherein they were produced.

The Cacique replied that his Indians would fish for pearls that very afternoon and night and that at eight o'clock of the next day the Governor might see how they took them from the shells. Then he immediately commanded that forty canoes be sent out with instructions to search as diligently as possible for oysters and to return the following morning. And on the ensuing day before the canoes arrived, he had a great amount of firewood piled up on some level ground alongside the river and lit so that many embers might be available. When the canoes returned, these embers were spread out and the oysters cast upon them. Thus the shells opened with the heat of the fire and one could search within their flesh for pearls. From among the first that opened, the Indians removed ten or twelve gems as thick as medium sized chick-peas. These were taken to the Curaca and the Governor, who had been watching together, and they observed that they were perfect in all respects except for the fact that the heat of the fire and the smoke had damaged their fine natural color.

Having witnessed the removal of the pearls, the Governor repaired to his lodging to dine. A short time after he had finished, Pedro López, a soldier who was born in Guadalcanal, entered and disclosed a pearl which he bore in his hand. "My Lord," this man said, "I carried to my lodging a few of the oysters which the Indians brought in today, and had them boiled. Afterward while eating, I bit down upon this pearl which might have broken my teeth. Since it seems to me to be good, I am bringing it to Your Lordship so that you personally may send it to my lady, Doña Isabel de Bobadilla."

"I am grateful for your good will," the Adelantado replied, "and shall regard as received both the gift and the kindness which you proffer Doña Isabel so that, whenever the occasion presents itself, I may reward you. However, it will be better for you to keep the pearl in order that it may be carried to Havana, where in exchange for it you may obtain two stallions and two mares as well as other things you need. But what I will do, because of the good spirit you have shown, is to pay from my own possessions the fifth of the value of the pearl which must go to His Majesty."

The Spaniards with the Governor examined this pearl, and those who prided themselves on knowing something about stones, gave an estimate of its value. They said that in Spain it was worth four hundred ducats[29] because it was the size of a thick hazelnut, shell and all, and again because it was perfectly round and of a clear and resplendent color, for not having been extracted with fire like the others, there had been no damage to its color and beauty. We are giving an account of these details even though they are so unimportant because through them one may comprehend the richness of that land.

One day while these Spaniards were in the town of Ychiaha, a tragedy occurred which grieved all of them exceedingly. It happened that a cavalier, Luis Bravo de Xerez, who was a native of Badajoz, while walking with lance in hand through a plain near the river, saw a dog passing nearby, and he threw his weapon, hoping to kill the animal and eat it; for with the general lack of meat in all that land, the Castilians ate as many dogs as they could lay hold of.[30] The lance, however, did not strike the animal but instead slipped forward across the plain and fell over the bluff to the river below. There it by chance penetrated the temples of a soldier who was fishing with a cane, and he fell dead immediately. Unaware that his throw had been so disastrous, Luis Bravo went in search of his lance, only to find it crossed through the temples of Juan Mateos (for this was the soldier's name), a native of Almendral. Of all the

---

[29] About nine hundred dollars.

[30] Elvas speaks of the great craving of the men for dog meat and the scramble which would result when the army arrived in a town where there were only twenty or thirty dogs. And woe be unto the successful hunter who did not share his catch with his captain.

Spaniards in the expedition, this man alone had grey hair, and everyone accordingly addressed him as "Father," respecting him as if he actually were their sire. So in general, our Castilians lamented the misfortune of this soldier, who, in going out to enjoy himself had been killed so miserably. But how near and how certain death is to us at all times and in all places!

The things related occurred in the camp during those ten days that the two companions spent going and coming in their expedition to the mines. Later these men reported that the mines contained very fine brass such as they had seen farther back, and that the disposition of the land led them to believe that they would not fail to find gold and silver if they but looked for its veins and sources. And they added that all the land they had seen was good for sowing and grazing, and that the Indians in the towns through which they had passed had received them with much affection and rejoicing. They had entertained and regaled them a great deal, even going so far as to send them each evening, after they had feasted, two beautiful young maidens to sleep with them and divert them during the night.[31] They claimed, however, that they had not dared touch these women lest when morning came they be shot. For it was their suspicion that the Indians in sending the women were seeking an excuse to take the lives of their guests. This is what our Spaniards feared, but it is possible that their hosts, on observing that they were young, were simply trying to provide them with lavish entertainment; for had the Indians wished to destroy them, they would have felt no need to look for excuses to do so.

---

[31] *les enbiavan dos mozas hermosas, que durmiesen con ellos, y los entretuviesen la noche*—The custom of presenting women to their guests was not unusual and was even prevalent among the Indians. As Garcilaso himself explains, the Indians had severe laws against cohabitation, but these laws apparently applied in the main to adultery and not to fornication in general, although there were cases of wives being permitted by law to commit adultery with the consent of the husband.

CHAPTER XXII

The army leaves Ychiaha and enters Acoste and Coza.[32] The hospitality offered them in these provinces.

HAVING received an account of the gold mines the two Spaniards went to examine, the Governor commanded the army to prepare to depart on the following day. This our Castilians did, leaving the Curaca and his principal Indians very happy with the gifts that both the Governor and his captains had bestowed upon them in recompense for their hospitality.

That day they traveled down the island, which as we have said, was five leagues in length. At its extremity, where the river turned to meet itself, there lay another town called Acoste which belonged to a lord quite different from the previous one. For this man received the Castilians in a manner very unlike that of the Cacique of Ychiaha, showing them no semblance of friendship. Instead he was arrayed for battle with more than fifteen hundred Indian warriors, all of whom were well provided with feather headdresses and with arms which they carried in their hands, none wishing to relinquish these arms even when the Spaniards had already been received in the town. And they proved to be so fierce and eager to fight that there was not one among them who, when speaking to a Spaniard, did not make a bold attempt to nail him in the eyes with his fingers. Moreover if they were questioned, they answered so arrogantly, shaking and brandishing their arms with clenched fists (signs that they make when they wish to fight), that their shamelessness could not be tolerated, nor could their words and gestures which so provoked everyone that many times the Castilians, having lost patience, were on the point of closing with them. But the Adelantado prohibited their doing so, instructing them to endure everything

[32] They are now in the present state of Alabama.

that the Indians might do, and under no circumstances to sever that thread of peace they had borne with them since leaving the bellicose province of Apalache. Accordingly they did as the Governor commanded, but both sides spent the entire night arranged in squadrons as declared enemies.

On the ensuing day, however, the Indians were more affable. The Curaca and his principal men came with a new attitude to offer the Governor all they possessed in the land and to give him corn for his journey. It was believed that this civility had been motivated by some favorable message that the lord of Ychiaha had sent concerning the Spaniards. The General thanked them for their offer and paid them for the corn, so they were content. Then on the same day, he left the town and crossed the river in canoes and rafts, of which there were great numbers. And all gave praise to God for delivering them from the town of Acoste without their having broken the peace which they had sustained until that point.

On leaving Acoste, they entered a great province called Coza. Here the Indians came out to receive them in peace, offering complete friendship and giving them supplies and guides for the road between the towns. The Curaca and lord of this province had the same name as the province itself. That part of it traversed by the Spaniards was more than a hundred leagues in length, and all of it was so fertile and thickly populated that on some days while traveling, they passed through ten and twelve towns, and there were more which lay on one side or the other of the road. The truth is that the towns were small, but the Indians came out from them with great happiness to receive the Christians. They offered them hospitality in their homes, giving them most willingly of what they had; and those of one town would accompany them along the way, serving them until they were received in the next town and then returning to their homes. In this manner they took them through the whole of the hundred leagues, the Spaniards lodging some nights in the villages and others in the country according to how the daily marches chanced to turn out, each of them being four leagues, more or less.

The lord of the province of Coza which lay at the next boundary, sent new emissaries each day who repeated the same message many times. This message congratulated the Governor on his safe arrival, begged him to travel through the land very slowly so as to enjoy and provide himself with all that he could, and stated that he, the Cacique, was waiting in the principal village of his province to serve his lordship and all of his men with such love and willingness as they would see.

There is nothing to say about the next twenty-three or twenty-four days that the Spaniards traveled, other than to tell over and over again of the fine reception they were given by the Indians until they came to the principal village of Coza, from which the whole province took its name. Here lived the lord of the land who, to receive the Governor, came out a full league from the town accompanied by more than a thousand noblemen, all of whom were magnificently clothed in robes lined with different skins, many of them fine marten, which gave off a strong odor of musk. Moreover they wore great feather headdresses, these being the adornments of which the natives of this great kingdom are most proud. Since these people were very comely (as in general all the Indians of that land are) and wore feathers of many different colors, which rose half a fathom in the air, and since they were placed in the field in the form of a squadron with twenty men in each row, they presented a beautiful and agreeable spectacle.

With this military and lordly pomp and ostentation, the Indians received the General and his captains and soldiers, making the greatest demonstrations they could to reveal the contentment which they said they felt at seeing the Spaniards in their land. They lodged the Governor in one of the three houses that the Curaca maintained in different parts of the town. These dwellings were constructed on the same model as others we have mentioned, and they were elevated so as to have the advantages a lord's habitation must have over those of his vassals. The village itself was located on the bank of a river, and its five hundred large and good houses well showed it to be the center of this province, which, as has been said, was so extensive and important. The half of the town near the Governor's lodging had been emptied, and here the captains and soldiers were quartered, there being room for all because the houses were capable of holding many people. For eleven or twelve days the Spaniards were served and regaled in this village of Coza by the Curaca and all his people as if they were beloved brothers. Certainly no exaggeration is sufficient to describe the affection, care and diligence with which these Indians ministered unto them, for they did so in such a way as to amaze the Spaniards themselves.

CHAPTER XXIII

The Cacique Coza offers his lands to the Governor to settle and populate. How the army leaves that Curaca's province.

ON ONE of the days that the Spaniards tarried in this town called Coza, the lord of the place, who was eating at the Governor's table, spoke of many things pertaining to the conquest and settlement of Florida; and to the great satisfaction of the Adelantado, he answered all that was asked concerning such matters. Then when he felt that the occasion was propitious, he arose, and after making a great bow of veneration to the Governor in the customary manner of the Indian people, he fastened his eyes upon the cavaliers stationed on both sides of the Governor and spoke in such a way as to address everyone. "My Lord," he said, "the affection which has increased within me for Your Lordship and all of your men during these few days I have known you, impels me to entreat that in the event you are seeking good lands in which to settle, you consider it expedient to remain in my land and establish a site here; for I believe this province to be one of the best that Your Lordship will have seen among all those you have discovered in this kingdom.

But I would have Your Lordship know that you by chance have passed through and seen the poorest and worst part of my land, and if you should care to examine it more at leisure, I myself will conduct you through better sections which will give you complete satisfaction, and from which you can choose whatever seems best for the populating and founding of your home and court. And if you do not desire to grant me this favor at the moment, at least do not refuse to pass the coming winter in this town since that season is already at hand. Here we shall serve you, as Your Lordship will see, for I shall ease your work, and Your Lordship then will be able to send out his captains and soldiers at leisure so that after having examined all parts of my land, they may bring for your greater satisfaction, a verification of what I have said."

Grateful for the Curaca's good will, the Governor replied that whereas he in no manner could settle in the interior before knowing what port or ports there were along the coast to receive those ships and people who might come from Spain and other places with livestock and plants and all additional things necessary for founding a town, he would always maintain friendship with the Cacique and when the proper occasion arose would accept his offer. But meanwhile, he said, let the Curaca Coza be content, for he was going to return without delay to populate that land, and then he would do whatever that chieftain might request for his pleasure and happiness. Kissing the Governor's hands, the Cacique answered that he accepted the words of his lordship as pledges of his promise, and that he would guard them in his heart and memory until he saw their fulfillment, which he desired in the extreme. The Curaca Coza was twenty-six or twenty-seven years of age and was very much a gentleman, as are most of the lords of that land. Furthermore he was a man of fine understanding and spoke with discretion, giving thoughtful consideration to everything asked of him. In fact, he appeared to have been brought up at court in an atmosphere of the best learning and culture.

When the Spaniards had rested ten or twelve days in the town of Coza, more to comply with the desire of the Curaca, who liked having them in his land, than to satisfy any need for rest, the Governor felt it wise to continue along the same route in search of the sea. For after quitting the province of Xuala, he had directed his course toward the coast, making a half-circle through the land in order to emerge at the port of Achusi, thus fulfilling his agreement with Captain Diego Maldonado, who had remained to explore the coast and was to come to that port at the beginning of the approaching winter (as we have already explained) with fresh supplies of people, arms, livestock and food. The Governor's principal purpose now was to reach this port and begin a settlement.

It was the desire of the Cacique Coza to accompany the Governor to the boundaries of his land, and this he did, bringing with him many noble warriors and a great amount of provisions as well as Indian porters to carry them. All traveled in the customary order for five days, and at the end of this time came to a place called Talise, which was the last settlement in the province and therefore its frontier and defense. This town was exceedingly well fortified, for in addition to the fact that it had a rampart of wood and earth, a great river almost completely encircled it and thereby made of it a peninsula.

Now the people of Talise were not very obedient to the lord Coza because of the double dealing of another lord called Tascaluza, whose state bordered upon that of Coza, and who was both an unsafe neighbor and an untrustworthy friend. It is true that the two Caciques did not wage open warfare, but Tascaluza was an arrogant and bellicose person who displayed much artfulness and trickery (which we shall see later) and, being such a person, had disquieted this particular town so that it was somewhat rebellious. Having been aware of this fact for some time, the Cacique Coza was pleased now to accompany the Governor, first to serve him on the road and in the town of Talise itself, and then to use the favor of the Spaniards to intimidate the inhabitants of that town and thereby impel them to obey him.

One of the Christians (if he was a Christian), named Falco Herrado, deserted the army in the town of Coza. The native land of this man was not known, but he was not a Spaniard; and since he was a very plebeian person, he was not missed until the army arrived at Talise. Efforts then were made to recover him, but they were of no avail, for he very shamelessly sent Indians with messages to inform the Governor that rather than see before him each day the captain who had reprimanded and verbally insulted him, he preferred to remain among the Indians, and that the Castilians, therefore, should not await him.

The Curaca replied more civilly and courteously to the Governor's request that he order his Indians to return this fugitive Christian, for he said that since all of the Spaniards would not stay in his land, he was very pleased that even one of them had chosen to do so, and he begged his lordship to pardon him for honoring this person exceedingly rather than forcing him to return. The Governor, realizing that Herrado was far away and that the Indians were not going to send him back to his people, insisted no further.

We have forgotten to mention that a sick Negro named Robles, who was a very fine Christian and a good slave, was left in this same town of Coza because he was unable to walk. He was entrusted to the Cacique, who undertook personally and with much love and willingness to restore him to health. Now all of these trifles we have considered worthwhile to give in minute detail so that when Our Lord God may be served by the land's being conquered and won, someone may be reminded to ascertain if there is any trace or memory of those who stayed among the natives of that great kingdom.[33]

[33] According to statements made to Tristan de Luna's colonists in 1560, both Falco Herrado and Robles lived on with the Indians for eleven or twelve years before death overtook them. See John R. Swanton, *The Indians of the Southeastern United States* (Washington, 1946), p. 60.

CHAPTER XXIV

*The fierce Curaca Tascaluza, who was almost a
giant, and the manner in which he
received the Governor.*

THE Governor remained ten days in Talise making efforts to
obtain news from every source as to how much of his journey
was yet to be accomplished, and what there was to be found in the
provinces lying on each side of the town. Meanwhile, there came
to him a son of Tascaluza, a boy of eighteen years and of such
goodly stature that from the chest up he was taller than any Spaniard
or Indian in the entire army. This lad, who was accompanied by
many noble people, bore a communication from his father in which
that Cacique offered his friendship, his person and his estate so that
with them the Governor might be served in the way that most
pleased him. Hernando de Soto received the messenger affably and
paid him great honor, not only because of his rank but also because
of his gentility and refinement. And when the youth had delivered
his message and learned that the Adelantado wished to visit his
father, he said: "My Lord, although it is no more than twelve or
thirteen leagues to the place where he now is, there are two routes.
I beg Your Lordship therefore to have two Spaniards go there by
one route and return by the other in order that they may ascertain
which is the better for your use. I myself will provide guides to
direct these men and bring them back safely."

Thus it was agreed, and one of the men who set out to explore
the two roads was Juan de Villalobos. He it was who had gone
to examine the gold mines where nothing but brass had been found.
He was always most eager to be the first of his companions to see
what there was in an exploration, and he was so fired now with this
passion that he offered to travel each route two and even three times.

Later when both companions had returned with an account of the
roads to Tascaluza, the Governor bade farewell to the good Coza

and his people, all of whom were very melancholy at the departure of the Castilians from their land. Then he set out by way of the road which he had been told was the most appropriate. Crossing the river of Talise in rafts and canoes, since it was too full of water to be forded, he traveled on for two days, coming very early on the third day in sight of the town where the Curaca Tascaluza was. This was not the principal town of his state, but another.

Now when Tascaluza learned from his runners that the Governor was approaching, he went forth to receive him at a place on a high little hill outside the town, an eminent spot from which much land could be seen in all directions. In his company he brought no more than a hundred noblemen, but they, conforming to the native dress and customs, were well adorned with great feather headdresses and rich robes of different linings. All were standing except Tascaluza himself who was seated in a chair such as those used by the lords of these lands. These chairs are constructed of wood and are a little more or less than one third of a yard high; they have a small concavity for a seat, are without backs or arms, and are all of one piece. Quite close to the chieftain, a standard bearer carried a great chamois banner which was yellow with three blue bands separating one part of it from another, and which was made in the same shape and form as the banners borne by troops of cavalrymen in Spain. It was a novel thing for the Spaniards to encounter military insignia, for up until this time they had not seen standard, banner or pennon.

The physical measurements of Tascaluza were like those of his son, for both were more than a half-yard taller than all the others. He appeared to be a giant, or rather was one, and his limbs and face were in proportion to the height of his body. His countenance was handsome, and he wore a look of severity, yet a look which well revealed his ferocity and grandeur of spirit. His shoulders conformed to his height, and his waistline measured just a little more than two-thirds of a yard. His arms and legs were straight and well formed and were in proper proportion to the rest of his body. In sum he was the tallest and most handsomely shaped Indian that the Castilians saw during all their travels in Florida.

Tascaluza awaited the Governor in the manner we have described, and although the cavaliers and captains of the army had gone ahead to where he stood, he made no movement toward them and offered them no sign of civility, acting rather as if he did not see them or as if they had not approached him. And he continued to conduct himself thus until the Governor arrived; then on seeing him near, he arose and advanced about fifteen or twenty steps from his seat to receive him.[34] At that the General dismounted and embraced the Cacique, and they remained where they were to talk while the army was being lodged both in and outside the town, there not being space for everyone within. Afterward the two men went hand in hand to the Governor's quarters, which were adjacent to those of the Cacique. Here the latter took leave and departed with his Indians.

The Spaniards rested two days in that town, leaving it on the third day to continue their journey. For the purpose of making a great show of friendship for the Governor, Tascaluza resolved to accompany him, explaining that he was doing so in order that his friend might be better served while traveling through his land. The Governor thereupon commanded that a horse be bridled for the Cacique to ride, for he had always provided mounts for the curacas, lords of vassals, who traveled with him, although we have forgotten to make mention of this fact until now. But no beast could be found among all those in the army capable of carrying the chieftain because of his great size; not that he was fat, for as we have said already, he had less than a yard of girth, nor that he was heavy because of age, for he was hardly forty years old. Finally, however, after making additional efforts to locate a suitable animal, the Castilians did find a nag belonging to the Governor, which because

[34] Biedma records that Tascaluza awaited the Spaniards quietly at his town and that on arrival the latter made much ado for him "with jousts at reeds and great running of horses, although the chieftain appeared to regard it all as small matter." One is reminded of a similar meeting in Peru when De Soto is said to have displayed his horsemanship before the impassive Atahuallpa, bringing his galloping steed to a sudden halt so near to the Curaca as to fleck the royal garments with the animal's perspiration and saliva.

of its strength was used as a pack horse and thus was able to bear the weight of the Cacique; but the Indian was so tall that when mounted not even a quarter of a yard remained between his feet and the ground. The Governor had not held lightly the fact that a horse must be found on which Tascaluza might ride lest the latter be insulted by their transporting him upon a mule.[35]

In this manner, they traveled three days at the rate of four leagues per day, and at the end of that time came to the principal town which was called Tascaluza, and from which both the province and its chieftain took their names. This town was well fortified, being located on a peninsula formed by the same river that passed through Talise. Here, however, the river was larger and more powerful, and the Spaniards, being poorly provided with boats, spent almost all of the following day in crossing it. Then they encamped in a beautiful valley a half a league beyond.

While in this encampment two Spaniards were found to be missing, one of whom was Juan de Villalobos, a person we have mentioned twice previously. What became of these men was never ascertained, but it was suspected that the Indians on encountering them far from the camp had slain them, for Villalobos, regardless of where he was, liked to run through the country to see what it held. This is a dangerous practice which costs the life of all those who indulge in it in time of war.

The loss of the two Spaniards was an ominous sign, and those who took note of it feared that the friendship of Tascaluza was not so true as he tried to show it to be. To this sign was added another even more ominous, for when Tascaluza's Indians were questioned about the missing Spaniards, they answered most shamelessly, asking if they had been assigned these men to guard, and what obligation they were under to give an account of them to the Castilians. The Governor did not want to be too insistent in demanding his men, for he believed them dead and that persistence

---

[35] Ranjel suggests that because of the Indians' terror of horses, Tascaluza would not have relished this ride any more than if he had been mounted upon the back of a tiger or a most savage lion.

would serve no other purpose than to irritate and drive away the Cacique and his vassals. It seemed well to him, therefore, to forego the verification and punishment of this deed for the sake of obtaining a better association with the Indians.[36]

At dawn of the ensuing day, the General sent out two soldiers whom he had chosen from among the best in all his army. One of them was Gonzalo Quadrado Xaramillo, an hidalgo who was a native of Zafra. He was skillful and practiced in everything and could be safely relied upon in all grave affairs of peace and war. The other was Diego Vázquez, a native of Villanueva de Barcarrota, who likewise was a trustworthy person of the finest character. Both men were ordered to find out what there was in Mauvila,[37] a town a league and a half distant from the encampment, for the Curaca had assembled many people in that place, spreading the rumor that they were there to provide better service and entertainment for the Spaniards. The two men were likewise instructed to await the Governor in Mauvila since he was to follow them at once.

CHAPTER XXV

The Governor arrives in Mauvila where he finds indications of treason.

AS SOON as the two soldiers had left the camp, the Governor commanded that a hundred cavalrymen and a hundred infantrymen be made ready to accompany him and Tascaluza, both of whom wished to be in the vanguard on that day. Meanwhile

[36] Other authorities do not picture the Governor as being so lenient and would lay the blame for the tragedy at Mauvila partly upon his action at this time, for De Soto is said to have threatened to burn the chieftain if he did not deliver up the assassins of these men. Tascaluza then promised to comply with his demand on reaching Mauvila.

[37] Mauvila—from which the present-day Mobile gets its name; but the Mauvila of the Inca was between the Alabama and Tombigbee Rivers in or near the present Clarke County. The actual site of the great battle has not been determined.

he left an order for the Campmaster to follow with the rest of the army soon after he had gone; but these men departed late and spread out over the countryside, hunting and enjoying themselves as they traveled, and taking no thought of battle because of the peace that had been theirs throughout the summer and up until that place.

The Governor, who traveled with great caution, came to the town of Mauvila at eight o'clock in the morning. Here there were not many houses, in fact scarcely eighty in all, but each was large, some being capable of holding fifteen hundred persons and others a thousand, while even the smallest had a capacity of more than five hundred. Now what we refer to as a house is a dwelling with a single floor like a church, for the Indians do not build by joining one story to another; on the contrary each structure, according to its function, consists of one main body like a hall and this in turn is divided into necessary apartments, a few of which are sufficient. Such single story dwellings as these are called houses. Since those of this town had been built as strongholds for the frontier and as proof of the grandeur of the lord, they were very magnificent, and the majority of them belonged to the Cacique as well as some of the most powerful and wealthy men of his whole estate.

Situated upon a very beautiful plain, the town of Mauvila was surrounded by a wall as high as three men and constructed of wooden beams as thick as oxen. These beams were driven into the ground so close together that each was wedged to the other; and across them on both the outside and inside were laid additional pieces, not so thick but longer, which were bound together with strips of split cane and strong ropes. Plastered over the smaller pieces was a mixture of thick mud tamped down with long straw, filling up all of the holes and crevices in the wood and its fastenings, so that, properly speaking, the wall appeared to be coated with a hard finish such as one might apply with a mason's trowel. At every fifty feet there was a tower capable of holding seven or eight persons who might fight within it, and the lower part of the wall, up to the

height of a man, was filled with the embrasures of a battery designed
for shooting arrows at those outside. There were only two gates to
the town, one on the east and the other on the west, and in its center
there was a great plaza around which were grouped the largest and
most prominent houses.

The Governor came to this plaza with the gigantic Tascaluza,
who, as soon as he had dismounted, summoned the interpreter Juan
Ortiz and while indicating with his finger said to him: "In that
large dwelling the Governor and all the cavaliers and gentlemen
that his lordship may wish to have with him are to be lodged,
whereas his servants and equipage will occupy the other one standing
nearby. And since the town is small and does not afford sufficient
room within for everyone, the rest of his people will remain at the
distance of an arrow shot outside, for there my vassals have constructed for them many very fine bowers of branches in which they
will be able to lodge themselves pleasantly."

The Governor replied that with the arrival of his campmaster
he would carry out the Curaca's orders in regard to lodging as well
as all other things, and Tascaluza thereupon entered one of the
largest houses in the plaza, where, it was afterward learned, he had
assembled the leaders of his council of war. Meanwhile the Governor remained in the plaza with both the cavalrymen and infantrymen
who came with him, but he commanded that the horses be taken
outside the town until it was ascertained where they were to be
quartered.

Gonzalo Quadrado Xaramillo, who, as we stated, had gone
ahead to investigate this settlement of Mauvila, came up to the
Governor as soon as he had dismounted and said: "My Lord, I
have examined this place carefully and the things that I have noted
within it give me no assurance of the friendship of this Curaca and
his vassals. Rather, they have aroused in me a strong suspicion that
these Indians have laid some treachery. In those few houses that
Your Lordship sees, there are now more than ten thousand people,
each one of them chosen, for among them there is not a single old

man or servant. All are warriors, nobles and youths, and all are provided with a great quantity of arms. And in addition to the weapons that each person possesses for his own exclusive use, many of these houses are filled with arms and are common depositories. Furthermore even though these Indians have many women with them, all are young and none possesses children; there is not a single child in the whole town, and these women are completely free of impediments. For the distance of a crossbow shot around the town (as Your Lordship will have seen) they have cleared the countryside in such a manner that even the roots of the grass have been pulled up by hand. To me each of these things appears to be evidence that the Indians desire to do battle with us and that they do not want there to be anything whatsoever to obstruct them. And to these unfavorable signs may be added that of the death of the two Spaniards who were missing yesterday from our camp. I feel, therefore, that Your Lordship, in consideration of each of these circumstances, ought to be very wary of this Indian and refuse to trust him. For even though there may be no more to this matter than the bad face and worse mien which he and his men up to now have shown us, and the arrogance and shamelessness with which they speak to us, still such things do suffice to warn us to regard his friendship as false and deceptive rather than good."

The General answered that he would pass the information as to what that town held from one to another among those present so that everyone might be secretly prepared. Then he gave a special command to Gonzalo Quadrado to inform the Campmaster on arrival as to what had been seen there so that he too might arrange whatever was best for all.

Alonso de Carmona, in his handwritten notes, gives a very lengthy account of the journey that he made with these Spaniards from the province of Cofachiqui to that of Coza, and he tells of the grandeurs of the latter province as well as the generosities of its lord. He names many of the towns along the route, although not all those I have named. And concerning the stature of Tascaluza, he asserts that this man lacked very little of being a giant and that he was excellently featured. Juan Coles too has the following to say of this tall, strong and robust individual: "When we had arrived in the province of the lord Tascaluza, he came out to us in peace. He was a mighty man who had as much bone between his foot and his knee as another very large person might have between his foot and his waist. His eyes were like those of an ox, and along the road he traveled upon a horse, but the horse was unable to sustain him. The Adelantado dressed him in fine scarlet cloth and gave him a very beautiful cape of the same material."

Having told likewise of this garment of fine red material, Alonso de Carmona adds: "When the Governor and Tascaluza entered Mauvila, the principal Indians, for the purpose of concealing their treason more adequately, came out to receive them with dances; and when they had completed their joyful demonstrations, they were succeeded by a group of marvelously beautiful dancing women.[38] For as I have said, the Indians, both men and women, are very well featured; in fact they are so handsome that afterward when we left that land and went to stay in Mexico, Governor Moscoso took with him a very beautiful and charming Indian woman from this province of Mauvila, and she was able to compete in pulchritude with the most exquisite Spanish women in all of Mexico. Because of her extreme loveliness the ladies of that land wished to see her and begged this governor to send her to them; and he agreed readily to their request, for it pleased him that so many people should be envious of her."

These are the words of Alonso de Carmona just as he himself has written them. I am pleased to refer to them and to all others that I have included in this history in the name of these two soldiers and eye-witnesses because by them one may see how clearly both accounts reveal themselves to be of the same cloth as my own. Although he does not name the man, Alonso de Carmona mentions

[38] Biedma and the Gentleman of Elvas both differ with the Inca in the details of the engagement at Mauvila, but all three give a similar picture of the dancing-girls.

a little later the information that we have given concerning the report Gonzalo Quadrado Xaramillo made to the Governor Hernando de Soto. And he adds that this man told the Governor how on that and many previous mornings the Indians had gone out to drill in the fields, and how on each of these days a captain had harangued them before their skirmish and military exercise.

As has been said, as soon as he and the Governor had entered the town, the Cacique Tascaluza went into the building where his council of war was waiting to conclude and determine the plan they were to follow in killing the Spaniards; for this Curaca had been determined for a long time to slay them in the town of Mauvila, and to do so had gathered together the fighting men that he had there—not only his own vassals and subjects but also people of the neighboring provinces, so that all might enjoy the triumph and glory of having slain the Castilians and at the same time share in the spoils their victims carried. Thus it was with this understanding that those who were not his vassals had assembled.

When Tascaluza found himself among his captains and the most illustrious leaders of his army, he told them to determine quickly how they would accomplish the deed—if they would slay those Spaniards immediately who were already in the town and then destroy the others as they approached, or wait until all arrived before killing any of them. For, finding themselves powerful and brave, the Indians expected to annihilate their enemies as easily when all were together as when they were divided into their three groups— the vanguard, the battalion and the rearguard, this being the order they followed when traveling. And Tascaluza asked that his council resolve this question immediately since he awaited only their decision.

CHAPTER XXVI

Tascaluza's council resolves to kill the Span-
iards. Herein is told the beginning of
the battle which occurred.

THE leaders of the council were divided in regard to Tascaluza's
proposal. Some said that lest the undertaking be made difficult,
they should not wait for the Castilians to reassemble but should kill
immediately those whom they had there and the remainder afterward as they arrived. Some of the more valiant, on the other hand,
maintained that the desire to destroy these people when they were
divided gave evidence of cowardice and fear, and even smelled of
treason; and they argued that since the Indians had the same advantage over the Spaniards in valor, skill and swiftness as they did
in number, they should permit them to collect their forces and then
destroy them all with one blow, for such would be a greater accomplishment and consequently more honorable and in keeping with the
nobility of Tascaluza. But the first group insisted that such a risk
was not wise since the Spaniards in combining their strength might
thus put up a better defense and kill some of the Indians; and they
said that no matter how few were slain, the grief occasioned by the
loss of these few would exceed the pleasure they might receive with
the death of all their enemies. It was sufficient, they reasoned, to
carry out the purpose they had in mind, which was to annihilate
them; and the more safely they did so, the better and more certain
would be the results. This last counsel prevailed, for although the
other was more compatible with the arrogance and fierceness of
Tascaluza, that chieftain's desire to see the Spaniards destroyed was
so intense that whatever delay, no matter how brief it might be,
seemed to him long. Thus it was agreed that any occasion should
be seized to put their determination into action; and if no occasion
arose, then they should create one since it was not necessary to look
for excuses to kill one's enemies.

During the time that Tascaluza's council was deliberating upon the death of the Spaniards, the Governor's servants who had hastened forward and lodged themselves in one of the large houses facing the plaza, had prepared breakfast (or dinner, for both meals were prepared at the same time), and they now informed their master that it was time for his lordship to eat. The General thereupon sent Juan Ortiz to tell Tascaluza to come and dine with him just as he had always done. Being refused admittance to the house where the Curaca was, Juan Ortiz left the message at the door, and when the Indians had carried it within, they replied that their lord would come out immediately. After waiting for some time, Juan Ortiz repeated his message, only to receive an identical reply. Then when a long interval had elapsed, he repeated it again, saying: "Tell Tascaluza to come forth, for the Governor is waiting for him with food on the table." At that an Indian who must have been the captain general, emerged from the house and with great pride and singular haughtiness said: "Who are these thieves and vagabonds who keep shouting 'come forth, come forth' to my lord Tascaluza with as little consideration as if they were talking with some such person as themselves? By the Sun and the Moon, no one can endure longer the insolence of these demons, and it is therefore only right that they die today, torn into pieces for their infamy, and that in this way an end be given to their wickedness and tyranny."

Scarcely had this Indian spoken when another, who came out after him, placed a bow and arrow in his hands to enable him to start the battle. Then that captain general threw back over his shoulders the folds of a magnificent mantle of marten fur which he had fastened at his throat, took the bow and, placing a shaft in it, aimed at a circle of Spaniards in the street. But Captain Baltasar de Gallegos, who chanced to be standing near one side of the door from which the Indian had emerged, perceived that he and his Cacique had been treasonous and that the whole town was raising a clamor at this point. So seizing his sword he struck the infidel on the left shoulder, and since the man bore no armor and was completely naked except for his mantle, he opened all that quarter of his body and disemboweled him. Thus the Indian fell dead immediately before having had a chance to release the arrow.

Now when this Indian had emerged from the house to pronounce his maledictions against the Castilians, he had already given his companions the signal for battle. The result was that six or seven thousand warriors now poured forth from all the houses (although chiefly from those around the plaza) and attacked the few Spaniards who were lolling about the principal streets by which they had entered the place. They fell upon them with such force and intrepidity that they very quickly and easily pushed them along without letting them put a foot on the ground, as they say, until they had hurled them beyond the gate and more than two hundred feet into the open country. Thus the flood of Indians that came out against the Spaniards was fierce, but it is a fact that in all of that time not a single Spaniard turned his back to the enemy. Instead all fought with the finest spirit, valor and force, defending themselves and retreating since it was not possible to take a stand and resist the cruel and arrogant onslaught of the Indians as they rushed forth from their dwellings and from the town.

Among the first to come out of the house where the Indian captain had been was a young nobleman approximately eighteen years of age, who fixed his eyes upon Baltasar de Gallegos and shot at him six or seven times with great fury and haste. And although he had more arrows, when he saw that those he had released had neither wounded nor killed the Spaniard, since he was well armed, this youth took his bow in both hands and, closing with his foe who was now near, struck him three or four blows on the head with such velocity and force that he made the blood spurt from under his helmet and run down over his forehead. Finding himself so abused, Baltasar de Gallegos, in order not to give the Indian an occasion to treat him worse, stabbed him twice through the chest as quickly as possible, and in consequence the youth fell dead. The Spaniards conjectured that this boy was the son of that captain who was the first to come out to do battle, and that it was because of a desire to avenge the death of his father that he had fought Baltasar de Gallegos with the great courage and lust to kill him that he had shown. But, everything considered, all of the Indians fought with the same urge to slay or wound the Spaniards.

The cavalrymen, who as we have said had tethered their horses beyond the wall of the town, went running out to get them when they saw the impetuosity and furor with which the Indians were attacking. Those who were the most skillful and put forth the greatest effort were able to mount, but others, who had not believed that the deluge of enemies was so extensive or that they would rush them as they did, could not mount, and they contented themselves with setting their horses loose, cutting the bridles and halters so that they could flee before the Indians were able to shoot at them. Still others, who were more unfortunate, had neither the time to mount nor to cut the halters; therefore they left their horses as they were, and the Indians hurled arrows at them with exuberance and joy.

Since the infidels were numerous, half of them hastened to fight the Castilians while the others occupied themselves with destroying the horses they found shackled and with picking up the vehicles and possessions of the Christians, for all of these effects had arrived and were either placed against the walls of the town or spread out over the plain waiting to be stored. Everything was now in the power of the foe, nothing having escaped them except the possessions of Captain Andrés de Vasconcellos, who as yet had not reached Mauvila. These spoils the Indians placed in their houses, leaving the Spaniards with no more than their clothes and their very lives. Nevertheless, our men fought with all the courage and will power that one needs in such an emergency, even though the long peace they had enjoyed after leaving Apalache had permitted them to grow unaccustomed to their weapons, and even though they had not anticipated fighting on this particular day because of the feigned friendship of Tascaluza. Neither circumstance was sufficient to deter them in their duty.

CHAPTER XXVII

The events of the first third of the battle of Mauvila are related.

THE few cavalrymen who had left the town and were able to mount their horses now joined forces with some of the others who were arriving by the road without any thought of finding such a cruel battle; and together they launched an attack to resist the onslaught and fury with which the Indians were pursuing those of their companions fighting on foot. For until their enemies saw the horsemen coming at them, these footsoldiers, in spite of their great efforts to hold their ground, were unable to avoid being pushed backward across the plain. At this point, however, a brief pause on the part of the Indians gave them an opportunity to collect themselves; and when the two groups, one of infantry and one of horsemen, had organized, they set upon the enemy with so much courage and with such humiliation at the previous affront that they did not stop until they had enclosed them once again within the town. And they would have pushed on into the town, but the barrage of arrows and stones raining upon them from the wall and the embrasures was so great that it behooved them to withdraw.

Then the Indians on seeing that the Spaniards were retiring returned with the same force they had exerted the first time, some coming out by the gate and others spilling over the wall. They closed with our men boldly even to the point of grasping the lances of the cavaliers, and badly as they suffered in doing so, succeeded thus in pushing them backward for a distance of more than two hundred feet from the wall.

As has been said, the Spaniards were retreating without showing their backs, fighting now with the utmost harmony and good form, for their safety depended upon their doing so because of their small number, the majority of them having remained with the rearguard which was yet to arrive. Then charging, they pushed the enemy back into the town, but when the Indians made a mighty offense against them from the wall, they came to realize that it was more to their advantage to fight on the plain at a distance from the town than to fight near it. Therefore, from then on when they withdrew, they were careful to retreat over more ground than they were forced to lose in order to take their places at a greater distance from the town and thereby give the cavalry more territory in which to use their lances against the enemy. In this manner, attacking and then retiring, first one and then the other, as if they were in a cane game instead of a very cruel and bloody battle, and at other times standing still, both sides fought for three hours, furiously afflicting each other with wounds and death.

Now in these attacks and withdrawals there was a Dominican friar named Juan de Gallegos[39] who traveled on horseback close in the rear of the Spaniards, not for the purpose of fighting, but because he wished to give his horse to his brother, Captain Baltasar de Gallegos. Moved by this desire, he shouted for his brother to come out and mount the animal, but that captain, who had never failed to be among the first, just as in the beginning of this battle it had fallen his lot to be, refused to respond since it was not commensurate with either his reputation or his honor for him to abandon the post he was occupying. At a sudden onslaught from the enemy when this good friar was rushing back and forth in his anxiety to assist his kinsman, an Indian fixed his eye upon him, and although far away, released an arrow which struck the Dominican in the back, for he by chance had turned and was in flight. Thus he was wounded, though slightly since he was clad in two cowls as well as in all of the numerous other accoutrements that men of his order are accustomed to wear (which is a great deal), and on top of everything else wore a large felt hat which hung over his back and was fastened with a cord to his neck. Because of all this protection, the wound inflicted by the arrow which the Indian had

[39] Perhaps the friar referred to by Ranjel as "Friar John the Evangelist." Garcilaso has spoken of him as both a Dominican and a Franciscan. See above, p. 23, and below, p. 639.

willfully shot at him was not mortal, but the experience taught this friar a lesson and, in his fear that more arrows might be forthcoming, he withdrew to a distance.

Many wounds and deaths occurred in this obstinate battle, but the one which moved the Spaniards to the greatest pity and sorrow, not only because of the unfortunate manner in which it occurred but also because of the person upon whom it fell, was that of Don Carlos Enríquez, a native of Xerez de Badajoz. This cavalier, whom we have mentioned previously, was married to a niece of the Governor, and because of his great virtue and affability was beloved by everyone. From the very beginning of the battle, he had fought as a most valiant soldier in each attack and withdrawal. Now Don Carlos had taken his horse from the last retreat with an arrow wound above the breastplate on one side of the chest. Because of having to remove the arrow, he had shifted his lance from his right hand to his left and grasping the missile had pulled at it while extending his body lengthwise along the neck of the animal. Straining thus he twisted his left shoulder so that his own neck was exposed at a very inopportune time, for at this point a stray arrow with a harpoon of flint fell and chanced to hit him in a small section of the throat which was exposed and unprotected even though the rest of his body was very well covered. Thus this poor cavalier was injured in such a manner that he immediately fell beneath his horse mortally wounded, although he was not to expire until the following day.

Amidst such events as these which are common to battles, the Indians and Castilians continued to struggle with a great amount of slaughter on both sides. The losses of the former were severer, however, because they bore no defensive arms. But when they had fought for more than three hours on the plain, they realized that because of the damage done by the horses, they were losing by contending in the open, so they agreed to withdraw to the town and, after closing the gates, station themselves upon the wall. This they did when they had summoned their people from all sides to assemble.

On seeing the infidels enclosed, the Governor commanded all men on horseback, since they were better armed than the foot-soldiers, to dismount and, with shields for their defense and axes for destroying the gates (most of them having brought axes with them), to attack the town like valiant Spaniards and do all in their power to gain it. Immediately a squadron of two hundred of these horsemen was formed, and they, after storming and breaking down the gate, did enter but with no small damage to themselves. Meanwhile, in order not to lose time from the conflict by being detained in the field, other Spaniards who were not able to pass through the gate because of its narrowness, struck great blows on the wall with their axes and tore down the mixture of mud and straw covering it. Thus they disclosed the lateral beams and the fastenings with which they were secured; then assisting each other they climbed over the wall by means of these beams and entered the town to aid their companions.

Seeing that the Castilians were within this place which had been considered impregnable, and that they were gaining in it, the Indians struggled desperately, not only in the streets but on the roofs, from whence they did much damage. But now in order to defend themselves from those who fought from the housetops, to provide security against attacks from the rear, and also to prevent their foes from regaining the houses that they were capturing, the Christians agreed to set fire to the buildings, and they promptly put their thoughts into action. And since these houses were constructed of straw, there arose instantly an immense flame and smoke which increased the great bloodshed, wounds and slaughter that this village, small as it was, afforded.

As soon as they had enclosed themselves in the town, many of the Indians hastened to the house set aside for the servants and effects of the Governor. This structure they had not attacked previously because it seemed to them a sure thing. Now, however, they went forward with great boldness to enjoy the spoils therein, but once arrived, encountered a very excellent defense in the persons of three crossbowmen and five halberdiers of the Governor's guard who were accustomed to accompany his equipage and servants, and in addition an Indian who was among the first to be captured in that land, and who now, as a faithful friend and slave, carried his bow and arrows to use whenever necessary in the favor and service of another people against men of his own race. Likewise within that house there chanced to be two priests (one a cleric and the other a friar), and also two of the Governor's slaves.[40] All of these people employed themselves in the defense of the place, the priests fighting with their prayers and the seculars with their arms; and they struggled so spiritedly that their enemies were unable to gain the door. The Indians decided therefore to enter by way of the roof, which they opened in three or four places; but the crossbow-men and the Indian archer performed so successfully that they killed on sight or badly wounded all who dared appear at the uncovered places. In this animated defense, these few Spaniards were thus engaged when the General and his captains and soldiers fought their way to the very door of the house and drove the enemy from it. Whereupon those within were free, and coming forth they went into the fields, while giving thanks to God for delivering them from so much danger.

CHAPTER XXVIII

A continuation of the battle of Mauvila through the second third of it.

THE Indians and Castilians had been fighting and destroying each other with great cruelty for more than four hours when that incident occurred which we related in the preceding chapter.

[40] Ranjel states that in addition to the friar, the priest and the soldiers, there were Indian women present as well as a number of pages. He adds that the women and even boys four years of age fought alongside the Christians, and that some Indian boys hanged themselves while others jumped into the fire rather than fall into the hands of the enemy.

For it seems that the more damage these people received, the more obstinate they became and the more they despaired of life. But instead of surrendering, they fought with a greater anxiety to annihilate the Spaniards, who, seeing their persistence, stubbornness and rage, wounded and killed them pitilessly.

The Governor had fought the entire four hours in front of his soldiers and on foot, but now he went outside the town and mounted a horse, by means of which he hoped to increase the fear of his enemies and at the same time to augment the spirit and strength of his own men. Afterward he re-entered the town in the company of the good Nuño Tovar, who also was mounted, and both horsemen while calling upon the name of Our Lady and the Apostle Santiago, and shouting loudly to their men to make way for them, broke through the squadrons of Indians fighting in the principal street and the plaza, and ran from one end of them to the other. Then they returned, and like the valiant and skillful cavaliers they were, lanced their enemies on both right and left.

During these goings and comings and at a moment when the Governor had lifted himself in his stirrups to give a blow with his lance, an Indian to the rear of him shot an arrow above his back saddlebow and in consequence struck him in that little space left exposed between the saddlebow and his cuirass. Although he wore a coat of mail, the arrow broke through this protection and a sixth of it entered his left buttock.[41] Not wishing it to be known that he had been injured lest his men be concerned about his wound, and having no opportunity to extract the shaft in the haste of the conflict, the good General fought on throughout the entire struggle, which lasted almost five hours, without being able to sit in his saddle, an accomplishment which was no small proof of his valor and dexterity in horsemanship.

[41] *asentadura*—Although both the 1605 and 1723 editions use this word, the Inca without doubt intended *asentadera* (buttock). Irving calls it the thigh, but the arrow was received in such a place as to make it inconvenient for the Governor to sit. A few pages later, Garcilaso refers to the *muslo* (thigh) and the *asentaderas* (buttocks).

Another arrow shot by the Indians struck the lance of Nuño Tovar. This lance being thin, the arrow passed through the middle of it, close to the hand, and its shaft proved to be of such fine material that it did not split. Rather it looked as if an auger had subtly bored through it; and afterward when the ends of the missile were cut off on both sides, the lance served just as before. This incident is of little importance, but it has been mentioned because such shots rarely occur, and also because by it one may see what we many times have told of the fierceness and dexterity which the Indians of Florida manifest with their bows and arrows.

These two cavaliers fought the entire day, many times breaking the squadrons which the Indians formed and re-formed at each step, and they entered into the most dangerous and critical moments of the struggle, but neither received any wounds other than those we have described, which was no small fortune.

The fire which the Spaniards had set to the houses increased each moment and caused much damage among the natives. For they being numerous and the space being limited, all of them could not fight in the streets and plaza, and as a result struggled from the flat roofs of the houses where they were caught by flames and either consumed or forced to fling themselves down in an effort to escape. Meanwhile the ravage of the fire was no less within the houses, which it took from the door; for as has been said, these dwellings consisted of large rooms with no more than one entrance, and the occupants of these rooms being unable to make an exit when the fire burst in upon them, were burned and stifled by the flames and smoke. In this manner many of the women enclosed within these houses perished. And again the fire did just as much damage in the streets; for because of the wind, the flame and smoke sometimes changed and blinded the Indians, thus aiding the Spaniards to carry them in a violent sally without their being able to resist. At other times, however, it turned in favor of the Indians and resulted in their regaining as much of the street as they had lost. Thus both sides were favored by these flames, and as a result the slaughter of the battle was increased.

With such cruelty and rage as has been seen, the fighting was sustained on both sides until four o'clock in the afternoon, seven hours having elapsed in which the struggle had gone on without ceasing. At this time, the Indians realized that many of their people had died of sword and flame, and that because of a scarcity of fighting men their forces were weakening while those of the Castilians were growing stronger; so summoning their women, they commanded them to take up arms from the many men who had fallen in the streets and with these weapons to avenge the destruction of their people. For even if they were unable to do so, they at least could bring death upon themselves and thus not become slaves of Spaniards. When this order was issued, many of them for some time already had been fighting valiantly alongside their husbands. But now none failed to join in the battle, and all seized those weapons which they found on the ground in front of them. In consequence they bore in their hands many of the swords, halberds and lances that the Spaniards themselves had lost, and they turned these things against their owners, wounding numerous men with their own arms. They also seized bows and arrows and shot them with no less ferocity and dexterity than their husbands. Furthermore, in fighting they took places in front of their mates and resolutely exposed themselves to death with much more temerity than did the males. Employing the weapons of their enemies, they attacked with utter rage and determination, thus showing well that the desperation and courage of women in whatever they are determined to do is greater and more unbridled than that of men. But the Spaniards on seeing that they were females and that they fought more with a desire to die than to conquer, abstained from wounding and destroying them.

While this long and obstinate battle lasted, the trumpets, fifes and drums never ceased to sound the call to arms with great insistence so that those Spaniards who had remained in the rearguard would make haste to come to the aid of their people. Meanwhile the Campmaster and his company had scattered out over the country-side as they traveled and were hunting and enjoying themselves, unaware of what was happening in Mauvila. But on hearing the sound of martial instruments and the shouting and clamor that went on both inside and outside the town, and on seeing the great quantity of smoke billowing up in front of them, they began to suspect what the trouble might be and consequently gave an alarm from person to person even to the last man of them. Then all pressed forward at full speed and came to Mauvila for the last quarter of the battle.

Among these men was Captain Diego de Soto, a nephew of the Governor and a brother-in-law of Don Carlos Enríquez, whose misfortune we have already described. Now this captain on learning the fate of his brother-in-law, whom he loved tenderly, felt the sorrow of such a great loss and resolved to avenge it. So throwing himself down from his horse and taking a round shield and a sword in his hand, he entered the town and came to the spot where the battle was raging most ferociously and cruelly. This was in the principal street, although it is true that in all the other streets there was no lack of blood, fire and slaughter, for the entire town was filled with savage fighting. Thus in that place and at four o'clock in the afternoon, Diego de Soto entered the conflict, but he was to imitate his brother-in-law's misfortune rather than to avenge his death. For this was not the hour for personal vengeance, but rather for the ire of military fortune, which, it would seem, in disgust for having afforded the Spaniards so much peace in a land of such cruel enemies, now wished to bestow upon them in one day all the warfare they might have experienced in a year. And, as we shall see later, such a concentration of battles would not have been so cruel as the one they experienced on this day alone; for there have been few or no struggles between the Indians and Spaniards in the New World which can equal this one, not only in the stubbornness of the fighting, but also in the length of time it lasted, unless it be that of the arrogant Pedro de Valdivia, which we shall describe in our history of Peru if God is pleased to grant us a few more days of this life.[42]

But as we were saying, Captain Diego de Soto arrived at the thickest part of the battle and had scarcely entered it when the Indians shot him with an arrow which pierced his eye and came out the back of his head. In consequence he fell to the ground at once and lay speechless in the throes of death until the following day when he succumbed without their having been able to remove the arrow. This was the way he avenged his relative Don Carlos to the greater sorrow and loss of the General and all the army, for these two cavaliers were men who worthily deserved to be the nephews of such an uncle.

CHAPTER XXIX

The end of the battle of Mauvila and the lamentable condition in which the Spaniards were left.

THE battle that took place in the fields, which had been cleared for the purpose even to the point of pulling up the grass and roots, was no less bloody. For having enclosed themselves in the town for reasons of self-defense only to realize that their great number made them a hindrance to each other in the fighting, and that the narrowness of the place prevented their taking advantage of their swiftness, many of the Indians decided to slip down over the walls and go out into the open country, where they fought with the finest spirit, strength and desire to conquer. But very soon they realized that their decision was not turning out to their profit, for even though their speed gave them an advantage over the Spanish footsoldiers, they were inferior to the men on horseback who now lanced them in this flat terrain whenever they wished and without

---

[42] The few more days were granted; the Inca died in 1616, approximately four years after completing the *Historia General del Perú.*

their being able to protect themselves. The only defense against horses is the pike, but Indians in spite of possessing this weapon, do not use it because they lack the patience to wait for the enemy to come within its range. Instead, they wish to have him shot full of arrows at a good distance before he reaches them, and it is principally for this reason that they use the bow and arrows more than any other type of arms. Many of them, therefore, died upon the field, ill advised by their ferocity and vain presumption. The whole Spanish rearguard, both cavalry and infantry, had now arrived, and they all attacked the Indians who were fighting in the open country. And when they had struggled for a long time, in which they received many deaths and wounds (for in spite of the fact that they came late, a very large portion of the casualties fell to their lot, as we have seen in the case of Diego de Soto and shall soon see in others), they defeated and slew the majority of their foes, though some did escape through flight.

It was now near the hour of sunset, but the shouting and clamor of men fighting within the village still resounded. Many of the cavalry, therefore, went inside to assist their companions, while others remained where they were for whatever need might arise. Previously, none of those on horseback except the General and Nuño Tovar had fought within the town because of its narrowness, but now a great number of them entered, and distributing themselves throughout the streets, since there was something to be done in each of them, routed and killed the Indians who were fighting there.

Ten or twelve horsemen rode into the principal street. Here the battle was fiercer and bloodier, and there was still one group of Indian men and women struggling with the utmost desperation, for these people had no other purpose now than to die in combat. Against this group the cavalry launched an attack. Taking them from the rear, they routed them with much facility, passing through them with such zeal that many Spaniards dismounted in their midst and fought on foot. In this way all of the Indians were slain, for none would surrender or give up his arms, preferring rather to die with them while fighting like good soldiers. But this was the last encounter, and when both sides had struggled nine hours without ceasing, our Spaniards ended the battle in victory just as the sun went down. It was the day of the blessed Saint Luke the Evangelist in the year 1540, and it was on this same day, although many years later, that the account of this battle was written.

Now among those who fought in the town was a single Indian, who, being stupefied by his struggle and passion, was unaware of the fate of his companions until the moment the battle ceased, at which time he regained his senses only to realize that all of his people were dead. Then when he found that he was alone and could not win, he resolved to flee for his life, and accordingly seized hold of the wall briskly and climbed with much agility to the top, thinking to escape through the open countryside. But when he beheld the Castilian footsoldiers and horsemen in the field and the carnage that had been accomplished there, he realized that escape was impossible and determined to take his own life rather than surrender. So seizing the cord from his bow with the greatest haste, he threw it to the branch of a tree growing among the stakes which had been driven in to form the fence. For on observing that the tree was alive, the Indians when walling in the town had purposely left it as it was. And this was not the only such tree in the fence, there being many others like it which had been preserved intentionally and which beautified it exceedingly. Now when the Indian had tied one end of the cord to the tree and the other to his neck, he let himself fall off the fence with such haste that the Spaniards, even though they desired to save him, were unable to reach him in time to do so. Thus this man was destroyed by his own hand, leaving admiration for his deed, but at the same time a certainty that he who hanged himself would have preferred to hang the Castilians had he been able to do so. And since the only male Indian who remained alive took his own life, one can imagine the temerity and desperation with which all of them fought.

The battle ended, Governor Hernando de Soto, in spite of the fact that he himself emerged from the strife badly wounded, took care to order that the dead Spaniards be gathered up so that they might be buried on the following day. And he commanded also that the injured be given medical assistance; but so much necessary to restore them was lacking that many died before being attended. For it was found by count that there were a thousand seven hundred and seventy-odd treatable wounds, and by this term was meant those which were dangerous and demanded the attention of a surgeon, such as wounds penetrating to the cavity, broken skulls, and arrow blows in the elbow, knee or ankle, from which there was danger that the victim would remain crippled or maimed. The number we have mentioned included only such injuries; for those which penetrated from one side to the other of the calf, the thigh, the buttocks, or the fleshy part of an arm or of any limb, even though inflicted by a lance, and those knife wounds or stabs which were not deadly dangerous, they did not consider cases for the surgeon. Instead, the men thus afflicted treated each other, even though some were captains and officers of the Royal Exchequer. There was almost an infinite number of these minor wounds, for scarcely a man among them was not injured, and most of them had five and six wounds whereas many had ten and twelve.

Having told, although poorly, of the bloody battle of Mauvila and the victory of our men in this engagement, from which, as we have also mentioned, they escaped with so many injuries, I now must submit my account to the consideration of those who may read it that they may supply with their own imaginations what I am not able to tell here of the affliction and extreme want that these Spaniards suffered for all the things necessary to heal themselves and save their lives—a want which would have been great for people who were well and rested, but which as we shall soon see, was even more so for men who had fought nine hours by the clock without stopping and had come out of the struggle with so many and such cruel wounds. And by this means, I wish to defend myself, for, in addition to my lack of talent, it is impossible for such great things to be recorded adequately or described as they happened.

Accordingly, in regard to the first type of injuries, one must reflect that if the men hastened to a surgeon to have such a multitude of wounds treated, there was not in the whole army more than one doctor, and he was not so skillful and diligent as was needed; on the contrary he was stupid and practically useless. Then if they asked for medicines, there were none; for those few that they carried along with the olive oil, which for days they had preserved for similar needs, and the bandages and lints which they always kept in readiness to put on sores, as well as all the other linen cloths such as sheets and shirts which could have been used to make dressings—all of these things along with the rest of the clothing that they carried, had been put in the town, as we have said, by the Indians, and had been consumed by the fire which the Spaniards themselves had kindled. Moreover if they wanted something to eat, there was nothing to be had because the flames had destroyed both the supplies that the Castilians had brought and those which the Indians themselves had had in their houses, not even one of which now remained standing, since all had been consumed.

In this plight our Spaniards now found themselves, without doctors, medicines, bandages or lints, without food and without clothing with which to cover themselves, or houses or even huts in which to take refuge from the cold and the night air, for the evil fortune of that day had deprived them of all help. And even though they might have wished to go in search of some remedy for their situation, the obscurity of the night, their ignorance as to where they might find assistance, and the very sight of themselves wounded and deprived of so much blood that most of them were unable to stand—all of these things hampered them. There remained to them now only an abundance of sighs and groans, which the pains from their injuries and the inadequate treatment of the same drew from the very depths of their being. Therefore from the bottom of their hearts and in loud voices they called upon God to shelter and assist them in their affliction, and Our Lord as a compassionate Father did come to their aid by bestowing upon them in that hardship, an invincible spirit, a spirit which has always enabled the Spanish nation above every other nation of this world to succour itself in its greatest necessities, just as these Spaniards did in their present want, as we shall see in the following chapter.

CHAPTER XXX

The efforts that the Spaniards made to aid them-
selves, and two strange occurrences
that took place in the battle.

OUR Spaniards on seeing themselves in the necessity, hardship and affliction that we have described, and realizing that their sole salvation lay in their own spirit and courage, rallied their forces. Then the least wounded hastened at once and with great diligence to aid those who had received the most injuries. Some sought a sheltered place in which to put them, and for this purpose rushed to the bowers of branches and the great huts which the Indians had constructed outside the town as lodgings for the Spaniards. From these bowers they made a few small hovels, which they placed against the walls that remained standing. Meanwhile others occupied themselves in opening the bodies of dead Indians and taking out the fat to use as unguents and oils for treating wounds. Still others brought straw on which to place the sick, and some took the shirts from their deceased companions as well as from their own selves to make bandages and lints. The linen dressings were not used for all but only for those whose wounds were of the most dangerous character; for the wounds that were less dangerous, they used less luxurious lints and bandages made of coarse cloth or of the lining of breeches and similar things they happened to have. Others set about skinning the dead horses so as to conserve their flesh for the most severely wounded in lieu of young chickens and hens, there being nothing else to offer them. And in spite of all the work they had to do, some stationed themselves as guards and sentinels so that even though very few of them were able to bear arms, if the enemy came he would not find them unprepared. In this manner they aided each other that night, all forcing themselves to bear with good spirit the hardship in which evil fortune had thrust them.

Four days they tarried, treating only those wounds which they judged dangerous, for there being but one surgeon and he not a very brisk one, these were all they could care for. During this time thirteen Spaniards died because of their inability to obtain medical attention. Forty-seven[43] had perished in the battle, eighteen of whom had been killed by arrows shot through their eyes or mouths, for the Indians, on perceiving that their bodies were protected, aimed at their faces. In addition to those Christians who died during the battle and afterward before they could receive treatment, another twenty-two succumbed later because of the inadequate supply of medicines and doctors. Therefore we may say that in all eighty-two Spaniards were lost in the battle of Mauvila. And to the loss of these men was added that of forty-five horses which the Indians slew during the struggle, and which the Spaniards lamented no less than they did their companions, for they realized that the greatest strength of their army lay in these animals.

But of all of their losses, great as they were, they felt none so deeply as that of Don Carlos Enríquez. Because of his great virtue and fine character, this man had provided the same comfort and ease to the Governor in his hardships and anxieties that good children provide their parents. Moreover, he had been a help to the captains and soldiers in their needs and a support in their negligence and failings; and he had brought peace and concord to them in their personal animosities and quarrels, intervening to placate them and adjust their differences. And not only had he done thus between officers and soldiers, but he had served as a mediator and sponsor for these people with the General himself, obtaining pardon and mercy for them whenever they had erred. And even the Governor,

---

[43] Ranjel says twenty-two, Elvas eighteen, Biedma twenty-plus.

when some dispute occurred in the army among grave persons, had remitted it to Don Carlos so that he might pacify such people and overcome the difficulty with his great affability and fine skill. Thus in addition to fulfilling completely the office of a good soldier, this true cavalier had occupied himself with these and similar things, favoring and helping with both actions and words everyone who had need of him. Therefore those persons who take pride in the titles of cavalier and hildalgo should feel pride also in the deeds of this man; for truly these titles sound inappropriate unless accompanied by such actions as his, which are their very essence, source and beginning. From like deeds true nobility was born, with them it sustains itself, and where there is no such virtue, it cannot exist.

Among other strange occurrences which took place in this battle, we shall relate two which were most noteworthy. One of these happened in the first assault the Indians made against the Castilians, when with that unpremeditated and extremely powerful fury with which they attacked, they threw them from the town and forced them to retreat through the open country. At this time there came running out of the village a very base, uncouth and loutish person, who was a native of some village of Badajoz, but whose name has not been remembered. He was the only man who fled with his back turned and had already reached a place of safety (although he himself must not have thought so), when he took a great fall. For the time being he arose to his feet, but a short while later dropped dead without a wound or any sign of a blow that the Indians might have given him. Since they could find no other reason for his death, all the Spaniards asserted that he had succumbed from fright and cowardice.

The other incident was just the contrary. It concerned a Portuguese soldier named Men Rodríguez, who was of the company of Andrés de Vasconellos de Silva. This noble man, who was a native of the city of Yelves, once had served in Africa along the frontiers of the kingdom of Portugal. Now he had fought all day on horseback, as the very valiant soldier he was, and had accomplished things in battle that were worthy of remembrance. But when he dismounted that night after the struggle was over, he was like a wooden statue, and after three days had passed in which he did not eat, drink, sleep or speak, he departed this life without a wound or any sign of a blow that might have brought about his death. Apparently this good hidalgo was exhausted by the great amount of fighting, and for this reason, in contrast to the previously mentioned individual, had been destroyed by his own valor and by the excess of his toil and struggle.

All that we have told in general and in particular about this great battle of Mauvila, both the facts concerning the time that it lasted (which was nine hours), and the events that occurred, Alonso de Carmona gives in his account. He speaks of the Governor's wound and the arrow blow on Nuño Tovar's lance, remarking that in this way the Indians made a cross for him. He tells of the unfortunate deaths of Don Carlos Enríquez and his brother-in-law Captain Diego de Soto, adding that he himself put one knee on the chest of the latter and another on his forehead while trying in vain with both hands to extract the arrow nailed through his eye. And he also speaks of the necessities and hardships all suffered in common. Though less lengthy in his account, Juan Coles says the same, and he refers particularly, as we ourselves have done, to the number of serious wounds that had to be treated. Both of these authors give identical reports as to the quantity of men and horses that died in this battle, for being so hotly contested, it remained well fixed in their memories.

CHAPTER XXXI

The number of Indians who died in the battle of Mauvila.

IT WAS believed that more than eleven thousand[44] Indian men and women were destroyed in this conflict either by fire or by sword. Spread around the outside of the town were upwards of

[44] Ranjel gives this number as three thousand plus; Elvas, two thousand five hundred (the same as the Inca's field count); and Biedma, five thousand.

two thousand five hundred dead, among whom was the younger Tascaluza, son of the Cacique; within the town, the streets could not be traversed because of the bodies, for here more than three thousand souls had perished by the sword; and within the houses themselves more than three thousand five hundred others had been consumed by fire, a thousand of them, mostly women, having died in a single dwelling when the flames seized it by the door, confining them within and so choking and burning them that it was a sight for compassion to see the condition in which they were left. Moreover, as the Spaniards ran through the land, they discovered nothing in the woods, ravines and streams within a radius of four leagues but dead and wounded Indians, two thousand of whom had not been able to reach their homes. And it was pitiful to find them howling in the forests with no remedy for their afflictions.

Just what happened to Tascaluza, the author of all this unfortunate business, was never ascertained. Some of the Indians said that he had escaped in flight; and others, that he had perished in the fire. This latter fate was held to be the more certain; and it is what he most deserved, since, as was later proved, he from the very day that he had received news of the Castilians and had learned that they were to come to his land, had resolved to destroy them while they were there. And it was with this determination that he had sent his son to receive the Governor at the town of Talise (as has already been said) so that this youth and his companions, on pretext of serving the Governor and his army might act as spies and take note of what military procedure the Spaniards observed both by day and by night. For according to their caution or carelessness, he would make his plans for the betrayal which he hoped would result in their death. It was discovered likewise that the Indians of the town of Talise (who, as we have said, were insubordinate to their Curaca) had complained to Tascaluza that their lord, at the Governor's request and without consideration for the welfare of his own people, had commanded that a certain number of them, both men and women, be given to the Spaniards, and had handed them over to these strange and unknown persons to be borne away as slaves. To their complaint, Tascaluza had then replied:

"Grieve not because you have delivered to the Spaniards the men and women whom your Cacique has ordered you to hand over to them, for very soon I shall return your people to you along with those Indians whom the Spaniards have brought captive from other places. Moreover I shall even give to you the Spaniards themselves so that they may become your slaves and serve in the labor and cultivation of your lands and estates, digging and plowing all the days of their lives."

Meanwhile the Indian women who remained in the power of the Castilians after the battle of Mauvila confirmed Tascaluza's statement and openly disclosed the betrayal that chieftain had prepared for the Christians. For they said that the majority of them were not natives of that town or even of that province but were from various other provinces of the vicinity, and that they had been induced to come there by the magnificent promises of the men whom Tascaluza had persuaded to gather for that battle. Some had been offered robes of fine scarlet cloth, and garments of silk, satin and velvet to wear in their dances and fiestas; others had been assured with solemn oaths that they would receive horses and as a sign of their victory would be permitted to ride these horses in front of the Spaniards. Still others came out saying that they had been promised the Spaniards themselves as servants and slaves, and each specified the number of captives she had been told she could take to her house. Another group confessed to having received numerous offers of linens, woolens and additional articles from Spain. And they declared likewise that many of those who were married had come in obedience to their husband's commands, whereas those who were single had come at the insistence of their brothers and other relatives who had assured them that they were taking them to see some high festivals and great demonstrations of joy to be solemnized and celebrated (after the death and destruction of the Castilians) as a thank offering to their great god, the Sun, for the victory he was to give them. A large number acknowledged that they had come at the request of their lovers and prospective husbands who had pled with them to accompany them and witness the valiant deeds they intended to perform in their service against the Spaniards. Such statements prove very clearly how much in advance this Curaca had planned the betrayal he perpetrated upon our people. Nevertheless, for his treachery, he and his vassals and allies were well punished, although with the great damage to the Castilians that has been observed.

The loss of the Spaniards was even more serious than that of the destruction of their companions and horses whom the Indians had killed; for there were other things which they esteemed even more when they considered the purpose for which they had been dedicated, such, for instance, as a small quantity of wheat flour (three bushels in all) and sixteen gallons of wine. This was all they possessed of these materials when they arrived in Mauvila, and for many days back they had guarded and preserved them for the masses to be said in their behalf. In order that they might travel in better care and greater safety, the Governor himself had brought them with his equipage. But all were burned along with the chalices, altars and sacerdotal vestments carried for divine worship. Hence, from that place on, it was not possible to hear mass, for they had no bread and wine for the consecration of the Eucharist. And although among the priests, the religious and the seculars there were disputes in theology as to whether or not they would be able to consecrate bread made from corn, it was agreed by common consent that the most certain thing that the Holy Roman Church, Our Mother and Lady, commands and teaches each of us in her sacred decrees and canons is that this bread must be of wheat and the wine of grapes. Thus these Catholic Spaniards made no efforts to find dubious substitutes because they held no doubt in regard to their obedience to their Mother, the Roman Catholic Church; and they also desisted because even had they possessed materials for the consecration of the Eucharist, they still lacked the chalices and altars for its celebration.

CHAPTER XXXII

What the Spaniards did after the battle of
Mauvila. An insurrection that was
discussed among them.

SINCE all of the provisions they had carried for saying the mass had burned in the conflict at Mauvila, the Spaniards from that time forward, by order of their clergy, constructed and adorned an altar on the Sundays and other feast days when it was obligatory to hear mass, and then a priest who was clothed in sacerdotal vestments of chamois (in imitation of the first garment in all the world which too was fashioned from the skins of animals) took his place at this altar, and without the consecration of the bread and wine, repeated the Confession, the Introit, the Prayer, the Epistle, the Gospel, and all other parts of the office until its close. Such ceremonies the Spaniards referred to as "dry mass." Afterward this same priest, or another, explained the Gospel and pronounced a discourse or sermon upon it. Thus by substituting this manner of ceremony for the office of the Eucharist, our men consoled themselves in the mental anguish they suffered at not being able to adore Jesus Christ Our Lord and Redeemer through the sacramental species. And in this way they were comforted during the intervening period of almost three years before they left the kingdom of Florida and came again to a land of Christians.

Our Spaniards spent eight days in the miserable huts they themselves had constructed in Mauvila, but when they were able, they moved into the lodgings previously prepared for them by the Indians, since these places offered more adequate accommodations. Here they remained fifteen additional days to treat the injured, which included almost everyone. Meanwhile those who were less afflicted went out to reconnoiter the land and seek sustenance in the towns lying in the vicinity. These towns were small but numerous and, as a result, yielded sufficient food.

In each of the settlements within a radius of four leagues, they encountered many wounded Indians who had escaped from the battle, but there was not a single man or woman among them to treat their injuries. It was believed therefore that the Indians came at night with supplies for the wounded and then returned to the forests during the day. Instead of maltreating such of them as were afflicted, the Castilians regaled them and shared with them the food they carried. But since none of those who were uninjured made their appearance in the open countryside, it was only with great effort that our horsemen, who were seeking them for the purpose of obtaining information, succeeded in seizing fifteen or twenty. When questioned as to whether their people were gathering in that district to make an attack, these captives replied that there was now no one to take up arms because the richest, noblest and most valiant of the province had perished in the previous conflict. And what they said appeared to be true, for in all the time that our men were in that particular encampment, no Indian appeared either by day or by night to make a sudden attack or alarm, which, just by upsetting the Spaniards, would have resulted in much damage and harm since they were so undone by the battle.

In Mauvila the Governor had received news of the ships in which Captain Gómez Arias and Captain Diego Maldonado were exploring the coast, and of how they were faring. This information came to him before the battle, and it was confirmed afterward by captives, who also informed him that the province of Achusi, for which the Spaniards were searching, and the seacoast were a little less than thirty leagues distant. This information pleased the Governor exceedingly because it meant that he now could put an end to his long wandering and begin the new settlement he was planning to make in that province. For, as we have said, his intention was first to found a town at the harbor of Achusi which would receive and offer haven to the ships that might come to it from all parts of the world, and then to found another twenty leagues inland, from which he might begin to make arrangements for converting the

Indians to the Faith of the Holy Roman Church and reducing them to the service and advancement of the Crown of Spain.

Having made certain that the roads were safe between Mauvila and Achusi, the Governor, as a compensation for the good word he had received, freed the Curaca whom Captain Diego Maldonado had brought captive from the harbor of Achusi. This man he had carried in his own company and had treated courteously; and he had not sent him back previously to his homeland because of the great distance lying between and because of the imminent danger that other Indians might kill or capture him while en route. And now, on learning that the Cacique was near his home and that he would be secure until arriving there, he gave him permission to depart, charging him gravely, however, to conserve the friendship of the Spaniards since he very soon was to have them as guests in his own land. The Cacique went away grateful for the Governor's favor, saying that he would be extremely pleased to see him in his land so as to render those services which he owed his lordship.

But all of the Adelantado's desires to populate the land, and all of those arrangements and plans which he had fabricated in his imagination, were destroyed and nullified by discord, for always when permitted to enter, discord is wont to rush in and demolish armies, republics, kingdoms and empires. And the entrée which it found among our men was the fact that some of them had participated in the conquest of Peru and the capture of Atahuallpa, and having beheld the wealth of gold and silver which was so great in that land, had given an account of it to those who were in this expedition to Florida. And since on the contrary no silver or gold had been discovered in this present kingdom, they were not at all content to populate or establish a site here, even though they had seen that the fertility of the soil and other favorable qualities of the land were exceedingly good. Then added to this disappointment was the incredible fierceness of the battle of Mauvila which had singularly frightened and terrified them into wanting to leave Florida as soon as they were able. They said that it was impossible to dominate such bellicose people or to subjugate men who were so free, and that because of what they had seen up until that time, they felt they could never make the Indians come under their yoke and dominion either by force or by trickery, for rather than do so these people would all permit themselves to be slain. There was no reason, they argued, to continue wasting away little by little in this land, and instead they should go on to other places such as Peru and Mexico which were rich and already won, for there they could gain wealth without so much labor. Hence it was their opinion that as soon as they came to the coast, they would be wise to leave that evil kingdom and sail for New Spain.

Some few of those we have mentioned muttered about these and similar things among themselves; but they could not discuss them so secretly as not to be heard by some of the Governor's loyal friends and comrades who had come with him from Spain. These men in turn gave their General an account of what was going on in his army, informing him of how certain of their companions were speaking resolutely of leaving that land as soon as they came to where they would be able to obtain ships or at least small boats.

CHAPTER XXXIII

The Governor makes certain of the insurrection,
and alters his plans.

IN A matter so grave as this, the Governor did not wish to give complete credence to his informers without first verifying the information himself. So taking this precaution, he began to investigate by walking around alone at night more often than he was accustomed and in disguise so as to avoid recognition. Wandering thus one night, he heard the treasurer, Juan Gaytán, and others who were in the hut with him, declaring that on reaching the Port of Achusi where they expected to find ships, they would depart for Mexico or Peru, or return to Spain since they could no longer endure such a laborious life just to gain and conquer so poor and miserable a land.

The Governor was very greatly upset by these words, for to him they were an indication that his army was disintegrating and that all of his men on finding where to go would desert him, just as at the beginning of the discovery and conquest of Peru others had deserted the Governor and Marquis, Don Francisco Pizarro, leaving him eventually on the island of Gorgona with no more than thirteen men. And he realized that if his present army should abandon him, there would be no possibility of recruiting another, and that so far as his pre-eminence, authority and reputation were concerned, he would be ruined, his money would have been spent in vain, and the excessive hardship which until that time his companions had passed through in the discovery of Florida would be lost. Such possibilities, when pondered by a man so zealous of his honor as the Governor, had upon him precipitous and desperate effects. So, in spite of the fact that he for the present concealed his anger and reserved his punishment for another occasion, he was unwilling to endure or to see and experience the malicious action which he apprehended from those whose spirits were weak and dejected. Therefore, with all possible ingenuity and without disclosing anything of his anger, he gave the command for the army to march inland and separate itself from the coast in order that he might remove the opportunity for those with malicious designs to bring shame upon him and cause insurrection among the remainder of his people.[45]

Now this order was the source and the principal cause of the ruination of this cavalier and his whole army. And from that day forward, as a discontented person whose own people had falsified

[45] Biedma states that De Soto's reason for turning inland at this point was to seek a country which afforded sustenance, now that winter was approaching. Elvas says that it was to guard the reputation of the land, for he feared that if it were learned in Cuba that he had found no riches in Florida (the pearls he had planned to send to Havana having been lost at Mauvila), he would not be able to persuade more men to come there when he had need of them.

his hopes, cut off the path to his good desires, and erased the plan he had formulated for populating and perpetuating the land, he never again succeeded in doing anything that might be for his own well-being, and it is believed that he never even attempted to do anything whatsoever. Rather, instigated by disdain, he continued from there on until he died, wasting both time and life fruitlessly and traveling always from one place to another without order or harmony like a man who abhorred life and, as we shall see later, desired to terminate it. He lost both his own happiness and his hopes; he deprived his descendants and successors of that which he already had accomplished and of the fortune he had spent in accomplishing it; and he caused all those who had come with him for the purpose of winning that land, to lose their fortunes. In like manner, he forfeited the honor of having given origin to a very great and beautiful kingdom for the Crown of Spain, and what he must have regretted most of all, of having augmented the Holy Catholic Faith.

In such a grave situation, it would have been wise for the Governor to have sought and accepted advice from those of his friends whom he could trust in order to have done prudently and harmoniously what would have been to the best advantage of all. Thus he could have prevented an insurrection by punishing its leaders and permitting the rest of the league, who were few, to take warning from the experience. In that way he would not have ruined himself and damaged all of his people by keeping secret the angry opinion which resulted in his own destruction. For although he was as circumspect as we have seen him to be in his own affairs, still, when enraged he could not maintain the clarity and liberal judgment that serious matters require. But let him who flees from seeking and accepting advice not hope to succeed.

Because of this fear of insurrection, the Governor now resolved to leave the encampment quickly and return inland, but through provinces not yet seen, lest by traveling the road that he had followed up to that point, his men might suspect his intention and succeed in their own design. So with a feigned spirit, which was foreign to what he had previously shown, he gave strength to his soldiers by urging them to convalesce quickly in order that they might leave that evil land where they had received so much injury, and he commanded that a proclamation be published for them to travel on a certain day which was approaching.

CHAPTER XXXIV

*Two laws that the Indians of Florida observe
in regard to adulteresses.*

SINCE I have promised to describe some or at least the most notable of the customs of the Indians of Florida, it will be well before leaving Mauvila to tell of those laws which the natives of Coza (a province we have left behind) and of Tascaluza (where our Spaniards at present are) observe in punishing the adulterous women found among them.

It is thus that throughout the whole of that great province of Coza there is a law which under penalty of life or of incurring a grave sin against his religion obliges any Indian who suspects a woman in his neighborhood of being adulterous (not because of having seen her evil deeds, but because of circumstantial evidence, and the law specifies what this evidence has to be both in quality and in quantity), first to confirm his suspicion and then report it to the lord of the province, or in his absence, to the magistrates of the town. After obtaining secret information from three or four witnesses and finding the woman guilty according to this evidence, the lord or his magistrates seize her. Then on the next feast day observed in their paganism, they command a public proclamation to be issued to the effect that all the inhabitants of the town must come out after eating to such and such a place nearby in the country, and there form a lane, the length of which will vary according to the number of persons present. At each end of this lane two judges station themselves, and the two at one end after commanding that the adulteress be brought before them, summon her husband and say:

"This woman in conformance with our law has been convicted by witnesses of being evil and adulterous. Do with her therefore what this same law demands of you."

The husband thereupon disrobes his wife, leaving her as she was on the day she was born; and then taking a flint knife (since in all the New World the Indians have never succeeded in inventing scissors), he cuts off her hair, thus bestowing upon her a most ignominious punishment which is common among the nations of the New World. Delivering her shorn and nude into the hands of the judges, he goes away with her clothes as a sign of divorce and repudiation. These magistrates next order the woman to proceed at once and as she is through the lane formed by the people so as to give an account of her transgression to the other judges. And she, after passing along the whole length of the lane, appears before these men and says:

"I come to you, condemned by your companions to suffer the penalty that the law exacts of adulterous women, for I am guilty of such sin. They send me to you so that you may command in this manner whatever appears to you to be appropriate for your republic."

"Return to those who have sent you here," these men reply, "and say by our order that it is most just that the laws of our fatherland which our ancestors ordained concerning chastity in women be guarded and carried out upon evil doers. We give our approval to what they have exacted of you in fulfillment of the law, and we order you never to violate their command."

With this response, the woman returns to the first judges. And her passing back and forth as she carries the messages between the rows of persons formed into a lane is ordained for no other purpose than to insult and shame her by forcing her to appear shorn and nude and guilty of such a sin amid the insults and vituperation of her people; for shame is a punishment peculiar to mankind. Thus while the wretched woman comes and goes from one judge to the other, all the inhabitants of the town, as an affront and expression of their scorn, shower her with clods of earth, pebbles, little sticks, straw, fistfulls of dirt, old rags, torn hides, pieces of rush mats and similar things, each throwing what he happens to bring for the purpose of punishing her transgression. This is what the law demands, giving it to be understood that she has been converted from a woman into a loathsome heap of rubbish.

Finally the judges condemn this woman to permanent exile, both from the town and from the whole province, this being the penalty designated by the law; and turning her over to her relatives, they admonish them under threat of the same penalty never to aid her to enter any part of the state either in secret or openly. On receiving her, the woman's kinsmen cover her with a robe and carry her to where she never again will be seen in either the town or the province. The husband, in the meantime, is given permission by the judges to re-marry. Such is the law and custom observed in the province of Coza.

There is in the province of Tascaluza a more rigorous law for punishing adulteresses. It is that the Indian who sees such evidence of evil as that of one man entering or leaving the house of another at an untimely hour must suspect that the wife of the latter is evil and guilty of adultery. And after his suspicion has been confirmed by his having seen the man enter or leave that house three times, he is required by his vain religion under penalty of a curse to tell the husband of this suspicion of his wife's behavior; but at the same time he must provide the husband with two or three other witnesses who have seen a part of what he affirms or similar evidence. The husband thereupon examines each witness separately, invoking great maledictions upon him if he is lying and great benedictions if he is telling the truth. Having found that his wife has fallen under that suspicion because she has provided damning evidence, he takes her to a field near the town and binds her to a tree, or in the event there is no tree, to a stake that he has thrust into the ground. Then he shoots her with arrows until she is dead. This done he goes to the lord of the town, or in his absence to his magistrate, and says: "My Lord, I have left my wife dead in such and such a place because such and such of my neighbors have informed me that she was an adulteress. Command them to be summoned, and if what they have told me is true, grant me my freedom, but if it is not, exact of me the penalty which our law demands."

Now this penalty is that the woman's relatives shall shoot her executioner with arrows until he is dead and then leave him in the field without a sepulchre just as he has left his wife, who being innocent must now be buried according to the law with all pomp and ceremony. But if the judges find that the witnesses corroborate each other and that the evidence is true, they grant the husband his freedom and permission to re-marry, and at the same time command that a proclamation be made publicly to the effect that under penalty of death, no person, whether relative, friend or acquaintance of the deceased shall dare give her burial or remove a single shaft from her body, but instead, they shall leave her to be eaten by the birds and dogs as an example and a punishment for her wickedness.

These two laws are observed particularly in the province of Coza and Tascaluza, and in general adultery is punished very rigorously throughout the whole kingdom of Florida. The penalty exacted of the woman's accomplice or of a married man who commits this act, I endeavored to learn, but the one who gave me my account was unable to tell me what it was because he heard only adulteresses and not adulterers discussed. It must be that always and in all nations such laws are rigorous in regard to women and favorable in regard to men, for as a dowager of this bishopric whom I have known once said: "Men and not women made these laws because they feared the offense; had women made them, they would have been ordained in a different manner."

CHAPTER XXXV

The Spaniards leave Mauvila and enter Chicaza.
They construct boats to cross a great
river.

RETURNING to the thread of our history, I must tell you that
when the Spaniards had spent twenty-three or twenty-four days
treating their wounded in the encampment at Mauvila, they left the
province of Tascaluza, having gained some strength to pass forward
in their exploration. At the end of a three-day march through peaceful though unpopulated lands, they entered a province called Chicaza.
The first town they encountered in this land was not the principal
one but another under the same jurisdiction. It was located on the
bank of a great and deep river[46] that flowed between high cliffs,
and it was on the same side of the river that they were traveling.
Here the Indians refused to accept the Governor peacefully, and
on the contrary showed very openly that they were his enemies by
informing his messengers that they wished a war of fire and blood.
So when our men arrived within sight of this settlement, they beheld
in front of it a squadron of more than fifteen hundred warriors,
who immediately came out to skirmish with them. But these Indians
put up very little defense, and after abandoning the town, which
they already had emptied of wives, children and property, retired
to the river. They had determined not to fight with the Spaniards
on an open battlefield, but rather to prevent their crossing the river,
for since this stream was very full and deep and flowed between
great, high cliffs, they felt that they would be able to block their
way and thus force them to seek another route. Hence when the
Spaniards rushed upon them with the utmost fury, they simply
plunged into the water and crossed over, some in canoes of which
they had many and very fine specimens, and others swimming, their

[46] Possibly the Black Warrior River. They were still in Alabama, but
were about to cross into Mississippi. Chicaza was in the latter state.

fear having moved them to haste. On the shore opposite the town, they had assembled their entire army, eight thousand men of war, who had vowed to defend the passage of the river and thus had spread their encampment out for two leagues along its bank so that in all that space the Castilians would not be able to cross.

In addition to setting up this defense against the Christians, the Indians molested them at night with sudden attacks and alarms. Groups of them would cross at different places in their canoes, and then all would rush upon the Spaniards at the same time, giving them in this way great affliction. But in defending themselves, our men employed a very excellent stratagem. This was that in the three landing places afforded by the river in the area occupied by their enemies and in that space where they now came to disembark, they made excavations at night in which their crossbowmen and arquebusiers could conceal themselves. Then when the Indians came again, these men permitted them to jump ashore and go some distance from their canoes, only to fall upon them afterward and do them great injury with their swords since there was no place to which they could flee. Three times they maltreated them in this way, and then the Indians learned from their rashness and ventured no more to cross the river, occupying themselves solely in a careful and diligent effort to keep our men from doing so.

The Governor and his captains, perceiving that it was impossible to make a crossing from where they were because of the strong defense of the enemy, and realizing that they were losing time by waiting for the Indians to grow careless, now gave the command for the hundred most diligent men of those who understood something of the art of shipbuilding to construct some large boats of the type known as pirogues, which are almost flat and are capable of conveying many people. And lest their foes be aware of what they were doing, the men detailed for the job betook themselves to a wood lying one league and a half up the river and another league from its bank. Here they worked so rapidly that they completed the pirogues in twelve days. In order to transport them to the river, they built two carts suitable for the purpose; and then with mules and horses pulling, while the men themselves pushed and in difficult passages even bore the boats on their shoulders, they came with them one morning before dawn to a very spacious quay which the river afforded, and opposite which there was also a good landing.

The Governor was present at the launching, for he had instructed his men to keep him advised as to the time; and he now ordered ten cavalrymen and forty artillerymen to enter each vessel and hasten over the river before the Indians came to prohibit their passage. The men on foot were to row, whereas those on horseback were to remain in their saddles in order not to be detained in mounting on the opposite shore.

In spite of the great silence the Spaniards attempted to maintain both in launching their craft and in embarking, it was impossible to prevent the five hundred Indians guarding the other bank from hearing them. Hastening now to where they saw the pirogues and the Spaniards who were attempting to cross, these Indians gave a very great shout to inform their people and ask for help, and then stationed themselves immediately at the landing for the purpose of defending the passage.

Fearing that more enemies would rush up, the Spaniards made every effort to embark, and the Governor himself attempted to go with the first boatload, but his companions prevented his doing so because of the great danger attendant upon this initial crossing before the landing had been cleared of enemies. With this urgency, our men applied themselves to the oars and did arrive at the opposite shore, but all were wounded since the Indians shot at them from the cliffs just as they pleased.

One pirogue reached the landing readily, but the other fell short of it, and because of the great cliffs along the river, its occupants for the time being were unable to jump ashore. It was therefore necessary for them to strain at their oars in order to attain the wharf. Meanwhile, however, those in the first vessel disembarked and the first man of them to do so was Diego García, son of the Governor of Villanueva de Barcarrota. This soldier was valiant and most determined in all deeds of arms; consequently, his friends called him Diego García de Paredes, not because he was related to that individual, although of noble blood, but because he was similar to him in spirit, strength and valor. Second of the horsemen to reach the shore was Gonzalo Silvestre. This pair now fell upon the Indians and drove them more than two hundred feet from the landing; then being in great danger because there were only two of them and the enemy was so numerous, they returned speedily to their companions. Afterward they attacked and retreated four times with no assistance from their friends, who meanwhile had got in each other's way and as a result had not managed to bring their horses ashore. But the fifth time they attacked, there were six of them, and they put more fear into the Indians who now returned with less fury to defend the crossing. The footsoldiers who came in the first boat, as soon as they landed, stationed themselves in a little town on the very cliff of the river and made no attempt to leave since they were so few and since all of them, as a result of having borne the greatest discharge of arrows, were wounded. The men in the second boat disembarked with greater ease, having found the landing place free of Indians; thus, without danger they hastened to the assistance of their companions who were fighting on the plain. In this second group, the Governor himself had crossed along with seventy or eighty other Spaniards.

When the Indians perceived that their enemies were numerous and that they could no longer hold them in check, they retired to a wood not far from the town and from thence rejoined their companions in their camp. Having heard the shouting and hallooing, the other Indians had hastened with great speed to defend the passage, but on encountering these runners and learning from them that many Spaniards had already succeeded in making a crossing, they too had returned to their army where they were reinforced. Meanwhile, they were pursued by the Christians who hoped to fight, but they remained passive, fortifying themselves with wooden palings and with the identical branches that had been used for their houses. Some who were very daring did come out to skirmish, but they paid for their pride, for, not being equal to the horses in swiftness, they were destroyed by our lances. The entire day was spent in this manner, but during the night the Indians went away and none of them appeared again. In the interim, the whole Spanish army passed over the river.

CHAPTER XXXVI

Our men camp in Chicaza. The Indians inflict
upon them a sudden and very cruel
nocturnal battle.

AMID the hardships and dangers we have described, our Spaniards overcame the problem of crossing the first river in the province of Chicaza; and on finding themselves rid of their enemies, they dismantled the boats, preserving the nails to make other craft when such should be necessary. This work done, they continued their exploration, and after marching four days through level country, which though populated contained only scattered villages of few houses, they came to Chicaza,[47] the principal settlement from which the rest of the province derives its name. This town was situated on a flat hill extending north and south between some ravines which contained little water but numerous groves of walnuts, liveoaks and oaks. At the base of these trees lay the harvest of two or three years, for having no livestock to consume it and not using it themselves because of possessing better and more delectable fruits, the Indians had left it to spoil.

It was in the first days of December of the year 1540 that the General and his captains reached the town of Chicaza. They found the place abandoned, and winter having already set in, they felt that

---

[47] In northeastern Mississippi, the exact location is by no means certain. The modern word Chicasaw is the same as the Indian's Chicaza.

it would be wise to pass the season here. Unanimous in their decision, they gathered together all necessary food supplies and brought from the neighboring hamlets a great amount of wood and straw with which to build houses, for even though the town contained two hundred dwellings, more were needed.

Our men remained in this camp with some tranquility and peace for almost two months, engaging in no activity during the time save that of running each day in the field with the horses. But they did capture some Indians, most of whom the Governor returned with gifts and messages to the Curaca for the purpose of enticing him with peace and friendship. To these overtures, the latter responded by offering hopeful promises of his coming, feigning excuses for his procrastination, and duplicating his messages from day to day in order to keep the Governor expectant. Furthermore, he sent fruits, fish and venison in exchange for the gifts he had received. In the meantime, however, his Indians continued to molest our men with sudden attacks and alarms which they gave two and three times each night. But they never waited to do battle, and when the Christians came out at them, took refuge in flight. Such a procedure was adopted purposely and as a military stratagem, for they planned thus to keep the Spaniards from sleeping and by a show of cowardice to make them careless and confident that things would always be as they were at present, so that when actually attacked they would be remiss in their military skill. But this display of cowardice the Indians did not keep up for long; rather, they to all appearances became ashamed of it, wishing now to reveal a contrary spirit and to make the fact clear that their previous flights had been performed with craftiness and with the idea of disclosing a greater strength and courage at the proper time. And this they did as we soon shall see.

On a certain night toward the end of January in the year 1541, the north wind blew furiously, and the Indians recognized how much this wind was in their favor. At one o'clock, therefore, three squadrons of them crept as silently as possible to within a hundred

feet of the Spanish sentinels. Then the Curaca, who led the center
and principal group, sent to find out the location of his two collateral
divisions, and on learning that they were in the same vicinity as his
own, gave instructions to sound a call to arms. This they did with
many drums, fifes, shells and other rustic instruments that had been
brought along for the purpose of making a greater noise, and then
all shouted at the same time so as to throw more terror into the
hearts of the Spaniards. In order to burn the town and create a
light by which to see their enemies, they had brought some faggots
of a certain native grass, which when woven into a thin rope or
cord and lighted, holds a flame like the wick of an arquebus, and
when swung in the air raises a flame that burns as continuously as
that of a wax taper. And indeed these faggots were so exquisitely
constructed that they looked like wax tapers with four wicks and
gave as much light. Of this same grass they had made little rings
for the tips of their arrows so that they might throw them while
burning and in this way set fire to the houses from a distance.

With such order and preparation the Indians now came and
attacked the town, swinging their faggots and shooting many lighted
arrows into the houses, which being made of straw caught fire
instantly with the strong wind that was blowing. Confronted with
such a sudden and fierce onslaught, the Spaniards rushed out as
quickly as possible to defend their lives. The Governor, who always
slept in his breeches and doublet in order to be prepared at all
times for these unexpected attacks, rode out to the enemy before
any of his cavaliers. But because of the haste occasioned by his foes,
he was unable to take along any defensive arms other than a helmet
and a loose quilted cotton coat three fingers thick, which is looked
upon as armor because it is the best defense our men have found
against arrows. With just this protection and with his lance and
dagger he went forth alone against such a multitude of enemies,
for he never knew what it was to fear. He was followed by ten
or twelve cavaliers, but not immediately.

The remainder of the Spaniards, both captains and soldiers,
hastened with their customary courage to resist the savagery and

fierceness of their foes, but they were unable to do battle because a strong wind was sweeping the flame and smoke back over them and thus damaging them extensively while contributing to the favor and defense of the Indians. In spite of all such obstacles, however, they came out of their quarters to fight in whatever way they could, some crawling on all fours to escape the flames and others running between the houses for the same purpose. In this way some reached the open fields while others hastened to the infirmary to assist the suffering, whom they had kept to themselves in a separate building. On perceiving the fire and hearing the shouts of the enemy, those of the sick who were able had fled, but the remainder perished in the flames before assistance arrived.

The cavalry evacuated the place only as the speed of the fire and the fury of their enemies permitted them to do so; for the attack being so sudden, they had no occasion to arm themselves or saddle their mounts. Some took their horses out by the halter and fled with them to save them from the flames; whereas others, who had no protection against the fire but flight, simply abandoned them. Several went now to aid the Governor, who had fought a long time with no assistance other than that of the very few men who had gone out with him at the beginning of the battle. He was the first to kill an Indian on that night, for he always prided himself on being first in all things. In the meantime the Indians of the two collateral divisions entered the town, and with the aid of the fire which was in their favor did a great amount of damage, killing a large number of horses and Spaniards before they had time to seek protection.

CHAPTER XXXVII

A continuation of the battle of Chicaza until its close.

FORTY or fifty Spaniards fled at full speed from the eastern quarter of the town where the fire and the violence of the enemy were greatest and most furious (a shameful flight such as had never been witnessed until that point in the whole of the expedition to Florida). Following these men was Nuño Tovar with his bare sword in his hand and wearing only an unbuckled coat of mail, the pressure of his enemies having given him no opportunity to obtain anything else.

"Return, soldiers, return!" this cavalier cried loudly, as he went in pursuit of his men. "Whither do you flee? There is no Cordova or Seville to offer you haven. Remember that the security of your lives lies not in flight but in the strength of your courage and in the force of your arms."

And now from the southern quarter of the town, which was as yet untouched by the fire, thirty footsoldiers emerged to intercept the fleeing men. These soldiers, who belonged to the company of Captain Juan de Guzmán, a native of Talavera de la Reyna, came from his lodging. Reprimanding their companions, they thus detained them; and then being unable to pass through the fire that lay between themselves and the Indians, all went around the town together and came out through the eastern part of the camp to encounter their enemies.

At the same time that these footsoldiers appeared, Captain Andrés de Vasconcellos, who likewise was lodged in the southern quarter, led forth twenty-four hidalgos from his own company, all Portuguese and chosen people, for most of them had served as horsemen on the African frontier. These cavaliers rode out through the western side of the town, and they were accompanied by Nuño Tovar, although he was not mounted. So now with some on one side of the town and some on the other, the Spaniards fought their enemies wherever they encountered them, forcing them to retire to their center squadron, which was the principal one. Here the fighting was the most intense; and here, because they had been so few and the enemy so numerous, the Governor and the men accompanying him had struggled until that moment with much exigency and at the risk of their lives. But when they saw companions coming to their assistance, they attacked with new zeal. The General, eager to slay a particular Indian who had been and was still very much favored in the conflict, now closed with him, and having succeeded in wounding the man with a lance, he leaned upon both his weapon and his right stirrup in an attempt to put an end to him. But because of the weight and effort he made, he pulled his saddle after him and tumbled with it into the midst of his enemies. On seeing their Captain General in such straits, both the Spanish cavalry and infantry spurred forward to his aid so quickly and fought so valiantly that they prevented the Indians from killing him. Then resaddling his steed they placed him upon it, and he returned once more to the struggle.

Now the Governor had fallen because his servants in the very sudden and furious assault of the Indians, and in their perturbation at the slaughter drawing near them, gave him his mount without fastening its girth. For the Spaniards who came later to assist him found the girth folded and laid in the place on the saddle where it ordinarily is left when a horse is unsaddled. At the time the Governor fell, he had fought for more than an hour in a saddle without girth, and he had been saved solely by his great skill in horsemanship.[48]

Perceiving the impetus with which the Spaniards were now hastening from all directions and the great number of horses coming with them, the Indians slackened the fury with which they had fought until that point; but they never ceased to persist in the battle, at times attacking with great animus and at others withdrawing in good order. Then when they could no longer withstand the force of the Spaniards, they called out to each other to retreat, and turning their backs, fled as fast as they could, pursued now by the Governor and his men on horseback, who went as far as the fires burning in the town lighted the way for them to do so. Thus, after more than

[48] Ranjel characteristically deprives the Governor of some of his glory here. He says that he fell over the first Indian at whom he thrust and who thrust at him; that he lost his saddle on this first essay; and that had the Indians known how to follow up their victory, "this would have been the last day of the lives of all the Christians of that army."

two hours, this battle, sudden and furious as it was, came to an end; and the General, when he had followed up his pursuit, ordered a call to reassemble and returned to determine what damage the Indians had done. This he discovered to be more serious than he had expected, for forty Spaniards and fifty horses had been slain.

Alonso de Carmona says that eighty horses were either dead or wounded, and that more than twenty of them had been burned or shot to death while tied in their very stalls. For their masters on finding them very spirited because of the great amount of food they had consumed in the encampment, had made them halters of large iron chains and shackled them for greater security. Then with the pressure of the fire and the Indians they had been unable to free the animals and thus had delivered them to the flames and the arrows of the foe.

In addition to the anguish our Spaniards felt for the loss of their companions and for the death of the horses, which were the very strength of their army, they were grieved further by a particular incident which occurred on that same night. For among them was one sole Spanish female,[49] Francisca de Hinestrosa, who was married to a good soldier named Hernando Bautista and was in her days of childbirth. Now since the attack of the enemy was so sudden, this woman's husband went out to fight, but when the battle was over and he returned to inquire about his wife, he found that she, being unable to escape the flames, was burned to charcoal.

Just the contrary happened to a worthless little soldier named Francisco Enríquez. This man, whom many of the Spaniards ridiculed, was, in spite of his good name, chicken-hearted and more of a scoundrel than a soldier. He had been sick and for a number of days had been carried on his back, but when he smelled fire and perceived the violent effort of the infidels, he fled from the infirmary. After he had taken a few steps in the street, an Indian came upon

[49] Another Spanish woman, presumably a serving woman of Doña Isabel de Bobadilla, claimed to have accompanied the army from the beginning of the expedition until it reached Mexico. See *Final Report, De Soto Commission,* p. 83.

him and shot him with an arrow that passed almost through his groin and left him extended on the ground. Here he lay apparently dead for more than two hours. But when day dawned he was given medical assistance and in a brief time was well, not only of the wound in his groin, which had been considered mortal, but also of his previous illness which had been long and annoying. For this reason, when those who customarily joked with him, teased him afterward, they said: "May misfortune protect you in adversity, for to you who are not worth two copper coins, it has given robust health and life, whereas to so many cavaliers and splendid soldiers who have fallen in these last two battles, it has brought only death."

Enríquez bore it all and said worse things to them.

We have told before of how the Governor brought swine to breed in Florida, and of how he took great care to nourish and increase these animals. In order to have them better protected at night in the encampment at Chicaza, his men had built within the town a wooden corral which consisted of many sticks driven into the ground and covered with a small roof of straw.[50] But since the fire on the night of the battle was so sweeping, it seized the swine also, and none of them escaped except the sucklings who were able to slip between the palings of the fence. Now these animals were so fat with the great amount of food they had found in that place that the lard from them ran for a distance of more than two hundred feet, and their loss was lamented no less than that of the men and horses because our Castilians suffered from a lack of meat and were saving the swine for the comfort of the sick.

Juan Coles and Alonso de Carmona agree in all their details of this battle, and both speak of the ravages made by the fire upon the swine. They praise highly the Governor's skill in the saddle, telling of his fall and of his having fought for more than an hour without a girth. Alonso de Carmona adds that each Indian brought three

---

[50] According to Elvas, De Soto gave some of the chieftains in this region a taste of pork, which they so relished that their Indians came every night to steal hogs. Three Indians were taken in the act; two were slain and the third was returned to his chieftain minus his hands.

cords wrapped around his body, one for a Castilian, another for a horse, and a third for a pig. And he says that our men were highly incensed when they learned of this fact.

CHAPTER XXXVIII

Notable deeds that occurred in the battle of Chicaza.

AS SOON as the dead were buried and the wounded treated, many Spaniards went out into the open country, where the battle had occurred, to examine and make note of the injuries the Indians had inflicted upon the horses with their arrows. For it was their custom to open the carcasses of the animals not only to see to what extent the shafts had penetrated but again to preserve the flesh for food. And they found now that almost all of the dead horses had received arrows through their entrails and lungs and near their hearts. Eleven or twelve in particular had shafts passing through the very center of their hearts, for as we have said elsewhere, the Indians, being able to do a horse the most damage here, aimed at no other spot. Moreover, four of them were discovered with two arrows through the middle of the heart, both of which had happened to be fired at the same moment from opposite sides. This was a marvelous coincidence and one that is hard to believe, but we are certain that it occurred thus, because, it being so unusual, all the Spaniards in the field were summoned to witness it. Another shot revealing unusual strength was received by the horse of Juan Díaz, a trumpeter who was a native of Granada. This animal had been killed by an arrow which pierced the thickest part of its shoulders and protruded the length of four fingers on the opposite side. Now since this shot had originated from so strong and fierce an arm (the horse being one of the broadest in the whole army), the Governor commanded that a written report be made of it, and that a royal scribe give witness thereto. Thus it was that a scribe called Baltasar

Hernández, a native of Badajoz whom I knew later in Peru, came at once. He was a very good and pious man, for it is fitting and requisite that all who follow his profession be so, since the property, life and honor of the republic are entrusted to them. An hidalgo both by birth and by virtue, Baltasar Hernández gave a written testimony of what he saw concerning that arrow, and his testimony concurs with what I myself have told.

Three days after the battle, the Castilians agreed to move their camp to a place a league distant, which seemed to them to be a better location for the horses; and this they did with much haste and diligence. From the neighboring settlements, they brought wood and straw, setting up to the best of their ability a town which Alonso de Carmona refers to as Chicacilla. Here, he says, they very hastily made saddles, lances and round shields, because the fire had burned all these things for them, and he adds that the men were like gypsies, some being without doublets and others without breeches. These words are all his.

In this town the Spaniards passed what remained of the winter. Here they endured much hardship because the season was rigorous with cold and ice, and they were naked. For they had no clothes with which to resist the weather except what they had brought out on their backs, none others having been saved from the fire.

Four days after the battle the Governor transferred the command from Luis de Moscoso to Baltasar de Gallegos. On making a secret investigation, he had learned that the officers of the camp had been negligent and careless in regard to the night patrol and sentry of the army, and that it was for this reason that the Indians had come upon them unheard and inflicted the damage that they did.[51] And the Spaniards themselves confessed that, in addition to those horses and

[51] Ranjel says that the Governor, sensing evil in the Indians on the day before the battle, had informed his men that he would sleep that night fully armed and with his horse saddled, and they in turn had promised to do the same. But neither De Soto nor his men kept the agreement. And he adds that, in spite of the fact that De Soto had told Moscoso to take extra precaution on that night in regard to sentinels, he had put the most useless horsemen and the poorest horses in the army on the morning watch.

companions lost on that night, all of them would have been overcome by the Indians but for the fact that the excellence of certain individuals and common necessity itself had forced them to recover a victory which they already had regarded as lost, although they had recovered it at great cost to themselves and with very little damage to their foes, not more than five hundred of whom had perished in that conflict.

All that we have related of this nocturnal and sudden battle at Chicaza, Alonso de Carmona gives at great length in his account, making considerable enlargements upon the danger that the Spaniards ran that night because the attack of the enemy had been so furious and unexpected; and he states that, as a result of the great pressure exerted upon them by the fire, most of the Christians came out in their shirts. In sum he says that they fled and were overcome; that it was the persuasion of a friar which caused them to return and miraculously recover the victory they had lost; that the Governor fought for a long time before his men came to his assistance; and furthermore that he carried his saddle without a girth. Juan Coles concurs with him in the majority of these statements, but he notes in particular that the Governor, as a good captain, fought alone. And Alonso de Carmona, in addition to the things he says about the battle which conform to our own account, adds:

"We remained there three days, at the end of which time the Indians decided to return and either conquer us or die. And indeed I have no doubt but that had their determination been put into effect they would have swept us completely off our feet[52] because of our lack of arms and saddles. But when they were on their way to engage us and were a quarter of a league from the town, God was pleased to send from His heaven a great deluge of water which wet the cords of their bows, and being unable to harm us, they departed. In the morning while traveling about the land, the Spaniards found their tracks and captured one of their number who told all his

[52] *nos llevaran a todos en las uñas*—literally, they would have carried us all in the nails.

people had planned to do, asserting that they had sworn to their gods to die in the attempt. This considered, the Governor decided to leave that place and go to Chicacilla where we very hastily constructed round shields, lances and saddles, for at such times, necessity makes a master of everyone. We built bellows of two bearskins, and, with the cannons that we carried, fitted out our forge, tempered our arms, and readied ourselves to the best of our ability." All these are words of Carmona taken to the letter.

Now when the Indians had verified their ravages among the Castilians, they collected more spirit and daring and occupied themselves nightly in disturbing our men with attacks and alarms. And they did not molest them in just any manner they pleased, but came in three or four squadrons from different directions, and all fell upon them at once with great shouts and outcries so as to cause more fear and confusion.

In order to prevent the Indians from burning their new encampment as they had done the one in Chicaza, the Spaniards spent every night outside the town arranged in four squadrons, with one squadron on each of the four sides. Sentinels were placed, but all kept watch, for there was no safe hour in which they could sleep since the Indians came two and three times a night and there were many nights when they came four. Most of their assaults were light, but they caused perpetual anxiety, never failing to wound or kill some man or horse. And although many of their own people were slain, they took no warning from the fact.

The Governor as a means of assuring himself that his enemies would not return on the following night, would send four or five groups of fourteen or fifteen cavalrymen each morning to intimidate them. Scouring the countryside about the town, these men did not spare an Indian, whether he were a spy or not, but lanced all of them and later returned at sunset to the encampment with a true report that there was not a single living Indian within a radius of four leagues of the town. But within four hours or five at the most, hoards of them were already stirring up disturbances with the Castilians, who were greatly amazed that they had collected their forces and come again to molest them in such a brief time.

Although there were always some dead and some wounded on both sides after these nightly affrays, nothing particularly notable can be told except an incident which occurred when a squadron of Indians came to attack the place where Captain Juan de Guzmán and his company were. With five other horsemen and some foot-soldiers, this captain rode out against the foe; and since these Indians were very near when they lit and swung their faggots, both foot-soldiers and horsemen were able to join and attack them simultaneously. Juan de Guzmán, who was a cavalier of great courage, although physically delicate, thrust his lance at an Indian standard bearer who came in the first row of his squadron. But this man, while still running, seized the lance in his own right hand, which he slid along its shaft until he had reached the hand of his assailant. Then letting go of the lance and taking Juan de Guzmán by the collar, he pulled him with a great tug from the saddle and kicked him without once releasing the flag he was carrying in his left hand. And all this was done with so much haste that it was difficult to judge just how it happened.

When the other soldiers saw their captain in such extremity they attacked the Indian and cut him to pieces before he could do further harm; then they routed his squadron and rescued Juan de Guzmán from peril. But the Spaniards did not escape without damage, for of the six horses that had gone out against the Indians, two were killed and two wounded. The loss of these animals our men regretted no less than the loss of their companions, and the Indians themselves were more pleased to kill one horse than four cavaliers, for they felt that it was solely on account of the horses that their enemies had any advantage over them at all.

CHAPTER XXXIX

*A protection which a Spaniard devised against
the cold suffered at Chicaza.*

THESE nocturnal skirmishes, because of being so numerous and continuous, resulted in unbearable annoyance and hardship, all of which our Castilians endured in that camp until the close of March; and here in addition to the persecution and anxiety inflicted by the Indians, they suffered also from the inclemency of the weather, which was most rigorous in that area. For since they spent every night arranged in squadrons, and since they possessed so few clothes that even the most fortunate among them had no more than some breeches and doublets of chamois, and practically none had either shoes or sandals, the cold which they endured was incredible, and it was only by a miracle of God that everyone did not perish.

In their need against the weather, they were aided by the contrivance of a completely clownish and gross person named Juan Vego, a native of Segura de la Sierra. There was an incident which occurred between this man and Vasco Porcallo de Figueroa on the island of Cuba at the beginning of our expedition—an incident which though humorous was injurious to Juan Vego. But since this story has to do with buffoonery and tricks, I shall say no more of it here other than that Juan Vego, even though coarse and vulgar, persisted in being funny, joking with everyone and making ridiculous and nonsensical statements that fitted the quiver from which they came, and that Vasco Porcallo de Figueroa, who also loved a joke, played an offensive trick upon this man, in recompense for which he gave him, while still in Havana where the incident occurred, a sorrel-colored horse. Afterward in Florida this horse turned out so well that Juan Vego's companions offered many times to give him seven and eight thousand pesos for it when they should receive their first division of spoils, for the prospects which our Castilians promised themselves in the initial and middle stages of the exploration were as rich and magnificent as this. But Juan Vego would never sell his horse, and he showed good judgment in not doing so, for there was to be no melting of metals, and instead only the death and loss of everyone, as our history will reveal.

Now in order to protect himself against the cold of the night, this Juan Vego wove a mat of straw, which is very good in that place since it is long, soft and pliable. This mat he made long, wide and four fingers thick, using half of it underneath as a mattress and the other half on top as a blanket. Then since he found himself comfortable, he made many other such mats for his companions, with their help, however, for everyone was eager to labor on common necessities. These things he carried to the garrisons where the Castilians were stationed every night in a squadron, and with them they resisted the cold of the winter, confessing afterward that all would have perished but for the assistance of Juan Vego. Juan Vego helped also during the bad weather to convey the great amount of corn and dried fruit which was to be found in that region, for even though the Spaniards suffered the severity of the cold and the molestation of the enemy, who would not permit them to sleep at night, they did have an abundance to eat and were never hungry.

End of the Third Book.

THE FOURTH BOOK

*Of the History of Florida by the Inca treats of the battle
at the fort of Alibamo; the death of numerous Spaniards
for want of salt; the arrival at Chisca and the crossing of
the Great River; the solemn procession made by both the
Indians and Spaniards to adore the cross and beseech
God's mercy; the cruel war and pillage between Capaha
and Casquin; the Spaniards' discovery of a means for
making salt; the fierceness of the Tulas both in stature
and in arms; and the comfortable winter which
the Castilians passed in Utiangue.
It contains sixteen
chapters.*

CHAPTER I

*The Spaniards leave the camp at Chicaza and
attack the fort of Alibamo.[1]*

ERCEIVING that the month of March had passed,
and that the time had now arrived to continue their
exploration, the Governor and his captains counseled each other to leave their encampment and
the province of Chicaza; and the remainder of the
army likewise wished to depart from that land where there had
been so much hostility and damage, always in the night; for in
the four months they were wintering there, the Indians had not
failed to attack and alarm them as many as four nights. So with
mutual determination our men set out again during the early days
of April in the year 1541. Then after they had traveled the first
day across four leagues of flat land where there were many small
towns of fifteen or twenty dwellings each, they halted at a site
a quarter of a league from all settlements, it appearing to them
that the people of Chicaza, who had annoyed them so extensively,
would cease this persecution when they saw them outside their land.
The thoughts of these Indians, however, were far different and quite
remote from all peace, as we soon shall see.

Now when the Spaniards paused to make camp, they sent horsemen in all directions to reconnoiter the vicinity. These men returned

[1] The tribe for which the fort was called has handed its name down to a
state and a river. This fort was, however, in the north-central portion of the
present state of Mississippi.

415

to say that nearby was a wooden fort garrisoned by some very select warriors, apparently about four thousand in all. So choosing a company of fifty cavalrymen, the General set out to inspect this fort, and, when he had seen it, returned to his men and said:

"Gentlemen, before darkness prohibits our doing so, we will be wise to hurl our enemies from their stronghold; for, not content with the annoyance and affliction they have bestowed upon us so persistently in their own land, they now wish, even though we are no longer there, to vex us further by showing us that they have no fear of our arms since they come to seek them outside their boundaries. Therefore, we will do well to punish them and prohibit their remaining this night where they are, for otherwise they will not permit us to rest and will come out by regiments, each in its turn, to hurl arrows at us throughout the entire night."

All approved this suggestion, and leaving a third of both the infantry and cavalry to guard the camp, the remainder of the army set out with the Governor to attack the fort of Alibamo. This fort was a perfect square with walls four hundred feet in length, made by binding pieces of wood together; and within this square, two additional wooden walls crossed from one extreme to the other. In the first wall were three little gates, so low that a person could not enter them on horseback, one being in the center and the other two on the sides next the corners. And directly behind these gates, in each of the other walls, there were three additional gates, so that in the event the Spaniards gained the first, the Indians still could defend themselves within those of the second, third, and even fourth walls. The gates in the last wall opened out to a river, which though narrow was very deep and flowed between high cliffs that could be ascended and descended only with difficulty on foot and in no manner on horseback. It had been the intention of the Indians to build a fort where they could be assured that the Castilians would not attack, either by bringing the horses through the gates or across the river, and where like themselves, they would fight on foot; for as we have already mentioned, they held no fear of our infantry and

felt equal if not superior to them. Over the river they had constructed wooden bridges which were fragile and dilapidated, and
could be used only with difficulty. On the sides of the fort there
were no gates.

Having examined and studied this structure thoroughly, the Governor ordered a hundred of his best armed horsemen to dismount and
charge it in three squadrons with three men to the line, while the
footsoldiers, who were less protected with armor, followed in their
rear. In this way all were to attempt to gain the portals. Instantly
everything was arranged. One gate fell to the lot of Captain Juan
de Guzmán, another to Captain Alonso Romo de Cardeñosa, and a
third to Gonzalo Silvestre; hence all three of these men now took
their places in front of their respective gates to attack.

Until that moment the Indians had secluded themselves in their
stronghold, but on seeing the Spaniards prepared to launch an attack,
a hundred of them came out through each entrance to skirmish.
They were wearing great feather headdresses, and to make themselves more ferocious, all had painted different colored bands across
their faces, bodies, arms and legs with ink or bitumen. Falling
upon our men with all of the gallantry that can be imagined, they
brought down with their first arrows Diego de Castro, a native of
Badajoz, and Pedro de Torres, a native of Burgos, both noble and
valiant men who flanked Gonzalo Silvestre in the front line. The
former was wounded with a flint harpoon in the large muscle above
the right knee, and the latter was pierced between the two shin bones
of one leg. On perceiving that his captain, Gonzalo Silvestre, was
alone, Francisco de Reynoso, a native cavalier of Astorga, stepped
up from the second line in order not to leave him thus.

In the second squadron, which was commanded by Juan de Guzmán, the Indians felled another cavalier, Luis Bravo de Xerez, who
strode at his captain's side. This they did likewise with a harpoon
of flint, wounding him in the large muscle of the thigh. Then from
the side of Captain Alonso Romo de Cardeñosa, who was on his
way to attack the third gate, they took one of his two companions,

Francisco de Figueroa, a native of Zafra, who was very noble in both blood and virtue. He too received a flint harpoon in the large muscle of the thigh, for these Indians, as men experienced in war, aimed at the Spaniards from the thigh downward, that being the portion of their bodies which bore no armor. Furthermore they used harpoons of flint because they could inflict more damage with them, for if the arrow failed to wound with its point, there was a possibility that it might cut with its edge in passing.

These three cavaliers, whose wounds had been of the same nature, died shortly after the battle and within an hour; and since they were noble, valiant and young, none having reached twenty-five years of age, their death caused much pity. In addition to the wounds I have described, there were many others, for the Indians fought most valiantly and shot at the legs of their enemies. But when our men had taken note of this fact, all with one accord shouted that they should close at once with their adversaries and not allow them an opportunity to use the arrows with which they were inflicting such extensive damage. So attacking now with the utmost haste and fury they carried the Indians in retreat to the gates of the fort.

CHAPTER II

A continuation of the battle of the fort of Alibamo until its close.

THE Governor had stationed himself to one side of his squadrons with twenty horsemen, and Captains Andrés de Vasconcellos and Juan de Añasco were on the other side with thirty more. All now set upon the Indians, one of whom discharged an arrow at the General as he rode in front of his men. This missile struck so forceful a blow on his helmet above the forehead as to bounce upward more than fourteen feet, and he confessed afterward that it made him see lightning. Then since both cavalry and infantry were attacking simultaneously, the Indians retreated to the wall of the fort, where great numbers of them were slain because the gates were too small to receive them within. But the Spaniards passed through these gates as furiously as they had fought on the plain, and in doing so, mingled so indiscriminately that no one was able to say which of the three captains had entered first.

The slaughter of the Indians within the fort was terrible, for our men on seeing their enemies enclosed and remembering the unceasing afflictions received from them in the previous encampment, pressed down upon them wickedly in their anger, and since they bore no armor, slew great numbers of them with their knives and daggers. Unable to pass through the gates to the river because of the pressure put upon them, and confident still in their swiftness, many Indians hurdled the walls only to fall prey in the open countryside to the horsemen, who annihilated them with lances. Numerous others who could reach the river by means of the gates, fled across the wooden bridges, but they hustled each other in such a manner that a number were pushed into the stream; and it was indeed a comic sight to see the splashes they made in the water since they fell from a great height. Still others who were unable to take the bridge because the fury of the Spaniards did not permit them sufficient time, plunged from the cliffs and swam the current. Thus all evacuated the fort very shortly, and those who could do so, crossed the river to a place of safety and formed a squadron. Meanwhile our men remained where they were.

One of the Indians who had escaped, on seeing himself outside the conflict, resolved to demonstrate his skill with the bow and arrow. Withdrawing from his companions and shouting to the Castilians, he gave them to understand by means of signs and a few words, that a crossbowman should come out and exchange a number of arrows with him in single combat in order to determine which of the two were the better marksman. At that, an hidalgo mountaineer named Juan de Salinas stepped forth quickly from among the Spaniards (who to protect themselves from the arrows had sought shelter behind some trees) and descended to the river to take his place opposite the challenger. A companion who was determined to go along and protect him with a shield shouted at him to wait, but he refused to do so, saying that since his enemy brought no odds, he himself wanted none. Soon after, he fixed a dart to his crossbow and aimed at the Indian, who in turn did the same with his bow, having selected an arrow from his sheath.

Both men released their missiles simultaneously. That of the mountaineer struck his adversary in the center of the chest and he would have fallen, but before he reached the ground, his comrades came and bore him away in their arms, more dead than alive, however, for the whole dart had penetrated his chest. But this Indian meanwhile had struck Juan de Salinas in the neck on a level with his left ear (for the latter had turned when firing so as to take good aim and present to his enemy the side of his body, which offers less to shoot at than the front), and the arrow had pierced the nape of his neck, protruding in one direction as far as it did in the other. And with this arrow thus crossed in his neck, the cavalier returned to his companions very content with the shot he had made. Meanwhile it would have been possible for the other Indians to have fired upon him, but they refused to do so since the challenge had been one against one.

The Adelantado, in a desire to castigate these people for their rashness and arrogance, summoned his cavalry and, crossing the river by a good ford lying above the fort, pushed them forward for more than a league across the open country, lancing them as they went. And the Spaniards would not have stopped this slaughter until they had finished with them all, had not night intervened and taken from them the light of day. At that, more than two thousand Indians[2] did die in this encounter, and they paid well for their daring, for no longer could they boast of the number of Castilians they had slain in their land or of the great annoyance they had inflicted upon them during the past winter. And now having pursued the battle to its

[2] Ranjel says "many," Elvas "three," Biedma "some."

close, the Spaniards returned to the encampment and treated their many injured. Since the wounded could not travel, they stopped here for four days.

CHAPTER III

Many Spaniards die for lack of salt. How they arrive at Chisca.

BUT let us turn back a little in our history to relate events in the time and place they occurred and thus avoid the necessity of referring to them later. You must know that when our Spaniards left the vast province of Coza and entered that of Tascaluza, they possessed no salt, and when they had traveled some days without it, their suffering was such that it became an absolute necessity. Some of those whose constitutions must have demanded salt more than others died a most unusual death for lack of it. They were seized with a very slow fever, on the third or fourth day of which there was no one who at fifty feet could endure the stench of their bodies, it being more offensive than that of the carcasses of dogs or cats. Thus they perished without remedy, for they were ignorant as to what their malady might be or what could be done for them since they had neither physicians nor medicines. And it was believed that they could not have benefited from such had they possessed them because from the moment they first felt the fever, their bodies were already in a state of decomposition. Indeed, from the chest down, their bellies and intestines were as green as grass.

In this manner, some commenced to die, to the great horror and consternation of their companions, many of whom out of fear now began to employ a remedy which the natives concocted to succour themselves in this same necessity. First they would burn a certain herb of which they knew, and from its ashes make a lye that served as a sauce in which to moisten what they ate. With this concoction they saved themselves from rotting to death as the Spaniards were doing. A number of our men because of their pride refused to take advantage of this remedy, for they felt that it was filthy and unbecoming to their quality, and that to imitate the Indians was base. But it was just such people as these who died; for when in their illness they did request lye, it was too late for it to be of benefit, since they had passed that crisis which must be guarded to prevent corruption from setting in. Once the body had begun to decompose, the lye was insufficient and thus of no avail to those who were late in requesting it. But the inability to find in a time of necessity that which has been scorned in prosperity is a just punishment for the proud. More than sixty Spaniards died in this manner during the time they lacked salt, which was almost a year. In its proper place we shall tell how they came to make salt and thus supplied their need.

You should be informed also that when the Governor came to Chicaza, ten, twelve and fourteen interpreters had been requisite for him to converse with the caciques and other Indians of those lands through which he had passed, for he had found a great variety of languages conforming to the numerous provinces, nearly all of which spoke a different tongue. Thus a message was passed from Juan Ortiz on to the last of the interpreters, all of whom were arranged according to their ability to comprehend each other and transmit what had been said. It was with just such labor and tediousness that the Adelantado asked for and received accounts of the proper things for him to know concerning all of that great land. But this difficulty was not present in the case of those individual men and women whom our soldiers had seized for their services, regardless of what province they came from, for within two months after they had been speaking with Spaniards, they comprehended what their masters said to them in Castilian, and they were able to make themselves understood in this same language when they talked of things necessary and common to all. Furthermore, when they had been with the Spaniards for six months, they served as interpreters between their masters and strange Indians. All of the inhabitants of this great kingdom of Florida disclosed this same skill in language and in anything else that they considered worthwhile.

When they had spent four days taking care of the wounded in the camp at Alibamo, which was their last in the province of Chicaza, the army departed; and after they had journeyed for three more days through an unpopulated region and toward the north so as to flee from the sea, they came to Chisca,³ a village lying near a great river. Now since this was the largest of all the rivers that our Spaniards discovered in Florida, they called it the Great River⁴ and never gave it any other name; but in his record Juan Coles says that in the language of the Indians this river was called the Chucagua. Later we shall speak more at length of its immensity, which is amazing.

Because of their continuous war with the people of Chicaza, and because of the wilderness lying between the two provinces, the Indians of Chisca knew nothing of the coming of the Spaniards to their land and as a result were not on the lookout. So when our men caught sight of the town, they charged upon it without order, and in addition to capturing males and females of all ages, pillaged everything that they found within the place just as if it had belonged to the province of Chicaza where they had been so maltreated.

Off to one side of the town was the dwelling place of the Curaca. It was situated on a high mound which now served as a fortress. Only by means of two stairways could one ascend to this house. Here many Indians gathered while others sought refuge in a very wild forest lying between the town and the Great River. The lord of the province, who like his land was called Chisca, was now old and sick in bed; but on hearing the noise and confusion in his village,

³ This is the Quizquiz of Ranjel, Elvas and Biedma. They are still in the present state of Mississippi.
⁴ *Río Grande.* This is the body of water which we know today as the Mississippi. Lest the reader confuse it with the river which forms a part of the boundary between the United States and Mexico, we will refer to it always as the Great River.

he arose and came from his bedchamber. Then beholding the pillage and the seizure of his vassals, he grasped a battle-ax and began to descend the stairs with the greatest fury, in the meantime vowing loudly and fiercely to slay anyone who came into his land without permission. Thus this wretched creature threatened when he had neither the person nor the strength to kill a cat, for besides being ill, he was very old and shriveled. Indeed among all the Indians that these Spaniards saw in Florida, they found none other of such wretched appearance. But the memory of the valiant deeds and triumphs of his bellicose youth, and the fact that he held sway over a province so large and good as his, gave him the strength to utter those fierce threats and even fiercer ones.

The Cacique's wives and servants now seized him, and with tears and entreaties and enlargements upon his poor health, persuaded him from descending. Then those Indians who came up from the town warned him that the strangers who had arrived were such as he had never seen or heard of before, and that in addition to being extremely numerous, they had brought with them some very large and swift animals. And they said that if he had determined to fight these people, he should consider first the lack of preparation of his own men, and that to avenge his injury he should summon the inhabitants of the district and await a better opportunity. Meanwhile, he would be wise to feign the most friendly appearance and adjust himself to such occasions as were offered, either of forbearance and suffering or of vengeance and wrath, and he should not inconsiderately attempt any rash act because of the great injury it would bring upon both himself and his vassals.

With these and similar reasonings the wives, servants and vassals of the Curaca detained him from closing with the Christians, but he was so enraged that when the Governor (on learning that he was in the chieftain's house) sent a message of peace and friendship, he refused to listen, remarking that he had no desire to hear the words of a man who had offended him but wished rather to wage upon that man a war of fire and blood, and that he thus was de-

claring such a war at once lest the fact be overlooked that he planned
soon to annihilate all of the Spaniards.

CHAPTER IV

*The Spaniards return what they have pillaged
to the Curaca Chisca and are happy to
be at peace with him.*

EXHAUSTED by all the inclemencies of the past winter, dis-
gusted with fighting, and burdened with many wounded and
sick (both men and horses), the General and his captains and soldiers had come to this place with a desire for peace and not war.
And since this desire was mingled with fear because of their having
sacked the town and angered the Curaca, they sent to Chisca many
additional messages, filled with all the suave words they were permitted to utter. For they perceived that in addition to the obstacles
they brought with them, almost four thousand armed warriors
had gathered around the Cacique within less than three hours after
their arrival in this town; and they were afraid that since these men
had assembled in such a brief time, many more would come later.
Again, they perceived that the site of the town, both inside and outside, was very favorable to the Indians and unfavorable to themselves,
and that because of the many streams and forests lying throughout
that region, they would be unable to use their horses to the extent
necessary for an offensive. But what caused them greater reflection,
and they came by it through much experience, was the realization
that they did not thrive on battles and instead were being consumed
by them, for the Indians from day to day were killing both their
men and horses. All of these things, therefore, moved them to seek
peace with great earnestness.

But among the Indians, on the other hand, there were many who
(after having met to discuss the messages of our men) wanted war,
for they were offended by the seizure of their wives, children and

other kinsmen, and by the pillage of their possessions. Being men of a bellicose nature, they felt that the speediest way to reimburse themselves for their losses was through arms, and that any other means would necessitate too much time. Desiring to start the conflict at once, they rejected the peace offers without giving any reason except that of their loss. Other Indians who had lost nothing they cared about regaining, but who, because of the natural inclination of their race for war, wanted to prove their strength and courage, also rejected the overtures of peace. Holding out for consideration the fact that this was a question involving their honor, they declared that it would be wise to learn by experience just what such strange and unknown people were like in arms, and what were the limits of their courage and strength, while at the same time letting these people know something of their own force and valor so that they and others would be warned against coming to their land in the future. There were still other more prudent and pacific Indians, however, who maintained that they should accept the Spaniards' proffer of peace and friendship; first, because by this means they were more certain of recovering their captured wives and children and their stolen goods than they would be by enmity and war, and then because they thus would be assured of avoiding the sight of damage that still might be done (such for instance as the burning of their towns and the desolation of their fields at a time when the grain was near ripening). And, they continued, there was no cause to discover by experience how valiant these people were since reason clearly told them that men who had passed through as much enemy territory as had these men before arriving at Chisca could not but be most valiant. Peace and concord with them were therefore better than war, for in addition to the ills already set forth, war would bring about the death of many of those present as well as that of their brothers, relatives and friends; and it would in itself give vengeance to their enemies among the neighboring Indians. For the reasons expressed, they concluded, it would be better to accept the friendship of the Spaniards and see how they fared with it, since in the event that it was not to their advantage, they could very easily and with more odds than they now held, take up arms again and succeed in their present aspirations.

This last counsel won over the others, and the Curáca bowed before it, reserving his anger for a time when he might be offered a better occasion to express it. Hence he answered the Governor's messengers by saying that first of all they should state what it was the Castilians desired. These men thereupon replied that since they were merely passing through this land and could not stop long, their Governor asked no more of the Indians than that they disoccupy their town for his camp and provide his men with what little food they might need. At that the Curáca responded that he was content to concede the peace and friendship requested, to disoccupy his town, and to supply food, but that he would do so only with the understanding that the Spaniards were to release his vassals at once and restore to them their possessions, not omitting so much as a single earthenware pot (these are his words), and that they were not to ascend to his house to see him. Under these conditions, he said, he would receive the Spaniards peacefully; otherwise, he was challenging them to fight at once.

Our men accepted the Cacique's stipulations because they had brought sufficient servants and had no need for these new captives, and again because the property they had seized consisted of no more than a miserable lot of chamois and a few robes. So all was restored according to the Curáca's specification, not so much as one earthenware pot being omitted. The Indians thereupon disoccupied the town and left the food they had in their houses for the Castilians, who because of their sick and their need to refresh themselves stopped six days in this town called Chisca. On the last of these days, the Governor, with the Cacique's consent, paid him a visit and thanked him for his friendship and hospitality. Then on the ensuing day, he set out once again upon his journey and exploration.

CHAPTER V

*The Spaniards leave Chisca and construct barges
to cross the Great River. They arrive
at Casquin.*

HAVING left Chisca, the army traveled on for four days, making short marches of only three leagues each since the indisposition of the wounded and sick did not permit longer ones. They proceeded always up the Great River and came at the end of the four days to where it could be crossed; not that it was fordable, but there was a pass by means of which the water could be reached. For all along that portion of the river bank they had traveled, there stretched a vast and dense forest, and on both sides of the water were lofty and deep cliffs which could not be ascended or descended. In this pass the Governor and his army stopped for twenty days, it being necessary to make barges or pirogues such as those used at Chicaza in order to cross the river. Moreover as soon as they had arrived here, upwards of six thousand Indian warriors, well equipped with arms and canoes, had appeared on the opposite shore to defend the passage against them.

On the day after the Governor pitched camp, four principal Indians arrived with a message from the lord of that same province, the name of whom I am omitting here because it has not been remembered. Stationing themselves before him without so much as uttering a word or showing any expression whatsover, they turned their faces to the east and with profound reverence made a bow to the sun; then turning to the west, they made a second but lesser bow to the moon; and finally addressing themselves to the Governor himself, they made a third and even less pretentious gesture. And everyone present took note of the degree of respect by the manner in which it was expressed. Then these men delivered their message, saying that the Curaca their lord, his cavaliers, and the

general populace of their land had sent them to welcome his lordship and offer him their friendship, co-operation, and whatever
service he would be pleased to accept. Afterward the Adelantado
made some very kind remarks and sent the Indians away quite
content with his affability.

During the entire twenty days or more that the Spaniards passed
in this encampment, the Indians ministered unto them with much
peace and cordiality. But the principal Curaca never came to visit
the Governor and instead continued to excuse himself with attacks
of ill health. The Spaniards concluded, therefore, that he had sent
the message and performed his services because of a fear that they
might lay desolate his fertile fields, in which the fruit was about to
ripen, or set fire to his towns, and not because of any love he might
bear for Castilians or any desire to favor them.

By putting a great amount of effort into building the barges (all
working equally and no distinction being made between captains
and soldiers, since he who was most diligent was regarded as the
leader), they at the close of fifteen days were able to launch two of
them, both of which were complete in every detail. These vessels
they guarded with much caution day and night lest they be burned,
for during the entire time the Spaniards were occupied in this work,
the Indians never ceased to molest them from their many finely
wrought canoes. Arranged in squadrons they would travel up and
down the river, showering them with arrows whenever they came
abreast. Meanwhile, however, our men defended themselves and
drove off the enemy with arquebus and crossbow. They succeeded in
inflicting great damage, for they dug excavations in the bank of the
river and concealed themselves therein so that the Indians would
draw near, and they fired from their defenses in such a way as not
to waste a single shot.

After laboring for twenty days in the construction of barges, the
Castilians had placed four of them in the water, a sufficient number
to provide space for a hundred and fifty footsoldiers and thirty
cavalrymen. In order that their enemies might see these vessels well

and in consequence despair of doing them harm, they took them up and down the river both by sail and oar. Thus it was made evident that the pass could no longer be defended, and the Indians decided to lift-camp and go to their towns. Without opposition, therefore, the Spaniards crossed the river[5] in their barges and a few canoes which they had won by noble industry. And when they had dismantled the boats to preserve the much needed nails, they continued on their way. Four more days they marched through uninhabited regions, and on the fifth came to the summit of some high hills where they beheld a town of four hundred houses, situated beside a river larger than the Guadalquivir at Cordova. Along the entire bank of that river and throughout the vicinity, there were numerous fields of corn and a great number of fruit trees, all of which proved the land to be fertile.

The Indians of this town had already noticed the approach of the Castilians, and they now came out in a body, but without anyone in particular being designated to acknowledge the Governor. Nevertheless, they offered him their persons, houses and lands, and assured him that they considered him lord of them all; then within a short time two principal Indians accompanied by many others came in behalf of the Curaca, and once more, in the name of their lord and all of his state, offered (as the first had done) their vassalage and service. The Governor in turn received them cordially and spoke kindly; thus they went away very content.

This town like the whole of the province and its Curaca was called Casquin. Because of the great quantity of food it afforded for feeding their people and restoring the sick as well as the horses, the Spaniards rested here six days. Then they continued for two more days to the town where the Cacique Casquin resided, a place situated

    [5] There are three theories as to where De Soto crossed the Mississippi; i.e., the Memphis theory, the Tunica theory and the Sunflower Landing theory. Because of the constant changes in the river, the exact place can never be known, but the United States De Soto Expedition Commission, after carefully weighing each theory, came to the conclusion that this crossing was made somewhere near Sunflower Landing, Mississippi.

on the same bank but seven leagues up the river. All of the land was very fertile and inhabited, though the villages were small and contained no more than fifteen, twenty, thirty and forty houses. The Cacique came out in the company of many noble people to receive the Governor, and he offered him his friendship and service as well as his own house in which to lodge. This dwelling was situated to one side of the town on a high mound, where there were in addition ten or twelve large structures that housed the chieftain's entire family of wives and his numerous servants. The Governor replied that he would accept the Cacique's friendship but not his house lest he prove an inconvenience, and that he would be content to occupy an orchard which Casquin himself had pointed out when he perceived that his guests did not want the houses. And since there was not a single good dwelling in this orchard, the Indians very hastily put together great bowers of fresh branches, which were necessary because it was already the month of May and the weather was hot. With a part of the army encamped in the town and a part in the orchards, all were most comfortable.

CHAPTER VI

A solemn procession of Indians and Spaniards is made to adore the cross.

THE army had bivouacked in the town called Casquin for three days, and there had been much good feeling among both Indians and Spaniards. Then on the fourth day the Curaca and all the nobility of his land, whom he had assembled for that solemn occasion, came before the Governor; and after each had made a great bow, this chieftain said:

"My Lord, since you have the advantage over us in strength and arms, we are of the opinion that yours is a better god than ours. Therefore these nobles of my land whom you see assembled here (and who because of their low estate and little merit have not dared appear before you) and I with them do now beseech that you deign to request your god to grant us rain, for our crops are very much in need of water."

To these words, the General responded that even though he and his entire army were but sinners, they would pray to God Our Lord, as the Father of mercy, to grant them this grace. Then in the presence of the Cacique, he ordered Maestro Francisco, a Genoese who was a great craftsman in carpentry and shipbuilding, to fashion a cross from the highest and thickest pine to be found in the whole of that region. And this tree, which was pointed out to him by the Indians themselves, was such that after being worked (by which I mean having the bark removed and the trunk rounded to gain more, as carpenters say), a hundred men were unable to lift it from the ground. Without taking anything from its height, the maestro made of it a perfect cross in the proportion of five and three, which because of its great height turned out to be magnificent. This cross was placed at the summit of a lofty mound which had been built on a cliff overlooking the river, and which served the Indians as a lookout, since it was higher than all the other hills of that vicinity.

Two days were spent in completing and planting the cross, and then on the third day a solemn procession was ordained. The Governor participated in this ceremony along with his captains and people of most consequence, but one armed squadron of infantry and cavalry was left on guard, it being necessary to do so as a protection for the army. The Cacique walked at the Governor's side and many of his nobles were scattered among the Spaniards. In front and off to themselves was a chorus of priests, clerics and friars, who sang the litanies while the soldiers made the responses. So it was that more than a thousand persons, including both Christians and infidels, proceeded a goodly distance to the site of the cross. Here in front of that symbol, all sank to their knees while two or three prayers were said. When they had arisen, the priests advanced two by two and, kneeling in adoration, kissed the cross. They in turn were followed by the Governor and the Cacique, and the latter, having come for a purpose and of his own accord, emulated his companion in all that he saw him do, even kissing the cross. Next came the rest of the Spaniards and finally the Indians, who also imitated the Christians in each of their acts of reverence.

Fifteen or twenty thousand human beings of both sexes and all ages had assembled on the opposite bank of the river where with arms outstretched and hands uplifted they stood watching the Christians. From time to time they raised their eyes to the heavens and made gestures with their hands and faces as if they too were beseeching God to give ear to the request of these strangers. Then again they uttered a low, dull cry as of people who had been hurt, at the same time commanding their children to weep; and this the children did. Thus on both sides of the river all of this ceremony and ostentation was being rendered for the purpose of adoring the cross, and the Governor and many of his men were moved to much tenderness on perceiving that in such strange lands and among people so far separated from the Christian doctrine, the symbol of our redemption should be adored with such an abundance of tears and great manifestations of humility. When all had worshipped in the manner we have described, they returned as they had come, observing the same order of procession while the priests chanted the *Te Deum Laudamus* to the close of that canticle. Only after four long hours was the ceremony of that day concluded.

Now God in His mercy desired to reveal to these pagans that he heeds those of his people who truly call upon him; for at midnight of that same day, a heavy rain began to fall and it did not cease for two more days. This circumstance afforded the Indians much happiness, so the Curaca and his cavaliers organized a procession such as they had seen formed to worship the cross, and in this manner went to thank the Governor for the great favor they had received through his intercession. In short, they assured him with very affectionate words that they were his vassals and would take pride in and boast of the fact from that time on. But the Governor replied that they should render their thanks to God, the Creator of heaven and earth, who not only had brought the rain but had bestowed upon them many other even greater blessings.

These things have been told in such detail because they did happen thus, and because the Governor and the priests who accompanied him had charged that the adoration of the cross be performed with all possible ceremony so that the pagans might witness the reverence with which the Christians regard that symbol. But all of this chapter concerning the adoration, Juan Coles relates at even greater length in his account, and in addition affirms that it rained for fifteen days.

When each of these things had been accomplished and the Spaniards had remained nine or ten days in that town, the Governor ordered the army to be ready to take up their exploration on the following day. The Cacique Casquin, who was fifty years of age, now begged permission to go along and to take with him his warriors and servants, the former to accompany the army and the latter to carry supplies and clear the roads (as they must go through uninhabited lands), and in the camps to provide firewood and bring grass for the horses. The Governor thanked the chieftain for his great kindness and told him to do whatever would afford him the most pleasure. With that this Indian went away very content; and either he already had a great number of warriors and servants prepared to go, or he now commanded that they be made ready.

CHAPTER VII

Both Indians and Spaniards go against Capaha.[6]
The location of this town is described.

FOR a better understanding of my history, you must know that for many centuries back this Cacique Casquin and his parents, grandparents, and more remote ancestors had waged war upon the

---

[6] In the book summaries this word appears as *Cafa* and again as *Capha*, but in the text, it is always *Capaha*. To avoid confusion we have emended the summaries and in each instance used *Capaha*. In all other accounts it is *Pacaha*.

lords of Capaha, a province bordering on their own. And since these lords were more powerful in both vassals and lands, they had pushed and were still pushing Casquin into a corner and almost to the point of surrender, for he dared not take up arms lest he anger and irritate the Cacique Capaha, who as a more powerful person could and might do him harm. Hence Casquin had remained passive and had contented himself with guarding his boundaries, neither going beyond them nor affording his enemies an occasion to attack, if it suffices not to give tyrants an excuse. But perceiving now that an excellent opportunity was being offered to avenge himself of all previous injuries with the strength of another if he were sagacious and astute, he had asked the permission of the Governor we have mentioned. Then with the latter's approval and with the idea of vengeance, he prepared to take with him not only his serving people but five thousand warriors, all of whom were well equipped with weapons and adorned with feather headdresses, for under no circumstances will the Indians leave their houses without these two things. Moreover, he made ready three thousand men who were loaded with food and at the same time armed with bows and arrows.

Thus equipped, Casquin departed from the town, having requested leave to go in advance under pretext of discovering enemies, if there were such, and providing lodgings with those things the Spanish army would need on arrival. His forces he carried in a squadron which, according to the best military procedure, comprised a vanguard, a battalion and a rearguard. Meanwhile the Spaniards came out at a quarter of a league behind and proceeded in this order throughout that day. Then when night fell, both groups camped with the Indians still in advance. They placed their sentinels as we did ours, and a night watch rode back and forth between the one and the other.

In this order they marched for three days, at the end of which time they came to a swamp that was very difficult to cross; for there were great morasses at its entrances and exits, and, in its center, water which though clean was so deep that for a distance of twenty feet it had to be swum. This swamp formed the boundary between the two enemy provinces of Casquin and Capaha. The men crossed it on some very unstable wooden bridges discovered there, and the horses swam, but with great difficulty because of the pools of stagnant water lying near the banks on both sides. The whole of the fourth day was occupied in making this crossing, and then both Indians and Spaniards camped in some beautiful and very peaceful pasture lands a half-league distant. The swamp now behind them, they traveled for two more days, and very early on the morning of the third day came to some high hills, from whence they caught sight of the principal town of Capaha.[7]

This town was the frontier and defense of the entire province against that of Casquin and in consequence was fortified in a manner I shall describe. It consisted of five hundred large and good houses, which were located on a site somewhat loftier and more eminent than its surroundings, and it had been turned into almost an island by means of a man-made ditch or moat ten or twelve fathoms deep and in places fifty feet wide, but never less than forty. The moat was filled from the previously mentioned Great River, which flowed three leagues above the town; and water was drawn into it by human effort through an open canal connecting it with the river, a canal which was three fathoms deep and so wide that two large canoes went down and came up it side-by-side without the oars of the one touching those of the other. Now this moat, of the width we have said, lay on only three sides of the town, for it was as yet incomplete. But the fourth side was fenced off by a very strong wall of thick wooden boards that were thrust into the ground, wedged together, crossed, tied, and then plastered with mud tamped with straw in the manner we have described further back. The great moat and its canal contained such a quantity of fish that all the Spaniards and Indians who accompanied the Governor ate them until they were surfeited, and still it appeared as if they had not taken out a single fish.

[7] The expedition, having crossed the Mississippi, is now in Arkansas. This is the northernmost point reached along the Mississippi.

The Cacique Capaha was within the town when his enemies, the Casquins, hove in sight; but feeling that his own forces were too few and unprepared to resist their adversaries, he gave way, and before they came into the place, entered one of the canoes which he kept in the moat and went out through the canal to the Great River to take refuge on a well-fortified island which he held there. Those of his people in the town who were able to obtain canoes followed their lord, and those who could not fled to the nearby forest. Others who were more dilatory and less fortunate remained where they were. Meanwhile the Casquins, on finding the place without defense, entered it; not suddenly, however, but cautiously and timidly lest there be some ambuscade of enemies within, for though supported by the Spaniards, they still were a people who had been conquered many times and as a result could not lose this fear of the inhabitants of Capaha. Thus their delay gave opportunity to many men, women and children to flee.

But once assured that there was no one within the town to oppose them, the Casquins made evident the rancor they felt for its inhabitants, for they slew whatever men they could lay their hands on, more than a hundred and fifty in all, and they removed the scalps of these men to take to their land as an evidence of triumph, for the scalp is a symbol which among all Indians signifies a great victory and vengeance for injuries. Afterward, they sacked the entire town and in particular the houses of the lord, which they robbed with more contentment and approbation than any others for no reason except that they were his. Furthermore, they seized numerous women and children, among whom were two of the many wives of Capaha, both very beautiful, who had not been able to embark with the Cacique because of the commotion and the great haste occasioned by the unanticipated approach and sudden attack of their enemies.

CHAPTER VIII

*The Casquins sack the town and the burial place
of Capaha, and then go in search of
the Cacique himself.*

NOT content with having sacked the town and the houses of
the Curaca and with having made what slaughter and seizures
they could, the Casquins moved on to the temple in the large public
plaza, which was the burial place of all who had ever ruled that
land—the fathers, grandfathers and other ancestors of Capaha. The
temples and sepulchres, as we have stated elsewhere, are the most
venerated and esteemed sites among the natives of Florida; but I
believe that the same is true in all nations, and not without good
cause, for these places are monuments, I would not say of saints,
but of those who have passed on, and such monuments recall the
dead to us as they were while living. Summoning all of their forces
so that everyone might enjoy the triumph, the Casquins went to this
temple and sepulchre, and since they realized how much Capaha
(proud and haughty because of their not having attacked previously)
would resent their daring to enter and desecrate this place, they not
only proceeded within but committed every infamy and affront they
could. Sacking it of all ornaments and riches, they took the spoils
and trophies which had been made from the losses of their own
ancestors. Then they threw to the floor each of the wooden chests
which served as sepulchres, and for their own satisfaction and vengeance as well as for an affront to their enemies, strewed upon the
ground the very bones and bodies the chests enclosed. Afterward
not content with having cast these remains to the ground, they trod
upon them and kicked them with utter contempt and scorn. Many
of the heads of Casquin Indians which the men of Capaha had
placed on the points of lances at the doors of the temple as a symbol
of victory and triumph, they now removed, substituting for them the
heads of citizens of the town whom they themselves had decapitated

on that very day. In sum, they did everything they thought of, and they even wanted to burn the temple as well as the Curaca's houses and the entire village, but they dared not do so lest they anger the Governor. For all of these things they accomplished before the Governor entered the town. Meanwhile, he, on learning that Capaha had retired to the island to fortify himself, had sent messages of peace and friendship by means of Indians whom his men had captured. But Capaha refused to accept peace and instead sent out a call to his people to avenge themselves upon their foes.

Now when the Governor was informed of this fact, he commanded both Indians and Spaniards to prepare to advance and attack the island. But the Cacique Casquin advised his lordship to wait three or four days until the arrival of a fleet of sixty canoes which he would command to be brought from his country, since these vessels were necessary for crossing over to the island. This fleet had to come by the way of the Great River, which also passed through the land of Casquin. Then the Cacique ordered his vassals to go at once and bring the canoes as quickly as possible, now that there was to be vengeance for them in the destruction of their enemies. Meanwhile the Governor continued to send messages of peace and friendship to Capaha, but on perceiving that they were of no avail, and that the canoes were already on their way up the river, he commanded his army to go out and receive this fleet and afterward proceed by water and land to the fortification of their enemies. Thus it was that on the fifth day after coming to the town of Capaha, the Castilians forsook it.

The Indians of Casquin, in order to damage the fields of their enemies while traveling, formed a wing half a league wide and thus devastated everything they encountered. Here they discovered many of their own people who had been captured and now served as domestics in the lands and fields of the inhabitants of Capaha. For the purpose of preventing these slaves from fleeing, their captors had injured each of them in one foot, as we have already told of others; and they had held them in bondage with these cruel and perpetual shackles, more as an evidence of their triumph than for the advantage and service they could obtain from them. The Casquins now set them at liberty and sent them again to their own land.

Arriving with their armies at the Great River, the Governor and the Cacique Casquin found that Capaha was fortified on the island with barricades of thick wood which crossed from one extreme of it to the other. And since there was a great undergrowth of brambles and bushes there, the island was difficult to enter and even worse to pass through; and this ruggedness, combined with the fact that he had with him many fine warriors, gave Capaha assurance that his enemies would not conquer. Even though confronted with all these difficulties, the Governor commanded two hundred Castilian foot-soldiers to set out in twenty of the canoes and three thousand Indians to embark in the remainder. Thus all were to attack the island at the same time and like good soldiers make an effort to take it.

At the Governor's command, the number of Indians and Spaniards we have mentioned set forth in the sixty canoes. When they landed, however, there was an accident which in general grieved all of the Castilians. This was that one of their number, Francisco Sebastián, a native of Villanueva de Barcarrota (who had been a soldier in Italy, was a gentleman in both body and countenance, and was of a very happy disposition), was drowned because of his haste to disembark by means of a lance. Thrusting the butt end of his weapon into the ground and not being able to reach the shore because the canoe moved back, he fell into the water, and since he wore a coat of mail, sank immediately to the bottom, never to appear again. A short time before, while crossing in the canoe, he had been very gay (as on other occasions) with his companions, and had uttered a thousand funny and foolish things, among which was the following:

"Evil fortune brought me to these hopeless regions, for God had placed me in Italy, a good land where, according to the usage of the language, I was addressed as your lordship, just as if I had been a lord of vassals. But you people here do not appreciate me sufficiently to address me as 'thou.' Furthermore the generous and charitable inhabitants of that place regaled and succoured me in my needs as if I were their own son. And in both peace and war I fared as follows: if I chanced to kill some Turk, Moor, or Frenchman, I never failed to despoil him of arms, clothing, or horses, which were always worth something to me. But here I have to fight with some naked individual who runs along ten or twelve steps in front of me, jumping and shooting arrows at me as if I were a wild beast, and I am unable to catch up with him. And if my good luck favors me and I do overtake and kill him, I find nothing to take off him except a bow and a feather headdress—as if these articles were of any value to me. And the thing that pains me most is that a famous astrological prophet called 'The Morning Star of Italy' has told me to avoid traveling on water since I am to die by drowning, and it appears that misfortune has brought me to a land where we never leave the water."

These and similar things Francisco Sebastián had uttered just a little while before he was drowned, and his death caused much grief among his companions.

In spite of their enemies, our men gained ground, and at their initial assault, won the first enclosure. Then they pushed back their foes to the second enclosure, and in the process so frightened the women, children and servants on the island that they ran screaming to their canoes to flee up the river. But the Indians who had been stationed to defend the second enclosure, when they saw their Cacique out in front and perceived the danger that their wives and children and everyone else ran of becoming the slaves of enemies, and when they realized that if they did not fight like men now and win this one battle, they would forfeit all the honor and glory they had gained in past conflicts, they attacked desperately and furiously, putting to shame those who had retreated and fled from the Casquins. Battling thus with great force, they wounded and detained many Spaniards with the result that neither they nor their Indian companions made any further progress.

CHAPTER IX

*The Casquins flee from the battle and Capaha
petitions the Governor for peace.*

O N PERCEIVING that they had checked the onslaught of their
enemies, the Indians of Capaha collected greater spirit and
force from their victorious performance and shouted to the people of
Casquin: "Advance, cowards! Seize and carry us away as your
slaves now that you have dared enter our town and attack our
prince in the manner that you have. But remember well what you
are doing and what you already have done, for when these strangers
have departed, then we shall see what manner of men you are in
battle."

The Casquins were an intimidated people who had been conquered
on many previous occasions, and these words alone sufficed to make
them cease fighting and indeed lose their courage altogether. With
backs turned, they sped to the canoes without regard for their
chieftain or fear of the shouts and threats the Governor and his
Spaniards raised in an effort to prevent their leaving unprotected
those two hundred Christians who had come with them. Fleeing
thus, as if being lanced by their foes, they seized their own boats
and would have taken those of the Castilians had they not found in
each of them two Christians who had remained on guard. It was
their desire to carry away all of the canoes so that their enemies
would have nothing in which to pursue them, but our guards defended the vessels with great blows of the sword. Thus with such
baseness and littleness of spirit, the Casquins were now fleeing,
whereas only a short time previously, they had believed that with
the kindness and aid of the Spaniards, they would gain the island
without their adversaries' having dared take up arms.

Our infantry, on realizing how few they were against so many
foes, and that they were without horses, their main force of resistance, began an orderly retreat to the place where they had left

the canoes. Then when the Indians on the island beheld these Christians alone and withdrawing, they rushed forward with great boldness to destroy them. But the Cacique Capaha, being a prudent and sagacious man, resolved to take advantage of the occasion to gain the Governor's favor as well as his pardon for the obstinacy and pertinacity he had manifested in refusing to accept his continuous offers of peace and friendship. For he felt that with such a courtesy, he would oblige the Governor not to permit the Casquins to do more damage in his town and his fields, a damage which had pained him exceedingly. With this thought in mind, he went out and commanded his men in a loud voice to leave the Christians unharmed and permit them to retire freely. Thus it was through the kindness of this chieftain that our two hundred infantrymen escaped death; for without his generosity and graciousness, all would have perished in that critical moment. The Governor was content at that time with having recovered his men alive, and he greatly appreciated the magnanimity of Capaha, later enlarging upon it considerably among all the Spaniards.

Very early on the following day, four principal Indians came to the Governor with a message from Capaha requesting pardon for the past, offering his service and fellowship for the future, beseeching his lordship to forbid his enemies to do more damage to his land than they already had done, and asking him to return to the town so that on the ensuing day he, the Cacique, might come in person to kiss his hands and offer the obedience due him. This in sum was what the message embraced, and the bearers delivered it with many words and with a great solemnity of ceremony and show of respect and reverence, which they paid to the sun and the moon.[8] But to the Cacique Casquin, who also was present, they offered no courtesy, acting rather as if they had not seen him and he were not there.

[8] Later in this chapter the Inca states that the Governor too received this gesture of reverence along with the sun and the moon.

The General replied that Capaha would be welcome at any time and should come whenever it suited him best to do so. He was happy to accept the Cacique's overture of friendship, he said, and would do no more harm in his land, not even to a leaf of a tree; but he reminded Capaha that he himself was to blame for what had already been done because of his unwillingness to receive the gestures of peace and good will so many times offered him. Then he urged the Cacique to say no more of the past and dismissed the messengers, who, having been regaled and soothed with fine words, were content. Meanwhile, however, neither the communication of this chieftain nor the Governor's reply contributed to the pleasure of Casquin, for he had desired that Capaha persevere in his obstinacy so that he, Casquin, with the assistance of the Castilians, might take revenge upon Capaha and destroy him.

As soon as the Governor had received Capaha's message, he set out for the town and en route commanded that a proclamation be issued to the effect that neither Indian nor Spaniard should dare take anything that might represent a loss to the inhabitants of that province, and that on reaching their destination the people of Casquin, both warriors and servants, were to go at once to their land, only some of them remaining to serve their Curaca, who wished to be with the Governor. Then at midday, while the army was still traveling, a messenger delivered a communication from Capaha beseeching his lordship to send word of his health and declaring again that he would arrive on the following day to kiss his lordship's hands. And afterward, at sunset, when they had reached the town, a second messenger arrived with the same words. Both communications were delivered, as had been the first, with the appropriate solemnities and ceremonies for the adoration of the sun and the moon and the Governor himself. These envoys, the General answered with much suavity, and he commanded his men to present them gifts so that they might understand that his feeling toward them was affable. Then on the following day, at eight in the morning, Capaha himself arrived in the company of a hundred noblemen, all of whom were arrayed in very beautiful feather headdresses and mantles of every kind of skins.

Before seeing the Governor, Capaha went to inspect his temple and place of burial. It may have been that this structure was along the route to the General's lodging, or that he felt the affront done him here more than all the others he had received. Nevertheless when he went within and beheld the destruction that had been wrought, he concealed his feelings, but lifting from the floor with his own hands the bones and bodies of his ancestors which the Casquins had thrown there, he kissed them and returned them to the wooden chests which served as sepulchres. After he had set the temple in order to the best of his ability, he proceeded to his own house where the Governor was lodged. The Governor came from his room to greet him, embracing him with much warmth, and when Capaha had made an offer of homage, he asked him many details concerning his land and the surrounding provinces. The Cacique's replies were satisfactory both to the General and to those of his captains present, for in his answers he revealed himself to be a man of good judgment. Capaha was twenty-six or twenty-seven years of age.

The Cacique Casquin had come out with the Governor to receive Capaha and had been present during the whole of their conversation; the latter however had disregarded him, treating him as if he were not there. But when Capaha saw that the Governor was through questioning him, and that there were no more answers to make, in other words that the field was calm, he was no longer able to repress his anger at the offenses he had suffered at the hands of Casquin, and, turning to that chieftain, he said:

"You must be exultant, Casquin, to have realized what you never dreamed or hoped to obtain with your own forces; that is, revenge for your injuries and affronts. For this be thankful to the power of the Spaniards. They will go away and we shall remain in our lands as we were before. Pray to the Sun and the Moon, our gods, that they give us good seasons."

CHAPTER X

The Governor twice supports Casquin and makes the two Curacas friends.

BEFORE Casquin replied, the Governor asked the interpreter what it was that Capaha had said, and having learned, he informed the latter that the Spaniards had not come to these lands to leave the Indians more inflamed in their wars and enmities than they had been before, but to bring them peace and harmony; and he again declared that Capaha had only himself to blame for the offenses he had received from the Casquins since he had not waited in his town when the Castilians came there and had sent them no messenger along the way. Had he done so, the Governor insisted, Capaha's enemies would not have entered that town or even crossed his borders. And he besought that Cacique, since the past damage had been occasioned by his own heedlessness, to agree to forget the anger and passion he and Casquin had harbored previous to that day, and from then on to be friends and good neighbors. This, he said, he begged and recommended as a partisan of them both, but he warned that if it became necessary, he would command it under penalty of imposing his own enmity upon the one who did not obey.

At that Capaha informed the Governor that since his lordship had so instructed and since it was his desire to serve him, he was resolved to be at peace with Casquin. Then the two Indians embraced like brothers; but neither the expression on their faces nor the look which they bestowed upon each other were of true friendship. Nevertheless, with whatever of such feeling they could feign, they discussed many things with the General concerning Spain and the provinces the Spaniards had seen in Florida. This conversation continued until they were advised that it was the hour to dine, and that they should pass to another room where a table had been laid for the three of them, it being the custom of the Governor always to honor caciques by placing them at his own table when they ate.

The Adelantado seated himself at the head of the table, and Casquin, who from the first day he had eaten with the Governor had sat at his right hand, now assumed his regular place. On perceiving him do so, Capaha, without any show of unpleasantness upon his face, remarked: "You well know, Casquin, that for many reasons that place is mine, the principal ones being that my rank is more illustrious, my title is more ancient and my estate is vaster than yours. Any one of these three should deter you from taking that seat, knowing as you do that because of each of them it belongs to me."

The Governor, who favored Casquin, sensed that what had happened was unusual and sought to know what Capaha had said. Then having understood, he addressed the Cacique as follows: "Even though all that you have declared may be true, it is only just that the age and grey hairs of Casquin be respected, and that you who are young should honor this man by giving him the most preeminent place; for to revere the aged is a natural obligation of youth, and in doing so youth honors itself."[9] To this Capaha replied: "My Lord, were Casquin a guest in my house, grey hairs or no grey hairs, I would give him the first place at my table and would pay him all the respect I could. But because we are eating at the table of another, I do not feel it is just for me to relinquish my pre-eminences, for they are those of my ancestors; and my vassals, particularly my noblemen, would not approve of my doing so. Now if it is the desire of Your Lordship that I dine at your table, I can comply only by your assigning me the place on your right since that place is justly mine; otherwise, I shall eat with my warriors, for to do so will be more to my honor, and they will be more content not to see me lowered from what I am and from what my parents left me." Then Casquin, who on the one hand wished to placate the past anger of Capaha and on the other perceived that all that Cacique alleged in his own favor was true, arose from his chair and said to the Governor: "My Lord, Capaha is indeed right and asks for justice. I

[9] Elvas says De Soto settled this affair simply by telling the chieftains that among Christians one place was as good as another.

beg you therefore to assign him his proper seat, which is this one, and I shall sit at your other side, for I am honored to occupy any place at Your Lordship's table."

Saying this, he crossed to the left and, without any displeasure, sat down to eat. Capaha, being thus conciliated, took his chair and, putting on the very best semblance, ate with the Governor.

Though it may seem that these things are trivial, they have been described minutely so that one may perceive how ambition for honor, more than any other passion, holds sway among all men no matter how barbaric or how far removed from every good teaching and wisdom they may be. Thus the Governor and the cavaliers with him were amazed to see what had come to pass between the two Curacas, for they had not believed that they would find such refinement in questions of honor among the Indians, or that these people would be so punctilious in such matters.

As soon as the Governor and both Caciques had eaten, Capaha's two wives, whom, as we have said, the Casquins had seized on entering the town, were brought before the three men and presented to their lord, the remainder of the captives taken with them having been given their liberty on the previous day. Grateful for the munificence being used with him, Capaha received these women but afterward told the Governor that he wished to offer them to his lordship and therefore begged him to accept them for his service. And when the latter replied that, having brought many serving people with him, he had no need for more, the Cacique suggested that he make a personal gift of the women to whatever captain or soldier he wished to favor in this way, since they could not be permitted to return to his house or remain in his land. It was believed that the chieftain now abhorred these two wives and was ridding himself of them because of a suspicion that they, having been seized by his enemies, could not possibly have escaped being defiled. So rather than show disdain toward Capaha, the Governor agreed to accept the women as a personal gift. Now these women were extremely beautiful and the Cacique was a young man; nevertheless, his suspicion alone was sufficient to make him despise and cast them from him. Thus by his behavior one may perceive how much the sin of adultery is abominated among the Indians; moreover, the exile and punishment of these women would seem to prove what we have said previously about Indian laws against this transgression.

CHAPTER XI

The Spaniards send men out to seek salt and gold mines; and they come to Quiguate.

THE Adelantado, on seeing the great necessity of his men for salt, since they were dying for lack of it, made great efforts while in the province of Capaha to learn from the curacas and their Indians where some might be had. Thus on inquiry he found among his men eight Indians who had been seized on the day the Spaniards entered the town. These people were not natives of this place but strangers and merchants who in their trading passed through many provinces and included salt among the things they customarily brought to sell. When taken before the Governor, they declared that in some mountain ranges forty leagues distant, there was a great quantity of very fine salt. And in answer to the repeated questions put to them, they replied that also in that land was much of the yellow metal about which the Spaniards had inquired.

Our Castilians rejoiced exceedingly over this news, and two soldiers volunteered to go with the Indians to verify what they had said. These men were Hernando de Silvera and Pedro Moreno, both natives of Galicia and both diligent individuals to whom any mission could be trusted. They were charged to take note of the disposition of whatever land they passed through and to bring information as to whether it were fertile and well populated. And in order to trade for the salt and gold, they carried pearls and chamois and some vegetable things called *frijoles,* given them at Capaha's command; furthermore they took Indians to attend them and two of the merchants to serve as their guides. With this accord, they departed, and at the end of an eleven-day journey returned with six loads of crystalline rock salt, which had not been made artificially but was formed naturally, and in addition brought a load of very fine and resplendent brass. They reported however that the lands they had seen were not good, but sterile and poorly populated.

Because of their urgent need for salt, our Spaniards were consoled by what they received of it for the deception they had suffered in regard to the gold. But the unfavorable report his two soldiers gave concerning the country they had seen led the Governor to decide to return to the town of Casquin and depart once again from that point, this time, however, heading toward the west so as to see what lands there were in that direction, for heretofore they had traveled from Mauvila always toward the north in order to escape the sea. So with this purpose our Castilians left the Cacique Capaha and returned with Casquin to his town, where they rested five days. Then setting out once more, they made a four-day march down the river through a fertile and well populated land. At the end of these four days they arrived at a province called Quiguate, whose lords and inhabitants came out in peace to receive the Governor. They offered him hospitality and on the following day their Cacique suggested that his lordship continue to the principal town of the province, there being more adequate provision in that town than in the present one for serving him.

The Governor now made a five-day march, going always downstream and through land which, as we have said previously, was densely populated and abundant with food. At the end of the fifth day, they came to the principal settlement, a place called Quiguate[10] from which the whole province took its name. This town was divided into three equal districts, in one of which the house of the lord occupied a position upon a high mound. The Spaniards were lodged in two of these districts and the Indians in the third,

---

[10] They are still in east central Arkansas, just north of the Arkansas River.

there being sufficient room for all. Two days after their arrival, the Curaca and all of the Indians fled without provocation; but when two more days had elapsed, they returned and asked pardon for their insidious behavior. The Cacique excused himself by saying that a certain urgent need had forced him to depart without his lordship's permission, and that he had thought to return on the same day, but had found it impossible to do so. After taking flight, he must have feared that with his departure the Spaniards might set fire to his town and fields, and as a result decided to return. According to appearances, he had left with an evil purpose in mind, for in his absence his Indians had rebelled and done all the damage they could, wounding two or three Castilians in their ambushes. Nevertheless the Governor overlooked everything in order not to break with them.

Now it came to pass that on a certain night while the Spaniards were in that encampment, the Adjutant General, Pablos Fernández, a native of Valverde, went to the Governor in the middle of the night and reported that when Juan Gaytán had been instructed to make the rounds on horseback during the second watch, he had been unwilling to do so, excusing himself with the statement that he was His Majesty's treasurer. The Governor was enraged because this cavalier was one of those who in Mauvila had muttered against the conquest and talked of returning to Spain or proceeding to Mexico when they should come again to where there were ships. Such talk as this, as we have said in its proper place, was the thing which had confounded the Governor's motives and blocked his fine plans for conquering and settling that land. And now since this present insubordination recalled to his mind his previous bitterness, he arose from his bed and went to the patio of the Curaca's house, which overlooked the village. Here he shouted in a loud voice, which, in spite of its being midnight, was heard throughout the entire place.

"Soldiers and captains! What is this? Do those conspiracies still prevail in which you discussed in Mauvila the subject of returning to Spain or proceeding to Mexico, so that now on pretext of being officers of the Royal Exchequer, you refuse to take the watch which has fallen to your lot? Why do you want to return to Spain? Did you leave family estates there to enjoy? Why do you want to go to Mexico? To disclose the baseness and littleness of your souls? Possessed now of the power to become lords of such a great kingdom as this where you have discovered and trodden upon so many and such beautiful provinces, have you deemed it better (abandoning them through your pusillanimity and cowardice) to go and lodge in a strange house and eat at the table of another when you can have your own house and table with which to entertain many? What honor do you think they will pay you when they have learned as much? Be ashamed of yourselves and bear in mind that officials of the Royal Exchequer or no, we all must serve His Majesty, and none shall presume to absent himself because of any pre-eminences he may possess, for should he do so, I will strike off his head, be he who he may. And be undeceived, for as long as I live, no one is to leave this land before we have conquered and settled it or all died in the attempt. Therefore, do your duty, and leave off your vain presumptions, for now is not the time for them."

With these words, uttered in great rage and heartfelt sorrow, the Governor disclosed the reason for the perpetual unhappiness which he had borne since leaving Mauvila, and which he carried with him until his death. Those who understood his words to be directed at themselves, did what he ordered from then on, not contradicting him in anything, for they realized that Hernando de Soto was not a man with whom one could trifle, and they were even more convinced of the fact now that he had declared himself to the extent that he had.

CHAPTER XII

The army arrives at Colima, discovers a process for making salt and passes on to the province of Tula.

SIX days the Spaniards passed in the town of Quiguate and then on the seventh departed. After a five day march downstream along the banks of the river of Casquin,[11] they came to the principal town of a province called Colima. Here the lord of the land came out peacefully and received the Governor and his army with much familiarity and many demonstrations of love, all of which pleased the Castilians no little because they had been informed that the natives of that province customarily carried poison on their arrows, and they were very much afraid of this poison. "For," they said, "if to the ferocity and savagery they manifest in shooting their arrows, these Indians add poison, what remedy will we be able to find for ourselves?" Hence when they discovered that the Colimas did not use poison, they received their friendship with even greater rejoicing. Their pleasure was short, however, for within two days these people rebelled without reason, and the Curaca fled to the forest with his vassals.

After the flight of the Indians, our men remained one day more in the town of Colima to gather provisions for the road; then they continued their journey, crossing some fertile and sown fields and some forests which were clear and pleasant to traverse. At the end of four days, they came to the bank of a river and pitched camp. Their quarters prepared, certain soldiers descended to the river, and while strolling along its shore, cast their eyes upon some blue sand which lay at the edge of the water. Taking some of this sand, one of them tasted it, and finding it brackish told his companions that in

[11] The Inca has the direction of the river wrong, presumably because he has confused the Arkansas and the White Rivers. At this point De Soto possibly is following what is now U.S. Highway 67 and 70.

his opinion they could make saltpetre of it for use in the manufacture of powder for their arquebuses. With this idea in mind they busied themselves in dexterously picking up the sand, endeavoring to take the blue without mixing it with the white. When some quantity had been collected, they put it in water and there rubbed it between their hands. Then draining off the water, they baked the residue and with intense heat converted it into a salt, which though somewhat yellow in color was very good in both taste and effect.

Happy over their discovery and pressed by an urgent need for salt, the Spaniards spent eight days in that camp and produced the salt in great quantities. There were some who felt such a craving for it that on finding it plentiful, they ate it in mouthfuls and alone as if it were sugar. And to those who reproved them they replied, "We are famished for salt, so let us glut ourselves upon it." Thus nine or ten of them did overeat it only to perish within a few days of dropsy, for whereas hunger kills some, satiety kills others.

Provided now with salt and joyful over having a means of producing it in time of necessity, the Spaniards broke camp, and, after traveling for two more days in an effort to leave this place, which they called the Province of the Salt,[12] they entered a province called Tula and continued four more days through uninhabited lands. At noon of the fourth day, they halted, for even though the guides declared that the principal town was no more than a half-league distant, the army had traveled for six days without stopping and the Governor wanted them to refresh themselves here until the following day. He himself, however, resolved to see the town on that very afternoon, and for the purpose selected sixty of the infantry and a hundred of the cavalry to accompany him.

The principal town of Tula was situated upon a plain between two streams. Its inhabitants were not on the lookout for the Castilians because they had received no news of their approach, but on catching sight of them, they sounded an alarm and rushed out to fight with all the bravery and strength that can be described. And

---

[12] *Provincia de la Sal.*

our men were greatly amazed to see women among them bearing weapons and fighting with the same ferocity as the males. But the Spaniards met this attack impetuously and routed the Indians. Then fighting in no order, all entered the town where the Christians indeed had something to do, for they found bold adversaries who battled without fear of death, and who though lacking in both arms and forces, preferred death to surrender. The women fought with the same determination and proved to be even more desperate than the men. During the struggle, Francisco de Reynoso Cabeza de Vaca, a cavalier from the kingdom of León, ascended to the upper room of a house which served as a granary. Here on finding five Indian women huddled in a corner, he instructed them by means of signs to remain calm since he intended them no harm. But they, on beholding this cavalier alone, rushed at him simultaneously and, like mastiffs on a bull, seized him by the arms, legs and neck; and one of them laid hold of his penis.[13] Then as the Reynoso shook his whole body and his arms with great force so as to free them and defend himself with his fists, he leaned too heavily upon one foot and broke through the floor of the room, which was made of a flimsy mat of cane. In consequence, he sank his foot and leg to the very termination of his thigh and thus remained seated upon the floor. At that the women completed his subjugation, and with their bites and blows held him at a dangerous advantage for killing him.[14]

---

[13] *y una de ellas le hizo presa del viril.*

[14] Indian women seem to have been well aware of the effectiveness of this method of attack. Ranjel tells of a garrulous young blade named Herrera who was "fatigued, subdued and very nearly killed" by a female savage who held him thus precariously by the genitals; and Captain Jonathan Carver in *Three Years Travels through the Interior Parts of North America* (Philadelphia: 1796), pp. 25–26, vividly pictures an Indian woman seizing her captor "by an exquisitely susceptible part" as he stooped to drink and "holding him fast till he expired on the spot." Somewhere in the annals of chivalry, knight errants must have encountered Amazonian women who were equally clever, but the code of the cavalier seems to have left him no more protection than that of courtesy; Amadis of Gaul would not lay hands on a woman though she stood a good chance of blotting out his life.

Even though he found himself in such straits, Francisco de Reynoso refused to cry out to his companions for aid since his struggle was with women. But at this point a soldier chanced to enter the room beneath which Cabeza de Vaca was being throttled, and on hearing the confusion above, raised his eyes, only to behold a leg suspended in mid-air. Now since this leg was bare, being without hose or footwear, the soldier thought that it might be the leg of an Indian and lifted his sword to give it a slash, but, suspecting at the same time what it could be because of the great noise heard overhead, he hastily called to two of his companions and the three of them ascended to the upper chamber. Here on seeing how the women were gripping Francisco de Reynoso, they attacked and killed them all, for not one would cease biting and pommeling her victim even though she were being slain. In this manner these men snatched that cavalier from the jaws of death, and in the present year of 1591 in which I am concluding my history, I have learned that Francisco de Reynoso is living still in his native land.

On that day a different but no better fate befell Juan Páez, a native of Usagre who was a captain of crossbowmen. Although not at all skillful while mounted and on the contrary rather good-for-nothing and stupid, this man was determined to do battle on horseback. Now when the struggle was in its last critical moments, he came upon an Indian who, while retreating, continued to fight. Juan Páez thereupon attacked the Indian, and even though lacking in time, craft and skill, hurled his lance at him. But as the Indian fled, he knocked the shaft aside with a piece of a stick more than six feet in length which he carried as a weapon. Then taking this stick in both hands, he struck Juan Páez such a blow in the center of the mouth as to break as many teeth as that cavalier possessed. And now leaving his victim stunned, he fled to safety.

CHAPTER XIII

*The strange fierceness of spirit of the Tulas, and
the battles that the Spaniards fought
with them.*

BECAUSE it was already late, the General commanded that the
signal be sounded to reassemble. Then leaving many of the
Indians dead and carrying some of his own men badly wounded, he
returned to the camp, not at all content with that day's expedition,
but instead irritated by the obstinacy and temerity with which the
Indians fought, and by the fact that their women possessed the same
courage and ferocity.

On the following day, the General entered the town with his
army, and finding it abandoned, pitched camp there. That afternoon, bands of horsemen reconnoitered the whole countryside to
see if there were gatherings of the enemy. They did encounter some
who were serving as lookouts. These they seized but were unable
to take back to the camp alive for questioning, for when put in
chains to be led away, they immediately fell to the ground and cried:
"Either leave us here or deprive us of our lives." They answered
not a single word to the questions put to them, and if the Spaniards
tried by dragging them to force them to arise, they merely permitted
themselves to be dragged. Hence, it was necessary to slay them all.

In the town (for we would give an account of its details) our men
found serving as bed covers a great number of cowhides which had
been softened and dressed without removing the hair; and there
were in addition many others ready to be dressed. Moreover, there
was beef; but no cows were to be seen in the fields, and it could
never be learned from whence the hides had been brought.[15] The
people in this province of Tula differ from all those our Spaniards
encountered previously; for, as we have said, the others are fine and

---

[15] Obviously from the American bison, or as it is commonly miscalled, the
buffalo.

handsome, whereas these, both male and female, have loathsome countenances. Even though naturally well featured, they render themselves hideous with devices wrought upon their persons. Their heads are incredibly long and taper off toward the top, having been made this way by artifice; for from the moment they are born their heads are bound and are left thus until they are from nine to ten years of age. Upon their faces they tattoo designs with points of flint, particularly on the exterior and interior of their lips, which they stain black, thereby rendering themselves extremely ugly and abominable. And this evil aspect of their countenances corresponds to the evil disposition of their souls, as we shall see in greater detail at a later time.

During the third watch of the fourth night that the Spaniards were in the town of Tula, the Indians came in great number and so silently that when first perceived by the sentinels, they had already mingled with them. They set upon the camp from three sides, and those who struck at the barracks of the crossbowmen, attacked so precipitately and with so much ferocity, impetus and haste, that even though awake, these men were given no opportunity to arm their weapons or indeed to make any resistance other than to flee with them in their hands to the barracks of Juan de Guzmán, which were nearest their own. Then the Indians pillaged the little that the archers possessed, and when the soldiers of Juan de Guzmán came out to resist them, they fought desperately with the new courage they had received from the fact that they apparently had seized victory from the hands of their enemy.

On the other two sides where attacks were made, the fighting was no less fierce; for there were dead and wounded everywhere, and there was great shouting and confusion because of the obscurity of the night which prevented all from seeing whether they were injuring friends or foes. As a result, the Spaniards issued a warning for each to go about calling upon the name of Our Lady and the Apostle Santiago so that they might be identified as Christians and thus not wound one another. And the Indians did the same, all of them carrying in their mouths the name of the province of Tula.

In place of the bows and arrows with which they customarily fight, many of these Indians on this particular night brought fragments of pikes two and three yards in length, a thing new to the Spaniards. The reason for their doing so was that the Indian who three days previously had broken the teeth of Captain Juan Páez had told his people of the success he had enjoyed with his cudgel. It had seemed to them, therefore, that this man's good fortune lay in the type of weapon employed and not in the dexterity of the one who used it so well, for the Indians in general are very superstitious. Therefore, on this night they brought many such sticks and with them gave very effective blows to a great number of soldiers, among whom was Juan de Baeza, a halberdier of the General's guard who happened to find himself at that time with a sword and shield. Two Indians caught this man between them, and one of them with his first blow broke his shield into pieces, while the other struck him so hard on the shoulder as to stretch him out at his feet. And they would have succeeded in killing him had not his companions come to his defense. In the same manner many other very comic incidents occurred, and afterward when talking about them among themselves, the soldiers laughed because the blows had been dealt with sticks. Nevertheless they were greatly benefited by the fact that these were bastinados and not arrow shots, which were more harmful.

The cavalry, which was the strength of the Spaniards and the thing their enemies most feared, now broke up the squadrons of Indians and routed them from the order in which they had come; but not for this did the latter cease fighting with a great courage and desire either to kill the Castilians or die in the attempt. Thus they continued to struggle for more than an hour with much stubbornness, and for the horsemen to ride back and forth among them many times and destroy them in great number (and they did lance them completely at will since the land was flat and cleared) was not enough to make these people leave off fighting and go away. At length, however, when they saw the light of dawn, they decided to retire, occupying as a defense and shelter against the horses the underbrush in one of the ravines which lay alongside the town.

The Spaniards were not a little pleased when these Indians did retire and cease fighting, for they had watched them battle desperately with such a great desire to destroy Christians that in exchange for the privilege of killing or wounding them, they had entered among their very arms. The struggle ended at sunrise, at which time our men, without going in pursuit, reassembled in the town to treat their wounded, for many had been injured, although no more than four were dead.

CHAPTER XIV

A fight between a Tula Indian and four Spaniards, three of whom were on foot and one on horseback.

SINCE the facts of history demand that we narrate the brave deeds of the Indians as well as those of the Spaniards, and that we not do injury to either race by recounting the valiant achievements of one while omitting those of the other, but instead tell all things as they occurred and in their proper time and place, it will be well for us to describe here a strange and singular feat performed by a Tula Indian shortly after the battle to which we have referred. But we beg that our listeners not be offended because we relate this incident in such detail, for since it happened as it did, it is necessary to record it thus.

It was on an occasion when some of those Spaniards who boasted of being more valiant than others had scattered out in pairs over the field of battle and, as was their custom, were examining the dead and taking note of grave wounds inflicted by powerful arms. This they always did when some great and much disputed struggle had taken place. Now a native of Medellín named Gaspar Caro had fought that night on horseback, and however it may have been, whether by the Indians knocking him off or by his falling off of his own accord, he lost his saddle, and his horse fled through the fields away from the conflict. This soldier then borrowed the horse of a friend to go in search of his own, and when he had found it, returned, driving the animal in front of him. Thus he came to where four other soldiers were examining the dead and wounded, and one of these men, Francisco de Salazar, a native of Castilla la Vieja, proceeded to mount the riderless steed in order to demonstrate his fine horsemanship, of which he was proud.

At this point, a native of Seville named Juan de Carranza, who was one of the three unmounted soldiers, cried out, "Indians! Indians!" His reason for doing so was that he had seen an Indian rise from behind some bushes and then conceal himself again. Believing that there were many Indians and not bothering to investigate further, the two men who were mounted rode out at a gallop in opposite directions for the purpose of cutting off others who might appear. Juan de Carranza, who had discovered the infidel, rushed to where he was hidden in the bushes, and he was followed quickly by one of his two companions, but the other, not having seen more than a single foe, came after them only by degrees.

Now when the barbarian perceived that he was cut off on all sides by both horsemen and footsoldiers, and that escape was no longer possible, he hastened out from the bushes to receive Juan de Carranza. In his hands he bore a battle-ax, which had been his portion of the sack and loot acquired that dawn from our archers. It had belonged to Juan Páez, and as the property of a captain of crossbowmen, possessed both a keen edge and a well-planed and polished shaft more than three feet in length. Clasping his weapon in both hands, the Indian struck Juan de Carranza with such force as to knock half his shield to the ground and badly wound his arm. So tormented was this Spaniard, both by the pain from the wound and the force of the blow, that he had no further strength to harm his assailant, who now turned upon a second Spaniard standing nearby and proceeded to deal him a blow equal in force to the one he had bestowed upon Carranza. For he split this man's shield into two parts and wounded him seriously on the arm, leaving him like his companion, incapacitated for fighting. This soldier was Diego de Godoy, a native of Medellín.

Presently Francisco de Salazar, he who had mounted Gaspar Caro's horse, perceived that these two Spaniards had been sorely wounded, and he attacked their assailant with extreme fury, but the Indian to escape being trampled took refuge under an adjacent liveoak. Not being able to ride his horse beneath this tree, Francisco de Salazar passed to one side of it and without dismounting made some very sad thrusts, none of which reached their mark. Meanwhile the infidel was finding it impossible to swing his ax effectively because of the branches, and he came out from beneath the tree to station himself to the left of the cavalier. Then lifting his weapon in both hands, he struck the horse across the shoulder and with the iron hook of the ax laid the animal open from the withers to the knee, thus rendering it incapable of stirring.

At this point another Spaniard approached, coming on foot and not making any more haste since it appeared to him that two unmounted Spaniards and one on horseback were sufficient for a single Indian. He was Gonzalo Silvestre, a native of Herrera de Alcántara. When the Indian saw him close by, he came forward to receive him with the utmost ferocity and savagery, having mustered new courage and strength with the three such triumphant blows he had bestowed. Seizing his ax in both hands, he now delivered a blow which would have achieved the same result as his first two had not Gonzalo Silvestre advanced more cautiously than the others so as to be able to step aside when the blow fell. Thus the ax merely grazed his shield without striking it and then because of its great force continued on to the ground. At that the Spaniard gave a backstroke from above to below and on reaching the Indian with his sword slashed him from the forehead down across the whole of his face and in the chest, and he even wounded his left hand in such a manner as to sever it completely at the wrist. Finding himself minus one of his hands and thus unable to swing his ax with both as he wished, the infidel placed the shaft of his weapon over the stump of his mutilated arm and lunged forward desperately in an attempt to wound his opponent with a sudden thrust in the face. But Gonzalo Silvestre turned the ax aside with his shield and then putting his sword beneath his shield gave his enemy a backhand slash through the waist. Because of the Indian's little or no protection of arms or clothing, or even of bones which the body might possess in that region, and moreover because of the good strength of Silvestre, everything was severed with such speed and keenness of the sword that after it had passed through him, the Indian remained standing and said to the Spaniard: "Peace be with you." These words uttered, he fell dead, severed in twain.[16]

At this moment Gaspar Caro arrived, it being his horse that Francisco de Salazar had brought to the fight. When he saw the condition of the animal, he took it without uttering a word, guarding his anger so as to express it elsewhere. And now that he had rescued his mount he led it to the Governor and said: "In order that Your Lordship may be aware of the wretchedness of some of the soldiers of his army, even though they boast of their valor, and that you may perceive at the same time the ferocity and bravery of the natives of the province of Tula, I would have you know that one of these Indians with three blows of an ax has incapacitated for fighting two Spaniards on foot and another on horseback, and that he would have succeeded in destroying them had not Gonzalo Silvestre arrived in time to give them assistance. For with the first slash of his sword, that cavalier opened the face and chest of this Indian and cut off one of his hands; and with the second, he severed his body at the waist."

[16] *Quedó el Indio en pie, y dijo al Español, quédate en paz; y dichas estas palabras, cayó muerto en dos medios.* Silvestre's prowess, at least in this passage, would lead us to believe that the narrator's recollection was stained with chivalric lore. Students of sixteenth century *libros de caballería* will recall that the Knight of Phoebus severed a giant in twain with a well-placed backstroke, and that Amadis of Greece was equally adroit, in one instance, if we may rely on Cervantes, achieving an identical result upon a "brace of huge and fearsome giants." Moreover, legend has supplied instances of miraculous utterances after such thorough mutilation, but Garcilaso has provided a certain uniqueness in having this unlucky pagan breathe such a benign and Christian blessing.

The Governor and those present marveled at the valor and dexterity of the Indian and likewise at the good arm of Gonzalo Silvestre. And since Gaspar Caro, in his rage at the mishap to his horse, was requesting that the first three Spaniards be branded as knaves and cowards, the Governor, in an effort to restore their honor, for indeed they were gallant men and worthy of any good deed whatsoever, told this soldier that he should lay aside his wrath and regard his companions as victims of fortune, which shows itself variable in nothing more than in the events of war, favoring one today and another tomorrow; that he should make haste to treat his horse, which in his own opinion would not die since its wound was not deep; and that being amazed at this story and believing it only right that many be able to bear witness to matters so heroic as these, he himself wished to go and behold with his own eyes what had happened. With these words, the Governor did go out in the company of many people to see the dead Indian and the heroic feats he had accomplished; and on learning from the wounded Spaniards themselves the particulars of what we have told, both he and all those who were listening were amazed anew.

CHAPTER XV

The Spaniards leave Tula and enter Utiangue[17] *where they encamp for the winter.*

THE Spaniards were in the town called Tula for twenty days treating the many wounded from the previous battle. During this time they made numerous runs through the whole province. The region being well populated, they captured many Indians of both sexes and of all ages; but regardless of how much cajolery or how many threats they used, it was not possible to persuade any of

---

[17] In the book summaries, this word is spelled once as *Utiange* and another time as *Utiangee*. Since the spelling in the text itself is always *Utiangue* we in each instance have rendered it thus. It is the *Autiamque* of the Elvas account.

these people to come with them. For when our Castilians attempted to take them by force, they simply fell to the ground without uttering a word, giving their captors to understand that their greatest desire was that they either slay them or leave them alone. Thus these Indians revealed themselves to be as stubborn and indomitable as we say, and for this reason it did become necessary to destroy the males, who were prepared to fight. The women and children, on the other hand, were permitted to go free, since it was not feasible to take them along.

One sole Indian woman from this province remained, however, in the service of a Spaniard called Juan Serrano, a native of León. She possessed such a malevolent disposition and was so evil-tempered and arrogant that if her master or any of his comrades spoke to her concerning what she must do in the cooking or indeed in any other of her duties, she struck them in the face with a pot or embers from the fire, or whatever else she could lay her hands on. It was her desire that they either permit her to do as she pleased or kill her, for, as she said, she was under no obligation to comply with their demands. In consequence, they did leave her alone and endured her, but with all that, she fled, and her master rejoiced to find himself delivered of such a shrew.

Because of the fierceness and inhumanity characteristic of the people of this province, they are feared by all the other Indians of the vicinity, who are thrown into a panic simply on hearing the name of Tula, even using this name to frighten and thereby quiet their children when they are crying. To illustrate, let us turn from the ferocity of the elders and tell of a game played by children.

It happened that when the Spaniards left the province of Tula, they took nothing from it other than a boy of nine or ten years of age belonging to the cavalier, Christóbal Mosquera, a native of Badajoz, whom I later knew in Peru. Now in those towns that the Christians discovered afterward, where the Indians were amicable, children gathered to play their games, which consisted almost always of battles wherein they were divided one against the other either according to surnames or to districts. And oftentimes they became so incensed in these contests that many emerged from them with their heads seriously battered. Once the Castilians commanded the Tula boy to join with one side and fight against the other, and he, happy over the opportunity, hastened to obey. Those of his band immediately elected him their captain, and accompanied by his soldiers he attacked his adversaries with great shouts and halloos, calling out the name of Tula, which in itself was sufficient to put his enemies to flight. Then the Spaniards commanded the boy to pass to the side of the conquered and fight against the conquerors. This he did, and again with the name of Tula was triumphant. Thus he always came out victorious. And the Indians asserted that his elders enjoyed a similar success since they were very cruel with their enemies, refusing to take them alive. Moreover, the neighbors of the Tulas said that the deforming of their heads, some of which were more than a yard in length, and the painting of their faces and their lips, both inside and out, were done to make themselves uglier than they naturally were so that the hideousness of their countenances might match the evil of their souls and the fierceness of their character, for in every respect they were most inhuman.[18]

Having passed twenty days in Tula, more because of the necessity of treating their wounded than for any pleasure to be derived in stopping in the land of such evil people, the Spaniards abandoned this town and after traveling for two days came out of its jurisdiction. They now entered a province called Utiangue where it was their intention to pass the winter if they should find conveniences, for that season was now approaching. Four days they continued through this province, observing that the land in itself was good and fertile, but that it was inhabited by few people and they very bellicose. For these people always came along the road and annoyed them with continuous alarms and sudden attacks, which they made at each half-league where they had gathered in groups of a

[18] These Tula Indians were of the Caddo tribes and were known for their ferocity long after De Soto's time.

hundred and never more than two hundred. But they did little damage to the Christians, for when with a great noise they had hurled a sprinkle or two of arrows at them from a distance, they put themselves in flight, and the land being flat, our cavalry very easily overtook and lanced them at will. They were not warned, however, by their experience, and when twenty of them were able to reassemble, they immediately resorted once more to the same acts. Moreover, in order to appear more unexpectedly and provoke greater surprise, they lay upon the ground and covered themselves with grass so as not to be seen. But they paid well for their daring.

Plagued by these attacks, which were more harmful to the Indians than to the Castilians, the army traveled for four days, coming at the end of that time to the principal town of the province, which also was called Utiangue[19] since the whole of this land took its name from the town. Here they camped without opposition, all of the inhabitants having abandoned the place. The Indians of this province have better features than those of Tula, for they do not paint their faces or taper their heads. But they revealed that they were bellicose, for they would never accept the overtures of peace and friendship which the Governor sent to them many times by some of their own people whom the Spaniards had succeeded in capturing.

Having observed that the town was large and walled-in, that it contained good houses with much food in them, and furthermore that it was situated between two streams and on a fine plain where there was an abundance of grass for the horses, the General and his captains determined to pass the winter there; for it was already the middle of October of the year 1541, and they did not know if in going forward they would find such good accommodations as those which the present site offered. Resolute in this determination, they repaired the fence, which being of wood was broken in some places, and gathered much corn with the utmost haste, though it is a fact that there already was so much of it in the town as to be

[19] Probably either the present day Camden or Calion. The expedition is now in the south-central part of Arkansas.

practically enough for the entire season. They provided themselves with a great amount of firewood and dried fruits such as nuts, raisins and prunes, as well as other varieties of both fruits and grains which are unknown to Spain. In the open countryside they found numerous rabbits like those of Spain, for even though these animals existed in all of that great kingdom, in no province were they so abundant as in the vicinity of this town of Utiangue. Here also there were many stag and fallow deer, and the Spaniards as well as their Indian domestics killed them in great number, going out to hunt for sport, although equipped to fight in the event that they should encounter enemies. And many times a deer hunt was converted into a battle of good arrow shots and lance blows, but always with more damage to the Indians than to the Spaniards.

There was much snow that year in this province, and for a period of a month and a half they were unable to venture into the countryside because of the extensive amount that had fallen. Nevertheless, with the great luxury of firewood and provisions, they passed the best of all the winters they experienced in Florida, and they themselves confessed that they could not have been more comfortable or even so comfortable in the dwellings of their families in Spain.

CHAPTER XVI

The good winter passed in Utiangue. A treason committed against the Spaniards.

BECAUSE of what we have told in the previous chapter concerning the ease and contentment with which our Spaniards passed the winter in the town of Utiangue, it is much to be lamented that they should have failed to conquer and populate a land so fertile and so abundant in all human necessities simply because they found no gold or silver there. For they did not take into consideration the fact that these metals were not to be found because the Indians did not seek or esteem them. I have heard from trustworthy persons that the natives of the coast of Florida on running across bags of silver from ships driven aground by storm, have been known to carry away the bags as something of more use to them and leave the silver on account of not valuing it or knowing what it might be. Because of such reports, and because it is true that the Indians of the New World, even when possessed of gold and silver, generally do not use it to buy and sell, there is no reason to doubt that Florida may have these metals, and that if sought for, mines of them will be found, as each day they are being found in Mexico and Peru. But should they not be found, it would suffice to establish an empire of such wide and long lands and of such fertile and abundant provinces as we have seen and will see, not only because of what the earth already yields but also because of the fruits, vegetables, grain and livestock that could be brought there from Spain and Mexico. And again there is no reason to doubt that for planting and cattle raising, better lands cannot be desired, and that with the riches of pearls already possessed by these lands as well as the great quantity of silk that could be produced immediately, one might trade with the entire world and enrich himself with such gold and silver as not even Spain obtains from her own mines, though she possesses such, but which are borne to her shores from outside—from those places in this very region which she has discovered and conquered since the year 1492. It therefore is unreasonable to leave off attempting this undertaking, and it should be carried out if for no other purpose than to plant the faith of the Holy Mother Church of Rome in this great kingdom and to take from the power of our enemies as many souls as are blind with idolatry. And for this achievement may Our Lord provide in the manner most to His service, and grant that the Spaniards may be inspired to gain and subjugate this land.

But returning to my history, I will say that the Castilians wintered in the good town of Utiangue in complete pleasure and comfort with food for both themselves and their horses. But the principal Curaca of the province, on seeing them settled, attempted with

feigned friendship and double dealing to cast them from his town.
For the purpose he sent envoys to the Governor with hypocritical
messages giving him to expect that he, the Curaca, would arrive
very soon to offer his services. These envoys acted as spies and came
only at night so as to see how the Spaniards conducted themselves
in their camp—if they kept watch and took caution or if they slept
carelessly and negligently, what manner of arms they had and where
they kept them, and what the horses were like. This they did so
as to take note of everything and to plan their attack in accordance
with what they had seen. And our men were indeed careless about
the messengers, for regardless of what hour of the night it might be,
when an Indian informed a Spanish sentinel that he bore a communication from his curaca, instead of being instructed to return in the
daytime, he was taken at once to the Governor and left to deliver
his message. Then having done so, he passed through the entire
town, examining in the meantime the horses and arms, observing
the way the Castilians slept and kept watch, and eventually carrying
to his cacique a long account of everything he saw.

Having news of such things through his spies, the Governor gave
orders for these messengers to come only in the daytime, but they
persisted in their evil purpose, continuing to arrive at night and furthermore at all hours of the night. In consequence the General many
times complained to his men of this effrontery, saying: "Is there not
some soldier who by giving a good knife blow to one of these nocturnal visitors could teach them by experience not to come here by
night, for although I have ordered them to come only in the daytime
my command has been of no avail?" These words aroused the wrath
of a soldier named Bartolomé de Argote. He was a noble man, who
had been brought up in the house of the Marquis de Astorga, and
he was a first cousin of the other Bartolomé de Argote, one of the
thirty cavaliers to accompany Juan de Añasco from Apalache to
the Bay of the Holy Spirit. One night while serving as sentinel at
one of the gates of the town, this cavalier killed a spy for trying to
pass against his will with a false message. Now the deed pleased

the Governor exceedingly, and he expressed his approval with praises; thus this soldier thenceforward was placed among the valiant, whereas until that time none had regarded him as such or considered him so worthy. But he had done what no one else in the army had been disposed to do; and with the death of the messenger, all messages and all plots of the Indians ceased, for they realized that the Castilians had seen through them, and that they could not take advantage of these people since they were on their guard.

The General and his men now occupied themselves in guarding their town and racing the horses each day throughout the whole neighborhood so as to have news at all times of whatever the Indians might be plotting against them. With such caution they passed the winter in much tranquility and comfort, for even though the natives did wage war upon them, never did they succeed in doing them harm. After the rigor of the snows was mitigated, one of the captains went forth with a group to make a foray and capture Indians, there being a need for servants. But eight days later he returned with few prisoners, and the Governor in consequence commanded another captain to set out with a second group. Accordingly this man made an identical foray, but when he had searched eight days, he also returned with but few prisoners.

Then when the General saw the little cunning that his two captains had demonstrated, he resolved to make an invasion himself. So selecting a hundred horsemen and a hundred and fifty footsoldiers, he traveled with them for twenty leagues, coming eventually to the boundaries of a province called Naguatex, a fertile and abundant land which was thickly populated with very handsome and well disposed people. In the first town of this province,[20] where the lord resided although it was not the principal one of his state, the Governor launched a sudden attack early one morning, and since he found the Indians unprepared, captured many of them, both men and women of all ages. Then after having spent fourteen days on his expedition, he returned with these people to his camp.

[20] Near the northern border of Louisiana.

Here he found that for four or five days, his men had been very much disturbed because of his delay, but now all rejoiced in his presence and shared in his spoils, which he divided among those captains and soldiers who were in need of servants.

End of the Fourth Book.

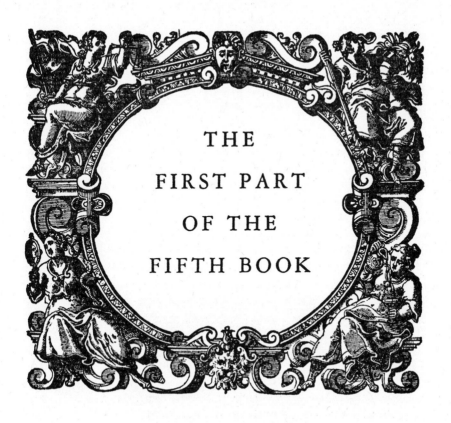

THE
FIRST PART
OF THE
FIFTH BOOK

*Of the History of Florida by the Inca where mention is
made of a Spaniard who remained among the Indians;
the efforts exerted to regain him; a long journey of the
Castilians across eight provinces; the enmity and cruel
war between the Guachoyas and Anilcos; the lamentable
death of the Governor Hernando de Soto and
the two burials that his men gave
him. It contains eight
chapters.*

CHAPTER I

*The Spaniards enter Naguatex where one of
them remains.*

HROUGHOUT the whole period that the Spaniards
were wintering in the town and camp of Utiangue,
which was more than five months, nothing momen-
tous occurred except what I have already related.
Then since the month of April of the year 1542
was beginning, the Governor felt it time to proceed with his exploration. With this purpose in mind, he left Utiangue and continued along the road to the principal town of the province of
Naguatex, a town which bore the same name since the whole of the
province was called after it. This road was different from that
described earlier when the Governor made his first expedition from
Utiangue to Naguatex, for where the Castilians now marched
there were twenty-two or twenty-three leagues of fertile and well
inhabited land which they covered in seven days without experiencing anything noteworthy other than attacks made by the Indians,
who came out in some of the narrow passes through the ravines or
the woods, only to take to their heels when confronted.

At the close of these seven days, the Spaniards came to the town
of Naguatex. This town having been deserted, they lodged themselves in the houses and remained here for fifteen or sixteen days,
in the meantime reconnoitering all parts of the vicinity and, with
little or no resistance from the Indians, seizing such food as was

needed. When six days had gone by, the local chieftain sent a message in which he begged the Governor's pardon and assured him that even though too embarrassed by his previous indiscretion to return at once, he would come within a few days to kiss his lordship's hands and acknowledge his sovereignty. Furthermore, he declared that in the interim he would instruct his vassals to serve the Governor in all that he might command. This communication was delivered with the same ostentatious ceremonies I have described in other instances. The Adelantado replied that he would welcome the Curaca at any time he should arrive and would be pleased to know and regard him as a friend, just as were most of the curacas through whose lands he had passed. Very content with these words, the messenger departed.

Early on the morning of the following day, a second messenger arrived in the company of four principal Indians and more than five hundred native servants. This envoy explained that the four noblemen, all of whom were close kinsmen of his master, had been sent to minister unto the Governor and carry out his lordship's commands during the time that would lapse before the Curaca himself should arrive, and he added that since his master had sent the most illustrious people of his house and state as a pledge of his coming, that event might be looked upon as assured. The Governor thereupon very eloquently expressed his appreciation of the chieftain's gesture and then ordered his men to seize no more people in their forays as they had been doing up until that time. But the Cacique never paid his promised visit, and by his failure to do so, it was understood that he had sent the Indians and the messages to save his fields and towns from devastation and burning and to prevent further seizure of his people. Nevertheless both the principal Indians and the domestics continued to minister unto the Castilians with a great desire to please.

Having been informed of what there was in the province and its vicinity through the accounts of the natives and those of his own men who went out to reconnoiter the land, the Governor and his

army left Naguatex, accompanied by the four principal Indians and
the many domestics whom the Cacique had sent with provisions they
were to carry until they had led the Castilians beyond their boundaries. But when they had proceeded two leagues, the Spaniards
missed Diego de Guzmán, a native of Seville. As a man of wealth
and nobility this cavalier had joined the conquest with a good supply
of costly and elegant clothes as well as fine weapons and three horses,
all of which he carried to Florida; and except for the fact that he
gambled most passionately, he had conducted himself in every respect as a gentleman. Now as soon as he was missed, the Governor
ordered the army to halt and hold the four principal Indians until
he could ascertain what had been the fate of this man, for it was
feared that the natives had slain him. When a thorough inquiry
was made among the Spaniards, it was learned that they had seen
the cavalier in camp on the preceding day, and that four days previously he had wagered all his possessions until losing his clothes,
arms, and a very excellent coal black horse. Then continuing in his
passion and blindness for gambling, he had forfeited a female domestic, who through her misfortune had fallen to him as his share
of those people whom, as we have said, the Governor seized in a
raid on another town of the same province of Naguatex, a raid in
which Diego de Guzmán himself had participated. It was learned
likewise that he had very honestly paid all his losses save that of
the girl and had agreed to send her to the lodging of the winner
within a period of four or five days. He had not kept that agreement,
however, and the girl was found to be missing along with her
master. From such evidence it was suspected that Diego de Guzmán had fled to the Indians because of his desire to withhold the
girl and again because of his shame at having wagered his arms and
horse, a wager which among soldiers is considered most contemptible. Soon afterward this suspicion was verified, for it was learned
that the girl was a daughter of the Curaca and lord of the province
of Naguatex, was extremely beautiful and was only eighteen years of
age. These were circumstances which could have so blinded this

man as to make him inconsiderately desert his own people and join the company of strangers.

The Governor thereupon commanded the four principal Indians to have the missing Spaniard brought immediately, saying that otherwise he would understand that they had killed him treacherously and that to avenge his loss, he would order them and all the people they had brought with them to be quartered. Fearing death, these Indians instructed messengers to go with the utmost haste to different places where they believed information concerning Diego de Guzmán might be obtained, charging them likewise to return with the same speed lest their delay provoke the Spaniards to do some grievance. The messengers departed but came again the same day with news that the fugitive was with the Cacique, who was offering him all the entertainment and pleasure possible, and that he had expressed his determination not to return to his people.

Since I have said that these Spaniards gambled but have not explained what they gambled with, you must know that after their playing cards were burned along with all the rest of the things lost in the bloody battle of Mauvila, they fashioned cards of parchment, painting them exquisitely; for whenever confronted by necessity, they were inspired to produce what they needed, and they succeeded with these cards as if all their lives they had been masters of that trade. Because they could not or did not wish to make any more cards than were necessary, they made just enough to suffice by serving for a limited time and being passed about by turn among the gamblers; from whence (or from some similar circumstance) we might possibly say that the expression was born which among professional gamblers it is the fashion to repeat while playing: "Let us make haste, gentlemen, because they are coming for the cards." Being of vellum these cards lasted a long time.

CHAPTER II

The efforts that were made to obtain Diego de
Guzmán. His reply and that of the
Curaca.

HAVING heard the news that the messengers brought, the
Governor told the four principal Indians that he believed it
to be a fact that they had killed the Spaniard and were lying when
they said that he was alive. Then one of them, whose countenance
was not that of a prisoner but was a grave and noble countenance
such as these people try to assume when oppressed, addressed the
Governor as follows:

"My Lord, we are not men who are obliged to deceive you.
Therefore, in order that the truth of what our messengers have
told may be seen more plainly, command that one of us be released
and permitted to go and bring back such testimony as will satisfy
Your Lordship in regard to what may have been done to the Spaniard; and demand that the three of us who remain give our pledge
that he whom you send will either return with the Christian or
bring definite news of his determination. And for the purpose of
assuring yourself that this man is not dead, have a letter written to
him in which you request that he come in person or answer your
communication, for by his handwriting, since we ourselves cannot
write, it may be seen that he still lives. In the event that our companion should not return with this satisfaction, then the three of us
who remain will pay with our lives for what he does not fulfill of
his and our promise. And it will be sufficient and even superfluous,
without Your Lordship's having to slay the rest of our Indians, for
three such persons as ourselves to perish because of the faithlessness
of one Spaniard who has deserted his own people without our
having forced him to do so or even known of his going."

All of these are the actual words of the Indian himself, and I have
added nothing to them other than to translate them into Spanish
or Castilian.

What that principal Indian had said and pledged in the name of the four of them appeared reasonable to the General and his captains; therefore, they ordered that he himself go for Diego de Guzmán, and that Baltasar de Gallegos, who was a friend of the fugitive and from his section of the country, write a message upbraiding him for his evil course should he persist in it, exhorting him to return and do his duty as an hidalgo, and promising to restore his arms and horse and even to bestow other horses upon him in the event that he had need of them. The principal Indian departed with the letter and also with an oral message in which the Governor entreated the Cacique to agree to send the Spaniard back without delay, and threatened otherwise to destroy his land with fire and sword, in sum to burn his towns, devastate his fields, and kill both the principal Indians and those of lesser rank whom he now had with him, as well as all others of that land whom he later might be able to seize. It was on the second day of the cavalier's absence that the Indian departed with these threats, and on the third day he came again with the identical letter he had carried. Upon this letter, however, the Spaniard had scrawled his name in charcoal as an evidence that he still lived. But that Christian answered not another word, and the Indian said that he neither desired nor planned to return to his own people.

The Curaca replied that his lordship could be very certain that he himself was not forcing Diego de Guzmán to remain in his land, but that at the same time he did not want to force him to return to his people and was not going to do so since such was not the desire of the man himself. Instead, he said, as a son-in-law who had restored to him a very much beloved daughter, this cavalier would receive from him all the luxury and honor possible, just as would each of the Spaniards or Castilians who might be pleased to remain in his land. And he added that his lordship would be in error and responsible for a miscarriage of justice should he attempt to lay waste his land and destroy his kinsmen and vassals just because he himself chose to do his duty in this matter. In sum, he assured the Governor that as a man of power he would do as he pleased and did not have to do any more than he had said.

Having spent three days in these efforts, and perceiving now that the Spaniard would not return and that the Cacique was right and asked only for justice, the Adelantado decided to proceed on his way, and he thereupon released the principal Indians and their domestics, all of whom continued to minister unto him with much affection and willingness until they had led him from their boundaries into another province.

Now this wretched cavalier had committed his indiscretion because of his blind passion for gambling and his affection for the woman; for rather than deprive himself of this woman by delivering her to the man who had won her, he preferred to remain at the disposition of his enemies. Herein, to conclude, one may see what is born of reckless gambling; and at this point I might deem it wise, were it my business to do so, to tell what of this passion I myself have seen, but let such matters remain for those whose duty it is to reprehend vices.

And returning to Diego de Guzmán, I will say that if continuing with the reputation and confidence with which he remained among the Indians of Naguatex, he afterward preached to them of the Catholic Faith, as ought a Christian and a cavalier, I not only could excuse his miserable behavior but could praise it highly; for according to the credence that the Indians generally give to those who hold with that faith, I could believe that he might have borne much fruit with this doctrine. But I have learned nothing further of him and therefore can tell no more of what came to pass at that time. What I have said of him, however, Alonso de Carmona records in his account, although not so copiously, and he refers to him as Francisco de Guzmán.[1]

---

[1] As does the Gentleman of Elvas, who places the incident after the death of De Soto. Two Francisco de Guzmáns have been listed in early accounts of the expedition, one from Toledo and one from Seville. The former is possibly the man referred to on page 471 of this translation.

After the loss of Diego de Guzmán, the Spaniards made a five-day march throughout the province of Naguatex, at the end of which time they came to another province called Guancane. Here the natives differed from those in the past, for whereas the others had been affable, these proved to be hostile and showed no desire for friendship. Instead, they demonstrated their hatred in every way possible, many times presenting themselves for battle. But the Spaniards refused to fight, for more than half of their horses having fallen victim to the Indians, they were determined to conserve those few that remained. As I have said many times, their greatest strength lay in their horses since the Indians paid no attention to the footsoldiers. The Spaniards took eight days to cross this province, not resting a single day within its confines because of their desire to avoid a conflict with these people who were so eager to fight.

Throughout the province of Guancane many wooden crosses had been placed on top of the houses, almost none being found without them. The explanation for this circumstance, according to what was learned, was that the people here had received news of the benefits and marvels Alvar Núñez Cabeza de Vaca and Andrés Dorantes and their companions had performed in virtue of Jesus Christ Our Lord within the provinces of Florida through which they had traveled during the years they were held in bondage by the Indians, as Alvar Núñez himself has recorded in his *Comentarios*.[2] And even though it is true that Alvar Núñez and his companions did not come to this particular province or to a number of others which lie between it and the lands where they traveled, still the fame of the deeds performed by God through these men eventually, by passing from hand to hand and from land to land, reached the province of Guancane. And since the Indians here had learned of these things and had heard it said that the Christians had brought the cross in their hands as a device, and that all benefits performed by them in curing the sick were accomplished by making above them

[2] Sometimes referred to as the *Naufragios*.

the sign of the cross, there arose the pious practice of putting this symbol over their houses, for they believed that just as it had cured those sick, so would it also deliver everyone from all evil and danger. Herein, therefore, one may see the readiness which the Indians in general had and these in particular do have for receiving the Catholic Faith if there were only someone to cultivate it, especially by good example, which commands their attention more than anything else.

CHAPTER III

The Governor leaves Guancane, passes through seven other small provinces, and arrives at the province of Anilco.

THE Governor departed from the province of Guancane with the intention of returning to that great river which he had left behind him;[3] not, however, by the same route pursued since crossing it, but by a different one in which he would make a large circle to discover lands and provinces other than those he previously had seen or planned to pass through. Now his reason for returning was to establish a town before the forces of his army should be expended, for he saw his strength diminishing from day to day in men as well as horses, more than half of both, or at least of the horses, having been depleted with the previous wars and illnesses. It grieved him exceedingly that, without advantage to himself or to anyone else, so much hardship as they had borne and were bearing should be wasted, and that such extensive and fertile lands should remain unsettled by the Spaniards and particularly by those Spaniards he had with him; for he did not fail to realize that if he himself should die or be lost before having begun the settlement of that land, then for a great number of years to come, there would not be assembled so

---

[3] The Mississippi, of course.

many and such goodly people or such a wealth of horses and arms as he had brought to the conquest.

So repenting his past anger, which was responsible for his failure to establish a settlement in the province and port of Achusi as he had once determined, he resolved now to make amends as best he could. And since he was far from the sea and would have to lose time should he go in search of it for the purpose of locating his settlement on the coast, he had proposed that on arriving at the Great River they establish a town at the best and most convenient site to be found along its bank and there construct two brigantines which he would send down the river to the Sea of the North with dependable persons chosen from among those whom he held as his most sincere friends. Thus they might give notice in Mexico, Tierra-Firme, the islands of Cuba and Hispañola, and in Spain itself of these provinces, so long and broad, which he had discovered in Florida; and then Spanish Castilians could hasten from everywhere with livestock and such seed as were not already to be found here, to settle, cultivate and enjoy this land. And as we shall see later, all of this could have been accomplished with much facility, had not death cut short his great and good plans just as it has done in the case of other greater and even better ones which have existed in this world.

I say that from Guancane the Governor set out toward the west in search of the Great River. But even though in this stage of my history as in others I have given the route that the army traveled when it left some one province for the purpose of going to another, I have not shown the latitude of each province or pointed out strictly the course that our men took. For, as I have already stated elsewhere, in spite of the fact that I have endeavored to learn these details, it has not been possible for me to do so because he who gave me the account was neither cosmographer nor mariner and as a result did not know them. Furthermore, the army carried no instruments to take the elevation of the land and had no one to obtain or consider it, for with the disgust that all bore at not finding gold or silver, they learned nothing well. Therefore, please forgive me this omission as well as the many others to be found in my work, for I should be happy if there were nothing for which to ask pardon.

Having left Guancane, the Governor crossed seven provinces, making now the longest daily marches he could and refusing to pause a single day in any one province, for he wished to come quickly to the Great River and accomplish in that summer the plans he harbored for beginning the settlement of the land and the founding of a town within it. In consequence no distinctive characteristics of these provinces were remembered other than that four of them, where our men found abundant food, contained fertile soil and great forests pierced by small streams and medium-sized rivers, and that the other three were poorly and sparsely settled and contained land not so fertile or pleasant. It was suspected, however, that since the guides were natives of these same provinces, they had led the Spaniards through the worst parts of them.

Some of the natives of the seven provinces came out to receive the Governor peacefully and some were hostile. But nothing occurred with either that should be told except that the Spaniards did attempt to maintain peace with those who presented themselves as friends and to avoid war and strife with those who were enemies, for our men were now trying as carefully as possible to escape a conflict. In this way they passed through the seven provinces which must have been at least one hundred and twenty leagues across. Then at the termination of a hurried journey, they came to the borders of a great province called Anilco from whence they traveled on for thirty leagues to its principal town,[4] which bore the same name. This town was situated on the bank of a river larger than our own Guadalquivir, and contained four hundred good and spacious dwellings, in the center of which was a magnificent plaza. The houses of the Curaca were located on a high mound which dominated the entire site.

[4] Presumably just south of Harrisonburg, Louisiana, probably on the site of what is now Jonesville.

This Cacique, who likewise was called Anilco, was armed and had placed fifteen hundred chosen warriors in front of the town to resist our men. The latter on seeing his preparedness, made a halt to await the arrival of the hindmost of the army and to put all in readiness for fighting; and in the meantime the Indians took their women and children and household goods to a place of safety. Some conveyed them in boats and canoes to the opposite shore of the river, and others carried them to the woods and underbrush lining the bank of the same stream. Then the Castilians arranged themselves in squadrons and advanced. But the Indians dared not await them, and without firing an arrow retreated to the town. From thence they went to the river where almost all crossed over to the opposite shore, some in canoes and boats and others by swimming. For they had not intended to fight the Spaniards but had desired only to delay them and prevent their entering so quickly, in order to have an opportunity to convey what was there to a place of safety. On seeing the Indians in flight, our men charged and took some of them prisoner as they were embarking; and in the town itself, they seized many women and children of all ages who had been unable to flee. Then the Governor dispatched messages with the utmost speed to the Cacique Anilco offering peace and friendship and begging for his own in return. He had sent such messages before entering the town, but the Curaca was so aloof that he had refused to answer the first communications, and now neither responded to the second nor spoke a word to the bearers, but as if mute, made signs with his hands for them to leave his presence.

The Spaniards camped in this town and were here four days procuring canoes and constructing large boats; and when they had a supply of these vessels, they crossed the river without opposition. Then they made a four-day march through some wilderness where there were great mountains, and at the end of that time entered a province called Guachoya.[5] The noteworthy things which occurred

[5] In the introductory summary to Part I of Book V, this word appears as Guacoya. Since this spelling is possibly due to a printer's error, we have changed it at that place.

in this province, I shall relate, God willing, in the chapter which follows.

CHAPTER IV

*The Spaniards enter Guachoya. Herein is told
how these Indians carry on perpetual
warfare with each other.*

THE first town of this province of Guachoya that the Spaniards beheld after passing the wilderness was the principal one. It bore the same name as the province itself and lay along one bank of the Great River, the river for which our men were searching. It occupied two high and adjacent hills, half of its three hundred houses being upon one and half upon the other. The level space in between served as a plaza, and on the summit of one of the hills stood the house of the Cacique.

Now the provinces of Guachoya and Anilco bore great hatred for each other, and a cruel war was being waged between them. For this reason it had not been possible for the Guachoyas to receive news of the coming of the Spaniards to their town, and as a result, the latter found them unprepared. Nevertheless, the Cacique and his vassals armed themselves in whatever way they could to defend the place. But when they saw the strength of their foe and realized their inability to oppose this strength, they assembled at the Great River, and in very handsome canoes, which they as hostile people kept in readiness for such occasions, crossed to the other side, taking with them their wives and children and all of the possessions they could carry. In this way, they abandoned the town. Then the Castilians entered, and finding within a great amount of corn and other grains as well as fruits which that land has in abundance, lodged themselves in complete comfort.

Since, as we have seen, almost all of the provinces that these Spaniards traversed were at war with each other, it will be appropriate to describe here the kind of warfare that was waged. One should know that this was not a conflict of force against force with an organized army or with pitched battles, except in rare instances, or a conflict instigated by the lust and ambition of some lords to seize the estates of others. Their struggle was one of ambushes and subtlety in which they attacked each other on fishing or hunting trips and in their fields and along their roads wherever they could find an enemy off guard. And those whom they seized on such occasions, they held as slaves, some in perpetual bondage with one foot maimed, as we have seen them in certain provinces, and some as prisoners to be ransomed and exchanged. But the hostility among these Indians amounted to no more than the harm they inflicted upon their persons with deaths, wounds, or shackles, for they made no attempt to seize estates. If sometimes the battle were more heated, they went so far as to burn towns and devastate fields, but as soon as the conquerors had inflicted the desired damage, they regathered in their own lands without attempting to take possession of the lands of others. It appears, therefore, that their enmity and hatred spring primarily from a desire for ostentation, or in other words a wish to show their valor and strength of spirit and to gain experience in military science rather than from a desire to obtain the property and estate of another. The prisoners, they easily ransom simply by a system of exchange, and then all return to their ambushes. This warfare, they now look upon as the natural order of things and, as a result, regardless of where they are found, are always provided with arms, for in no place are they secure from enemies. And the circumstance of their being so practiced in continuous fighting gives rise to that of their being of such a bellicose nature and so skillful with their weapons, particularly with the bow and arrows, for these being shooting arms with which they can be effective from a distance, they, as hunters who go in search of both men and animals, use them to a greater extent than they do others. Moreover a cacique does not carry on warfare with just one of his neighbors, but with all who share his boundaries, for whether there be two, three, four or more, all wage war upon each other—a practice which is indeed praiseworthy in soldiership, for no one becomes careless and each can demonstrate his individual gallantry. Such is the common enmity of the Indians of the great kingdom of Florida, an enmity which in itself would be an excellent reason why that land might be won with facility, because "the whole kingdom divided, etc."[6]

By the time our men had spent three days in the town of Guachoya, its lord, whose name was the same, having learned what had happened between the Indians and Spaniards in the province of Anilco and how the Curaca of that land had been unwilling to receive the Governor peacefully (instead scorning his friendship by refusing to answer his messages), determined not to lose the opportunity now offered to avenge himself upon his enemies, the people of Anilco. As a man who was tricky and full of astuteness, he dispatched a solemn message at once to the Governor by four illustrious Indian cavaliers and many servants who were loaded with great quantities of fruit and fish. With these things he sent to say that he begged his lordship to pardon him his inadvertence in not having awaited and received him in the town and to grant him permission to come now and kiss his hands; and he asserted that should the Governor allow him this favor, he would arrive within four days to salute him in person, and that he thenceforward was offering him his vassalage and service.

Pleased with these words, the Governor told the bearers to inform their Curaca that he appreciated exceedingly his fine spirit and friendship, and that he should come without any qualms, since he would be well received. These men thereupon returned content with the reply; and the Cacique, during the three days that he delayed in coming, sent each day seven or eight communications, all of which contained the same words—words to the effect that his lordship should advise him of his health, and of whether there were any way in which to serve him, along with other nonsense of no

[6] *porque todo reyno diviso, etc.*—The Inca no doubt refers here to the old proverb "Divide and conquer."

moment. Such messages Guachoya sent as a cautious and astute man to see if with them he might discover anything extraordinary or ascertain how the Adelantado received them. But when he perceived that the Governor accepted them with gracious civility, he gained confidence and on the fourth day arrived before dinner as he had advised on the preceding day he would do. In his retinue he brought a hundred noblemen, all very magnificently arrayed, according to their custom, in large feather headdresses and beautiful robes of marten skin and other much esteemed fur. Moreover all brought their best bows and arrows, which they make for their greater adornment.

CHAPTER V

How Guachoya visits the General and both return to Anilco.

ON LEARNING that Guachoya was approaching, the Governor, who was lodged in that Cacique's house, went to the door to receive him. And to the chieftain and all his people, he spoke affectionately, while they in turn were much favored and pleased with his words. Then everyone entered a great sala, and the General by means of the many interpreters placed in fixed order, conversed with the Curaca, informing himself thereby of what there was in that land and its neighboring provinces in favor of and contrary to his conquest. During this conversation the Cacique Guachoya gave a great sneeze, at which his noblemen, who were leaning against the walls among the Spaniards, simultaneously lowered their heads, and then opening and closing their arms and making other gestures of great veneration and courtesy, saluted him with different words, all of them, however, directed toward one end. Thus they said, "May the Sun protect you, be with you, enlighten you, exalt you, shelter you, favor you, defend you, prosper you, save you," and other similar things, each speaking as the word presented itself to him; and for a long time the murmur of their voices continued among them. Amazed at this, the Governor said to the cavaliers and captains who were with him: "Do you not see how the whole world is one?" This instance of conduct was well noted among the Spaniards who did perceive now that the same or greater ceremonies are used among barbarous people when sneezing as are observed by those who are considered to be most civil. From whence one can believe that this mode of salutation is natural among all nations and does not result from a corruption of manners as it is in general customary to say, even though there is no lack of people who might contradict such a statement.

The Cacique dined with the Governor while all of his Indians stood around the table, and even though the Spaniards told them to go and eat, they would not do so until their lord had eaten. This was a courtesy, however, which was observed likewise among our own men. Then they fed them in another room, for the meal had been prepared for all of them. To provide quarters for the Curaca, they vacated one of the sections of his own house. Here he remained with a few servants, while his noblemen crossed at sunset to the other side of the river, coming again, however, on the following morning. This they did each day that the Castilians were in that town. Meanwhile the Curaca Guachoya persuaded the Governor that the Spaniards should return to the province of Anilco. He offered to go in person with his people to serve his lordship and said that to facilitate the passage of the river of Anilco, he would command eighty large canoes to be brought and in addition some small ones, all of which would descend the Great River for seven leagues until reaching the mouth of the Anilco, and from thence go up that river until they came to the village of Anilco itself. The whole journey through both rivers, he said, would amount to about twenty leagues of navigation. And he added that while these canoes were descending the Great River and ascending the Anilco, they themselves would go by land in order that all might arrive simultaneously at the village of Anilco.

The Governor was easy to persuade to this trip because he wanted to know what there might be in that province of advantage and assistance to his project for making the brigantines. At the same time he wished through peace and friendship to attract the devotion of the Curaca Anilco, so that without the hardship and afflictions of war he might establish a base between those provinces (which to him had seemed abundant in food) where he could await the outcome of the two vessels he planned to send down the river.

The Governor's purpose in returning to the town of Anilco was what we have seen, but that of the Curaca Guachoya was quite different, for his was to use the forces of another to avenge himself upon his enemy, Anilco. He, who in their continuous wars and disputes had always been and was now being brought under subjection and vassalage, hoped on this occasion to take retribution for past injuries. With this idea in mind and with all possible dissimulation, he induced the Governor to return to the village of Anilco, and he urgently and hastily ordered the necessary things to be made ready for the journey.

As soon as they were prepared and the canoes had been brought, the General commanded Captain Juan de Guzmán and his troops to go along with these vessels for the purpose of governing and giving organization to the four thousand Indian warriors who were to travel within them and to the oarsmen who likewise carried bows and arrows. And as a time limit for their navigation he decided upon three complete days, this seeming to him sufficient time for both groups to arrive concurrently in the village of Anilco. At the Governor's command, Captain Juan de Guzmán set out down the Great River; and at the same time, the Governor himself with his Spaniards, and Guachoya with two thousand men of war and another great multitude of Indians carrying supplies, departed by land. Then without anything of moment occurring to either party, all arrived simultaneously within sight of the town of Anilco. Here, though the Cacique of the town was absent, the inhabitants sounded an alarm and with all possible courage and strength, arranged themselves to prohibit the passage of the river; but being unable to resist the fury of their enemies, who were both Indians and Spaniards, they eventually turned their backs and abandoned the place.

The Guachoyas entered this town as they would a settlement of such hated enemies; and as do offended people who desire revenge, they sacked it and robbed the temple and burial place of the lords of the state. Here in addition to the bodies of their dead, the Cacique kept the best, richest, and most prized of their possessions, as well as the spoils and trophies of the greatest victories his people had enjoyed over the Guachoyas themselves, trophies which consisted of a large number of flags and weapons and of the heads of their most illustrious victims, placed now on lance points at the doors of the temple. The Guachoyas replaced the heads of their own people with those of Anilcos; and their military insignia and arms they carried away with great happiness and contentment at seeing them once again in their possession. The corpses within the wooden chests they threw upon the ground, and in retaliation for past injuries, trampled upon these bodies with all the scorn they could demonstrate.

CHAPTER VI

An account of other cruelties of the Guachoyas.
The manner in which the Governor
attempts to solicit aid.

THE wrath of the Guachoyas was not assuaged by what they did to the possessions and the dead of Anilco, nor were these people satisfied with seeing their banners and weapons restored. Their madness urged them on to worse things and they became so rabid that they would not take any person alive that they encountered in the town regardless of sex or age. Instead they slew them all, and with those most deserving of pity, such as women now in extreme age and infants at the breast, they employed even more severe cruelty; for dispossessing the old women of what scant clothing they wore, they killed them with arrows, shooting at the pudenda more readily than at any other part of the body. Moreover the smallest of the children they seized by a leg and throwing them high, shot them while they were still in the air with five or six arrows more or less, according to the number that happened to strike the mark.

With these cruelties and all additional ones that they were able to perpetrate without the knowledge of the Spaniards, the Guachoyas manifested the hatred that they as offended people held for the Anilcos. But when these things were witnessed by some of the Castilians (for the Indians were not able to conceal them to the extent that they wished), they immediately gave notice to the Governor, who was greatly enraged that an injury should be inflicted upon the people of Anilco when his purpose had been to gain their friendship and not to do them harm. Therefore, lest the cruelty of the Guachoyas continue, he gave a command to signal to them to reassemble as quickly as possible. Then he reprimanded the Cacique for what his people had done, and to prevent their accomplishing further damage, ordered a proclamation to be published to the effect that it would be under forfeiture of life for anyone to dare set fire to the houses or harm the persons of the Indians. And then lest the Guachoyas be ignorant of this proclamation, he instructed the interpreters to declare it in their language. And since he feared that they still would do what damage they could, while secreting themselves from the Spaniards, he departed from the town of Anilco with the utmost haste and went to the river, having first issued orders that the Castilians should carry the Indians before them so that they not remain to burn the town and kill the people hidden within it. With these precautions, some evil was averted, and the damage was not so extensive as it might have been.

The General now embarked with all his people, Spaniards as well as Indians, and crossed the river to return to Guachoya. But they had not proceeded a quarter of a league when they saw smoke pouring from the town and many houses lighting up in flames.

The reason for this was that the Guachoyas, being unable to bear the idea of not burning the town and having been prohibited from openly doing so, had endeavored to set fire to it in whatever manner they could. For the purpose, they had left live coals placed in the wings of the houses, and since these dwellings were built of straw and with the summer had become excessively dry, there was little need for wind to kindle them quickly. The Governor resolved to return and keep the town from burning completely, but at this point he saw many of the inhabitants rushing with the greatest possible haste to extinguish the fire, and he therefore left off and continued on his way to the village of Guachoya, meanwhile concealing his anger lest he lose the friends he possessed for the sake of people whom he had not yet been able to win.

When he had reached the town and made an entry with his army, the Governor left all other charges to the officers of his camp and took upon himself the responsibility for constructing the brigantines. These he planned and worked upon day and night. He gave orders to cut the necessary wood, which was very abundant in that province; and for the rigging, he had all the cordage collected that could be obtained in that town and its vicinity. He told the Indians to bring him all the resin from the pine, plum, and other trees which were to be found throughout the countryside, and he commanded that many new nails be made and that those which had served in the previous pirogues and boats be put in shape for use. Moreover, in his own mind he selected the captains and soldiers whom he regarded as his most faithful and trustworthy friends to return in the brigantines when he should send them to request the assistance he had contemplated.

Until such time as the vessels should be sent, he had determined to cross over to a large province called Quigualtanqui;[7] which lay on the opposite side of the Great River. He had received news of this land through certain runners whom he had sent out both on horseback and on foot, news to the effect that it was abundant in food

---

[7] Occupied by the tribe that was presumably in the next century to be called the Natchez Indians.

and thickly populated, that its principal town, which contained five hundred houses, was near the town of Guachoya, the river lying between the two, and furthermore that its lord and cacique, who likewise was called Quigualtanqui, had replied unfavorably to the message he had sent requesting peace and offering friendship. For with much disrespect that chieftain had uttered many affronts and vituperations as well as great and fierce threats in which along with other offensive words he had said that he would exterminate the Spaniards in one battle, as they should soon see, and that he would separate them from the evil life they engaged in, lost in another's lands and thieving and killing like highway robbers and vagabonds; moreover that he had sworn by the Sun and the Moon not to offer them friendship as the rest of the curacas had done through whose lands they had traveled, but rather to slaughter them and place their bodies in the trees.[8]

At this stage, Alonso de Carmona has the following to say:

"A little before the Governor was to die, he issued an order to assemble all the canoes of that town. Joining the largest in pairs, they put the horses within them, and then taking the people in the others, they crossed over to the opposite side of the river where they found many extensive settlements. But since the inhabitants had moved out and gone away, the Spaniards returned without having accomplished anything. Aware of this fact, the principal men of those places dispatched a messenger to warn the Governor that he should not be so bold as to send Spaniards again to their lands, since in that event none would return alive; that he might thank his own good reputation and the gracious treatment he had afforded the

---

[8] According to the Elvas account, the reply of this particular Cacique was no less an affront than a challenge. Announcing himself as a child of the Sun, De Soto had suggested that the Indian follow the usual custom of paying him a visit, bringing along something of value to signify his love and obedience. Quigualtanqui answered that everybody he ever heard of came to visit him with a tribute either voluntarily or otherwise and that if the Spaniard wanted to see him, he could do the same. And he added that he would believe what De Soto said about his being the child of the Sun when he saw him dry up the Great River.

inhabitants of his present location, since it was because of these things that their own Indians had not emerged to destroy all of the Spaniards who had come there; that should the Governor now attempt something in their land, they would all meet person to person; that they would have him realize the lack of courtesy and respect he had demonstrated in sending men to raid them; and finally, that they had sworn by their gods, in the event another raid should occur, to kill him and his entire army or die in the attempt."

All these are the words of Alonso de Carmona, and since they are practically the same as what we have said of Quigualtanqui, I desire to transcribe them to the letter.

To these affronts, the Governor had replied with much gentleness and suavity, wooing Quigualtanqui with pleasantness and friendship; and although it is true that because of the Governor's great courtesy that chieftain changed his evil words to good ones, giving manifestations of peace and concord, it was understood that he did so with falseness and deception in order to catch the Spaniards off guard; for through spies the Governor learned that he went about machinating treasons and wickedness and that he was calling together his people and those of the neighboring provinces for the purpose of killing the Christians treacherously under the guise of friendship. All this our General was aware of, but he guarded it in his heart in order to punish it in its time, for he still possessed a hundred and fifty horses and five hundred Spaniards, with which, after having sent away the brigantines, he planned to cross the Great River and make his seat in the principal town of Quigualtanqui where he would spend the present summer and the coming winter until he had the assistance he planned to ask for—assistance which could have been supplied very easily from the whole coast and the city of Mexico, and from the islands of Cuba and Santo Domingo by sending ships up the Great River, for that river could have held all the ships that might attempt to ascend it, as we shall see further on.

CHAPTER VII

*An account is given of the Governor's death and
of the successor whom he appointed.*

DESIRING as a good father that the many hardships he and
his men had experienced and that the expenditures they had
incurred in the exploration should not be wasted and without fruit
for them, this heroic cavalier was absorbed day and night in the
cares and aspirations we have described, when on the twentieth of
June of the year 1542 he felt a slight fever. On the first day this
fever was slow, but on the third very severe; and, observing its in-
ordinate increase, the Governor realized that his illness was mortal.
So he prepared himself at once for dissolution, and as a good
Catholic Christian, arranged his will, almost in cipher, however,
because of his not possessing an adequate supply of paper.[9] Then
in sorrow and repentance at having offended God, he confessed his
sins.

As his successor in the position of governor and captain general
of the kingdom and provinces of Florida, he selected Luis de Moscoso de Alvarado, that gentleman whom in the province of Chicaza
he had deprived of the office of campmaster. For the ceremony of
appointment, he summoned before him his cavaliers, captains, and
soldiers of higher rank, and then on the part of His Imperial Majesty, he begged and charged these men that out of respect for the
virtue, rank and merits of Luis de Moscoso, they look upon him as
their governor and captain general until such time as His Majesty
should send another decree.[10] Afterward he took their solemn vow
that they would thus comply. This task completed, he called before

[9] This will has never been found, but there was another which De Soto
had drawn up in Cuba on May 10, 1539.

[10] According to the Elvas account, De Soto asked his officers to select
his successor, but they signified their desire through Baltasar de Gallegos that
the Governor make the appointment.

him the noblest of his army in groups of two and three; and later he instructed the remainder of his people to come to him in groups of twenty and thirty. To these men he bade farewell with much sorrow on his part and copious tears on theirs, and he charged them with the conversion of the natives to the Catholic Faith and with the augmentation of the Spanish Crown, declaring that death was depriving him of fulfilling these ambitions. Then he very earnestly besought them to keep peace and affection among themselves.

Five days Hernando de Soto consumed in this matter, during which time his raging fever was increasing; and then on the seventh day, the fever deprived him of this present life.[11] He died as a Christian Catholic, beseeching mercy of the most Holy Trinity, invoking in his favor and protection the blood of Jesus Christ Our Lord, and calling for the intercession of the Virgin and all the Celestial Court as well as the Faith of the Roman Church. With such words, which he repeated numerous times, this magnanimous and never conquered cavalier who was worthy of great titles and estates and undeserving that his history be written by an Indian, thus rendered his soul to God. He died at the age of forty-two.[12]

[11] The great wilderness of sixteenth-century Florida provided ample opportunity for even so young and vigorous a person as De Soto to contract a physical illness of mortal consequence, but he was too important a figure for his contemporaries not to speculate on the nature of his fatal affliction. Some attributed it to despondency over the seeming impossibility of reaching the sea or sustaining his men until help should arrive; and some said that he merely pined away in shame, embarrassment and disappointment at the outcome of the expedition and his failure to find wealth. Others asserted that the Indians put an end to him, and still others that he died with what was known as a "bloody flux." Both his course of action throughout the expedition and historical evidence of the sad fate that sometimes awaited a conquistador who returned to Spain with an empty purse would lead us to believe that his fatal illness did not find its origin in a germ. Nevertheless, whether the cause were physical or mental, either could have produced in this cavalier a raging and consuming fever, so the Inca rather diplomatically leaves it at that.

[12] It is said that during his illness De Soto had been haunted by the prediction of an astrologer that he would not live to be older than Vasco Núñez de Balboa was when he met his death. Balboa had been executed at the age of forty-two. Guachoya, where De Soto died, is believed to have been near the present site of Ferriday, Louisiana. The date of his death was May 21, 1542.

The Adelantado Hernando de Soto was, as we stated in the beginning, a native of Villanueva de Barcarrota and an hidalgo in all four successions of his ancestry. When His Caesarean Majesty was informed of this fact, he sent him the order of Santiago, but this honor he never enjoyed, for by the time the decree reached the island of Cuba, he had already entered upon the discovery and conquest of Florida. More than medium in stature, and graceful, he appeared well both on foot and mounted. He had a dark but merry face and was skillful in both saddles, more so however with the short stirrups than the long.[13] In hardships and want, he was very patient, indeed so patient that the greatest comfort of his soldiers at such times was to behold the suffering and forbearance of their captain general.

Hernando de Soto was fortunate in those particular expeditions which he undertook personally, although not in the principal one since he lost his life at the moment of his greatest opportunity. He was the first Spaniard to see and speak with Atahuallpa, a tyrant king who was the last of the Incas to rule Peru, as I shall disclose in my history of the discovery and conquest of that empire if Our Lord God vouchsafe to lengthen my life, which already grows feeble and tired. Severe in punishing transgressions of military science, he pardoned others freely. He esteemed highly those of his soldiers who were strong and brave, and he personally was most courageous, in fact so courageous that wherever he entered a battlefield fighting, he cut a path through which ten of his men could pass. Thus all confessed that ten lances from his entire army were not of such worth as his own.

This valorous captain possessed one very notable and memorable characteristic, which was that in the unexpected attacks made on his camp by day, he was always the first or the second to rush forth

---

[13] *diestro de ambas sillas, y más de la gineta que de la brida*—Cunninghame-Graham (*op. cit.*, p. 218) says: "The saddle *á la gineta* was the Moorish saddle with short stirrups, and was the very opposite of the saddle *á la brida*, which was but the modification of the older saddle *á la estradiota*, with the straight seat of armour-clad knights. To ride well in both saddles (*ser ginete en ambas sillas*) was a great feather in a man's cap. Sometimes it was mentioned in his epitaph."

at the alarm, and never the third. But in those assaults which the enemy made by night, he was the first and never the second. So it appears that it was only after having prepared himself to go out to a battle that he gave his men the alarm. With such promptness and vigilance as this, he always conducted himself in war. In sum he was one of the best lancers who have gone to the New World; and there were few as good and none better, unless it were Gonzalo Pizarro, to whom by common consent was invariably given the honor of first place.

In this exploration, Hernando de Soto spent the more than one hundred thousand ducats which he had obtained in the first conquest of Peru from the division of that rich ransom the Spaniards had collected at Cajamarca.[14] Moreover, he paid with his life, and, as we have seen, died in action.

CHAPTER VIII

The two burials that they gave to the Adelantado Hernando de Soto.

THE death of the Governor and Captain General, Hernando de Soto, a death so worthy of being mourned, brought great sorrow and pain to all of his people,[15] not only because of their having been orphaned by his loss, for they looked upon him as a father, but also because of their inability to afford him the sepulchre which his body merited or the obsequies which one would wish for

---

[14] The Elvas account states that De Soto, on his death, left two male and three female slaves, three horses, and seven hundred swine. This property was sold at auction. Money was to be paid at the first melting of gold and silver, or at the division of vassals and territory.

[15] De Soto, of course, had his enemies. According to the Elvas account some were even glad when he died and welcomed the change in leadership, "holding it certain that Luis de Moscoso, who was given to leading a gay life, preferred to see himself at ease in a land of Christians rather than continue the toils of war, discovering and subduing, which the people had come to hate."

so beloved a captain and lord. This pain and sorrow was doubled
when they realized that it was necessary instead to bury him in silence
and secrecy lest the Indians learn where he lay; for they feared that
those people might commit upon his body such outrages and dis-
honors as they had inflicted upon other Spaniards. Disinterring and
dismembering their victims, they had placed them in trees, each
joint upon a separate limb; and it was easy to believe that these
Indians, in order to insult the Spaniards further, would offer to the
Governor, as their commander in chief, even greater and more
abusive affronts. And our men declared that since their commander
had not received such treatment in life, it would not be right that
through their negligence he receive it in death.

For this reason, therefore, they agreed to bury him at night with
sentinels so placed that the Indians would not see him or know
where he was. Thus they selected as a sepulchre one of the large
and broad excavations on a plain near the town where the Indians
had removed dirt for their dwellings, and here they interred the
remains of the illustrious Adelantado Hernando de Soto amidst the
abundant tears of the priests and cavaliers who found themselves at
his sad obsequies. Then to conceal their grief as well as the place
where he lay, they spread news among the Indians on the following
day that the Governor's health was improved; and with this falsehood they mounted their horses and, galloping across the plains,
through the holes and over the sepulchre itself, made a show of
great festivity and rejoicing. They would have entombed this beloved and esteemed man in the Mausoleum or Needle of Julius
Caesar; and to trample his sepulchre as they now did to their greater
sorrow was far from what they felt in their hearts. They took
such action, however, to prevent the Indians from offering him even
grosser indignities. And that all evidences of the sepulchre might
be completely obliterated, they were not content just with trampling
it, but before the celebrations, gave orders for much water to be
thrown on the plain and in the excavations with the excuse that
otherwise the horses on running would raise dust.

All of these precautions our Spaniards took to convince the Indians of a lie and to veil their grief. Nevertheless, as pleasure can be but poorly feigned, and as sorrow cannot be hidden so well but that it will be detected from afar in the person who suffers, so our men could not conceal their feelings to such an extent that the Indians did not suspect both the death of the Governor and the place they had laid him. Passing over the plain and through the excavations, they would pause and look very attentively in all directions and then talk with each other and point with their chins and wink with their eyes toward the place where the body lay.

When the Spaniards became aware of these gestures, their first fears and suspicions increased, and they resolved by common consent to remove the body from its present location to another where its discovery would not be so certain and where the Indians would have more difficulty finding it in the event of their trying. For, they said, the infidels, on suspecting that the Governor was there, would dig up that whole plain to its very center and not rest until they had found him. They felt therefore that it would be wise to give him the Great River as a sepulchre, but before putting their decision into effect, they wished to determine if the depth of its waters were sufficient to conceal him. Accordingly, the Comptroller, Juan de Añasco, the Captains, Juan de Guzmán, Arias Tinoco, Alonso Romo de Cardeñosa, and the Ensign General of the army, Diego Arias, took charge of examining the river. Carrying with them a Biscayan called Ioanes de Abadía, who was a seaman and a great engineer, they went out one afternoon to make some soundings. With all possible dissimulation, lest the Indians perceive what they were doing, they acted as if they were fishing and enjoying themselves in the water. Thus they found that the stream was nineteen fathoms deep in the center of its channel, and a quarter of a league wide; and with this discovery, they determined to bury the Governor within its depths. Now since in all that neighborhood there was no stone which could be thrown in with his body to carry it to the bottom, they hewed down a thick liveoak and hollowed it out on one side to the height of a man. Then on that night, they disinterred the Governor as silently as possible and placed him in this tree trunk, nailing boards over the aperture and leaving him enclosed as if in a chest. Afterward with many tears and much sorrow on the part of the priests and cavaliers present at this second burial, they lowered him in the center of the river, and commending his soul to God, watched him sink at once to its depths.[16]

Such were the sad and lamentable obsequies which our Spaniards gave to the body of their captain general, the Adelantado Hernando de Soto, Governor of the kingdoms and provinces of Florida— obsequies which were unworthy of so heroic a man, yet which when viewed closely appear similar in almost all respects to those which the Goths, who were ancestors of the Spaniards, gave one thousand one hundred and thirty-one years before to King Alaric when they buried him in the river Busento at a place close to the city of Cosenza within the Italian province of Calabria. I said similar in almost all respects because the Spaniards are descendants of those Goths; both burial places were rivers; the deceased were chiefs and leaders who were much beloved by their people; and both were valiant men who, in leaving their own lands and seeking places to settle and establish a site, performed great feats in foreign kingdoms. And even the purpose of both peoples was the same, for it was to bury their captains where their bodies could not be located by enemies even though they were sought. They differ only in that the obsequies offered by our men originated in their compassion for their captain general and in their fear that the Indians might mutilate his body, whereas those offered by the Goths sprang from their vanity in wishing to reveal to the world the glory and majesty of their king.

[16] The Elvas account states that De Soto's body was kept secretly for three days and then buried just within the gates of the town. Later when the Indians became suspicious, it was disinterred and after being wrapped in some shawls along with an abundance of sand, was committed to the river.

In the will drawn up in Cuba, De Soto had provided for the construction of a chapel for Our Lady of Conception in Jerez de los Caballeros, and in this chapel his remains were to have rested.

And now that the similarity may be seen more clearly, it will be well to describe here for those who do not know it, the burial which the Goths gave King Alaric. That famous prince having performed numerous heroic feats with his people throughout the world, and having sacked the imperial city of Rome (this was the first sack that it suffered after its empire and monarchy, and occurred one thousand one hundred and sixty-two years after its foundation, and four hundred and twelve years after the virginal parturition of Our Lady), resolved to cross over into Sicily; and when he had been in Reggio and attempted the passage, he was forced by a great tempest at sea to return to Cosenza, where in a few days he expired. His Goths, who loved him passionately, celebrated his obsequies with numerous and excessive honors and magnificent events, among which was conceived a most solemn and admirable one. They commanded many of the captives whom they carried with them, to divert the river Busento from its bed, and then in the center of its channel to build a grand sepulchre, where along with unlimited treasure they placed the body of their king. (These words are from the Collenuccio;[17] but all other historians, both ancient and modern, Spanish and otherwise, who write of those times, say the same). Later when they had covered the sepulchre, they gave the order to turn the river back into its former course, after which they slew all of the captives who had labored there lest they at some time reveal where King Alaric lay.

It has seemed appropriate to me to touch here upon this story because of its great similarity to my own, and also to say that the nobility of those Spaniards and of all the people of present day Spain comes without any question whatsoever from those same Goths; for since the time of the Goths no other race has entered into Spain except the Moors of Barbary when they conquered it in the days of King Don Rodrigo. But the few remaining survivors of those Goths drove the Moors little by little from Spain and populated it as it is today. Even the lineage of the kings of Castile

[17] Pandolfo Collenuccio, *Compendio de le Istorie del Regno di Napoli.*

comes directly from the Gothic kings and without their blood having been lost; and in this well known antiquity and sovereignty, they surpass all the kings of the world.

Of everything which I have told concerning the will, the death, and the obsequies of the Adelantado Hernando de Soto, Alonso de Carmona and Juan Coles report neither more nor less in their accounts. Both add, however, that when the Indians failed to see the Governor, they inquired about him, but that the Christians told them that God had sent for him to command of him great things that he was to perform when he should return; and they said that with this explanation, which all repeated, our Spaniards rendered the Indians less troublesome.[18]

[18] According to the Elvas account, the Cacique Guachoya, on being told that De Soto had departed for a somewhat lengthy sojourn in the skies, generously provided two well proportioned young men to accompany him. In order to save the necks of these youths, it was necessary to assure the chieftain that the Governor not only was not dead but had been adequately supplied with companions for his journey.

End of the First Part
Of the Fifth Book

THE SECOND PART OF THE FIFTH BOOK

Of the History of Florida by the Inca tells of how the Spaniards decided to abandon Florida, and the long journey they made in an effort to do so; the unbearable hardship they suffered both in going and returning until they came once again to the Great River; the seven brigantines they constructed for the purpose of leaving that kingdom; the league of ten Caciques formed against the Spaniards and the secret information which they obtained concerning this league; the promises of General Anilco and the fine qualities of this man; a severe rise in the Great River; the efforts involved in making the brigantines; a challenge of General Anilco to the Cacique Guachoya and the reason for this challenge; and the punishment inflicted upon the messengers of the league. It contains fifteen chapters.

CHAPTER I

The Spaniards decide to abandon Florida.

ITH the death of the Governor and Captain General Hernando de Soto, not only did the fond hope which he had nurtured for settling and establishing a site in that land cease, but his captains and soldiers retracted and turned against his plan, as is wont to happen wherever the head of a government is lacking. For since all of the officers and soldiers of the army were discontent at not having found the spoils in Florida that they had anticipated, even though it did possess the other qualities we have mentioned, and since they had wanted to abandon this kingdom and had refrained solely because of their respect for the Governor (the one dead), the most influential of them now agreed that they should leave it as quickly as possible. Their decision was one which they afterward lamented all the days of their lives, as those things customarily are lamented which are decided upon and executed without wisdom or counsel. The Comptroller, Juan de Añasco, as the King's Minister of the Exchequer and, apart from that, as a cavalier and nobleman who had labored most in this exploration, was under obligation to support the very fitting opinion of his captain general by proceeding with the undertaking and conquest, if for no other reason than to avoid wasting what already had been accomplished, since as we have seen it was of so much honor and advantage to everyone, and of such splendor, dignity and increase to the Royal Crown of Spain. But he too failed to oppose those captains and cavaliers who favored leaving Florida, and on the contrary offered

to lead them in a brief time to the boundary and jurisdiction of Mexico; for he prided himself on being a cosmographer and boasted of his ability to put them very quickly in safety, not reflecting upon the long provinces, swollen rivers, rugged forests where there was no food, and troublesome swamps which had to be crossed. Instead, he erased all difficulties, for when this ambition and desire of ours wanders, it is wont to facilitate hardships and remove obstacles from its aspirations with the result that we later perish in them.

A recollection of certain false information which the Indians had supplied during the past winter and the preceding summer to the effect that other Castilians were conquering provinces not far to the west gave these men more courage and daring for their decision, and in calling those rumors to mind they converted them into truths, saying that people must have gone out from Mexico to conquer new kingdoms, and that according to the report of the Indians those people ought not to be far distant. And as if they themselves had found nothing to conquer or settle, they declared that it would be wise to go in search of those people, and, on locating them, assist in their conquest and settlement. With this mutual decision, arrived at so unfortunately, our Spaniards left Guachoya on the fourth or fifth of July and directed their steps to the west with no idea of turning either to the right or left.[1] They felt that by following this route they would of necessity come eventually to Mexico; for they failed to remember that according to their cosmography they were in a much higher latitude than the lands of New Spain. But in their eagerness to see themselves in those lands, they traveled more than

[1]The Elvas account states that Luis de Moscoso asked for the written opinion of all captains and principal personages as to what direction they should take in leaving Florida. For several reasons they decided on the westward course. First, they had heard that the country lying in that direction was well inhabited whereas only a short distance downstream it was desert and of little sustenance. Again, a voyage by sea was held to be hazardous and of doubtful accomplishment since they could not build vessels of sufficient strength to weather storms, they were without captain, pilot, needle, or chart, and they did not know how far they were from the sea or whether there were turns and falls in the river. And finally, they felt that in going by land they still had a chance to find riches.

a hundred leagues, making the longest daily marches possible through strange provinces where there was less food and fewer people than in any they had seen before. I am not able to say what these provinces were called; for the Spaniards, having no intention of colonizing at that time and desiring solely to pass through them as rapidly as possible, made no effort to learn their names or obtain information concerning their quality. And, not having taken their names, they were unable to give them to me.

CHAPTER II

Some superstitions of the Indians of Florida as
well as those of Peru. How the Span-
iards come to Auche.

BUT turning back in our story to a somewhat earlier stage, I should tell you that when the Spaniards left the town of Guachoya, there came with them of his own volition an Indian sixteen or seventeen years of age, a lad noble in body and handsome of face, as are most of the natives of that province. When they had traveled three or four days, the servants of Governor Luis de Moscoso noticed that this boy had joined them and were surprised not only at seeing him but also by the fact that he came without having been forced to do so. Fearing that he might be a spy, they gave an account of him to the General, who thereupon sent for him and, by means of interpreters, among whom was Juan Ortiz, asked his reasons for leaving his parents, relatives, friends and acquaintances and coming away with these Spaniards whom he did not know. The Indian answered as follows:

"My Lord, I am a poor orphan. At their death, my parents left me very young and unprotected, but a principal Indian of my native village, who is a relative of the Curaca Guachoya, took compassion upon me and, receiving me into his house, reared me among his own children. At the time of Your Lordship's departure, this chieftain was ill and in despair of his life, and as soon as his wife, children and kinsmen realized the fact, they determined that on my master's death they would bury me with him, alive as I am; for they said that my lord had loved me very much and that because of his affection it was appropriate that I accompany and serve him in the other life. And even though it is true that I am obligated to him for having reared me and that I love him well, still my affection at the moment is not so great that I should be pleased to share his grave. So resolving to escape this death and not finding a better remedy, I decided to come away with Your Lordship's people, for I preferred being your slave to seeing myself a victim of such a fate. This is the reason for my coming and there is no other."

The General and his companions were amazed when they heard the Indian, for they perceived that the abominable practice of burying living servants and wives along with a dead chieftain was observed in that land just as it was in all other parts of the New World which at that time had been discovered.

In the whole of the empire of the Incas, who ruled Peru, it was for a long time the custom to entomb with kings and great lords their most beloved wives and their most favored and intimate servants; for in their paganism they believed that their souls were immortal, and that after this life there was a similar though not spiritual one which afforded punishment for the wicked, and glory, reward and honor for the virtuous. Thus for the word heaven, they say *hanampacha,* which signifies the upper world, and for hell, they say *veupacha,* which means the lower world; and the devil, with whom they affirm the wicked walk, they call Zupay. This subject I shall treat more at length in a history of the Incas.

But returning to our Castilians whom we left anxious to travel far, and who are to be so regretful later for having done so, I will say that when they had proceeded more than a hundred leagues across the provinces which because of our not knowing the names we have been unable to identify, they at length reached a province called Auche.[2] The lord of this place, who came out to receive them,

---

[2] They are in Texas now, possibly at the present site of San Augustine. Auche, incidentally, is the only province traversed by Moscoso to which the Inca gives a native name.

performed many acts of endearment and welcomed them with demonstrations of affection, saying that it gave him great happiness to behold them in his land. But, as we shall see later, all was false and feigned. Two days the Spaniards rested in Auche, which was the principal town of the province, and while informing themselves of those things suitable for their expedition, they learned that a two-day march hence there lay a great wilderness which required four days to cross. For this journey, the Cacique Auche gave them Indians loaded with sufficient corn for six days and an old man to take them through the wilderness to a populated land. Moreover, feigning great friendship, he commanded this aged person in their very presence to lead them along the best and shortest route that he knew.

Equipped in this manner, our men left Auche and, after a two-day march, reached the wilderness, through which they proceeded three more days along a broad road that appeared to be a highway. But by the end of two days this road gradually began to narrow, and eventually it faded out altogether. Then without a road, they continued for six more days wherever the Indian wished to lead them, for he had told them that he was taking them by short cuts in order that they might reach settlements more quickly. But at the termination of eight days of travel through deserts, forests and craggy lands, the Spaniards realized that they were having no success in coming out of these places, and they now observed something they had not noticed before. This was that the Indian had led them in circles, guiding them sometimes to the north and sometimes to the west and south, and at other times returning to the east. The deception had not come to their attention previously because of their great desire to advance and their belief that the guide would not mislead them. They now noted likewise that they had been traveling three days without corn or any food other than grasses and roots, and furthermore that their difficulties were increasing by the hour. Hence their hopes for coming out of those deserts were diminishing, for they had neither sustenance nor road.

CHAPTER III

*The Spaniards kill the guide. A particular act
of an Indian is told.*

GOVERNOR Luis de Moscoso ordered that the Indian serving
as his guide be called before him, and by means of his interpreters, he inquired of this man as to why it was that after eight days
of wandering in that wilderness he did not take them out of it, since
on leaving the town he had promised to cross the desert and reach
a settlement in half that time. The Indian did not reply to the
point but instead offered some foolish remarks which he felt exon-
erated him of the charge made against him. This response, however,
added to the sight of the army brought to such straits through the
man's malice, so enraged the Governor that he issued an order to
bind him to a tree and subject him to the large mastiffs which they
had with them; and one of the mastiffs thereupon shook him
violently. Seeing himself wounded, and fearing that the Spaniards
would indeed kill him, the Indian now begged that the dog be
removed and vowed to reveal the truth concerning everything which
in this particular instance was happening. Then having been relieved
of the animal, he said:

"My Lords, my Curaca and true sovereign commanded me at the
time of your departure to do what I have done, for opening his
heart to me, he declared that since he did not have the forces to
exterminate you in one battle as he should like, he had determined
to destroy you all with astuteness and trickery by putting you in these
forests and terrible deserts to perish of hunger. And in order to
realize his desire, he selected me as one of his most faithful servants
to mislead you to a place from whence you would never manage to
reach a settlement. Moreover, he said that he would confer great
honors upon me should I accomplish this task, but that otherwise he
would slay me cruelly. Being a vassal, I did what my lord demanded
of me just as I believe any one of you would do should your lord
so command. Thus I was impelled to act as I did out of respect for

and obedience to a superior, and not through any wish or intention I might have had to destroy you, for indeed I have not desired your death and do not now desire it, since you have given me no reason to do so. And well considered, the greater part of the blame which you place upon me is your own because you have very carelessly permitted yourselves to be misled without uttering a single word to me in regard to the road. If on the first day you were lost, you had asked some of the questions you now ask, I would have told you all, and the present unfortunate predicament would have been avoided beforehand. And even now it is not too late, for if you wish to grant me my life (since I was commanded to do what is past and could not do otherwise), I will amend the error that all of us have made. I now offer to lead you out of this wilderness into a populous country before the next three days have elapsed, for by traveling always toward the west without turning aside we can soon leave this desert. And if within that period of time I fail to fulfill my promise, you may destroy me, for I will submit myself to punishment."

General Luis de Moscoso and his captains were so incensed on learning of the wicked intention of the Curaca and of the deception wrought upon them by this particular Indian that they were unwilling to accept these good reasons as to why his transgressions should be pardoned or concede to his pleas that they spare his life and put faith in his promises. Instead all remarked in unison that "he who has been so malicious to us heretofore will be even worse from now on," and then gave the order to release the dogs, who in their ravenous hunger tore the man to pieces and devoured him in a short time.

Such was the vengeance that our Castilians wrought upon the miserable Indian who had misled them, as if it were of some satisfaction to them for their past hardship or some remedy for their present ill. And after having done so, they found that they still were unavenged and in fact more entangled than they had been before, for they now were entirely without a guide, since on consuming the corn brought by the other Indians, they had given these people permission to return to their homes. Hence they were utterly lost.

Placed as they were in this extremity, the Spaniards were confused and repentant at having slain the guide, for had they permitted him to live, it might have been that he would have led them out, as he promised, to a settlement. But perceiving that there was no other recourse, they seized upon the one the Indian himself had suggested, which was to travel westward without deviation. Thus after that man's death, they gave credence to what they would not accept when he was alive. Three more days they journeyed in great hunger and necessity for during the past three days they had eaten nothing save grasses and roots. And it was very lucky for them in their difficulty that the forests of this wilderness were open and not closed like a wall as are those in other parts of the Indies; for had they been, our Spaniards would have perished of hunger before leaving their confines.

Under these difficulties they continued always toward the west. Then at the termination of the three days, they beheld settlements from the top of some hills where they were traveling, and this sight gave them such contentment as one may imagine, although on coming to these places they found that the Indians had fled to the woods and that the land was weak and sterile, with towns which, unlike previous ones, consisted merely of houses sprinkled about the countryside in groups of four and five. Moreover these houses were constructed badly and arranged worse, and they appeared more like the huts of melon growers than dwelling places. Nevertheless the Spaniards assuaged their hunger with great quantities of beef which they discovered within the houses along with recently skinned hides. But still they found no cows on the hoof, and the Indians would never say from whence they had brought these things.

On the second day of their travel through that sterile and sparsely populated place which our men now referred to as the Province of the Herdsmen[3] because of the beef and cowhides, one of the natives attempted to demonstrate his courage by a strange deed madly

[3] *La Provincia de los Vaqueros.*

performed. It happened that the Spaniards had completed that day's march and were bivouacked on a plain in perfect peace when they observed a lone Indian with magnificent plumage on his head emerge from a nearby forest and come toward them, his bow in his hand and his sheath of arrows resting on his back and leaning slightly toward the right shoulder as the natives always carry it. Having perceived that the Indian was alone and so tranquil, those present where he came out from the trees were undisturbed. In fact they believed that he bore some message for the Governor from his Cacique and as a result they permitted him to draw near. But when the man found himself less than fifty feet from a circle of Spaniards who were standing about talking, he fixed an arrow to his bow with extreme gallantry and swiftness, and aiming at those in the group who were watching him, released the missile with great force. The Christians, on realizing that he was firing, scattered hurriedly to right and left and some dropped to the ground. In this way they escaped being shot, but the arrow sped forward to a group of five or six native women who were beneath a tree preparing food for their masters. One of these women it struck in the back and, after passing completely through her, plunged into the breast of the woman facing her. This second victim it penetrated likewise but stayed fixed in her body. Both women immediately fell dead. Having accomplished his savage shot, the Indian fled once more to the forest, and he ran with such swiftness and nimbleness as to show well that in coming to do what he did, he had possessed confidence in his speed.

The Spaniards sounded an alarm, and being unable to follow the Indian, shouted at him instead. Then Captain Baltasar de Gallegos, who happened to be mounted, rushed to the scene of the outcry, and when he beheld a man in flight and heard shouts of "kill him, kill him," he suspected what that man must have done. So hastening in pursuit, this cavalier overtook the fugitive near his place of safety and put an end to his life. Thus that unfortunate Indian failed to enjoy his heroic exploit, which was rash, as are all feats perpetrated in battle.

CHAPTER IV

*Two Indians give the Spaniards to understand
that they challenge them to single
combat.*

THREE days after this occurrence, there befell in that same
province, which they called the Province of the Herdsmen,
another and no less singular incident, which was as follows. The
General and his captains and soldiers had left off traveling one day
to recuperate from the hardships of the long marches made up to
that point, when at ten o'clock in the morning they saw coming
across a beautiful plain two Indian noblemen who were adorned with
magnificent plumes and were carrying their bows in their hands and
their arrows in sheaths upon their shoulders. When these men
arrived at a place two hundred feet from the camp, they began to
walk about in the vicinity of a walnut tree. Now they did not walk
close together and shoulder to shoulder but with one passing the
other so that each in turn might guard the rear of his companion.
In this manner they proceeded for almost the entire day without
deigning to notice the Negroes and the Indian men, women and
children who passed near them bearing water and firewood. Thus
the Castilians came to understand that the two Indians were not
behaving as they were for the benefit of the servants, but for the
Spaniards themselves, and they thereupon gave an account of their
conduct to the Governor, who immediately commanded that a
proclamation be issued to the effect that none of his soldiers should
approach them, and that all should avoid them as if they were
lunatics.

The Indians continued to do nothing but walk until the afternoon,
for it was their hope that two of the Spaniards might come out and
offer to fight. Then when the sun was near setting, there rode up a
company of horsemen who had gone out in the morning to reconnoiter the countryside. The lodgings of these men were not far

from where the Indians were walking, and when they saw them, they inquired as to who they might be. On being informed and on learning the order that had been published concerning them, that is, that they were to be avoided as though mad, all acquiesced save one man who, to display his courage, was determined to disobey. Shouting, "Plague take it, is it not wise for there to be someone more lunatic than they who might punish them for their foolishness?" he went running toward the Indians. This soldier was Juan Páez, a native of Segovia.

When the Indians perceived that only one Castilian was attacking, the man nearest came forward to receive him in order to make it clear that he had asked for single combat. Meanwhile the other Indian drew apart and stationed himself beneath the walnut tree, thus confirming their intention of fighting one against one and making it understood that his companion desired no assistance with a single Castilian even though that Castilian were mounted. At that Juan Páez attacked with the utmost zeal in order to overpower his adversary with a sudden stroke. But the infidel was awaiting him with an arrow placed in his bow, and on perceiving him within range, released this arrow, which struck him at the left elbow and after piercing the sleeve on both sides remained transfixed in his arm. Because of the violence of the blow and the wound inflicted, Juan Páez was unable to move his arm; in consequence his reins slipped from his hands, and his horse, realizing that they had fallen, immediately halted. For it is a very common thing for horses to behave thus when they feel the reins fall, and it likewise is the counsel of good riders to release the reins suddenly when a horse is running away and will not stop.

When Juan Páez' companions, who had not yet dismounted, beheld him in such peril, they attacked in a group and as quickly as possible, hoping to aid him before his enemy should bring about his destruction. Then both Indians, on perceiving so many Castilians advancing upon them, fled to a nearby wood; but before they reached it, our men lanced them, thus failing to respect the proper ethics of warfare. These two infidels had refused to fight as they were against a single antagonist, and it was not just that so many Spaniards on horseback should attack only the two of them, neither of whom was mounted.

Although not typical, we mention these events because no more important ones occurred. The Castilians proceeded for upwards of thirty leagues across this land called the Province of the Herdsmen;[4] and then at the end of that distance, the sparsely populated region terminated, and they saw to the west of them some large mountain ranges and forests which they learned were completely uninhabited. Warned by the hunger and toil suffered in the wilderness behind them, the Governor and his captains resolved not to go forward until they had found a road out to a settlement, and also to know beforehand what inconveniences there might be. For the purpose they commanded that three divisions of cavalry with twenty-four horses in each division, set out through three separate districts toward the west to ascertain what there might be in that direction. Moreover they insisted that these men go just as far as they posssibly could in order to bring an account not only of what they might actually behold but also of what there might be further on. For interpreters they were provided with Indians from among those domestics of the Spaniards who were best versed in the language.

With this charge the seventy-two cavaliers left the camp and in fifteen days returned, almost all of them with the same story. Each division reported that it had penetrated these lands more than thirty leagues[5] and had found them very sterile and sparsely populated, and moreover even worse the farther they advanced. This, they said, was what they had actually seen, but that they brought still more unfavorable news of what lay farther on. For many of the Indians whom they had captured, and others who had received them peacefully, had informed them that there were indeed Indians ahead but that they did not live in settlements or even in houses, and did not sow their lands. Instead they were unattached and roved about

[4]The main body of the expedition is presumed to have reached the Trinity River.

[5]In short, they may have gone as far as the Brazos River.

in bands, picking the fruit, grasses and roots that the land naturally afforded them and maintaining themselves by hunting and fishing as they moved from one place to another according to the advantage the season offered. Each of the three groups brought this information with little or no variation. And to it Alonso de Carmona adds that the Indians told them that on ahead to the west of the province where they now were, they would find great settlements of very flat and sandy lands where the cows were raised whose hides they had seen, and that there were many more of these animals.

CHAPTER V

*The Spaniards return to search for the Great
River. The hardships they experienced
along the way.*

WHEN they had heard a proper account of the route by which they had been assured they could reach the land of Mexico and had discussed it and considered the difficulties of their journey, Governor Luis de Moscoso and his captains agreed to go no farther, lest cut off in those deserts without knowledge as to where they terminated, all should perish of hunger. Rather, they decided to turn back in search of that same great river they had left behind them, for they now felt that to escape from the kingdom of Florida, there was no means more certain than that of making their way downstream to the Sea of the North.[6] With this determination they strove to obtain information as to a route that would enable them to escape the waste lands and wildernesses previously traversed. They learned that the shortest way was to proceed in an arc to the right

---

[6]Additional reasons given in the Elvas account for the decision to return were that they knew there was corn in Anilco and that they could pass the winter building brigantines for use the following spring. Again, they had no interpreters for traveling ahead by land, and, what may have been more significant, Luis de Moscoso longed to be where he could get his full measure of sleep rather than govern and conquer a land so full of hardship.

of the road by which they had come, but that this route would oblige them to pass through many additional deserts and unpopulated regions. And they found on the other hand that if they wished to return to the left, making the same arc, they would pass at all times through settlements where there were food and guides, but that their journey would thereby be lengthened.

With such information in their possession, they hastened to depart from those miserable lands of the Herdsmen, traveling now in an arc toward the south and obtaining information always of what lay ahead in order to avoid falling into any wilderness from which they would be unable to escape. And even though these Castilians took care while en route not to commit any grievances against the Indians which might incite them to war, and furthermore accomplished long marches each day so as to get out of the provinces quickly, the natives did not permit them to pass in peace but surprised them at all hours of the day and night with alarms and attacks. For the purpose of causing even greater consternation, they hid in the forests when there were such near the road, and when not, lay on the ground and covered themselves with grass. Then as the Spaniards passed, careless now that they saw no one, these Indians rose up and shot them maliciously with their arrows, only to plunge into flight when their victims retaliated. So frequently and so continuously did the infidels strike that they had scarcely been driven from the vanguard, when others of them rushed upon the rearguard, and many times they struck in three or four places simultaneously. They never failed to inflict damage, killing and injuring both men and horses; and the Spaniards without coming to blows received greater harm in the Province of the Herdsmen than in any others through which they passed. On the last day that they traveled here, the Indians gave them particular affliction, for the road, besides being rough, lay through forests and streams, thus affording very suitable passes for such footpads as these people were. Entering and leaving at their safety, they continued their attacks ceaselessly throughout the entire day, and in this way killed and wounded many Castilians as well as their Indian domestics and horses.

In the last onslaught, made while the Spaniards were crossing a stream where there were many trees, the Indians wounded a soldier named Sanjurge, a native of Galicia. This man we mentioned at the beginning of our history, and since he was a notable person it will be appropriate to tell some particular facts about him, for they all pertain to our story. But because these facts are singular, I submit what I have to say concerning them and concerning whatever else I may mention here or in any other place, to the correction and discipline of the Holy Mother Church of Rome whose most Catholic son I through God's mercy am, although I am unworthy of such a Mother.

While Sanjurge was passing through the center of a stream, an Indian shot at him from among the bushes. The blow received was so fierce that the arrow broke through his breeches of mail, penetrated his right thigh, his saddletree and saddle blanket, and sank into his horse to a depth of two or three fingers. At that the horse came running out of the stream with great kicks and humps in an effort to free itself if possible from both shaft and rider. The Spaniards nearby rushed up to render assistance, but on perceiving that Sanjurge was nailed to the saddle, and that they were not far from their camp, they carried him to his quarters, pinned as he was to both saddle and steed. Once there, they lifted him from the saddle, cutting the arrow between it and his thigh. Then on removing the saddle itself with great circumspection, they perceived that the horse's wound was superficial; still they were amazed that the arrow had penetrated to the extent that it had, since it was of the common variety that the Indians make without tip, solely for ammunition. This type of arrow, they make of reed grass, fashioning a point of the cane itself by cutting it obliquely and toasting it in the fire.

Sanjurge was now left stretched out flat on the ground to the benefits of his own skill, for among his many talents was that of healing wounds with oil, dirty wool and incantations. In this exploration he had effected numerous cures which had incited great admiration, for it appears that he possessed the special God-given grace of healing. Nevertheless after the battle of Mauvila, in which his oils and dirty wool, as well as all other things carried by the Castilians, were burned, he had given up his cures, even though he himself had been wounded on two separate occasions, once when an arrow entered his instep and came out at the heel, inflicting an injury from which he was more than four months in recovering, and again when another struck him in the knee joint and its surrounding flesh. The head of this second shaft, which was of deer horn, had remained broken off in his knee, and in order for it to be extracted, he had endured great martyrdoms. Yet with all that, he would no longer minister to himself or any other wounded person, because it was his belief that treatment without oil and dirty wool would be of no avail.

Although aware of his present emergency, Sanjurge would not summon the surgeon because of a grudge resulting from the harshness and cruelty with which the latter had treated his knee. Enraged at the clumsiness of that gentleman's hands, he had most insultingly told him that even though he knew himself to be dying, he would never call upon him again. To this remark the surgeon had complacently replied that it would be useless for Sanjurge to call upon him again at a time of need since he would refuse to treat him even if doing so might mean saving his life. Because of the magnitude of this hatred, Sanjurge therefore would not ask for the surgeon, and the surgeon, even though aware of his condition, would not deign to go and administer to him. It was expedient, therefore, that the wounded man assist himself with those things about which he had knowledge. So instead of the oil, he used pork lard, and instead of dirty wool, he used the ravellings of an old blanket belonging to the Indians, for it had been many days since there had been a shirt or anything of linen among the Castilians. And the treatment he concocted for himself was so beneficial that he recovered during the four days that the army, because of its many wounded, was resting in that camp. Then on the fifth day, while our men were traveling, he mounted his horse, and for the purpose of proving to his comrades that he was in good health, ran from one side to the other of the army, shouting in a loud voice: "Give me death, Christians, because I have been a traitor and an evil companion, for believing that the strength of my cures lay in oil and dirty wool, I have made no attempt to heal you and in consequence have permitted more than a hundred and fifty of you to perish."

With the events we have related, the Castilians left the Province of the Herdsmen and for twenty days traveled in long marches through other lands, the names of which they did not learn. They carried their journey now in an arc toward the south, and then it seeming to them that they were falling much short of the province of Guachoya to which they desired to return, they veered toward the east, never forgetting however that at all times they must point their course northward. Proceeding thus, they eventually crossed the road followed on coming but failed to recognize it because of the scant attention they had paid previously to the lands they were leaving behind them. When they reached this stage of their journey, it was already the middle of September, and they had traveled almost three months since leaving the town of Guachoya. And in the whole of that time and along all of that lengthy road, even though they experienced no open conflicts, never did they lack for unexpected events and surprise attacks. The Indians assaulted them at any hour of the day or night and always inflicted damage, particularly upon those who strayed from the camp. Like footpads, they would lie in ambush and, on seeing our men separated from their troop, shoot them at once with arrows. In just such instances in this journey alone they killed more than forty Spaniards. Moreover they would enter the camp at night on their hands and knees, and without being heard by the sentinels, would draw themselves along the ground like snakes, shooting both watchmen and horses. Taking them from behind in penalty for their not having seen or heard them, they one night killed two sentinels in this way. Thus with such continuous afflictions, they harassed our Castilians exceedingly.

Once during this journey, some of the Spaniards, because of their need for servants, petitioned the Governor to permit eighteen of them to remain behind in ambush for the purpose of seizing ten or twelve of the Indians who at each departure of the army were accustomed to come and search the camp for whatever of value might have been left within it. So it was that with the General's permission, twelve horsemen and another twelve footsoldiers stationed themselves among some dense trees, in the highest of which they placed a lookout to inform them when there were Indians about. In this way, they on four occasions very easily captured fourteen Indians, none of whom made any resistance. Then when they had divided their catch among them, they resolved to depart, but the Genoese, Maestro Francisco, at whose request the permission had been sought, was not content with the two captives who had fallen to his lot, but declared that he had need of a third and would not go away until he had seized another. His companions thereupon admonished him to be satisfied for the time being with what he had, and they promised to accompany him on some future day in an effort to seize more. Nevertheless, Maestro Francisco persisted in his purpose, replying that since he was in need of an Indian, he would not leave that place until he had taken one, even though it were necessary for him to remain there alone. And in spite of the fact that each of his companions offered him his own share in the division, hoping thereby to placate him since all understood that there soon would be need for him to construct the brigantines, he refused to accept their courtesy, remarking that he would not be so rude as to take another man's allotment and that he was resolved to capture an Indian in his own name. Thus with this obstinacy, he forced his companions to remain in ambush, though all did so against their will, for they sensed a woeful outcome.

Shortly after, the lookout gave notice that one Indian had arrived, and the Castilians in their eagerness to be off, waited for no more. Juan Páez, a native of Segovia whom we have already mentioned, now galloped forth and, without having profited by his previous experience, launched an impetuous attack. To avoid being trampled, the Indian took refuge beneath a tree and awaited his assailant with loaded bow. As Juan Páez passed alongside the tree, he thrust ineffectually with his lance; and when he came abreast of the Indian, the latter nailed an arrow near his left stirrup, thus causing his horse to stumble forward for more than twenty feet and fall dead. Close behind Juan Páez rode Francisco de Bolaños, a comrade from his own land. This cavalier now made at the Indian, but being likewise unable to pass beneath the tree, he threw his lance from the side, sending it over his left arm. The weapon had no effect. Then the Indian, who prided himself on being able to employ his arrows more skillfully than the Castilians did their lances, nailed the second horse in the same spot as he had the first, and this animal likewise reeled forward for the same distance as had the other only to fall dead at the feet of its executioner. Both of these shots were felicitous, but on releasing his third arrow, the Indian encountered an obstacle which cut the thread of his good fortune. A similar incident we related as having occurred in the province of Apalache.

CHAPTER VI

The intolerable hardships that the Spaniards suffered before reaching the Great River.

A CAVALIER named Juan de Vega (a man whom I knew in Peru and later in Spain), who was a native of Badajoz and from one of the very noble families of that city, had gone out behind these men but had paused along the way because of his belief that two Castilians on horseback were adequate for a single Indian on foot. But seeing the Spaniards stretched out on the ground with their horses dead, he made at the Indian with the utmost fury in an effort to kill him, and as he did so the two soldiers themselves arose and charged with their lances from the opposite side. Perceiving himself assailed from both directions, the Indian came running out from beneath the tree to receive the cavalier, for he considered this man of more import than those he had converted into footsoldiers or pedestrians. It was his feeling that because of the general advantage the Indians hold over the Spaniards in running, he would be free to take to his feet without molestation from any one of the three if he could but destroy this third horse as he had destroyed those other two. And his plan would have succeeded as he had intended, had not Juan de Vega come so well prepared, bringing on his horse a breastplate of cowhide, three layers deep and a half-yard wide. Diligent Spaniards made these protections for their horses from whatever skins of cows, lions, bears and deer they could obtain. Having emerged from beneath the tree with all the fine courage that a man placed in such danger could show, the Indian fired at the horse of Juan de Vega, and his arrow after passing through the three thicknesses of leather left a wound four fingers deep in the animal's chest. Had it not been for the breastplate, the arrow, being so very straight, would have penetrated to the heart, but the fortunes of war would not permit so much to this Indian.

Juan de Vega now lanced the man and killed him; but with his death, our Castilians were not relieved of the sorrow they felt at having lost two horses upon such a dismal occasion and at a time when, because of their carrying few, they needed them desperately. Moreover, when they came to examine the Indian, their anger and pain were doubled, for in physical proportion he was unlike the other people of Florida, who in general are well built and strong. This man, on the contrary, was small, thin and wizened, and his stature gave no indication of valor. Nevertheless his fine spirit and strength had rendered him so heroic that he had amazed his enemies and left them to weep. Cursing their misfortune and Maestro Francisco who had occasioned it, they set out upon the road and overtook the army. Here everyone lamented anew the loss of the horses, for in these animals they held their greatest strength and their profoundest hopes for overcoming whatever hardship they might encounter.

Harassed by these annoyances, so numerous and continuous, that the Indians inflicted upon them, the Spaniards journeyed on in search of the province of Guachoya and the Great River until the close of October of the year 1542 when a very rigorous winter set in with much rain, cold and strong winds. Being anxious now to reach their objective, they traveled each day without fail, no matter how bad the weather, and they came each day to their camps laden with mud and water. Here they found no food unless they went in search of it, gaining it most of the time only by dint of arms and in return for their very lives and blood. Because of such necessities and the inclemency of the weather, they felt the harshness of the road more than ever before. Moreover as time passed, the rains poured, the snows fell, the rivers rose, and the difficulty of crossing them so increased that even the small streams could not be forded. Consequently, in almost every day's journey it was necessary to construct boats; and in crossing some of the rivers, they were detained five, six, seven and eight days because of the perpetual opposition of their enemies and the scant provisions they found for making vessels. Such circumstances increased and lengthened their labors.

But in addition to what they suffered throughout the day, their difficulties many nights were so extreme that the horsemen, not finding ground on which they could rest because of the great quantity of mud and water, did not even dismount but slept, or rather passed the night, on their steeds. And let it remain to the imagination of those who read this passage as to how the footsoldiers would spend such nights since they had water up to their knees, and when it was shallowest, halfway up their legs. Furthermore their clothes, which were made of chamois and similar skins, and which consisted of a moderate jacket that served as shirt, doublet, cloak and cape, they always wore wet because of the many rains and snow and the fording of the numerous rivers, and because it was only by a miracle that this garment ever dried upon them. Moreover, they went bare-legged, without hose, shoes or sandals.

Since to these particular necessities and the inclemencies of the heavens, there was added bad food and lack of sleep as well as the great weariness of such a long and laborious journey, many Spaniards and many of the Indian domestics whom they took with them, fell sick. And this illness did not confine itself to the people, but spread to the horses, and as it continued to increase among all, both men and beasts began to die in great number. Each day two or three Spaniards perished, and on one day as many as seven died. Almost none of the domestics escaped, and since they represented such a loss to their masters, whom they served like sons, they were mourned no less than were the companions themselves. One Spaniard was accompanied by four Indians, all of whom died. Because of the haste to advance, there was scarcely time to bury the dead; the result was that many were left without a grave, and many who did receive burial were only half covered, for the majority of them having perished along the road, no more could be done for them. The sick had traveled afoot, there being nothing on which to convey them since some of the horses themselves were ill and the remainder were withheld from them so that they might be ridden out to resist the enemy who continued to offer unexpected attacks and alarms. While suffering these miseries and afflictions, our men did not become careless in their watches either by day or by night, but as soldiers, stationed their sentinels and body guards in order that their enemies might not find them unprepared, although for such caution they had so little health and so many infirmities, as has been stated.

Here at this stage, Alonso de Carmona, after telling at length of the miseries and hardships of this journey, adds that they came upon a sow which had been lost on their trip out, and that this animal had dropped thirteen pigs, all of which were now large and marked on the ears, each with a different mark. It must have been that the natives had distributed these pigs among themselves and identified them with their own particular signs, from whence one may deduce that this livestock has been preserved.

With the inclemencies of the heavens and the persecutions of air, water and land; the obstacles of hunger, sickness and death among both men and horses; the care and effort, though weak, of taking precautions and guarding against their enemies; and the continuous disturbance of alarms, sudden assaults and battles that the Indians inflicted upon them, our Castilians traveled throughout the months of September and October and on until the close of November. Then they came to the Great River. They had yearned for this river since that day when in the midst of such adversities and anxieties of heart they had determined to search for it, although only a short time previously they had so hated and despised it that with the same adversities and anxieties they had fled and separated themselves from it. And now on viewing this stream, they wished each other joy, it seeming to them that with their arrival here, their toils and miseries were at an end.

In this last expedition, which our men accomplished after the death of Governor Hernando de Soto, they traveled, going and coming and including the trips of the runners, more than three hundred and fifty leagues, in which distance there died at the hands of the Indians and from disease, one hundred Spaniards and eighty horses. Such was the profit derived from bad counsel, and even though they had reached the Great River, their losses did not cease; for, as we shall discover later, fifty more Christians were to perish in the encampment.

CHAPTER VII

The Indians abandon two towns, and the Span-
iards take lodgings within them for
the purpose of passing the
winter.

OUR Spaniards gazed upon the Great River with the utmost contentment and joy in their hearts, because in their opinion this river offered an end to all the hardships of their journey. Along its bank, where they happened to emerge, they found two towns, one near the other and each comprising two hundred houses. Furthermore, a moat with water drawn from the river itself encircled both places and made an island of them. It seemed well to both Governor Luis de Moscoso and his captains to lodge that winter in these towns in the event that it were possible to win the natives either through war or peace, for though not in the province of Guachoya, which they had been seeking, they felt it enough to have arrived at the Great River since this body of water constituted the most essential element in the fulfillment of their intention, which was to depart by means of it from that kingdom.

With this decision, although they did not come prepared to fight, they arranged themselves in squadrons, there still being among them more than three hundred and twenty footsoldiers as well as seventy horsemen. Then they attacked one of the towns, whose inhabitants abandoned it without putting up any defense. Afterward they left men here and went on to the second town, which was gained with the same facility. It was believed that the reason the Indians had not defended themselves was that they thought the Spaniards had come this time as valiantly as on the two other occasions when they had explored the banks of that river. For even though our men had not traveled as far as this province previously, their fame must have, along with the news of what they had accomplished in the lands of Capaha and Guachoya, and this fame no doubt so cowed these Indians that they would not now defend their towns.

On entering these places, the Castilians found a great quantity of corn and other grains and vegetables as well as such dried fruits as nuts, raisins, prunes, acorns and some additional ones unknown to Spain. Truly, had they, with the idea of wintering in these towns, busied themselves throughout the whole of the preceding summer in gathering supplies, they would not have collected so much. Alonso de Carmona declares that on measuring the corn found in both settlements they discovered that there was by count eighteen thousand bushels of it, and he adds that the Spaniards were exceedingly astonished to see this much corn and other grains in such a small settlement. But all of this food and the great readiness with which the Indians had abandoned their towns, our Christians attributed to God's desire to bestow a special favor upon them in that necessity. For had they not found these settlements as agreeable and well supplied as they did, all most certainly would have perished there in a few days since they had arrived so maltreated, weak and ill. Indeed they confessed to having been at this time in such a condition that they could do nothing to benefit their lives and health. And in spite of the discovery of the comfort and largess we have mentioned, more than fifty Castilians and an equal number of Indian domestics did die after they came to these towns, for being so exhausted on arrival, they were unable to recover.

Among those to perish was Captain Andrés de Vasconcellos de Silva, a native of Yelves through whose veins coursed the extremely noble blood of the two Portuguese families bearing his surnames. Also, Nuño Tovar died.[7] This cavalier was a native of Badajoz and a man no less valiant than noble. He was unfortunate, however, in having drawn such a harsh superior, for being forced by an error of love to marry without the Adelantado's permission, he had always received from him a disfavor and disdain very contrary to what he deserved. Furthermore Juan Ortiz died—that faithful interpreter and native of Seville.[8] Throughout the entire exploration he had served no less with his forces and strength than with his tongue, for he was an excellent soldier and of much help on all occasions. In sum, there were many very generous cavaliers and many noble soldiers of great valor and courage who perished, for more than one hundred and fifty persons died on this last trip. And the fact that so many and such fine people should have been lost without benefit because of the imprudence and bad management of their leaders occasioned great compassion and sorrow.

Having once gained the towns, the Spaniards agreed for their greater comfort and safety to combine the two places in order that

---

[7]And what was the fate of the beauteous Doña Leonor de Bobadilla, whose clandestine liaison with Nuño Tovar was so devastating to his political fortunes? She afterward contracted a second marriage with a Spaniard named Lorenzo Mexía de Figueroa, and their son, Gonzalo Mexía de Figueroa, became a boyhood companion of Garcilaso in Cuzco. (See Aurelio Miró Quesada y Sosa, *op. cit.*, p. 49.)

[8] The Inca is in error here. Juan Ortiz died in Utiangue during the winter of 1541–42.

their strength not be divided in whatever might offer itself to them. Putting their decision into effect immediately, they leveled one of the towns to the ground and conveyed to the other all of the food, wood and straw it had contained. In the best way they were able, they enlarged and fortified the second place and then proceeded to lodge themselves within it. And because they were weak and debilitated and as a result unable to work as much as they wished or as much as was necessary, they took twenty days to complete these activities. But with the shelter of good houses and the pleasure of abundant food, the sick (and these included almost all) began to convalesce. Moreover, the natives of that province were so peaceful that though holding no amity with the Spaniards, they at the same time occasioned them no bother or opposition, attempting neither to lay ambushes in the countryside nor to give them alarms and assaults in the night. Everything, however, the Spaniards attributed to the special providence of God's mercy. This town, like its province, was called Aminoya. It lay sixteen leagues upstream from Guachoya, the place for which our men had been searching.

Having now gained some health and strength, and perceiving that the moon had already begun to wane in this month of January of the year 1543, our Spaniards gave the order to cut wood for making the brigantines in which they would sail downstream to the Sea of the North, there being a great abundance of this wood throughout the vicinity. And they also made an effort to obtain other necessary things such as rigging, oakum, tree resin for use as tar, blankets for sails, oars and nails. And in all of these efforts, each assisted with great promptitude and willingness.

In his account, Alonso de Carmona states that on entering the town of Aminoya, he and Captain Espíndola, the Governor's captain of the guard, encountered an old woman who had been unable to leave with the remainder of her people, all of whom had fled. And he says that this aged person inquired of them as to why they were there, and on learning that they had come to pass the winter, asked where they planned to quarter themselves and their horses since the Great River overflowed its main channel every fourteen years, thus flooding the entire land and forcing the natives to take refuge in the upper part of their houses. And, she added that this was the fourteenth year. But, he continues, all scoffed at what the old woman said and cast it to the wind.

These are Alonso de Carmona's own statements, just as he gave them in his *Peregrinación*. This title he affixed to the small amount he wrote, which was not intended for publication.

CHAPTER VIII

*Two Curacas come in peace. The Spaniards talk
of constructing seven brigantines.*

ALREADY during this time and previously, news of how the Castilians had returned from their journey and were encamped in the province and town of Aminoya had been proclaimed throughout that whole district. When this information came to the ears of the Curaca and lord of the province of Anilco, whom we have mentioned before, he was afraid that the Spaniards might damage his land in the same way they had done on other occasions; and lest his enemies, those people of Guachoya, being favored by the Spaniards, come now to avenge themselves upon him and to perpetrate those abominations he had suffered at their hands in the past, he resolved to make amends for the error which he had committed at that time with his rebellion and obstinacy, an error which to him had proved so damaging. Not daring, however, to trust his person to the Spaniards, he summoned a very near relative who for many years had been and now was the captain general and governor of all his estate. This man he addressed as follows:

"Go in my name to the leader of the Spaniards and tell him that because of my lack of health, I do not come in person to serve his people and am sending you in my place, that I beseech them with the utmost sincerity to receive me into their fellowship and favor, and that I give my pledge to be their loyal and obedient servant in everything of which they wish to avail themselves in my house and state. Deliver these words in my name; and as for yourself and the rest of the Indians in your company, obtain the best results possible in whatever these Castilians command of you so that they may have faith in my purpose and in your own willingness to gratify them in all that may be to their advantage."

With this communication, Captain General Anilco (we give him the same name as his Curaca since we do not know his real name) left his land in the company of twenty-four noblemen magnificently arrayed in feather headdresses and fur robes; moreover, he brought a number of Indians who were loaded with fruits, fish and venison, and still two hundred others who were to attend to the needs of the whole army. Coming before Governor Luis de Moscoso, he delivered his message with a good countenance and with the utmost respect, repeating the identical words that the Cacique had said and afterward offering his person as a token of the fine spirit and the willingness of all his people to minister unto this governor. Then at the termination of his offerings he remarked: "My lord, it is not my desire that you give credence to my words, but to the deeds which you will see us accomplish in your service."

The Governor received this man affably and rendered him the same honor that he might have bestowed upon the Cacique himself. He expressed very great appreciation for his fine words, his spirit and his willingness; and he gave him many complimentary messages for the Curaca, saying that he valued that chieftain's friendship and held it in high esteem. Furthermore, he offered numerous expressions of endearment to the remainder of the Indians, all of whom were thereby rendered very happy. Anilco thereupon forwarded the Governor's message to his lord, and in the meantime he himself remained to serve the Spaniards.

Two days afterward, the Cacique Guachoya came to kiss the Governor's hands, and for the purpose of confirming their previous friendship, brought a great gift of such fruits, fish and game as were to be had in his land.⁹ This Cacique the Governor received likewise with much affability and many acts of endearment. But it gave Guachoya no pleasure to behold Captain Anilco among the Spaniards, and it gave him still less to see all of them honoring this man as they did, for as has been noted before, the two Indians were mortal enemies. Nevertheless he concealed his displeasure as best he could, only to show it in due time.

Both chieftains, Guachoya and Anilco, ministered unto the Castilians during the whole time they were in the province of Aminoya, returning each week to their homes only to come again with new gifts and luxuries. And even when the two of them were absent, their Indians continued to attend the Spaniards, who having placed their hope for leaving that kingdom in the brigantines which they proposed to construct, now occupied themselves with the utmost diligence in arranging the things requisite for them. In order to realize their plans, they placed the work in charge of the Genoese, Maestro Francisco, who was a skilled artisan in the construction of ships; and he, having computed the size the vessels must be according to the number of people who were to embark in them, found that seven were needed. Then they planned what was necessary for this number of vessels, and furthermore, lest the winter disturb their operations with its waters, they built four large sheds to serve as dockyards. Here everyone without distinction worked on an equal basis, and each without being ordered hastened to do what he ordinarily did most skillfully—some to saw wood into boards and others to work it with the adze; some to pound iron into nails and others to make charcoal, while others made oars and still others twisted riggings. And the soldier or captain who labored most on these things was the man who received the most respect.¹⁰

⁹ The Elvas account states that Guachoya's gift of fish was so great as to "cover the town" and that the Indians also brought hogs which had been produced by sows lost in that region the previous year. See above, Book V, Part II, chapter VI.

¹⁰ According to the Elvas account, the lumber was sawed by a Portuguese of Ceuta who had learned the art while a prisoner in Fez; the brigantines were built by a Genoese (the only man in the crowd who knew how to

Our men were occupied in such activities throughout the months of February, March and April without being disturbed in their work by the Indians of that province, who thus did them no small favor. Moreover, in all of this time and afterward, General Anilco proved to be most friendly, for he hastened with great promptitude to comply with their requests for things needed in the construction of the brigantines. He brought many old and new blankets, thus supplying a want which the Spaniards had feared would not be filled, there being so few of these articles in the kingdom. So it was that the friendship and fine efforts of this noble Indian made easy that which our men had thought would be most difficult. The new blankets they kept for sails, and the old ones they converted into string to be used as oakum for calking the ships. The Indians of Florida made these blankets of a certain grass like mallows which has a fiber similar to linen, and with which they do make linen also, coloring it exquisitely with such hues as please their fancy.

Anilco brought likewise a great quantity of thick and thin ropes for riggings, tacks and cables. But of all those things and others supplied by this amiable Indian, that which was most to be esteemed and appreciated was the good will and generosity with which he offered them; for always he arrived with more than they requested, and he came with so much punctuality within the limit of time that he undertook to provide this and that, he was never overdue. Moreover he went about among the Spaniards as one of them, assisting in their labor and telling them to ask for what they needed since he desired to serve them and to demonstrate the love which he held for them. For these considerations, General Luis de Moscoso and his captains and soldiers rendered Anilco the same respect that they might have rendered Governor Hernando de Soto himself, had he been alive. And Anilco merited this honor as well for his virtue as for the fine aspect of his face and his person, for he was in every way a gentleman.

---

construct vessels) with the help of four or five Biscayan carpenters and two calkers, one a Genoese and the other a Sardinian. The only cooper sickened to the point of death, but by the grace of God rallied in time to make two half-hogsheads for each brigantine.

CHAPTER IX

*Ten Curacas form a league against the Span-
iards, whom the Apu Anilco advises
of the fact.*

ALTHOUGH the Curaca Guachoya served the Spaniards and
provided them with things necessary for their ships, he did
so with much delay and with such niggardliness that one saw even
from afar how contrary his spirit was to that of Anilco. Furthermore, one noted the pain and anger he bore on observing the esteem
and honor the Spaniards rendered Captain Anilco, who was poor
and vassal to another, and that this honor was greater than they paid
to himself, who was rich and a lord of vassals. For he felt that it
should be the reverse, and that honor should be rendered a man
according to his possessions and not his virtue. And now from
this feeling, there was born within him an envy so intense as to
gall him exceedingly and permit him no rest, until one day, not
being able to endure his passion, he revealed it quite openly, as we
shall see later.

It is appropriate that we tell now what the Indians of this district
were scheming while the Castilians were at work on their caravels.
You must know that located in front of the town of Guachoya, on
the opposite shore of the Great River, as we have said previously,
was an immense province called Quigualtanqui where there was an
abundance of food and a large settlement. The lord of this province
was a youthful and bellicose person who was beloved and obeyed
throughout his own estate and, because of his great power, feared in
others. On perceiving that the Spaniards were constructing ships
for the purpose of descending the river, this Cacique reasoned that
they, having seen as many and such good provinces as they had
found in that land, would carry away news of its riches and fine
qualities, and then, as covetous people who were seeking a place
to settle, would return in greater number to conquer and seize it for

themselves, thus taking it from its rightful lords. It seemed to him, therefore, that it would be wise to forestall these Spaniards by issuing an order that they were not to be permitted to leave that land and that all of them should die there, for thus they could not give information in any place of what they had seen in the kingdom of Florida. With this evil objective, he commanded that the nobles and the illustrious people of his own land be summoned, and declaring his intention, asked their opinion. They in turn concluded that what their Curaca and lord desired to accomplish against the Castilians was most appropriate, and they thereupon advised him that his design should be put into effect with all brevity, and that they would serve him unto death.

With this common determination on the part of his own people, Quigualtanqui, to make his plan more secure, now sent messengers to the neighboring Caciques and lords, informing them of his fixed resolution against the Spaniards and stating that since the danger he feared and desired to avoid extended to all, he begged and exhorted them to lay aside those enmities and ancient passions which had always existed among them, and to hasten, unanimous and agreed, to obstruct and cut off the evil that could come upon them should strange peoples arrive to take their lands, wives and children, thereby making slaves and tributaries of them all. Each of the curacas and lords of that vicinity individually received the messengers of Quigualtanqui with much applause and many demonstrations of joy; and with the same ceremony they approved that chieftain's opinion and counsel, lavishly praising his discretion and prudence, not only because of their feeling that he was right in what he said but also because of their desire not to vex and anger this man whom all feared on account of his superior power.

So it was that ten Curacas from both sides of the river formed an alliance, and all agreed that each should summon what people he could in his land with great diligence and secrecy, collect the canoes and other apparatus that were needed to wage war against the Spaniards on land and water, and feign peace and friendship with these strangers for the purpose of rendering them careless and thereby taking them unprepared. Moreover, it was decided that each cacique individually should send his emissaries, and that these men should go separately lest the Spaniards suspect something of their league and in consequence take precaution against them.

The conspiracy completed, Quigualtanqui, as its principal author, sent emissaries at once to Governor Luis de Moscoso, offering him his loyalty and whatever of his service he might wish to receive. Then the remainder of the caciques did likewise, and the General responded by expressing his appreciation for their kindness and stating that the Spaniards were much pleased to have their peace and friendship. And in truth, being unaware of the treachery that this friendship concealed, they were pleased. The General himself was happy, since for many days his people had been surfeited with fighting.

Although invited, neither the Cacique Anilco nor his captain general, whom we also call Anilco, entered this league. Instead it pained them to know that the rest of the curacas would attempt to slay the Castilians, for they loved them well. And because of this love and of his desire to fulfill the pledge of loyalty that he had given the Spaniards, Captain Anilco, in the name of both his Cacique and himself, brought the Governor an account of what the Indians of the vicinity were plotting against him, and then, having done so, said that he again offered the service and allegiance of both himself and his Cacique and that they would attend his lordship with the same affection and loyalty that they had demonstrated previously. Moreover, he promised to inform the Governor in the future as to what was being plotted among the conspirators.

With many fine phrases, the Governor thanked General Anilco for what he had said, and he sent the same message of appreciation to his Curaca, placing great value on his friendship and loyalty. It is noteworthy, however, that the Cacique Anilco, although he, as we have said, offered his friendship and service to the Spaniards, would never visit the General and continued to excuse himself by stating that his health was bad. But the truth of the matter is that he confessed to his people that he was ashamed of not having accepted the peace and friendship the Castilians had offered when they came the first time to his land, and that this embarrassment would not permit him to appear before them.

Whether or not the Curaca Guachoya, who was also making demonstrations of loyalty to our men, had entered the league, could not be ascertained; but it was suspected that since he brought no news of it, he had consented to its formation and would join in due time. This suspicion was increased by another unpropitious sign, that of the hatred and rancor he disclosed for Captain Anilco, and the great pain occasioned him by the extensive honor and esteem the Governor and indeed all the Spaniards bestowed upon that Indian. This they did out of gratitude for Anilco's assistance in the construction of the brigantines and in addition for his loyalty in telling them of the uprising in that land. Guachoya was not mindful of this indebtedness and, instigated now by his past enmity and present envy, went about tearing down and discrediting Anilco with the Governor, saying in private all the evil things concerning him that he could. But Luis de Moscoso and his captains assumed that the chieftain was making a subtle effort to prevent their believing Anilco should he already have informed them of the league, or were he to inform them of it now. For they felt that the Indian's unwillingness to join forces with the other caciques had led Guachoya to suspect his opposition and fear his betrayal, and that the chieftain thus was secretly arranging in advance whatever seemed to be appropriate for his purpose.

CHAPTER X

Guachoya speaks ill of Anilco in the presence
of the Governor and Anilco responds
with a challenge to single
combat.

FOR some days Guachoya continued to struggle against both his old and his new passions lest he reveal them in public. But in these feelings he had no command of himself and eventually lost his patience as well as all proper civility. He now addressed many words to the Governor openly and in the presence of the numerous captains and soldiers with him, including Anilco himself—words which according to the interpreters were as follows:

"My Lord, for days it has pained me deeply to behold the excessive honor Your Lordship and these cavaliers, captains and soldiers bestow upon this man, for it appears to me that honor should be rendered each according to his estate, his rank and his wealth. In this individual there is little or nothing of any of these things, for he is poor, and he is the son and grandson of poor parents and grandparents. Moreover, it is the same with his lineage, for his rank is no better than that of a servant, and he is the vassal of another lord such as myself, for I have subjects who are his equal and who have an advantage over him both in rank and possessions. I have told Your Lordship these things that you may realize upon whom you are bestowing your favor and credit, and that from this day forward you may not put so much faith in his words, which could succeed in contributing to the injury of another. For being poor and having no lineage to respect, he will deceive Your Lordship readily unless you are distrustful of him."

This in sum was what the Cacique Guachoya said, yet the expression on his face and the many other superfluous and injurious words he uttered showed well the hatred and envy he bore for Captain Anilco. The Spaniards noted, however, that while Guachoya was speaking, Captain Anilco made no semblance of interrupting him, but without a word or move permitted him to say everything he wished. Nevertheless, when he perceived that the Cacique had finished, he rose to his feet and informed the Governor that since Guachoya had maligned his honor in the presence of his lordship and so many captains and soldiers, and had done so without regard to them, he now implored his lordship to grant him the privilege of restoring his honor with truth and justice in the presence of the same people. And he declared that he would be pleased to have Guachoya contradict him in anything that might not be as he told it, so that the facts of their case would be verified and brought out clearly, for in this way one might see the little or no reason Guachoya had had for abusing him. And since his lordship was governor, captain general, and supreme judge of them all, both in war and peace, he continued, then let him not deny this petition, for it was a just one and concerned his honor, which he valued so much.

Luis de Moscoso informed the captain that he might say whatever he pleased, but that he must do so without abuse and disrespect to Guachoya since to this he would never agree. Moreover, he commanded his Indian interpreters to translate whatever the captain might say, without omitting anything, so that it could be seen if he made any remark which was discourteous to Guachoya. Then Anilco, after having bowed most solemnly to the Governor, declared that he would speak the truth without disrespect to anyone, and he begged that his lordship pardon his having to be prolix. With these words, he seated himself once again and, turning his face to Guachoya, addressed to him the following discourse, in fragments, however, to enable the interpreters to translate as he spoke.

"Guachoya, you have sought without provocation to belittle and abuse me before the Governor and his cavaliers when you ought to be paying me honor for what you know (and which I shall tell later) I have done for you and your state. But now that I have the Governor's permission to answer you and thus restore my honor, do not contradict me in anything I say that is true, for I shall prove my statement with your own vassals and servants to your greater confusion and shame. That which may not be a fact or that which in my vanity and pride I exaggerate more than is just, I shall be glad to have you deny because it is my desire that the Governor and all his army know the truth or falsity of what you have said, and that they perceive the lack of reason you have had for saying it. Therefore do not interrupt me before I have ended.

"You say that I am poor and that my parents and grandparents likewise were poor. It is true that my ancestors were not rich, but they were not so poor as you make them out, for they always held their own property and with it sustained themselves. Moreover, I, with the aid of my good fortune in wars against you and other lords equally as powerful, have gained copiously what I have needed to maintain my household and family according to the quality of my person, so that now I can be numbered among those rich whom you so greatly esteem. And as to what you say about my being of vile and base lineage, well you know that you have not spoken the truth, for even though my father and grandfather were not lords of vassals, my great-grandfather and all of his ancestors were, and their nobility has been preserved even to my own person without having been corrupted in any way. Therefore, insofar as my quality and lineage are concerned, I am as good as you and as all of the lords of vassals in this entire district. You declare that I am vassal to another, and you speak the truth; for not all can be lords, since the eldest son of a lord carries on the estate and the younger ones continue as his subjects. Yet it is true that neither my lord Anilco nor his father nor grandfather has treated me or mine as vassals, but as near relatives who are descendants of the second son of his house and of his own flesh and blood. As such we have never served him in low and menial offices but rather in the most prominent positions of his house. You know that in my own particular case I had scarcely passed twenty years of age when he selected me for his captain general and shortly afterward named me as lieutenant and governor of his entire estate and sovereignty; therefore, for twenty years I have ranked second to my lord Anilco both in war and peace.

"You know likewise that since becoming my lord's captain general, I have won all the battles I have waged against his enemies. To be specific, I conquered your own father in battle and afterward all of his captains whom he from time to time sent against me. And finally when approximately six years ago you inherited your estate and for the sole purpose of revenge collected all of your forces and came to seek me, I went out to the encounter and in the ensuing battle conquered and captured you and your two brothers as well as all of the noble and rich men of your province. At that time, had I so desired I could have seized your land as my own, for there was no one within the whole of it to contradict me, and it is possible that the common people among your subjects would have been pleased rather than sorry had I done so. Yet I not only made no such attempt nor even thought of it, but instead regaled and served you in your bondage as if you were my lord and not my captive. Moreover I acted in the same manner toward your brothers, your vassals and your servants, even unto the least of them; and in the stipulations concerning your own liberty as well as that of your men, I was a useful mediator in your behalf, it being through me that all of you left your prison. Even though not valuing very highly the pledges and promises you made at that time, I served as your guarantor and surety; for when you should violate these promises, as you did during the past summer, it was my intention to return you to prison as I will after the departure of these Spaniards, with whose assistance, since they did not comprehend your wicked heart, you came to desecrate the temple and burial place of my lord Anilco and his ancestors, and to burn his houses and his principal town, all of which will be well claimed against you. This I promise.

"You state in addition that it is unwise that the honor and esteem due a lord of vassals be rendered one who is not such. You are correct even though that man may deserve to be the lord. But in connection with this, you are aware also that many subjects deserve to be lords, and many lords are worthless, even for becoming the servants and vassals of others. And this estate which so inflates your vanity and pride, had you not inherited it, you would not have been man enough to gain; whereas I, who was born without it, might have had it simply by taking it from you had it been my desire to do so.

"But since it is for women and not men to quarrel with words, let us avenge ourselves with arms, that it may be proved by trial which of the two of us deserves because of his efficacy and strength to be a lord of vassals. Let us, you and I alone, enter a canoe. By this Great River, one descends to your land, and by another which flows into it seven leagues hence, one enters my land. Let that man of us who is the more powerful along the route, carry the canoe to his own home. Should you slay me, you as a man will have avenged your grievances, since for you they have consisted in the favors bestowed upon me by my good fortune and the honors and grace these cavaliers have rendered and do now render me; moreover, you will have satisfied the envy and rancor which transport you against me beyond reason. And in the event that I slay you, I shall have dispatched you undeceived as to whether the merit of men consists in their being rich and having many vassals or in their deserving these things because of their own efficacy and courage.

"This is my answer to the words you have uttered so unreasonably against my honor and lineage without my having abused you in any way, unless you still take as an offense my having served my lord Anilco with loyalty and good fortune. But judge now if you have something in which to contradict me, for I shall submit myself to the test for the purpose of proving to these Spaniards that what I have said is the truth. And if you have sufficient manhood to accept the challenge I make in regard to the canoe, I shall gain satisfaction for all the malevolent words you have uttered."

CHAPTER XI

The Spaniards wound an Indian spy; the complaint which the Curacas lodged concerning the incident.

THE Cacique Guachoya made no response whatsoever to all that Captain General Anilco had said, but he did reveal by the expression on his face that he was ashamed of having started the conversation (for it does happen many times that a man who attempts to offer an affront finds himself affronted). Hence the Governor and those with him inferred that what Anilco had said was true, and thenceforward all held him in even greater esteem. But meanwhile, having concluded that the hostility of the Caciques, if permitted to continue, would redound to his own injury since it would keep them from providing those things necessary for the construction of the brigantines, General Luis de Moscoso told them that both being equally his friends, it was not wise for them to quarrel among themselves since the Castilians thus would not know to which of the two they might have recourse for aid. And on this basis he begged that they forget whatever enmity they might bear between them and become friends. The Curacas thereupon responded that they would be pleased to obey his lordship and vowed to say nothing further about what had occurred. But holding no faith in Guachoya's word, the Governor feared that he might lay some ambush along the road for Anilco and thus obtain revenge when the captain should return to his home. Consequently, when four days after the incident just related Anilco resolved to take leave, thirty horsemen were ordered to accompany him until they had placed him in safety. Anilco declined this courtesy and revealed his little fear of his rival by denying any need of the horsemen; and although he did eventually accept them out of obedience to the Governor, he traveled to and from his home many times afterward in the company of no more than ten or twelve Indians. This he did to give the Spaniards to understand that he had little or no fear of his adversaries.

While these things were happening in the camp of the Castilians, the Curaca Quigualtanqui and his conspirators were persisting in their wicked design and in line with it sent many envoys day and night with gifts and false messages. These men, after having delivered their communications, proceeded throughout the whole Spanish camp as if they were friends, in the meantime taking care to observe how the Christians guarded themselves at night, how they kept their arms, and what security there was for the horses. This they did to take advantage in their treachery of whatever carelessness our men might reveal. And the fact that the Governor gave frequent orders for them not to come by night was of no consequence whatsoever; rather, they behaved even worse, for they felt that as friends, which they made themselves out to be, they had license for anything.

Gonzalo Silvestre, whom we have mentioned at other times, was exasperated with their behavior. Like the rest of the Spaniards, he had been ill and many times at the point of death, but being now convalescent, was serving the second watch on a certain night at one of the gates of the town. At exactly midnight, he beheld two Indians approaching in the bright moonlight with great plumes on their heads and their bows and arrows in their hands. These men crossed the moat by way of a fallen tree and then headed straight for the gate. At that Gonzalo Silvestre turned to Juan Garrido, a native of Burgos, who was sharing his watch. "Here come two Indians," he said, "and I intend to slash the face of the first one of them that passes through this gate. Then they will not be so arrogant about visiting the camp at night when the Governor has forbidden them to do so."

"Let me render the blow," his companion insisted, "for I am a little the stronger, now that you are very debilitated."

But Gonzalo Silvestre replied: "The blow will be sufficient to frighten them regardless of how it is given." And with that he prepared to receive the Indians. Meanwhile, they, on seeing the open gate, which was a small wicket, entered it as if they were entering their own house, neither asking for permission nor uttering a word. When the Spaniard beheld their arrogance and temerity, his anger was doubled. So he slashed the first Indian across the forehead and knocked him to the ground; but scarcely had the man fallen when he arose and, collecting his bow and arrows, fled as fast as he could. It had not been Gonzalo Silvestre's desire to kill this Indian even though he could have done so, for he felt that what he had accomplished was sufficient to warn him.

The second Indian, at the sound of the blow, raced off without learning the fate of his companion. On reaching the tree spanning the moat, he crossed to where he had left a canoe on the Great River. Then without awaiting his friend, he embarked and passed over the river, sounding an alarm as he proceeded. Meanwhile the wounded Indian, because of the blood streaming over his eyes, or possibly because of a fear that the Spaniards might pursue and finish killing him, plunged into the moat and swam across, shouting to his companion who was already safe. When the people on the opposite shore heard his cries, they came out to give assistance, gathering him up and carrying him away.

At sunrise of the following day, four principal Indians came to the Governor to offer a complaint in the name of Quigualtanqui and all of his neighbors and fellow citizens of that district. They declared that the peace and fellowship which they had regarded as established among them had been violated and that in doing so the Spaniards had offended them exceedingly and shown general contempt for each of them because the wounded Indian not only was one of their most illustrious men but was a relative of them all. And since their kinsman was mortally wounded, they continued, it was Quigualtanqui's plea that his lordship give satisfaction to each and every one by issuing an order immediately for the public execution of the soldier or captain who had inflicted the blow. Then at noon, four other principal Indians arrived with the same demand, affirming now that the Indian was dying; and at sunset the original four returned with an identical complaint, asserting this time that the Indian was dead and that they asked satisfaction for his death with that of the Spaniard who had slain him so unjustly.

CHAPTER XII

The efforts of the Spaniards to make the brigantines. A very severe flood in the Great River.

ON EACH of the three occasions, General Luis de Moscoso replied that the Indian had not been wounded at his command because it was his desire to preserve the peace and friendship he had established with Quigualtanqui and the rest of the curacas, but that a man who prided himself very much on his soldiership and his observance of military regulations had done this thing while on duty. Therefore, he continued, should he wish to punish this person for the sake of satisfying the caciques, the remainder of his soldiers and captains would not tolerate his doing so; for strictly according to justice or to military law, a soldier could not be blamed for having performed his duty well, and the fault was that of the wounded or dead Indian, who had entered the gate without addressing the sentinels, and of the caciques, who had dispatched him at such hours after having been advised against sending their communications at night. And now, he said, since there was no remedy for what had already been done, the caciques in the future should act as he had advised them in order that there might be no reason for disrupting the peace and destroying the fellowship which existed among them.

Enraged at this reply, the messengers departed to repeat it to the caciques, who in turn were incited to even greater wrath by the boldness and scorn of the Spaniards. In consequence all of them agreed that while concealing their indignation so as to avenge it at the proper time, they should hasten to put into execution what they had schemed against their adversaries. And there was one captain within the ranks of the Castilians who was in sympathy with the complaint of the infidels, declaring it unwise to leave the death of a principal Indian unpunished and thereby give occasion for the friendly caciques to rise in rebellion against them. Indeed some of the Spaniards might have quarreled violently on this subject had they not been forestalled by the most discreet and least impassioned of their number, for the matter had arisen as a result of a certain secret rancor existing among them.

At the time of the incident just mentioned, the first days of March had already begun; and the Castilians, in their desire to leave that land, for the days were becoming to them as years, did not pause for a moment in their work on the caravels. The majority of those who labored at the forges and in the carpentries were very noble cavaliers who had never imagined themselves doing such jobs; but they were the men who ordinarily did them with the most skill, because their mental powers were naturally the best, and their need for better workmen made them masters of that which they themselves had not learned. The ships under construction we sometimes call brigantines and at other times caravels, conforming to the general language of those Spaniards who referred to them thus. And in truth they were neither the one nor the other but just some large boats constructed according to the weak and miserable capability that our men possessed for making them. In this work Captain General Anilco was the outstanding person because of the magnificent provision he made of everything requested, and he brought his offerings so profusely and so quickly that these same Christians confessed that had it not been for the kindness and help of this good Indian, they would never have been able to depart from that land.

Some of the Spaniards who possessed no talent for working with iron or wood were able to perform other duties of equal importance, such, for instance, as seeking out food for the entire group. These men made particular efforts to obtain fish from the Great River, there being need for them now that it was the season of Lent. They devised large and small hooks for the purpose, and one among them ventured to fashion his hooks so skillfully and subtly that it looked as if he had made them all of his life. Baited and set in long lines, these hooks were cast into the river at nightfall, and when taken in on the following morning were found to have ensnared very large fish, the heads alone of some of them weighing forty pounds (of sixteen ounces each). Because of the valiant efforts of the fishermen, there was fish to spare on most days, and because of the abundance of corn, vegetables and dry fruit found in the two towns called Aminoya, there was sufficient food for the entire time they were in that province and even a surplus to carry away afterward on the brigantines.

While this work on the caravels was in progress, Quigualtanqui and the other curacas of that region were not idle, for each individually was raising in his own land the greatest number of warriors that he could, it being their purpose to amass among themselves thirty or forty thousand fighting men and to make a sudden attack in which they would kill all the Spaniards or at least burn all the machinery and equipment they had completed for their boats, so that for the time being they might not be able to depart from the land. For the Indians were of the opinion that with the continuous war they intended to inflict afterward upon our people, they would gradually and easily consume them, because already they saw among them only a small number of horses, these animals being their main strength, and they perceived that the men themselves were now so few that according to what they had been told, two-thirds of those who had originally entered Florida were missing. Moreover, they had learned that their captain general, Hernando de Soto, who was worth the whole of them, was now dead. This news increased the desire to put their wicked scheme into effect, and they awaited only the arrival of the day which they had set for their treason.

And that day must already have been near, for some of those Indians who customarily conveyed the gifts and false messages of the curacas, on finding themselves alone with certain women who served Captains Arias Tinoco and Alonso Romo de Cardeñosa, said:

"Be patient, sisters, and rejoice in the news that we bring you, for very soon we are going to release you from the captivity in which you are held by these wandering thieves. For know you that we have agreed to decapitate them and impale their heads on great lances for the glorification of our temples and burial places; and we will cut their bodies into small pieces to be placed on the trees, this being all that they deserve."

The women immediately carried their masters an account of what those Indians had said. And in addition to this warning, they heard the noise made by the natives on calm and serene nights in different places along the other side of the river, and they saw the light of many separate fires. Such things made it clear to them that regiments of warriors were gathering to carry out their treachery.

But this treachery, Our Lord God forestalled temporarily with a very powerful rise in the Great River, for in those same days, which were the eighth or tenth of March, its water began to move swiftly out over some immense strands that lay between the main channel and its cliffs. Afterward the water rose gradually to the tops of these cliffs and overflowed to the fields with the greatest speed and volume, encountering no obstacle to keep it from inundating the land since the surrounding terrain was flat and there were no hills. Then on the eighteenth of March, 1543, (which has been computed to be Palm Sunday of that year, since the date precedes the reformation of the ten days in the calendar)[11] while the Spaniards in spite of all their labors and in conformance with the ceremonies of Our Mother and Lady, the Holy Roman Church, were making a procession in honor of Our Redeemer's entrance into Jerusalem, the river entered the gates of the little village of Aminoya in the wildness and fury of its flood, and two days later one could not pass through the streets of this town except in canoes. The flood was forty days in reaching its crest, which came on the twentieth of April. And it was a most magnificent spectacle to behold. That which previously had been forests and fields was converted now into a sea, for from each bank the water extended across more than twenty leagues of terrain. All of this distance was navigable in canoes and nothing was visible except the pine needles and branches of the highest trees. In his passage describing the rising of this river, Alonso de Carmona says: "And we recalled the good old woman who predicted this flood." These are his very words.

CHAPTER XIII

In order to complete the brigantines, a Spanish commander is sent to the Curaca Anilco for assistance.

BECAUSE of similar inundations of the Great River and other rivers we have mentioned in this history, the Indians attempt to settle where there are hills; and where there are no hills, they build them by hand, especially for the dwelling places of their lords,

[11] He refers to the change brought about by the Gregorian calendar.

both to give grandeur to the houses and to prevent their being submerged. The individual structures are placed eighteen to twenty-four feet off the ground on thick beams which serve as pillars. From one of these pillars to another, they cross additional beams, on which they build a wooden floor, and then above this floor they raise a dwelling with corridors on each of its four sides. Here they store their food and other valuables, and seek refuge from the great floods. Now these floods did not occur each year, but only when in the regions and sources of the rivers there had been snows during the previous winter or rains during the previous summer. Thus the flood of that year of 1543 was very great because of the many snows that we saw fall during the preceding winter, if it were not as the old woman said that the river rose each fourteen years. But this is a point which can be determined by experience if the land is conquered, as I trust it will be.

During this particular flood, it became necessary for the Spaniards to send out a squad of twenty soldiers, who were to travel in four canoes, tied two by two, lest in going singly they be overturned by striking against trees beneath the water. These men were to proceed to the village of Anilco, twenty leagues distant from Aminoya, for the purpose of requesting old blankets from which to make oakum for calking the brigantines, cordage for the riggings, and tree resin for use as pitch; for in spite of the fact that the Spaniards had provided themselves with all such things, they did not have sufficient to complete their work. Gonzalo Silvestre was chosen to accompany these twenty men in the capacity of commander because of his excellence as a soldier and captain and again because of the fact that he a few days previously had performed a great service and favor for the Curaca Anilco. For it happened that in the expedition which, as we have said further back, Governor Hernando de Soto made the preceding year to the town of Anilco when the Guachoyas committed such cruelties and set fire to the place, Gonzalo Silvestre had seized a lad twelve or thirteen years of age who by chance was the son of the Cacique Anilco himself. This boy he had taken with him along the whole route that the Spaniards had covered to the region known as the Land of the Herdsmen, eventually bringing him back to the province of Aminoya where they now were. And of all the five Indian domestics who had accompanied him on that journey, this boy alone had remained to him and escaped the past illnesses. When the Spaniards came again to the Great River, the Curaca Anilco had made inquiry about his son, and learning that he was alive had requested his return on the basis of friendship. And in recompense for the numerous benefits the Cacique had conferred upon his companions, Gonzalo Silvestre had restored the youth most willingly, although he, boylike and accustomed now to the Spaniards, had declined to go with his own people when delivered to them. So it was that because of this service rendered the Curaca, the Governor selected Gonzalo Silvestre, for he felt that with Anilco under obligation to him for the restitution of his son, that cavalier would obtain from the chieftain more benefits than any other person in the Spanish army.

Silvestre departed with the twenty men of his squadron, taking with him also some of Anilco's own people as guides and oarsmen. When he came to the town, he found that it had been converted into an island, and that the flood had passed on five or six leagues beyond. Thus at this point the river had overflowed its channel some twenty-five leagues. As soon as the Cacique Anilco learned that there were Castilians in his village, who the commander was, and what they came to request, he summoned his captain general and said to him:

"Because of the love that we bear all of these Spaniards, and because of the particular obligation this commander has placed us under with the restitution of my son, you, my Captain, will demonstrate our spirit and willingness to serve them by ordering our people to feast and regale them more than they would their own chieftain, and by giving them the provisions they request for their brigantines as plentifully as if they were our very selves. And note that I commit this matter to you especially rather than attempt it myself because I know that in every way and in all things, you will give better care than I since you always do so with whatever is entrusted to you."

This command issued, the Cacique ordered that Gonzalo Silvestre be summoned, but that none of his men be permitted to accompany him; for he said that not having received the Spaniards courteously the first time they had come to his land, he was so ashamed that for the remainder of his life he would feel the pain and sorrow of the cowardly disgrace and stigma he had brought upon himself, and that because of such guilt he dared not appear before these people. But he came outside his house to receive Gonzalo Silvestre and embraced him with great affection. Then he took him within and sought to keep him there during the whole time the Castilians were in that town. It pleased him exceedingly to talk with this man and to learn of what the Spaniards had experienced in that great kingdom, what and how many provinces they had crossed, what battles they had fought, and many other details concerning the events of their exploration. With such subjects as these they amused themselves during the days that Gonzalo Silvestre was there, and the Cacique's own son whom the Spaniard had restored served as their interpreter.

Among these and other conversations which they carried on continuously, the Cacique during one of the last days that Gonzalo Silvestre was with him, said: "It is enough, Captain, that without any of them ever having possessed the courage to put their feet on any part of my estate and sovereignty, Guachoya and his people did dare with the assistance of the Castilians to come to my town and enter and sack my own house with much impudence and with none of the respect he should have shown me. Moreover, in a never-anticipated vengeance for his injuries, he did other insolent and cruel things to the very young and the aged. Then not content with what he had inflicted upon the living, he proceeded to abuse the dead by removing the bodies of my parents and grandparents from their sepulchres and casting them to the ground, only to drag, tread upon, and kick their bones which I so greatly revere. And lastly, he dared set fire to my village and my house, contrary of course to the will of the Governor and of all his Spaniards, for I am well informed of everything that came to pass at that time. To this I have nothing more to add other than to say that whereas you will depart from this land, we shall remain here; and perhaps some day I shall exact satisfaction for the lost match."

These are the very words that the Cacique said to Gonzalo Silvestre, and he uttered them with a vehemence and sentiment of affront and rage that cannot be overstated. It was understood, therefore, that this chieftain had acted and was now acting so courteously toward the Castilians, first, because he did not want them to be inclined to favor Guachoya against him, and then because he wanted them to leave his land quickly in order that he might avenge his injuries. And it was for this reason that he had been giving and was now giving so liberally the things sought for the brigantines. He made every effort and exertion possible; and the blankets, cordage and resin they had sought, he quickly brought in even greater quantity than they had requested or even expected, for such things being scarce, they had feared he would not be able to provide them.

In addition to these materials, the Cacique presented them twenty canoes, some Indian warriors and domestics, and a captain to serve and guide them to safety. And at their parting, he embraced Gonzalo Silvestre and said that he should exculpate him with the Governor for not having gone in person to kiss his hands, and that in regard to the things which concerned the league of Quigualtanqui and his confederates, he would warn the Governor in time of what was being plotted against the Castilians.

With this message Gonzalo Silvestre returned to give Governor Luis de Moscoso an account of what had occurred on that journey.

CHAPTER XIV

*The incidents which occurred during the rising
and falling of the Great River, and
the information that Anilco
supplied concerning
the league.*

DURING the entire time that the rise in the Great River lasted,
which was forty days, the Spaniards did not halt in their
construction of the brigantines, even though the water was a hindrance to them. Instead they went up into the large structures,
which we have said they built high off the ground and referred to as
dockyards, and here did all tasks with most excellent skill and
industry, even going so far as to produce charcoal for the forges in
the wooden lofts of those places. This they made of limbs cut from
the trees which stuck up out of the water, for at that time everything
was submerged and there was no other timber or firewood to be had.
And in these tasks, which must have comprised the labor of the
forge, carpentries and calkeries, the men who helped most notably,
not only as assistants but also as maestros, were two brothers named
Francisco and García Osorio. These cavaliers were very close kinsmen of the house of Astorga; and in Spain, Francisco was a
feudatory lord. But noble as they were, they assisted so promptly,
skillfully and dexterously in everything necessary for the work to
be done that all of the other high-born Spaniards as well as men of
low birth were inspired by their fine example to do the same; for
producing results is more effective than commanding when it comes
to being imitated.

Since the inundation that came with the rise in the Great River
was so excessive, the warriors raised by the caciques of the league
against the Spaniards now dispersed; for it was necessary and even
obligatory that all repair to their towns and houses to give attention
to the things they had within them and to put these things in a place

of security. Thus it was that Our Lord, for the time being, prevented these Indians from carrying out their wicked plans for destroying the Spaniards or burning their ships. But even with their people scattered, the curacas never abandoned their evil design, concealing it by continuing to send false messages of friendship; and to these messages, the Governor himself replied with all possible dissimulation, permitting the Indians to believe that he was unaware of their treason. Never, however, did the Spaniards leave off being cautious and guarding themselves in every way necessary to prevent their enemies from doing them harm.

During the closing days of April, the river began to recede but just as slowly as it had risen, so that by the twentieth day of May the Castilians still could not walk about the town except by going barefooted and bare-legged through the mud and water in the streets. Now among all those hardships which our Spaniards suffered in the discovery, the one they felt most was that of going about with their feet and legs bare; for after the battle of Mauvila when so much of their clothing and footwear was burned, they were forced to do without shoes or hose. It is true that they did make shoes, but they made them of untanned leather and chamois, and the soles being of the same material or of deerskins were immediately converted into tripe on becoming wet. And even though by employing their skill for greater and more difficult matters, they were capable of producing sandals like those the Spaniards produced in Mexico, Peru and other places, they could not do so in the expedition to Florida because of not finding hemp or anything else with which to make them. And the same circumstance befell them in the matter of clothing, for encountering no woolen or cotton cloth, they dressed in chamois with only a short garment serving them as shirt, doublet and cloak. And traveling across rivers or working while the rains fell upon them from the heavens without woolen clothing to protect them from the water, they were forced almost always to go about wet and, as we have seen, dead with hunger, eating grasses and roots because of having nothing else. So from this little we have told in our history and shall tell to the very end of it, any judicious person will be able to deduce the innumerable and never adequately or even moderately extolled hardships which our Spaniards have suffered in the discovery, conquest and settlement of the New World— experiences so without profit to themselves or to their sons, a fact to which I as the offspring of one of them, can certify well.

At the close of May, the river receded to its bed, having gathered together those waters which had spread so extensively throughout that country. And then as soon as the land could be tread upon, the caciques began to recall to the campaign the warriors whom they had prepared, and each came forth determined to give quick execution to their enterprise and wicked design. This fact being made known to the good Captain General Anilco, he went in his usual way to visit the Governor, and on the part of both himself and his Cacique gave in secret a very special account of all that Quigualtanqui and his confederates planned for the damage of the Spaniards. He told how on a day soon to come each curaca separately would send emissaries to the Governor, and he said that they would do thus in order that the Governor might not suspect the league and their treason as he would in the event all came at the same time. And as a greater proof that he was speaking the truth and did know the secret of the caciques, the captain related what each messenger was to say, and described the gift that each was to bring as a token of his friendship. Moreover, he said that some would come in the morning and some at noon, whereas others would come in the afternoon, and that the messages would continue for four days, this being the period of time that the confederating caciques had allotted to finish assembling the people and to attack the Spaniards. Their idea, he explained, was to exterminate them now, but if they could not succeed in doing so, at least to burn their boats and thus prevent their leaving the land, so that afterward they might destroy them by degrees with the continuous warfare they would wage against them.

Having revealed those things which concerned the treason of the curacas, General Anilco continued: "Your Lordship, my Cacique Anilco, offers you eight thousand chosen warriors. With these men, who are feared by all in his district, you may resist and attack your enemies; and I myself am willing to come with them and die in your service. Furthermore, my master has said that should you wish to withdraw to his land, it is yours immediately for anything that may befit your service, and he very strongly urges that Your Lordship accept his person, state and seigniory to use as if they were your own. And Your Lordship can be certain that if you do retire to the state of the Cacique Anilco, your enemies will not dare attack you there, and you will be able to arrange whatever may be to your best advantage."

CHAPTER XV[12]

The punishment given the messengers of the league and the efforts made by the Spaniards until they embarked.

HAVING heard from Captain General Anilco the news concerning the treason of the caciques and the offers which he made on the part of his own chieftain as well as himself, the Governor was filled with gratitude for both and replied in terms of great affection. "I cannot accept the assistance of your warriors," he said, "because I do not want your Curaca to be detested and regarded as an enemy in the future by the other curacas and Indians of the district as a result of his having favored the Castilians so openly, and again, because it is unnecessary for me to wage war on my adversaries since I plan to set out down the river so shortly. Moreover, for the same reasons, I cannot accept your own agreeable company as a captain general even though I am aware of your great value and of how much consequence your favor and assistance would be to the Spaniards should they have to subdue their enemies by

---

[12] The 1605 edition states in both the table of contents and the chapter head that there are sixteen chapters. This mistake results from the fact that the Inca skips a number (VI) in enumerating his chapters.

sword. For since I am to depart from your land, I desire not to leave you hated and despised by your neighbors or to have them know anything of your having provided us with information concerning the league. Likewise I cannot withdraw to Anilco's land because it at present is not convenient for me to make a settlement in this kingdom. But," the Governor continued, "even though I am not able to receive the material effects which both you and your Cacique offer, I at least am going to accept your good intentions, that I may be mindful of them and of the obligation under which your words and deeds have placed both myself and the entire Spanish nation, for the Castilians will try to repay this obligation if occasion should be offered at some future time for them to do so. Moreover, the King of Castile, who is the emperor and leader of all Christian kings, lords and princes, will be informed of what your people have done for his vassals and servants, for I myself intend to command that a memorandum of it be written for His Majesty so that both he and his royal descendants may make recompense for it. This pledge and promise I leave to the Indians of your land and to their sons and successors in return for the kindness you have rendered the Spaniards."

With these words, the Governor bade farewell to Captain Anilco and, having consulted his own captains and most illustrious soldiers concerning the approaching event, held himself in readiness for it.

Four days after the receipt of this advice, which came during the early part of June in the year 1543, the emissaries of the various caciques of the league arrived in the same order and manner that Anilco had predicted, some in the morning, others at noon, and still others in the afternoon; and each brought the same statements and gifts that Anilco had given as proof of their treason. This circumstance being noted by the Governor, he commanded that his men seize them and place each off to himself that they might be examined concerning their league and conspiracy. And arriving at the fact, the Indians made no denial of it, but instead confessed very openly to everything they had planned for the purpose of killing the Spaniards and burning their ships.

Then the General, to prevent the punishment which he was awarding the emissaries from falling upon as many as it would if he awaited the arrival of them all, instructed that it be carried out quickly upon those seized that day so that they in turn could convey news to the others that their treason had been discovered and that no more of them should be sent. Thus, on the same day that these Indians came, when the Spaniards had finished taking their confessions, they punished them for the malevolence of their caciques; and the reward they gave for their mission was to chop off the right hand of thirty of them. These thirty came up with so much resignation to receive the penalty assigned, that one had scarcely removed his severed hand from the block before another had placed his hand there to be cut off, all of which provoked great pity and compassion among those who beheld it.

With the castigation of the messengers, the league of their curacas was disbanded, for they now said that since the Castilians had received notice of their desire to harm them, they would take caution and prepare themselves against attack. Therefore each cacique returned to his land, exasperated at not having carried out his wicked purpose. But all guarded this intention in their breasts, hoping to show it in whatever might offer itself in the future; and since they believed that they were more powerful on water than on land, they arranged for each to make ready as many people and canoes as he could for the purpose of pursuing the Spaniards when they should leave to go down the river, for there they thought to slay them all.

The Governor and his captains having seen that the curacas had indeed formed a great league against them felt now that it would be wise to leave the lands of their enemies quickly and before they might ordain a worse conspiracy. With this accord, they made even greater haste than previously to perfect the brigantines, although until then they had not been idle. Now our Spaniards made seven caravels, but not having an adequate supply of nails to construct decks that would shelter them completely, they covered in each of them only a part of the poop and the prow where they could place ship stores. In the center they carried some loose boards which provided a floor, and by removing one of these boards they were able to drain the water collected.

Then with the same diligence displayed in building the ships, they gathered whatever supplies they felt would be necessary, asking the friendly Caciques, Anilco and Guachoya, to assist them with corn and other grains and dry fruits that they might have in their lands. They butchered the hogs, which in spite of all past hardships had been preserved until that time for breeding purposes; but they still held on to a dozen and a half of these animals, for they had not lost hope of settling near the sea in the event that an agreeable site should be found. To each of the friendly caciques, they presented two sows and one boar, thus making it possible for them to raise swine. The meat of those killed, they stored in salt for the journey; and with the lard, instead of oil, they tempered the harshness of the resin used to tar the brigantines, in this way rendering it soft and liquid.

They procured some canoes to convey the remaining horses, of which there were a few more than thirty in all. These vessels were tied in pairs to enable the animals to travel with their forefeet in one and their hindfeet in another. And in addition to the canoes used for the horses, another was carried at the poop of each brigantine to serve as a ship boat. At this point, Alonso de Carmona states that of the fifty horses remaining, they slew the twenty which because of lameness were more useless; and that to kill them, they tied them one night to heavy stakes and opened their veins, thus leaving them to bleed to death. And he says that this was done to the great sorrow of their masters and with the compassion of all because of the excellent service these animals had rendered. The meat of the horses, he adds, they boiled and put in the sun for preservation. In this way they were able to keep it as ship stores for their navigation.

And now having concluded the things we have told, they cast the brigantines into the water[18] on the day of that great precursor, Saint

---

[18] According to the Elvas account, they were able to float the brigantines to the river because of the flood. Had these vessels been dragged over the ground, there would have been danger of tearing open their bottoms, for the planks were thin and the spikes were short.

John the Baptist; and afterward during the five days that intervened before the eve of those princes of the Church, Saint Peter and Saint Paul, they were occupied in loading ship stores and horses, and in dressing the sides of the brigantines and canoes with boards and animal skins as a protection against arrows. Two days before embarking they bade farewell to the Cacique Guachoya and to Captain General Anilco, thus permitting these princes to return to their lands. They pled with these men to live in true friendship with each other, and both in turn promised as much. Then on the very day of the Apostles, our Spaniards embarked, having first ordained that those whom we shall name in the following book and chapters should command their seven ships.

End of the Fifth Book

THE

SIXTH BOOK

Of the History of Florida by the Inca contains an account of the selection of the captains for the navigation; the multitude of canoes opposing the Spaniards; the order and the manner of their fighting, which continued for eleven days without ceasing; the death of forty-eight Castilians because of the mad action of one of them; the return of the Indians to their homes; the arrival of the Spaniards at the sea and a skirmish they had with the people on the coast; the events of their fifty-five days of navigation before reaching Pánuco; the many quarrels which took place among them there, and the reason for these quarrels; the fine reception given them by the Imperial City of Mexico; the way in which they dispersed through different parts of the world; and the wanderings and hardships of Gómez Arias and Diego Maldonado, with which our history ends.

It contains twenty-two chapters.

CHAPTER I

The Spaniards choose commanders for the caravels and embark upon their journey.

UIS de Moscoso de Alvarado embarked in the admiral ship as governor and commander-in-chief of the entire group, just as he had been on land, and his two brothers, Juan de Alvarado and Christóbal Mosquera went as co-commanders of the vice-admiral's ship. These two brigantines or caravels were designated the admiral's ship and the vice-admiral's ship respectively, but the others were simply referred to as the third, the fourth, the fifth, the sixth and the seventh. The Comptroller Juan de Añasco and the Factor Biedma[1] were in command of the third caravel; Captain Juan de Guzmán and the Treasurer Juan Gaytán, of the fourth; Captains Arias Tinoco and Alonso Romo de Cardeñosa, of the fifth; Pedro Calderón and Francisco Osorio, of the sixth; and finally Juan de Vega, a native of Badajoz already mentioned at other times, and García Osorio, of the seventh and last. All of these cavaliers were men of noble blood and famed for their exploits, and as such had given a good account of themselves in the events of this journey and discovery. Two commanders were selected for each brigantine

[1] Luis Hernández de Biedma (erroneously called "Antonio" by Elvas) was factor or accountant to the expedition. He was author of the shortest of the four main narratives of the expedition, a report which he presented to Charles V in person before the Council of the Indies in 1544.

so that when one should go out to perform some deed on land the other might remain aboard to govern the ship.

With the captains just named and under their command and leadership, there embarked fewer than three hundred and fifty Spaniards, almost a thousand having entered originally into that land. And embarking with them were up to twenty-five or thirty men and women whom they had brought as servants from distant provinces. These latter were the only Indians who had escaped the illness and death that the past winter had offered, for though originally more than eight hundred in number, the remainder had perished. And now the Spaniards took them aboard and carried them away, for they had not wanted to remain with either Guachoya or Anilco because of the love they professed for their masters, with whom they preferred to die rather than dwell in alien lands. No effort, therefore, was made to force them to remain, it seeming to our men very ungracious not to offer a suitable return for the affection the Indians had shown them, and at the same time very cruel to abandon them outside their own lands.[2]

This group of Spaniards and Indians set sail as the sun was sinking on the very day of the Apostles—a day so celebrated and joyous for the whole of Christendom, although for our Castilians a sad and lamentable one because of the particular thing they now were doing, for they were abandoning the fruit of the numerous hardships they had experienced in that land, and were forfeiting the guerdon and reward for the magnificent and heroic deeds they had accomplished. Without receiving any molestation whatsoever from the Indians, they rowed and sailed that entire night and on through the following day and night. Each brigantine carried seven oars to the side, and at these oars, all persons aboard, without exception unless it were the commanders, took turns rowing their hours. It is believed that the distance traveled during these two nights and a

[2] The Elvas account states that they took only those Indians belonging to persons of condition whom Moscoso could not refuse. The rest, all of whom were now Christians of their own will, were left weeping and lost among strange tribes.

day comprised the district and boundary of the province of Guachoya, which as we have stated further back, lay downstream, and
that the Indians might not have wished to harm the Spaniards while
they were in the limits of this land, either because the Cacique
Guachoya had shown himself to be their friend, or because the
natives themselves were observing some superstition and ritualistic
practice concerning the waxing and waning of the moon which at
that time was approaching its conjunction, a superstition such as
the Germans held according to what Julius Caesar writes in his
Commentaries. But the real cause as to why they did not pursue
the Castilians during those first two nights and a day is not known.
Nevertheless on the second day, there began to appear in pursuit a
most magnificent fleet of more than a thousand canoes which the
curacas of the league had amassed against the Spaniards. Now
since the canoes of this great river were the largest and best that
our men saw in the whole of Florida, it will be well to give a special
account of them here, for henceforward we have no battles to
describe other than those which occurred on the water.

CHAPTER II

Types of rafts made by the Indians for crossing the rivers.

THE word canoe, in the language of the Indians of the island of
Hispañola and all of its vicinity, means the same as boat or
caravel without deck; for these people call all of their vessels by this
name unless it is those of the Río Grande de Cartagena which, being
the largest, are referred to as pirogues. The natives of each of the
regions of the New World, and especially those of islands and
lands near the sea, make their craft large or small according to their
means for doing so. For instance, they search for the thickest trees
to be found, and by hollowing them out in the shape of a trough,
make boats of one piece, for they have not yet hit upon that very

meticulous device of fashioning them with boards joined and nailed along their sides. Neither do they have iron or a knowledge of how to make nails; and they know even less about providing forges and doing the work of calkers, or looking after such matters as pitch, oakum, sails, riggings, cables, anchors, and the rest of such things as are necessary for building ships. They take advantage only of that which nature points out to them and not that which they might obtain by their mental faculties. Thus, for the purpose of crossing rivers and of navigating what little they did by sea, the Indians throughout Peru and along the coast, wherever they failed to find wood as thick as canoes demand, made rafts of light woods such as that of the fig. They said that these trees were to be found in the provinces near Quito, and that they carried them from thence to all of the turbulent rivers of Peru by order of the Incas. Their rafts were made of five beams tied one to the other, with the center beam the longest, the first collateral ones shorter than the center, and the second ones shorter still, for in this way they could break the water better than when the whole front was the same length. I myself crossed in some of these rafts which still existed from the time of the Incas.

The Indians of Peru also make such rafts with a round bundle of reeds the thickness of the body of a horse. This bundle they tie very securely and, to make it cut the water, taper it a great deal, leaving the forward end raised like the prow of a boat and only two-thirds the width of the stern. At the elevated part of it they construct a little flat spot or table upon which to put the cargo or man they are to send from one side of the river to the other. Each passenger is placed face downward with his head resting on the raft and his hands grasping its cords, and he is warned with the greatest earnestness not under any circumstances to shift his position, lift his head, or indeed even open his eyes to look at anything. Once when I was crossing a very swift and turbulent river in this manner (and it is only in such rivers that the Indians issue their admonition, for no attention is paid to those which are calm and shallow), the native bargeman cautioned me overmuch not to open my eyes, and since I was just a boy, he thus planted some apprehensions within me as to how the earth would sink or the heavens fall, and as a result made me curious to look up and see if I might behold some enchantments or things of the other world. So when it appeared that we were traveling in the middle of the river, I lifted my head slightly and gazed upstream. And in truth it did seem to me that we were falling from the skies. Moreover because of the tremendous current of the river and the fury with which the raft was cutting the water and yielding to its current, the sight was enough to make me dizzy, and I was forced to close my eyes and admit that the natives were right in commanding me not to open them. In addition to the passenger or cargo only one Indian travels on each of these reed vessels. He, in order to navigate, mounts it at the very end of its poop, and throwing himself across it on his chest, proceeds to row with his hands and feet, thus directing it in the current until he has brought it to the opposite side of the river.

In some places the Indians make rafts of gourds which they entwine and tie one to the other until forming a slab more or less a yard and a half square. To this they affix a breast leather as to the saddle of a horse. Here the bargeman places his head and begins to swim, and as he does so bears his raft and its load upon himself until he has crossed the river, bay, lake, or arm of the sea. And if necessary he takes one or two assistants behind him to swim along and push.

In other places where because of their great current and ferocity the rivers are not navigable, or where because of the many crags and rocks and the lack of beaches there are no spots to embark or land, the Indians extend a thick cable of hemp from shore to shore, anchoring it to large trees or immense stones. A great basket with a wooden handle like an arm moves quickly along this cable and is capable of carrying three and four persons. It has ropes attached to two sides and by means of them is tugged from one extreme to the other. Being long, the cable sags a great deal in the middle; thus the basket on descending to the center must be loosened gradually, and afterward as it ascends the other half, must be pulled by hand from the opposite shore. In this procedure there are Indians who are responsible for getting travelers across, but at the same time the passengers themselves seize the cable and assist both in descending and ascending. I myself remember having crossed in baskets two or three times. Being just a boy of less than ten years of age, I was carried along the roads upon the shoulders of the Indians.

The Indians convey their native livestock by this same means, but with much difficulty, since to do so they must manacle the animals and throw them into the basket. They do likewise with smaller animals from Spain such as sheep, goats and hogs, but not with larger ones like horses, mules, donkeys and cows, because of their strength and weight. These more cumbersome beasts are taken by other passages such as bridges or fords, for the method of crossing in a basket on a cable is just for people on foot. Moreover, it is not to be found along the highways, but only on those private roads maintained by the natives between their towns.

Such devices for crossing the rivers are what the Indians of Peru possess in addition to their bridges, which they make of willow and reeds or rushes, as we shall show in its proper place[8] if God is pleased to grant us life. But in all of the land of Florida through which our Spaniards traveled, the Indians, because of the great advantage of having large trees appropriate for canoes, used no other means, although the Spaniards, as we have seen, did build rafts in some places.

CHAPTER III

The size of the canoes and the splendor and order the Indians manifested in them.

BUT returning now to the topic of our history, let us say that among the numerous canoes which appeared in pursuit of the Spaniards on the morning of the second day of their navigation,

---

[8] This he does in the *Comentarios Reales,* Book I, Part I, chapters xv–xvi.

some were observed of such unusually large size as to cause our people to marvel. The command ships and others like them were so immense that they supported twenty-five oarsmen on each side, and in addition, held twenty-five or thirty warriors placed successively from poop to prow. Thus many of these canoes had a capacity for seventy-five and eighty passengers with each of them placed in such a manner as to be able to fight without obstructing the others. Moreover, the oarsmen added to the supply of munitions for the canoes by bringing their own bows and arrows. But though so large, these vessels were made of only one piece of wood. Hence one may see what very handsome trees are to be found in that land.

From the size we have described, which were the largest, the canoes graduated down to the smallest, which carried fourteen oars on each side, none smaller being found in the fleet. In general, the oars are six feet in length, rather more than less, and their paddles are four and a half feet long and two feet wide. They are all of one piece and so shiny and polished that they could not be more so even if they were the lances of horsemen. When one of these vessels moves with all hands rowing together at full strength, it attains so much velocity that a horse running at top speed will hardly have an advantage over it.

In order for all to row simultaneously and in rhythm, the Indians compose various songs of different tunes, the length or brevity of which depends upon the haste or slowness with which they are moving. In these songs they tell of deeds accomplished in war by their own as well as other commanders, with whose recollection they are incited to battle and triumph. And there is still another curious detail to relate concerning the canoes of the admirals and of the rich and powerful men in this particular fleet. This is that each individually came tinted within and without even to the oars with a single color, such as, let us say, blue, yellow, white, red, green, scarlet, purple, black or some other hue if there are more; and this color conformed to the heraldry, or the fancy of the captain, curaca, or rich and powerful man who owned the craft. Furthermore, the oarsmen and oars, and the warriors even to the feathers and skeins of thread worn around their heads, and their bows and arrows—all were tinted with a single color without mixture of any other whatsoever. Thus had they been bands of cavaliers who with much fastidiousness wished to hold a tournament of canes, they could not have sallied forth with more exquisiteness than they now achieved in their canoes, for since these boats were numerous and of so many colors and in such an arrangement as they observed, and since the river was very broad and they could spread out in all directions without breaking rank, they made a magnificent spectacle to behold.

With such beauty and grandeur the Indians followed the Spaniards until twelve o'clock of the second day without occasioning them any trouble, so that they, being unmolested, might observe with more consideration the magnificence and strength of the armada. And as they followed, they rowed to the sound of their songs, which, among other things, according to the interpreters whom the Spaniards carried with them, praised and aggrandized their own strength and valor, vituperated the pusillanimity of the Castilians, and vaunted that even though these cowards and thieves now fled their arms and strength and feared their justice, such an effort to escape from the land would avail them naught since each of them would soon die in the water. For, they said, whereas on land the Spaniards were to have provided sustenance for birds and dogs, the Indians would now convert them into food for the fish and marine animals of the river, thus bringing to a conclusion the wickedness and damage they had inflicted upon everyone.

These and similar things they uttered as they rowed to the sound of their songs, at the close of each of which they gave tremendous shouts and outcries.

CHAPTER IV

*The manner of fighting which the Indians em-
ployed with the Spaniards as they
traveled down the river.*

HAVING closely examined the armada of the Spaniards, which
was small in number but mighty in quality and strength,
the Indians pursued it until midday without inflicting any harm,
but that hour having passed, their canoes separated into three
equal groups, thus forming a fleet with both vanguard and rearguard. Taking the lead in the first group were the canoes of the
Curaca Quigualtanqui, who was captain general of the league of
caciques on both land and water. It was not ascertained if the
chieftain himself came with the canoes, but the Indians did call out
his name very often both in the songs they sang and in the separate
shouts they gave.

Divided thus into three groups, all of the canoes now drew near
to the right shore as they proceeded downstream. Then those of
the vanguard, which had formed a long narrow squadron, made at
the caravels of the Castilians, not to ram them, but to pass in front
and leave them to the left so as to be able to hurl arrows more
freely. Cutting across the river in this manner, they moved from
one shore to the other, meanwhile throwing such a rain of arrows
as to cover the caravels from top to bottom and wound many Spaniards, for the shelter of their round and oval shields failed to provide
protection.

When the first canoes had crossed to the shore on their left, they
straightway returned to a place near the right bank and took the
front position. Meanwhile the canoes of the second group assailed
the brigantines in the same fashion as their companions, and having
discharged their arrows and arrived at the bank on their left, returned at once to the right to take a position in front of their
predecessors. Hardly had this second squadron finished passing

before the brigantines when those of the third assailed them in the same order and form as had the others, and when they had thrown another shower of arrows upon them, returned to the right shore to station themselves in front of the second squadron. Since the caravels had not ceased navigating in spite of the molestation of the Indians, they now came abreast of the first group of canoes, who, seeing them at such a point of vantage, set upon them again to do the same as they had done before. Afterward both the second and third groups acted likewise, returning when they had discharged their arrows to station themselves along the right shore. Thus in the manner of a very methodical tournament of canes, entering to hurl their missiles and leaving to return and take their places again at their posts, these Indians pursued the Castilians that entire day without permitting them to rest for an instant. And when night came, they did the same, although not so continuously, for they were content with making only two attacks, one at the close of the evening and the other at the break of day.

Notwithstanding the fact that the canoes in which the horses traveled were carried fastened to the poop, the Spaniards, when the Indians first assailed them, placed men within these vessels for their defense, for they believed that this was to be a hand-to-hand struggle. But on observing that the Christians traveling in these canoes were ineffective since the Indians attacked from a distance with arrows and would not come within range of a sword, and that these men on the other hand were receiving a great deal of damage because of their scant defense, they took them again into the brigantines and left the horses to the little protection of the oval shields and covers made for them from the skins of animals.

With the same perpetual struggle that they had borne with the Spaniards on that first day and night, and without any innovation or change in order, the Indians followed them for ten consecutive days and nights; but since I wish to avoid prolixity, and also since no particular incidents befell other than those I have mentioned as occurring the first day, I do not write of these days and nights separately. Only it is necessary to say that during this time the

Indians killed almost all of the horses with their arrows; there remained no more than those eight which happened to be better protected than the others.

Even though the Spaniards in general were wounded, none escaping, they defended themselves with their round and oval shields and attacked with their crossbows since they had used the arquebuses to make nails for the brigantines. For in addition to the fact that a lack of iron had created a need which forced them to do so, these weapons had been of little effect in that whole expedition and discovery because of the scant practice and experience our men had had at that time, a circumstance not greatly ameliorated by the poor provision they found for making powder after all that they had brought had been burned in the battle of Mauvila. In consequence the Indians not only had held no fear of the arquebuses but had scorned and ridiculed them; and as a result our men had not brought them.

CHAPTER V

What happened on the eleventh[4] day of the navigation of the Spaniards.

THESE ten days of continuous warfare and fighting with the Spaniards having passed, the Indians now left off and withdrew their canoes a little more than a half-league from the brigantines. Meanwhile our men passed forward and, as they continued their journey, beheld near the shore of the river a small town of up to eighty houses which appeared to them to have been abandoned. They now felt that they must be near the sea, for they believed that they had traveled more than two hundred leagues in those days, because even while resisting their enemies, they had continued to navigate with both sail and oar, and the river made no turns by

[4] At the close of this chapter, the Inca states that this was the twelfth day, and his subsequent dates indicate that it was the twelfth.

which they could have been detained. For this reason, they resolved to provide themselves in advance with food for the sea, and they issued a proclamation among the brigantines that all who were willing to go for corn should proceed to the town with the commander selected. At that a hundred soldiers disembarked, taking with them the eight remaining horses to permit them to regain strength and vigor and if need be to fight upon them.

Seeing that the Spaniards were coming to the town, the Indians who were there abandoned it and fled through the fields, in the meantime sounding an alarm and calling for help with much shouting and noise. Then our men after having hastened forward as quickly as possible, reached the houses, which were something like two arquebus shots from the river. Here they found an abundance of corn and different varieties of dry fruit, a large quantity of chamois, some of which was white and some tinted with all colors, and many blankets of different and very finely dressed skins. Among the last was a very broad strip of marten skins eight yards long and a yard and a third wide. Being folded widthwise, it revealed two facings, and thus came to have the breadth of silk. All of it was decorated at intervals with ropes of pearls and seed pearls, each type of gem being fashioned separately into little bundles like tassels and placed with much regularity. It was believed that this article served as a standard or some other insignia for their fiestas, merrymakings and dancing since it was not for the adornment of a person or room, or even a bed.

This strip of marten fur was in the possession of Gonzalo Silvestre, the leader of those men who went ashore, and with it as well as with what corn, fruit and chamois they could carry on their backs, all now returned quickly to the brigantines, from whence the trumpets were calling them most insistently because the Indians in the canoes and also those in the open countryside, having been summoned by the shouting of the people in the town, were hastening to their assistance. And since the natives on land were few, many had come out from the canoes to join them and thereby reinforce their number and their spirit for battle. Thus Indians were rushing up by both land and water with great impetus and ferocity to defend the town and attack the Spaniards, but the latter with the same haste they had borne on land now embarked in their canoes and proceeded with similar speed until arriving at the brigantines. It was necessary, however, to abandon the horses, for with the hurry and fury of the Indians, it was only under penalty of all being cut off and perishing that they could have got these animals aboard ship. And as it was, they ran so much risk that had either the Indians on the river or those on land advanced so much as a hundred feet more, it would not have been possible for anyone to have reached the brigantines. But God came to their assistance and delivered them from the death of that day.

And now the enemies, on perceiving that the Spaniards had reached safety, turned their fury upon the horses that had been left ashore. Removing their headstalls and halters to prevent their being hindered in running, and taking off their saddles to leave them unprotected from arrows, they set them loose in the open countryside. Then, as if these animals were deer, they hurled arrows at them with great fiesta and rejoicing, continuing to do so until they saw them all fallen. Thus came to an end on this day those three hundred and fifty horses which had entered Florida for its discovery and conquest; and on none of the expeditions which to date have been made in the New World have so many and such fine horses been seen together. Beholding their mounts pierced with arrows and being unable to go to their assistance, the Castilians experienced extreme sorrow, weeping for these animals as if they were their sons; but at the same time perceiving that they were that much less encumbered,[5] they gave thanks to God and continued their voyage. This incident occurred on the twelfth day of the navigation of our men.

[5] The Elvas account states that the horses had become a nuisance. The men in the canoes would weary of rowing and get behind, thus slowing up the entire fleet.

CHAPTER VI

The Indians almost succeed in overcoming a caravel. The folly of a vainglorious Spaniard.

WHEN the Indians had discovered through experience that by pursuing the Spaniards extensively they were not accomplishing their desire, which was to destroy them all, and on the contrary were causing them to navigate with more order and concord without separating one from the other, they resorted to a military stratagem. This was to withdraw to a greater distance from the brigantines or caravels in the hope that some, being relieved of care, might stray from the others and thereby give occasion for their defeat. So with this cunning they remained upstream, allowing it to be understood that they would no longer molest the caravels, which were now navigating with a favorable wind. Then as our vessels proceeded on their way, one of them, for no purpose whatsoever, separated from the others, and breaking the formation which all were observing, remained less than a hundred feet behind. The Indians, on perceiving that their trickery and deception had not been in vain and being unwilling to lose the opportunity offered them, rushed upon the errant caravel from all sides with the greatest fury and went on board to subdue and take it in hand.

When the remaining six caravels, which were moving ahead, became aware of the carelessness of their companion ship, they lowered their sails and returned with the utmost haste to give assistance; but although no more than a short distance away, they reached it only with a great amount of difficulty and labor since they were traveling against the current of the river. On arrival they found those Castilians aboard so pressed by the inundation of Indians which had charged upon them that they were defending their lives with their swords. They had been unable to rush to as many places as was necessary when their enemies were entering the caravel;

therefore some Indians were already within the vessel, whereas many others were holding on to its sides. But with the arrival of assistance, the Indians withdrew, taking with them the canoe from the ship's poop and five of the sows which had been reserved for breeding in the event that a settlement should be made. Now this was the outcome of the thirteenth day of the navigation of our Spaniards, and they, attributing to the mercy of God their not having lost their vessel, warned and charged each other anew to take care not to stray or get out of order lest they find themselves again affronted and endangered in the same manner. And with this warning they sailed two more days while the Indians followed less than a quarter of a league behind, waiting to take advantage of some confusion that might occur among them.

Observing how much on the lookout their enemies proceeded lest they lose any occasion wherein they might be able to attack, our Spaniards navigated with much circumspection and vigilance. But the great diligence enjoined was not sufficient to prevent a most pitiful and grievous misfortune from befalling them on the sixteenth day of their journey—a misfortune so much the more to be lamented since it was occasioned by arrogance and foolishness rather than by any danger which might have forced or necessitated their running the risk of losing their lives, as did forty-eight of the best and most valiant Spaniards who traveled in the armada. But there is no authority which suffices to gainsay the headiness of one overbold person, and a single fool destroys more than a hundred wise men can build. That the miserable outcome of our men may be better understood, permit me to tell at length how it came to pass and who was responsible for so much evil and destruction.

Among the Spaniards of this armada, there traveled a yokel named Estévan Añez, a native of Villanueva de Barcarrota. This individual brought a horse to Florida, which although of comic shape, was nevertheless strong and robust; and because of being so, or more likely because no arrow had struck it in the proper place, the animal had served until the end of the expedition and was one of the few that had been loaded aboard the brigantines for the journey we are describing. And since Estévan Añez had always traveled on horseback and had found himself in many past dangers, though without having accomplished anything of note, he had gained a reputation for valor. With this reputation, aided by his bucolic and clownish nature, he was becoming swollen with presumption and getting to be a fool. And now as an example of his madness, he left his caravel and entered the canoe at its poop, explaining that he wished to speak with the Governor who was traveling in front. Accompanying him were five other Spaniards whom he had beguiled with a statement that the six of them were to perform a heroic deed which would be the most notable and celebrated of all that might be accomplished in the entire discovery; and all five of them, being youths, had been easily persuaded. Among these young men was a cavalier twenty years of age, a natural son of Don Carlos Enríquez, who had perished in the battle of Mauvila. This lad bore the same name as his father and was as gentlemanly in person and as handsome of face as any human can be; and at his tender age, he had proved himself to be the offspring of such a sire, both in the force of arms and in the moral goodness of his life and habits. But now he and four other cavaliers, with a lust for gaining the honor that Estévan Añez promised, entered the canoe with that man, and on pretext of speaking with the Governor drew away from the caravel. Then perceiving themselves at a distance from their vessel, they assailed the Indians and shouted at them in loud voices to flee.

When the Governor and the other commanders of the caravels beheld the folly of these six Spaniards, they gave orders for the trumpets to sound a signal with the utmost haste for them to halt, and then with shouts and signs, they urged them to consider their danger and return to their ship. But the louder the cries of his people, the greater was the obstinacy displayed by Estévan Añez in his madness and folly, and he refused to return, on the contrary making signs for all the caravels to follow his lead. Having witnessed the disobedience of this fool, the Governor commanded thirty or forty Spaniards to pursue him in the canoes carried by the brigantines at their poops, for he had determined to order that the man be hanged as soon as he had been brought back. It would have been better, however, to have remitted the punishment to the Indians for them to cure his madness, as they did cure it, rather than to send to perdition many others who were lost for the sake of this one profligate.

CHAPTER VII

Because of the lack of prudence of one Spaniard, the Indians kill forty-eight of them.

ON HEARING the Governor's command, forty-six Spaniards sprang quickly into three canoes for the purpose of bringing back Estévan Añez. One of these men, Captain Juan de Guzmán, was exceedingly fond of traveling by canoe and he liked to manage his craft himself. And even though all of the soldiers in his caravel pled with him to hold back, they were unable to persuade him to do so. On the contrary, enraged by their insistence and especially by that of Gonzalo Silvestre, who as his most intimate friend had been the one most to oppose his going and had offered to go in his stead, he had retorted angrily: "You have always opposed me, and you would gainsay me the joy I receive from traveling in canoes by predicting some woeful outcome for me as a result of it. Well, for this reason alone, I am obliged to go, and you must remain behind because I do not want you with me." With these words he leaped into the canoe, only to be followed by Juan de Vega, another cavalier and great friend of his, who was a native of Badajoz and a first cousin of that Juan de Vega now in command of one of the caravels.

The Indians had continued to follow the Spaniards in a squadron of boats which were so numerous that they covered the river from one bank to the other and concealed the water for a quarter of a league behind. But when they caught sight of the canoe of Estévan Añez, which was approaching them, and the three others which in turn were pursuing him, they advanced no further and instead with much ease and uniformity pulled back on their oars, hoping thereby to lure the canoes of the Spaniards from their brigantines. For the men on the brigantines had lowered their sails and were now contending with their oars (although with much labor since they were moving against the current) in an effort to come to the assistance of the canoes. Meanwhile, blind in his folly, Estévan Añez on seeing that the Indians were backing up, mustered greater courage in his rashness, and instead of proceeding with caution, pushed forward with more speed to reach his adversaries, shouting now louder than previously: "They are fleeing, they are fleeing! Let us at them for they are fleeing!" Thus he obliged the three canoes in his wake to increase their speed, either to detain him or if possible to come to his assistance.

Finding the Castilians near at hand, the Indians opened their squadron in the center and let it take the shape of a new moon, continuing in the meantime to move back so as to encourage and afford the Christians an opportunity to place themselves in their midst. Then when they saw them enclosed and powerless to withdraw, even though they might wish to do so, they assailed them from the right horn, ramming all four canoes from the side and with so much impetus and furor that each was overturned and its occupants tossed into the water. And now since such a multitude of canoes passed over them, all of the Spaniards sank, and if any one of them happened to be seen swimming, the Indians killed him with arrows or with blows on the head with their oars. Thus without their being able to protect themselves, forty-eight of those Spaniards who had set out in the four canoes miserably perished on this day, for of the original fifty-two, only four escaped.

One of the four to survive was the mestizo, Pedro Morón, a native of the island of Cuba whom we have already mentioned; for he was a very fine swimmer and, having been born and brought up in canoes, was most dexterous in handling them. Therefore, even though he had fallen into the water, he was able with his skill and strength to retrieve his vessel and escape, taking with him three companions. One of these three was Alvaro Nieto, a most valiant soldier who as we said came very near killing the interpreter Juan Ortiz by accident when at the beginning of the expedition he had gone to the village of Mucozo with Captain Baltasar de Gallegos in search of the captive. Discovering himself in his present extremity, Alvaro Nieto, as the very fine soldier he was, fought alone in his canoe (if one can say this) against the whole armada of Indians, in imitation of the famous Horatio at the bridge and the brave centurian, Sceva, at Dyrrachium. Thus he detained his enemies while Pedro Morón piloted the canoe to a place of safety. But neither the strength and valor of the one nor the diligence and dexterity of the other would have been of any avail had they not found the caravel of the courageous Captain Juan de Guzmán nearby. For when this man had entered the fray, his soldiers, because of the love they bore him, had exerted more strength with their oars than had the others in order to save him if they could. His caravel, therefore, was proceeding in front and consequently was able to retrieve and save from death those two valiant companions, Pedro Morón and Alvaro Nieto (who were arriving with many though not mortal wounds) as well as two other Spaniards. And this caravel likewise picked up poor Juan Terrón, whose disdain for the fine pearls he carried, I mentioned further back. He had been able to swim to the vessel, but before he could clamber over its side, expired in the arms of those who had reached out to lift him aboard, for he carried more than fifty arrows thrust into his head, face, chest, shoulders and back.

Juan Coles states that he participated in this nonsensical peril; that almost sixty men, including Captain Juan de Guzmán, died in it;[6] that he himself was traveling in one of the three canoes, which he affirms were forty and some odd feet long and more than four feet wide; and that he escaped with two wounds which resulted from two arrows piercing the coat of mail he was wearing. All of these are his own words.

[6] The Elvas account records that those who escaped claimed to have seen the Indians take Juan de Guzmán into one of their canoes, but none could say whether he was carried away dead or alive.

This was the outcome, so sad and costly both to Estévan Añez and his companions, of that vain arrogance and presumption which he had assumed was bravery in himself, and which caused the death, so useless and unfortunate, of forty-eight other Spaniards who were better than he, since most of them were noblemen. And in fact they were more valiant than he, and being so, had offered to assist this madman. The Governor now assembled his caravels to the best of his ability, and after putting them in order, resumed his voyage, keenly pained, however, by the loss of his men.

All of the most noteworthy perils we have described in the voyage of these seven brigantines, Alonso de Carmona mentions likewise in his *Peregrinación,* and he especially notes the incident in which we said the brigantine found itself in danger of being lost. Moreover he adds that the Indians had gained this boat up to the poop deck, but that when the Spaniards expelled them with the aid of their companions, they slew thirty of them with knife blows and pushed the remainder into the water, where they were picked up by their own canoes. He tells of how the Castilians abandoned the horses because of pressure put upon them by the Indians in embarking, and he mentions the death of Captain Juan de Guzmán and that of Juan Terrón, which he says occurred on the side of the caravel, although he does not give the man's name. And finally he states that the Indians followed the Castilians to the sea, where they left them.

I am always pleased to present what these two eyewitnesses offer me in their accounts, for they were on this very journey. But neither tells much more than I have told and will tell in mentioning them, for they wrote very little, in fact no more of the most noteworthy things than what they could remember as having experienced themselves. For example, they do not say a word about all of these incidents, numerous as they are, in which I make no mention of them.

CHAPTER VIII

The Indians return to their homes and the Spaniards sail on until they recognize the sea.

THE Indians, after this fine occasion which they turned in their favor on that sixteenth day of the journey of the Spaniards, continued their pursuit throughout the remainder of that day and night, shouting and crying out at our men continuously as they taunted them with their victory. Then with the dawn of the seventeenth day, they worshiped the rising sun, making a joyous salvo with a great clamor and clatter of voices, trumpets, drums, fifes, shells and other noisy instruments; and when they had rendered thanks to it, as their god, for the victory gained, they withdrew their forces and returned to their lands, it seeming to them now that they had come a far distance. For according to what was believed, they, with these continuous combats and attacks, which they inflicted upon our Spaniards day and night, had followed them downstream more than four hundred leagues; and always in their songs and shouts, they had called out only the name of their captain general, Quigualtanqui, never uttering that of any other cacique, as if to say that it was this great prince alone who was waging all of that warfare upon them. Afterward when these Spaniards came to Mexico and related the events of this unhappy expedition to Don Antonio de Mendoza, then viceroy of that kingdom, and to his son, Don Francisco de Mendoza, who later was commander-in-chief of the galleys of Spain, and particularly when they told of the dangers experienced on the Great River and the savage persecutions inflicted upon them by the subjects of that famed cacique while crying out his name, the Viceroy, in such conversations and elsewhere and wherever he encountered some captain or soldier of consequence, would always say in a gracious though sententious manner: "Truly, my lords, Quigualtanqui must have been a real man."[7] And with this remark he revived the grandeurs and eternized the name of that Indian.

---

[7] *hombre de bien*—or in other words "what a man!"

On seeing that the infidels were gone, our Spaniards concluded that the sea was nearby, and that it was for this reason that their enemies had withdrawn and returned to their homes. At this place the river was already so wide that from its center no land could be seen on either side. Along its banks nothing was visible save some marshes of very tall rushes which appeared to be, or really were, forests of great trees. According to what could be determined by sight, the river must have been more than fifteen leagues across at this point, but even so, our men dared not approach its shores or leave the center of its current lest they encounter some swamps or sand banks where they might be lost. Furthermore they did not know whether they were still traveling on the river or if they were already in the sea.

With this uncertainty, but with the aid of a good wind, they proceeded for three more days by sail and oar, these being the seventeenth, eighteenth and nineteenth days of their navigation. Then when the sun rose on the twentieth day, they fully recognized the sea. Here to the left of them as they traveled they descried a very great quantity of timber which the river in its floods had carried there and piled up in such a way that it appeared to be a massive island. A half-league beyond this wood was an uninhabited island which they judged must be of the type formed by large rivers at their outlet, and they therefore came to the conclusion that they had already reached the sea.

And now not knowing where they were or what distance lay between them and the land of Christians, they agreed to examine their brigantines or caravels before entering the sea. Accordingly, they unloaded them with great diligence and placed their cargo on the island of wood in order to careen them if necessary or to determine if there were something in the joints to mend. Furthermore they butchered nine or ten sows which they were still carrying alive. Three days were occupied in these activities, though it is true that more time was spent in resting from previous toil and taking on new vigor and strength for what was to come than in repairing the caravels, for there was very little to do on them, and the greatest need of our Castilians was for sleep, since the continuous vigil the Indians had forced them to observe day and night had left them very weary. As a result, they slept during those three days as if they were dead.

Just precisely how many leagues our Spaniards covered during those nineteen complete days and one additional night en route to the sea where they now were, could not be learned; for fighting continuously with the Indians as they did, they had had no opportunity to compute the distance they were navigating. But when eventually they found themselves free of enemies, they talked with each other of such matters and afterward in Mexico discussed them in the presence of persons experienced in the navigation of oceans and rivers. And there were many opinions and arguments; for some declared that they traveled twenty leagues each twenty-four hours, and some said it was thirty, while others said forty, and still others said more and others less. But the majority agreed that twenty-five leagues should be allowed for each complete day and night because they had navigated always by means of both sail and oar, had never lacked wind, and had never encountered any bends in the river which might have detained them. According to this reckoning our Spaniards found that they had traveled a little less than five hundred leagues between the place they embarked and the sea. In making a calculation, anyone can form his own opinion and give the number of leagues he may wish, but with the warning and presupposition that in addition to aid received from the wind, the men themselves did their utmost with the oars to press forward and leave behind them the land of those enemies who had been so anxious to destroy them.

Juan Coles says that in all there were seven hundred leagues; therefore he must be giving the opinion of those who allowed thirty-five leagues of navigation for each twenty-four hours of time.

CHAPTER IX

The number of leagues that the Spaniards journeyed inland.

SOME may be amazed to read that our Spaniards went as far inland as I have affirmed, and they perhaps will doubt what I have stated. But my reply to such people is that they should not be surprised to learn that the Spaniards traveled much farther inland, for they reached the very fountainheads of the Great River. At the site where they embarked afterward in the province of Aminoya, which was near that of Guachoya, the river was nineteen fathoms deep and a quarter of a league wide, the same as I said it was when they sounded it for the purpose of lowering into its depths the body of the Governor and Adelantado Hernando de Soto. Again, those who presume to understand something of cosmography have declared that there were three hundred leagues between the place of embarkation and the source of the river, and I am giving the most conservative opinion, for others have said many more. Thus it was estimated that this river in its course to the sea flowed for a distance of eight hundred leagues, and our Spaniards traveled its entire length into the land. Therefore, when it may please God for the kingdom of Florida to be won, we may judge by the length of the Great River just how far our men did separate themselves from the sea, although I at present can offer no more proof of my account than what I have written. And indeed it is difficult to bring to light even this little since so many years have gone by and the purpose of the people involved was not to mark off land, even though they were exploring it, but to search for gold and silver. Consequently, it will be necessary to accept here the plea I have given elsewhere concerning the discrepancies of my account in matters of cosmography.

But I should like for my history to have been recorded with great accuracy in order to have given more and better information concerning the kingdom of Florida since my primary aim in this task,

which has proved no small one for me, has been none other than
to present a report to my lord the King and to the Republic of Spain
of what Spaniards have discovered so near to their own land. This
I do that they may not permit themselves to lose what their predecessors struggled for, and instead may strive and become inspired to
conquer and populate a kingdom as extensive and fertile as Florida
is. And the essential thing is the augmentation of the Catholic
Faith, for here is a place where it can be disseminated extensively
among people who, because of having few ceremonies and super-
stitions in their paganism to abandon, are disposed to receive it with
facility. Now it is the duty of Spaniards more than other Catholics
to spread this faith since God in his mercy has chosen them to preach
his gospel in the New World, which they already hold in sovereignty; and it would be much to their dishonor and disgrace should
other peoples gain control of these pagans even though it were by
this same divine office of preaching. Moreover, this obligation is
magnified by the fact that almost all of our neighboring nations are
infected with the abominable heresies of these unhappy times, and
it is profoundly to be feared that they may inseminate their doctrines
within such simple people while attempting as they already have
done to settle among them. And should the enemy now, because of
our carelessness and our having fallen asleep, plant snares and
cockles in the great kingdom of Florida, which is such an essential
part of that new world belonging to Spain, our nation would be held
to account; for Jesus Christ our Lord and the Roman Church, His
Wife, Mother and Our Lady have given to Spaniards the seed of
truth and the faculty and power to sow it as they have sown it for
a hundred and ten years and are sowing it in the most and best
parts of this new world.

But in addition to those things which pertain to religion, Spaniards of today if just for their individual honor and profit ought to
force themselves to the conquest of an empire whose lands are as
long and broad and as fertile and suitable for human life as we
have seen these to be. For in regard to the mines of gold and silver
which are so greatly desired, it is impossible that they will not be

found if looked for prudently; they have not been lacking in any province of the New World and will not be lacking in this one. And while they are being discovered, one can enjoy the wealth of pearls, so abundant, large and beautiful as we have reported them, and of silk, for the culture of which we have seen such a quantity of mulberry trees. Moreover for the propagation and care of all species of livestock, a greater abundance of pasture land and fertility of soil than that which this kingdom affords cannot be desired.

Let us beseech the Lord, therefore, to encourage Spaniards not to be amiss in this respect or lose zeal in their good fortunes since each day in all other parts of the New World additional kingdoms and provinces are being discovered and conquered which are more difficult to gain than those of Florida. In order to enter and subdue that kingdom they have an easy journey from Spain, it being possible for the same ship to make two voyages within a year; and to obtain horses, they have the whole of the land of Mexico where many very excellent steeds are to be found. Moreover, should help be needed, it could be brought from the islands of Santo Domingo and their surrounding territories, as well as from New Spain and Tierra-Firme, for they have the advantage of the Great River, which is capable of receiving any armada whatsoever, and can be ascended easily whenever one might wish.

As for myself, I can say that had the Lord given me wealth conformable to my spirit and desire, I should be pleased to spend it along with my life in this heroic undertaking. Such an achievement, however, must be reserved for some very fortunate person, as that man will be who accomplishes it. And when it is done, those doubtful points in my history, for which I have often apologized, will be cleared. But let us return now to my story. Because of my passionate desire to see it completed, I neither shun the labor, which is now intolerable to me, nor do I spare my feeble health, which already is very much spent, or indeed desire health now for any other purpose; for should I die before publishing this story, Spain, to whom I am so indebted, will be deprived of it.

CHAPTER X

*A battle that the Spaniards had with the Indians
of the coast.*

AS I have said, the Spaniards were three days in taking care of the
caravels and restoring their bodies, for their greatest need was
to satisfy a drowsiness which had wearied them exceedingly. Then
in the afternoon of the third day, they caught sight of seven canoes
setting out toward them from some rushes, and in the first of these
canoes they beheld an Indian very different in aspect and color from
those they had left inland, for he was as large as a Philistine and as
black as an Ethiopian. The cause of this exceptional swarthiness in
the coastal Indians is the salt water in which they are continually
fishing, for the land being sterile, they sustain themselves by this
means. Furthermore, the heat of the sun, which is more intense
along the coast than inland, contributes toward making them dark.
Standing in the prow of his canoe, this Indian shouted to the Castilians in a gross and pompous voice: "Thieves, vagabonds and
loiterers who without honor or shame travel along this coast dis-
quieting its inhabitants, depart from this place immediately by one
of the two mouths of the river, if you do not want me to destroy
you all and burn your ships. And see to it that I do not find you
here tonight, for if I do, no man of you will escape with his life."

The Spaniards were able to comprehend what this individual was
saying by the many words which their servants interpreted, and by the
gestures which he made with his arms and body as he pointed to the
two entrances of the Great River that formed the island which, as
we have stated, lay ahead. But when he had spoken, the Indian,
without awaiting a reply, returned to the rushes. At this place, Juan
Coles reports the following words in addition to those I have given:
"If we possessed such large canoes as yours (he means to say ships),
we would follow you to your own land and conquer it, for we too
are men like yourselves."

Having considered the remarks of this particular man and noted the pride disclosed in them as well as in his countenance, and having observed in addition that these Indians were returning to join others who from time to time had begun to appear from among the rushes as if lurking in ambush, the Spaniards agreed on the wisdom of making it clear that they did not fear these people so that they would not muster the courage to come out and hurl arrows or throw fire over the caravels. Such things the Indians could do better at night than by day, for they knew how to attack and flee to safety both by land and sea, whereas the Spaniards were unfamiliar with any of the terrain. Therefore, with this decision, a hundred of our men entered the five canoes reserved for the service of the brigantines, and went forth under the command of Gonzalo Silvestre and Alvaro Nieto to search for Indians.

They found a great number concealed in the rushes with a fleet of more than sixty small canoes amassed for an attack. But undismayed by such a large force of men and boats, they assailed them with all of their fine strength and courage. On the initial encounter, they by good fortune overturned three canoes, killed ten or twelve warriors and wounded many more, for among our men were twenty-two crossbowmen and three archers. One archer was a Spaniard who from childhood to the age of twenty had been reared in England, and another was an Englishman by birth; therefore as men experienced in the arms of England and skillful with the bow and arrow, they would use no weapons but these throughout the whole expedition, and for this reason were carrying them at present. The third archer was an Indian, a servant belonging to Captain Juan de Guzmán, who had captured him immediately after coming to Florida. This Indian had grown so fond of his master and the Spaniards that he had persistently used his bow and arrows against his own people as though he himself were a Castilian.

Thus with the skill of these archers as well as the strength of their entire group, our men destroyed the canoes and forced the enemy to flee; but they themselves did not emerge from the conflict unscathed, for the majority of them, among whom were two captains, were injured. One soldier was wounded with a weapon which the Castilians in the Indies call an arrow, but which I shall call more appropriately a dart since it is thrown with a wooden strip or a cord.[8] Our Spaniards had never seen this weapon before that day in any part of Florida through which they had traveled. But the Indians in Peru use it extensively. It is six feet in length, and is fashioned from a reed, firm on the outside though spongy within, from which arrows are also made. As a head it bears the tip of a deer horn worked with the utmost perfection on four sides, or a harpoon made from palm or other available woods which are as strong and heavy as iron. And in order that the reed of the arrow or dart not be split when a blow is given, they put a knot of thread where it receives the tip or harpoon and another on the opposite end at the place which archers call the "battle" in an arrow, that place where the shaft receives the cord of the bow or the strip with which it is hurled. The strip is of wood two-thirds of a yard in length, and is capable of sending a dart with such great force that it has been seen to pass completely through a man armed with a coat of mail. In Peru, the Spaniards feared this weapon more than any others the Indians possessed, for the arrows there were not so fierce as those of Florida.

The dart or arrow with which the Indians wounded the Spaniard of whom I was speaking, had three prongs instead of one, like the three longest fingers of the hand. That in the center was a quarter

---

[8] *un amiento de palo, o de cuerda*—An "amiento" is a leather strap which is customarily fastened to a javelin for the purpose of giving it more force when it is hurled and retrieving it afterward. Since in his first reference the Inca speaks of a "strap" of wood or of cord then later specifically states that the "amiento" is of wood, it is possible that he had in mind something like a pliable vine or a piece of the bark of certain types of trees. On the other hand, he could have meant simply a strip of wood. In case of the latter, he no doubt is picturing here the ancient atlatl, a good description of which may be found in A. Hyatt Verrill, *The American Indian* (New York: 1943), pp. 184, 185, 195; and in William S. Webb and David DeJarnette, "An Archeological Survey of Pickwick Basin," *Smithsonian Institution Bureau of American Ethnology*, Bulletin 129 (Washington: 1942), pp. 270–286.

of a yard longer than those on the sides, so whereas it passed completely through the man's thigh, the other two remained buried in the flesh. Since these were prongs and not smooth points, it was necessary, in order to remove them forcibly, to make a great shambles in the leg of this miserable creature; and such was the carnage that before they might cure him, he expired, not knowing of whom to complain most, the enemy who had inflicted the wound or the friends who had hastened his death.

CHAPTER XI

The Spaniards set sail. The outcome of the first twenty-three days of their navigation.

SINCE we have not yet left the Great River whose canoes I have spoken of protractedly in the previous chapters, it will be well to mention at this point the skill which the natives of all the land of Florida have for righting a canoe when it has been overturned in their naval battles, fishing expeditions or howsoever it may be, for I forgot to describe this skill in its proper place. Thus it is that being very great swimmers, twelve or thirteen Indians, depending more or less upon the size of the canoe, take their vessel between them and turn it so as to have its mouth straight downward. Then as it comes up full of water, all simultaneously give it a shake, and when the water in falling is collected on one side, they immediately give a shake in the opposite direction. After two such shakes, not a drop of water remains in the canoe, and the Indians re-enter it. And all of this they accomplish with such haste and facility that the vessel has hardly been upset before they have it turned over and put in position again. Our men were greatly amazed at this trick because they themselves were never skillful at doing it in spite of the many times that they tried.

While the one hundred Spaniards went out to fight with the Indians, the remainder reloaded the things taken from the caravels; and they were able to do so without the aid of the canoes because their ships were moored to the driftwood, which, as we said, formed an island and made no movement other than to rise and fall with the ebb and flow of the sea. Then when the enemy had been conquered and cast from the rushes, all reassembled; but fearing that the Indians might return by night and set fire to them or do other mischief, they boarded the caravels and proceeded to the desert island at the mouth of the Great River. Here they cast anchor, and after landing, explored the entire island without finding anything worth mentioning.

That night all slept aboard the caravels lying at anchor and, as soon as the following day dawned, agreed to continue toward the west in search of the coast of Mexico, carrying the land of Florida always to their right and not separating themselves far from it. But when they lifted anchor, one of their cables snapped, for having been made with mended rope, little was needed to part it. Since they had not attached cable buoys, an anchor was lost; and it being essential, they were unwilling to proceed without it. So the best swimmers among them plunged into the water, but regardless of the great amount of toil they put forth, their efforts to locate the anchor were of no avail until three o'clock in the afternoon, when at the termination of nine or ten hours of diving, they managed to recover it.[9]

At that hour they set sail, not daring, however, to venture out into the gulf,[10] since they did not know where they were or in what direction they might proceed to reach the islands of Santo Domingo or Cuba; for they had neither sea chart, compass or astrolabe to take

[9] This anchor, according to the Elvas account, was never found. A substitute was made of a stone used for crushing corn, and the bridles that remained to some of the hidalgos.

[10] The Elvas account states that opinions differed as to whether they should follow the coast or head out to the open sea. Moscoso, overpersuaded by Juan de Añasco, favored the latter course, but later when they did attempt such, they encountered difficulty and fled once more to the shore.

the altitude of the sun, nor forestaff for that of the north star. They understood only that by continuing westward along the coast, even though it were extensive, they eventually must reach the coast and land of Mexico. With this determination, they traveled all of that afternoon and night and then on until near sunset of the second day. In the whole of that distance they encountered fresh water from the Great River and were amazed to find this water so far out at sea.

At this stage, Alonso de Carmona says the following, which I have transcribed to the letter: "And thus we were traveling more or less near the coast because the Indians had burned the instruments of navigation, or rather they were burned when the Indians set fire to us in Mauvila. Meanwhile Captain Juan de Añasco, who was a very cautious man, had taken the astrolabe and looked after it, for being of metal it had not suffered much damage. Moreover he made a sea chart from a parchment of deer skin, and with a ruler he made a forestaff by means of which we were guiding ourselves; but the mariners and others with them, having pondered the fact that this man was not a seaman, and indeed he had never embarked in his life except for this expedition, ridiculed him. Then when he learned that they were making fun of him, he threw all of these things into the sea except the astrolabe. But they were rescued by another brigantine which came behind, for the chart and the forestaff were bound together. Thus we traveled, or better said, navigated, seven or eight days, when a storm coming up, we took shelter in a cove." Up to here is of Alonso de Carmona.

The weather for their voyage being good, our Castilians journeyed fifteen more consecutive days without anything worthy of mention offering itself save that during this period they landed five times[11] to take on water, for there being no large flasks and only small pots

[11] According to the De Soto Expedition Commission they spent the second night among the islands at the mouth of Terre Bonne Bay and reached Texas soil at the end of eight days. They possibly entered the mouth of Matagorda Bay and remained longer at Corpus Christi or Aransas Pass than at any other place.

and pitchers in which to carry the water, it was consumed rapidly. This handicap, along with their lack of navigating instruments, was one of the principal reasons that they dared not cross to the islands or travel any distance from the mainland, for it was necessary to take on water every three days. And when they did not encounter a river or spring from which to obtain it, they dug into the ground ten or twelve feet from the sea where at less than a yard in depth they found very fresh water in great quantities. Thus in the whole voyage they never lacked water. At the close of the fifteen days of navigation, they came to four or five small islands, not far from the mainland, where they discovered innumerable marine birds which breed on these islands and build their nests upon the ground. These nests were so numerous and so close together that our men found no place to put their feet, and when they returned to the brigantines they were loaded with eggs and with young birds which were so fat that they could not be eaten. These birds, like their eggs, tasted very much of shellfish.

The following day they came to anchor and to take on water at a magnificent beach which was clean and free of reeds, having on it only a forest of many massive trees separated one from the other and formed into a light and beautiful wood without bushes or underbrush. Some of the Spaniards landed to gather shellfish along the shore, and here they found some slabs of black bitumen, almost like tar, which the ocean had cast up among its refuse. This substance must come from some spring which flows into the sea or which is born in the sea itself. The slabs weighed eight, ten, twelve and fourteen pounds; and they were found in quantity. Seeing the assistance that good fortune offered them in their necessity, for the caravels were leaking and they feared that in the future they would continue to do so in more quantity and as a result be lost, and not knowing what remained for them to travel or having any hope of reaching the land of Christians other than by means of these vessels, they decided to repair them, now that they had material and a good beach where they could take them out on land. So with this determination they stopped eight days in that place. Each day they unloaded a brigantine and by dint of arms took it ashore and tarred it; and then in the afternoon they cast it again into the sea. And in order that the tar might run, for it was very dry, they put in it the grease of the small amount of pork they were carrying to eat, holding it better to use this grease on the ships than in their own food because of their belief that in these vessels lay their salvation.

CHAPTER XII

An account of the navigation up to the fifty-third day. A storm which strikes the Spaniards.

DURING the eight days that our men were occupied in repairing their ships, eight Indians came to them on three separate occasions. Approaching very peacefully they presented ears of corn which they had brought in quantity, and the Spaniards in turn gave them some of the chamois they were carrying. But even with this good will existing between them, our men did not ask the name of that province, their only desire being to attain the land of Mexico. It therefore has not been possible for me to ascertain what region they were in. The same Indians came on all three occasions and, though they brought their bows and arrows, proved to be most friendly.

When they had delayed eight days tarring the caravels, our Castilians departed from that cool and peaceful shore, and as they continued on their way, took care always to stay near land lest some north wind blow them out to the high sea, for the winds are most tempestuous along that coast. But they did this also because of their need, which we have seen, of taking on water every three days. And now whenever they found conditions suitable, they set themselves to fishing, for after they had used the lard in repairing the caravels, there was nothing else on board to eat except corn. Forced by necessity, therefore, some cast their hooks into the sea, while others went ashore to search for shellfish; and they always returned with something of benefit. They fished also because of their need to rest from the great amount of labor shouldered in rowing, for whenever the sea permitted them to use oars, everyone aboard except the captains took his turn doing so. Thus it was that twelve or thirteen days were spent at various intervals in fishing, for when the fishing was good, they would tarry for two and three days at a time.

In this manner the Spaniards navigated many leagues (although just how many I cannot say) with the greatest desire now to reach the River of the Palms,[12] for it appeared to them that according to the distance they had traveled, they were not far from that place. Those who boasted of being cosmographers and great mariners fed and gave assurance to this hope, but the truth of the matter is that the most informed man among them knew no more about the sea or the region through which they were traveling than that it seemed to him (and to him it thus was a fact) that by continuing that route forever, finally, finally, if the sea did not swallow them up, they would come to the land of Mexico. And it was this certainty which enabled them to suffer the excessive hardships which they bore.

Fifty-three days had elapsed since our Spaniards had left the Great River where it flows into the sea. Thirty of them had been spent in travel and the other twenty-three in repairing the brigantines and relaxing by means of the fishing that they did. But then in the afternoon of the fifty-third day, a north wind came up with the ferocity and power that it is wont to exert on this coast more than any other, and it drove them out to sea as they had always feared it might. The five caravels traveling together, among which was that of the Governor, saw the storm before it struck, and they drew near to land, touching it with their oars as they traveled along in search of some shelter wherein to take refuge from the tempest. But the two other vessels, which included that of the treasurer, Juan Gaytán, who through the death of the good Juan de Guzmán had remained as its sole commander, and that of the captains, Juan de Alvarado and Christóval Mosquera, had not judged the weather so

[12] *Río de las Palmas.*

wisely as the other five, and were traveling rather far from shore. Because of this carelessness, they were exposed that whole night to a violent tempest in which the fury of the wind so increased for hours that they proceeded with the Creed in their mouths.

The caravel of the Treasurer was in greater danger than the other because its largest mast on being disjointed by a gust of wind came out of a mortar box where it was inserted in the keel; and only with great labor and difficulty were they able to return it to its place. But during the entire night both vessels went on resisting contrary winds and struggling against the tempest in an effort not to separate far from the shore. And though all aboard had judged the wind would abate with the dawn, it blew even more wildly and furiously, and, without slackening in its rage, brought them foundering until the middle of the day. Then at this hour both caravels perceived that the other five had entered an estuary or river and were now safe from this tempest in which they themselves were still struggling. At that they forced themselves anew to contend with the wind in order to see if they could reach the place where their companions had found shelter, but they could not do so regardless of how much they toiled because the wind was forward and so very vehement that no efforts were of any profit. On the contrary, by struggling they placed themselves in even greater danger and many times were seen to be in grave peril; yet with all this, they contended with the storm until three in the afternoon. Then realizing that they not only were laboring in vain but also were increasing the danger, they concluded that the lesser evil would be to allow themselves to run forward along the coast in the hope of finding some refuge there. With this decision they turned their prows to the west and ran with a side wind, but with a wind that was unwilling to temper itself for them in any way. All were now naked except for loin cloths, and their boats, because of the many waves falling into them, were half swamped. Therefore, while some hastened to man the sails, others bailed out water, for the brigantines being without decks, whatever was thrown within them remained, and our men as a result were walking in water halfway up their thighs.

CHAPTER XIII

A wild storm which two caravels ran, and how they were grounded.

THE two caravels ran the aforementioned tempest for twenty-five or twenty-six hours without its subsiding in the least; to those who were subjected to it, it seemed on the contrary to increase by the hour. All of this time our Spaniards continued to resist the wind and the waves without sleeping or eating so much as a mouthful, for death being as imminent as it was, fear dispelled their drowsiness and hunger. Then when the sun was setting, they beheld land to the fore which was found to be of two kinds.

That coast descried directly ahead, which veered off to the right of where they were traveling, was white and appeared to be sand, for they saw many hills of it being easily and quickly moved from place to place by the strong wind that was blowing. On the other hand that which turned off to the left looked to be as black as tar. Then a twenty-year-old youth called Francisco, who was traveling in the caravel of Juan de Alvarado and Francisco Mosquera, said to these captains: "My lords, although I do not know this land or to whom it belongs, I am acquainted with its shoreline, having sailed it twice while serving as a ship's page. The black coast to our left is a land of flint. It is rugged and extends over a vast distance to Vera Cruz. And along the whole of it there is neither port nor shelter which may be of assistance to us but instead slithers of stone and razor-like edges of flint, where, if grounded we shall all be dashed to pieces between the waves and the rocks. The other coast which is visible straight ahead and swerves back to our right is sandy and therefore appears white. All of it is soft and clean, and for this reason it behooves us to try to run aground there before daylight fails and night closes in upon us; for should the wind drive us from this coast and cast us upon the black one we will have no hope left of escaping with our lives."

Captains Juan de Alvarado and Francisco Mosquera thereupon commanded that notification of what the boy Francisco had said be imparted at once to those on board the caravel of Captain Juan Gaytán so that they too might be forewarned of the impending danger. Now the waves were so lofty as not to permit the occupants of the ships to address or even see each other; nevertheless it became possible for them to communicate by signs and shouts given at successive intervals when the vessels happened to appear on the crests of waves in such a way that men might see and talk from one to the other. Then they agreed by common consent to ground the ships upon the white shore. Only Juan Gaytán, acting in his official capacity as treasurer and not as a commander, opposed their doing so, contending that it was not wise to lose a caravel, since it was worth money. At these words, all of the soldiers sprang to their feet and cried in one voice: "What more have you in this boat than any one of us? If aught, you have less; for, presuming upon your position as the Emperor's treasurer, you would neither cut wood nor work it, nor would you make charcoal for the forges or help there in beating the iron into nails, and again you would not perform the role of caulker or do any other thing of moment. With the royal office, you excused yourself from all the labor that we ourselves underwent. Now this being true, what have you to lose in the destruction of the caravel? Will it be better for the fifty of us who travel in it to perish?" And there was not a man among them who failed to say to him also: "Cursed be he who gave you that slash on the neck for not cutting to the root."

These remarks were uttered very freely, and since the captain gave none in reply and did not attempt to issue an order in that matter, the leading soldiers began briskly to man the sails. Then a Portuguese called Domingos de Acosta threw his hand to the rudder or helm, and all directed the prow of the ship toward land, meanwhile making themselves ready with their swords and shields for whatever might confront them there. Tacking from one side to the other so as not to fall to leeward upon the black coast, they with much peril and labor struck the white one just a little before the sun went down.

Since I have made mention of the knife wound of the treasurer, Juan Gaytán, it will be well, although it is not a part of my history, to tell here how it occurred. To understand, you must know that our Juan Gaytán was a nephew of that Captain Juan Gaytán who because of the marvelous deeds he performed everywhere with his sword and cape gained sufficient importance to be named above all others in the adage, "the sword and cape of Juan Gaytán." Now this nephew of the famed swordsman found himself in the war of Tunis when in the year 1535 our lord the Emperor seized that place from Barbarossa, the Turk, and presented it to Muley Hacén, the Moor, who was his friend. Over his share of the spoils received in that sack, Juan Gaytán engaged in a quarrel with another Spanish soldier whose sword must have been no less worthy than that of the renowned uncle, for this soldier gave Juan Gaytán a great slash on the neck which almost put an end to his life, and even after he recuperated left a scar two fingers deep. One of those individuals who found himself parting them in the quarrel, chided the man who had inflicted the wound, saying that he had done wrong in maltreating a nephew of Captain Juan Gaytán and that he would have been wise to respect him because of the fame of his kinsman. But in reply, this soldier, who was unrepentant of his deed, cried: "All the worse because he is not a nephew of the King of France, for thus I would be so much the more pleased at having killed or wounded him since there would be that much more honor and fame for me." This statement the Treasurer Juan Gaytán, himself, repeated as a witty saying of the man who had wounded him.

CHAPTER XIV

*What the commanders and the soldiers of the
two caravels ordained.*

BUT let us return to our story. Juan Gaytán on sensing that the
caravel had touched land plunged into the water from the
poop, either because he was angered at the opposition of the
soldiers, or because he wished to boast of having learned by experience that it was less perilous in such jeopardies to enter the sea
from that part of the vessel rather than from any other. But on
coming to the surface, he struck his back against the rudder, and
being naked, was injured, hurting his shoulders badly. All the
rest of the soldiers stayed where they were in the caravel, which
because of the great size of the waves when it first struck ground,
remained more than ten feet out of the water as the surf receded to
the sea. And when the waves came again to assail this vessel, they
turned it upon its side. Then those within jumped overboard at
once, being unhampered from doing so by clothing. Some rushed to
one side and some to the other to set the boat upright and hold it
straight lest it be destroyed by the lashes of the sea. Meanwhile
others busied themselves in unloading the corn and throwing out the
ship's cargo, whereas still others conveyed this cargo to land. With
such diligence they unloaded everything in a very brief time, and
then since the boat was light and they were assisted by the beating of
the water against it, they carried it almost suspended in the air and
easily put it on dry land. Afterward they shored it that they might
return it later to the sea should they feel compelled to do so.

The same thing which came to pass in the caravel of the Treasurer,
Juan Gaytán, occurred in that of the captains, Juan de Alvarado and
Christóval Mosquera. For this vessel struck the coast something
like two arquebus shots from the other, and with an effort and haste
identical to that exerted in the companion ship, its occupants unloaded it and took it to land. Then when the captains and soldiers

of both brigantines found themselves free of the tempest and the hazards of the sea, each sent at once to inquire personally as to how the others had fared in the shipwreck. Just as if signals had been given, both messengers set forth at the same instant and thus met halfway. After exchanging words of interrogation and reply, they returned to their respective companions with a favorable account of everything, for which both groups rejoiced exceedingly and gave thanks to God who had liberated them from so much toil and peril. But their ignorance as to what had been the fate of the Governor and the remainder of their companions afforded them new anxiety, for it is the particular reward of mankind that we have hardly survived one misery when we find ourselves confronted with another.

For the purpose of discussing what they should do in that necessity, the three captains and the most illustrious soldiers of both ships met immediately and decided among themselves that it would be wise for some energetic soldier to go at once on that very night to learn of the Governor and the caravels which had been seen ascending the estuary or river, and at the same time to provide him with an account of what had happened to their two vessels. But upon considering the great amount of labor these men had undergone in the storm at sea, and realizing that they had not eaten or slept during the more than twenty-eight hours that the tempest had raged, and furthermore had not rested so much as a half-hour since coming out of the water, they lacked the courage to name anyone in particular for the mission. To them it seemed a great cruelty to select a man for a new task at this time, and no less foolhardy to send him to where he so manifestly might perish along the way. For whoever undertook that task must walk on that same night the thirteen or fourteen leagues which in their estimation lay between where they were and the place where they had seen the caravels ascending the river, and furthermore, he must traverse a land unfamiliar to him, without knowing whether there were other rivers or creeks en route, or whether his path would be secure from enemies, because as has been said, they were ignorant as to what land they were in. But the perturbation of our captains and soldiers, and the adverse arguments of the hardships and proposed dangers were surmounted by the generous and valiant spirit of Gonzalo Quadrado Xaramillo, whom we mentioned particularly on the day of the great battle of Mauvila. Placing himself before his companions, this man said:

"In spite of past difficulties and of those which now may confront me at the imminent risk of life, I am offering myself for this mission because of my love for the General, who is of my own land, and because I would deliver you from the perplexity in which you find yourselves. If there is another who wishes to join me, I propose to walk this entire night without pausing and to be with the Governor tomorrow at the break of day or die in the attempt. And if none will join me, I hereby declare that I will go alone."

The captains and soldiers were most pleased to see this fine spirit, which Francisco Múñoz, another valiant Castilian who was a native of Burgos, wished to emulate, for stepping out from among his companions and taking a place at the side of Gonzalo Quadrado Xaramillo, he asserted that whether it were to live or die, he was resolved to accompany him on that journey. Then at the same moment and without any delay, they gave these men some saddlebags with a small amount of corn and saltpork, both poorly prepared, however, because as yet there had not been time to cook them well. Thus equipped with this simple luxury as well as swords and shields, and barefooted and barelegged as we have said all the Spaniards were, these two courageous soldiers departed at one o'clock and walked throughout the rest of the night, following the shore of the sea since they knew no other route. But here we shall leave them in order to tell what their companions were doing in the interior.

As soon as these two men had been dispatched, the others returned to their caravels and slept, first stationing sentinels, however, because of not knowing whether they were in the land of enemies or of friends. But with the dawn of the next day, they united once more and chose three squadron commanders who were to set out in different directions with twenty men apiece for the purpose of exploring that place and ascertaining what land it might be. We refer to these men as commanders of squadrons and not as captains because of the small number of people they were leading. One of them, a man named Antonio de Porras, followed the coast to the south, and another, Alonso Calvete, followed the same coast but to the north, whereas Gonzalo Silvestre turned inland and went west. All carried the order not to go far so that those who remained could come to their assistance should they need them, and each man of them bore a great desire to return with good news on his part.

CHAPTER XV

What happened to the three captain explorers.

WHEN those commanders who set out along the coast in one direction or the other had traveled for more than a league, they returned to their companions, one group bringing a half of a plate of white clay of the very fine kind that is worked in Talavera, and the other a little broken bowl of gilded and painted clay such as is worked in Malasa. They declared that they had found nothing else, but that these fragments were very good indications of their being in the land of Spaniards because the clay in both pieces was from Spain. All of our men therefore rejoiced exceedingly and made a great celebration over the fragments, regarding them as both certain and fortunate signs since they conformed to what they wanted to believe.

But Gonzalo Silvestre and the group traveling inland fared even better, for when they had left the sea a little more than a quarter of a league behind and had crossed a small hill, they beheld a lagoon of fresh water which extended more than a league into the distance. Here there were four or five canoes of Indians fishing; so lest these people see them and give a warning, the Spaniards concealed themselves among some trees and then in wing formation, as if searching for hares, moved alongside the lagoon under cover of the trees for a quarter of a league. While proceeding in this manner and looking in one direction and another with great care and attention, they perceived ahead of them (at a distance of two arquebus shots from where they were) two Indians who were gathering fruit under a large tree known in the language of the island of Hispañola as a *guayavo*[13] and in my own language of Peru as a *savintu*. At that all passed the word from one to the other and threw themselves upon the ground to avoid being discovered. Then they gave the order that while moving in a circle with some going in one direction and some in another, they should drag themselves along the earth like lizards and approach the Indians in such a manner that they would not flee, and furthermore that those who were in the rear should not rise from the ground until the men in front had surrounded their prey. With this injunction, all now moved forward, chest to the ground, but those in the lead advanced on hands and knees for a distance of almost three arquebus shots to get the start of the Indians, each man of them having made it a point of honor not to let the game escape on his account. Then when they had surrounded the Indians, all rose up simultaneously and rushed at them, but in spite of this great effort one Indian eluded his assailants, and plunging into the water, swam away.

The captured Indian gave loud cries, repeating over and over again the word "Brezos"; but our Spaniards, in their haste to get back to their companions before other Indians should rush up and seize their victim, paid no attention to what he was saying, and concerned themselves solely with making a hasty departure. With the utmost speed they seized two baskets of guavas which the Indians had gathered, a little corn discovered in a hut, a turkey of the species found in the land of Mexico though not in Peru, a rooster and two hens such as we have in Spain, and a little conserve made from some prickly leaves of a tree called the maguey, leaves which are like those of the thistle.

This maguey tree the Indians of New Spain use for many things. For instance, of a certain sweet liquor which the leaves (the trunk

[13] The guava.

removed) exude at a particular time of the year, they make wine, vinegar, honey and syrup; and the tender leaves themselves when cooked and left in the sun are delicious to eat, being similar in appearance to the candied pumpkin, although nothing like so good. Moreover, of these same leaves (which are like those of the thistle), when they have been dried on the tree, the Indians make a hemp which is very strong and good; and of the stalk of the maguey (which is similar to the reeds of Spain in that no more than one springs from each base), they make the roofs and floors of their houses when better wood is lacking, for though in itself spongy, its outer covering is hard.[14]

All that we have said the Castilians found in the hut, they carried away along with the Indian, whom they tied well lest he escape them. Meanwhile they asked him with signs and Spanish words what land this was and what is was called. And he, by their gestures, which they made as if he were a mute, did comprehend that they were questioning him, but he failed to understand by their words just what it was they wanted to know, and in his ignorance as to what to answer, simply repeated the word "Brezos," many times mispronouncing it as *bredos*.[15] And since he did not answer them properly, they said, "Go to the devil, you dog. What should we want with *bredos?*" What the Indian meant was that he was a vassal of a Spaniard named Christóval de Brezos, but since in his perturbation he did not manage to say Christóval and sometimes said "Brezos" while at others *bredos*, the Castilians were unable to comprehend him. So they took him away for the purpose of questioning him more at leisure concerning those things they wanted him to tell them; and they forced him to make haste lest his companions come and seize him from them.

[14] In the *Comentarios Reales,* Part I, Book VIII, chapter XIII, the Inca gives an even more extensive account of the various uses of the maguey. Indian women, for instance, employed it in dying their hair.

[15] The *bredo* or *bledo* is a plant known as the wild amaranth or wild spinach. The word is used to indicate a thing of the lowest value. For example: *No me importa un bledo* means "I don't care a straw."

Apropos of the questioning by the Spaniards and the unsatisfactory response of the Indian (for they did not understand each other), I had put here the derivation of the name Peru, for the Indians of that nation did not have this word in their language, and it came about as a result of an incident similar to the present one. But the printing of this book having been delayed more than I imagined, I have transferred that information to its proper place,[16] where it will be found at great length along with many other names mentioned at random. For already in this year of six hundred and two,[17] I by divine favor am in the last quarter of that history and am hoping that it soon will appear.

CHAPTER XVI

The Spaniards learn that they are in the land of Mexico.

GONZALO Silvestre and his squadron of twenty hastened on with the captured Indian, asking him questions which he poorly understood and receiving his replies which they interpreted worse. Thus they proceeded until they reached the coast where the rest of their companions were making a great fiesta and demonstration of joy over the pieces of plate and the small bowl which the other explorers had discovered. But when they saw the turkey and hens, and the fruit and other supplies that Gonzalo Silvestre and his men brought, they could not refrain from excessive manifestations of joy, jumping and leaping like madmen. Moreover, to the greater happiness of all, it chanced that the surgeon administering unto them had been in Mexico and knew something of the Mexican language, in which he now spoke to the Indian, saying, "What are these?" And they were some scissors which he held in his hand.

[16] See the *Comentarios Reales,* Part I, Book I, chapters IV–VI.
[17] Sixteen hundred and two. The Inca frequently abbreviates dates in this manner.

The Indian, who meanwhile had recognized that these people were Spaniards, was now more himself, so he answered in Spanish, saying *tiselas*.[18] And when he spoke this word, although he pronounced it badly, our men were completely assured that they were in the land of Mexico, and in their joy at this realization, they persisted in embracing and kissing the face of Gonzalo Silvestre and all of his men. Then lifting them in their arms and setting them on their shoulders, they carried them from place to place while telling them grandiose and complimentary things without either prudence or consideration, as if these men had brought to each one of them the seigniory of Mexico and all of its empire. But when this gay celebration and the most joyous of their merriment had subsided, they inquired of the Indian with more tranquility and purpose as to what land they were in and what river and estuary the Governor had entered with the five caravels. And to their questions, he replied as follows:

"This land belongs to the city of Pánuco, and your Captain General entered the river of Pánuco which flows into the sea twelve leagues hence. The city itself lies twelve more leagues upstream and is ten leagues by land from where we now are. I myself am a vassal of a resident of Pánuco called Christóval de Brezos. A little more than a league from here there is an Indian lord of vassals who can read and write, since from his childhood he was reared by the priest who instructs us in the Christian doctrine. If you wish I will go and summon him, for I am confident that he will come at once and inform you of all that you may desire to know."

The Spaniards rejoiced over the good report of this Indian and presented him gifts from among the things they had brought. Then they dispatched him at once for the Cacique, advising that he bring or send them a supply of paper and ink for writing. The Indian made such good time on the journey that in less than four hours he had returned with the Curaca himself. For as soon as that chieftain had been apprised that the ships of the Spaniards had

[18] Again the Indian's Spanish is bad, for he should have said *tijeras*.

run aground on his land, he had felt a desire to visit them personally and take them some gift. Thus he brought eight Indians loaded with Spanish hens, bread made of corn, fruit, fish, and in addition ink and paper; for he prided himself on his ability to read and write, and he placed great value on such skill. Everything that he brought, this Curaca presented the Spaniards, and furthermore offered them his person and his house with much affection. Our men thanked him for his visit and his gifts, and in recompense gave him some of the chamois they had brought. Then they sent an Indian at once to the Governor with a letter bearing an account of all that had happened to them up until that time, and requesting instructions for the future.

The Cacique remained throughout that day with the Spaniards, questioning them concerning the events and adventures which had occurred on the expedition, and taking much pleasure in what he heard; but he was amazed at seeing them so lean, sunburned and broken, for the hardship they had suffered was revealed clearly in both their persons and their clothing. When night approached he returned to his home, but he visited the Spaniards on each of the six days they were on that shore, never failing to bring them gifts of those things he had in his land.

CHAPTER XVII

The Spaniards unite in Pánuco. Bitter quarrels
spring up among them. The reason
for these quarrels.

GONZALO Quadrado Xaramillo and his companion, Francisco Múñoz, whom we left walking along the coast, did not stop during the entire night and at dawn came to the mouth of the river of Pánuco. Here they learned that the Governor and his five caravels had entered the river safely and proceeded upstream. Encouraged by such agreeable news, the two men refused to rest even though they had traveled for twelve leagues that night without pause, but instead increased their gait and journeyed on for another three leagues. Then at eight o'clock in the morning, they came upon the Governor and his men who were waiting with much anxiety and sorrow because of their fear that the two caravels which had continued in that great storm at sea might have been destroyed, for the tempest had not yet abated and as a matter of fact did not abate during the five days which followed. With the arrival of the two good companions and the report they brought, this grief and anxiety was converted into happiness and joy, and all gave thanks to God for delivering them from death. On the following day they received the letter which had been sent with the Indian, and the Governor replied by saying that as soon as the missing Castilians had rested to the extent they felt wise, they should come on to where he was awaiting them in the city of Pánuco so that he might determine the course of action of them all.

Eight days after the shipwreck, our Spaniards rejoined their governor in Pánuco, there being now a little less than three hundred of them in all. They were well received by the inhabitants of that city, who though poor, offered them as much courtesy and gracious hospitality as they were able. Among these people were very illustrious cavaliers who were distressed to see their countrymen so haggard, sunburned, lean and shrunken, and, what is more, barefoot and nude, for they were wearing no clothes save chamois and cowhide and the skins of bears, lions and other savage beasts. Indeed they appeared more like wild animals than human beings. The Corregidor immediately forwarded word to the Viceroy, Don Antonio de Mendoza, who resided sixty leagues distant in Mexico, that almost three hundred of the one thousand Spaniards who had entered Florida with the Adelantado Hernando de Soto had now emerged from that kingdom. And the Viceroy in turn commanded his informant by messenger to treat these men as he would the Viceroy himself, and when they were ready to travel to provide them sumptuously and direct them on to him. Later he sent shirts, sandals, and four mules loaded with conserves and other gifts as well as medicine for the sick, for it was his belief that the Spaniards were suffering. But the truth of the matter is that they bore an excess of health and a lack of everything else necessary for human life. At this point, the accounts of both Juan Coles and Alonso de Carmona state that these gifts were sent at the Viceroy's command by the Brotherhood of Charity of Mexico.

One should know now that when General Luis de Moscoso de Alvarado and his captains and soldiers had found themselves united and had rested ten or twelve days in that city, the wisest and best informed of them had scrupulously considered the mode of life of its inhabitants, which at that time was miserable enough; for these people possessed neither gold nor silver mines nor any resources they might value other than a sustenance eked out from what the earth yielded and from the production of some few horses which were sold to persons coming from elsewhere to buy them. Moreover they had seen that most of these people wore cotton, whereas only a few wore clothes from Castile; that the wealthier citizens and the most illustrious of their feudal lords possessed just the resources we have mentioned, along with the beginnings of some stock farming on a very small scale; that they busied themselves in planting mulberry trees for the production of silk and in setting out other trees from Spain in order to have fruit to enjoy in the future; that still more in keeping with what has been said were their household furnishings and equipment, and that the very houses themselves were poor and humble, most of them being constructed of straw. In sum, these Spaniards realized that the whole of what they had seen in that town was no more than a start at settling and miserably cultivating a land which, with its many fine qualities, was inferior to the one they themselves had forsaken; that instead of wearing cotton clothing like the citizens of Pánuco, they could dress in very fine chamois of such numerous and diverse colors as they at the moment were wearing or in capes of marten and other very handsome and elegant furs (for as we have said the furs in Florida are

magnificent); and again that they themselves had no need to plant
mulberries to raise silk since, as we have seen, they had found such
a great quantity of these trees along with the groves of walnut of
three varieties, cherry, oak and liveoak and the abundance of grapes
that they saw growing in the open countryside. And now as they
compared certain things with others, the glory of the many fine
provinces they had discovered increased (there being forty provinces
among just those that have been named, not to mention others forgotten and still others whose names they had not tried to learn);
they recalled the fertility and abundance of all these places, their
natural fitness for bearing the seeds, grains and vegetables that they
could bring to them from Spain, and the advantage offered in their
pasture lands, woods and rivers for raising and multiplying whatever
livestock they might wish to breed.

Finally, they remembered the great wealth of pearls and seed
pearls they had scorned, and the splendors in which they had seen
themselves, for each man of them had fancied himself as the lord of
a great province. And as they compared those riches and noble
estates with these present miseries and paucities, some discussed their
visions and melancholy thoughts with others, and with most sorrow-
ful hearts and self pity remarked: "Could we not have lived in
Florida as these Spaniards are living in Pánuco? Were not the lands
we left better than these where we at present are? Where, if we
should attempt now to stop and settle, might we become richer than
these people who are our hosts? Do they by chance have more gold
and silver mines than we found? Or even the riches that we scorned?
Is it well that we have come to receive alms and hospitality from
people poorer than ourselves when we might have been able to
offer entertainment to the whole of Spain? Is it just or befitting our
honor that from feudal lords which we might have been, we have
come to beg? Were it not better to have died there, than to live
here?"

With these and similar words born of their grief over the good
they had lost, some were enkindled against others with so much fury
that, desperate with repentance for having abandoned Florida,

where they could have been possessed of so many riches, they fell to slashing one another with rabidness and a desire to kill. And their greatest anger was amassed against the officers of the Royal Exchequer and the captains and soldiers of Seville, noble and otherwise, for it had been they who after the death of Governor Hernando de Soto had insisted most that Florida be abandoned. Moreover these were the men who had obstinately importuned and eventually forced Luis de Moscoso to undertake that long journey to the Land of the Herdsmen, wherein, as we have seen, so many inconveniences and hardships were suffered that a third of both their men and horses had perished. And it had been this lack of both men and animals that had brought about the ultimate ruin of all, for it had necessitated their leaving that land quickly and prevented their awaiting or requesting the aid that the Adelantado Hernando de Soto had once thought to solicit by sending two brigantines down the river to give notice to Mexico, the islands of Cuba and Santo Domingo, and Tierra-Firme of what had been found in Florida so that they in turn might forward assistance for making a settlement in that land. And this aid, because of the opportunity afforded by the Great River for any ship or fleet either to enter or leave it, could have been brought to them most easily.

All such things were examined and considered carefully by those who had been of an opposite opinion; that is, of the opinion that they should carry forward the plans of Governor Hernando de Soto and establish a settlement in Florida; and realizing now through experience the justification that they had had for remaining, and at present had for being indignant with the officers and those of their factions, they were inflamed with so much fury that, having lost respect for these people, they went slashing after them in such a way as to leave both dead and wounded. The captains and officials of the king dared not come out of their quarters, and the soldiers were so infuriated with each other that all of the people in the city were unable to pacify them. But these and other such consequences do result from decisions made without prudence or counsel.

CHAPTER XVIII

How the Spaniards went to Mexico. The fine reception given them by that remark-able city.

ON WITNESSING so much dissension among our Spaniards and perceiving that it was increasing from day to day without his being able to provide a remedy, the Corregidor of Pánuco gave a report of affairs to the Viceroy, Don Antonio de Mendoza, who in turn commanded that these men be sent promptly to Mexico in groups of ten and twenty, advising however that all individuals of each group be of the same faction and not adversaries lest they slay one another en route. So with this arrangement and mandate our Spaniards left Pánuco twenty-five days after arriving there.

Along the roads a very great concourse of people, Castilians as well as Indians, thronged to see them; and the crowds were amazed to behold Spaniards afoot, bare-legged, and clothed in animal skins, for the gains of those among them who had fared best consisted of little more than the sandals which had been bestowed upon them as alms. Moreover the onlookers were shocked at seeing our people so sunburned and haggard, and they declared that they showed clearly in their appearance the labors, hunger, miseries and persecutions they had suffered. Already Rumor performing its mission had proclaimed the condition of these men loudly throughout the kingdom, and as a result both Indians and Spaniards offered them hospitality with much affection and great acts of endearment, serving and entertaining them along the way until each successive group had entered that most renowned city of Mexico, a city which because of its splendors and excellencies has today the reputation and prestige of being the finest of all the cities of the world. Here they were received and lodged by the Viceroy and the rest of the citizens, cavaliers, and wealthy men of the city, with so much enthusiasm that each, emulating the other, took them in groups of five and six to their houses and entertained them as if they were their own sons.

At this stage, Juan Coles says that an illustrious cavalier and citizen of Mexico named Xaramillo took eighteen men to his house, all of whom were from Estremadura, and that he dressed them in twenty-four cloth of Segovia,[19] and in addition gave to each a bed with mattresses, sheets, blankets and pillows, as well as a comb and brush and everything else that a soldier requires. And he adds that the entire city, being much distressed to see these men dressed in chamois and cowhide and knowing them to have suffered many hardships, offered them both respect and charity, whereas they had refused to bestow any favor upon the followers of Juan Vásquez Coronado[20] (a citizen of Mexico, who, a short time previous to Hernando de Soto's entrance into Florida had set out to explore the Seven Cities), for that group had been unwilling to settle and in consequence had returned to Mexico when there was no need for them to do so. All of these statements are taken from the report of Juan Coles, a native of Zafra; and Alonso de Carmona is in agreement in every respect, though he does add that among those whom Xaramillo took to his house was a relative of his. This man must have been our Gonzalo Quadrado Xaramillo. But that one may see how much in accord these two eyewitnesses are in many passages of their accounts, I feel it wise, since I have already given the remarks of Juan Coles, to include here those of Alonso de Carmona, which are as follows:

"I have already said that we left Pánuco in groups of fifteen or twenty, and that we entered the great city of Mexico in this manner, not in one day, however, but in four, since each group entered separately. And the kindness bestowed upon us in that place was such that I shall not know how to explain it here. For when a company of soldiers came into the city as it did, the inhabitants rushed at once to the plaza, and he who arrived there first considered himself to be in great luck, for each was trying to outdo the other.

---

[19] *paño veintequatreño de Segovia* was a fine cloth whose warp consisted of twenty-four hundred threads. Juan Coles, being himself a tailor, could appreciate the quality of the material.

[20] Again the Inca errs. See above, Book I, chapter II, note 13.

Thus they took these men to their houses and gave every one of them a bed; and then after ordering sufficient black twenty-four cloth of Segovia to cover their bodies, they clothed them. Moreover, they gave them everything else they needed, such as pleated shirts, doublets, caps, hats, knives, scissors, hair ribbons, bonnets and even combs with which to dress their hair. After providing them with clothes, they took them one Sunday to mass, and later when they had partaken of food together, exclaimed: 'Brothers, you can find success here because the land is abundant; therefore, let every man look to his own resources.' There was in this place a citizen of Estremadura called Xaramillo who, on going out to the plaza, found a company of twenty soldiers, among whom was a kinsman; but he treated each of these men most graciously, giving preference to no one. All of those in my company decided to go and kiss the hands of the Viceroy, Don Antonio de Mendoza, and even though other citizens invited us to their houses, we would not accompany them. The Viceroy, after we had paid our respects, ordered that we be given food and then lodged us in a large room where each was offered a bed with mattress, sheets, pillows and blankets, all of which were fresh. Only after we were provided with clothes were we permitted to leave that place, but then we again kissed the Viceroy's hands and departed, expressing our gratitude for the favor and kindness he had bestowed upon us. Later all of us went to Peru, not so much for its riches as for the changes that were taking place there when Gonzalo Pizarro was in the process of making himself governor and lord of that land."

With the above statement, Alonso de Carmona completed the account of his peregrination; and all these are his words transcribed to the letter.

The Viceroy, as such a fine prince, seated each person who was to eat at his table with much tact, making no distinction between captains and soldiers or cavaliers and commoners; for he said that since all had been equal in their heroic deeds and tasks, they ought likewise to be equal in that small honor he was paying them. And he not only favored them at his table but issued an order to proclaim throughout the city that no officer of justice other than himself should judge the cases which might occur among these men. This he did, not only through a desire to honor and favor them but also because of his having learned that a regular magistrate had seized and cast into the public jail two soldiers from Florida who had been slashed in the squabbles that had sprung up at Pánuco. And now these quarrels were being kindled afresh in Mexico with even greater smoke and flames of anger by the high value which the cavaliers and the illustrious and wealthy men of that city were seen to place upon those things that had been brought from Florida; such, for instance, as fine chamois of all colors. For it is a fact that as soon as these people saw the skins, they converted them into very elegant breeches and doublets. Moreover, they regarded with much esteem those few pearls and strands of seed pearls that had been brought, for they were of great price. But when they beheld the robes of marten and other furs that our men were wearing, they prized them above everything else; and even though these robes were resinous and filled with tar from the ships because of their having served as mattresses and blankets for lack of other bed clothing, and were dirty with the dust and mud received when trampled on the ground, they had them washed and cleaned, for they were extremely good. With them they lined their best clothing and then wore them in the plaza as a very rich adornment. And he who could not manage to line his entire cape or cloak, contented himself with a collar of marten or some other fur which he wore disclosed with the ruffle of the shirt as a thing of much value and esteem.

All of this was cause for great despair, pain and rage among our men—this realization that such rich and illustrious people placed so high a value upon what they themselves had scorned. For they recalled that without consideration whatsoever they had abandoned lands which had been so laborious to explore, lands where there was such an abundance of these and other things as fine. This recollection brought to their minds the words that Governor Hernando de Soto had spoken to them in Quiguate concerning the conspiracy in which at Mauvila they had discussed the subject of abandoning Florida and departing for Mexico, and they remembered that among other things he had said: "Why do you wish to go to Mexico? To disclose the baseness and littleness of your souls? Possessed now of the power to be lords of such a great kingdom as this, where you have discovered and trodden upon so many and such magnificent provinces, have you deemed it better (abandoning them through your pusillanimity and cowardice) to go and lodge in a strange house and eat at the table of another when you can have your own house and table with which to entertain many?"

It would seem that these words were an accurate prediction of that pain and sorrow which now was tormenting them and inciting them to destroy each other by knife blows without respect to or even remembrance of their former comradeship and brotherhood. And in these quarrels which took place in Mexico, some were killed and some wounded, just as they had been in Pánuco. But the Viceroy, realizing that these men were more than justified, placated them with the utmost suavity, and as a consolation, vowed to make the same conquest should they wish to return to it. And it is true that he, having heard of the fine qualities of the kingdom of Florida, did want to undertake such an expedition. Thus to many captains and soldiers from among our men he gave a monetary income along with additional gifts over and above their wages, and furthermore provided them with charges in which they were to occupy themselves while he made ready for the journey. Many accepted this emolument, but many would not lest they obligate themselves to return to a land they abhorred, and also, as is proved by the following incident which occurred during those same days, because they had set their eyes on Peru.

A soldier named Diego de Tapia (whom I knew afterward in Peru where he served His Majesty well in the wars against Gonzalo Pizarro, Don Sebastián de Castilla and Francisco Hernández Girón), while clothes were being made for him, was walking through the city of Mexico dressed in nothing but skins, just as he had come out of Florida. And when a wealthy citizen saw him thus appareled and noted his diminutive size, he felt that this man must be one of the most forlorn of the group and thereupon said to him: "Brother, I have a cattle farm near the city where, if you wish to serve me, you may spend your life in tranquility and repose; and furthermore, I have a competent salary to offer you." At that, with the appearance of the lion or the bear whose skin he happened to be wearing, Diego de Tapia replied: "I am going now to Peru where I plan to have more than twenty farms. If you wish to go along and serve me, I will accommodate you on one of them in such a way that you may return rich in a very short time." The citizen of Mexico retired without saying another word, for it seemed to him that with a few more remarks, he might not extricate himself from his suggestion agreeably.

CHAPTER XIX

They give an account to the Viceroy of the most noteworthy incidents that occurred in Florida.

AMONG those citizens and illustrious cavaliers of Mexico who entertained our men was the Factor Gonzalo de Salazar, whom we mentioned at the beginning of this history. Now it happened that this man took Gonzalo Silvestre to his house, and while the two of them were talking of the many things which occurred in the discovery, they came eventually to speak of the beginning of the journey—of what befell them on that first night after leaving San Lúcar, and of how the two generals had found themselves in danger of being sunk. And in this conversation, the Factor learned that it was Gonzalo Silvestre himself who had issued the order to fire the two cannon shots, and that these shots had been leveled at his ship because of its having gone in advance of the armada and to the windward of the admiral's ship, as we treated at length in the first book of this history. For this reason, he from that time forward paid even more honor to Gonzalo Silvestre, declaring that the latter thus had performed as a good soldier, but adding that it would give him pleasure to encounter Governor Hernando de Soto and talk with him about what had happened on that night. Afterward the Factor learned from other soldiers of the good fortune Gonzalo Silvestre had enjoyed in the province of Tula and of the Indian whose waist he had severed with one slash of his sword; and when he saw this sword, which was old and would now be considered antique, he asked for permission to add it to his collection of articles of great value. Moreover when he learned that in recompense for hospitality rendered in Pánuco the captain had given his host that long strip of marten furs adorned with pearls and seed pearls (which I said he seized during the voyage down the Great River when the Spaniards stopped in a village to obtain food and abandoned the horses because of the pressure put upon them by the Indians), the Factor was pained, declaring that he would give fifteen hundred pesos just to have in his collection an article as interesting as was that pennon, for he was indeed very curious about such things.

On the other hand, all of the city of Mexico in general and both the Viceroy and his son Don Francisco de Mendoza in particular were exceedingly pleased to hear of the events of the exploration of Florida, and they asked that these things be related to them in the order of their occurrence. They were amazed when they heard of the very numerous and cruel torments inflicted upon Juan Ortiz by his master, Hirrihigua; the generosity and spiritual excellencies of the good Mucozo; and the terrible pride and savagery of Vita-chuco, as well as the constancy and strength of his four captains and the three young sons of lords of vassals who were taken half-drowned from the lagoon. They commented upon the fierceness and unconquerable passion disclosed by the Indians of Apalache; the flight of their handicapped Cacique; the strange events which occurred in that province during the dangers of battle, and the tedious journey made by the thirty cavaliers in leaving and returning to that place. And they marvelled at the great riches of the temple of Cofachiqui (its splendors and sumptuousness, its abundance of different kinds of arms with the multitude of pearls and seed pearls which they found there) and at the hunger our Spaniards had suffered in the wilderness before arriving at that temple. It gave them joy to hear of the courtesy, discretion and beauty of the mistress of the province of Cofachiqui, and of the Curaca Coza's civilities and splendors, and his offers of his estate as a site for the Spaniards. They were astonished by the gigantic size of the Cacique Tascaluza and of his son, who was like his father; the bloody and obstinate battle of Mauvila and the unexpected attack at Chicaza with the slaughter of men and horses in both; and the battle of the fortress of Alibamo. They were pleased with the laws against adulteresses, but were pained by the need for salt which our men suffered and the horrible death caused by the lack of it, as well as by the long and useless wanderings made as a result of the secret discord which arose among them and prevented their settling. They were profoundly impressed by the adoration of the cross made in the province of Casquin, and the peaceful and comfortable winter passed in Utiangue; but they abhorred the monstrous deformities that the Indians of Tula made artificially upon their heads and faces, as well as the fierceness of their souls and tempers, which was similar to that of their external appearance.

The death of Governor Hernando de Soto afforded them great sorrow. They grieved over the two burials he received, but on the contrary were much pleased to hear of his heroic feats and invincible spirit, his promptitude in battles and attacks, his patience in hardship, his strength and courage in fighting, and his caution, counsel and prudence in both peace and war. And when they told the Viceroy of his intention, cut short by death, of sending two brigantines down the Great River to solicit assistance from His Excellency, and of how very easily (according to what they themselves had observed while navigating to the sea) that help could have been rendered, Don Antonio was deeply moved, and placed much blame on Luis de Moscoso and his captains for not pursuing and carrying forward the plans of Governor Hernando de Soto, since they were so much to the honor and advantage of them all. And he vowed most solemnly that he personally would have taken help to the mouth of the Great River in order to have had his assistance reach there the more quickly and efficiently. And all of the cavaliers and illustrious people of the city of Mexico said the same.

The Viceroy was pleased likewise to learn of the beauty and good disposition in general of the natives of Florida; their strength and valor; the fierceness and dexterity they disclosed in shooting their bows and arrows, and the very strange and amazing shots they made with them; the temerity of spirit which many revealed individually, and which all in general possessed; the perpetual warfare they waged upon each other; the point of honor found in many of the caciques; the fidelity of Captain General Anilco and his challenge to the Cacique Guachoya; the league of Quigualtanqui with the ten Caciques who conspired with him, and the punishment given his messengers; the hardship our men endured in constructing the seven brigantines; the severe flood in the Great River; the embarking of the Spaniards; the multitude and beauty of the canoes that appeared upon them early one morning; and the cruel persecution these canoes inflicted until casting them from the whole of their confines.

Moreover, the Viceroy wanted to know in particular about the quality of the soil of Florida and was pleased to hear of the great abundance of such fruit trees in that land as were to be found also in Spain—trees like the numerous varieties of plum and the three species of walnut, one of which produces a fruit so oily that when its kernel is pressed between the fingers, oil runs out through them; of such quantities of acorns from the oak and liveoak; of the beauty and large number of the mulberry trees; and of the fertility of the wild grape vines and the many fine grapes that they bear. And finally it made him very happy to hear of the spaciousness of that kingdom, the opportunity that it holds for raising all kinds of livestock, and the fertility of the land for corn, grains, fruits and vegetables. And because of these things, his desire to make the conquest increased, but however much he endeavored, he could not succeed in getting the people who had come out of Florida to remain with him for the purpose of returning to that kingdom; rather, within a few days after they had entered Mexico, they scattered to many places, as we presently shall see.

CHAPTER XX

Our Spaniards spread out into divers parts of the world. What Gómez Arias and Diego Maldonado did in order to obtain news of Hernando de Soto.

THE Comptroller Juan de Añasco and the Treasurer Juan Gaytán, and the Captains Baltasar de Gallegos, Alonso Romo de Cardeñosa, Arias Tinoco, and Pedro Calderón, as well as other men of less note, returned to Spain, preferring to come back to that country poor rather than remain in the Indies, for they had amassed a hatred within them as a result of what they had suffered as well as what of their estates they had lost, a loss which in the case of most of them had brought ruin without any gain. Gómez Suárez de Figueroa returned to the house and estate of his father, Vasco Porcallo de Figueroa y de la Cerda, and others who were more judicious took the habit of a religious order, thus following the good example set by Gonzalo Quadrado Xaramillo, the first one of them to do so. For this man had wished to heighten his nobility and his past achievements by making himself a true soldier and cavalier of Jesus Christ Our Lord, and thus had bound himself as an apprentice under the banner of such a field marshal and general as the seraphic Father San Francisco, in whose brotherhood and profession he died, having proved by his action that in ecclesiastical orders one acquires the true nobility and the highest valor that God esteems and rewards. And this action, because it was taken by Gonzalo Quadrado, was noted and admired much more than if it had been taken by any other person. But many of our Spaniards did likewise, adopting the habits of various religious orders so as to dignify all of their past life with such a fine end.

Still others, and they were the fewest, remained in New Spain; among these was Luis de Moscoso de Alvarado who married a rich and illustrious kinswoman of his in Mexico. But the majority went to Peru, where as men who had undergone the hardships we have mentioned (and it is so true that we have not told a tenth part of those difficulties they actually experienced), they ennobled themselves in the service of the Crown of Spain in all that they encountered during those wars against Gonzalo Pizarro, Don Sebastián de Castilla, and Francisco Hernández Girón. I knew many of these cavaliers and soldiers[21] in Peru who were highly esteemed and who gained many possessions, but I do not know that any of them has succeeded in obtaining allotments of Indians as he could have done in Florida.

And now for the purpose of bringing my history to a close, since by virtue of the favor of the Creator of Heaven I find myself at the end of it, there remains nothing more for me to tell save what Captains Diego Maldonado and Gómez Arias did after Governor Hernando de Soto sent them to Havana with the order they were to carry out during that summer and the following autumn, as was reported in its place. It will be well, therefore, to give here an account of what these two fine cavaliers executed in fulfillment of the Governor's instruction and of their own obligation so that their loyalty for their captain general and the generosity of their souls may not be forgotten but instead be enshrined in memory and thus become an honor to them and an example for posterity.

As I have already stated, Captain Diego Maldonado went to Havana with the two brigantines under his command to visit Doña Isabel de Bobadilla, wife of Governor Hernando de Soto. He was

---

[21] Within the text of the *Florida,* the Inca tells us that among those survivors whom he later encountered in Peru were Diego de Tapia, Baltasar Hernández, Christóval Mosquera and Juan de Vega, the last of whom he knew also in Spain. For some unknown reason, he never mentions his subsequent friendship with Gonzalo Silvestre. See introduction.

to return with Gómez Arias, who had made the journey a short time previously, and the two captains between them were to take the two brigantines and the caravel, in addition to whatever other ships they might be able to purchase in Havana, and load them with food supplies, weapons and ammunition. Then during the following autumn, which was in the year 1540, they were to conduct these ships to the port of Achusi, which this selfsame Diego Maldonado had discovered; for here Governor Hernando de Soto was to appear, after having made a great swerve through the interior of the land for the purpose of exploring it. But the appearance of the Governor never took place, for he happened to discover the dissension and the secret rebellion that his men were plotting and as a result fled the sea and went inland where all eventually lost their way.

Therefore you must know now that when Gómez Arias and Diego Maldonado had united in Havana and fulfilled their obligation by seeing Doña Isabel de Bobadilla, and when they had sent a report throughout all those islands of what they had found in Florida as well as what the Governor needed for settling the land, they purchased three ships and loaded them with food, arms and ammunition, and in addition with calves, goats, ponies, mares, sheep, wheat, barley and garden stuff, all of which would enable them to start raising cattle and planting seed. Moreover, they loaded the caravel and two brigantines, and had there been two more ships, they would have had sufficient for them all, since the inhabitants of the islands of Cuba, Santo Domingo and Jamaica, because of the fine report they had heard of Florida and because of their own interest as well as their love for the Governor, had made an effort to assist him as much as they could.

With these things Diego Maldonado and Gómez Arias went to the port of Achusi at the appointed time, but failing to find the Governor there, departed in the brigantines, each on his own, and sailed along the coast in opposite directions to see if the Spaniards had appeared at some place to the east or the west. Wherever they arrived they left signs on the trees; and in the hollows of trees they placed written messages giving an account of what they had done

and planned to do the following summer. Then when the severity
of the winter no longer permitted them to navigate, they went back
to Havana with the sad news that they had received no word of
the Governor. But not for this did they fail to return to the coast
of Florida in the summer of 1541 and sail along it to the land of
Mexico and Nombre de Dios and later on the eastern side to the
Land of the Codfish in order to determine if in some way or some
manner they might be able to have news of Governor Hernando de
Soto. Being unsuccessful, they came again that winter to Havana.
Then in the following summer of the year forty-two they set out on
the same quest, but after spending almost seven months making
similar efforts, were forced by the weather to return and pass the
winter in Havana, from whence, just as soon as the spring of the
year forty-three made its appearance, they set forth once more in
spite of the fact that the past three years had yielded no news. And
this time they persisted in the undertaking and quest with a determination not to desist until they had obtained news of the Governor
or perished; for they could not believe that the land had swallowed
up all of these Spaniards, and they felt that some of them must appear somewhere. So with this perseverance they continued throughout that summer as they had the previous summers, suffering the
hardships and privations which one can imagine, but which, for the
sake of avoiding prolixity, I will not relate in detail.

CHAPTER XXI

A continuation of the peregrination of Gómez Arias and Diego Maldonado.

AND now traveling with this anxiety and care, they came to Vera
Cruz in the middle of October of this same year of forty-three.
Here they learned that their companions had left Florida, that those
who had escaped were fewer than three hundred, and that Governor
Hernando de Soto had perished along with all the others that were

missing from the almost one thousand who had entered that kingdom. Moreover, they learned the details of the whole unfortunate
issue of that expedition. Then these two good and loyal cavaliers
returned to Havana with this sad and lamentable news, which they
conveyed to Doña Isabel de Bobadilla. And since to the pain and
anxiety she had suffered for three continuous years because of her
failure to receive word of her husband, there was now added the new
anguish of his death and of the unfortunate outcome of the conquest,
the destruction and loss of his property and consequent fall of his
estate and ruin of his house, the lady soon after expired.

This tragic story, worthy as it is of tears because it embodies the
outlay of so many and such excessive labors on the part of the
Spanish people without profit or increase to their fatherland, was
the progress and the termination of that exploration of Florida made
by the Adelantado Hernando de Soto with so much expenditure of
his possessions, so much equipment of arms and horses, and such a
number of noble cavaliers and valiant soldiers. For as I have said at
other times, never has there been gathered together for any other
conquest of all those which until today have been made in the New
World such a magnificent and dazzling band of people or one so
well armed and arrayed, or again such a great number of horses as
were assembled for this one. And yet all these things were consumed and lost fruitlessly for two reasons: first, because of the
dissension that sprang up among these Spaniards and prevented their
settling in the beginning, and then because of the early death of
the Governor. For had he lived two more years, that magistrate
would have repaired the first damage with the assistance he was to
have requested, assistance which could have been afforded him as
he had planned to receive it, by way of the Great River.

And it may have been that with such assistance, he would have
begun an empire that could have competed today with New Spain
and Peru; for in the broadness and fertility of that land and in its
fitness for planting seed and raising livestock, it is inferior to none
other. Rather, it is believed to be superior, for among its riches
we have seen already the incredible amount of pearls and seed pearls

that were found in just one province or one temple along with marten and other fine furs which appertain solely to kings and great princes, as well as the rest of the splendors which we have referred to at length. Furthermore, it could be, and I myself do not doubt it, that by searching slowly for mines of gold and silver, these Spaniards in time would have found them, for when Mexico and Peru were first won, neither possessed the mines that they have today. Those of the Cerro de Potosí were discovered fourteen years after the Governors Don Francisco Pizarro and Don Diego de Almagro began to undertake the conquest of Peru. Therefore these Spaniards could have done the same in Florida, while enjoying in the interim the remainder of the riches which, as we have seen, that land possesses. For not everywhere are there gold and silver, yet people do live in all places.

And for this reason, I many and many times shall supplicate our lord the King and the whole Spanish nation as well, not to permit a land which is so excellent and which has been trodden upon and possessed by their own people to remain without their empire and sovereignty, but rather to make an effort to conquer and settle that land: first, that they may plant within it the Catholic Faith which they profess, just as their people have already planted it in the other kingdoms and provinces of the New World which they have conquered and populated; second, that Spain may enjoy this kingdom as she has enjoyed the rest of them; and finally, that this land may not remain without either the light of the Evangelic doctrine (which is the principal thing we should desire) or the other benefits the Spaniards can render it both in bettering its moral life and in perfecting it with those arts and sciences which flourish today in Spain. The natives of Florida have a great ability for these things, for without any instruction other than that of their natural intelligence, they have said and done such good things as we have seen and heard. Many times I have dreaded to find such courteous, magnificent and excellent deeds and utterances in the discourse of this history lest it be suspected that they were figments of my own imagination and not products of the land itself. Nevertheless Our Lord God is my witness that I not only have added nothing to the account given me, but, I confess with shame and humiliation, have not come anywhere near describing the heroic achievements as they were told to me or as they actually occurred. For this I therefore beseech the pardon of the entire kingdom of Florida and of all those who shall peruse this book.

But let it suffice that just the credit which is due be bestowed upon one who (without hoping for the reward of great lords and kings or of anyone else, or without pretending to any interest other than that of having spoken the truth) has taken the trouble to write this history, wandering from land to land, sick and exceedingly weary, solely to report what has been discovered in that great kingdom in order that our Holy Catholic Faith and the Crown of Spain may be augmented and understood. These are my primary and secondary purposes, for inasmuch as those who go on the conquest bear them both in mind, so will they be sure of divine favor.

May Our Lord for the glory and honor of His name, lead us in this conquest so that the multitude of souls who live in that kingdom without the truth of His doctrine may be converted to it and not perish. And may He grant to me His mercy and support so that from this day forward I may utilize what remains of my life in writing the history of the Inca kings who were of Peru—their origin and beginning, their idolatry and sacrifices, and their laws and customs. In sum I shall write of the whole republic as it was before the Spaniards won that empire, and indeed the greater part of my account is already placed in the loom. I will tell of the Incas and all the things I have outlined as I heard them from my mother and her uncles and aged kinsmen and from people in general of that country; and I will tell of what I myself managed to see of those antiquities which during my childhood had not as yet vanished, there being then still some shadows of them in existence. Furthermore, I will tell of the discovery and conquest of Peru, giving what I heard from my father and his contemporaries who won it; and in this same account I will describe the general uprising of the Indians against the Spaniards and the civil wars that occurred over the dissension between Pizarros and Almagros, for thus those factions were named who rose up against each other to the punishment of themselves and destruction of them all. Of the rebellions which occurred afterward in Peru, I will tell briefly what I heard from those who found themselves participants on one side or the other, and also what of them I saw personally, for though a mere boy, I knew Gonzalo Pizarro, his campmaster, Francisco de Carvajal, and all of his captains, as well as Don Sebastián de Castilla and Francisco Hernández Girón. Moreover, I have information concerning the most noteworthy things that the viceroys have accomplished since that time in the government of that empire.

CHAPTER XXII[22]

The number of Christians, both secular and religious, who died in Florida before the year 1568.

SINCE I have given extensive notice of the death of Governor Hernando de Soto and in addition of such illustrious cavaliers as the great Spanish Portuguese captain, Andrés de Vasconcellos, the good Nuño Tovar of Estremadura, and numerous other noble and valiant soldiers who died on the expedition, as we have been able to observe at length throughout this history, I have felt it unworthy not to commemorate the priests, clerics and other religious who accompanied these men to Florida and died with them, and furthermore those who since their time have gone to that kingdom to preach the Faith of the Holy Mother Church of Rome. For it is only right that these people not remain in oblivion, since captains and soldiers, as well as priests, monks and friars died in the service

[22] The edition of 1605 includes twenty-two chapters in Book VI while stating that there are only twenty-one. This same error occurs also in the introductory summary to Book VI of the 1723 edition. Such an obvious mistake we have felt it wise to correct in our translation.

of Christ Our Lord, both having gone out with the same zeal to disseminate His holy gospel—the cavaliers to force the infidels with arms to subject themselves and enter to hear and obey the Christian doctrine, and the priests and religious to oblige and compel them by their virtuous life and example to believe in the Faith and to imitate them in Christianity.

So starting with the seculars, let me say that the first Christian to die in this attempt was the first explorer of Florida, Juan Ponce de León, a native cavalier of León who in his childhood served as a page to Pedro Núñez de Guzmán, lord of Toral. But all those who went with this man also perished, for having been wounded by the Indians, none survived. Just how many of them there were could not be ascertained, but it is known that they numbered more than eighty. Next came Lucas Vázquez de Ayllón, who likewise died at the hands of the Floridians, along with the more than two hundred and twenty Christians who accompanied him. Later Pámphilo de Narváez brought four hundred Spaniards, all but four of whom were lost, some being killed by enemies, some drowning in the sea, and those who escaped from the sea dying of pure hunger. Then ten years later the Adelantado Hernando de Soto went to Florida with a thousand Spaniards gathered from all the provinces of Spain, and more than seven hundred of these men died. Thus it is that the number of Christians who previous to this year have perished in that land along with their commanders exceeds fourteen hundred.

It remains now for me to tell of the priests and the religious who have died in that land. But I have information about those only who accompanied Hernando de Soto and who have journeyed to that kingdom since. For in the accounts of Juan Ponce de León, Lucas Vázquez de Ayllón, and Pámphilo de Narváez, there are no records of such men, and it is as if they had not gone. But as I said in chapter six at the beginning of this history, twelve priests did travel with Hernando de Soto; eight of them clerics and four of them friars. Four of the clerics died the first year that they entered Florida and as a result the record does not contain their names. Two clerics, Dionisio de París, a native of the great city of Paris, and

Diego de Bañuelos, a native of the city of Cordova, and one friar, Francisco de la Rocha, who was a member of the Advocation of the Most Holy Trinity and a native of Badajoz, all died of illness during the life of Governor Hernando de Soto; for there being neither doctor nor apothecary, if nature failed to cure the man who fell sick, there was no help for him from human skill. The other five to perish were the cleric priests, Rodrigo de Gallegos, a native of Seville, and Francisco del Pozo, a native of Cordova, and the three friars, Juan de Torres, a native of Seville who belonged to the order of the Seraphic Father San Francisco; Juan de Gallegos, also a native of Seville, who was of the order of the divine Saint Dominic; and Luis de Soto, a native of Villanueva de Barcarrota, who too was a Dominican. Each of these men of virtuous life and example perished after the death of the Adelantado Hernando de Soto and during the great hardships encountered in going to and fro on that long and ill-advised journey made for the purpose of reaching the land of Mexico, and also after that journey until the time they embarked. For although as priests they were cared for in every possible way where comfort was so lacking and there was such an excess of hardships, they were unable to survive and thus remained in that kingdom. Now these men in addition to their holiness and priestliness were all noble and, while they lived, performed their ecclesiastical office admirably, receiving the confessions of those who were dying and giving them courage to die well, and furthermore instructing and baptizing the Indians who remained in the service of the Spaniards.

After the year 1549, five friars of the Dominican Order went to Florida. The Emperor Charles V, King of Spain, paid the expenses of these men because they offered to go alone and preach the Gospel without benefit of armed forces so as not to offend the Indians. But the pagans, already provoked by previous expeditions, refused to hear the doctrine of these friars, and, when three of them disembarked, slew them with both cruelty and rage. Among those who died on this occasion was their leader the good Father Friar Luis

Cancer de Balbastro. Fired by a desire to augment the Catholic Faith, he personally and most insistently had petitioned the Emperor for that mission, and as a result had given his life for the Faith as a true son of the Order of Preachers. I did not ascertain from what land he came or the names of his companions, and I regret that I cannot include each of them.

In the year 1566, three religious of the Holy Company of Jesus crossed over to Florida with the same zeal. He who went as their superior was Maestro Pedro Martínez, a native of the famous kingdom of Aragón—a kingdom renowned throughout the world in that, small as it is, it has been so distinguished for the valor and strength of its sons who have accomplished such magnificent achievements as those which its histories and the histories of others reveal. This man, who was a native of the town of Teruel, was destroyed by the Indians immediately upon disembarking, and his companions, one a priest named Juan Rogel and the other a brother named Francisco de Villa-Real, withdrew to Havana in great distress at not being able to fulfill their desires to teach and preach the Christian doctrine among the pagans.

In the year five hundred and sixty-eight, eight more religious of the Holy Company of Jesus, two of them priests and six of them brothers, sailed for Florida. He who went as their superior was Bautista de Segura, a native of Toledo, and the other priest was Luis de Quirós, a native of Xerez de la Frontera. I did not learn the birth places of the six brothers, but their names are as follows: Juan Bautista Méndez, Gabriel de Solís, Antonio Zavallos, Christóval Redondo, Gabriel Gómez and Pedro de Linares. These men took in their company an Indian lord of vassals who was born in Florida, and it will be well for me to give here the following account of how this Indian came to Spain.

Between the years five hundred and sixty-three and five hundred and sixty-eight, the Adelantado Pedro Meléndez sailed three times to Florida for the purpose of evicting from that coast certain French corsairs who were attempting to settle and populate it. From the second of these trips he brought seven Florida Indians who were perfectly friendly and were wearing the same clothes that, as we have said, they wear in their native land. Moreover, they carried their bows and arrows, which were of the very excellent kind that they fashion for their greater adornment. Now when these Indians were being taken to Madrid to be shown to His Majesty the King, Philip II, they traveled through one of the towns of Cordova where the author who gave me the details of this history was residing, and he, on learning that Florida Indians were passing near, went out to the open countryside to see them. Then he inquired of them as to what provinces they came from, and in order that they might realize that he too had been in Florida, asked if they were from Vitachuco, Apalache, Mauvila, Chicaza or other places where the Spaniards had fought great battles. The Indians thereupon recognized that he was one of those who had accompanied Governor Hernando de Soto, and regarding him with evil eyes, replied: "Having left those provinces as desolate as you did, do you want us to give you news of them?" And they would not answer him another word, but in speaking among themselves they did say (according to the interpreter who was accompanying them): "We would more willingly give him arrow blows than the information he requests of us." Then two of them (in order to make this man realize their desire to shoot arrows at him and the skill with which they might do so) discharged great arrows high into the air with so much force that they were lost from sight. In telling me of this incident, my author admitted that he feared they might shoot at him, since Indians are foolish and rash, especially in matters that concern arms and valor.

All seven of these pagans were baptized in Spain, but six of them died within a short time. Then the seventh, who was a lord of vassals, requested permission to return to his land, making great vows to act as a good Christian in converting his subjects as well as the rest of the inhabitants of his kingdom to the Catholic Faith. Hence the religious admitted him into their fellowship, believing that he was to assist them, since he had promised to do so. Later they went to Florida and journeyed many leagues inland, crossing great swamps and marshes, and refusing to take soldiers lest they give offense to the natives with their arms. When the Cacique had led them far enough into his land to feel that he could kill them with safety, he told them to wait where they were while he went forward four or five leagues to prepare the Indians of that province to listen to the Christian doctrine complacently and amicably; and he promised to return within eight days. These men therefore waited for fifteen days, and when they saw that the Cacique did not return, they dispatched Father Luis de Quirós and one of the brothers to the town where he had said he was going. But here the Cacique with many of his people, on seeing Don Luis and his companion before him, as a traitor apostate and without uttering a word, slew them both with great rage and cruelty. Moreover on the following day, before the other Spaniards might learn of the death of their companions and depart for a neighboring province to find protection, he fell upon them with great impetus and fury as if he were attacking a squadron of armed soldiers. On hearing the noise of the Indians and beholding the weapons they carried in their hands, these religious, for the sake of expounding the Faith of Christ Our Lord, merely knelt to receive the death that was to be inflicted upon them. At that the infidels struck them most cruelly, and they as devout religious departed this present life to enjoy that of eternity.

The Indians, after having killed these men, opened a chest in which they had carried books of the Holy Scripture, breviaries, missals, and sacred vestments for saying mass; and each Indian took the vestment he liked and put it on as he pleased, ridiculing that richness and majesty and regarding it as something poor and base. Then while the others jumped about and danced in these sacred garments, three of them seized a crucifix from the chest, and as they gazed upon it, suddenly fell dead. At that all of their comrades cast the holy vestments to the ground and fled. Of this incident Father Maestro Pedro de Ribade-Neyra likewise writes.

Thus these eighteen priests, ten of whom represent the four orders we have named, the eight clerics, and the six brothers of the Holy Fellowship, in all twenty-four, are those who before the year fifteen hundred and sixty-eight perished in Florida while disseminating the Holy Gospel, and they are over and above the fourteen hundred secular Spaniards who went to that land on four expeditions. And I do trust God that the blood of these men is not crying out and pleading for vengeance like that of Abel, but for mercy like that of Christ Our Lord, so that these pagans may come into the knowledge of His Eternal Majesty under the obedience of Our Mother the Holy Roman Church. Thus we may believe and hope that that land which has been watered so frequently with so much Christian blood, may yield fruit in proportion to the irrigation of this Catholic blood that has been poured upon it.

May glory and honor be given to God Our Lord, the Father, Son, and Holy Ghost, Three Persons and the only true God. Amen.

The End.

LEAF OF PRIVILEGE

From the 1605 Edition

I have seen this volume of six books by the Inca, Garcilaso de la Vega. It treats of the discovery of Florida and contains therein nothing contrary to our Holy Faith and good customs; rather, it is a history which merits reading since it relates many curious things concerning divers unknown peoples and nations, very notable events of war, and numerous other matters worthy of being brought to the attention of all.

In Lisbon, in San Francisco   FR. LUYS DOS ANJOS.
d'Enxobreguas, November 16, 1604.

In view of the above information, this book entitled *The Discovery of Florida* may be printed but afterward must be returned to this council to be compared with the original and given license for publication. Without this license it must not circulate.

In Lisbon, November 23, 1604.   MARCOS TEIXEIRA.
                                     RUY PIREZ DA VEIGA.

In view of the license which it holds from the Holy Office, and of its having been seen by the Council, this book may be printed.

In Lisbon, February 21, 1605.   DAMIÃO D'AGUIAR.
                                        SOUSA.

As is to be seen in the document executed at Lisbon on March 8, 1605, and the provision attached, etc., His Majesty has agreed that any printer or bookseller who within a period of ten years prints or sells this book without the author's permission will be subject to the penalties ordained.

INDEX

THIS BOOK is set in twelve point Intertype Garamond, two point leaded. The paper is Warren's Olde Style India Laid, fifty pound basis. The type ornaments, tail-pieces and other decorative devices were reproduced from the 1723 Madrid edition of *La Florida* and from specimens of seventeenth and eighteenth century Spanish printing in the private collection of Dr. Carlos E. Castañeda. The initial letters were reproduced from a set of the 1598 London edition of *The Principal Navigations, Voiages, Traffiques, and Discoueries of the English Nation,* by Richard Hakluyt, which is in the Rare Book Collections of The University of Texas.